M

EVANSTON PUBLIC LIBRARY

3 1192 01199 5477

725.83 Siry.J

Siry, Joseph, 1956-

The Chicago Auditorium
Building : Adler and
c2002.

W9-BIS-517

The Chicago Auditorium Building

CHICAGO ARCHITECTURE AND URBANISM

A series edited by   ROBERT BRUEGMANN

JOAN DRAPER

WIM DE WIT

DAVID VAN ZANTEN

THE CHICAGO AUDITORIUM BUILDING

Adler and Sullivan's Architecture and the City

JOSEPH M. SIRY

UNIVERSITY OF CHICAGO PRESS   *Chicago & London*

EVANSTON PUBLIC LIBRARY
1703 ORRINGTON AVENUE
EVANSTON, ILLINOIS 60201

JOSEPH M. SIRY is professor of art history and American studies at Wesleyan University. He is the author of *Carson Pirie Scott: Louis Sullivan and the Chicago Department Store*, published by the University of Chicago Press, and *Unity Temple: Frank Lloyd Wright and Architecture for Liberal Religion*.

The University of Chicago Press, Chicago 60637
The University of Chicago Press, Ltd., London
© 2002 by Joseph M. Siry
All rights reserved. Published 2002
Printed in Italy

11   10   09   08   07   06   05   04   03   02   1   2   3   4   5
ISBN: 0-226-76133-9 (cloth)
ISBN: 0-226-76134-7 (paper)

Library of Congress Cataloging-in-Publication Data

Siry, Joseph, 1956-
  The Chicago Auditorium Building: Adler and Sullivan's architecture and the city / Joseph M. Siry.
      p. cm. — (Chicago architecture and urbanism)
  Includes bibliographical references and index.
  ISBN 0-226-76133-9 (cloth: alk. paper) — ISBN 0-226-76134-7 (pbk.: alk. paper)
      1. Chicago Auditorium Building (Chicago, Ill.) 2. Adler and Sullivan. 3. Multipurpose building—Illinois—Chicago. 4. Chicago (Ill.)—Buildings, structures, etc. I. Title. II. Series.

NA4178.C48 C487 2002
725'.83'0977311—dc21

                                                                    2002017374

This book is printed on acid-free paper.

This publication of this book was supported by a grant from the Graham Foundation for Advanced Studies in the Fine Arts.

To my mother, Jennie D. Siry, and to the memory of my father, Joseph W. Siry, and my sister, JoAnne Michaele Siry

CONTENTS

ILLUSTRATIONS

ACKNOWLEDGMENTS

Although research and writing for this book began in January 1996, its roots go
back to my earlier work on Chicago's architecture that began in 1981. Throughout the past twenty years, I have much appreciated the support of professors Robert
Bruegmann of the University of Illinois at Chicago and David Van Zanten at Northwestern University, both of whom are also editors for the Chicago Architecture and
Urbanism Series. In recent years, Professor Richard Etlin of the University of Maryland has been a source of encouraging interest. In Chicago, Timothy Samuelson,
Curator of Architecture at the Chicago Historical Society, helpfully responded to
questions about the building and sources, as did Bart Swindall, tour coordinator
and archivist for the Auditorium Theater Council, and Kathleen Roy Cummings,
whose research on the Auditorium Building's art glass resulted in the exhibition at
Roosevelt University's Albert A. Robin Campus in 2000. Miles L. Berger generously
shared his research files on Ferdinand W. Peck. Charles Laurier, formerly at Roosevelt University Library, and Rebecca Stark were especially helpful in guiding me to
the different parts of the Auditorium Collection in Roosevelt University's Archives
and in locating photographs. Ward Miller, at the Office of John Vinci, AIA, facili-
tated access to the Richard Nickel files there and helped with obtaining photographs.
Fred Zubb of the Archives of the Circuit Court Clerk of Cook County located and
photocopied probate records for Philip F. W. Peck and Ferdinand W. Peck. Andrea
Telli and her colleagues at the Chicago Public Library's Department of Special Collections were most helpful, as were librarians throughout the Library of Congress.
Natasha Derrickson and Susan Perry at the Ryerson and Burnham Libraries of the
Art Institute of Chicago and Tessia Whitehead, Caroline Nutley, and Jessica Meyer
at the Chicago Historical Society patiently searched for requested photographs.
Roosevelt University, through its Provost and Vice President, Vinton Thompson,

and its Director of Public Relations, Thomas Karow, expressed support for this project, whose completion coincides with further restoration of the Auditorium Hotel and Theater. The Society of Architectural Historians granted me permission to use materials from my earlier article on the Chicago Auditorium Building in the society's journal. For their valuable comments, I thank the two anonymous readers of that article manuscript and the two anonymous readers of the book manuscript at the University of Chicago Press. Acquisitions editor Susan Bielstein, her assistant, Anthony Burton, and senior manuscript editor Alice Bennett were most helpful through the stages of review, editing, and production.

Wesleyan University continues to provide superb institutional support for scholarship, including two semesters' sabbaticals and one semester's leave, a project grant for travel to Chicago, and supplementary grants over seven years to help defray costs of research and photographs. At Olin Library, Kathleen Stefanowicz and Katherine Wolfe of Interlibrary Loan found many sources that otherwise would have been inaccessible. Daniel Schnaidt of Information Technology Services and John Elmore at the Center for the Arts kindly instructed me in Photoshop so I could draft several figures. Wesleyan's Center for the Humanities offered a semester's faculty fellowship in spring 2000. The interdisciplinary conversations there stimulated me to respond to perspectives from many fields. My colleagues and students in the Department of Art and Art History elevated this work through the example of their own. Susanne Grace Fusso, my colleague and friend, could not have been kinder or more helpful.

To my mother, Jennie D. Siry, I continue to owe great gratitude for her encouragement and support. This study is dedicated to her and to the memories of my father, Joseph W. Siry, and my sister, JoAnne Michaele Siry, both of whom were always supportive of us all.

Rarely in the modern period, either in Europe or in the United States, has a major city's identity been so strongly associated with the creation of a single monumental building as when Chicago's Auditorium opened in December 1889. Not only did the city's capitalist newspapers—of diverse political loyalties—represent the structure in this way, but so did reports of the Auditorium's advent elsewhere in the United States and in Western Europe. These accounts emphasized that the Auditorium represented a defining moment for its city, the most important since the Great Fire of 1871. When completed, the Auditorium marked Chicago's emergence as a focus of international interest, a city whose significance was confirmed for a world audience with the World's Columbian Exposition of 1893. Indeed, the Auditorium's creation provided a model of the local cooperation that would create the fair. The building was the cultural center for Chicagoans concerned with their city's well-being in an era when radical working-class politics challenged civic leaders to respond to economic and social inequities. In these ways the Auditorium's architectural history is intertwined with Chicago's dynamic and difficult urban history. As the major civic project of its period, this monument and its city were linked on many levels.[1]

Yet a contextually premised history of the Auditorium is not sufficient. From its celebrated opening, the structure has been considered a major work of American and early modern architecture. Its main theater is among the world's great rooms of its kind, while its monumental exterior has remained one of its era's defining images. Because of its technical and aesthetic innovations, Chicago's Auditorium occupies a central place in the oeuvre of its architects, Dankmar Adler and Louis Sullivan. It was the building that initiated their national and international reputation as creators of highly innovative American architecture for large public buildings. Almost

1

all of Adler and Sullivan's later works referred in important ways to the Auditorium. More broadly, the Auditorium, as one of the most complex structures of its time, probably did more than any other single building to launch Chicago's reputation as a major center for modern architecture. The monument's centrality in its city's architectural canon demands analysis of its forms in terms of Adler and Sullivan's inventive development and in relation to those contemporaneous works in and beyond Chicago that served as these architects' points of departure. The Auditorium's story is inextricable from, but irreducible to, those urban social conditions it was meant to engage. This monument stands historiographically at the intersection of multiple narratives—architectural, technical, urban, cultural, and political—that reveal its meanings for its patrons, architects, and audiences.[2]

When looking at the Auditorium today from the southeast across Michigan Avenue, it is difficult for an observer to reconstruct the building's original physical and historical context. When it opened, the Auditorium stood less than one hundred yards from Lake Michigan to the east, before the expansion of the nineteenth-century Lake Front Park into the twentieth-century Grant Park (fig. 1). Michigan Avenue to the south was almost exclusively residential, and though prime hotels stood north of the Auditorium, the avenue's commercial development lagged behind the city's

Figure 1

Dankmar Adler and Louis Sullivan, Auditorium Building, Chicago (1886–1890), with houses to south on Michigan Avenue. View looking north over Lake Front Park toward Inter-state Industrial Exhibition Building and tracks of Illinois Central Railroad along lakefront leading to Central Depot, originally built 1856. From Garczynski, *Auditorium*. Courtesy of the Library of Congress.

other major north-south arteries. In retrospect, those who knew Michigan Avenue in the 1880s maintained that its architectural development began with the Auditorium. Along the lakefront ran the tracks of several major railroads; one Italian visitor in 1893 told his Milanese readers he counted thirty-eight trains passing in a single hour, "and all of the hours are alike, it is the same night and day."[3] These trains ran along the surface, not out of view beneath the parkscape as they do today, so that the Auditorium was the first major monument their passengers saw when they arrived in Chicago, as after the eighteen-hour trip from New York City. Although later structures dwarfed the Auditorium's 240-foot tower, when completed it was the tallest in Chicago. The original observation platform atop the tower (later dismantled) offered unobstructed panoramic views in all directions over city, lake, and prairie. As an observatory, the tower fulfilled a local need for commanding vistas, with citizens and visitors alike surveying Chicago's urban expanse.[4]

As the southernmost of Michigan Avenue's major buildings, the Auditorium anchored a monumental blockfront stretching north from Congress to Adams Street, as seen in a view of about 1893 (fig. 2). This blockfront had special significance for the Auditorium's principal patron, Ferdinand W. Peck, whose parents' home had stood on this block in Michigan Terrace, a row of the city's most prestigious prefire townhouses. These were the southernmost structures on Michigan Avenue to perish in the Great Fire of 1871, which swept north along the lakefront from Congress Street. In Peck's Auditorium, Adler and Sullivan's Romanesque-inspired front aligned stylistically with Solon S. Beman's Studebaker Building (1885–1886) to the north, built for the manufacture and sale of carriages by what was then the

Figure 2

Michigan Avenue, south from Van Buren Street, showing east front of Auditorium Building, south of Studebaker Building (1886, before remodeling in 1898 as Fine Arts Building), by Solon S. Beman, and Art Institute of Chicago (1885–1886; demolished 1923), by Daniel Burnham and John Wellborn Root. Photograph by J. W. Taylor. Courtesy of the Chicago Historical Society, ICHi-04455.

world's largest maker of wheeled vehicles. Farther to the north was Daniel H. Burnham and John Wellborn Root's Art Institute of Chicago (1885; demolished 1923). After the Studebaker brothers built a new building nearby in 1895, Beman's first Studebaker Building was remodeled in 1898 as the Fine Arts Building. Emulating the Auditorium, it contained studios, music schools, and two theaters. In the larger rearmost theater, a local opera company gave performances. Burnham and Root's Art Institute, with only three upper stories, was low enough to allow sufficient light for the north side wall of this theater. Although they were designed by different architects and for different uses, these three adjacent buildings constituted a collective architectural showpiece that, in the eyes of one eastern visitor, "would be conspicuous and admired in any city in the world."[5]

While all three displayed a round-arched style based on the work of Henry Hobson Richardson, Adler and Sullivan's elevation was the largest and the only one of the three with a nearly flat horizontal cornice. Although the Auditorium Building marked Sullivan's first large-scale engagement with Richardson's style, it was the Auditorium's patrons who had directed their architects to design the stone exterior finally built. The base of Minnesota and Maine granites and the upper stories clad in Indiana limestone signified Chicago's regional dominance as a center of consumption for the many materials used in its construction. Farther north on Michigan Avenue stood major hotels and one of the city's corporate headquarters, that of the Pullman Palace Car Company in Beman's Pullman Building (1882–1883) on the southwest corner of Adams Street. Yet Michigan Avenue and Lake Front Park had also been the sites of repeated socialist rallies and marches through the mid-1880s, so that the Auditorium and similar structures marked a capitalist reclamation of this symbolically central urban space. The lithic solidity of these fronts signified Chicago's recovery after the Great Fire and conveyed an image of indestructibility in the face of continual threats of social violence through the 1880s, when dynamite was the weapon of choice among the city's radical labor leaders.

Concern for Chicago's architectural and cultural reputation relative to New York City prompted Ferdinand Peck to build the Auditorium. In October 1888 he had invited Cornelius Vanderbilt, who owned the New York Central Railroad, one of the chief lines connecting the two cities, to tour the nearly completed building. Vanderbilt admired it, and one of his Manhattan colleagues, United States senator and orator Chauncey Depew, extolled the Auditorium as "the most impressive structure in the world." He concluded that it was "the architectural wonder of the nineteenth century."[6] In December 1889 Peck escorted President Benjamin Harrison on a tour of the Auditorium Theater on the day of its opening (fig. 3). Upon entering the great room, Harrison, an Indianan, termed it "surpassingly beautiful." Turning to his vice president, Levi P. Morton, a prominent Manhattan banker, he asked, "I say, Mr. Morton, New York surrenders, eh?" And Morton replied yes.[7] These interactions and their broadcasting in local publicity typified the kind of regional competition that prompted the Auditorium's creation as a symbol of Chicago's identity as the leading city of the Midwest. New Yorkers' praise of the Auditorium

Figure 3
Auditorium Theater, interior showing elliptical ceiling arches, main organ screen to left of stage (with portraits of Wagner and Haydn in arch spandrels), and iron-and-plaster reducing curtain framing stage. Face of proscenium arch shows mural by Charles Holloway. Photograph by J. W. Taylor. Architecture Photograph Collection, Courtesy of the Art Institute of Chicago.

and its theater was especially meaningful in light of the completion in 1883 of Manhattan's Metropolitan Opera House, the building that Chicago's Auditorium Theater was meant to surpass. Adler and Sullivan's interior marked not only the culmination of over a decade of experience in theater design, but also Peck's intention of creating a civic space whose great size and flexibility would make it a public hall where a broad audience could have access to high culture. As conceived by Chicago's capitalists, the Auditorium Theater represented democratic outreach to the city's skilled workers, whose political views Peck and others identified as key to the future of their urban society. As Peck often stated, "It is not primarily a money-making organization, but a center of music, art and education."[8] As a building "of Chicago to the smallest detail," the Auditorium Theater and the Auditorium Hotel encasing the theater exhibited the skills of local artists and craftsmen.[9] These spaces displayed not only Adler and Sullivan's architectural imagination but also the capabilities of the city's building industry as a form of regional cultural expression.

It is said that great buildings have a way of disappearing behind their reputations.[10] This is not wholly true of the Auditorium, for it has held a prominent place in accounts of Adler and Sullivan's work and in architectural histories of Chicago, America, and the early modern period. Yet the Auditorium's historical situation presents a rich opportunity to link different fields of study in its analysis. The most frequently invoked frame of reference for Adler and Sullivan's work has been an art historical perspective that identifies their originality as precursors of the modern movement in architecture of the twentieth century. Adler as a technical innovator and thinker and Sullivan as a creative artist and theorist were cited as central figures in the first "Chicago school" of commercial architecture in the 1880s and 1890s. As a phrase that has itself become a kind of artifact, the "Chicago school" as defined by Sigfried Giedion and Carl Condit celebrated the protomodern, nonhistoricist masonry and metal buildings of postfire Chicago's central Loop. More recently, a series of revisionist accounts have demonstrated the relation between Chicago's architectural culture and that of New York City and major European cities, particularly for the first generation of Chicago's tall office buildings, among which Adler and Sullivan's works from 1890 to 1895 figured prominently.[11]

Apart from studies of Chicago's architecture rooted in art history, there are rich traditions of writing about the city's political, economic, and social history that need to be integrated into accounts of its architecture. For example, the building trades were at the center of Chicago's labor disputes from the 1850s, but there has been little effort to connect the extensive accounts of the city's labor history with architectural histories of the period.[12] As the Auditorium's story illustrates, the cycles of workers' political activities and capitalist architectural responses were closely connected through the postfire decades as continuations of prefire urban tensions. The postfire reconstruction in the 1870s engaged issues of class conflict.[13] Rather than focusing primarily on architects as innovative artists and technicians, recent histories that treat the first generation of tall buildings in the 1880s have shown the importance of the social and cultural agenda of these buildings' patrons.[14] The case of Ferdinand Peck shows how Chicago's capitalist elite saw economic progress and cultural amenities as complementary priorities to be pursued through the creation of architecture and landscapes. In advancing this agenda, Chicago's leaders were emulating the philanthropic efforts of their counterparts who were endowing cultural institutions in eastern cities.[15]

Yet to understand the urgency that prompted Peck and his peers to act, one has to examine the counterculture of the city's politicized working class, which created its own journalism, rituals, and entertainment. These workers' events had their characteristic urban sites, including streets and parks as well as buildings owned or used by labor groups. Moreover, these workers were predominantly foreign-born Germans, whereas Chicago's business leaders were then mainly Anglo-Americans, to whom such workers were ethnic "others." In the 1880s, when Germans were the city's largest ethnic immigrant group, differences in language often, though not always, coincided with differences in class. Class itself was understood not only in terms of occupation and income, but also in terms of the characteristic leisure activities of different groups. In this light the workers' own political and social events as a whole exemplified a process of class self-representation no less central to Chicago's history than its capitalists' self-representation in monumental architecture. As one labor historian has written, "working-class culture" is understood as "the reservoir of traditional patterns of thought, behavior, and representation available to German workers in their encounter with the processes of industrialization and in their efforts at integration into American society."[16] In Chicago of the early 1880s, these patterns had violent currents that erupted publicly. It was into this highly charged, fluidly unstable historical moment that Peck inserted the Auditorium Building as a bastion of capitalist politics and culture, whose theater's moderately priced performances were to attract middle-class and working-class audiences.

Architectural and social histories together provide complementary frames of reference for examining the Auditorium. These viewpoints converge in the study of how Adler and Sullivan's structure responded to the conventions of theaters and hotels as two of the most prominent building types of the late nineteenth century. Chicago had many gradations of both kinds of structures, whose histories provide windows onto the ways the city developed as a segmented society. In addition to politically conscious workers' events, Chicago's middle-class and working-class people patronized nonpolitical theater of all kinds, in a period of considerable debate about what constituted publicly acceptable entertainment. As with the city's elite philanthropy, the local systems of public entertainment and their spatial settings exemplified national trends of the period. In Chicago of the 1880s, as earlier elsewhere in the United States and in Europe, the question of amusement, especially in the fields of music and drama, was an important constituent of class identity. Public theaters in London, Paris, New York, and elsewhere had long been major sites of urban conflict.[17] Hotels similarly functioned as settings for many types of local social gatherings, in addition to representing the city to its many out-of-town guests. The architecture of theaters and hotels was keyed to their users' expectations, based on their continual comparisons between different variations on these building types throughout the central city. In commissioning and designing theaters and hotels, Chicago patrons and architects looked carefully at models of these types in the eastern United States and Europe, selectively adapting from these sources to create a distinctive regional tradition in works like the Auditorium. For Peck, Adler, and Sullivan, adapting certain models and rejecting others was an ideologically structured process. Their choices were based on the messages about urban society that they wanted their buildings to convey.

From these perspectives, the achievements of Adler and Sullivan emerged within the guidelines of their patrons' agenda. It was the vision of clients such as Peck that structured the situations in which these highly original architects developed their approach to their field. Yet both Adler and Sullivan had richly creative minds that were totally committed to architecture as a profession and as an art. Their intentions for their medium developed from project to project, guided by preoccupations expressed in their writings. Issues of type and patronage provided a framework within which they developed their thinking, but these issues did not determine their precise expressive direction. Their work had its own intellectual priorities, and it was their skill in realizing their ideas that made the Auditorium the outstanding building in a series of architectural experiments in Chicago that Adler and Sullivan pursued in related commissions through the years before and after Peck's great project. These structures also engaged issues of patronage and use that

linked their architecture to its city's larger historical situation. It was perhaps because Chicago's future was so contested, both internally because of class tensions
and nationally because of interregional rivalry, that their work was so vigorously
defined.

This book traces the development of Adler and Sullivan's architecture in
Chicago before and after the Auditorium Building, from 1880 to 1894. Yet their
works through this period were embedded in other narratives of urban politics and
culture that had their roots in the city's history before the Great Fire of 1871 and in
the tumultuous decade of the 1870s, before they began their continuing architectural collaboration in 1880. Histories of Adler and Sullivan's and Chicago's architecture focus on their contributions to the tall office building from 1880 to 1895 as a
paradigm of early modern construction. Yet this book's focus is on their theaters
and other major public interiors in buildings that were then at the center of discussions about Chicago's character as an urban society. The central analytical theme
running through the following chapters is the relation between elite efforts like
Peck's to shape the course of the city's cultural development and resistance to those
efforts by working-class groups that sought, in many ways, to take Chicago in a very
different direction. Also important were the contests of ideas not only between
highly empowered citizens and less empowered ones, but also between competing
elites, who had different social priorities and cultural agendas. It was within this on-
going dynamic of rival visions for their city's future that Adler and Sullivan developed their distinctive architecture. To recover its meanings, one not only has to explore these architects' intentions but must also reconstruct those facets of Chicago's
life that their buildings were meant to accommodate and define.

Ferdinand Peck, Chicago Politics, and Chicago Theaters to 1880

In histories of modern and American architecture, the Auditorium Building is usually presented as the first of Adler and Sullivan's major works, prefacing their tall office buildings of the early 1890s. Yet when the Auditorium Theater opened in December 1889, these architects' contemporaries saw this structure as the culmination of Chicago's earlier tradition of theater architecture (fig. 4). Guidebooks of the period listed over thirty theaters throughout the city, of which eleven had productions regularly reviewed in newspapers. Five were centrally located, with others on the Near North, West, and South Sides.[1] Together these theaters constituted a middle- and upper-class entertainment network that was central to Chicago's cultural and architectural history. Their productions shaped popular taste for drama and music, while their facilities provided a rich body of precedent that informed Adler and Sullivan's own theater architecture of the 1880s as an important contribution to local development of this building type. Chicago's drama and music, and their architectural settings, evolved interactively with New York City's and with those of other midwestern cities, especially Cincinnati. This was notably the case with opera, the principal medium for which the Auditorium Theater was built.

The Auditorium's origins have always been credited to Ferdinand W. Peck (1848–1924), who initiated the project in 1885, by which time Adler and Sullivan had perfected their novel architectural approach to theater design. Peck's personal history reveals the ideological and architectural attitudes he brought to this project. His ideals found expression not only in the Auditorium but in a range of civic activities. Because of his family's large real estate interests, Peck was at the center of Chicago's building activity and civic development, whose major theme was the contest for political supremacy between a properted elite and a variably empowered

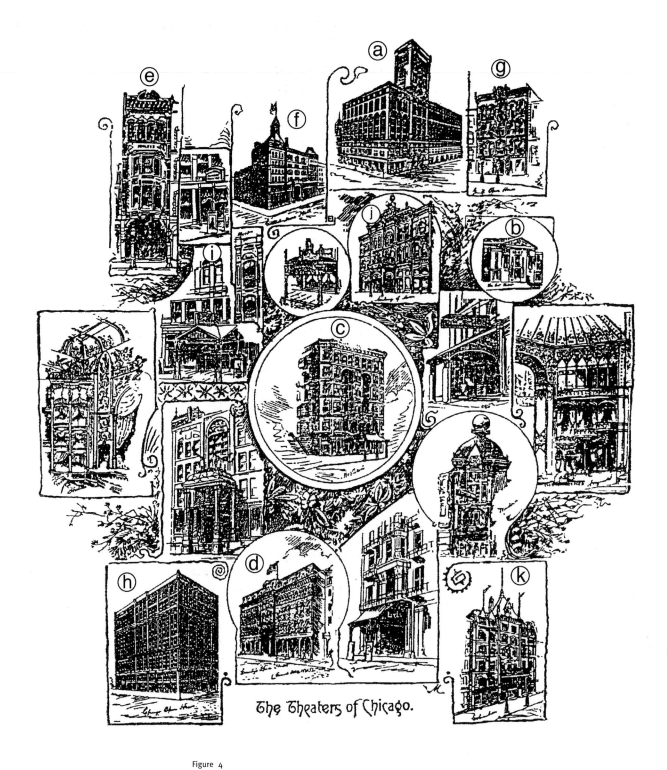

Figure 4

Chicago's major theaters to 1890, including (a) the Auditorium; (b) the original Rice's Theater of 1847; (c) McVicker's as remodeled in 1885; (d) Crosby's Opera House, opened in 1865 and destroyed in the Great Fire of October 1871; (e) Hooley's; (f) the Central Music Hall, opened in 1879; (g) the Grand Opera House; (h) the Chicago Opera House; (i) the People's Theater; (j) the Academy of Music, and (k) the Columbia. From Auditorium Supplement, *Chicago Daily Inter Ocean*, 11 December 1889. Graphic notations by author.

working class. Within this struggle, Chicago's social classes developed varied musical and dramatic cultures as extensions of their economic and political positions. Different class and language groups attended different theaters and music halls, not only for commercially staged entertainments, but also for social events and political gatherings. Study of these rituals and their buildings reveals how urban interests defined themselves through spaces for collective experience. The Auditorium emerges from multiple histories that unfolded within and beyond Chicago, many of which intersected in the life's work of Ferdinand Peck as the building's patron.

The Chicago of Philip F. W. Peck, 1830–1857

Ferdinand Peck's outlook was powerfully shaped by his unusual social situation, rooted in his family's earlier history in Chicago. His father was Philip Ferdinand Wheeler Peck (1809–1871), whose career illustrates the interrelated processes of capital formation and urban development that shaped early Chicago. Born in Providence, Rhode Island, Philip Peck was a seventh-generation Anglo-American whose forebears came from Suffolk County, England, to Hingham, Massachusetts, in 1638. His father was a prosperous wholesale merchant in Providence, and Peck trained there before going to New York City where, while still a minor, he spent a few years with a mercantile house. When he turned twenty-one, Philip Peck went to Chicago in the summer of 1830, just after the federal government had made a grant of public lands to open canal navigation that was to link the Great Lakes and the Chicago River westward to the Illinois River, leading on to the Mississippi. After deciding to settle permanently on the site of the future Chicago, Peck returned to New York City, where credit extended by his former employer enabled him to procure a supply of goods. He loaded this stock of general merchandise at Buffalo and sailed on a lake schooner to the settlement of Chicago, still known as Fort Dearborn. At that time, "but for the presence of the fort and a few log or frame houses the entire place was as unoccupied and desolate as Marquette had found it in 1673."[2]

Peck opened his store in the fort, then moved it to a log house he had built nearby in 1831. Local records indicate that this was the only house built in the settlement in that year. At an auction of lands in the newly platted town, for $78 he bought his first piece of real estate, a standard lot 80 feet wide by 100 feet deep at what became the southeast corner of LaSalle and South Water Streets (later Wacker Drive). There, in spring 1832, he built a two-story wood-frame building that became his store and home. Chicago then had no sawmills, so the black walnut lumber had to be brought from Detroit by boat. The building was later claimed to be the first of its kind in the village and formed a conspicuous landmark. In 1886 Philip Peck's sons commissioned Adler and Sullivan to design a six-story warehouse on this site, which stood there until construction of Holabird and Root's twenty-three-story LaSalle-Wacker Building in 1930, a century after Philip Peck's arrival.[3]

Philip Peck began as a commission merchant, buying and selling goods for others for a fee. Given Chicago's early role as a point of transshipment of goods between eastern manufacturers and western settlers, merchants crowded the city, yet most failed quickly and soon left town. Peck's business prospered, and like other merchants who survived, he began to invest his profits to acquire town lots in the nascent settlement. Peck's initial capital came from his former employer in New York and from other eastern friends who entrusted him with funds to invest in land speculation. He bought the lots his eastern clients requested, and others for himself, but only those he could pay for. Chicago town lots were initially bought from the federal government at the then standard price of $1.25 an acre. By 1835, expectations for the Illinois and Michigan Canal dramatically boosted local land prices to an average of $60 an acre. Land along the canal route west of Chicago was also sold, and Peck was among the first to invest in it. This land boom drew population and investors and prompted a small group of locals, including Peck, to charter the township of Chicago in 1833.[4]

Peck's flow of capital enabled him to pay for more land as he acquired it, keeping initial payments and later installments within his means. Most men who bought land in times of rising prices, as in the 1830s, were speculators hoping for quick and profitable resale. Peck bought land to hold for its eventual rental income once it was improved with commercial buildings. Federally owned land had to be paid for in full at the time of purchase, so speculators borrowed heavily from local banks to meet the sale price. Other lands were sold with a down payment of one-quarter of the price, with the balance to be paid over three years. Speculators acquired such properties with a small initial outlay and often with scant resources to meet later payments. In financial panics, like those of 1837, land values dropped, and new buyers at high prices were scarce. Overextended speculators could not meet their payments and lost their holdings. Many banks that had extended mortgages also failed. In 1837 every payment on canal lands was in default except Philip Peck's. He was remembered as the only man who never forfeited on city land purchased for himself where a second or third payment was required. The elder Peck selected his lots wisely, paid for them in full, then held most of them until his death.[5]

In 1838, at age twenty-nine, Peck "retired from active trade" as a merchant to devote full time to managing his real estate holdings and to continue in speculation for out-of-town clients. In this period most of those few merchants who ascended to the status of full-time landlords did not retire from the highly uncertain world of merchandising until their forties. In the depression following the Panic of 1837, Peck, who had faith in the city's ultimate prosperity, was in a position to buy temporarily undervalued properties, whose prices recovered as Chicago continued to grow rapidly. According to the city's tax rolls for 1849 and 1850, only 2,454 of the city's total population of 29,000 owned taxable property, and 105 had property with an assessed value of more than $10,000. Philip Peck's wealth included some twenty-four parcels of land in and beyond what later became the Loop. These holdings made up almost all of his assessed real and personal property, valued at just over

$73,000. This made Peck the fifth wealthiest Chicagoan at a time when land was routinely assessed at only 40 to 50 percent of its actual salable value. Peck's conservative approach to building up his estate enabled him to pass through the Panic of 1857 "such that he met with no reverses of consequence during his business career and his fortune grew steadily from the date of his coming to Chicago to that of his death," just after the Great Fire of 1871. At that time the inventory of Philip Peck's estate listed over $1,170,000 worth of local real property in his name, not including lands previously transferred to his sons' ownership.[6]

Like those of other leading landlords, Philip Peck's properties were on the city's South Side, which had developed as the central district since the 1830s. At that time most overland trade came to Chicago from the southeast, before bridges were built across the Chicago River to link to the North Side (via Clark Street in 1842) and to the West Side (via Lake and Randolph Streets in 1846–1847). Peck's holdings were concentrated at what became central sites on Lake, South Water, and Clark Streets and on Wabash Avenue (fig. 5).

Although the city was then primarily a shipping center, Chicago's early fortunes were based on real estate and its architectural improvements. As one scholar has observed: "Wealth and class in early Chicago cannot be understood without also looking at buildings, for these were the principal instruments of capital accumulation."[7] Philip Peck's career epitomized this pattern. Like other central property owners, he commissioned substantial buildings on his holdings, including three in the 1860s from Chicago's first architect, John Van Osdel, on South Water Street and Wabash Avenue.[8] In an era when most of the city was built of wood, these were brick and stone buildings whose materials were a measure of urban progress at a time when a higher class of activities was identified with the most substantial structures, much like the Auditorium Building half a century later. Brick was pressed from clays dug along the banks of the Chicago River's north and south branches, while limestone was first quarried in 1851 at Lemont, then about twenty miles southwest of the city. By 1857 Chicago had more than four hundred masonry buildings, over 90 percent of them commercial structures rented by merchants. Although these tenants routinely failed, their landlords prospered as new merchants flocked to the growing city. This rental system was the foundation of most elite wealth. By 1890 Philip Peck's landholdings formed the core of what had grown into Chicago's fourth largest private fortune, with the wealth of his descendants estimated at $10,000,000.[9]

In 1835 Philip Peck had married Mary Kent Wythe, a Philadelphia native who had come to Chicago a little earlier and had run a local school before her marriage. Four of their eight children died in infancy, and a fifth died as a young adult in 1884. The surviving sons, Walter (1839–1908), Clarence (1841–1916), and Ferdinand (1848–1924), all played important roles in the Auditorium's creation. Their parents' houses marked notable stages in Chicago's early architectural development. In 1836 Philip Peck had commissioned Van Osdel to design one of Chicago's first brick buildings as the Peck home on the southwest corner of LaSalle and Washington Streets, where his sons commissioned Adler and Sullivan to design the Chicago Stock Exchange in

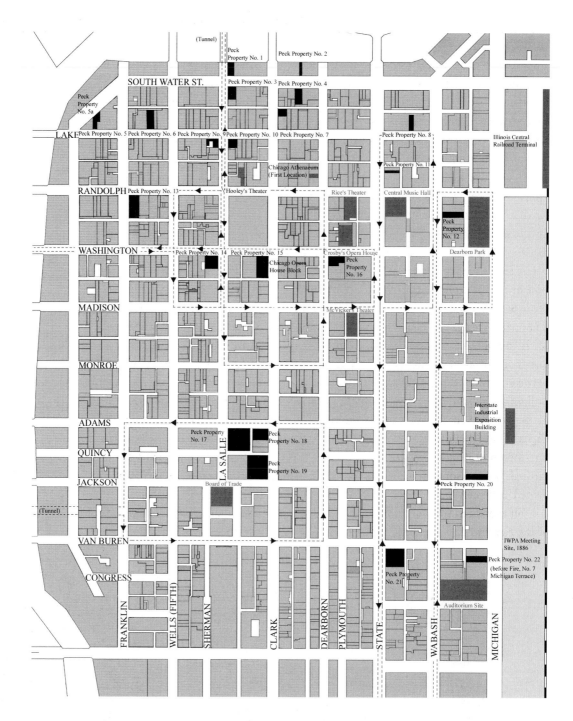

Figure 5

Chicago theaters and related sites to 1886 (in dark gray) and properties of Philip Peck and Peck estate to 1897 (in black), numbered as in the appendix listing Peck properties in central Chicago (p. 401), which notes sources for identification of Peck properties. This map also shows cable car lines of 1881 and sites of Dearborn Park (1833); Rice's Theater (1847); McVicker's Theater (first built 1857); Illinois Central Railroad Depot (1856; demolished 1912); Michigan Terrace (1856; destroyed 1871); Crosby's Opera House (1865; destroyed 1871); Hooley's Theater (1872; demolished 1926); Inter-state Industrial Exposition Building (1873; demolished 1893); Central Music Hall (1879; demolished 1900); Chicago Athenaeum, first site at 48–54 Dearborn Street (1878; demolished); Chicago Board of Trade (1882–1885; demolished 1929); Chicago Opera House (1884–1885; demolished 1912); International Working People's Association meeting site at Van Buren and Congress (1886); and Chicago Auditorium Building site. Drawing by author.

1893–1894.[10] By the time of Ferdinand's birth in 1848, the family had moved to a villa on a garden estate extending along the north side of Jackson Boulevard from Clark to LaSalle Streets, which became the site of the Grand Pacific Hotel in 1869. Of his childhood in this house, Ferdinand recalled: "The great amusement of the boys was skating. What is now the Lake-Front was a basin. It was our skating pond, and there we would assemble on Christmas day for high old times. I was able to cross lots between our house and the basin, for there was only open ground between the two. There wasn't a paved street between Clark and the lake. We had fun, too, coasting down a bank between Michigan Avenue and what we called the inner basin."[11] From his youth, Peck felt a personal and proprietary tie to Chicago's lakefront, an attitude that shaped his proposals for the Auditorium Building.

After the construction of a lakeshore protection barrier in 1851 and the conclusion of negotiations to accommodate the Illinois Central Railroad along the lakeshore in 1852, Chicagoans developed an elite district along the lakefront. Philip Peck was one of eleven citizens who joined to acquire the site and fund construction of Michigan Terrace in 1856 (fig. 6). Designed by William W. Boyington (1818–1898), this block of eleven limestone-fronted row houses stood along Michigan Avenue between Van Buren and Congress Streets, partly on the site of the Auditorium Building. Peck and his family lived there, at 203 South Michigan, until the Great Fire of 1871 destroyed this block. Michigan Terrace was the architectural symbol of Chicago's antebellum era when all the city's real property was owned by fewer than one-fourth of its adult white males. Contrary to the myth of an egalitarian frontier through the Jacksonian period, tax records in 1850 show that 1 percent of Chicagoans owned 52 percent of the city's wealth.[12]

Yet even then the lakefront served not only as a recreational ground for the sons of the rich but as a setting for protests against economic inequality. Landlords like

Figure 6

William Boyington, Michigan Terrace, including house of Philip F. W. Peck, on west side of Michigan Avenue from Congress Street north to Van Buren Street, Chicago (1856; destroyed in Great Fire of 1871), where the Auditorium Building later stood, with Central Depot in background at right. Philip Peck owned and occupied with his family the seventh house from the terrace's south end, with each house marked by a width of three windows and an enlarged cornice bracket. Lithograph by Charles Shober from a drawing by Edward Whitefield, 1863. Courtesy of the Chicago Historical Society, ICHi-18510.

Peck were at the top of society and merchants who rented built space were in a volatile middle position, but the skilled tradesmen who built these structures were the first to stage urban demonstrations for better conditions. On Saturday, 6 August 1853, at four o'clock in the afternoon, 3,000 to 4,000 building workers walked off construction sites and assembled in Dearborn Park on Michigan Avenue south of Randolph Street, the city's first and then still only public park, where the old Chicago Public Library was built in 1893 (fig. 5). Led by fife and drum, these workers marched through the streets to demand a reduction in the Saturday workday from ten to eight hours, ending at 4:00 P.M., with no reduction in pay. For two weeks the lakefront protests continued, with the mayor pleading for calm in the face of abolitionist speeches that implied a parallel between Negro slavery in the South and the condition of northern white workers. Yet builders refused to yield, and the cause of the eight-hour day was initially lost. The issue fueled labor protests for the next thirty years through the Haymarket clash of 1886, whose violence prompted Ferdinand Peck's proposal to build the Auditorium Building. In 1886 the first site he wanted for this structure was the still unoccupied Dearborn Park.[13]

Because Peck's fortune and similar ones derived from the appreciated rental values of land as building sites, early Chicago capitalists took an active interest in government. They had a large and real stake in their city's social and economic well-being, since it affected the value of their properties. In Chicago's earliest days, Philip Peck had joined the town's first military company, organized to fight in the Black Hawk War of 1832. In a treaty with the United States signed at Chicago the next year, local tribes sold their lands east of the Mississippi in Illinois. Peck was also a member of Chicago's "Hook and Ladder Company No. 1 . . . who used to run to the fires, dragging their engines after them, in the Forties and Fifties."[14] He also helped to organize the city's first post office and voted in the city's first election in 1837. Chicago's first regular religious services in 1832 were held on his store's second floor, where the minister boarded. For the next thirty years the nascent municipal government was designed to serve Peck and other local landowners. With low property assessments, low taxes, and low budgets, antebellum Chicago was modeled on a business corporation that acted chiefly to benefit property owners as analogous to stockholders. Major expenditures for urban improvements were funded by special assessments of affected property owners and by bond issues. Almost all mayors and most aldermen were from this landed class, which led in municipal affairs through the Civil War.[15]

In the 1850s this political situation created the framework for the beginning of ethnic conflict that would shape the city's social history for the next generation. In 1854, 35,857 of Chicago's 65,872 residents (about 54 percent) were foreign born, and the percentage increased steadily through the nineteenth century. The largest ethnic minority was German. From 1846 to 1855 more than a million Germans immigrated to the United States. Immigration peaked in 1849 after the failed European revolutions of 1848. By 1854 the nativist Know-Nothing movement had gathered national momentum, and its effects generated Chicago's first full-scale rioting. Nonnatural-ized immigrants who had not lived in Illinois in 1848 could not vote. Thus almost all local German immigrants were disfranchised. In March 1855 the Know-Noth-ings' American Party elected its candidate as mayor, and the entire city government was in the group's hands. Every applicant for a municipal position, including the new police force, was compelled to prove he had been born in the United States. The new nativist administration's agenda focused on a temperance crusade in-tended not "to conserve the ends of public morality; but purely and simply to strike at the habits and customs of one class of foreigners—the Germans."[16] Accordingly, the city's liquor license fee was raised from fifty dollars to three hundred to drive out the small beer dealers who served the city's German community concentrated on the North Side, where land was less expensive. The new nativist mayor selectively enforced laws on Sunday closing of alcohol-selling establishments, ordering police to close German beer gardens while saloons frequented by native-born Americans were untouched. The Germans organized, comparing such harassment to the con-ditions of southern chattel slavery. In April 1855 a climactic clash between the police and armed German mobs storming across new bridges into the South Side left sev-eral dead, with scores temporarily imprisoned. Afterward the excesses of the Know-Nothings were locally repudiated, and they subsided the next year when Chicago's Germans joined the nascent antislavery Republican Party.[17]

The city's political battles were fought not only on its streets and squares, but through its cultural institutions, notably its theaters. While energetic and enterpris-ing in the extreme, the local landowning elite had interests that depended on the continuing rise in their properties' rental values, made possible by Chicago's rapid growth. Such growth depended on these citizens' ability to continually attract the interest and investment of nonresident capitalists from the eastern United States. Leaders saw civil order and physical infrastructure as foundations of local urban development, but they also viewed Chicago's cultural life as an asset to be developed to make the city more attractive to outside interests and new wealthy residents. As one founder of the Chicago Historical Society said in 1856, Chicago must have "cul-ture, taste, beauty, art, literature, or there is danger that our city will become a town of mere traders and money getters; crude, unlettered, sharp, and grasping."[18] From this era through the Auditorium's creation thirty years later, economic and cultural developments were not competing but complementary priorities, both intersecting with local politics.

The conjunction of political and cultural interests appeared in the histories of Chicago's first theater buildings as both places of entertainment and urban monu-ments. In 1847 the city's boosters outbid St. Louis to host the national River and Harbor Convention, whose aim was to draw eastern private investment to Chicago, particularly its railroads. Approximately 20,000 delegates converged on the city during the two weeks before their meeting on 5 July. This was the first conclave that drew representatives to Chicago from throughout the Union. These representatives included Abraham Lincoln, who visited the city for the first time. An impressive parade of Chicago's firefighting companies suggested the safety of outside investment in local buildings. Anticipating the convention, theatrical manager and actor John B. Rice (1809–1874) arrived in Chicago and created the city's first permanent building for public amusement, known as Rice's Theater, on the south side of Randolph Street west of State (fig. 5). It was constructed in fifty-four days, and Rice opened his theater on 28 June 1847, a week before the River and Harbor Convention, at the height of the influx of its delegates. His hall was a two-story wood-frame building, externally plain yet with an ornamental interior that featured furnished boxes surrounding a central pit, with all seats affording a good view of the stage. Puritanical prejudice against the theater induced the city council to impose a heavy license fee of twenty-five dollars a month, yet Rice's Theater drew consistently large audiences with a respectable dramatic repertoire offered by its own stock company. Rebuilt after a fire in 1850, this structure housed the city's first season of opera in that year, and the house had no effective competition until 1857. By then financial success enabled Rice, like Philip Peck and other successful merchants, to retire from trade and tend to his investments in urban real estate.[19]

Rice's Theater served the English-speaking community, yet Chicago's immigrant Germans established a semiprofessional theater as early as 1849. Soon after the urban warfare of April 1855, Germans responded to the harassment of the Know-Nothings by erecting a social center, Deutsches Haus, at the corner of Wells and Indiana Streets on the Near North Side. The structure was the capstone of Chicago's first ethnic neighborhood, surrounded by German churches, hostelries, shops, and trade unions of workers in nearby small-scale industries, notably furniture making, metalworking, and printing. German was the language of all local activity, as it was in Deutsches Haus's spacious theater, which opened in spring 1856 with a performance of Schiller's *Kabale und Liebe* (Intrigue and love), preceded by a festive prologue read by a local German poet. The same cultural impulse underlay the creation of Adler and Sullivan's Schiller Theater Building, which opened in 1892 for similar productions serving the German-speaking community.[20]

The early success of the Schiller repertoire at Deutsches Haus preceded the creation of the city's first architecturally ambitious theater, built in 1857 by James H. McVicker (1822–1896), another actor turned impresario, on the South Side at Madison Street west of State (figs. 5 and 7). Born in New York City, McVicker had an itinerant acting career in the southern United States before coming to Chicago in 1848 to join Rice's company, where he became the leading comic actor. Continuing to tour regionally and in England, McVicker became a theatrical manager in St. Louis, returning to Chicago in 1857 after Rice's retirement from his theater early that year. With financial backing from St. Louis, McVicker built his first theater, which opened in November 1857 after that year's financial panic.[21] Costing $85,000, this structure was "the most substantial, convenient, safe, and costly theater building then standing in the West," with a seating capacity of 2,500. The plan included a

Figure 7

McVicker's Theater, on south side of
Madison Street west of State, Chicago
(1857), before rebuilding of February
1871. From Andreas, *History of Chicago*,
vol. 2. Courtesy of the Chicago Historical
Society, ICHi-31470.

parquet with a rear dress circle and balcony, while boxes flanked the proscenium arch. To aid the theater financially, the building's front housed rentable stores and offices, as would Adler and Sullivan's later structures for McVicker on the same site. A local reporter concluded: "For the first time since Chicago took rank as one of the first cities of the Union, she has a Theater worthy of her citizens who patronize the drama."[22]

As with Rice's Theater, the scale and timing of McVicker's investment were keyed to Chicago's regional economic growth. The city had had a fourfold increase in population (to 93,000) since Rice's Theater opened a decade earlier. During the early 1850s, Chicago began to emerge as a rail center for agricultural products, with major lines connecting to the west and south, giving the city an advantage over St. Louis. In 1856 competition with St. Louis for the grain trade prompted Illinois leaders to complete the first railroad bridge across the Mississippi River for the Chicago and Rock Island Railroad to reach Iowa's farmlands. In the same year the Illinois Central Railroad connected southward to Cairo, Illinois, near the juncture of the Mississippi and Ohio Rivers, below St. Louis. North along this line came cotton, sugar, and other southern products for shipment east. In 1856 the city's role as a concentrated regional market for agricultural production prompted the Chicago Board of Trade to adopt standardized procedures for inspection and grading of grains. These efforts laid the foundations for Chicago's regional dominance, making it the opportune city in which to open a new theater; hence McVicker's return from St. Louis in 1857. On the drop curtain of his new stage, a painting depicted the cities of Rock Island, Illinois, and Davenport, Iowa, connected by the new railroad bridge. McVicker's was Chicago's first cultural showpiece whose patrons included passengers on new railways converging at the city.[23]

In contrast to the German theater, McVicker's became the regional center of English drama. McVicker was a generational contemporary of Junius Brutus Booth, a member of the famous family of American actors known for their roles in Shakespearean tragedies. Their success reflected a widespread tradition of popular appreciation of Shakespeare and other English dramatists central to the vitality of American theater before the Civil War. Having been schooled in this tradition, McVicker frequently played roles in productions of the stock company he formed when he built his first theater in Chicago. Soon after his theater opened in 1857, its attractions included Edwin Booth (who later became McVicker's son-in-law) acting in *Richard III*.[24] McVicker's stock company regularly presented the eighteenth-century plays of Richard Sheridan and Oliver Goldsmith, countering the German community's staging of Schiller's works. Before the Civil War, McVicker's Theater was a standard of local cultural identity. Yet the war soon transformed Chicago's economic and political life, prompting new investment in theaters before 1865.

Crosby's Opera House and Elite Political Decline

The early phase of the Civil War depressed Chicago's economy as connections to the South were cut at a time when much of the city's capital was invested there. Yet by 1863 the demand for midwestern food products to feed the Union armies and to export to Europe, which was suffering from poor harvests, turned Chicago's fortunes around. As the war progressed, the city for the first time became a major manufacturing center whose factories produced all manner of goods and equipment for the North's armies. War profiteering flourished, and Chicago became a magnet for immigrant laborers whose presence began to alter the balance of political power in the immediate postwar years. As in the antebellum period, the influx of capital was channeled into commercial buildings concentrated in the city's center. The leading investors were usually established landowners, since even by the 1850s the prices of such sites had advanced beyond the means of most newly wealthy citizens. Although the Panic of 1857 and the start of the Civil War temporarily depressed land values, still very few citizens could afford to make the socially decisive transition from merchant to landlord, which remained the defining mark of elite status. In this situation, major proprietors like Philip Peck remained prominent as members of a relatively closed club.[25]

Among those who did cross this line before the war years was Uranus C. Crosby, who made a unique contribution to Chicago's cultural life by building Crosby's Opera House, the antetype of Ferdinand Peck's Auditorium. Although they were pioneering for their period, neither Rice's Theater nor McVicker's attempted to become a comprehensive urban cultural center. This ideal did inspire Crosby's monument, which opened in April 1865 (figs. 5 and 8). An observer of 1890 recalled that Crosby's Opera House was "the finest building erected in Chicago up to that time, and held its preeminent position up to 1871, when it was destroyed."[26]

Although this structure was not rebuilt after the Great Fire, so strong was its hold on local collective memory that it was illustrated along with extant theaters in 1889 (fig. 4). As one editor wrote in that year: "The opening of the Auditorium is to the Chicago of today what the opening of Crosby's Opera-House was to the Chicago of 1865."[27] Crosby, who lived to attend the Auditorium Theater's opening, had a career that typified the city's rapid growth during the war, when its lumberyards, stockyards, and meatpacking houses became the world's largest such operations. Before and especially during the war years, Crosby profited enormously from distilling and selling alcohol. Long a supporter of local music, theater, and visual art, by 1863 he chose to invest his fortune in a structure that would realize "his desire to foster a love of the higher ideals in art, and in music, and in drama."[28] Much like Peck's Auditorium, Crosby's Opera House was architecturally extraordinary yet financially problematic.

Crosby sought not only to build Chicago's first edifice explicitly for grand opera, but also to include a lecture and concert hall, an art gallery, studios for artists and musicians, and stores for related businesses. He obtained 140 feet of frontage on the north side of Washington Street, midway between State and Dearborn, leasing the property from John B. Rice. With the support of Chicago's business leaders, Crosby pursued his project by hiring one of their architects, William Boyington, with whom he "visited the principal cities of the Union, with a view to gaining a practical knowledge of how to construct an opera house."[29] Crosby and Boyington also visited Italy, several of whose opera houses inspired the decorative program of their Chicago building. One United States model for both patron and architect was likely the New York Academy of Music, opened in 1854 (fig. 9). This building's relation to Crosby's Opera House prefigured that of New York's Metropolitan Opera House to Chicago's Auditorium, exemplifying the interactive dynamic with Manhattan that shaped Chicago's aspirations for music and architecture.

Figure 8

Boyington, Crosby's Opera House, on north side of Washington Street midway between State and Dearborn Streets, Chicago (opened April 1865; destroyed October 1871). Drawing by James W. Sheahan, published by Jevni and Almini, 1866. Courtesy of the Chicago Historical Society, ICHi-01727.

Figure 9

Alexander Sältzer, New York Academy
of Music, northeast corner of Fourteenth
Street and Irving Place, New York City
(1854; remodeled 1866; demolished
1926). Reception of Russian Grand Duke
Alexis at a performance of Gounod's
Faust by Strakosch Italian opera troupe,
December 1872, showing proscenium
boxes and family boxes in balcony as
remodeled 1866. Harvard Theatre
Collection, Houghton Library.

Like its counterparts in Boston and Philadelphia, the New York Academy of
Music was a private commercial project with no government subvention, unlike the
European state opera houses that were among its models. Manhattan capitalists organized to sell stock in the venture, which was financed by public subscription.
Their effort responded to repeated indications of local popular demand for Italian
opera at moderate prices. The attempt to include large numbers may also have been
a reaction to antielite riots of May 1849, when crowds had attacked the nearby Astor
Place Opera House as a bastion of privilege. This had been the worst civil distur-
bance in New York City's history, with one of its focal issues being popular access to
this theater, which seated 1,500 to 1,800.[30] Even the name *opera house,* with its elite
and foreign association, was replaced by the term *academy,* which conveyed emphasis on musical education as an institutional purpose. The Academy's sponsors also
valued an opera house as a social setting for the city's financial elite and an attraction
to traveling businessmen who frequented those cities with the most appealing entertainment. With its European court origins, opera in New York City was culturally
prestigious, yet it was also acceptable as a family amusement before its respectability
eroded with changed repertoires of the 1860s. Limited private capital meant that

investors put minimal resources into purchasing a site, securing only enough ground to accommodate a large auditorium and its necessary spatial appendages. They commissioned a volumetrically simple theater with a relatively unadorned exterior and favored including or being adjacent to revenue-generating facilities controlled by the same investors.[31]

The architect selected for New York's Academy of Music was the German-trained Alexander Sältzer (1814–1883), who designed the theater for a site on the northeast corner of Fourteenth Street and Irving Place, one block east of Union Square and directly adjacent to Tammany Hall on the east. A number of theaters were later built nearby.[32] Inside its Rundbogenstil (round-arch style) exterior, the New York Academy of Music displayed a distinctly American arrangement of seating in its auditorium. To the 1850s, with few exceptions, European opera houses followed the seating conventions of their premodern counterparts at royal courts. From the prototype of Milan's La Scala (1776–1778), opera houses for Europe's bourgeoisie featured horseshoe-shaped auditoriums whose main floor or parquet was surrounded by five or six tiers of private boxes, with each box seating six to eight. The boxes were owned privileges of prominent local families who, when they chose not to attend themselves, could rent the boxes to others or allow guests to use them without charge. Boxholders were an opera house's principal patrons, with occupants of boxes making up a high proportion of the total audience, typically numbering about 2,000 in major European houses to the 1850s. In the English-speaking world, the prime example of this type was London's Covent Garden, redesigned by Sir Edward M. Barry in 1856–1858 after a fire (fig. 10). The convention of multiple box tiers, with proscenium boxes, prevailed at Paris's Opéra National, opened in 1847 as a democratic alternative to the state-run Paris Opera (officially called the Académie de Musique) and to the Opéra Comique.[33]

Figure 10

Edward M. Barry, Royal Italian Opera House, Covent Garden, London, as rebuilt 1856–1858. From *Builder* (London), 22 May 1858. Courtesy of Watkinson Library, Trinity College, Hartford, Connecticut.

When the directors of New York's Academy of Music announced the architectural competition for their new building in 1853, they decided on a larger opera house of a different type. To achieve the goal of affordable opera, meaning low prices for individual seats, the house had to have a large seating capacity to generate enough revenue to cover the productions' costs. The architect was asked to make plans for a building holding 5,500 with tiered balconies of open seating rather than private boxes above the parquet to accommodate such a huge audience. To approximate the required number of seats for the new Academy, Sältzer made a horseshoe-shaped plan with the auditorium twice as deep as the stage. The house had many gradations of seating, beginning with the parquet (whose rows had no aisles and had to be entered at the sides) and extending to family boxes at the back of the first and second balconies. The floors of both parquet and balconies inclined downward toward the stage, which was flanked by a small number of proscenium boxes framed by pilasters. Originally there were also boxes on the stage itself. Both types of boxes were to be showcases for members of Manhattan's wealthy families.

At the Academy's opening on 2 October 1854, its interior struck one observer as "a tolerably faithful copy of the Opera House in Berlin," designed by Georg W. Knobelsdorff in 1741–1743 and remodeled in 1843–1844 by Carl F. Langhans, whose earlier acoustic studies Sältzer later cited in his book on acoustics.[34] While imitating the basic spatial shape and proscenium design of this royal opera house for the much larger New York Academy of Music, Sältzer replaced its box tiers with hundreds of balcony seats around his horseshoe's sides. Many of these seats had either no view or only a partial view of the stage, which could be clearly seen only from the parquet, the parquet circle under the lowest balcony, and the central section of the balconies. Thus the conventional horseshoe plan proved ill adapted to the democratic ideal of relatively few boxes. Although the Academy was largely a blunder in its sight lines, it nevertheless earned a reputation for superb acoustics, partly owing to the depth of the proscenium arch, which helped to contain and direct sound emerging from the stage. Sältzer wrote that he had immersed himself in existing literature on acoustics (some twenty books), which had developed continually in Europe since the late eighteenth century. He credited his Academy's acoustic success to his lining its walls and ceilings with wood boards "tongued and grooved so that every part formed a sound-board." The galleries also descended an unprecedented eight feet from the rear middle down toward the stage on either side so "the sound reaches directly to every spot without interruption."[35]

Created in a period of economic prosperity before the Panic of 1857, the New York Academy of Music's architectural merger of a European court opera house with a democratic American commercial theater signified opera's range of social appeal. As Lawrence Levine has written, Americans in the mid-nineteenth century viewed opera as "an art form that was *simultaneously* popular and elite. That is, it was attended both by large numbers of people who derived great pleasure from it and experienced it in the context of their normal everyday culture, *and* by smaller socially and economically elite groups who derived both pleasure and social confirmation from it."[36] Yet the Academy only slowly fulfilled such expectations. Initially its unprecedentedly capacious auditorium could not be filled, even as ticket prices were reduced, and it was not until the Civil War that the Academy consistently yielded a profit and became Manhattan's social center.[37]

In 1866 a New York reporter wrote that the Academy of Music had "led to the erection of similar opera houses in all the principal cities of the East and West."[38] What had given the Academy its distinction among Manhattan's several operatic theaters was its resident company of performers, which included the most notable Italian singers of the period. In the 1850s and 1860s, opera in the United States meant almost exclusively Italian opera, the emerging Wagnerian tradition not yet having become popular. It was thus the Italian opera troupe managed by conductor Jacob Grau that came to Chicago to open Crosby's Opera House on its completion in April 1865, just after Grau's company finished an opera season at the New York Academy. Crosby's Opera House and its land had cost $700,000, compared with $335,000 for New York's Academy. Unlike Sältzer's exterior of stucco over brick, Boyington's five-story front was entirely of locally quarried "Athens marble, in the modern Italian style," with a projecting central pavilion below a mansard attic.[39] Flanking its two-story arched doorway were four street-level stores, each 30 by 180 feet, rented by Chicago's two premier piano and musical instrument manufacturers, the city's leading music publisher, and its most fashionable restaurant. Above were three stories of offices and artists' studios. In niches between windows on the third and fourth floors, local sculptor Leonard Volk carved six life-size allegorical figures, four of which represented Music, Painting, Sculpture, and Commerce. He also rendered Italianate cherubs in high relief in the spandrels around the main entrance's arch. Before Chicago had public art museums, Crosby's skylit fourth-floor art gallery displayed his own large and valuable collection of paintings and sculptures, including works by such recognized American masters as Jasper Cropsey and Albert Bierstadt. The gallery also displayed works on loan from local and eastern collections. In 1866 the Chicago Academy of Art and Design, precursor to the Art Institute of Chicago, held its first meetings in Crosby's Opera House.[40]

As a cultural center the building's frontal lecture rooms and its music hall facing east onto State Street were used by many groups. Although the New York Academy of Music's charter provided for establishing a music school to train singers and instrumentalists to support the opera company, such a school was never developed. By contrast, Crosby's Opera House became "the home of music in Chicago," where "the great singing societies held their exercises" and where local musicians had their headquarters. The opera house's painters of scenic art and its stage architect were the local leaders in creating theatrical backdrops. In the music hall, concerts were "held even while opera was going on in the main structure, and the strains of the two entertainments sometimes mingled."[41] This room also hosted nontheatrical events, such as meetings of the city's public school teachers. In 1868 the main theater also held the Republican national convention, where Grant was nominated for president. With such a range of civic functions, the building was seen retrospectively by Chicagoans as "certainly a worthy forerunner of the Auditorium."[42] This was the case in part because neither of these opera houses had received government funding. As one contemporary said of Crosby: "Here is a private citizen of the Republic who has done for Art, what in monarchies is done only by Emperors and Kings."[43] Twenty years later Ferdinand Peck would seek to do likewise.

Accessed by stairs leading to the second-floor grand foyer behind the frontal block, Crosby's main theater (90 feet wide and 150 feet deep) held over 3,000 in a parquet and dress circle on the main floor, a second-level balcony with fifty-six boxes in two central tiers, and a third-level gallery called the family circle, which was reached by a separate entrance. There were also six proscenium boxes framed by tall Corinthian half columns flanking the stage. This opera house was Chicago's first theater to have such boxes, their inclusion consistent with Crosby's intention of creating an elite cultural center. Prices were "on the same scale as at the New York Academy of Music," with the least expensive gallery reserved seats for the opening costing fifty cents. Yet even at this price, opera was then expensive relative to plays at local theaters, whose lowest-priced seats cost fifteen cents.[44]

The interior of Crosby's Opera House was extravagantly praised in numerous accounts (fig. 11). Those who saw it "agreed that it had the charm and elegance of a European theatre."[45] Across the ceiling above the proscenium was a copy of Guido Reni's fresco *Aurora,* showing the goddess riding her chariot through the clouds, with images of Comedy and Tragedy on each side. Above, a set of twelve sunken panels containing composers' portraits encircled the ceiling's central crowning dome, lit by hundreds of concealed gas lamps whose light reflected up into the canopy. With its white and gold walls and light blue upholstery, the house was commended for "the tone and harmony of the coloring. All is quiet, subdued; very favorably contrasting with the glaring reds, whites, and yellows of most public structures. There is nothing to offend or fatigue the eye."[46] Claiming it was the handsomest auditorium in the country, the opening program stated that "American Opera houses generally, being of recent construction, possess advantages and conveniences which are not to be found in any of the well-known establishments of the Old World." Boyington's interior had superb stage lighting, dressing rooms, mechanisms for changing scenery, and ventilation and was "a model in its acoustic qualities, and in the range of vision which, from every part of it, it gives to the spectator. These merits are so marked and peculiar that every one who enters the auditorium of this building will be able to see and hear PERFECTLY."

Figure 11

Boyington, Crosby's Opera House, interior, showing parquet (with armchairs behind orchestra), parquet circle, balcony, and gallery, with proscenium boxes flanking stage, at concert in honor of the presidential party, 6 September 1866. Courtesy of the Chicago Historical Society, ICHi-18413.

Grau's production standards were high, so the house was to serve Italian opera as "the most exalted, delightful and refining amusement of the age, and the only one where fashion, wealth and taste reign supreme."[47]

Emphasis on the elite character of Crosby's building and its entertainments contrasted with workers' culture in prefire Chicago. In the face of rising living costs during the Civil War and unemployment owing to the postwar economic slowdown, local ironmongers, machinists, blacksmiths, those engaged in the building trades, and other groups had organized vocationally and politically. Many of these workers were Germans whose trade groups had united in 1857 to form the Chicago Workers' Association, or Chicagoer Arbeiter-Verein, whose membership grew to 1,000 by 1865. Its centrally located rented quarters housed performances, meetings, and festive gatherings in keeping with the society's educational and social goals. A notable feature of this facility was its library of three thousand books, at a time when Chicago did not yet have a public library. This collection helped to support the union's educational program of lectures and an evening school. On Sundays whole families gathered at the hall to drink beer and sing songs, apart from the reproving attitudes of some Anglo-Americans who objected to both alcohol and theater on the Sabbath. In October 1864 a branch institution of 130 members, the Social Workers' Association of the West Side (Sozialer Arbeiterverein der Westseite), had built the city's first worker-owned structure with its own meeting hall. In the late 1860s these societies' emphasis on nonradical politics and educational opportunities epitomized the aims of the eight-hour movement. This was meant to bring workingmen "more time for moral, intellectual and social culture," like that available for the more privileged at Crosby's Opera House.[48]

Two events in the winter and spring of 1867 highlight the contrast between bourgeois and workers' culture in postwar Chicago. Although the opening of Crosby's in April 1865 had been hailed as a major civic event, its opera house was not in continuous use, since no regular company was employed. By May 1866 Crosby announced that, in the face of financial failure, he and his local supporters would organize a public lottery to recover costs. The grand prize would be the building itself, while its collections of art, totaling 302 objects, would also go to lottery winners. The event was heavily publicized, and approximately 175,000 tickets were sold for five dollars each. The scheme aroused great regional public interest. Large numbers of middle-class ticket buyers were entranced by the fantasy of owning a monument to upper-class taste. A ticket-holding visitor to one of the house's last opera performances "glanced complacently about, between the acts, and viewed the noble edifice which soon might be his own."[49] The drawing itself, on 21 January 1867, drew large numbers of visitors to Chicago. The event took place on the opera house's stage, where winning tickets drawn from one wheel were matched with prize tickets drawn from another. The winner of the building was not present but was notified, and he agreed that for $200,000 he would sell the opera house back to Crosby, who relinquished its management. The theater was extensively renovated for a reopening on 9 October 1871, but the local public never saw the new interior, since the Great Fire destroyed the structure that same evening.[50]

The opening and the selling of Crosby's Opera House revealed the tendency of Chicago's middle class to identify with the cultural initiatives of local high capital. Yet the city's politicized workers in this period focused their energies on defeating the local elite through municipal elections. The workers' hand was strengthened by new voting rules adopted in February 1865, which dropped the requirement that nonnaturalized immigrants had to have been residents in 1848 if they were to vote after residing in the state for one year. The new rules of 1865 granted the vote to all white males age twenty-one or over who had lived in Illinois for at least a year and in Chicago for six months. In this period, former theater manager John Rice's public visibility and popularity commended him to the local Union Party, which mainly represented Chicago's property holders, and it supported his election as mayor in 1865 and 1867. In this office he defended the party's interests against the political efforts of the nascent trades assembly, which organized to elect candidates for the city council who supported a legally limited eight-hour workday.[51]

The election of March 1866 was the first to place friends of labor on the council, which then advanced an ordinance limiting the local workday to eight hours for all laborers and mechanics hired by the city. Mayor Rice opposed the measure, yet attempts to block it were overcome by political pressure on the council. This electoral victory moved the Illinois legislature to follow in March 1867 with passage of the nation's first statewide eight-hour law for all mechanical trades and arts. This statute marked the first major defeat of Chicago's business leaders, yet these employers developed various means of opposing its implementation. In protest, on 1 May 1867, the day the eight-hour law officially took effect, thousands of Chicago's workers representing forty-eight unions staged their first major demonstration, a "grand civic procession" including banners, floats, and models, that moved from Lake Street on the West Side to the lakeshore. Stretching "more than a mile long, the procession made a deep impression on the thousands of onlookers who had gathered along the streets and especially at the intersections." They saw each major trade with its own display, so that "the marble cutters [over half of whom were German] were represented by a four-horse wagon carrying various monuments and marble products."[52] The bricklayers marched behind, 230 strong, the sign of hammer and trowel embroidered on their white aprons. They carried an American flag, a French tricolor, and their association's banner, but not yet the red flag as a symbol of socialist or communist revolution. The event culminated in speeches at the main rally on the lakefront, held just north of the block of Michigan Terrace, where Philip Peck and other wealthy families lived. There Mayor Rice again implored the workers to compromise, while their leaders successfully urged them to stand firm. The citywide strike that began the next day was broken within two weeks, and the eight-hour issue remained dormant until the mid-1880s. Yet the procession did initiate a local tradition of protest on May Day, long before it became the internationally recognized date for mass demonstrations of labor's solidarity.

The Great Fire's Aftermath and the Inter-state Industrial Exposition Building

Politically and culturally, Chicago's urban society was divided along class lines before the Great Fire, an event with numerous consequences. For Ferdinand Peck, the fire was doubly tragic. After passing through his local public elementary school, Peck had transferred to the city's one high school, where his schoolmates included the future architect Daniel H. Burnham. Graduating as salutatorian in 1865, Peck went on to study literature at the old University of Chicago and then graduated from that university's Union College of Law in 1868, being admitted to the bar in 1869 at age twenty-one. The following year he married Tilla Spalding, who subsequently had an active civic role in Chicago.[53] Before the fire, Ferdinand had entered private legal practice. The fire destroyed his family's home on Michigan Terrace as he and relatives rescued possessions and dragged them to the lakefront, watching their whole block destroyed by the blaze as it swept northward. Philip Peck had been seriously ill for several months, and he died at Ferdinand's home (then farther south on Michigan Avenue) after an accident on Saturday, 21 October, twelve days after the fire.[54] These events hastened the redirection of Ferdinand's career. After the Great Fire, he and his older brother Clarence assumed management of the Peck estate, whose value, like that of other Chicago properties, dropped with the loss of nearly all built improvements in the city's center. Yet the Chicago the Pecks faced as large property owners had changed politically from their youth, and Ferdinand Peck was among those who responded actively to its postfire social dilemmas.

By the time of the Great Fire, the efforts of labor groups to achieve political supremacy in municipal elections had succeeded as they endorsed candidates for office who were friendly to labor's interests. This process ensured that large proprietors like the Pecks were effectively shut out of local government, which was now dominated by a city council of ward-based politicians. These officeholders managed an extensive network of political patronage that had begun to emerge during the war. Whereas Chicago's original landowning elite had been Anglo-American, the new ward leaders were mostly Irish and German, representing those immigrants who made up 72 percent of the city's population by 1860.[55] As a number of historians have detailed, after the fire local holders of large wealth like the Pecks continued to exercise disproportionate influence over urban life, but they would do so most effectively in economic and cultural affairs, operating outside direct political channels of officeholding and government leadership.[56]

The structure that emerged as a statement of capital's power after the fire was the Inter-state Industrial Exposition Building, completed by September 1873 on Michigan Avenue's east side, centered at Adams Street (figs. 5 and 12). This project was the first of the postfire period to demonstrate "the power of syndicates or of consolidated money interests to bring forth large buildings."[57] It had grown out of what had originally been two distinct efforts: one to create a permanent home for an annual regional exposition in Chicago, and the second to stage a singular special

Figure 12

Boyington, Inter-state Industrial Exposition
Building, east side of Michigan Avenue
centered on Adams Street, Chicago (1873;
demolished 1893); Blomgren Brothers
and Company. From Andreas, *History of
Chicago*, vol. 3. Courtesy of the Chicago
Historical Society, ICHi-31742.

event to commemorate the city's rapid reconstruction after the fire. A series of
meetings led to the formation of a joint stock company in March 1873, the first local
organization of this kind to erect a major building. Over five hundred subscribers
raised a capital stock of $250,000. Officers and members of this company's executive
committee included Joseph Medill, publisher of the *Chicago Tribune,* who was elected
as a reform mayor immediately after the fire; Potter Palmer, a real estate magnate;
Wirt Dexter, a corporate lawyer for the Illinois Central Railroad; and Nathaniel
Fairbank, a lard manufacturer, who played a key role on the finance committee.
These men were also among the leaders of Chicago's Relief and Aid Society, a private organization entrusted with dispensing the considerable funds donated from
beyond the city to aid Chicago's recovery. Dexter and Fairbank were among the exposition's supporters who later played leading roles in the Auditorium Building's
realization. As in the Auditorium, purchases of stock in the exposition were promoted as nonremunerative and civic contributions rather than as profitable commercial investments, and the exposition operated with a deficit for its first two
years. The project's goal was to assert Chicago's leadership over its midwestern rivals,
St. Louis and Cincinnati, which also held annual expositions.[58]

Initially persuaded of the exposition's public value, the city council permitted
the company to use a portion of Lake Front Park north of Van Buren Street to erect
the Exposition Building, whose plans William Boyington had developed. At that
time the site was described as "a quiet part of the city, exposed to the view of but
few who pass it and repass it on suburban trains. Michigan Avenue, in that part of
its course, is not explored by many."[59] In this place Boyington's structure was designed to "exclude every appearance of temporary building or ground" that had

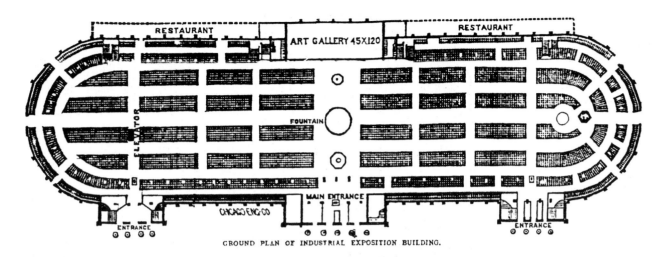

GROUND PLAN OF INDUSTRIAL EXPOSITION BUILDING.

characterized Chicago's earlier annual livestock shows, long held on the lakefront because of its proximity to the railroads. Instead, the new building was "to satisfy the country that the Chicago Exposition is to be not only greater than any other, but is to be permanent."[60] Accordingly, Boyington's plans called for the largest enclosed space yet built in Chicago; it would be 800 feet long and 200 feet wide, crowned by a central dome 200 feet high (fig. 12). Most of its almost 244,000 square feet of floor space was allocated to exhibits of local producers, whom the exposition company drew by charging no fees for space or utilities. As the main floor plan shows, the exhibition space was arranged "as at Paris in 1867, in concentric ellipses," with galleries running around the whole interior. Musicians stationed on this level performed periodically for visitors. A central art gallery and flanking restaurants on the east front were among the hall's specially enclosed rooms (fig. 13).[61]

In its overall scale and form, Boyington's iron-and-glass Inter-state Industrial Exposition Building was Chicago's essay in a type that had originated with London's Crystal Palace (1851) and New York City's building of the same name (1853) and that recurred in Paris and in Vienna. Chicago had built the large Union Hall in Dearborn Park for events in the Civil War era, like the Sanitary Commission's Northwestern Sanitary Fair of 1865. Yet the postfire Inter-state Industrial Exposition Building was a hall whose floor area was almost twice as large as that of New York's Crystal Place of 1853. To solicit funds for the costly project, Chicago's newspapers emphasized "how, on the whole, a Crystal Palace had now become as necessary an adjunct of a first-class American city as a court house or a corn exchange."[62] Chicago's new aspiration to permanence had dictated a structure substantially more monumental than its precursors. Though erected in just over three months, it was nevertheless "the biggest structure ever built for any such purpose in America—a structure altogether unique in its architecture."[63] Boyington's hall stood on oak pile foundations, which supported a brick wall twenty-four feet high skirting the whole building and upheld the huge iron trusses that spanned its main spaces. The central and side projecting entrances on Michigan Avenue were domestic in style, with bracketed

Figure 13

Boyington, Inter-state Industrial Exposition Building, ground floor plan. From *Chicago Tribune*, 25 September 1873.

gabled roofs, balconies, and porticoes, so that the building was called "'the cottage by the sea'—the big house by the lake," in keeping with the residences that then lined the avenue's west side.[64] The central twelve-sided dome and the simpler squared end domes were crested and ornamented in galvanized iron, the same material that formed the decorative railing along the roof's crowning ridge. The central dome formed an imposing eastern terminus for Adams Street, like the central entrance to the Art Institute of Chicago's building, which replaced the Exposition Building on the same site in 1893. Yet the most impressive views of the mammoth hall were from along the lakefront as one approached the city by rail, much as the later Auditorium was to be seen. Like the Auditorium's tower, the Exposition Building's dome served as an observatory, from whose summit "one can get about the best view of Chicago and the lake that can be found anywhere in the city."[65] The dome's allusion to a capitol signified the exposition's claim to regional preeminence and centrality.

The monumentality of Boyington's structure was consistent with his clients' aim of giving Chicago's exposition "a more cosmopolitan character" than those of St. Louis and Cincinnati.[66] The day plans were adopted, one of the exposition company's leaders remarked that "if so handsome a building was ever erected on the Lake Park, it would remain there, not merely because it was good-looking, but since it could be put to so many uses, expositions in autumn, concerts in summer, and party conventions and mass meetings at all times."[67] This assessment proved prophetic. Most important among the hall's cultural functions was its art gallery, which effectively replaced that of Crosby's Opera House, lost in the fire. In Boyington's hall, the gallery displayed not only paintings and sculpture but also architectural drawings and photographs. The painting collection initially included works by the same masters represented in Crosby's gallery. By 1877, for the fifth annual exposition, energetic local efforts had brought to the hall's gallery paintings by well-known American artists, French impressionists, and painters of the Barbizon school.[68] These annual exhibits took place in the same structure that housed displays of agricultural and industrial production, including all manner of mechanical inventions displaced from their usual working environs. As one contemporary wrote in 1873, "Here, too, even the heaviest and most practical machinery attracts, for it is one thing to see it in a greasy, smoky shop, and another thing to view it in operation in the splendid hall of the Exposition building."[69] In that year about 60,000 people toured Boyington's interior, which provided a setting for their visual consumption of objects of art and industry. The enormous hall thus experientially linked economic and cultural production in a single civic space for a middle-class audience, like the international exposition buildings of the period.

Built in just ninety-six days, the Exposition Building was inaugurated on 25 September 1873 in a triumphal event marking the city's recovery from the Great Fire near its two-year anniversary. As many visitors noted, the reconstructed city outside Boyington's hall was the most impressive exhibition. Yet the moment's promise was quickly superseded by the onset of the Panic of 1873, which began in eastern banks earlier that same month. The Exposition Building was popularly identified with those Chicago capitalists who continued to head the Relief and Aid Society, whose mission to aid the newly destitute broadened with the depression following the panic.[70] The winter of 1873–1874 saw large numbers of the homeless and hungry sleeping in police stations. In late December 1873, the 400-member International Workingmen's Association (IWA) organized unemployed laborers in staging marches and rallies to call on the city for a public works program to provide jobs and accused the Relief and Aid Society of harboring substantial funds that were not being appropriately dispensed. Predominantly but not exclusively German, the IWA modeled these mass demonstrations on those of Berlin. The focus of the Chicago protests was City Hall, then at Adams and LaSalle Streets (site of the later Rookery Building), which Philip Peck had sold to the city. For the first time in local memory, the red flag appeared above the IWA's marching columns of workers as a new symbol of their political discontent. They borrowed the red flag from the Paris Commune of 1871, whose first anniversary the IWA had celebrated in March 1872. To the *Chicago Tribune*'s editors, the rallies of December 1873 threatened "the entire edifice of our present state of society . . . [and] the distribution of wealth."[71] The city council, now dominated by populist ward politicians, joined labor leaders in approaching the Relief and Aid Society, which agreed to help the genuinely impoverished but refused to fund a public works program. In winter 1874, workers responded by staging their most unruly demonstration to date outside the society's offices on LaSalle Street. With the crowd chanting "bread or death," its leaders threatened not only to demolish these offices but also to seize the Exposition Building, whose symbolic importance would not be forgotten by either workers or capitalists in the coming years before the Auditorium's construction. Its then singular monumentality and prominent location made it a contested site in the struggle for local political dominance.

Elite Responses to Postfire Class Strife: The Citizens' Association and the Athenaeum

The confrontations of spring 1874 were the most visible highlights of issues of urban rebuilding created by the Great Chicago Fire. From the viewpoint of property owners, the need to attract eastern and European capital for the city's reconstruction demanded a reformed municipal government in which these investors could have confidence. In November 1871, less than a month after the fire, Medill's mayoral administration had come into office at the head of a reform ticket that pledged incorruptible government. Among its first proposals was an ordinance to prevent erection of flammable wood buildings within the city, yet workers protested that the ordinance would make new dwellings unaffordable. Even brick buildings were not wholly fireproof, but they were more valuable than wood structures, hence the proposed city of brick enhanced property values for landowners. Such an urban transformation would effectively push poorer workers out to Chicago's periphery, mostly toward its Southwest Side near the Union Stockyards.[72]

In 1872, after heated debate, and much to the dismay of propertied interests, the law requiring brick construction was limited to the central city. Workers had continued to gain ground in local politics with the onset of the Panic of 1873 that dramatically slowed rebuilding. In February 1874 local German workers began publication of their first postfire political newspaper, the weekly *Der Vorbote* (the Harbinger), and in March they offered their first slate of candidates for offices in municipal elections, though none was successful. Yet another runaway fire in July 1874 shifted the political momentum back in favor of the property owners. The fire had begun in the workers' district of wooden shanties south of the limits of fireproof construction, then spread north to destroy the rebuilt business center. Within weeks of the fire, the eastern insurance industry issued an ultimatum that it would not do business in Chicago unless fireproof construction was extended to the city's limits, a stringent new building code was adopted, and the fire department was placed beyond the reach of corruption. This threat to the flow of capital into Chicago aroused its leading property holders to form the Chicago Citizens' Association in August 1874 as the city's first political organization of businessmen. Although they did not meet all the conditions of the insurers' ultimatum, the association's efforts sufficiently restored confidence so that these eastern companies continued to send capital to Chicago.[73]

The Citizens' Association's founding president, Franklin MacVeagh, sought to return local political control to property owners. In September 1874 he asked the association, "How can you be sure of finding a set of men severely anxious about the protection of property who themselves have no property to protect?"[74] In this spirit, by 1876 the association succeeded in reorganizing the city's government, bringing the police and fire departments directly under control of the mayor, and making the city council more responsive to propertied interests. The association also lent continuing support to the militia unit that later became the First Regiment of the Illinois National Guard, which had been organized in August 1874. The unit's purpose was to protect local business properties from workers' riots like the one that had occurred the previous winter. Funded and equipped by Chicago's commercial leaders, and composed of youths from the city's upper and middle classes, this regiment was first mobilized to forestall a workers' protest in February 1875, again aimed at increasing disbursements of the Chicago Relief and Aid Society. Unlike the spring of 1874, this time local business interests were ready with a show of armed force, combining police and militia units sufficient "to thwart an insurrection of a whole continent." In the face of this exhibition, the workers' demonstration did not materialize.[75]

Like many of the leading capitalists who later financed the Auditorium, Ferdinand Peck was a member of the Citizens' Association, serving on its executive committee from November 1876 through October 1877 and again from November 1878 through October 1879. At the time the Auditorium was built, it was said of Peck that "apart from the care of his estate, his entire time is devoted to public interests of an aesthetic, moral, and educational character."[76] Yet unlike many wealthy Chicagoans who owned extensive urban properties, Peck was neither an industrialist nor a merchant who dealt directly with workers or their associations. This distance from capital-labor confrontations may have fostered the more charitable outlook toward workers for which he was well known. Though born to wealth, Peck had "always been outspoken in his defense of the rights of workingmen, and he heartily despises all forms of snobbish aristocracy."[77] He was recalled as "very sympathetic towards the man who could not afford to indulge his propensities in the direction of culture without pecuniary aid."[78]

Peck's outlook on his relationship to Chicago derived from the history of his family's real estate. Although his father, Philip Peck, had commissioned a number of prefire buildings from architect John Van Osdel, at the time of the Great Fire most of the Peck lands in Chicago were unimproved, meaning that either no buildings or only temporary structures had been erected on them. Most of Philip Peck's holdings were still in either "whole blocks or corner lots, which for the most part were acquired at times when prices were very low, say from $2 to $4 a front foot for lots, and less in proportion for acreage." The elder Peck tenaciously retained these holdings through all the local financial vicissitudes of his lifetime, "and with every year he saw them increase in value as rapidly as the population increased. He lived to see the selling value of the bare land of more than one of his corners raised to $1,000 a foot, and had he lived a few years longer he would have known them worth $500 an inch."[79]

From the perspective of socialist theory in Chicago in the 1870s, these increases in the value of real estate represented an "unearned increment" of wealth for the land's owners. Because of the prevailing system of taxation, this wealth remained in the hands of the few, even though the increased value had been due to labor of the overall working population of the city, whose concentrated industries had spurred the rise in land prices. Many socialists proposed that the answer to this unequal distribution of wealth would be a "single tax," meaning a tax to be levied on land and natural resources, as a substitute for all other forms of taxation such as income or sales taxes. In keeping with Marxist theory, such a tax would be aimed at those who controlled land and natural resources as the essential means of all economic production. Louis Sullivan recalled that in 1873–1874, before he went to the École des Beaux-Arts in Paris, the architect and later anarchist John Edelmann, his close friend, made impromptu speeches on the virtues of the single tax while he and Sullivan were draftsmen in the architectural office of William Le Baron Jenney.[80]

When Ferdinand Peck took over the management of his father's estate in late 1871, he too was interested in political questions, as he was throughout his life. Once in control of the family's resources, so much of which derived from the rise of land values, Ferdinand Peck adopted what was later called "a policy of reciprocation." This meant that "vast numbers of people, by settling in Chicago, had given immense value to the Peck estate and now the Peck estate was to do what was right and handsome by the people of Chicago." With "a cultivated mind and an artistic temperament," Peck "early perceived the desirability of having in Chicago institutions specially designed to stimulate a love of various knowledge, and of the arts, in the people. He had turned over in his mind, even before 1871, several plans for one and another institution of such a nature."[81] After the fire, the institution that Peck helped to found and was most closely identified with was the Chicago Athenaeum, originally created by business leaders in October 1871 as a distribution point of merchandise for the dispossessed and as a social center for unemployed fire victims. With direction from local clergy, the institution's original name was the Young Men's Christian Union of Chicago, modeled after an organization of the same name in Boston. In May 1874, after the workers' protests of February targeting the Chicago Relief and Aid Society, the organization renamed itself the Chicago Athenaeum. Newly chartered as a private, nonprofit corporation for education, Chicago's Athenaeum reinvented itself as an institution more like New York City's Cooper Union and English workingmen's colleges. The Athenaeum's founders "gave their thought to providing a home-like place for young men, wherein encouragement might be given them in the work of mental and moral culture." Peck was "closely identified with the institution from the day of its organization, and for sixteen consecutive years in an official capacity," serving as the Athenaeum's secretary (1874–1881) and vice president (1881–1886), and later as its president for four one-year terms (1889–1892).[82]

By spring 1878, after moving through three temporary locations, the Athenaeum acquired its first permanent home in a new four-story building built for it at 48–54 Dearborn Street, on its west side north of Randolph (fig. 14). The Athenaeum stood just north of Adler and Sullivan's later Borden Block, on whose top floor these architects had their offices from 1881 to 1890, where they and Peck conferred about the Auditorium Building's design. From its founding the Athenaeum had been "*entirely unsectarian* in its spirit and aims," with its facilities and programs open to men and women regardless of "nationality or religious belief."[83] The Athenaeum had a library, reading rooms, and classrooms that served a variety of local educational needs. Its instructional program was partly meant to provide skills to make students employable by local businessmen whose philanthropy heavily subsidized the costs of instruction. Indigent mechanics and their children were given instruction in mathematics, drawing, and other fields so they could be rehired or promoted. Women who sought teaching positions in public schools studied here for certification or advancement. There were also college preparatory courses in science, history, elocution, and classical and modern languages, helping young men and women gain access to universities. Yet such offerings were also to provide a place where "the adult student may repair the neglect of earlier years."[84] In its educational opportunities, access, and affordability, the Athenaeum was a regionally unique enterprise, drawing students not only from Chicago and its suburbs but from elsewhere in Illinois and nearby states.

Figure 14

Chicago Athenaeum, 48–54 Dearborn Street, Chicago, 1878, as five-story building north (right) of Adler and Sullivan's six-story Borden Block, northwest corner of Dearborn and Randolph Streets (1880–1881; demolished 1917). To left (west) of Borden Block is Adler and Sullivan's seventeen-story Schiller Building (1890–1892; demolished 1961). Photograph from 1914. Courtesy of the Chicago Historical Society, ICHi-19454.

Styling itself "the People's College," the Chicago Athenaeum was to be a unifying, upbuilding urban institution. Its many programs included a "Dime Course on Art Topics," a subsidized lecture series that featured distinguished local practitioners like the architect William Le Baron Jenney (1832–1907), whom Peck knew and later commissioned to design his own house. Supporters and participants included such liberal clergy as Frank Lloyd Wright's uncle the Reverend Jenkin Lloyd Jones, Rabbi Emil Hirsch, and the Reverend David Swing. As one of the Athenaeum's "steadfast friends," Peck was committed to its goals of providing educational opportunity of high quality to those whom financial constraints had prevented from acquiring the kind of complete schooling he had enjoyed, which was then unusual even for Chicago's elite. In urging support for its programs, Peck stated that "whoever looks into the work of the Athenaeum will see in what a friendly way it meets inquirers for instruction. Sometimes they are timid ones, sometimes they are those who have deep regrets that they know so little. But all these are made to feel our respect for them because of their *desire* to learn."[85] In 1890 Peck directed the acquisition, remodeling, and expansion of a new building for the Athenaeum in the same block as his Auditorium, completed the same year. Earlier he had thought that the Athenaeum was going to move into the Auditorium Building. Like the Auditorium, the Athenaeum was to provide workers with a capitalist-structured alternative to leftist political culture.

The Central Church and Chicago's Rebuilt Music Halls after the Great Fire

Peck was a prime supporter of another postfire institution, Chicago's Central Church, which sought to counter the city's political divisions and enhance its cultural life in ways that were religiously inspired and socially directed. This church largely inspired the creation in 1878–1879 of Chicago's Central Music Hall, Dankmar Adler's first major independent building and Chicago's most important private architectural work of its period. The convergence of ideology and architecture in this hall made it a key model for the Auditorium. Yet the Central Music Hall also emerged from a larger urban pattern of siting entertainments for different social classes around the city in similar structures, whose designs and uses informed the Central Music Hall and the later Auditorium. Throughout the 1870s, Chicago's music halls and theaters were focal points not only for amusements but for the city's politics of class struggle. These buildings' siting and their architecture were socially activated statements, anticipating the monumental Auditorium.

The Central Church emerged from the career of a unique personality, the Reverend David Swing (1830–1894), acknowledged in the postfire era as the foremost preacher in Chicago and the western United States. Educated at Miami University in Oxford, Ohio, where he was a classmate of President Benjamin Harrison, Swing came to Chicago in 1866 to accept a ministry and soon became pastor of the Fourth Presbyterian Church on the city's Near North Side. When this congregation's building was destroyed along with many other churches in the Great Fire of 1871, it resumed services in the new McVicker's Theater, the first large structure to be rebuilt after the fire, opening in August 1872. Rising again on its old site on the south side of Madison Street west of State, the centrally located hall drew a broad audience to Swing's sermons, yet by 1873 he decided to return to the Fourth Presbyterian Church's new postfire building on the North Side.[86]

As his liberal theological views drew wide recognition, in April 1874 Swing was arraigned for heresy by Presbyterian denominational leaders. Though acquitted, Swing, facing the prospect of having to defend himself in further appeals, resigned his pulpit in October 1875 and briefly left the city. Ferdinand Peck was among his congregational supporters who greatly valued his ministry and organized to bring him back to Chicago. Their initiative derived from their belief in Swing's value to the city and from the widely held awareness that Chicago's rapid postfire growth had accelerated the prefire pattern of church relocations to what were then the city's outskirts. In their view, religious life needed to be reasserted in the center of the city. In November 1875 Swing's supporters drafted an agreement that called on him to "continue his public teachings in some central and commodious place."[87] The same elite concern for strengthening cultural institutions in Chicago's historic core underlay later discussion about the Auditorium Building. Fifty supporters, including Ferdinand Peck, his brothers Walter and Clarence, Nathaniel Fairbank, Joseph Medill, Wirt Dexter, McVicker, and others who would later invest in the Auditorium each subscribed $1,000 to launch a new church. Its organization and policies they left to Swing, who drew up a covenant and statement of faith for "a Christian Society to be known as the Central Church of Chicago."[88]

Swing articulated his new institution's rationale in a sermon titled "The Reasons for a Central Church," at its inaugural service in December 1875. He argued that a church was needed at Chicago's center that was accessible where streetcar lines from the North, West, and South Divisions merged. The central focus of urban transport was at the intersection of State and Madison Streets, half a block east of McVicker's. Swing observed that "when all the places of worship that stood near the center of this great city were torn down and removed, the destroyers of these temples took worship away from the place where all the carriageways meet."[89] Yet there, where Chicago's business was "massed into one solid square mile . . . there are thousands of young business men, who are quite far removed from the family churches, and who would be quite near to some central church."[90] Within a few blocks of McVicker's there stood perhaps a dozen comfortable hotels that, given the destruction of houses downtown, had come to serve as homes for hundreds of men who once attended the old centrally located churches. Swing initially proposed to direct his ministry to this group, though his audience consistently included the city's best-known business leaders, who also supported the Chicago Athenaeum.

Swing argued that his church's urbanistic centrality should parallel its theological centrality within the denominational spectrum. He proposed a simple, humane statement of faith that would include beliefs held in common by different churches and leave aside those points of doctrine that divided them. As its other founders directed, the Central Church was "for all time to be kept separate and apart from any religious creed."[91] Such a church's guaranty for its freedom of thought would be its congregational governance and eventual ownership of its place of worship, without denominational control of a mortgage, so that its "property should at all times hereafter be under the entire control and direction of the members."[92] Such an independent church's liberty of thought was to compensate for its loss of denominational support. To meet expenses, the Central Church initially sold annual tickets for rental of individual seats in McVicker's Theater, with many other seats free. Although prices varied according to a seat's position in the theater, these prices were much lower than pew rents in local churches. Because it rented an existing theater, the Central Church had a smaller annual budget of about $15,000. With this theological and financial policy, and the fame of Swing's preaching, his church had five hundred members at its outset when it met in McVicker's Theater. It never ran a deficit, so that its initial guaranty fund was never used.[93]

Swing's ideas won support from a younger man who typified those he sought to reach. George B. Carpenter (1845–1881) was a native of New York City who met Swing when they both first came to Chicago in 1866. Soon known as an editor of religious periodicals, Carpenter had been a prime supporter of the postfire Inter-state Industrial Exposition Building. With his partner E. L. Sheldon, Carpenter organized lectures and concerts in Chicago's South and West Sides to compensate for the lack

Figure 15

Gurdon P. Randall, Union Park Congregational (now First Baptist) Church, 60 North Ashland Avenue, Chicago (1868–1869). Stereoscopic photograph by Copelin and Son, c. 1872–1877. The pipe organ, built in Boston and encased in solid black walnut, was completed just before the Great Fire of 1871. Courtesy of the Chicago Historical Society, ICHi-22322.

of entertainment before the city's central theaters and music halls were rebuilt and before the Panic of 1873 triggered a depression.[94] One of the two regular venues for Carpenter's events was the Union Park Congregational Church (1868–1869), designed by Gurdon P. Randall on Chicago's West Side (fig. 15). Swing modeled his own effort on such Congregational churches, whose name signified each parish's control over its affairs with minimal denominational oversight. Architecturally, Union Park was a prime example of Chicago's auditorium churches, which replaced the basilican spatial convention of a long nave leading to a frontal altar with a square room whose curved pew rows on a main floor and balcony faced a frontal pulpit backed by a large organ.[95] This room's spatial emphasis on the audience's collective visibility and musical participation anticipated the Central Music Hall.

This project took shape in Carpenter's mind by 1874. After Swing's heresy trial that year, it had been Carpenter who led in organizing Swing's supporters to contribute to the Central Church's guaranty fund. In 1875, after Swing's congregation started meeting at McVicker's Theater, Carpenter and Sheldon managed the church's sales of annual tickets for seats. Yet McVicker's lacked an organ and other features desirable for the Central Church's Sunday and weekday services. The church's need for a new permanent home fused with Carpenter's ambition to construct a centrally located music hall that was architecturally superior to those built just after the fire. In that period he and Sheldon had to repeat the same performances or lectures in several parts of the city in order to meet requests for them. This had multiplied their expenses for productions while dividing their audiences and receipts.[96] Chicago's immediate postfire music halls were either spatially insufficient, like Burling and Adler's Kingsbury Music Hall (the first to open downtown in October 1873), or not centrally located, like Boyington's much larger McCormick Hall on the Near North Side, which opened the next month. The opening of such facilities had depressed Carpenter and Sheldon's business in small outlying halls.[97]

Carpenter imagined a new Central Music Hall that would accommodate the Central Church's nondenominational services and separately managed commercial musical events. The hall would combine the spatial types of church and theater. As early as 1873 Carpenter had identified the southeast corner of State and Randolph Streets as the most desirable for his project, since every streetcar from around the city ran directly to that corner or within two blocks of it (fig. 5). For financial support, he approached leading capitalists with this idea and found a friend in Nathaniel Fairbank, who had helped to fund the Exposition Building and who would later support the Auditorium Building. From early 1875, Carpenter and Fairbank worked jointly with Burling and Adler on planning the new Central Music Hall. As "a passionate lover of music," Fairbank was the project's chief supporter, holding the unbuilt plans for about two years until the worst of the depression of 1873 had passed and after the tumultuous events of 1877.[98]

Workers' Turner Halls and the Great Railroad Strike of 1877

The middle- and upper-class music halls of rebuilt Chicago had their working-class counterparts in the halls of the city's *Turnvereine,* or German gymnastic societies, which had long served as social, cultural, and political havens for those whose lives were tied to manual labor, either skilled or less skilled. Along with local German *Männerchor* or male singing societies, the gymnastic associations were American transplantations of similar groups developed by trade guilds in German cities. These groups' roots went back to the Napoleonic occupation of Berlin, though their radical politics dated from the 1840s, and they were brought to America with German immigration to the United States after the revolution of 1848. In both countries, workers' associations served as socially self-protective enclaves where laborers created their own cultural space. As in many American cities, Chicago's *Turnvereine* thrived as social and political organizations from their founding in the 1850s. Between the Civil War and World War I, the city had more *Turnvereine* than any other in the United States. By 1896 there were twenty-four societies listed in Chicago, equally divided between the North, West, and South Sides. These organizations grew in a period when between 25 and 30 percent of the city's population consisted of first- or second-generation German immigrants and about 70 percent of that German population was working-class. The older Chicago Turner societies, founded in the 1850s in the wake of mass immigration, were more conservative and middle class, indifferent to or opposing left-wing politics. Yet several of Chicago's later *Turnvereine* became closely associated with the labor movement, especially after Bismarck's antisocialist legislation of 1878 drove many radicals to the United States in the 1880s, when more than 1.4 million Germans entered the country. Regardless of their politics, though, all of Chicago's *Turnvereine* attempted to maintain German cultural traditions and enhance the position of German workers in the face of nativist opposition, which took the form of temperance movements. At these societies' gatherings, German was the sole language of speech and song. Yet what gave the Chicago *Turnvereine* their urban presence was the architecture of their halls, which served a range of purposes and became a focus for outside attacks.[99]

In Chicago from the late 1860s, the *Turnvereine* built several halls for their members in German workers' neighborhoods around the central city's periphery. These *Turnhalle* were distinct as enclosed structures housing workers' events, in an era when gatherings of less empowered citizens were mostly held outdoors. Temporary possession of a hall marked a first step to empowerment, which culminated in full ownership of a purpose-built structure. After 1871 the most prominent of these

Figure 16

August Bauer and Robert Löbnitz,
Concert Hall, Chicago Turngemeinde
(North Side Turner Hall), 255 Clark Street
and Chicago Avenue (1872–1873).
From Janssen, *Geschichte der Chicago
Turngemeinde*.

halls was that of the more conservative Chicago Turngemeinde, organized in 1853, the city's oldest and strongest German society, with a postfire membership of over 400. This society owned Turner Hall on the North Side at 255 Clark Street and Chicago Avenue, opened on 3 January 1873, replacing the society's earlier building on the same site occupied in 1863 and destroyed in the Great Fire. In addition to a thoroughly equipped gymnasium where 500 children were instructed in gymnastics, the building contained a three-thousand-volume library with many standard German works, a reading room with the leading German periodicals, and meeting rooms where an evening school was conducted. Designed by German-trained architects August Bauer (who had been Dankmar Adler's first employer in Chicago in 1861–1862) and his partner Robert Löbnitz, this building's most impressive interior was its concert hall (fig. 16), the main performance space of German singing societies. Less elaborate but comparably multiuse buildings included those of the smaller but more radical Aurora Turn Verein (organized 1864), built in 1867–1868 on the corner of Huron Street and Milwaukee Avenue, and the similarly politicized Turn Verein Vorwärts on the West Side at 251 West Twelfth Street at Halsted. The Aurora and Vorwärts Turner Halls were built and owned by their societies, which by 1887 had sold the properties but still leased the halls as tenants.[100]

Though architecturally unknown, Chicago's *Turnhalle* were key neighborhood centers. As early as 1867, the year of the city's first major labor demonstration, one German local said: "I feel at home wherever Turners erect a temple, for I know that they dedicate their churches only to the causes of freedom and progress. Every new Turner [hall] that we build . . . is a barricade against narrow minded ideas, a fortress of progress."[101] The halls distinguished German workers from those of other ethnicities. As one Anglo-American unionist declared in 1876: "Our German citizens are the owners of five or six magnificent halls in the city," while mechanics of all other nationalities "combined are unable to point to a single structure which stands as a monument to their independence which they can claim as their own property—or which they can use as a resort, without the payment of rent to any landlord." In these buildings, equipped with lecture and music halls in addition to their gymnasiums, German workers "can meet in social intercourse, discuss the political situation, enjoy an intellectual treat and improve their physical conditions without money and without price—because the revenue received from rent more than covers all necessary expenses."[102] From this perspective, Ferdinand Peck's Chicago Athenaeum served as a comparable institution for the city's non-German workers, who lacked such halls.

As the American unionist observed, the *Turnhalle* hosted a range of events staged by rent-paying organizations. Many of these were dances sponsored by local nonradical trade unions. Other events included concerts by local orchestras, such as those of Hans Balatka at the North Side Turner Hall. Louis Sullivan later recalled that "his fine orchestra gave a concert every Sunday afternoon." It was at such concerts in spring 1874 that Sullivan heard performances of his favorite Wagnerian music. Significantly, he had attended these concerts with his best friend, the architect and later anarchist John Edelmann.[103] Yet the most characteristic events in these buildings were the Sunday gatherings of members. As one reporter described a later such event at the Vorwärts Turner Hall: "Few Americans, born and bred, know what it is that our German and Bohemian cousins do in their own halls." In an effort to educate his non-German readers, presumably to counter prevailing suspicion that these halls were dens of labor radicals, this reporter described a Sunday evening where two or three thousand people were gathered around hundreds of little tables, mostly complete families, from babes in arms to grandparents, all in their Sunday best with flowers in hand or on their breasts and glasses of beer or soda water before them. In the gallery above were another thousand or more "similarly happy people," with "smiles on their faces and many words of gay social converse on their lips." Throughout the room, "everybody seemed to know everybody else, good nature ruled supreme," and "there was no disorder, no boisterousness, not one thing unseemingly [*sic*] said or done."[104]

The evening's main event took place on the hall's stage, "quite as large as that of a first-class theatre, draped by a handsome curtain and the proscenium ornamented with figures of Germania and Columbia holding aloft the flags of the [German] empire and [American] republic." After an orchestral overture, this curtain rose to reveal seventy-five boys on stage, ranging in age from four to ten, who, under the guidance of their adult teacher, began a gymnastics display with feats of rapid pole climbing from the stage floor to the proscenium's crown. Between musical interludes, subsequent events included individual routines on the horse and parallel bars, followed by fencing. Emphasis was not on display but on disciplined development of the male child from a young age, "for, be it known, the German system of gymnastic training, as taught in the practice rooms attached to the German and Bohemian turner halls of Chicago, is the best ever devised for development of the human body."[105] Exercises emphasized order and propriety as a time-honored Old World technique for personal development and socialization of youths.

The political role of more radical *Turnhalle* emerged vividly during the great strike of Chicago's workers in late July 1877, whose scope of industrial disruption and violent suppression by police and militia proved a turning point in the local labor movement. The Chicago action began as an extension of a national strike of railroad workers that reached the city by Monday, 23 July. Through the course of that workweek, striking local railroad workers sparked sympathetic walkouts of many trades in manufacturing and construction, to the point where the city's industries were largely shut down. Marches, demonstrations, and large meetings, addressed by socialist leaders, aroused the fear of local and national authorities and a middle-class public, whose anxiety and hostility were raised by accounts of events in the capitalist press. Police actions were forceful, with fighting ranging over two days, especially near key rail yards, leaving between twenty-five and fifty civilians dead and some two hundred seriously injured. The scale and level of violence prompted the first use of federal troops to suppress a labor uprising. United States Army troops, returning from Indian fighting in the Dakotas, were ordered to stop at Chicago. Cheered by nonworker audiences, they marched through the central city to quarters in the Inter-state Industrial Exposition Building, which workers had threatened to seize three years earlier.[106]

During the week's violence, one of the worst episodes occurred at Vorwärts Turner Hall on West Twelfth Street. Like other such buildings around the city, this hall had been used for labor rallies in earlier years. On 21 December 1873, as the panic of that fall had deepened, a meeting of the unemployed drew about 6,000 to

Figure 17

Vörwarts Turner Hall, police attack on German socialist cabinetmakers' meeting, 26 July 1877. From *Harper's Weekly* 21 (18 August 1877), titled "Driving the Rioters from Turner Hall." Courtesy of the Chicago Historical Society, ICHi-14018.

the hall, where a platform of relief measures was adopted. In the tumult of 1877, Vorwärts Turner Hall was the meeting place rented by the Harmonia Association of Joiners, the German socialist furniture workers' union. On the afternoon of 26 July, several hundred union members then on strike met there to confer with employers about wages and the eight-hour day. Though the meeting inside was peaceful, in the street outside boys stoned regular and special police, who charged the crowd and then continued inside and up the stairs. After smashing the doors to the auditorium itself, the police opened fire and clubbed at random and without warning, killing one worker, wounding others, and driving most into panicked flight down the stairs or out the windows (fig. 17). Outside, a bayonet charge by the Chicago militia's Second Regiment dispersed the workers. Later the courts held that the police action had grossly violated the right of free assembly, yet the officers responsible were only lightly fined. The nationally reported and locally embittering event highlighted the pivotal role of Chicago's *Turnhalle*, which the days of urban rebellion in July 1877 had temporarily transformed from workers' havens into political battlegrounds.[107]

The great railroad strike, although tragic and largely without results in terms of better conditions, briefly boosted the political fortunes of Chicago's socialists. By fall 1878 they had elected three state assemblymen and one state senator, who lobbied to create the Illinois Bureau of Labor Statistics. In municipal elections of spring 1879, the mayoral candidate favorable to workers made a creditable showing, while additional aldermen were elected to the city council.[108] Throughout this period, local labor leadership made effective use of public space as a counterweight to its control by capitalists. Like their counterparts in German cities, Chicago's workers could not afford to build major structures to hold large numbers, so ceremonial venues for laboring masses were mostly open-air sites. Frequent Sunday picnics were organized at Ogden's Grove, the Chicago German community's favorite rentable beer garden on Clybourn Avenue, along the eastern banks of the Chicago River's north branch, north of North Avenue, a site then northwest of the city limits. Processional parades to this grove were organized and staged as public rituals. At the grounds there were musical and dramatic performances, poetry readings, and other ideologically shaped cultural events in addition to speeches exhorting political action.[109] These picnics prepared the way for the largest rally of Chicago's workers on 22 March 1879, the date commemorating the start of the 1848 revolution in Germany and the Paris Commune of 1871. Equally significant was the rally's location at the Inter-state Industrial Exhibition Building, rented for the occasion for only $100 by the local branch of the Socialist Labor Party against the wishes of Chicago's Board of Trade. The two-day event, in which the Aurora Turn Verein took a leading role, drew an estimated 25,000 to 40,000 people into the hall, while thousands more were kept outside for lack of room even in this enormous space. This rally's unprecedented size, and its elaborate program of speeches, with music and dancing, demonstrated the local labor movement's popularity and vitality, even though the program did not proceed as scheduled, largely owing to the crush of bodies in the hall.[110]

Even more influential was the display of newly organized self-defense groups created by German, Bohemian, and Irish immigrant workers. These had paraded through the city's streets to the hall in colorful uniforms, marching as paramilitary units armed with rifles, cartridges, and bayonets. Although such units predated the strike of 1877, they had grown quickly in response to treatment of workers in that event and as a counterweight to capitalist-supported militia like the First Regiment. Afterward, members of these German *Lehr- und Wehr-Verein,* or education and defense societies, drilled regularly, even staging mock battles simulating confrontations with police and militia. Their headquarters were in Aurora Turner Hall.[111] Although they professed peaceful intentions of self-defense, these groups' displays aroused sufficient fear to place political pressure on local government for their control. After the rally of March 1879, the Citizens' Association effectively lobbied the Illinois legislature to prohibit private militia companies and ban armed drilling without the governor's permission. Peck was on the Citizens' Association's executive committee during this period, as he had been through the troubled summer of 1877, after which the association had recommended that Chicago's taxpayers help support the local militia. The courts' ultimate upholding of the state laws against workers' militia groups effectively gave the police and capitalist-supported state militia a monopoly on military activity in Chicago, a situation that helped turn the city's socialist movement toward anarchism in the 1880s.[112]

The Central Music Hall and Labor's Decline to 1880

Within weeks of the strong socialist showing in the state elections of November 1878, a group of Chicago's capitalists held their first major organizational meeting to raise funds for building the Central Music Hall. After the Inter-state Industrial Exposition Building, this project was the next major demonstration of their collective power to bring forth large buildings by associating as a joint stock company. By 1878 Boyington's hall had become a contested site, not only because of events in 1874 and 1877 but also because of pressure from a more worker-oriented city council to begin charging the exposition's directors rent for the building's use of its site, which the city had initially let them use free.[113] The huge socialist rally held there in March further politicized the facility. For the first time its great space, the largest interior in Chicago, was filled with communist adherents and sympathizers. In this context, it is not surprising that promoters of the new Central Music Hall found ready financial support after they began building in May 1879.

While the Central Music Hall went forward in this period's highly charged political context, the project's advancement was also presumably prompted by the opening of Cincinnati's monumental new Music Hall in May 1878 (fig. 18). While living in New York City, Carpenter had heard concerts by Theodore Thomas's orchestra, the foremost of its period and the leading American interpreter of Wagner's music. Thomas most often performed at Steinway Hall on East Fourteenth Street after its opening in 31 October 1866, shortly after the fire that had damaged the nearby New York Academy of Music. The Thomas orchestra's first midwestern concert had been at Cincinnati in 1869 to coincide with the city's Sängerfeste of local German choral groups. In 1870, for these annual festivals, Cincinnati's leaders had built a 5,000-seat temporary wooden hall, where Thomas's orchestra performed for biennial festivals three times from 1871 to 1875. The musical and financial success of these concerts was so great that local leaders funded the permanent Music Hall to replace the temporary structure on the same site. Designed by the Cincinnati architect Samuel Hannaford, the Music Hall, whose auditorium seated 3,632, opened to hold the May Music Festival of 1878, for which Thomas returned (fig. 19). The Music Hall's auditorium was on a raised second floor, above a main floor used for industrial expositions. Wings were also added to the lower levels in 1879. Externally, Hannaford's building was a massive Victorian Gothic edifice 372 feet long, which Thomas described as "unlike any structure devoted to festival uses in America."[114]

The monumentality of Cincinnati's Music Hall reinforced its city's reputation not only in music but in architecture. On a visit to Cincinnati before 1872, Dankmar Adler wrote home to a friend that the city "is much better built than Chicago both as to the solidity and good taste displayed by the external appearance of the buildings."[115] The Chicago architect Peter B. Wight wrote that before 1880 Cincinnati had "always been the best-built city in the West," being superior to St. Louis and Chicago

Figure 18

Samuel Hannaford, Music Hall, Cincinnati (1878); lateral south (left) and north (right) exposition wings added 1879, as shown in main floor plan at upper left. Courtesy of the Cincinnati Museum Center, B-89-061.

Figure 19

Hannaford, Music Hall, Cincinnati, at opening concert of 14 May 1878, showing organ with ornamental casing designed by Robert Rogers, before addition of stage and proscenium in 1895–1896. Courtesy of the Cincinnati Museum Center, B-88-162.

in the construction and outward design of business structures.[116] As late as 1885 Chicagoan William Penn Nixon, one of the Auditorium's supporters, "alluded to the gifts of enterprising citizens of Cincinnati, which had resulted in a grand music hall and grand music. Chicago had nothing to compare with it."[117] The Cincinnati Music Hall's identification with Thomas particularly concerned Carpenter, who had brought his orchestra to Chicago for several series of concerts from 1872 to 1875 in the city's much smaller postfire theaters.[118]

On 23 December 1878, within weeks of the first notable socialist political gains in the state's November elections, Fairbank chaired a meeting of local capitalists who agreed to initiate the project of building a new hall primarily for Swing's church and for any traveling concert troupe or lecturer. The vacant site that Carpenter had identified on the southeast corner of State and Randolph Streets was just north of Field, Leiter, and Company's new store of 1878 in the Singer Building on the northeast corner of State and Washington. Marshall Field's brother, Henry Field, and Levi Leiter were founding supporters of the Central Music Hall, whose presence would enhance these merchants' own location. Initial stockholders also included Ferdinand Peck, among other members of the Central Church, which had incorporated in November 1877 as a preliminary legal step to issuing stock and owning a site and building. The land was bought rather than leased, whereas later projects like the Auditorium were usually built on leased ground to lessen initial capital expenses. Twenty-year bonds totaling $125,000 were issued to cover the purchase of the site, while the structure's eventual cost of $210,000 would be met with stock purchases. Despite the Music Hall's location and promise, there was no direct local precedent for such an enterprise. The level of risk partially inspired the "great opposition to the construction of the building," whose "financial collapse was dolefully predicted."[119]

By the time the stockholders met in December 1878, Edward Burling and Adler had largely completed final drawings for the new hall, before these two architects formally separated early in 1879. Adler recalled that he then devoted himself to the building's realization as his first major independent work.[120] His and Burling's earlier Kingsbury Music Hall had originally seated fewer than 1,000, whereas Carpenter thought that an optimally sized music hall would seat about 2,000. He claimed to have "visited and carefully inspected every hall and theatre of prominence from Portland [Maine] to San Francisco, besides studying the plans of the leading continental theaters."[121] In the United States, among Carpenter's probable sources would have been New York's recent concert venue, Chickering Hall, on the northwest corner of Fifth Avenue and Eighteenth Street, designed by George B. Post to seat 1,450 and opened in 1875. Carpenter's European models may have included concert halls in Berlin. To knowledge of such models, Carpenter added ideas from over a decade of experience as a theater manager in Chicago. For his Central Music Hall, Carpenter worked with Adler, who supervised "six different sets of plans, each embodying novel features and improvements suggested by [Carpenter's] personal examination of the many important auditoriums in the country."[122] Of Central Music Hall, Adler recalled: "It is but just that I should acknowledge my obligations for the success of this building to the innumerable suggestions of my dear friend Geo. B. Carpenter," who died in January 1881 at age thirty-five, just over a year after his unique structure opened in December 1879.[123]

The Central Music Hall's auditorium featured several key innovations for Chicago theaters that Adler later developed in designing the Auditorium, where the Central Church met for a time after the Central Music Hall's demolition in 1901. Whereas Cincinnati's Music Hall had been built for festival purposes, Carpenter's aim had been to create "a compact, cozy, brilliant and convenient concert auditorium, suitable for every-day wear and ordinary occasion."[124] As its plans indicate, his hall had 1,677 numbered seats arranged on a main floor (including the frontal parquet near the stage and the rear parquet circle), a first balcony or dress circle, and a second balcony above (fig. 20). All these levels had richly furnished boxes on either side, which together seated 120. Standing room enabled the hall to hold a total of over 2,000, so that it housed what "was then considered to be the largest church congregation in the middle West."[125]

The Central Music Hall's floor plans reveal the ways its design complied with Chicago's Theater Ordinance passed by the city council on 14 June 1878. This law's

Figure 20

Dankmar Adler, Central Music Hall, southeast corner of State and Randolph Streets, Chicago (1879; demolished 1900), showing main floor plan with parquet and dress circle (left), and balcony or third-floor plan (right). Courtesy of the Richard Nickel Committee Archive, Chicago, Illinois.

Figure 20

Dankmar Adler, Central Music Hall, southeast corner of State and Randolph Streets, Chicago (1879; demolished 1900), showing main floor plan with parquet and dress circle (left), and balcony or third-floor plan (right). Courtesy of the Richard Nickel Committee Archive, Chicago, Illinois.

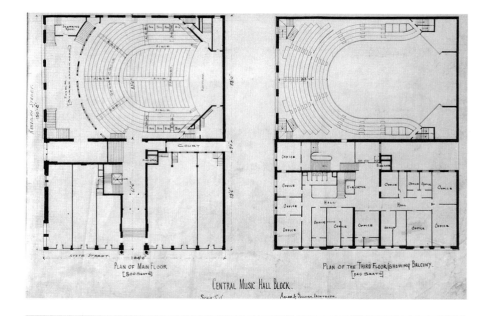

Figure 21

Central Music Hall: (left) sixth floor plan, showing Apollo Hall in southwest corner, with (a) trusses spanning north-south; (b) columns supporting trusses; (c) central vaulted ceiling with skylight; (d) east and west semidomes; and (right) longitudinal section looking east, showing main floor with rear north foyer and balcony and gallery levels. Courtesy of the Richard Nickel Committee Archive, Chicago, Illinois.

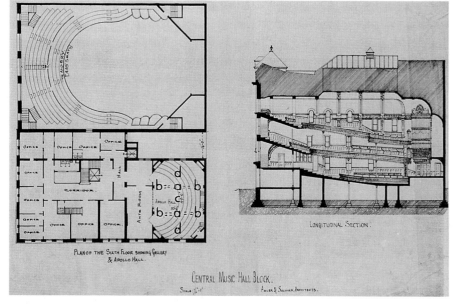

provisions derived from a report on theater safety by L. D. Cleaveland, superintendent of buildings under Mayor Monroe Heath, who had requested a survey of such buildings in the wake of a disastrous theater fire in Brooklyn, New York. Cleaveland had observed that means of egress from the main floors of local theaters were occasionally sufficient but that none had provided adequately for egress from their galleries, where life-threatening panic most easily took hold of an audience. Accordingly, he had recommended that there should "be stairways from the galleries near to the proscenium, where the stage boxes are usually placed," that "the *exits* for the different galleries should be *separate*," and that "the main floor should be provided with exits, so that an audience there could readily escape without meeting the stream of people from the galleries." Finally, "there should be no long flights of straight stairs, but the stairs should have many landings and change direction at each landing," to break falls. Cleaveland wrote: "The more separate and distinct the exits from a building are the more security there will be for the audience in case of fire. People in a panic, whether from a real or imaginary cause, have no judgment, and should be provided with ample safe-guards, protections and exits, when such occurrences happen."[126]

In January 1881 the Chicago Citizens' Association charged its newly formed Committee on Theatres and Public Halls to examine the city's theaters, of which two had been largely reconstructed and most others had been improved, to see how well theater owners had met the ordinance's requirements. The committee, which included architects Edward Burling, Peter B. Wight, and Frederick Baumann, filed its report in January 1882. It concluded that "although several theatres and halls have been erected since the passage of the Theatre Ordinance, there has been no regard paid to the essential provisions of that law, except in one instance—the Central Music Hall."[127] Comparison of the Central Music Hall's floor plans for the main parquet, dress circle, and balcony levels shows that all levels had exit stairways on both sides of the house in front and rear, that stair runs were short with frequent turns and landings, and that stairs were wider toward the lower levels to ease passage of more people there (figs. 20 and 21). There were a total of sixteen exits, made more accessible by dividing seating into small sections with a maximal number of aisles to permit egress. Cleaveland had advised that means of egress should be adequate for standees as well as for seated patrons, hence the Central Music Hall's rear north foyers on the main and balcony levels were served by wide exit stairs on both sides.

As Charles Gregersen has shown, the Central Music Hall was Adler's first auditorium whose design was based primarily on acoustic principles. Among the most widely cited papers in architectural acoustics, and the only one Adler referred to in his own writings, was that of John Scott Russell (1808–1882), a Scottish physicist and mechanical engineer whose principal field of study was the mathematical theory of wave motion in fluids. In 1838 Scott Russell read his paper "Elementary Considerations of Some Principles in the Construction of Buildings Designed to Accommodate Spectators and Auditors." The paper grew out of his experience as a lecturer in different halls at the University of Edinburgh. His most fundamental idea, later revisited in subsequent lectures to the Royal Institute of British Architects, was that optimal seating meant securing the best possible conditions for both hearing and seeing a speaker, because auditory and visual conditions were inseparable. As Adler later did, Scott Russell sought designs that provided uniformly good seats throughout a hall, whose architectural perfection meant minimizing differences in the quality of experience among all audience members.[128]

With these criteria in mind, Scott Russell diagrammed a "building for public speaking" in which each listener should feel "as if the speaker were speaking principally to and for him . . . as if there was no one else in the room but himself and the

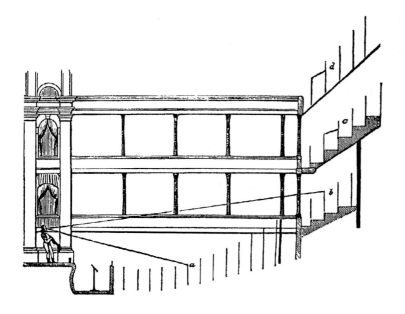

Figure 22

John Scott Russell, diagram of an auditorium derived from optimal elevation of seating rows to create an isacoustic (equal-hearing) curve (1838). Forty years before Adler adapted his ideas to theaters, and later to convention halls, Scott Russell had envisioned that application of the isacoustic curve in a hall seating 10,000 where the speaker on a raised central platform addressed rising tiers of listeners viewing him and each other from all sides. From Scott Russell, "Elementary Considerations of Some Principles in the Construction of Buildings Designed to Accommodate Spectators and Auditors."

speaker." Ideally "each individual should see and hear without interruption from any of the rest of the audience, with equal comfort." This emphasis on optimizing every individual's access to sight and sound meant that rows of seats should form a rising slope, one row behind the other. The slope's incline should be sufficient to ensure that each spectator's head would be fifteen inches above that of the person in front. Assuming seating rows that were about two and one half feet apart, Scott Russell calculated the points that indicated the heads of spectators sufficiently elevated above those in front of them. These points lay along "a very beautiful curve which may be termed *the equal seeing or equal hearing curve, the iseidomal or isacoustic curve.*" Based on this curve, Scott Russell developed a schematic design for an interior that could become a model for a lecture room, church, or music hall (fig. 22). In such a space, he proposed seating rows rising successively to ensure that everyone could see and hear without interruption. The design would minimize both dissonance from sound reflected to listeners off walls and echoes in the ears of speakers from sound reflected back to the stage from the auditorium's rear walls. Because of the elevation given to rear seats, "the great proportion of the house walls of the building were covered with auditors, and the sphere of sound and sight almost wholly occupied in useful effect."[129]

In the Central Music Hall, Adler implemented this idea, setting seating rows on a curved rise steeply ascending from front to back (figs. 21 and 23). To further ensure that everyone could see and hear well, chairs in each row were set between chairs in rows in front and behind, so that no one would be seated directly behind another's head. To contain sound and reduce its reverberation time, Adler also decreased the auditorium's overall spatial volume by keeping its vaulted plaster ceiling as low as possible above the upper gallery. Echoing Scott Russell's ideal for such a room's configuration, Carpenter described how "the entire auditorium opens out, widening like a bowl. This will be the first audience room constructed in this way, and the effect will be most brilliant, the sweeps of the auditorium rising and widening out like a parterre, each part visible to all the other parts of the hall."[130] When the room opened as a music hall in December 1879, an impromptu instrumental test of its acoustics was arranged. The notes of a difficult piano solo "rang out round, and pure, and unbroken to the remotest corners of the vast space above and below, delighting each listener with the perfect acoustic properties which the Hall possessed." The Reverend David Swing's own preaching voice was habitually quiet to the point of inaudibility, yet in the new hall, the "faintest words of the orator

Figure 23

Central Music Hall, auditorium looking north, showing alternating position of seats in successive rows, columns supporting balcony and gallery, and medallions of composers in stained glass at rear. From *Central Music Hall* (Chicago, c. 1880). Courtesy of the Chicago Historical Society, ICHi-01718.

were heard as distinctly as though each individual in the large assemblage were standing at his elbow."[131]

At the auditorium's north rear wall, three tall windows of colored "cathedral" or art glass included medallions of famous composers: Beethoven, Haydn, Mendelssohn, Mozart, Bach, and Handel.[132] The light from these three-story windows complemented that of the ceiling's central art glass skylight, a feature especially important for daytime services and performances in a room that had exterior windows only on the north side. Burling and Adler had employed such skylights in earlier theaters like the Kingsbury Music Hall, and Adler and Sullivan set a large one in the Auditorium Theater, which lacked any exterior windows. In the Central Music Hall, the skylight's rolled stained glass had "an exquisite combination of pale orange tints relieved by blue, green, deep orange, and red," in a design of conventionalized natural forms that was then locally unrivaled. Sullivan's longtime collaborators in decorative art, George L. Healy and Louis J. Millet, listed the Central Music Hall among their works, and they located their office as partners in this building by 1881. They may have been responsible for designing both the skylight and the stage's stenciling. In this effort they may have worked with Sullivan, since the skylight's description recalls those of his earlier ornamental ceiling frescoes for Sinai Temple and the Moody Tabernacle, both of 1876, the former project having been his first collaboration with Adler.[133]

Ferdinand Peck knew the Central Music Hall well, for "although holding no decided religious views of his own, he may be seen with his family at Central Music Hall nearly every Sunday, listening to the logical and symmetrical discourses of Prof. David Swing."[134] Chief among this auditorium's innovations was its rear foyer (26 feet wide by 80 feet long) on its north side (fig. 24), the precursor to the Auditorium Theater's foyer arrangement (fig. 125). From this innovative space, people

Figure 24
Central Music Hall, main north foyer at
rear of auditorium looking east, showing
bust of founder George B. Carpenter.
From *Central Music Hall* (Chicago, c.
1880). Courtesy of the Chicago Historical
Society, ICHi-31468.

could pass down into the seating rows of the main floor's U-shaped parquet circle
or to the parquet nearest the stage. Alternatively, stairways in the foyer's rear corners
led up to the rear main balcony and gallery above. For Carpenter the key innovation
was the balcony's relation to the parquet below. In earlier theaters the balcony's
curving front projected over the dress circle, placing seats in these rows under the
balcony's shadow, "where they can neither see the audience nor hear the performance with comfort." These conditions rendered nearly worthless the rear dress circle
seats, which constituted almost half the first-floor seating.[135] As the Central Music
Hall's section shows, the rear foyer allowed Adler to set the balcony back so that it
did not deeply overhang the parquet circle (fig. 21).

In a room meant for church services, this architectural device had a social purpose. By making the main balcony curve "more like the shape of a horseshoe, and
extending it back over the lobby or foyer, the entire dress-circle is exposed, and is almost without posts or constructions to intervene between the sitter and the stage.
This will enable the entire audience to see itself."[136] For Carpenter, who had proposed the balcony's setback, "the more an audience can see of itself, the more it
dresses, the more enthusiastic it becomes, and the more it individually and collectively enjoys an entertainment."[137] The effect of the collective audience appeared in
the hall's dedication service as a church on 5 January 1880, the first Sunday of the
new decade. Just before 11:00 A.M., the singing master led the congregation in its first
hymn. The house was full, with upward of 2,000 persons attending, and "when the
vast audience rose to its feet, it was a sight worth seeing."[138] By enabling the audience
to see itself as a totality, the room's architecture supported the Central Church's unusual tradition of congregational singing without the lead of a separate choir.

For their music, Central Church's members "had been very anxious to secure a
place where they can have an organ, and better accommodations than at McVicker's
Theatre."[139] The Central Music Hall's organ (fig. 25) was designed to surpass that of

Figure 25

Central Music Hall looking south to
stage framed by raised organ screens
at sides and organist's gallery above,
with ornamental cherrywood work
and stenciling probably designed by
Louis Sullivan. The organ pipes themselves were originally painted in gold
and colors. From *Central Music Hall*
(Chicago, c. 1880). Courtesy of the
Chicago Historical Society, ICHi-31467.

Cincinnati's Music Hall (fig. 19), then the largest in the United States, in order to
provide support for large choral concerts. This organ's fame also derived from its
huge screen of carved wild cherry wood. Designed by Robert Rogers, this screen
was commissioned as a major work to display local proficiency in the art of wood-
carving. Its motifs, based on natural forms, were hand carved over nine months by
more than one hundred students from the Cincinnati Art Academy. Visible during
performances as it towered sixty feet above the stage, the screen had fifteen panels
each dedicated to an individual composer, epitomizing the Music Hall's goal of
conjoining local civic pride and universal musical culture.[140]

The Central Music Hall's organ was donated by Swing as his auditorium's only
piece of stage equipment, since neither opera nor drama was to be performed there.
Of this instrument, its organist said: "Though not so large as the great Cincinnati
organ, it is vastly more effective, being both finer in quality of tone and better balanced."[141] The Central Music Hall's organ was also encased in carved cherry wood,
yet unlike its Cincinnati counterpart, the Chicago instrument was used mainly for
church services. Its casing was "very neat in its architectural design, and, without
being extravagant or showy in character, is prettily carved and disposed, and forms
a beautiful setting for the ornamental dummy pipes of the front," whose decoration
in gold and colors harmonized with the hall's. Louis Sullivan is said to have designed these decorative organ casings and the pipes' polychromy flanking the stage,
as well as the open loggia-like screen across the central organ loft. His continuous
association with Adler began about May 1880, before the organ was installed for its
dedication late in October of that year.[142] Sullivan may have designed the mural

Figure 26

Adler and Sullivan, Hooley's Theater, Chicago (first built 1872); remodeling of 1882, showing ornamental box tiers at right designed by Sullivan. Architects H. R. Wilson and Benjamin Marshall remodeled this interior as the Powers Theater in 1893 and 1897–1898 (demolished 1926). From Flinn, *Chicago, the Marvelous City of the West.*

motifs, probably stenciled, below the flanking organ casings and central loft screen. Their rapid rhythm of vertical forms echoed the organ pipes, so that the instrument and its architecture constituted a visual whole as the permanent frontal *scenae* of the house. The stage had no proscenium, no scenery, and no curtain, hence the concentration of ornament across the stage's walls themselves. One account noted: "The Central Music Hall was designed for the higher and more intellectual class of entertainments, such as classical concerts and lectures. It has no facilities for theatrical or operatic presentations."[143]

As the visual focus for the Central Music Hall's stage, Sullivan's decorative forms were characteristic of his and Adler's other theatrical interiors of the period. These included the ornamental designs for the proscenium and boxes of the remodeled Chicago Opera House, opened in September 1880; the Academy of Music at Kalamazoo, Michigan, opened in May 1882; and the remodeled Hooley's Theater, Chicago, opened in August 1882 (figs. 4 and 26). This last project entailed the installation of a new proscenium and adjoining tiers of paired boxes made of ornamental cast iron and colored in gold and bronze. Yet when asked about the style of these motifs, Sullivan responded: "I have not given study to the nomenclature of the peculiar art forms developed in these boxes or carried out in that proscenium crown. These are unclassified forms, and stock terms will convey no adequate idea of the successful treatment under a formula that is a new phase in the art view of architecture. . . . I prefer that you speak of it as the successful solution to a problem."[144] Presumably he had brought the same idea to the design of motifs surrounding the Central Music Hall's stage. As in the later Auditorium, his forms at Hooley's were appropriate to the social function of boxes, yet their style was not historically derivative.

Like the earlier Crosby's Opera House and the later Auditorium, the Central Music Hall was a concentration in one structure of related cultural facilities previously "scattered in a variety of places throughout the centre of the city."[145] On the first floor, along both the State and Randolph Street fronts, there were rentable stores, above which were five floors with seventy-five offices, including those rented by the Chicago Musical College, then the city's foremost institution of its kind. Above the main auditorium's stage on the hall's south side there were skylit studios, claimed as the postfire city's first designed explicitly for artists. On the upper floors of the block's west front on State Street there was a recital hall, known as Fairbank Hall, seating 600. Yet other than the main auditorium, the most distinctive room was the

Figure 27

Central Music Hall, Apollo Hall looking north, showing (a) trusses spanning north-south; (b) columns supporting trusses; (c) central vaulted ceiling with skylight; and (d) east and west semidomes. From *Central Music Hall* (Chicago, c. 1880). Courtesy of the Chicago Historical Society, ICHi-31469. Graphic notations by author.

small rehearsal hall seating 400 known as Apollo Hall (fig. 27), set in the southwest corner of the top (sixth) floor. This interior had a relationship of invisible structure to visible surfaces prophetic of Adler and Sullivan's later theater interiors. Comparing the interior view and the sixth-floor plan shows that two trusses, invisibly encased in the ceiling, spanned the hall from north to south (figs. 21a and 27a). These trusses were supported by columns (figs. 21b and 27b) partly visible in the room. Between the trusses arched a vault whose central panels formed a crowning skylight (figs. 21c and 27c). On either side of this central space were plaster semidomes also crowned with skylights (figs. 21d and 27d). The central vault and side semidomes, hung below the ceiling's invisible trusses, shaped the space as a container of sound. The Apollo Hall's design integrated function, structure, light, acoustics, and ornament into a unified statement whose sweeping curved lines in three dimensions presaged the Auditorium Theater's (fig. 95 and plate 6).

The room's seating sloped down to its north frontal floor as the performance space for the Apollo Musical Club, for which the hall had been designed and named. To the hall's north were the club's parlors, creating a suite of spaces whose generous daylight meant that the "general air of the place is light, cheerful, and homelike."[146] Founded in 1872 as an all-male chorus or *Männerchor* on the model of Boston's Apollo Club, Chicago's Apollo Club was in part an Anglo-American response to the city's numerous German singing societies. By 1896 there were at least eighty-seven such groups, including many German workers' and socialist singing societies. Yet Chicago's oldest and largest German chorus was the socially conservative Germania Männerchor. It had been founded in May 1865 after 300 German-Americans gathered to mourn Lincoln's assassination by singing dirges while the president's body lay in state at the Chicago Court House. Growing into a permanent singing society of 400 voices, the Germania Männerchor gained recognition through its large-scale performances of German opera at Crosby's Opera House in 1870. Just after the fire, the Germania Männerchor and its offshoot, the Concordia Society, "formed the nucleus of all choral work of a pretentious or public character, and great was the impetus given to musical affairs in Chicago by their public spirited assistance and co-operation."[147]

Before the Central Music Hall was built, the Apollo Club performed in McCormick Hall on the corner of North Clark and Kinzie Streets, on the Near North Side, nine blocks south of the North Side Turner Hall, at North Clark and Chicago Avenue, where the Germania Männerchor often sang. With the completion of the Central Music Hall, the Apollo Club gained a focal South Side location. Under William L. Tomlins, its extraordinary conductor from 1877, the club soon developed into a chorus for mixed voices, with some 266 members in 1885. By then it had become the city's most accomplished and celebrated singing society, performing works for chorus and orchestra. Since its beginning, the membership had included many of those prominent in local music, and the club performed on many civic occasions, including the openings of the Central Music Hall in December 1879 and of the Auditorium Theater ten years later.[148] When Sullivan first visited England in 1874, he had been "astonished at the brilliance of the demi-monde" at London's music halls, whose entertainment and architecture were keyed to a popular audience.[149] But Chicago's Central Music Hall was civic and elevated in character, like the later Auditorium. In 1885 an English critic visiting the city described the hall to his compatriots as "an edifice which, having regard to the object it serves, even mighty and wealthy London cannot match." He pronounced the Apollo Club's chorus "to be one of the best in America; further than this, its rendering of Rossini's and Mendelssohn's music on the occasion of my visit was absolutely the finest choral performance I heard during my stay in the country."[150] In the later Auditorium Theater, Tomlins directed subsidized series of choral concerts for workers, realizing Peck's vision of broad access to elite culture.

The Central Music Hall's exterior contrasted with earlier local preference for a modern French or Second Empire style for commercial architecture, represented by the Field, Leiter, and Company store to the south on the same blockfront (fig. 28). For contemporaries, the change in style was associated with the return of prosperity by 1879, whereas the Second Empire style of the immediately postfire monuments built in the early 1870s was by then negatively associated with the intervening depression. As one local observer wrote, the Central Music Hall was a modern building that "outlines, in a measure, the utilitarian ideas which architects were forced to follow within a short time and forms the link or divide between the columnated [*sic*] or pilastered stone fronts of former years and the gigantic brick fronts of later days."[151] The massive street fronts on State and Randolph were of gray limestone quarried nearby at Lemont. The lower two floors were of red and gray granite framing the store windows, with monolithic columns of polished red granite flanking the central two-story arched entrance, which recalled that of Crosby's Opera House. Of Adler's work, John Wellborn Root later said that it "shows a certain strength, simplicity, and straightforwardness, together with a certain refinement, which reveal the true architect."[152] Adler regarded the Central Music Hall as the foundation of his independent professional reputation, and one of its red granite Corinthian columns was ultimately set above his grave after his death in 1900. In that year the building was torn down to permit construction of part of Marshall Field and Company's new retail store on the site.

The Central Music Hall's connections to the Field enterprise provide a clue to the exterior's significance. Although symmetrically self-contained, Adler's front, with its central portal, projecting corner blocks, and crowning central tower, also balanced the symmetrical front of the Field, Leiter, and Company store at the south end of the same block, designed in 1878 by Edward S. Jennison. Both Field and Leiter were major property owners in the vicinity, and both had invested in the Central Music Hall, as had Adler. Field occupied one of its auditorium's boxes,

Figure 28

Central Music Hall from the northwest, showing cable cars along State Street and Edward S. Jennison's Field, Leiter, and Company Store of 1878 at right. Photograph of 1888. Courtesy of the Chicago Historical Society, ICHi-22298.

Figure 29

George B. Post, Western Union Building,
northwest corner of Broadway and
Dey Streets, New York City (1872–1875;
demolished). © Collection of the
New-York Historical Society, negative no.
48522.

while Leiter had presided over the hall's inaugural ceremonies. Though undertaken financially "with the greatest fear and trembling," the Central Music Hall turned out to be most profitable.[153] The building's location and design had made it a successful investment. Even after the Auditorium Theater opened in December 1889, at the Central Music Hall "there is never a night in the season when it is vacant, and here [came] all the great artists and lecturers who have visited Chicago since 1879."[154] By 1890 its stockholders were receiving annual dividends of 20 percent, with the stock valued at $375 per share on a par of $100. When Adler died in 1900, his own shares in the Central Music Hall Company's stock had risen to $550 on a par of $100, and Marshall Field bought these shares from Adler's widow.[155] Many of the hall's supporters would later commit much larger resources to the Auditorium, which was also a joint stock venture, yet a building that was not meant to be comparably profitable.

From this perspective the Central Music Hall was part of a network of investments aimed at concentrating people and trade downtown, with Adler's building and the Field, Leiter, and Company store together defining Chicago's cultural and mercantile core. When built, both structures were served by horsecar lines converging from the city's three outlying divisions. By 1881 Field, Leiter, and others would direct the Chicago Street Railway Company that built new cable car lines (shown in fig. 5) to improve access to their urban center.[156] The Central Music Hall's crowning tower with its four-faced clock both announced the building's location and told those coming off the horsecar lines how many minutes there were before the starting times of events inside the hall. Adler's clock tower with its pyramidal cupola perhaps recalled the one atop George B. Post's Western Union Building in Manhattan's lower Broadway, completed in 1875 as New York City's tallest structure (fig. 29). Adler admired Post, whose later New York Produce Exchange similarly provided a model for Adler and Sullivan's Auditorium tower, also conceived by Peck and Chicago's leading capitalists as a central civic symbol.[157]

Construction of the Central Music Hall, from the laying of foundations in May 1879 to the building's opening that December, coincided with a dramatic shift in local political power away from the Socialist Labor Party. Its candidates had made strong showings at the polls in November 1878 and April 1879, a week after the party's huge rally at the Exposition Building in late March. Yet by the elections of fall 1879 the

SLP's vote total had dropped by 60 percent, from 12,000 the year before to 4,800. By the year's close, national party membership had declined to less than one-third of what it had been nine months earlier. The city's only radical newspaper in English, the *Socialist,* launched in September 1878, had suspended publication a year later. This decline in Chicago workers' support for leftist politics has been attributed to the sudden growth of the national and regional economy in 1879, when employment was again plentiful and wages rose. Yet labor's local electoral efforts were also discouraged by a record of flagrant voter fraud against socialist candidates, as in the municipal elections of spring 1880.[158] Thus, as the 1870s closed, the opening of the Central Music Hall as the finest building of its kind in Chicago represented the renewed power of local capitalists after the threats of 1877 had subsided. This monument also marked the beginning of Adler and Sullivan's joint career as theater architects, whose work through the early 1880s gave distinctive local definition to structures of this type before they designed the Auditorium Theater.

Theater Architecture and Social Conflict **2**
in Chicago, 1880–1886

In his autobiography Sullivan recalled that "the year 1880 may be set as the zero hour of an amazing expansion, for by that time the city had recovered from the shock of the panic of 1873." He wrote that "in Chicago, the progress of the building art from 1880 onward was phenomenal," especially in the business district, whose structures featured an array of new constructive techniques, ornamental materials, and interior equipment.[1] The technical progress Sullivan recalled is widely known as the core achievement of the first Chicago school of architecture, particularly in the creation of tall office buildings. Yet this transformation of the building art occurred in years of uneven economic prosperity and continuing social strife. Connections between Chicago's architectural and social history of the 1880s are also visible in the development of the city's theaters, which have received less historical attention than the tall office buildings. Before the Auditorium, it was in theater design that Adler and Sullivan made their most distinctive mark. These theaters included remodelings of several of Chicago's major central halls: the Grand Opera House (1880), Hooley's Theater (1882), Haverly's Theater (1884), and McVicker's Theater, whose renovation was commissioned as early as January 1883, then redesigned in fall 1884 before being executed in spring 1885.[2] Although none of these buildings survive, when completed they were Adler and Sullivan's most publicly discussed works, whose success led to their commission and solution for the Auditorium. Like other architects in Chicago, Adler and Sullivan worked with an eye on developments in New York City of the same period. As regional variations on an architectural type then central to urban cultural life, their theaters displayed distinctions that emerge when they are compared with influential models in Manhattan.

In social terms, Adler and Sullivan's theater designs of the early 1880s were uniformly for high-grade, centrally located playhouses with upper- and middle-class

patronage. The buildings' spatial planning, mechanical systems, and decorative surfaces were all keyed to standards of interior architecture for these audiences. As
such, their theaters were the settings for a dramatic and musical culture that contrasted sharply with the characteristic working-class amusements around the city,
which had their own buildings and outdoor settings. After 1880 Chicago's labor
movement, not having succeeded in its leftist electoral efforts, turned toward radical political agitation. With the local rise of socialistic anarchism through the early
1880s, the entertainments made by and for laborers were in some cases statements
of class consciousness. It was this chasm between bourgeois and workers' cultural
opportunities that Ferdinand Peck sought to bridge in creating the Chicago Grand
Opera Festival of 1885, whose temporary hall became the visible model for the Auditorium Theater. His ideas for the Auditorium emerged partly in response to a
sharp rise in extreme political activity among workers that culminated in 1885–1886,
when Peck appealed to fellow capitalists to support his vision of broader access to
high culture.

McVicker's Theater and Its Transformations to 1885

When the Central Music Hall opened in December 1879, James H. McVicker,
Chicago's most eminent theatrical manager, acknowledged that "it surpasses anything of the kind he ever saw" and that "after a thorough examination of the whole
building, he could not think of a single feature in which he could suggest an improvement."[3] This full endorsement of Adler and Sullivan's work came from the
man who not only had built his own theater in 1857 but had reshaped it three times
before 1879. With the economic downturn at the outset of the Civil War, McVicker's
was the only theater offering legitimate drama to survive in Chicago, and it remained the city's main theater through the economic upturn of the later war years.
Until 1865 McVicker's offered a mixed repertoire of canonical English dramas, new
plays with elevated social themes (like *Uncle Tom's Cabin*), and a gradually declining
proportion of comic farces, whose low moral tone drew dramatic and also clerical
criticism. By 1866, when McVicker's had new competitors in a city of about 110,000,
some 2,500 people attended theater each night, or about one of every forty
Chicagoans. In this context McVicker thoroughly remodeled his theater's interior in
summer 1865, in large part to keep it competitive with the new Crosby's Opera
House that opened in April. The number of private boxes doubled to eight, while
the ceiling was "beautifully frescoed, containing figures of Apollo, Bacchus, and
great dramatists. The proscenium is also highly ornamented."[4] Though operas
played at McVicker's for only one to four weeks each year, the theater's new interior
conveyed a social cachet more like that of an upscale opera house.

If McVicker's renovation of 1865 competed with the local standard of Crosby's,
his rebuilding in spring 1871 was modeled on actor Edwin Booth's new theater in
Manhattan, which was the country's most architecturally ambitious theater when it

opened in 1869. McVicker's ties to the Booths had continued through the war years, when John Wilkes Booth had enjoyed great success on Chicago's stage as a Shakespearean tragic actor. In New York his brother Edwin was master of that tradition, and he commissioned architects James Renwick and Joseph Sands to design a monumental building on the southeast corner of Sixth Avenue and Twenty-third Street, well north of Union Square as the center of Manhattan's theatrical life (fig. 30). Inside, this building featured a marble vestibule and staircases, a classically ornamented 1,750-seat auditorium with optimal sight lines through three levels of balconies above the parquet, fan-powered ventilation, and a novel stage equipped with hydraulic lifts and devices for handling scenery. The architecture was to convey Booth's advertised credo that "I never permit my wife or daughter to witness a play without previously ascertaining its character."[5] Thus the theater's 120-foot tall granite exterior proclaimed a fashionable propriety in its Renaissance detailing and mansard roof, and also in its statuary. High above the main arched doors "are three large alcoves, framed in Ionic pillars, which are to contain enormous statues in white marble. Shakespeare will stand in the central arch, and Tragedy and Comedy will occupy the others."[6] Since canonical drama was not financially self-sustaining, Booth's Theater also innovated with its rentable stores, acting studios, and offices in a five-story section on the west side facing Sixth Avenue.

The next year, McVicker commissioned the Chicago architect Otis L. Wheelock to create a regional variation on Booth's monument. Like its Manhattan counterpart, the new McVicker's built in spring 1871 was a salient urban structure, higher than nearby buildings and crowned with a mansard roof (fig. 31). A central bust of Shakespeare atop its arched entrance certified the social acceptability of the productions within. Inside, beyond a spacious vestibule, an auditorium seating 1,400 (reduced from 2,000 in the previous building to enhance fire safety and proximity to

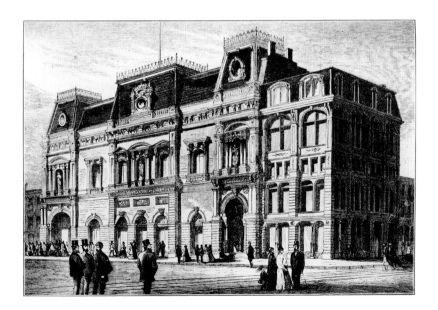

Figure 30

James Renwick and Joseph Sands, Edwin Booth's Theater, southeast corner of Twenty-third Street and Sixth Avenue, New York City (1869). Courtesy of the Hampden-Booth Theatre Library at the Players Club, New York City.

the stage) would have a parquet, dress circle, and balcony above, all with sight lines to encompass a stage separately designed by Wallace Hume to McVicker's specifications. McVicker did away with an upper gallery, whose low-priced tickets attracted lower-class patrons. To attract middle-class patrons to balcony seats, this level "in every respect, is as good as any other portion of the house. It is seated, carpeted, and upholstered in precisely the same manner, has its spacious and elegant lobby, and, as far as vision and acoustics are concerned, is even preferable to the lower part of the house."[7] Usable boxes flanked the stage, near new purely ornamental proscenium boxes, where no one sat and that were faced with mirrors, recalling usable proscenium boxes where the wealthy were on view in houses like Crosby's and Booth's. The Great Fire destroyed this McVicker's six weeks after it opened on 29 August 1871, yet its successor was the first public structure to rise again in postfire Chicago, opening in August 1872. Edwin Booth, by then McVicker's son-in-law, was a major creditor to enable rapid rebuilding. As before, "in general appearance the interior resembles Booth's Theatre in New York more than any other, though of course the frescoing and decorations are entirely different."[8] McVicker's Theater, in its program and architecture, was a regional echo of its Manhattan model, a situation the Auditorium Theater was meant to change.

Through the 1870s, McVicker's rebuilt theater was renowned as the setting for his stock company's productions of plays by Richard Sheridan, Oliver Goldsmith, and other English dramatists in addition to Shakespeare, as well as comedies by American playwrights. If this repertoire had little hold on a lower class of theatergoers, such performances, which increased in frequency and attractiveness through the decade, consistently drew literate, salaried white-collar audiences in addition to

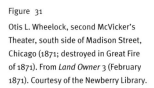

Figure 31

Otis L. Wheelock, second McVicker's Theater, south side of Madison Street, Chicago (1871; destroyed in Great Fire of 1871). From *Land Owner* 3 (February 1871). Courtesy of the Newberry Library.

the city's upper class. A bizarre incident highlighted the nature of McVicker's clientele. On 23 April 1879, the 315th anniversary of Shakespeare's birth, Edwin Booth played the lead role in *Richard II*. In the balcony's first row, where seats were less expensive, there sat a St. Louis dry goods clerk named Mark Gray, who read one published text of the play while listening to Booth's rendition of his part, which followed another edition of Shakespeare's drama. By the fifth act, McVicker believed, Booth's departures from the text Gray had in hand had so upset Gray that he drew a pistol and fired two shots at Booth "to kill the man that could, as he thought, so murder Shakespeare."[9] Evidently Gray had a history of animosity toward Booth, and his attempt on Booth's life recalled John Wilkes Booth's assassination of Lincoln fourteen years earlier. Gray's shots missed, but his attack on Edwin Booth while on stage was unprecedented in American theater, and the intense local reaction underscored the central place that McVicker's held in Chicago's collective culture.

By 1877 McVicker's was the last remaining resident stock company among the city's theaters. The system of traditional plays performed by a salaried troupe of local actors was being replaced by less dramatically elevated shows produced under the "combination system," which soon became nearly universal in the United States. Under this system, one well-known star performer traveled with his or her supporting cast, scenery, and properties. Such a traveling company contracted with local managers for a fixed percentage of gross receipts in exchange for furnishing a complete play. The local theater owner was relieved of the costs of maintaining a resident company yet also lost a large measure of control over the plays staged. This system rapidly increased the variety of plays produced but concentrated their production in New York City. The combination system grew with the railways, over twenty of which converged on Chicago, making it a prime venue for traveling companies whose productions were aimed at the broadest audience. The new pattern brought short engagements by varied companies, so that from its reopening in 1872 until its remodeling in 1885 McVicker's was "probably the only theater in the country that has averaged forty-eight weeks to the season for the last twelve years."[10] Its repertoire by then did not usually include canonical English dramas, whose restricted appeal and reduced revenues marked the demise of local resident stock companies like McVicker's. His theater continued to feature such plays for smaller audiences only a few weeks each year, usually in summers. McVicker acknowledged that actors might prefer the old stock companies, yet he felt that the combination system better served the public, "which have far better performances as a rule than under the old [stock company system]."[11]

The change in the character of plays brought on by the combination system rekindled debate in Chicago between theater managers and some clergy, who objected to the sudden prevalence, particularly on Sundays, of what they considered to be lewd productions. An increasing proportion of non-English immigrants narrowed the audience for old English dramas, so that, as one Chicagoan wrote, "we have sensuous show-pieces, roaring and essentially vulgar farces and farce-comedies, broad burlesques, and minstrelsy."[12] One leading local critic was Dr. Herrick

Johnson, a theological conservative who had succeeded the Reverend David Swing as pastor of Chicago's Fourth Presbyterian Church and who pointedly attacked McVicker's in the press in 1881–1882. When McVicker challenged Johnson, the minister gave the names and plots of plays presented at that theater to which he objected. A joint interdenominational committee of ministers and laymen met to discuss halting Sunday productions. After visiting with local managers, the committee did not pursue the issue.[13] Yet the controversy put McVicker publicly on the defensive (not for the first time in his Chicago career) and forced him to articulate his views on the social role of the theater in modern urban society.

In November 1882 McVicker chose the Central Music Hall, identified with intellectual entertainments, as the venue for his response in a lecture titled "The Press, the Pulpit, and the Stage." He quoted one clerical attack asserting that "ninety-nine of every hundred opera-houses have a saloon, gambling-hell and brothel attached." Another claimed that "the patrons of the grog-shop are the patrons of the theater. The patrons of the house of the strange woman are the patrons of the theater. The patrons of the gambling hells are the patrons of the theater and they go there because they find what they want there; because their depraved appetites are whetted there." McVicker criticized such pervasive generalizations, deeming it unfair "to place all theaters, all actresses, all actors, and all plays upon the same degraded level as the low saloons and halls which our municipal governments license as theaters and permit to exist among us."[14] He renewed his rebuttals in a lecture on the history of local theater, given at the Chicago Historical Society in February 1884, where he argued that Shakespeare's instructive insights about human spiritual nature had made this dramatist's influence as valuable as that of Martin Luther. Such dramas did not threaten social values but were a moral force for good, "co-equal with the pulpit and the rostrum, the school and the studio in shaping the intellectual course and determining the aesthetic plane of corporate society."[15]

In the context of this debate, McVicker viewed theater architecture as a means of shaping public perception of his theater and similar ones as different from those halls for working-class audiences that fit the image of clerical critiques. He spoke out in a period when Chicago, like New York, had more theaters than the city's population could support economically. In May 1884 McVicker was perhaps among those Chicagoans who advocated an increase in the city's license fee for theaters from $200 to $1,000, "the calculation being that this will be to the interest of the more pretentious houses by closing up some of those in which popular prices prevail. The high liquor-license has reduced the number of saloons by about six hundred, and it is thought that a high theatrical-license may cut down the number of theatres in even greater proportion than one-tenth."[16] Unlike lower-class halls, McVicker maintained, theaters like his had the capacity to deepen moral consciousness and broaden mental vision, so much so that "the character of its theatres should be one of the chief tests of a community's culture and refinement."[17] For McVicker, the artistry of his theater's designed interiors should correspond to the cultural level of its stage productions.

The same attitude informed George M. Pullman's (1831–1897) plans for the theater that architect Solon S. Beman (1853–1914) designed in the Arcade Building of Pullman's factory town (fig. 32). Opened on 9 January 1883, this theater seated 1,000 on its main floor and in its single balcony. Its opening was a major Chicago social event that signified the completion of the town of Pullman. The theater had been perfected in its sight lines so that "there [was] a full view of the stage to be had from every seat in the house." The Pullman Company's own woodworkers fabricated the carved ornamentation in balustrades, colonnades, and other surfaces, while walls were richly polychromed with painting and stenciling by the English scenic artist Hughson Hawley, who had decorated New York City's Madison Square Theater. For Pullman's playhouse, "the decoration of the auditorium [was] oriental in style, the designs employed being for the most part Moorish, Arabic and Persian." This stylistic theme culminated in the painted drop curtain, on which Hawley worked for eleven weeks to create a perspectively realistic view of "an oriental pavilion on the shores of the Bosphorus, with a view of a small Turkish town in the distance and boats upon the far away waters." What looked like rich brocaded drapery to the side of this scene was actually painted as "an exact copy of a costly piece of material loaned to the artist by Marshall Field." Other rugs, vases, and accessories in the painted curtain were copied from models of these luxurious objects, creating the image of a material culture far removed from Pullman's everyday work of manufacturing railroad cars. Such an effect on audiences of laborers was the interior's calculated intention: "In this artistic work there is not the remotest hint of cars, railways, and locomotives. The beholder easily realizes that something besides the mechanical holds sway here, and that for a time the hum, clatter and clang of machinery fades into silence, and even from memory, while the mind is busy with the pleasing environment of art."[18]

Although created for patrons drawn principally from Pullman's own population of industrial laborers, skilled workers, and foremen, this theater interior's richness was to be comparable to that of any house for upper- and middle-class audiences in central Chicago. In this spirit there were "ten beautifully arranged boxes, five on each side of the theatre. Curtained, adorned and elegantly furnished, they are like a dream of summer houses in oriental gardens."[19] The elaborately carved and spatially conspicuous boxes could be opened to each other to accommodate larger groups. Who were they for? Presumably not for Pullman's employees but for his peers among Chicago's wealthy, including Marshall Field and others, whom he transported to Pullman by special train for the theater's opening night and envisioned as his guests on later occasions. Pullman hired no manager but rather chose to direct the theater himself.

Figure 32

Solon S. Beman, Arcade Theater, Pullman, Illinois (1882–1883). Historic Pullman Collection, photograph no. 1.43. Chicago Public Library, Special Collections and Preservation Division.

The theater was open only three or four times a month during the theater season. As a devout Universalist, Pullman intended "to permit only first-class performances upon the stage, only such as he can invite his own family to enjoy with the utmost propriety, following a rule of selection no less severe than that which maintains the standard of McVicker's Theater." The latter was then known as "the leading and eminently respectable place of amusement of the city, the patronage coming from the better class of our citizens."[20] As Peck would do at the Auditorium, Pullman shaped architecture as a sign of high culture accessible to workers, who were presumed to want it but who often felt financially and socially excluded.

Pullman's selection of Hughson Hawley as the interior painter of Pullman's Opera House reflected not only a stylistic preference but also an ideological commitment to the vision that created the Madison Square Theater, which had opened in February 1880 on the south side of Twenty-fourth Street west of Fifth Avenue in Manhattan (fig. 33). It was the Madison Square Theater's company that opened Pullman's theater in 1883. The New York house's patrons were two brothers, the Reverend Dr. George S. Mallory and Marshall H. Mallory, both pious Episcopalians, who owned and coedited a religious periodical, the *Churchman.* In a time when the great majority of churchgoers were deeply prejudiced against the whole world of the theater, these brothers sought to prove "not only that a good theatre is a profitable speculation, financially, but that it is an important moral factor, and may be run in connection with the church and with church papers." New to the theatrical business, these capitalists "poured out their money like princes" to enable the theater's visionary creator, the impresario and playwright James Steele MacKaye, to create an architecturally ideal theater consistent with their religious and financial aims. The theater was to fulfill MacKaye's ideals for a stock company whose quality of performances and whose profit-sharing among playwrights and actors were modeled on Paris's Théâtre Français. In short, patrons and playwright created an alternative to the combination system. MacKaye dedicated the new Madison Square Theater to Edwin Booth, whose theater of 1869 a few blocks away failed financially after the depression of the 1870s.[21]

Designed by noted theater architects Francis H. Kimball and Thomas Wisedell and decorated by Hawley and Louis C. Tiffany, the Madison Square Theater was famous for its vertically movable two-tiered stage, patented by MacKaye in 1879. This elaborate mechanism permitted one scene to be played on a stage visible to the audience while a second scene could be set on a stage above, then lowered into the audience's view for the subsequent scene like a large hydraulically powered elevator.

Figure 33

Francis H. Kimball and Thomas Wisedell (architects), with Louis C. Tiffany (decorator), Madison Square Theater, for James Steele MacKaye, on West Twenty-fourth Street, just west of Fifth Avenue, New York City (1879–1880; demolished). Drawing by Hughson Hawley, showing one tier of double-tier stage set and musicians' gallery above stage. From MacKaye, *Epoch*, vol. 1.

The first stage, then lowered into a twenty-five-foot pit below the main visible level, could be readied for yet another scene while out of the audience's sight. Claimed to be the first mechanical moving stage ever built (predating revolving stages developed in Munich), this device minimized the time between acts usually required for setting the stage. The impetus for MacKaye's invention had been the general tendency toward more elaborate scenic detail and stage surroundings in American and English theaters. This trend had been partly inspired by the early performances of Wagner's operas in his Festspielhaus at Bayreuth, whose opening in August 1876 had been reported in enthusiastic detail by New York City newspapers.[22] To keep the audience's view of the stage from the parquet unobstructed, MacKaye raised the orchestra from its usual location in front of the stage's apron up to a "pavilion" over the stage opening, within the proscenium arch. The orchestra was held aloft like a singing gallery in a palatial household, or like a church's choir or organ in a raised central gallery.

The Madison Square Theater's design replaced the conventional horseshoe-shaped balcony (whose relatively large number of side seats had poor views of the stage) with a deeply sloped central balcony that gave almost all patrons a frontal view of the stage. To enable the theater to stay open in summer, the house was cooled by passing air over blocks of ice, like the method later used to cool air in Chicago's Auditorium Theater. The interior included proscenium boxes designed after a Moorish style of decoration. With such features, Madison Square Theater became a prominent national model. A native of New York City, McVicker returned there regularly and presumably had such a source in mind when he proposed to renovate his own Chicago house by combining "the good qualities of other famous theaters in Europe and America" with his own original ideas.[23] He may have approached Adler and Sullivan by January 1883 because of their extensive transformation of the Chicago Opera House (1880), which had been a partial model for Beman's Pullman Opera House, and their limited but admired renovation of Hooley's Theater (1882), McVicker's oldest and leading competitor in Chicago. Yet McVicker also supported the Central Church and had invested in Adler's Central Music Hall, which he praised.[24]

A view of McVicker's Theater in 1881 shows the interior before Adler and Sullivan's remodeling (fig. 34). In rebuilding this interior Adler, as he had done in the Grand Opera House, raised the ceiling higher above its second balcony or gallery, whose configuration, along with the first balcony's, was not otherwise changed. The higher ceiling "added wonderfully to the desirability of the [first] balcony and gallery seats," which, as the least expensive levels, were usually taken by the least privileged patrons. The improvement of these levels ensured that "there is not a seat in the entire house, from pit to dome, but commands a good view of the stage and is extremely comfortable."[25] To the public, McVicker proclaimed: "I believe that those who pay 25 cents for a seat should have the conveniences provided for those who pay $1.50. To make cleanliness and comfort prevail in the gallery will, I think, render the theater attractive to many who would otherwise seek the cheap accommodations of

Figure 34

McVicker's Theater, 1881, before Adler and Sullivan's remodeling of 1885. From *Interior Views (with Seats Numbered): Chicago Theatres* (Boston, 1881). Courtesy of the Chicago Historical Society.

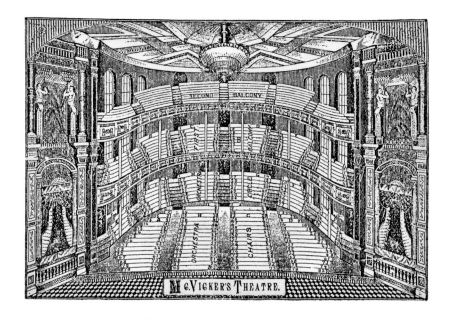

variety dives."[26] A uniformly high grade of seating was consistent with the public image McVicker sought for his house in the face of clerical criticism and with his financial need to attract a broader patronage. As he had said earlier: "Theaters would be bankrupt and the public deprived of a favorite pastime, if managers were to defer to the pretensions or demands of any one class."[27]

McVicker's efforts to optimize seating for all patrons were consistent with those of Steele MacKaye at the Madison Square Theater, but the remodeled McVicker's went beyond its New York model in acoustic design. As Adler had done in the Grand Opera House, he took several related steps in McVicker's to achieve acoustic control by reducing the room's overall spatial volume. First, Adler removed the old central dome and gaslit chandelier. As one critic wrote: "One can say good-by to the cumbrous ornament without a pang, for people in the body of the house never looked up at it without thinking of the sword of Damocles."[28] Adler then rebuilt the ceiling as gradually lowering toward the proscenium, whose arch was also lowered and widened. Its span of thirty-four feet made it the largest freestanding brick arch in the city. Between the lowered proscenium and ceiling, Adler added an upward- and outward-slanting sounding board to contain sound as it emerged from the stage and direct it outward. To either side of the stage were six private boxes arranged in two tiers slanting inward toward the stage. McVicker's new interior was thus "more compact than of old," with "a more intimate connection established between auditorium and stage."[29] The new acoustic environment was such "that the ordinary conversational tone of voice can be distinctly heard in every part of the house."[30]

Within McVicker's transformed interior, Adler devised an innovative system of mechanical ventilation for heating and cooling the house, which previously lacked such equipment. This improvement was essential not only to make seating on upper levels bearable in warm weather but to convey this theater's identity as an upper-class house, since stale, vitiated air, often laden with odors of food and alcohol, had long been identified with theaters catering to lower-class audiences. In the Madison Square Theater, mechanically warmed or cooled fresh air was introduced from the basement, rising through seating levels to be drawn upward through the hall's volume and out through the central ceiling, equipped with a powerful exhaust fan.[31] Yet this system carried exhalations from the parquet's patrons up to those on the first and second balconies. Since vitiated air was 50 percent heavier than fresh air, more energy was needed to force such stale air up through the theater. For the renovated McVicker's, as for the Auditorium, Adler designed a system that instead supplied fresh filtered air, warmed or cooled, from the ceiling. The vitiated air was then drawn out from below each seating level by exhaust fans that pulled it into the basement, enabling complete changes of air through the house every fifteen minutes.[32]

A few years after it opened in February 1880, New York's Madison Square Theater was among the city's first playhouses with a stage equipped with electric footlights, though the interior was otherwise illuminated by gaslights, whose open flames not only risked fire but flickered unevenly, creating a harsh, dim light. Introduced in Manhattan in 1881, Edison's incandescent electric light was more expensive than gaslight but had the triple advantage of being even, bright, and flameless. In Chicago incandescent electric light first appeared in selected public interiors of major hotels like the Grand Pacific (1881) and the Palmer House (1882). McVicker's as renovated in 1885 was the city's first theater to be equipped with such illumination, powered by the building's own generators. Moreover, Sullivan pioneered the idea of integrating the new lighting into his architectural ornament, making the light "a positive and integral part of the decoration." Over the walls and ceiling were perforated rosettes and bosses of cast plaster that "admit the mellow, beautiful light which permeates the house without the source of the combustion being seen, not a bulb in sight." Throughout the renovated McVicker's were 1,235 incandescent bulbs, with 105 in the proscenium's sounding board "shining through the apertures concealed by its elaborate ornamentation."[33] The warm color of the interior's incandescent lights contrasted with the harsh bluish white light of outdoor arc lamps that then lit Chicago's streets. Thus, in the evenings, McVicker's audiences would come from the sidewalk's garish older illumination into the auditorium's softer modern lighting. This incandescent technology helped to further distinguish urban reality outside from theatrical fantasy inside.

Sullivan developed a coloristic treatment for the renovated McVicker's that took fullest advantage of its brighter, more even lighting and created a gradation of color from entrance through auditorium. One observer wrote of the new incandescent interior: "The effect produced by this method of lighting cannot be described. The whole interior of the theater seems bathed in a luminosity which, while intensely penetrative, is so softened and refined that no glare can possibly hurt the vision or interfere with the fullest appreciation of the most delicate tints and the most subtle gradations."[34] Acutely sensitive to color, Sullivan here collaborated with decorative artists George L. Healy and Louis J. Millet to design and realize a decorative "symphony" of graded color. The entrance "presents rich reds and metal effects; as you pass to the foyer it changes to blue and gold, and presently from the blue and gold there bursts on the eye a pale red brown, which floats up in mellowing metamorphosis—like the sun from the filmy veil of dawn—to cream color in the ceiling. In this beautiful transformation act in pigments not fewer than twenty-seven different shades blend into each other and so imperceptibly that the boundary lines are indefinable."[35] The color was to signify the house's renewal and its respectability. Before Adler and Sullivan's transformation, McVicker's postfire interior was deemed "old fashioned," so that its remodeling "promised that the atmosphere of gloom which has brooded over it for some years past will be effectually dispelled."[36] Moreover, "night and pollution have no color, no beauty," whereas the color scheme of McVicker's new room was "like the opening day preparing for the full burst of sunrise, without a cloud," signifying "his dedication to the public of the west."[37] Unfortunately, no views of the remodeled 1885 interiors are known.

The allusion to regional character based on nature recalled Sullivan's own theory of architecture, articulated in his first public speech of October 1885, "Characteristics and Tendencies of American Architecture," which he gave at the second annual meeting of the Western Association of Architects in St. Louis. There he emphasized that, given the relative youth of the United States, it would be premature to expect, as some critics proposed, the sudden flowering of an original, highly developed American style. Instead one should "look rather for the early signs of a spontaneous architectural feeling arising in sympathy with the emotions latent or conspicuous in our people." Sullivan saw the beginnings of a national style as of utmost interest, concluding that those whose work approaches most nearly "the qualities inherent to our race and potential to [sic] a national style, will come nearest to the hearts of our people." He saw in American architecture of the 1880s not a lack of references to foreign historic styles, but rather each of these "being quietly divested of its local charm, and clothed in a sentiment and mannerism unmistakably our own."[38]

This dual process of articulating native sentiments and adapting foreign styles presumably underlay Sullivan's designs for the renovated McVicker's. On one level, its coloristic and ornamental scheme was hailed as wholly new. One local observer claimed: "Nothing like it, or anything even approaching it, has ever before been seen in this country."[39] This assessment is consistent with Sullivan's view of the inventive forms he had designed for Hooley's Theater in 1882, which he had identified as "a new phase in the art view of architecture."[40] Yet at the same time, accounts of the opening of McVicker's termed the ornamental scheme as "after the Moresque pattern, and everything conforms, with slightly varying degrees in different parts of the house, to this general idea."[41] Sullivan's adaptation of Moorish architectural forms may have been his variation on their use in the Madison Square Theater and in Kimball and Wisedell's Casino Theater, opened in 1882. There the Islamic motifs were more literal, on both the interior and the exterior (fig. 35), where they were profusely rendered in terra cotta. The appearance of the Moorish style in Manhattan followed its use in the 1882 remodeling of London's Royal Panopticon from an exhibition hall into a music hall, known as the Alhambra Theater, whose interior recreated the theme of a palatial Islamic "pleasure dome." MacKaye had similarly described the Madison Square Theater as "a castle in Spain," perhaps alluding to Moorish palaces there.[42]

Several notable buildings in Chicago of the mid-1880s adapted Moorish motifs. Yet in the renovated McVicker's, Sullivan, though reportedly inspired by this style, had a different agenda for architecture than did his contemporaries who replicated its forms literally.[43] One admirer of Kimball and Wisedell's Casino Theater in New York argued that "as for the people who clamor for a 'new style' and demand that the architect of a building like this should invent not only the details of decoration, but a decorative system, without any reference to any historical architecture, it is safe to dismiss them with the single remark that they do not know what they are talking about. Architectural styles grow, they are not invented."[44] Sullivan sought to do precisely what this writer dismissed. His aim was to invent a decorative system that went beyond traditions of ornament. As he suggested in his speech of 1885, he sought to transform a distant historical style, known for its rich ornamental effects, into an expressively American idiom animated by his individual artistic invention. In McVicker's he created his first theatrical interior to integrate lighting, materials, and ornament in a way that he later developed on a larger scale in the Chicago Auditorium. As Sullivan wrote, "The architectural treatment of the interior of McVicker's Theater is based upon a single consistent scheme or plan which is differentiated into form, color and illumination."[45] Given McVicker's electrification, one architectural review of its remodeled interior noted that Adler and Sullivan's motto was, "Let there be light."[46]

The emphasis on electric light inside the theater had its parallel in their remodeling of its exterior front, whose six floors contained seventy-two offices (fig. 37). This is here compared with the four-story front before Adler and Sullivan's renovation of 1885 (fig. 36). The office rents in the expanded structure were to help sustain the theater financially, in part to enable McVicker to pursue his sometimes unremunerative stagings of classic English drama. The rental value of these north-facing offices depended on adequate daylight. Taking the existing postfire front as their point of departure, Adler and Sullivan added two stories, introduced a central projecting galvanized iron bay between the earlier structure's masonry bays, and connected the central and flanking bays by balconies with ornamental railings at the level of the fifth floor. The continuous crowning story tied these bays together

Figure 35
Kimball and Wisedell, Casino Theater, southeast corner of Broadway and Thirty-ninth Street, New York City (1882; demolished); photograph of 1888, showing a playbill at base of corner tower. Theater Collection, Museum of the City of New York.

across the front, beneath a decorative cornice of galvanized iron, unlike the pre-1885 carved-stone bracketed cornice. It had a stone balustrade with crowning finials on either side of a central segmental pediment framing a relief of Shakespeare, below an eagle, like the prefire theaters (figs. 7 and 31). At the front's base, Adler and Sullivan kept the existing two-story projecting loggia as a publicly familiar sign of McVicker's, whereby a "light and graceful canopy invites you to glance within and examine the wide and handsome entrance."[47] The four statues above the loggia were also retained, yet the new doorway below was fashioned as a double arch framing the ornamental tympana, with a central statue much like a trumeau figure on a medieval church portal, as if to signify the moral acceptability of the entertainment offered within. The renovated exterior proclaimed the continuity and renewal of its patron McVicker's presence on his central site, marking his theater as the choice venue for the highest caliber of plays for a broad urban audience.

The renewed McVicker's was to be the architectural setting for an experiment with a new stock company. McVicker had disbanded his old troupe because its productions had not been profitable, yet after investing in the renewed house, if "he finds that there is sufficient encouragement to maintain such an institution, his theater will continue to have a stock company. Otherwise he will complete negotiations now pending to present the regular run of combination attractions."[48] McVicker temporarily engaged a company of players to produce Goldsmith's *She Stoops to*

Figure 36

McVicker's Theater, Madison Street front as rebuilt after the Great Fire of 1871, before Adler and Sullivan's renovation of 1885. Courtesy of the Chicago Historical Society, ICHi-01757.

Figure 37

Adler and Sullivan, McVicker's Theater, Madison Street front designed for renovation of 1885, showing outdoor emergency exit stairs on east alley side leading down from theater's upper seating levels. Rendering by Paul C. Lautrup. From *Inland Architect and News Record* 5 (May 1885). Architecture Photograph Collection, Courtesy of the Art Institute of Chicago.

Conquer and Sheridan's *School for Scandal.* Like his architects Adler and Sullivan, McVicker was known for his idealistic commitment to art, selecting plays for their dramatic merit rather than their profit potential. As far as commercial conditions permitted, McVicker "always maintained a standard at his own theatre which enabled him to look to the greatest purist in theatrical matters straight in the face—without evasion and without apology."[49]

Unfortunately, local patronage was not sufficient to support productions of this stock company, which McVicker disbanded in August 1885, within two months of the theater's reopening. One critic wrote that the decision "makes all sorry that the gorgeous theatre is to be turned over to Burlesque Bluffers, and the usual combination slop-work which has already demoralized the whole theatrical world of America, and is doing its best to utterly ruin all correct taste and bring the stage back to the coarse buffooneries of traveling booths and country fairs." He felt that "refined and educated people have been driven from the theatre by the influx of such dramatic rottenness."[50] Such debate over the quality of local amusements prompted Ferdinand Peck to promote popular access to Italian opera, partially in response to the opening of New York's Metropolitan Opera House in October 1883.

Chicago Opera and New York's Metropolitan Opera House, 1879–1883

When McVicker commissioned Otis L. Wheelock to design his prefire rebuilding in 1871, he claimed that "the theatre will be adapted to opera as well as to drama."[51] From the earliest operatic performances in Chicago of the 1850s, McVicker's stage had served as one of the main local venues for short seasons presented by traveling companies before the construction of Crosby's Opera House in 1865. With the destruction of Crosby's in the Great Fire, McVicker presumably envisioned that his postfire theater would succeed to Crosby's role as the city's center for opera. This McVicker's largely did, but in a period when Chicago's tastes ran much more toward light opera. By the later 1870s the American tradition of Italian grand opera, centered in New York, had been profoundly affected by the new standards for scenic staging and choral support of Wagner's productions at Bayreuth. The first season of grandiose Italian opera in Chicago was that given in January and February 1879 by Col. James H. Mapleson's company on tour from Her Majesty's Theater, Covent Garden, London. His engagement was at Haverly's Theater (formerly the New Adelphi Theater), until then the largest theater in Chicago. Its interior, seating 2,500 before it was entirely reconstructed and redecorated in summer 1878, was far larger than McVicker's (1,800) or Hooley's (1,200).[52] To this renewed Haverly's, Mapleson brought a troupe, orchestra, and chorus double the size of previous performances in the city. With the productions attracting packed houses of over 3,000 including standees and yielding receipts of $58,000 in two weeks, Mapleson's initial success was the most spectacular in local operatic history, so that afterward Chicago "was in the throes of a grand opera furor."[53] He returned annually, with less success, in 1880,

1881, and 1882. Then in January 1883 Mapleson brought Adelina Patti, the foremost prima donna of the day, to McVicker's, where he repeated his initial triumph.[54]

During this period Mapleson was also the manager of New York's Academy of Music, which had remained that city's leading venue for Italian grand opera. In 1883 its preeminent position in Manhattan was challenged by the Metropolitan Opera House, which had opened in October. Unlike the earlier Academy of Music, the Metropolitan was financed by individual stockholders who purchased boxes in the projected theater for their private use. Although the Academy seated 2,700 after its renovation in 1866–1867, it had only eighteen proscenium boxes, which had long been occupied by families whose commercial wealth predated the Civil War. Those whose fortunes derived from such newer industries as the railroad were effectively excluded from owning a box, a conspicuous sign of social prestige. The issue came to a head after Mapleson revived Italian opera at the Academy in 1878 and 1879, bringing to New York his company from Her Majesty's Theater in London, which he also continued to manage. Mapleson's initial operatic tour to Chicago in the winter of 1879 was an extension of his transatlantic Manhattan venture.[55]

In spring 1880 the Academy of Music offered to add thirty-one boxes to the auditorium's main gallery to accommodate local nouveaux riches, who deemed this insufficient. Those excluded from the Academy's existing proscenium boxes led in forming the Metropolitan Opera-House Company to fund a new building.[56] Seventy patrons eventually donated $17,500 each by buying shares of stock in the new company in order to own a box. Among the leaders of this effort were Mr. and Mrs. William K. Vanderbilt, whose house at 660 Fifth Avenue was designed by Richard Morris Hunt and completed in 1882. Responding to perceptions that they were nouveaux riches, the Vanderbilts conspicuously imitated the fashions of European nobility in their entertainments and their architecture. Their house, for example, was styled after the chateaus of Francis I. In this spirit the Vanderbilts and their allies wanted "a new Opera House which should compete in costliness and splendor with those of the great European capitals."[57] Led by such families, fund-raising for a new opera house netted about $1,200,000, which, together with a loan of $600,000, met the $1,800,000 cost of the building. In May 1883, as the Metropolitan Opera House neared completion, its subscribers drew lots for its boxes.[58]

The patrons of Manhattan's new opera house gave their organization a name whose connotations bespoke the greater social acceptability of opera since the Academy of Music had been built. In New York, the popularity of Italian operas had supported the importation of leading European musical artists since the 1850s.[59] Yet some of these performances were seen as so emotional in appeal as to border on the disreputable. This view became dominant with changing repertoires of the 1860s, when plots of new operas dealt more with personal mores.[60] Such concerns underlay the name of New York's Academy of Music as an acceptable label for a theater chartered by the state as an educational institution but where opera had been staged since its opening. Leopold Eidlitz's building for the Brooklyn Academy of Music (1859–1861) also looked like a church, externally disavowing its operatic repertoire.

Yet by the 1880s architectural critic Montgomery Schuyler wrote that "it is quite certain that when these edifices were built, it would have been as difficult to obtain the money for an undissembled opera-house as twenty-five years later it has proved easy to obtain ten times as much."[61] The new Metropolitan Opera House would be a social institution for the elite. In its first season of 1883–1884, the Metropolitan hosted concerts, a major society ball, and some nonmusical events in addition to opera. The Metropolitan Opera House's name not only declared its theatrical purpose but adapted the term *metropolitan,* with its intended suggestions of cultural centrality. This idea had inspired the Metropolitan Museum of Art, whose building, dedicated in 1880, had been financed by many of the families that soon supported the new opera house.[62]

The Metropolitan's concept of audience shaped its architecture. In 1880 its patrons appointed a committee, which invited four architects to submit plans for an initial site about 200 feet on each side. Those of Josiah Cleaveland Cady were selected. Yet leases covering parts of the site banned nonresidential buildings for amusement.[63] This led to the purchase of a larger site fronting 200 feet along Broadway between Thirty-ninth and Fortieth Streets and extending 260 feet back to Seventh Avenue. Before Cady's selection, the chair of the Met's building committee wrote: "There is no Theater or Opera House in this country that can be taken as a model for what we intend to have."[64] Though he was an accomplished organist and musician, before he became the Met's architect Cady had never designed a theater, seen an opera, or traveled to Europe. His selection prompted him to tour European opera houses (including London's Covent Garden) in 1881 before producing his final plans. In developing his designs, Cady also relied on the technical expertise of his German-trained associate Louis de Coppet Berg, whose sister had studied music in Italy and provided pictures and details of European opera houses.[65]

As Cady explained: "In this country, where the government is not 'paternal,' aid has been found in another quarter: the wealthy, fashionable classes, who, even if not caring especially for, nor appreciating deeply the music, find [the opera house] a peculiar and valuable social feature. Its boxes afford a rare opportunity for the display of beauty and toilet[te]s. They also give opportunity for the informal exchange of social courtesies, being opened to select callers through the evening; the long waits between the acts especially favoring such interchange."[66] This method of financing "in no small degree determines the size and character of the house," where provision had to be made "for accommodating liberally and elegantly the boxholders who have built this house, guarantee it against loss, and receive their special accommodations as a return for the same."[67]

In Cady's plan for the Met, the auditorium housed a ring of equal-sized boxes in the tradition of La Scala in Milan (1776–1778) and Edward M. Barry's Covent Garden in London (1856–1858). Yet the Met's larger auditorium was a slightly modified version of their horseshoe-shaped plans. To ensure good sight lines from boxes near the stage, Cady shaped the boxes in plan as a lyre that flared outward where it met the stage (fig. 38). Indeed, he named his original competition project "Lyre," alluding to the musical instrument of Apollo as the god of music, whose image appeared in the mural over the proscenium. The auditorium's large overall area and its distended curvature enabled Cady to include a total of 122 boxes in three full tiers around the horseshoe and in an additional half tier of boxes beneath the lowest full tier. This half tier of *baignoire* (bathtublike) boxes was near the stage, where the lowering of the parquet permitted its insertion (fig. 39). As in La Scala, each box at the Met had an anteroom or salon used by boxholders' servants or for receiving visitors. The box itself seated up to six, yielding a capacity of 732 in boxes. Stockholders purchased only the boxes on the two lower full tiers. Those on the lowest half tier and the upper full tier were rented, at first for $12,000 a season. When the Metropolitan opened, newspapers printed diagrams showing who owned which boxes. To ensure adequate ticket revenues, the Met's entire auditorium was to seat 3,045, making it larger than major European theaters like the Paris Opera, with 2,156 permanent seats.[68]

Figure 38

Cady, Berg, and See, Metropolitan Opera House, New York City (1881–1883); half-plans of (right) first story and (left) second story. From *Harper's Monthly* 67 (November 1883).

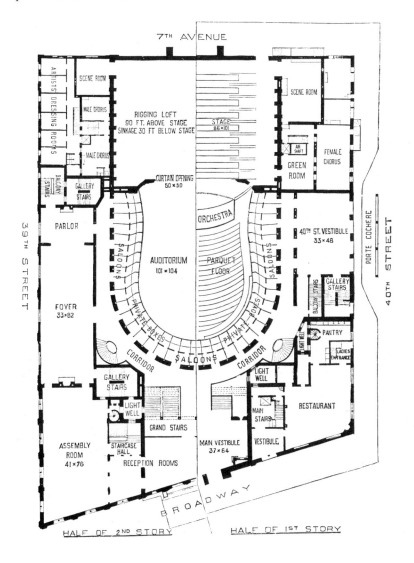

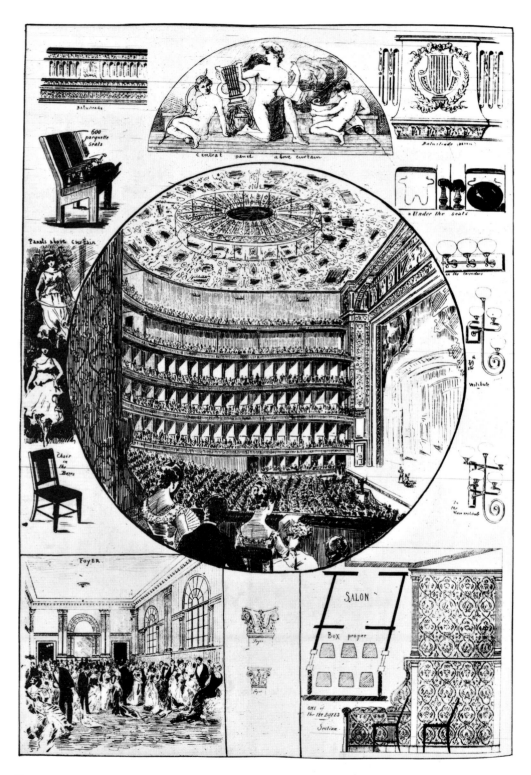

Figure 39

Metropolitan Opera House, original interior showing parquet rows, lowest half tier of *baignoire* boxes, three full tiers of boxes, and balcony below gallery. From *New York Daily Graphic*, 23 October 1883. Courtesy of the Library of Congress.

To lessen social competition, Cady omitted visually prominent boxes close to the stage in the side walls of the proscenium, characteristic of earlier opera houses like the Academy of Music. To make all the boxes equally desirable, "sight lines were drawn from every part of the house in each tier [of boxes] to the sides and the rear of the stage, to ascertain how much of the view of the stage would be lost from that point, and the contour of the auditorium and the pitch of each tier [of boxes] were modified in conformity with the results of these studies to the arrangement actually adopted."[69] In optimizing sight lines from boxes, the Metropolitan converted its wealthiest patrons "into a republic of oligarchs with no precedence among themselves, nodding on equal terms all around Olympus."[70]

After a fire in August 1892 gutted Cady's interior, it was remodeled by architect John B. McElfatrick, and again transformed by Carrère and Hastings in 1903. At the time of its closing and demolition in 1966, accounts of the Metropolitan's hall praised its acoustics, especially for the voice. Yet in the old Met's first season (1883–1884) some deemed the theater too large to be an acoustically optimal space because its huge volume made it difficult to hear performers from the uppermost galleries (especially those with less strong voices).[71] Also, though Cady's office prepared several hundred drawings to adjust sight lines, such studies did not perfect the quality of views from seats in the balcony and top gallery above the three full tiers of boxes. In the topmost gallery, only a fourth of the seats had a view of the stage, while in the theater overall, 700 seats had only partial views. At the close of the Met's first season, one editor concluded that "the problem of providing over three thousand good seats—that is to say, seats in which all the occupants can hear well and see well—in a theater of which three tiers are given up to less than seven hundred people [in boxes] is an insoluble problem. The Metropolitan Opera-house is probably the last attempt that will be made at its solution."[72]

Figure 40

Metropolitan Opera House, view of original stage and proscenium, showing frieze with central mural of Apollo flanked by individual figural portraits of the Muses and paintings *The Ballet* and *The Chorus* by Francis Maynard to either side of the frieze above topmost gallery. From *Century Magazine* 28 (July 1884).

The Met's concept of audience determined the volumetric form of the auditorium. When viewed from the stage, the house appeared as an encompassing wall of box tiers. On the parquet, the Met's seating rose in a shallow curve up from the stage. The total volume of space was largely determined by its three full tiers of boxes. Above these, the old Met had a gallery and an uppermost balcony around three sides. Above the upper balcony, the ceiling had a height of 80 feet over the stage. The high ceiling demanded a tall frontal opening or proscenium consistent with the overall proportions of the room. Cady's proscenium was as tall as it was wide, about 50 feet in both directions, and crowned by an attic (fig. 40). As one contemporary wrote, the need for boxes in many tiers increased the theater's height to create "an enormous unoccupied space within the auditorium." As a result, "the voice becomes diluted, its quality changes, and as the singer forces his tones to make them reach his distant hearers, half the pleasure is lost."[73] In short, the social demands of the patrons had resulted in a functionally compromised hall.

In the Metropolitan's auditorium as first built, trussed iron beams spanned 108 feet across the theater above its ceiling, whose design as a low dome gave no hint of these major structural elements, unlike Adler and Sullivan's later solution for the Chicago Auditorium Theater's ceiling. The Met's domed ceiling featured richly ornamented plaster coffering centered over the parquet and radiating out to the box tiers (fig. 39). Instead of a conventional chandelier, the original ceiling had concentric circular rings of gaslights, echoing the ringed tiers of boxes below. Working with the architect E. Prentice Treadwell of Boston, Cady chose blue green for the ceiling, with arabesques and gold medallions. The cast iron box fronts and proscenium were white tinged with yellow, with ornamental relief highlighted in gold, all seen under the flicker and glare of the original house's gaslights. Departing from the conventional deep red upholstery for boxes, Cady had these lined in a yellow silk with dark red threads. Their effect was festive, yet critics decried the boxes' pale color because it did not "supply a good background to the audience," meaning especially that it did not contrast sufficiently with the sparkling costumes of ladies in these boxes.[74] To correct this, its box interiors were redecorated before the theater's second season of 1884–1885 in a rose-colored satin. Only after its subsequent remodeling in 1903 did the old Met have its widely recalled red interior.[75]

Beyond the scheme of color, the architectural treatment of the Metropolitan's interior focused on the auditorium's front surrounding the stage (fig. 40). Above the proscenium, large brackets appeared to hold up the hidden iron trusses, each 15 feet deep, that spanned 80 feet across the stage. These brackets flanked a frieze above the stage, where Francis Lathrop painted a mural showing Apollo as the ancient deity of poetry and music, holding a lyre and being crowned by the comedic and tragic Muses, reclining to either side. This mural was flanked by individual arched niches representing eight of the nine Muses. Also, to the sides of the proscenium and above the topmost gallery were figural paintings by Francis Maynard, *The Ballet* and *The Chorus*. Across the top of the proscenium were the names of six composers (not visible in fig. 40): Gluck, Mozart, Beethoven, Verdi, Wagner, and Gounod. Although elaborate for New York City's theaters, the Met's iconographic program was simple and conventional relative to those of such European state opera houses as the Paris Opera (1861–1874) or the Viennese Imperial Opera House (1860–1869). The Met also lacked their ample foyers and grand stair halls.[76]

Not only was the Met to be structurally fireproof, with walls of solid masonry and spanning beams and trusses of iron, it was to be devoid of flammable materials for its ornamental surfaces. For the proscenium's splayed walls, Cady designed pilasters and ornamental panels of cast metal to minimize the carved wood that had contributed to earlier theater fires. Curved box fronts were of bent rolled iron, with cast ornamental relief.[77] Montgomery Schuyler regretted that Cady had treated the Met's interiors "in the conventional manner," concluding that "no doubt a more expressive treatment would have been desirable. But it is almost too much to require of a single architect that he should develop a decorative construction suitable to an opera-house from the modern construction of clay and metal which has been employed here. There are almost no precedents in point."[78]

The Met's exterior also lacked American precedents, since no opera house of its size, construction, or social pretension had previously been built in the United States. Cady stated that the interiors of a large opera house were so complex and expensive in their construction, equipment, and ornament that "there is little money left with which to make it a noble work of art, or a monumental work." Thus it would be best "if the architect acknowledges the situation frankly, and meets it in a simple manner . . . following some honored and appropriate style, especially adapted to the economy he must exercise."[79] Cady chose a round-arched style centered on a portico of three bays as the main entrance on Broadway (fig. 41). To the sides were corner blocks that rose to seven stories. Only the first two of these stories were part of the opera house internally, articulated as such by larger windows. The corner blocks' ground floors contained rentable spaces, with the Met's assembly rooms on the second floor. These could also be rented to supplement income from the theater, whose operations alone were not expected to be profitable. Supplemental incomes were also expected from the corner blocks' upper stories, which were initially identified as apartments for bachelors.[80] The residential corner blocks were

Figure 41

Metropolitan Opera House, on west side of Broadway between Thirty-ninth and Fortieth Streets, New York City (1881–1883; demolished 1966), looking from the southeast, showing Eidlitz and MacKenzie's New York Times Tower (1904; externally rebuilt 1964) at right, at Forty-second Street, Broadway, and Seventh Avenue. Photograph (c. 1905) by Detroit Publishing Company. Courtesy of the Library of Congress, negative no. LC-D401-18310.

crowned by a bracketed cornice and balustrade, so that the round-arched exterior style was distinctly Italianate, seen as appropriate to a theater initially intended for Italian opera. Since funds were insufficient for costly stone and marble, Cady's walls were of a pale yellow brick with ornamental terra cotta trim of the same color.[81]

The Metropolitan's exterior conveyed its institutional identity with Italian grand opera as a legitimate entertainment. To certify its social acceptability, the Met's sober fronts were meant to contrast with those of the Casino Theater of 1882 (fig. 35), standing opposite on the southeast corner of Thirty-ninth Street and Broadway. Designed as a concert hall, the Casino became Manhattan's main center for light opera and burlesque, successfully specializing in musical comedies. Its second-floor auditorium, which seated 1,300, also hosted Sunday evening concerts. The Casino's productions were famed for their women dancers such as Evelyn Nesbit, who, like a number of her colleagues on the Casino's chorus line, eventually married a millionaire.[82] Kimball and Wisedell's design for the Casino Theater's exterior was highly eclectic and picturesque. Its round corner tower and bowed loggia curving out above the arched entrance on Thirty-ninth Street combined with Islamic motifs to evoke exotic fantasy that bespoke the productions within. As one observer wrote when it opened in October 1882, a year before the Met, "The architectural forms are Moorish, and the soaring round towers and bold outlines of the exterior are sure to strike the eye of all visitors to the vicinity of Broadway and Thirty-ninth-st."[83] The north front's outwardly bowed loggia signaled the presence of a roof garden, the first space of its kind in Manhattan, meant for informal musical performances.[84] Communicating an appropriate urban character was also a central issue for the Chicago Auditorium's design, yet it was to be a different kind of theater, shaped by its city's social and cultural situation.

Anarchism in Chicago and the Bricklayers' Strike of 1883

When the Metropolitan Opera House opened in October 1883, its uniqueness and prominence made it among the most celebrated buildings in the United States. The completion of Cady's structure quickly stirred Chicagoans to act. As Adler recalled: "The wish of Chicago to possess an Opera House larger and finer than the Metropolitan, a hall for great choral and orchestral concerts, a mammoth ball-room, a convention hall, an auditorium for mass meetings, etc., etc., all under the same roof and within the same walls, gave birth to the auditorium proper."[85] Despite its theaters and music halls, and though it had grown to be the country's third largest city, Chicago was still without a building created specifically for staging grand opera. From at least 1883, newspapers called for the realization of such a project. It was also in this period that Chicago became the national center of the radical labor movement identified as anarchism. In the face of this highly charged situation, the city's capitalists who were the likely patrons of such an opera house continued to increase financial support for high culture as a force for social pacification.

In November 1880, seven months after Manhattan's nouveaux riches organized the Metropolitan Opera-House Company, the first American revolutionary socialist club was established in New York City. In October 1881 the first Social Revolutionary Congress in the United States convened in Chicago, after the International Social Revolutionary Congress at London in July. The much smaller Chicago meeting drew just twenty-one delegates of revolutionary clubs from eastern and midwestern American cities. Almost all the delegates were German immigrants, so the congress, organized by August Spies, an editor of the labor paper *Chicagoer Arbeiter-Zeitung,* met for three days in the North Side's Turner Hall. These radical local meetings belatedly countered the Republican national convention, held in Chicago's Inter-state Industrial Exposition Building in June 1880, where James A. Garfield became the party's presidential nominee.[86] Whereas the earlier Socialist Labor Party had been committed to political gains through elections, the congress avowed support of "armed organizations of workingmen who stand ready to resist, gun in hand, any encroachments upon their rights."[87] In October 1883, the month the Met opened, a second national congress of revolutionary socialistic clubs convened in Pittsburgh, the city whose violent railroad strikes in July 1877 had triggered comparable upheaval in Chicago.

This congress created the International Working People's Association (IWPA), which was committed to the "destruction of the existing class rule, by all means, i.e., by energetic, relentless, revolutionary and international action," and to the "establishment of a free society based upon co-operative organization of production."[88] These and other principles of what was widely published as the Pittsburgh Manifesto became the founding aims of the IWPA as the organizational framework for the movement soon known as anarchism. In Chicago, in addition to Spies and other German immigrants, its leaders included Albert Parsons (1848–1887), a typographer who became publisher of the city's main English-language socialist newspaper, the *Alarm,* launched in 1884. Well known for his radical speeches during the railroad strike of 1877, Parsons afterward had been a leading socialist political candidate. Yet the repeated failure of leftist electoral efforts had helped to convert him to revolutionary anarchism as the violent overthrow of capitalist society and its replacement by a postcapitalist world based on freedom, equality, and brotherhood.[89]

At the Pittsburgh congress, Parsons and Spies articulated what proved to be a powerful thesis, known as the "Chicago idea," which saw existing trade unions not as co-opted and ineffectual players in the capitalist order but as the organizational nuclei of revolutionary struggle and postcapitalist anarchism. With this idea, Parsons and Spies were able to link their revolutionary politics with Chicago's existing structure of trade unions, converting many working-class unionists to their radical views. Their cause was abetted by another recession of 1883–1886, which, though less severe and protracted than the depression of the 1870s, caused similar layoffs and wage reductions in skilled trades, with consequent misery for many. In Chicago, the *Alarm* estimated that 34,000 men lost employment, amid high levels of new immigration. Economist Richard T. Ely wrote: "Never before had there been seen in

America such contrasts between fabulous wealth and absolute penury."[90] The IWPA's extremist politics provided a frame of reference within which many of Chicago's dispossessed workers engaged militantly with its capitalist order.

No institution in the city was so strongly identified with this order as Chicago's Board of Trade. From its founding in 1848, this organization had developed into the most influential of its kind in the United States. With a membership of about 2,000 in the 1880s, the Board of Trade's key historical contribution had been the development of a system for managing the region's vast trade in grain. Since the 1850s, midwestern harvests of wheat, corn, and other cereals had come to Chicago's huge grain elevators. Receipts for quantities of these grains, specifying their type and grade, were then traded by hand on the exchange floor of the Board of Trade, whose leadership had established rules to which all its trading members had to conform. Although it was a private organization, the board's size and its location in Chicago made its standards of operation an influential norm for trade in grain and other commodities throughout the central United States. Its trading floor was the national center for speculation in buying and selling key agricultural products, an activity whose daily intensity had become legendary. Locally the board's membership, which included many of Chicago's most energetic business leaders, sought to promote the city's national commercial supremacy in its railway, manufacturing, and marketing systems.[91]

So influential was the Board of Trade that its decision to build a new structure had a major effect on patterns of urban development in central Chicago. Situated in a postfire building at Lake and South Water Streets, the Board of Trade decided in 1880 to buy properties at the juncture of LaSalle Street and Jackson Boulevard. The board's decision to relocate followed a general shift in Chicago's wholesale trade from the northeast corner of the South Side (near the mouth of the Chicago River) to the southwest part of what became the Loop. Once the city agreed to close LaSalle in the block south of Jackson, the Board of Trade controlled this site that became the southern terminus of LaSalle Street (fig. 42). The siting of the Board of Trade transformed LaSalle Street to its north into Chicago's central financial axis, immediately elevating land values and thus prompting construction of an array of tall office buildings in the 1880s. These included William Le Baron Jenney's Home Insurance Building (1883–1885; demolished 1931), Burnham and Root's Insurance Exchange Building (1884–1885; demolished 1912), and their Rookery (1885–1887).[92]

Even before its completion, the Board of Trade Building's embodiment of local high capital made it a prime target of labor unrest. Like other commercial buildings before the advent of the iron and steel frame, the Board of Trade's walls of solid masonry demanded the skills of the city's bricklayers. They could halt all progress on an expensive structure whose timely completion was essential to minimize investors' rental payments on the land before income-producing tenants occupied offices. As the largest and most powerful of Chicago's building trades unions, the local United Order of American Bricklayers and Stonemasons was organized in 1879. Early in

Figure 42

William Boyington, Chicago Board of
Trade Building (1882–1885; demolished
1929), with Jenney's Home Insurance
Building (1883–1885; demolished 1931),
left foreground; Burnham and Root's
Rookery (1885–1887), left background,
opposite Burnham and Root's Insurance
Exchange Building (1884–1885;
demolished 1912), right background.
Courtesy of the Chicago Historical
Society, ICHi-00255.

1883 this union's leadership served notice upon the city's builders, who employed the bricklayers, that the wage schedule after 1 April would be four dollars for a ten-hour day. The builders, confident that they could employ nonunion men if need be, ignored the notice, and the union initiated a citywide strike of the building trades by pulling bricklayers off the Board of Trade Building, whose cornerstone had been laid in December 1882. As builder Henry Ericsson recalled, this structure "was by all odds the most important project then under way, and the strike was looked upon as a challenge to the industrial and financial might of the city."[93]

Because of the indispensability of bricklaying to the building process before the advent of the metal frame, the union strike of 1883 was partially effective. Wage demands were largely met, though builders as employers refused to recognize the bricklayers' union, in that builders continued to insist on the right to employ nonunion bricklayers. Ultimately the strike was unsuccessful in this respect because many bricklayers negotiated their own agreements with builders independent of the union. Yet the action's duration of several months, its partial success, and the spirit of defiance it aroused set a local precedent for mobilization in other trades, including the efforts of the IWPA. The Chicago bricklayers' strike also provoked the federal Bureau of Labor to begin to compile data on the history of strikes nationwide. Through the strike period of 1883, sites of local conflicts were those of prestigious large commercial structures, nine of which were near the Board of Trade.[94] No previous building season in Chicago's fifty-year history had experienced such extensive and prolonged disruptions, affecting as they did the heart of the city's real estate interests, which included Ferdinand Peck's. His family owned the east half of the Grand Pacific Hotel's site diagonally across Jackson Boulevard from the Board of Trade, whose construction greatly enhanced the hotel property's value.[95] The struggle between labor and capital played itself out not only in strikes but also in protests over access to Chicago's cultural amenities, and it was within this arena that Peck chose to concentrate his energies.

Working-Class Life, Popular Access to Musical Culture, and the Chicago Opera House

Two events in the winter of 1883–1884 reveal how deeply segmented Chicago's urban society was and how the histories of its different classes interacted in the realms of musical culture and architecture. During that season, the social problems accentuated by the business recession prompted the Citizens' Association to fund an investigation of living conditions in workers' districts. Headed by a prominent local socialist and followed in the socialist press, this investigation revealed the extent of dilapidated, unsanitary, unheated, and overcrowded dwellings and of inadequate, filthy food and related disease that shocked and overwhelmed even the investigators. Tenement districts were without drainage, utilities, or minimal standards of housing for thousands of workers and their families, among whom exposure and starvation were not uncommon. Conditions at Chicago in the 1880s recalled those that Engels had described at Manchester, England, in the 1840s. A leading anarchist, Michael Schwab, asked of Chicago's situation: "Is it not horrible in a so-called civilized land where there is plenty of food and riches?"[96]

In its report of September 1884, the Citizens' Association's Committee on Tenement Houses noted that of Chicago's population of 630,000, some 250,000 adults were then "wage workers in the different trades, railway employe[e]s, factory hands, laborers and the like." The three-man committee, which included Adler and Sullivan's architectural colleague Frederick Baumann, noted that workers had effectively organized into trade unions, clubs, and societies that "comprise distinct bodies for nearly every trade and calling." These groups had central administrative leaders for negotiations with capitalists, property holders, and manufacturers, whom the report recommended "should likewise, by combination, be in a position to meet the questions of the hour in a practical manner, and apply the proper remedies for the general discontent and occasional popular outbreaks that a long period of mercantile depression is apt to engender." Baumann and his colleagues argued that trade unions sought solutions through increased wages, that socialists had fallacious theories, and that communists advocated destructive principles. The committee instead proposed "to reach down to the root of the matter" and "advance the idea that the betterment desired can be accomplished more easily by reducing, at the outset, the cost of living."[97] Among these costs, socially conscious capitalists saw that of homeownership as the most politically crucial, arguing that "the man who has a home is always on the side of law and order; the man who has a family has given hostages to fortune. The man who has no home envies those who have. Envy leads to hatred. Hatred leads to that state of mind in which a man is ready to take by violence what he has not, and as a preliminary step is anxious to abolish the existing order of things because he imagines that government does nothing but protect the individual in the possession of what he has . . . . Every home-owner is a recruit from the very soil in which the Upas tree of Anarchy grows." In this era, savings banks were widely mistrusted and not yet strongly regulated. Instead, workers saved for homes through building and loan associations, which worked well. Yet workers' difficulty in saving enough for homes discouraged frugality and encouraged reckless consumption of income. One capitalist argued that, given intelligent state banking laws, "Chicago ought to have $40,000,000 deposited in savings banks; instead she has 4,000 saloons."[98]

Though mainly concerned with designing and financing decent housing at an accessible cost, Baumann's committee perceived that a lack of alternatives led workers to prefer alcohol-centered recreation. It argued that "one of the reasons why 4,000 saloons flourish in Chicago [is] that their patrons have no better place for meeting and recreation."[99] Such patterns grew through the depressed year of 1884, when about 30,000 Chicagoans were unemployed and many of those employed worked only seasonally. Only 20 percent of Chicago's workers had full-time jobs, and one-third were idle for more than half the year. In these circumstances, the neighborhood saloon became in some instances more than a center of working-class recreation. These buildings, with their halls rented by local radical groups for meetings, became a focus for middle- and upper-class fear of losing social control over the interrelated processes of industrialization, urbanization, and immigration. In this light, temperance campaigns directed against saloons took on an overtly political cast. By 1880 Chicago's reformers were pushing for high license fees for saloons, to which the local radical labor movement was perceived as a direct appendage. Conversely, for German and other immigrant workers, saloons could become centers of resistance to the city's dominant political and recreational culture. As a sociologist of the period wrote, a saloon was often the "social and intellectual center of the neighborhood" and "a clearinghouse for the common intelligence."[100] In saloons, workers found the *Chicagoer Arbeiter-Zeitung* and other labor and trade union papers. Over time, some labor groups went beyond habitually renting space for meetings in a given saloon and tried to acquire title to the saloon's property so as to secure a permanent meeting hall that would be a headquarters for job placement, organizational business, or occasional strike mobilization. Continually meeting in the same place was an important element of a group's solidarity.[101]

Saloons were publicly identified with the increasingly popular program of the radicals. In November 1883, immediately after the Pittsburgh congress that created the IWPA, Albert Parsons founded the English-speaking American Group in Chicago, whose anarchist membership of about forty-five met on Wednesdays and Sundays from its founding until the Haymarket clash of May 1886. Parsons and his group were the most dynamic agitators in the city. The venue for their Wednesday evening meetings was Greif's Hall at 54 West Lake Street, across the Chicago River's south branch, near the center of the streetcar network and industrial area on the Near West Side. As the prime meeting place for many German unions and the Central Labor Union, Greif's Hall stood within blocks of the Peck family's original property on the southeast corner of Lake and LaSalle. This hall, with its public saloon in front and its rentable meeting room in back, was later described as "a place with a reputation for fostering anarchy." At Greif's Hall, Parsons's American Group heard papers on social and economic topics, followed by discussion.[102] Another similar meeting place was Neff's Hall, where German workers gathered on the North Side. This was a two-story frame building with a saloon on the lower floor in front and a meeting room in the rear (fig. 43), shown here set up for a festive occasion. The hall appeared as simply furnished with tables and chairs for small discussion groups and surrounded with framed pictures and busts presumably of working-class heroes, while overhead festoons swung between the walls and the central skylight. This engraved view was one of a series published by a police official in order to document workers' meeting places before the Haymarket clash of 1886. At the 1887 trial of the Haymarket conspirators, a detective testified that Neff's Hall was "known under the name of the Communisten-Bude. Different Socialistic and Anarchistic organizations met there."[103] Often, when workers' groups rented such spaces from their proprietors, leaders would pass the hat at the end of a session to meet the owner's fee. Alternatively, a labor group might compensate the saloon owner by promising to purchase a large stock of beer.

Figure 43

Neff's Hall, Near North Side, Chicago, as meeting hall for German workers' organizations before Haymarket. From Schaack, *Anarchy and Anarchists.*

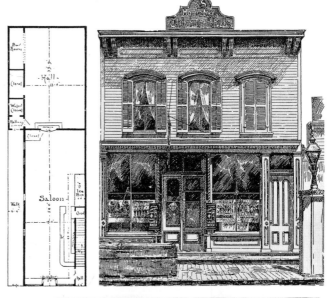

Saloons as centers of labor activism epitomized those aspects of workers' culture that Chicago's propertied classes identified as most threatening to their interests and that some civic leaders sought to counter with alternative systems of amusement. In the winter of 1883–1884, coinciding with the highly publicized probe of Chicago workers' poor living conditions and following the state of Illinois's first comprehensive statistical study of these workers' earnings, expenses, and living conditions, there emerged a controversy over the pricing of the city's leading musical entertainments. This new local debate engaged for the first time the issue of access to high culture for those with working-class incomes. The controversy emerged in the wake of the first season of grand opera performed in Chicago by the new Metropolitan Opera-House Company, which had traveled from New York after its fall premier to tour other cities before returning to Manhattan in the early spring of 1884. Unlike Mapleson's earlier Chicago tours of grand opera, the Met's company was managed by Mapleson's rival, impresario Henry Abbey (1846–1896). Abbey's company began its two-week engagement on 21 January 1884 at the new Haverly Theater, one week before Mapleson's troupe from the New York Academy returned to McVicker's on 28 January.[104]

Chicago's critics considered Mapleson's performances to be musically and dramatically superior to Abbey's, whom they viewed as a "consciousless [*sic*] speculator" funded by New York's millionaires to manage the Met so as to destroy Mapleson's chances of deserved success at the Academy of Music. Basing his scale of productions on the new Metropolitan, Abbey had brought with him an orchestra of eighty and a chorus of eighty. To support such shows, Abbey charged what Chicagoans viewed as "unreasonable and distortionate prices . . . which no one in Europe would have the temerity to demand," for "in older countries the lover of music, however poor in this world's goods, may hear the great singers at a trifling expense."[105] Abbey's profiteering made prices prohibitive for workers, including Chicago trade union groups that were then the focus of the IWPA's increasingly successful propaganda and organization. One editorial concluded: "Why should not every great city have constantly within easy reach of all classes of its citizens these ennobling divertis[s]ements? Music halls and art galleries, accessible to the poorest, promote peace and good order, elevate the general social tone and abound in all exalting influences."[106]

Such stirrings for an opera house came indirectly from the city's large manufacturers of musical instruments, who supported publication of local music trade papers. These papers' editorials promoted the project of an opera house to enable mass audiences to experience grand opera. Yet the fundamental problem with such a structure's realization was financial. The building's capacity had to be much larger than any existing Chicago theater so that the cost of operatic productions could be divided over a large number of ticket holders. For example, Mapleson's company had staged grand opera festivals in Cincinnati in late 1881 and 1882, bringing Adelina Patti from New York. When Mapleson's troupe played in Cincinnati, whose Music Hall seated 4,900, a ticket for eight performances, with three Patti appearances, cost

$14. When Mapleson came to Chicago with Patti in January 1883 and played at McVicker's (seating 1,865), a ticket for six nights, with only one appearance by Patti, sold for $20. If the price of opera tickets, as their cost to the public, were to be reduced, Chicago capitalists would have to invest in a sufficiently capacious permanent structure. Some observers maintained that such an auditorium could yield its stockholders an annual interest of 5 percent. Yet as others believed, "The Academy of Music needed must be erected by public spirit alone, for no one pretends to think or say that it will be a good financial investment. It must be large, with excellent acoustics, central in location, with exits on three sides possible—nothing else can give satisfaction or benefit the community. Such a building devoted to art and music would make it possible for the middle classes to hear opera and not become paupers."[107] As the venue of choice for large events, Chicago's imagined Academy of Music would replace the Inter-state Industrial Exposition Building, since that structure's enormous hall, "built for mechanical exhibitions alone," had acoustic difficulties, and since it had recently come to be used for socialist rallies.[108]

As early as January 1883, another editor had observed that "two or three Chicago gentlemen are ready to take hold of this work and contribute even more than their proportion to the construction of an opera-house, but they have not yet met with the encouragement which they had the right to expect from others."[109] Among these capitalists was Nathaniel K. Fairbank, the prime supporter of the Central Music Hall's construction, who had initiated the idea of an opera house and public hall for the city. In 1880 he had offered to donate $100,000 for its construction if nine other supporters would each match this pledge. With his strong interest in music, Fairbank served as president of the Chicago Music Festival Association for Theodore Thomas's concerts at the Exposition Building in May 1882 and 1884. From 1882 to 1885 Fairbank, with Thomas's prompting, "made many brave but ineffectual efforts to convince a number of [Chicago's] wealthy citizens and her supposed leaders in culture and refinement to join in giving Chicago a great public hall and opera house." During these years Adler and Sullivan made a series of "comprehensive studies" that "had enabled them to show that adaptation to a multiplicity of uses could be attained in the construction and equipment of an Auditorium without imperiling its utility or its beauty."[110] No record of these studies is known, yet they were apparently done for Fairbank. Sullivan later recalled that about 1885 Fairbank started the movement for building an opera house and that Adler and Sullivan "made some sketches, but somehow the thing did not pull through. It lagged along. No one took a special interest in it, that is, interest enough to put up the money."[111] Sullivan recounted that for several years before the start of Peck's Auditorium project in 1886 "there had been talk to the effect that Chicago needed a grand opera house; but the several schemes advanced were too aristocratic and exclusive to meet with general approval."[112]

Fairbank's unrealized proposals were presumably a stimulus for Peck's project for the Auditorium Building, yet another completed local structure provided Peck with

Figure 44

Henry Ives Cobb and Charles S. Frost,
Chicago Opera House, southwest corner
of Washington and Clark Streets, Chicago
(1884–1885; demolished 1912). At right
(west) is Edward Baumann and Harris
Huehl's Chamber of Commerce Building,
on the southeast corner of LaSalle and
Washington Streets (1890; demolished
1928). Photograph by J. W. Taylor.
Architecture Photograph Collection,
Courtesy of the Art Institute of Chicago.

a model for his monument's financial and architectural planning. This was the Chicago Opera House on the southwest corner of Washington and Clark Streets, finished in 1885 (fig. 44). In January 1884 several local capitalists had announced their intention to finance this structure. Their leaders included Charles Henrotin, a stockbroker and founder of the Chicago Stock Exchange in 1882, and William D. Kerfoot, among the city's most prominent real estate dealers.[113] Their effort presumably responded not only to the Metropolitan Opera House's opening in October 1883, but also to a publicly alarming report of the city council's Committee on Public Buildings issued in December of that year. Charged with inspecting Chicago's theaters and public halls for their safety in case of fire, the committee detailed extremely hazardous conditions prevailing in Haverly's Theater, then the city's largest. Its stage was not sufficiently insulated against fire spreading to the auditorium, and its two large balconies were served by narrow staircases and few exits.[114] The report came just weeks before Abbey's Metropolitan Opera Company was scheduled to play at Haverly's. After their arrival, one editor wrote: "Can any one, after reading this report, and thus being aware of the true condition of this fire trap, stand in the auditorium and view the immense throng which is gathering there each night during the opera season, without shuddering for the jeopardy of precious lives through the criminal negligence of provision for their safety . . . without a horrible foreboding that the (European) theatre horror [of fire] is sooner or later to be repeated in Chicago?"[115]

In this context, the supporters of the Chicago Opera House block commissioned architects Henry Ives Cobb (1859–1931) and Charles S. Frost (1856–1932) to design a theater seating 2,300 set behind a ten-story L-shaped office block fronting on Clark and Washington Streets. Its capacity would not enable low prices for opera, but its construction was to ensure a degree of safety not found in Haverly's. The site, the single most valuable piece of property owned by Philip Peck at his death in 1871, was leased from the Peck estate, though Ferdinand Peck and his brothers were not among the project's chief investors. Its location directly across Washington Street from the Chicago City Hall and Cook County Courthouse made it an optimal location for a large volume of rentable space, including twelve stores along the sidewalk and 240 offices on upper floors, which soon filled with lawyers and other professionals. The Chicago Opera House was "one of the first of the buildings erected on the joint-stock plan, and the success of its promoters led to the erection of the Auditorium."[116] A joint stock arrangement meant that the project's capital was held in a common fund but that individual stockholders could sell their shares or transfer them to others. The building's cost of $600,000 was met with an issue of $350,000 in closely held capital stock and an issue of $250,000 in bonds paying 6 percent annually. The site was rented at 6 percent of the land's value, to be reappraised every five years. By 1889, four years after the Chicago Opera House opened, its stockholders received dividends of 10 to 15 percent annually on their investment, and the land's value had risen, though stockholders and the Peck family disputed its reappraised value.[117]

The Chicago Opera House theater was designed specifically for the productions of impresario David Henderson, which were arranged "upon a basis never before seen in this country of spectacular extravaganza." As a former drama editor and newspaper founder, Henderson, seeking to become wealthy as a theatrical manager, became known for his elaborate staging of "musical burlesque, on a scale beside which everything else in that line ever attempted in America shrinks to pigmy proportions."[118] As one guidebook noted: "This house is the scene of triumph of the Amazon show, and here the tinseled marching host has scored its greatest success in America, and summer after summer the richest of spectacles and the sorriest of dramas draw crowded houses with no change of bills."[119] About twenty-six weeks of each year were devoted to Henderson's musical extravangazas, the first of which was "Arabian Nights," produced shortly after the Chicago Opera House's opening in August 1885. For such shows, Cobb and Frost had designed the city's most completely equipped stage, one of the finest "in the country for plays requiring machinery to produce spectacular effects." During the other half of the year, Henderson offered a repertoire of reputable drama and opera staged by traveling companies on the combination system. His program made the Chicago Opera House "essentially the representative theater of Chicago, and a visitor there is always assured of high class entertainment."[120]

Constructed from May 1884, the Chicago Opera House was steadily promoted as having "the only fireproof theater in Chicago" and the only entirely fireproof theater in the country outside New York City, where the Metropolitan Opera House had set a new standard.[121] The whole building, including the theater, was to have incandescent electric lights. Spanning structures were to be iron beams resting on masonry walls, including a wall three feet thick at the proscenium separating the stage from the audience, since most theater fires began on the stage and then spread into the house. To further reduce risk to the audience from fire, all heating and ventilating machinery was placed outside the theater in the adjoining office building. Unfortunately, the theater's great size, with seating for 2,300, led to excessive crowding of rows, hampering entrance and egress. The interior "impresses one as less open and airy than most of the other city theaters, more compact, something of agreeable appearance having been sacrificed to the purpose of getting as many people as possible close to the stage."[122] Another critic wrote of the scene on opening night in August 1885: "By the way the people on the sides of the balcony stand up and crane their necks to look at the stage it is evident that the construction of the many seats in that quarter will have to be revised." That evening and later, the ventilation system failed to supply the house with adequate cooled air, so that "long before the play is over many seats in the parquet and balcony are deserted because of the heat."[123] Like New York's Metropolitan, the Chicago Opera House had images of Apollo and the Muses over its proscenium arch. In the auditorium, green, dull red, and buff tones toward the floor lightened to white and gold above, surrounding the ceiling's central skylight of stained glass.[124] One editor criticized this decorative scheme, whose gaudiness corresponded to the character of the productions. There "every advantage has been taken of the color scale, so as to obtain the greatest amount of glitter and glare. There is a want of repose—some cool spot to rest the eye upon. An endeavor has been made to gild refined gold and paint the lily, and the feeling aroused is more one of astonishment than admiration."[125]

Owing in part to its faulty design, the Chicago Opera House's first season from August 1885 to June 1886 proved financially disastrous, and the theater was then closed for a comprehensive remodeling by Adler and Sullivan before reopening in August 1886. They reduced the number of seats to ease movement along the aisles, raised the ceiling above the topmost gallery, and reshaped that gallery's and the balcony's seating to improve sight lines. The stage's squared proscenium was given an acoustically improved round-arched form, and the ventilation system's defects were corrected. Sullivan also redesigned the interior's ornamental scheme, and the theater reopened to much praise. One account noted that the remodeled auditorium "now appears as round and compact as it was formerly long and narrow."[126] Adler had achieved this effect by bringing the main balcony forward over the parquet. This provided more seating in the balcony yet reduced the auditorium's apparent volume forward of the balcony, as shown on the floor plans of these levels (fig. 45). Presumably the balcony's new frontal addition was high enough so that the rear parquet seats beneath it were not deeply overshadowed by the expanded balcony above.

Externally the Chicago Opera House had its auditorium set inside the block of office floors, an approach to planning commercial theaters on valuable real estate also then typical of New York. The Chicago Opera House's steel frame was externally clad in pressed brick articulated by an arcade whose vertical piers rose from the fifth floor through the eighth. Wider piers marking vertical lines of structural columns alternated with narrower piers. Above, ornamental terra cotta capitals marked the springing line of the arches, which had molded brick frames above. One critic called it "an exceedingly practical building; in fact, it is nothing but a big box, pierced with square holes. It is said to be very well built, and is certainly very satisfactory in arrangement, but one cannot but wish it was treated in a more artistic manner." The Chicago Opera House's rigorously functional exterior, with maximal light afforded by its windows, contrasted with the elaborate neo-Renaissance Chicago City Hall and Cook County Courthouse across Washington Street (fig. 194), finished in 1885.[127] In Peck's later Auditorium, Adler and Sullivan combined commercial functionality and civic monumentality in a single structure of even larger scale.

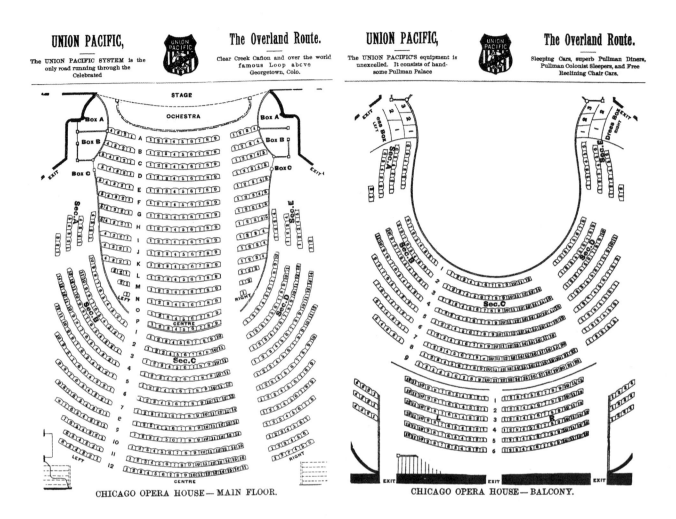

CHICAGO OPERA HOUSE—MAIN FLOOR.   CHICAGO OPERA HOUSE—BALCONY.

Even more so than the Auditorium, the Chicago Opera House fronts gave almost no hint of the theater inside. Only its entrance was well marked, with an iron canopy extending over the sidewalk to the curb on Washington Street (fig. 46). This canopy's incandescent lamps advertised the interior's electrification as they lighted the playbills astride the doors, so that this entrance's "illuminations at night make it a landmark of the city."[128] After Adler and Sullivan's renovation, Henderson's Chicago Opera House reopened on Saturday, 14 August 1886. In his autobiography, Frank Lloyd Wright recalled his arrival in Chicago by train from Wisconsin, giving the date as May 1887. Yet Wright offered an alternative clue when he described his first evening walking into the city through a cool rain, until he stood "shivering now in front of the Chicago Opera House on Washington Street." There "under a great canopy that made a shelter from the rain were enormous posters—"SIEBA"—Extravaganza by David Henderson, Grand Corps de Ballet."[129] Announcements from the time record that Henderson staged this production in the week beginning Sunday, 29 August 1886. As an urban neophyte, Wright recalled being impressed with "Sieba" as his first experience of Chicago theater. He wrote that "the Henderson

Figure 45

Chicago Opera House, floor plans of (left) parquet and (right) balcony levels after Adler and Sullivan's remodeling of 1886. From E. L. Lomax, *Diagrams: Chicago Theatres*, 2d ed. (Chicago, 1890). Courtesy of the Chicago Historical Society.

Figure 46

Chicago Opera House, theater entrance
canopy on Washington Street. From Flinn,
Chicago, the Marvelous City of the West.

extravaganzas were duly extravagant. This one took the roof off an unsophisticated mind." Wright's response echoed that of many rural midwesterners. One account of 1887 noted: "It is no uncommon sight to see a party of honest country folks appearing, gripsacks in hand at the doors of the Chicago Opera House, having come straight from the train to the theater to witness the show, the fame of which had penetrated to their homes in the country."[130] Presumably Wright did not know that this remodeled playhouse, the first interior he entered in Chicago, was the most recent theater of Adler and Sullivan, whom he would soon assist in the design of the Auditorium Theater.

The May Music Festivals and Chicago's Anarchists, 1882–1884

As rebuilt, the Chicago Opera House provided an architectural and financial model for a permanent auditorium of about 2,000 seats. Yet before 1885 local demand for grand opera on a scale sufficient to fill a hall seating 4,000 or more had yet to be proved. This was presumably why Fairbank's project of the early 1880s for such a structure had not attracted support. Fairbank's May Music Festivals of 1882 and 1884, held inside the temporarily remodeled Exposition Building, were to counter this perception, as the first Chicago musical events to attract the kind of mass audience that Peck envisioned for opera. Their musical standards, and their scale as performances, made them prime precedents for Peck's development of his idea for the Auditorium Building as a home for high culture.

The central figure in the May Festivals was Theodore Thomas, whose orchestra played similar engagements in other cities, principally New York and Cincinnati. Thomas was the prime American example of an orchestra leader who had successfully cultivated a middle-class, though not a working-class, following. He was devoted to classical rather than popular music. As his wife recalled, Thomas, unlike Peck and his supporters who built the Auditorium, concluded that "neither children nor what are called 'wage-workers' were sufficiently advanced intellectually to be able to appreciate the class of music that was his specialty."[131] In this role of entertaining and instructing a middle-class audience, Thomas's career had forerunners in European traditions of public concerts of classical and popular music earlier in the nineteenth century. London, Paris, and Vienna were among those cities with traditions of such concerts going back to the Biedermeier period before the revolution of 1848. Large choral performances had also been held at London's Crystal Palace, built for the Great Exhibition of 1851. After being rebuilt at Sydenham in

1853, the Crystal Palace housed more such large events. These concerts later found a home in the Royal Albert Hall (1867–1871) in South Kensington, London, where Adelina Patti sang, and whose capacity Chicago's Auditorium was to surpass. Early in the life of France's Third Republic, for the Paris international exposition of 1878 the architect Gabriel Davioud designed the large Palais du Trocadéro as a popular concert hall where opera could also be staged. In New York City, Thomas's orchestra played at Steinway Hall and others, but not in an auditorium large enough for choral events, like Cincinnati's Music Hall.[132]

Since 1869 Thomas's orchestra had come to Chicago at least once every year except 1871, when it had been scheduled to open Crosby's Opera House on the night that the Great Fire broke out. George B. Carpenter arranged Thomas's Chicago concerts through the 1870s, including a series at the Exposition Building in summer 1877. These concerts began on 18 June and continued through the city's great railroad strike in late July, during which attendance dropped, making the whole series financially marginal for Thomas. On 27 July, as the strike was being forcibly suppressed, Marshall Field, Wirt Dexter, and Nathaniel Fairbank, who had been among those capitalists who supported the efforts of public and private militia against the workers, wrote to Thomas to request his return the next year. They noted that "in the way of pleasure and musical instruction there has been nothing in Chicago comparable to your summer garden concerts."[133] Thomas replied that "Chicago is the only city on the continent, next to New York, where there is sufficient musical culture to enable me to give a series of fifty successive concerts."[134]

In early May 1882 Thomas had staged what he termed a "monster" music festival, including presentation of large choral works, at New York City's Seventh Regiment Armory. This was the model for similar events held in Cincinnati and Chicago later that same month. Preparations in Chicago had taken definite form in February 1881 with the organization of the Chicago Music Festival Association, of which Fairbank was elected president. Marshall Field, George Pullman, Potter Palmer, and others subscribed to a guaranty fund ensuring that Thomas and his orchestra would be paid even if performance receipts did not cover his expenses. The Chicago festival of 23–26 May 1882 consisted of seven concerts, with a large proportion of the works performed in German. The same format was repeated in 1884, when the program was largely given over to Wagnerian music, including solo artists imported directly from Wagner's Festspielhaus in Bayreuth.[135]

Neither festival was financially successful, in part because the music was strange to most listeners and because the orchestra was imported, so that both the scores and the players lacked the local significance usually associated with a music festival. This element was supplied by the chorus under the direction of William Tomlins, whose Apollo Musical Club was the core of the chorus of nine hundred voices that Tomlins rehearsed for eight months before it performed at the festival of May 1882. Other members were recruited from Chicago's churches, at a time where there was "a growing inclination for large chorus choirs in the city's principal churches," some led by Tomlins.[136] The 1882 festival was to "decide the question whether Chicago in the future will have a chorus distinctively its own, and as intimately identified with the city as the Cincinnati chorus is with that city."[137] Leading rehearsals in the Central Music Hall, Tomlins drilled huge groups to create a unified precision and collective refinement that astonished festival audiences. The result was a mass presentation that provoked new thinking about local cultural possibilities. A chorister wrote: "While in the absorbing commercial city men will go on piling up fortunes into millions without a thought of music or art, still some will be found who like the gentlemen at the head of this Festival Association, and others who subscribed to the guarantee fund, who believe that there are other investments as well as railroad shares and stocks and bonds; investments bringing princely returns in happy hearts and smiling faces."[138]

The May Festival of 1882 took place in the Exposition Building just two months after this hall had hosted the "monster" rally of the Socialist Labor Party, so that Thomas's orchestra performances, supported by a local chorus, effectively reclaimed this prime civic space for middle- and upper-class musical culture. Although not built for such uses, the Exposition Building's appropriation for these events gave this hall an enhanced local meaning. As Thomas recalled its appearance in 1877, the building

> was an immense structure, two Chicago blocks long, and proportionally wide, and innocent of either partitions or interior finish. One end only was used for concert purposes, and was converted into a sort of German garden by evergreen trees planted in tubs, and tables for refreshments in the rear part of the building. Common wooden chairs were placed in rows upon the rough flooring of the front part for seats, and the passing of many railroad trains outside at times completely drowned out the music. In short, it was the last place in the world in which one would have expected orchestral concerts to succeed. Nevertheless, there was something in the very size and informality of the building which made these concerts always delightful, notwithstanding its unsuitability for musical purposes.[139]

Accounts of the May Music Festivals of 1882 and 1884 show how difficult it was to shape the Exposition Building's interior for transmission of sound. For the 1882 festival, held in the hall's south end, Fairbank commissioned Adler and Sullivan to set a large sounding board behind the frontal platform to enhance the acoustics for both orchestra and chorus. Seating for 6,500 was built in sections on raised levels, and the whole hall was electrically lit. Yet its cavernous volume made performances "little removed from outdoor singing in the matter of space to be overcome."[140] One critic wrote of the 45,000 who attended the four days of performances: "The people were there; but they did not hear the music . . . . It may be reasonably doubted that more than ten percent of those who were present heard any soloist as they should all have been heard, or felt the chorus and orchestra [carry] to their ears the complement of harmony necessary for genuine pleasure." Locomotives passing just outside also occasionally ruined concert moments with their screaming and snorting engines. This observer concluded: "The readiness with which business men advanced the cost of the festival, and the actual popularity of the concerts, even in severe weather, indicated that Chicago people are eager to enjoy music of the highest character. They have not yet had an opportunity to do so . . . . The opportunity cannot arrive until a suitable structure, like that of which Cincinnati justly boasts, shall be erected."[141]

To correct this problem, for the 1884 festival the Exposition Building's north end was redesigned with a stage for the orchestra and an amphitheater behind for the chorus, now enlarged to include 1,000 local children. According to one account: "The management, profiting from the experience of the past, where these concerts had been partial failures, because of the lack of proper acoustic arrangements, engaged architects Adler and Sullivan with the view of making the hall, as far as the nature of the building would permit, perfect in this respect, as well as to seat the vast audience with comfort and safety." The architects responded first by reducing the hall's volume and shaping a section of the interior as a room 150 feet by 400 feet long. Within this reduced space, they then "by an ingenious arrangement of inclines, distributed the seats so that all gave a perfect view of the stage." For the acoustic arrangement, "at either end were placed immense sounding boards, that above the singers being 120 x 150 feet, and so adjusted that the sound waves were kept down and swept out over the vast auditorium, while the immense amount of timber in the ceiling, so laid as to cut off all chance of speaking below and to take up the slightest sound, and cooperating with the sounding boards, gave a pure, clear quality to the sound that made every word distinct. The effect was most clearly noticed by the audience when the words of the director, with his back to the audience, were often clearly heard when only intended for the ear of those nearest him." The rear sounding board aided acoustics by reflecting sound back toward the audience. Although one hundred private boxes were set to either side of the stage, the rear sounding board made the rear gallery seats the best location in the house for hearing the music. Adler and Sullivan's acoustically enhanced interior served the Republican and Democratic national conventions held there in June and July 1884.[142]

Yet despite these elaborate architectural improvements, acoustic imperfections persisted for the 1884 music festival, whose goal, as in 1882, was to elevate standards of public taste. To achieve this goal, seating prices for the 1884 festival were graded, "giving all an opportunity to attend."[143] Though the festival was held in late May, unseasonably cold, snowy weather dampened attendance. With the hall's seating capacity of 9,130, even with concerts that drew 6,000 the space appeared empty. Also, the hall continued to prove too large for the best orchestral and choral results. The refitted Exposition Building's defects inhibited the festival's capacity to fulfill its social purpose, which was to spiritually elevate its mass audience through the psychological effects of the music. One critic wrote: "The inspiration that comes from a musical festival is very great if the performances are of the highest character." Yet he noted that artists who sang in Adler and Sullivan's refitted space reported that while audiences responded visibly to loud and powerful passages, the acoustics caused them to experience the "loss of those delicate shadings that make music so deeply representative of the various emotions that belong to the tone art. If a listener had followed the training of the chorus in their rehearsals in the small halls, and observed the shading that Mr. Tomlins was so careful in having done, and then marked the performance of those pieces at the concerts, he could not but have noticed that much of the intended effect was lost." As in 1882, the 1884 May Music Festival, though much enhanced, closed at a slight financial loss. This failure was regretted, since such festivals "have too much bearing on the future culture of the city to be treated simply as a passing amusement."[144]

Attaching social significance to the May Music Festival of 1884 and urging a permanent architectural solution for such events were presumably parts of the local response to the radicalization of the Chicago labor movement that same spring. As the Socialist Labor Party had declined after 1877, the Knights of Labor arose to supplant its influence, with a rational program for amalgamating unions to gain leverage for achieving the goals of individual member trades in their contractual bargaining with employers. The Knights discouraged random strikes and radical politics. Under their influence the city's central labor organization became the Amalgamated Trades and Labor Assembly, whose orientation toward political success at the polls had differentiated it from the revolutionary IWPA. Through the early 1880s, the assembly's moderating effect had a strong political ally in Chicago's popular Democratic mayor, Carter Harrison, who temporarily united the diverse ethnic and political components of Chicago's working class under his leadership. In local political discourse, class issues went from being marginal and threatening to central and legitimate. Together with the city council, Harrison protected labor organizations from employers, enacted pro-labor ordinances, tolerated demonstrations in public places around the city, and was lax in enforcing municipal laws against gambling and prostitution in workers' districts. Chicago police even cooperated with workers during orderly strikes. As one of Harrison's labor supporters wrote in 1881, Chicago was becoming "a working class democracy, the like of which had never existed before."[145]

Yet the depression that began in 1883 strained local forces of moderation and reignited polarized politics. By June 1884 the IWPA's program of transforming the unions into agents of radical change led four unions of predominantly German workers (the metalworkers, butchers, cabinetmakers, and carpenters and joiners) to secede from the Trades Assembly and establish a new Central Labor Union. Its principles called for every worker to "cut loose from all capitalist political parties" and "stand ready to resist the encroachment of the ruling class upon our liberties."[146] On 24 May 1884, while the Thomas festival went on at the Exposition Building, anarchist and communist leaders debated their respective visions of a postcapitalist order. Speaking before a large audience in Steinmuller's Hall at 45 North Clark Street, two blocks south of City Hall, they agreed that anarchist emphasis on individual autonomy and communist faith in collective solidarity were compatible ideals, enabling adherents to both positions to join forces against the capitalists. Their debate, conducted in German, was published and distributed by the *Chicagoer Arbeiter-Zeitung,* whose editors helped to organize this event and similar ones.[147]

Since November 1883, Parsons's English-speaking American Group of anarchists had continued to meet weekly on Wednesday evenings at Greif's Hall on the Near West Side. For their much larger Sunday afternoon meetings, in good weather the American Group went to the lakefront, specifically a large grassy area on the shore of Lake Michigan on the east side of Michigan Avenue at the foot of Van Buren Street (fig. 5). This gathering place was just a block south of the Exposition Building. The site, together with Market Square and the Haymarket, was among the few places a large outdoor meeting could be held. There Parsons and others asserted that "the private ownership of the means of production gave the employing class absolute power over the propertyless class." Regularly, literature was distributed and new members were enrolled in the IWPA.[148] As one witness recalled of the lakefront meetings: "The speeches were very nearly alike; they spoke about dynamite and fire-arms to be used against the police, and any one who opposed them in their designs; they wanted things their way and to regulate society. The speeches were alike Sunday after Sunday."[149] Rhetoric of the period targeted by name a number of high capitalists such as Marshall Field, whose famous dry goods store on State Street some leaders had proposed to loot in order to obtain clothes for workers' families. Field was also among the city's largest real estate owners.[150] As one speaker told his audience of workers: "The owner of the land was the owner of the inhabitants. Land in Chicago [once] worth $1 an acre was now, in some localities, worth perhaps $1,000,000 an acre. The people made this value, but the land-owner reaped the benefit of the advance the people had created." Anarchists claimed that their Sunday lakefront meetings drew 1,000 or more, yet police reported attendance of at most 150.[151] The numbers increased as the recession deepened all through the summers of 1884 and 1885, with twenty-six lakefront meetings held on one site between May and November 1885.

The meetings were staged just south of the Exposition Building and almost directly east across Michigan Avenue from the future site of the Auditorium Building. Their speakers' tone was threatening, and business leaders turned against Harrison's policy of tolerating such gatherings. By early 1885 there were reports of businessmen arming themselves and their clerks, and the city's leaders prepared the National Guard to counter expected demonstrations on 1 May, the deadline for a general strike if labor's demands were not met.[152] For Ferdinand Peck, among the city's largest real estate owners, these lakefront scenes must have been not only ideologically threatening but personally poignant, for they took place on a site that had been visible from the front windows of his boyhood home in the prefire Michigan Terrace, on the west side of Michigan south of Van Buren. The stretch of lakefront that had been his playground had became a rhetorical battleground. Yet Peck's response to the radical labor movement's gains in 1884–1885 was not to denounce them but to lead a new local initiative to give all classes access to high musical culture.

Ferdinand Peck's Chicago Grand Opera Festival, 1885

In April 1884 Peck led in organizing and incorporating the Chicago Grand Opera Festival Association. Its guarantors included many of those who were simultaneously supporting the May Music Festival, including Fairbank, George Pullman, Potter Palmer, Marshall Field's brother Henry Field, and newspaper publishers Joseph Medill and William Penn Nixon. The group developed its agenda in response to several factors. First, the high prices for tickets to Chicago performances of Abbey's Metropolitan Opera Company in January 1884 had effectively excluded the non-wealthy. After the May Music Festival of 1884 failed to meet expenses, it was clear that a costly remodeling of the Exposition Building was not financially practicable for a solely musical event. Yet a full operatic series for large audiences had never been produced in Chicago. The association's goal was to stage such a series and demonstrate local demand for opera sufficient to justify investment in a permanent hall far larger than any of the city's existing theaters.

Nine of the eleven directors of the Chicago Grand Opera Festival Association were members of Chicago's Union League Club, formed early in 1880 as an organization of wealthy Republican businessmen. Union Leagues had emerged in eastern cities during the Civil War in support of the federal government. From these organizations emerged New York City's Union League Club and Chicago's original Union League Club, inactive by 1880. Chicago's new Union League Club revived this name, associated with the Civil War, in the postwar period, which was dominated politically by Democratic control of urban politics and the specter of radical labor revolt. The club's first organizational goal was "to encourage and promote by moral, social, and political influence, unconditional loyalty to the Federal Government, and to defend and protect the integrity and perpetuity of this Nation," now threatened not by the Confederacy but by anarchistic socialism. In this era there was a rhetorical link made between radical workers and Southern rebels.[153] The club's earliest goal was to renominate Ulysses S. Grant for a third presidential term in 1880. Such agendas were not lost on leftist labor leaders, whose rhetoric sometimes targeted this individual club. The Union League Club sought to end fraudulent election practices that favored Democratic candidates of nonpropertied classes and shut out Republicans supported by League members. Voter fraud peaked in the municipal elections of April 1885, the same month as the Chicago Grand Opera Festival. Later that year the club finished a successful legislative and legal effort to reform local balloting. The opera festival corresponded to this political initiative, being led by the same men. As one local account noted in 1890, "probably more enterprises have been started and corporations organized at the Union League Club than have emanated from any other source."[154] Peck was the club's first vice president (1891–1892) and then president (1893), while Adler and Sullivan were among the architects who were members, as were a number of their clients.

Among Peck's allies in the Grand Opera Festival Association was a local composer, Silas G. Pratt, later nationally known, and earlier the first conductor of the

Apollo Club. Pratt edited the booklet that described the Grand Opera Festival Association's aims. Presumably alluding to the Metropolitan's opening in October 1883, Pratt wrote: "Those who have observed operatic events for the last decade in America, have noted the gradual withdrawal of Grand Italian Opera from the enjoyment and patronage of the masses, and its limitation as a luxury to the favored few of wealth and fashion." The renowned vocal artists of the period, epitomized by Adelina Patti, demanded high fees, so managers often sought to balance their books by retrenching on the expenses of orchestra and chorus, to the detriment of the performances' artistic effects. Peck's association was meant "primarily to remedy this evil, and provide Grand Italian Opera for the people at popular prices, within the reach of all, and, at the same time, to raise the performances to a higher level of excellence."[155]

Sullivan later recalled that Peck, in projecting the Grand Opera Festival and the Auditorium Building, was "an emotionally exalted advocate of that which he, a rich man, believed in his soul to be democracy."[156] Peck's emphasis on democratic access to high culture in music and theater, and especially opera, may have been partly based on his familiarity with European efforts that predated the Auditorium. When he first imagined the project is not known, yet Peck was said to have traveled repeatedly to Europe, where he had cultivated his lifelong enthusiasm for Italian grand opera, whose repertoire predominated in the later Auditorium Theater's first opera season of 1889–1890. Early in 1889, speaking on Chicago's cultural life, Peck remarked that he had "traveled the world over."[157] He was not alone among wealthy Chicagoans in acquiring musical culture from European travel. For example, Philo A. Otis, one of the key supporters of the Chicago Symphony Orchestra and the author of its history, noted church services, concerts, and operas he attended in an account of his European journey of 1874.[158] For Otis, as for many of his American contemporaries, one prime link to European operatic culture was the productions of the Royal Italian Opera Company at London's Covent Garden. By then this was the home of Patti, who also sang in New York from 1881 and at the Auditorium's opening.[159] Yet as early as the 1850s the London impresario Edward T. Smith, while a manager at Covent Garden, had initiated the idea of "Italian opera for the people." At the end of one of his productions there, he informed the public that he intended to open a new theater to provide this class of entertainment that had been too long exclusively given for the benefit of, as he put it, "Mr. Lord Tomnoddy." Fearing Smith's proposal, his colleagues at Covent Garden offered him a generous sum not to open such a house, but he eventually did so, at London's Drury Lane Theater, whose building Adler studied in the course of his European trip of 1888 while Chicago's Auditorium Theater was being planned and built.[160]

In France, the revolution of 1789 initiated a prolific development of popular theater in Paris. Numerous new buildings for public commercial theater were built there before the Bourbon restoration. By 1847 the growth of Parisian popular theater led to the creation of the Opéra National, whose repertoire, staging, seating, and pricing were intended to attract workers. Democratic ideas also informed Charles Garnier's building for the Paris Opera of 1861–1875, where the architect carefully orchestrated the spatial system of arrival and circulation to accommodate a range of ticket holders.[161] A comparable goal informed the design of Parisian municipal theaters built under the Second Empire for popular audiences, where auditoriums were encased within rented shops and apartments. The most prominent were Gabriel Davioud's Théâtre du Châtelet and the Théâtre Lyrique (the latter built for a reincarnated Opéra National), sited on the Place du Châtelet, highly visible along the north bank of the Seine, both commissioned by the city in 1859 and inaugurated in 1862.[162]

As Roula Geraniotis has shown, perhaps the most direct architectural and ideological precedent for Chicago's Auditorium was one of the most innovative new European opera houses, Richard Wagner's Festspielhaus in Bayreuth. Its architects, Otto Bruckwald and Carl Runkwitz, worked with the theater's technical director, Carl Brandt, to design a setting specifically for Wagner's works of musical drama. The Bayreuth project grew from Wagner's earlier collaboration with architect Gottfried Semper to design a comparable theater in Munich, which was never built.[163] At Bayreuth, Wagner selected the site and specified the Festspielhaus's plan. Built from 1872 to 1876, this famous hall featured an amphitheaterlike sweep of seating designed to give spectators a broad view of the stage (fig. 47). The theater seated about

Figure 47

Otto Bruckwald and Carl Runkwitz, with Carl Brandt, Festspielhaus, Bayreuth (1872–1876), showing scene from Richard Wagner, *Das Rheingold*, on the theater's opening night, 13 August 1876. Drawing by L. Bechstein. From Robert Bory, *Richard Wagner: Sein Leben und sein Werk in Bildern* (Frauenfeld: Huber, 1938). Courtesy of the Deutsches Theatermuseum, Munich.

1,500, including its rear boxes and a rear gallery above. Bayreuth had neither a single main foyer nor aisles running to the stage between seating groups. Instead, the audience entered the theater proper from vestibules along its sides through five doors on the right and five on the left. Each of these led to a certain number of seating rows entered from the sides, leaving an unbroken curvature of seating in front of the stage. As with Semper's projects for Munich, the Festspielhaus at Bayreuth explicitly recalled the shape of ancient Greek amphitheaters. The architecture's classical allusion was consistent with Wagner's ideal of musical drama rooted not in Italian court opera but in ancient Greek theater. The Bayreuth Festspielhaus's deemphasis on boxes in loges or tiers fulfilled Wagner's aim of shaping a democratic and unified experience for the audience. He felt that Europe's ruling classes, with their box-filled theaters, had removed musical drama from its popular origins in antiquity and that partial restoration of ancient theater architecture signified the public's reappropriation of musical drama. In this goal Wagner was carrying forward Semper's earlier intentions for the Court Opera House at Dresden (1837–1841). Similar democratic impulses had underlain the amphitheaterlike main hall of Schinkel's Royal Theater or Schauspielhaus at Berlin (1818–1824), where each tier or loge had a higher level of more open boxes and a lower level of nonboxed seating.[164]

The opening of Wagner's Festspielhaus in August 1876 was an international event described in detail in New York newspapers. By the mid-1880s Americans were among the many non-Germans who traveled to Bayreuth. In 1880 one design for the Metropolitan Opera House incorporated Bayreuth's idea of a deeply sunken orchestra pit. After its first season of 1883–1884, the Met adopted a program of German opera modeled closely on Bayreuth's, hiring Wagner's protégé Anton Seidl to conduct the performances in New York.[165] Yet the Met's directors did not choose to build a theater whose form imitated Wagner's at Bayreuth. Instead, by modeling the Met on Covent Garden and La Scala, Manhattan patrons recalled the court opera houses to which Bayreuth's Festspielhaus was opposed. In effect, the Met imported a Wagnerian program into a non-Wagnerian building. By spring 1884 Bayreuth was also much on the mind of Chicago audiences. At the May Music Festival, soloists from Bayreuth and Vienna rendered Wagner's music, including selections from early operas like *Lohengrin* and *Tannhäuser* as well as from recent works. One Chicago critic believed that these later Wagnerian operas, like *Götterdämmerung* and *Die Meistersinger von Nürnberg,* needed to be heard in their entirety, with dramatic action and stage scenery added to convey their aesthetic totality. He proposed that at the next festival they be performed "in their original form upon the operatic stage."[166]

The immediate precedents for Peck's efforts were Cincinnati's Grand Opera Festivals of 1881 and 1882, whose impresario, James H. Mapleson, was still the manager of Italian opera at the New York Academy of Music. Mapleson's Chicago tour in winter 1884 followed that of Abbey and the Met's company. By then, owing to competition from the new Met, Mapleson was in an embattled situation, not only vis-à-vis Abbey, but with the Academy's directors. Mapleson had increased his expenses to mount more competitive shows, but these outlays were not being met by higher revenues from ticket sales, so he was eventually forced out of his position at the Academy, which produced vaudeville shows after 1888. Yet when Peck organized his association in spring 1884, he approached Mapleson, whose Academy programs still represented the accessibility of Italian opera to popular audiences in Chicago, which the new Met threatened to destroy.[167]

To certify Mapleson's willingness to stage a festival in Chicago in April 1885, Peck went to New York in May 1884, where Mapleson reassured him that he retained contracts with Patti and other leading artists. Given his situation in New York, Mapleson regarded his Chicago agreement as the most important he had ever had. He was thus "prepared to give the grandest of operas, furnish a chorus of 400, and an orchestra of 150" in order to create "the most successful operatic season the world had ever seen."[168] Mapleson's claim turned out to be more than promotional bombast. He and Peck were serious in their aim to do something unprecedented. They proposed a two-week series of thirteen operatic performances, all of different works from German as well as French and Italian masters, including a variety of comic, lyric, dramatic, and tragic operas, with elegant costumes, new scenery, and stage effects. Early in 1885 the Met's company brought its new program of German opera to Chicago, with well-received productions copied from Bayreuth and conducted by Wagner's protégé Seidl. Yet Peck's festival that spring was based on the assumption that "there are a great number of people in Chicago who admire the singing of the Italians, and in order to hear them are content to listen to the old familiar operas again and again."[169] In an obituary of 1924, it was said that Peck himself "preferred the old operas" and "loved [Gounod's] *Faust,* [Verdi's] *Trovatore,* and [Puccini's] *Bohemian Girl,*" the last first produced in 1896, all of which emphasized melodic vocal effects characteristic of the Italian tradition. Thus, for the festival seven performances were of Italian opera, four of German, and two of French.[170]

Peck's preference for Italian opera was consistent with American tastes going back to the mid-nineteenth century in New York City, where an elite patronage sought to use such opera as a social divider. There being few Italian-born residents meant that Italian opera lacked a popular base of ethnic support, so that for native-born Americans, as one scholar has noted, Italian opera "provided something of an intellectual exclusivity and a dilettantish appeal" that maintained itself up to the 1880s.[171] By contrast, in its early years about three-fourths of the Metropolitan's general audience were German speakers from New York City's population of 250,000 German immigrants, then the city's largest ethnic group. Germans, who made up 15 percent of Chicago's population, enthusiastically supported the Met's first Wagnerian tour of the city in 1885, just as they had enjoyed Wagnerian selections rendered by their fellow national Theodore Thomas in the May Music Festivals. Yet in the Chicago of the 1880s, part of what made the anarchist movement so threatening to propertied Chicagoans was its German element. The city's oldest socialist newspaper remained the *Chicagoer Arbeiter-Zeitung,* begun in 1876 and edited by two leading anarchists who were later among those tried for the Haymarket bombing, August Spies and Michael Schwab. In the period 1880–1886, since 63 percent of the city's anarchists were Germans and another 16 percent German-speaking Bohemians, German was the language of the radical speeches and banners prominent at anarchist gatherings (fig. 48). Much of Albert Parsons's reputation derived from his rarity as an English-speaking radical.[172] In this context Peck's emphasis on Italian opera reasserted a cultural standard that was identified nationally with elite Anglo-American patronage and removed from the then politically charged German language. With almost all of his festival's directors and many of its guarantors drawn from the Union League Club, Peck's choice of a mainly Italian operatic repertoire signaled capitalist control of musical culture in the socially divided city.

The festival represented a large financial risk for Peck and his allies. The architectural transformation of the Exposition Building for the program in mind would cost $60,000, just about the total receipts of each May festival, on top of which would come the production costs. Yet by lowering prices Peck's group gambled that they could fill the hall and meet expenses, thereby demonstrating their association's long-term aim, noted in its motto, "Music for the People." Peck and the festival's guarantors were "prominent citizens who are willing to assume any loss which may occur in order that the people may have opera at reasonable prices." The lowest-priced ticket for a reserved seat in the main balcony cost $1 for a single performance. During Abbey's tours with the Met's company in 1884, Chicagoans "constantly complained that they have been kept away by the high prices, and that they could not afford to pay all the way from $3 to $6 for a seat." Yet for the Grand Opera Festival of 1885, "the action of the association and the public spirit of the guarantors have now made it possible for them to attend fourteen performances for $12 by buying season seats, and to obtain the best seats in the house for the season for a little over $2 a performance. If they fail to avail themselves of this extraordinary privilege they will have no right to complain in the future."[173] One of Peck's collaborators said that the idea "was to show citizens where they could invest money, and while the profits would not come back to the investors, it would benefit the citizens."[174] Peck later repeated this argument in soliciting local investment for the Chicago Auditorium.

For the opera festival, Peck hired Adler and Sullivan to again refit the Exposition Building's north end. Undoubtedly Peck chose these architects because of their earlier renovations of the same building, but he may have also been interested in

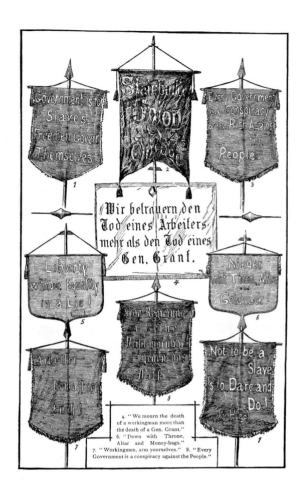

Figure 48

German- and English-language banners carried in Chicago workers' demonstrations before Haymarket. From Schaack, *Anarchy and Anarchists*.

Figure 49

Adler and Sullivan, Chicago Grand Opera
Festival Hall, (1885), in north end of
Inter-state Industrial Exposition Building
(1873) by William Boyington. Rendering
by Paul C. Lautrup. From Pratt, *First
Chicago Grand Opera Festival.* Courtesy
of the Chicago Historical Society,
ICHi-00086.

their concurrent remodeling of McVicker's Theater. By 1887 Peck knew McVicker
personally, since they lived three doors apart on South Michigan Avenue. For Peck's
Grand Opera Festival, as Sullivan recalled, Adler and he were to create "a vast temporary audience room, with a huge scenic stage."[175] For this event Adler built new
interior walls to lessen the room's volume so that "the entire opera hall will be in-
closed, and also the stage."[176] He also built a massive sounding board extending upward from the stage's arched proscenium and outward 80 feet into the auditorium
(fig. 49). Fan-shaped seating focused on the stage, whose area (120 by 80 feet) was as
large as that of the Central Music Hall's entire auditorium. Adler arrayed seats in
rows whose curvatures were segments of circles, the common central point of
which was at the stage's rear. Sounds produced near the stage's front were thus not
reflected back to that point, avoiding echoes that annoyed performers. Curved seating rows complemented the curvature of arches overhead to give the whole hall its
fan shape focused on the stage, which was flanked by splayed walls fitted with boxes.

Adler's sounding board ensured that the least strong voices of singers carried to
the rear of the house, and when tests were made of sound's transmission in the
empty hall, Peck asserted that "the seats most remote from the stage are in as good
hearing as those near the stage."[177] Another observer who heard these tests wrote
that "the clearness with which the softer sounds carry to the extreme back of the
hall is simply wonderful."[178] Once the hall filled for performances, however, the audience acted as an absorber of sound, so that observers noted it then became hard
to hear solos and recitatives from the rear. Some lateral seats also lacked a full view

of the stage. Yet Mapleson recalled that the festival's auditorium was "probably one of the finest ever constructed for such a purpose. The acoustic properties were simply perfect; sounding boards, stage drop reflectors, and other scientific inventions being brought to bear."[179] Much later Sullivan recalled that "6,200 persons saw and heard; saw in a clear line of vision; heard, even to the faintest pianissimo. No reverberation, no echo,—the clear untarnished tone, of voice and instrument, reached all."[180]

The democratic character of the festival demanded that systems of entrance and egress accommodate a varied audience. The main floor had three separate pedestrian entrances, vestibules, and staircases: for the least expensive gallery, for the moderately priced dress circle, and for the most expensive parquet, along with a carriage entrance for the boxes (fig. 50). To promote public perceptions of safety, Peck claimed that "the exits from the various portions of the house are more extensive in proportion to the size of the hall than in any theatre in the world."[181] Peck's goal was to stage performances that brought Chicago's wealthy and modest citizens together in the same hall. On one level, artists like Patti expected attention from local elites, and Peck led delegations of Chicagoans who personally greeted Mapleson's artists with ceremonies when they arrived in the city and when they left. An audience worthy of such artists meant a concentration of the host city's elite in boxes facing the stage. Thus, for the festival's opening Illinois's governor, Chicago's mayor Carter Harrison (who was a guarantor of the project), Marshall Field, Potter Palmer, and other notables were on view to each other, to the stage, and to the rest of the audience.[182]

Figure 50

Chicago Grand Opera Festival Hall (1885), main floor plan showing entrances for (a) the least expensive gallery, (b) the moderately priced dress circle, and (c) the most expensive parquet, along with (d) a carriage entrance for the boxes. From *Chicago Tribune*, 1 March 1885, 7. Graphic notations by author.

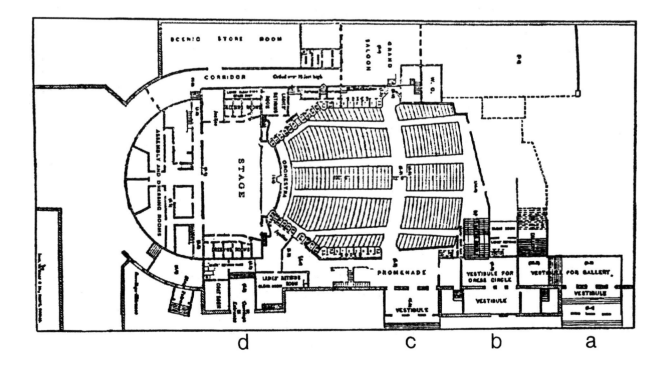

Yet while star vocalists on stage were socially equated with the boxholders, the opera festival's enormous chorus, largely organized from Chicago talent and not supplied by Mapleson, corresponded to the local citizenry who constituted most of the festival's average attendance of over 8,000 per performance. Twenty-minute intermissions afforded everyone intervals for exchange of social courtesies, so that "each time the curtain descended, over half the immense audience rose to promenade and to greet their friends. During these intermissions the auditorium resembled a vast reception room."[183] For one observer, these scenes evoked memories of comparable intervals in the prefire Crosby's Opera House. The spectacle within the hall was one of civic unity, with a vast middle class peaceably assembled for entertainment guaranteed by the city's wealthy. German citizens thronged performances of German opera. For evenings of Italian opera when Patti sang, seats were priced lower than hitherto customary for her appearances. One witness recalled, "The enthusiasm of the public upon her nights was something long to be remembered, the vast hall being a sea of heads and a flower-garden of brilliant costumes."[184]

The visual spectacle of the audience complemented the spectacle of the opera on stage. For the festival of 1885, the immense size of the newly built stage "gave the opportunity for the most magnificent scenic effects," making performances "remarkably brilliant as stage pictures."[185] One hundred new scenic backdrops were specially painted for the festival's thirteen operas. For example, the rendition of Verdi's *Aida* included a stage scene portraying the banks of the Nile, where "even the twinkle of the distant stars came softly through the moss laden trees, and the glimmer of the moonlight on the water was delicately managed, and the observer forgot the painted canvas in the sense of the reality that the delusion excited." Such captivated reactions to operatic stage sets were consistent with Chicagoans' enthusiasm for the period's gigantic panoramic paintings of historical events. These large-scale paintings on canvas employed many local artists, including some of the same individuals who painted the sets for local theaters and for the Grand Opera Festival.[186]

As continuations of a long nineteenth-century tradition of panoramas in European and American cities, Chicago's cycloramas were a popular form of entertainment with which the imagery of Peck's festival competed. A crucial part of this imagery was Sullivan's ornamental design for the architectural frame of the stage and its array of spectacular sets. Frank Lloyd Wright later recalled how Sullivan himself would vividly describe his favorite operatic scenes. For the opera festival's hall, the scenery on stage served as a point of departure for Sullivan's decorative treatment of the stage's architectural frame. Its principal focus was "the transition from the proscenium to the auditorium," meaning the sounding board's diagonal surfaces above and the splayed walls to the sides of the stage (fig. 51). The sounding board was "richly ornamented by color decoration and plastic forms," rendered in papier-mâché as extensions of the elaborate theatrical scenes on the stage.[187] Sullivan's ornamentation was "in bright and harmonious colors," calculated to make "the auditorium *itself an attractive feature of the festival.*"[188]

Figure 51

Chicago Grand Opera Festival Hall (1885), view toward stage with stenciled ornament over sounding board projecting from proscenium. Photograph by C. M. Hobart, published in Shafer, "First Chicago Grand Opera Festival."

Peck's goal was to ensure that the festival hall's music and architecture were accessible to as many Chicagoans as possible. One evening too many tickets were sold for general admission, so that many who bought them could not even enter the theater and stood crowded in its west foyer. On learning of this, Peck ordered the sale of tickets stopped and "directed all doors to be thrown open to allow those in the foyer to crowd in and see the stage if possible, and announced that those who could not would get their money back." His effort to create impromptu standing room and to deal honestly with all ticket holders was uncommon for theater managers, so that it "was hailed with delight on the part of the hundreds of unfortunates who could not see the stage, and as they went out they gave President Peck three hearty cheers."[189]

The incident not only served as a metaphor for Peck's broader aim of opening the doors of musical culture to the masses, it highlighted the financial liberality that permeated the whole enterprise. Peck spent generously on many details of the hall to ensure the comfort and enjoyment of the whole audience, such as padding the wooden floors of the Exposition Building's aisles to decrease the distraction of footfalls during performances. To the expenses of renting and remodeling the hall were added those of paying stage carpenters, scene painters, lamplighters, ushers, trumpeters who announced the end of intermissions, and many other temporary employees, apart from the contractually defined payment to Mapleson's company. Yet

Peck's judgment of the event's potential proved correct, for when the festival ended, its low-priced general audience tickets had attracted over 115,000 and receipts exceeded $170,000. This yielded a small surplus even after the association paid the large costs of the productions and of refitting the hall, so that the association's guarantors paid no deficits. Local taste was educated and the audience for grand opera much broadened. At the end of the last performance, Peck, in response to repeated calls to the stage, came forward and declared that the festival "had shown what Chicago would and could do, and he hoped that people would look upon this as a stepping stone to a great permanent hall where similar enterprises would have a home. The continuation of this annual festival, with magnificent music, at prices within the reach of all, would have a tendency to diminish crime and Socialism in our city by educating the masses to higher things."[190]

Anarchist Counterculture, the Board of Trade Building, and Haymarket, 1885–1886

Peck spoke those words on 18 April, just ten days before Parsons and others led the most dramatic socialist demonstration Chicago had yet seen. Peck's vision of access to cultural amenities was meant partly to counter the increasingly effective campaign of the IWPA, which crested in 1885–1886. As a part of the international anarchist movement, the IWPA not only opposed oppression of working people by propertied classes but also decried authority, privilege, and hierarchy in culture as in politics. An important part of the IWPA's program in Chicago was the nurturing of a working-class counterculture that provided a prerevolutionary model of the future utopia they imagined. The IWPA organized orchestras, choral groups, theater clubs, concerts, dances, lectures, and plays, all as politically motivated alternatives to their bourgeois counterparts. Annually a series of musical and theatrical fetes focused on revolutionary rhetoric and anarchist speeches. The events were intended as socialist rituals, offering politicized working people a collective identity that they did not find in bourgeois theater and music. As historians of this era write: "German working-class culture was above all performed culture . . . . Workers' festivities—parades, picnics, celebrations—were momentary transfigurations of everyday life."[191] Such events were to provide organized sociability, usually suppressed in the workplace, and to strengthen group solidarity for serious political work, with its conflict and suffering in the face of empowered opposition.

Outdoors, the combination of parade and picnic recurred from the 1850s through the 1890s. On 29 June 1884, in the depths of a slack work year, the IWPA organized a parade that began with marching groups carrying American and red flags assembling in Market Square at Greif's Hall, 54 West Lake Street. Between bands marched trade unionists carrying signs that announced "Private Capital Is Exploitation" and "Workers of the World Unite." Among the decorated floats, one showed workers enslaved in want and misery, kept down by a policeman's club, while the era's paragons of robber baron capital, such as Jay Gould and the Vander-bilts, were seated above, representing the Rule of Money. Among such mobile tableaux, the parade of about 3,000 marchers wound its way to a picnic at Ogden's Grove, which the IWPA had rented for the day. There speeches by labor leaders prefaced ball games, shooting contests, dancing, and beer, all continuing late into the evening. As one editor noted: "The overworked proletarian and his modest wife, worn out by worries and cares, can seldom enjoy an hour of amusement, relaxation, and entertainment. At best, this happens but once or twice a year; at worst, not for years on end. But when it does happen, they enjoy this hour thoroughly, though moderately—to the extent that their means allow."[192]

For indoor events, workers rented local auditoriums, especially Turner Hall on the North Side and Vorwärts Turner Hall on the West Side, both outside the central city, where middle-class theater buildings and music halls predominated. Labor's limited resources and lack of professional actors made the tableau vivant, long a part of the European theatrical tradition, a favorite dramatic device of the anarchist cause. In such a tableau, a frozen moment was portrayed with the curtain rising on a stage of still actors, whose arrangement formed a condensed symbol of the complex political rhetoric of the period. In this way the tableaux vivants staged indoors were analogous to the fixed scenes of oppression set atop the horse-drawn floats in workers' urban parades. For the Commune's fifth anniversary in March 1876, at the North Side Turner Hall, the audience witnessed a dimming of the house lights, then a softly ringing bell, whose sound signaled the start of the curtain's slow rise to reveal the scene of the tableau. Observers gasped in amazement at the scene, bathed in red calcium light, of Commune fighters battling troops from Versailles who aimed a fusillade to crush the communards, all set against a backdrop of ruins. This tableau vivant was "so delightful and illustrating such a sympathetic motif, that the enthusiastic applause of 2,500–3,000 people made the huge building tremble. The curtain had to be raised time and again, and time and again the same burning sympathy for the group of workers murdered in May, 1871. The highlight of the evening, it was a means of agitation which won't easily find its way out of the spectators' hearts."[193]

On 18 March 1882, the Paris Commune's eleventh anniversary, Wilhelm Rosenberg's play *Die Nihilisten* (The Nihilists) was staged at the North Side Turner Hall. The play dramatized the trial of a group of revolutionary Russian Nihilists who are exiled to Siberia, then liberated by their comrades after the czar's deposal. For this performance in Turner Hall, amateur actors (including August Spies) came from Chicago's anarchist community. The climactic liberation scene featured members of Chicago's Lehr- und Wehr-Verein, the workers' armed defense society, live on stage. Such fusion of fictive and real revolutionary personae fueled the play's popularity with its labor audience, and it was repeated at a West Side hall for those lacking public transportation to the North Side.[194]

In 1885, about two weeks before Peck's Grand Opera Festival began, there was a major celebration of the Commune's fourteenth anniversary. Chicago members of the IWPA rented the North Side and Vorwärts *Turnhalle,* which were "filled to over-flowing with delighted thousands of working people, bent on celebrating in a befitting manner that great event of March 18, 1871." At the more radical Vorwärts Turner Hall, ceremonies began with a performance of a play titled *The Rich and the Poor, or Life on the Streets of New York City.* After this, "the grand hall was cleared, and to the soft strains of enchanting music the dance began, which was participated in by all, and kept up till the early morning hours." At the North Side Turner Hall, "some splendid singing was given by the Socialistic singing societies," followed by a series of political speeches extolling the Commune.[195] The stage sets and music of Peck's Grand Opera Festival offered a powerful counterweight of popular nonradical entertainment to such politically charged spectacles.

The IWPA's activist program was not the only alternative to capitalist high culture. Many politically conservative trade unions also had their own programs of conventional entertainment. These were usually balls held in larger rented halls, mostly on the city's West and North Sides. Dancing preceded or followed supper, sometimes at nearby hotels. Chicago's tugboat captains, plasterers, steamfitters, theatrical mechanics, and many other trades organized and funded these events, which attracted large numbers of men and women. These dances were major social occasions, sometimes attended by mainstream local politicians. The gatherings were meant to affirm respectability and solidarity among working people, who wished to show themselves and others that their occupations did not prevent them from having their own recreational culture. Like the elite, the workers could have good times on their own terms. One account of the West Side Street Railway employees' ball asserted "that it is never in the ball-rooms of the rich that one will see really good, enjoyable dancing. There wasn't a clawhammer coat, nor a décolleté costume among the whole 600 couples, nor were there any Frency [*sic*] dishes with unpronounceable names and garlicky flavor at the midnight supper, but there was a heap of fun to the square inch just the same—a good sight more than there is at the bong-tong balls that 'society' amuses itself with."[196] Accounts of workers' social events often emphasized the beauty of the women in attendance, as if to counter prevailing assumptions about the correlation between attractiveness and wealth.

Both the politically radical and socially conservative workers' gatherings were special events that demanded planning and funds. They were organizationally sponsored and publicly reported. Yet the day-to-day lives of poor male and female workers included their high rates of individual attendance at nonpolitical and much decried amusements and leisure activities prevalent throughout Chicago. These facets of working-class life were portrayed in the period's popular short novels, such as Shang Andrews's *Chicago after Dark* (1882), and in the writings of religiously inspired middle- and upper-class social reformers, such as George Wharton James's *Chicago's Dark Places* (1891). Both kinds of sources described the city's widespread poverty and demoralization, represented by saloons and brothels as centers of general public immorality throughout those peripheral districts where most workers lived. In such areas, many smaller theaters and music halls were closely tied to alcohol and prostitution. Like his contemporary, the Englishman William Stead, James painted a bleak picture of the lewd entertainments staged at these theaters to warn his readers of an alarming degree of social degradation.[197]

Capitalists like Peck and anarchists like Parsons both sought to provide alternatives to cheap, nonpoliticized, and depraved amusements for Chicago's workers. Both valued the symbolic dimension of control over highly visible public space in the city. In spring 1885 the most symbolically charged monument in Chicago was the new Board of Trade Building, whose construction had been the focus of strikes in 1883. As designed by William Boyington in 1881–1882, the Board of Trade's outward form recalled that of John McArthur's Philadelphia City Hall (begun 1872), with a tower rising above its frontal northern pavilion and a ten-story office block behind to the south. Yet Boyington's exterior did not aim for the stylistic consistency of McArthur's neobaroque edifice. Instead, the Board of Trade was meant to be unlike any structure in the world, with a style that was "a combination of various schools of architecture, the better elements of each being preserved."[198] Eclectic in its detail, the building was monolithic in its construction, with bearing walls made of enormous blocks of Maine granite to convey institutional stability and permanence (fig. 52). In May 1883 the largest single stone ever used in a Chicago building until then was put in place as one of the twenty-ton monolithic granite columns flanking the Board of Trade's entrance on Jackson Boulevard. These columns were only the most visible of the imported materials that led to the building's total cost of over $1,700,000, making it "the most splendid and costly structure of the kind in the world."[199]

The Board of Trade's crowning tower integrated national and civic symbolism. Its apex was 304 feet high, making it then the tallest structure in the United States other than the Washington Monument, dedicated in February 1885. On a clear day, the outdoor platform atop the tower provided a magnificent view of Chicago and the surrounding countryside. The commanding gaze from this level reflected the Board of Trade's proprietary self-image relative to the city and its region beyond the horizon. The clock mechanism in the tower duplicated that installed at Philadelphia's City Hall for the national centennial in 1876. Fifty feet above the clock was the lantern, whose bell sounded the hours for citizens outside and announced the opening and closing of the trading day for members inside. As a construction, the tower had massive Phoenix iron columns rising through each of its four masonry corners. Yet so great was the tower's weight on

Figure 52

Boyington, Chicago Board of Trade Building before removal of tower in 1895. Kaufmann and Fabry Company, Photographers, Chicago. Courtesy of the Chicago Historical Society, ICHi-31483.

notoriously poor bearing soils that it was dismantled above the main block in 1895 because of excessive settling. Thus truncated, Boyington's Board of Trade anchored the south end of LaSalle Street until Holabird and Root's building of the same name replaced it in 1930.[200]

At the tower's base on the north front, visitors entered a portico framed by squared polished granite columns upholding a massive lintel, crowned with allegorical statues of Commerce and Agriculture. Inside, the vestibule led to a double grand staircase that one ascended to reach the main trading room on the second floor (fig. 53). This rectangular hall was 144 by 170 feet in area and 80 feet in height. In 1882 Boyington's plans had been selected over those of another architect who proposed a circular shape for this room. Coming into this space, "one is struck with something akin to awe, transfixed as it were with the vastness, and splendid immensity of the most beautiful public interior thus far completed in this country."[201] Around the hall were twenty-four great windows, rising through four stories as seen on the building's street fronts. These afforded ample daylight throughout the hall, where traders not only exchanged receipts for grain but also needed daylight to inspect samples of grain on marble tables around a peripheral balcony. Ringing the hall were twenty-six immense marble columns supporting an arcade below a flat paneled ceiling. On the cornice between the columns were the coats of arms of

Figure 53

William Boyington, Chicago Board of Trade Building, main trading room looking north, showing marble columns and pilasters, allegorical paintings in arched lunettes, state seals in arcade spandrels, and central art glass skylight by John La Farge. A stenciled frieze below the main cornice ringed other walls. Architecture Photograph Collection, Courtesy of the Art Institute of Chicago.

every American state and territory, between repeated shields of the United States. The ceiling's central section was a stained-glass skylight, said to be the largest and most elaborate in Chicago. Over most of the peripheral windows there were also stained-glass transoms designed by John La Farge of New York City after a national competition. Around the hall's upper walls was a set of twenty-six allegorical paintings. Toward the four corners of a square on the exchange's ashwood floor, were a telegraph counter and pits for trading wheat, corn, and other provisions. At the floor's center was the official market reporter's box "from which the tickers of the world are put in operation."[202]

As a symbol of the local power and international connections of capital, the Board of Trade's main hall served as the setting for the building's inaugural banquet on 28 April 1885. The board issued 4,000 invitations to the banquet, to cost $20 a plate, with the most distant guests coming from San Francisco and Liverpool, at a time when Chicago's anarchist leaders had threatened to march on grocery stores to obtain food for workers' hungry families. To them the Board of Trade epitomized the system of production and distribution they felt labor had created, yet from whose material rewards it was excluded. The most radical agitators reportedly now talked of sacking the Board of Trade on its inaugural evening. Since 1883 the IWPA had staged massive urban workers' parades, which wound their way through the streets of the capitalist city. Lines of 3,000 to 4,000 workers marched to music, waving the flags of socialist groups. Parades and rallies often took place on Sundays, or as countercultural events on Thanksgiving and other "capitalist holidays." On the evening of 28 April 1885, just ten days after Peck closed the Grand Opera Festival and two days before the annual workers' May Day parade, Albert Parsons led a protest march to the Board of Trade to disrupt the inaugural banquet. As guests arrived at Boyington's building, Parsons's procession began in Market Square, a few blocks to the west. Singing an anarchist adaptation of the "Marseillaise," the workers marched to cheers from sidewalk spectators. Finally they approached what they termed the "Board of Thieves" who had erected a "Temple of Usury," every stone of which had been "carved out of the flesh and blood of labor, and cemented by the sweat and tears of the women and children of toil."[203] Police lines blocked their approach at every street, so the parade marched around the building, its tower ablaze with electric lights against the night sky. Protesters' voices were audible inside the exchange room fitted as a banquet hall. The marchers eventually gathered in front of the offices of the *Arbeiter-Zeitung*, where speaker after speaker decried unemployment and want amid Chicago's great wealth.[204]

Demonstrations like these continued through spring 1886, when the workers' cause focused on the eight-hour day, an idea supported by the American Federation of Labor, which declared that it should go into effect nationally on 1 May. Chicago was the center of this national movement, the city being home to almost one-third of the 352,000 American workers who took part. Their labor actions were large and numerous. In 1881–1885, an average of 6,357 Chicago workers engaged in thirty-five strikes a year. But in 1886 this activity increased about tenfold, as the city experienced 307 strikes, with over 88,000 workers participating. On 24 April, Easter Sunday, a week before the eight-hour law was supposed to go into effect, the Central Labor Union, representing mainly German trade unionists, organized and led the largest workers' demonstration in Chicago's history. A procession estimated at 15,000, stretching over two miles and viewed by some 50,000 citizens, passed through the German districts of the North Side to the lakeshore. Marchers carried red flags and banners in various languages displaying the rhetoric of class struggle as a conflict between capital and labor. At Lake Michigan, Parsons and other representatives of the IWPA spoke on the need for unity and action, comparing the rise of class solidarity to a resurrection. The next Saturday Parsons led the main May Day march of 80,000 workers along Michigan Avenue, past the future site of the Auditorium. In this era his ally Samuel Fielden vowed to "march with the black flag [of revolution] down Michigan Avenue and strike terror to the heart of the capitalist."[205]

Strikes and other demonstrations followed to force employers to yield to the eight-hour demand. One labor action developed into a violent clash at Chicago's large McCormick Reaper Plant, over half of whose employees were German, where police shot several workers on Monday, 3 May. It was in the wake of this event that the labor rally at the Haymarket, an urban square on Chicago's Near West Side, took place on the evening of Tuesday, 4 May. Mayor Harrison reported that the meeting was peaceable as speakers addressed the crowd. As the meeting wound down, police arrived and ordered the group to disperse. A few moments later, someone (never identified) hurled a dynamite bomb toward the police. After the explosion and ensuing gunfire, seven officers and at least four civilians were fatally wounded, and scores more were seriously injured. As workers scattered, an alarm called additional police from around Chicago, who then swept the streets near the Haymarket, clubbing and arresting any man deemed suspicious. The event was tragic in its loss of life, bystanders hurt and abused, and the deep social rift it caused.[206]

Novelist Robert Herrick recalled: "The morning after the fourth of May was sizzling with excitement. From what the papers said you might think there was an anarchist or two skulking in every alley in Chicago with a basket of bombs under his arm . . . . There was every kind of rumor flying about; some had it that the police had unearthed a general conspiracy to dynamite the city; others that the bomb throwers had been found."[207] The shock of the violence at Haymarket devastated civic morale throughout Chicago. Its labor movement retreated in the face of a wave of reactionary rhetoric and legal action. In the weeks and months that followed, the city continued to experience a kind of mass hysteria, with widespread fear of anarchist plots to disrupt civil order and destroy property. Radical labor leaders like Parsons, whose newspaper the *Alarm* had long been advocating the use of dynamite, were arrested, even though there was no evidence that they had hurled the deadly weapon. Police shut down radical newspapers and conducted mass arrests of suspected radicals around Chicago. On 11 November 1887, after a politically charged trial, Parsons, Spies, and two other local anarchists were executed for their suspected link to the bombing. A fifth man who had been similarly sentenced killed himself in his cell. Others convicted were pardoned by Illinois's governor Richard J. Oglesby, who received thousands of petitions for clemency from throughout the United States on behalf of all the condemned.

In Chicago the bombing represented an urban society divided not only along class lines but between foreign born and native born. Newspapers other than socialist ones, and most clergy, condemned the violence. More broadly, they decried the depth of social division within the city. The Reverend David Swing, whose liberal ministry Peck supported, had seen the need for a symbolic counterweight to structures like the Board of Trade, noting, "There is perhaps only one city in the world having population of half a million along whose streets no traveller or citizen can find a single structure built by local benevolence. Chicago has the honor of being that city."[208] Peck also envisioned access to cultural privilege as a politically effective counterweight to labor agitation and violence. By May 1886 his philanthropic program converged with his city's social disruption to create the moment for publicly launching the Auditorium project.

Initiating and Designing the Auditorium Building   3

The Auditorium Building's design evolved from Adler and Sullivan's first known project of early 1886 through their definitive drawings of April 1887, well after construction began in January. There continued to be significant changes in both the interior and exterior form as different parts of the building opened through 1890. The process of design reveals how the architects responded not only to their own view of what was technically and aesthetically appropriate but also to what Ferdinand Peck thought was socially and symbolically necessary. As an urban monument and a cultural statement, the Auditorium was Peck's building, much as Henry Hobson Richardson's slightly earlier Marshall Field Wholesale Store was closely identified with the client it was named for. Peck set the financial and the ideological frame of reference within which his architects worked. Responding to their client's aspirations and limits, Adler and Sullivan fashioned technical and formal solutions that advanced their own architectural ideas. Both were concerned with giving the Auditorium a distinctively American and modern character. In doing so, they responded to Peck's priorities, to local architectural taste of the period, and to the conditions of Chicago's building industry, whose trades they coordinated.

Peck's Original Proposal of 1886

In the wake of the Grand Opera Festival of 1885, Chicago's Democratic mayor Carter Harrison proposed that a new permanent hall be built on the lakefront, since those grounds historically were accessible to all people. In 1882 the Trades and Labor Assembly had appealed to the city council for a grant of lakefront property as a site for a central hall to be used by its constituent unions. This project was not carried out, but the idea of a mammoth hall by the lake accessible to all was the compelling image that animated discussions of Peck's project and similar ones. One plan was to convert the Exposition Building into a permanent opera house and music hall. For the opera festival of 1885, Adler and Sullivan's interior design had "given the public an auditorium which is as elegant in its decoration and as attractive to the eye as if it were a permanent structure devoted to lyric art," and some hoped their interior could be preserved.[1] The hall could become "a grand polytechnicon of art, music, industrial museum and place for technical teaching of all kinds, where the greatest music festival can be held all year round." It could be "a place where on Sabbath and holidays, our people can enjoy higher things than are to be found in dime museums, variety dives, saloons, and skittle alleys. As a financial success it would be a marvel, and as great moral teacher of inestimable benefit to the whole city."[2]

As president of the Chicago Opera Festival Association, Peck hosted its annual meeting on Saturday, 2 May 1885, the day before Parsons led many local workers in the IWPA's first large open air mass meeting on the lakefront, at the east end of Van Buren Street. Among those at Peck's luncheon was Fairbank, and Adler and Sullivan attended as the festival's architects. Peck announced that a committee had been formed to press for a permanent building.[3] To save the expense of land acquisition, Cincinnati's Music Hall had been built on public land, and Peck's group initially sought a comparable publicly owned site for Chicago's opera house. The plot they eyed then was the federally controlled Dearborn Park at the southwest corner of Michigan Avenue and Randolph Street (fig. 5), where the Chicago Public Library would be built in 1893. Reserved for the public from Chicago's early days, Dearborn Park was claimed by both the library and veterans' groups. Through the fall of 1885, Peck worked with them on the idea of building one structure that would house the library and the opera house, though his effort was criticized as proposing a semiprivate venture for a public site.[4] Peck and his association pursued partial public funding for the structure, but by early 1886 they began to plan for a totally private effort.

After Haymarket, Chicago's political conditions favored Peck's aim of recasting the type of the opera house, long associated with urban elites, into a novel building aimed at the cultural inclusion of workers. On Saturday, 29 May 1886, less than four weeks after Haymarket, Peck outlined his vision of a permanent Auditorium Building at the Commercial Club's first meeting after the tragedy, which addressed the topic "The Late Civil Disorder: Its Causes and Lessons."[5] Founded in fall 1877 after the violent railroad strikes of that summer, the Commercial Club was a group of sixty leading businessmen. Many of them also belonged to the much larger Citizens' Association, for which the Commercial Club functioned as a kind of elite caucus. In 1886 the club's president was Franklin MacVeagh, founder of the Citizens' Association. Modeled on Boston's Commercial Club, Chicago's club had earlier supported a range of initiatives to boost the city's competitive position. In spring 1880 the Commercial Club devoted a meeting to "the fostering of art, literature and science" in Chicago. Another session in that year was devoted to "the cultivation of art, literature, science, and comprehensive charities, and the establishments of art museums, public libraries, industrial schools and free hospitals." In 1882 the Commercial Club's members founded the Chicago Manual Training School.[6] Six of the Commercial Club's thirty-nine charter members were guarantors of Peck's Chicago Grand Opera Festival of 1885.[7] Yet as traveled Chicagoans well knew, after Haymarket their city still had no monumental art institute, public library, museum, or opera house.

On the evening of Peck's speech, the club's guest was Gen. William T. Sherman, who gave one of several talks on the recent civil strife. The meeting was held in the Grand Pacific Hotel, long the prime gathering place for local Republicans. The speaker preceding Peck ascribed the labor troubles to alcohol and proposed regulating it. Then Peck detailed his proposal for the program, siting, and financing of a new civic structure that, from the viewpoint of property owners, would aid social stability by housing cultural events for mass audiences. Such a hall would not be for one purpose alone but would be an enabling location, hosting outside organizations rather than being an institution in itself. Peck called for "a large public auditorium where conventions of all kinds, political and otherwise, mass-meetings, reunions of army organizations, and, of course, great musical occasions in the nature of festivals, operatic and otherwise, as well as other large gatherings, could be held."[8] He noted that "the large cities of Europe all have great halls and gathering places," as did eastern American cities. Yet the Auditorium would be the only permanent hall in the United States large enough to hold national political conventions, thus attracting them to Chicago, whose location and railways made it accessible near the national center of population. Peck argued for a permanent convention hall based on economy. Between 1860 and 1886, Chicago had hosted seven national party conventions and built temporary auditoriums for six, four of them remodelings of existing structures and two of them completely new buildings. The Exposition Building had been internally refitted four times for music festivals. Total expenses for these temporary auditoriums had been $480,000, of which $440,000 had been spent in the previous five years.[9] These events showed Chicago's need for what would be the city's most expensive permanent building. But how would it be paid for?

Peck proposed the ambiguous concept of a building that financially was at once a philanthropic and a profit-making enterprise. The structure would be a gift to the city yet would yield a return on its investment, even if that return was modest compared with those expected of commercial buildings. This dual character would define the Auditorium project and would help to shape its architecture. On one level, Peck thought there would be sufficient local private capital to pay for construction. The project would be civic, culturally motivated, and not designed to be profitable. Yet funds would not be forthcoming if the project was purely philanthropic. Peck assumed that the proposed hall alone could not provide a monetary return. By 1886 central properties large enough for such a structure had become so expensive that, unless a public or a free site could be secured, the land would be too costly to buy and would have to be leased for a long term. A lakefront site east of Michigan Avenue, like that of the Exposition Building, was not optimal because of legal uncertainty surrounding the city's ownership of the land and thus its right to lease it to

Figure 54

Chicago buildings and sites related to the Auditorium, c. 1890, including Hotel Brunswick (built 1883; occupied by hotel after 1886; demolished 1910); Pullman Building (1882–1883; demolished); Leland Hotel (1872; remodeled 1891; demolished 1924); Richelieu Hotel (1885; demolished); Victoria Hotel (1875; burned 1882; rebuilt; remodeled 1892; demolished 1909); Borden Block (1880–1881; demolished 1917); Home Insurance Building (1883–1885; demolished 1931); Insurance Exchange Building (1884–1885; demolished 1912); McCoy's (later Victoria) Hotel (1884–1885; demolished); Rookery Building (1885–1887); Marshall Field Wholesale Store (1885–1887; demolished 1930); IWPA meeting site at Van Buren Street east of Michigan Avenue; Art Institute (1885–1886; demolished 1923); Studebaker Building (1885–1886; remodeled 1898 as Fine Arts Building); Farwell Wholesale Block (1886; demolished); Union League Club Building (1885–1886; demolished 1927); Monadnock Building (1891); Walker Wholesale Store (1888–1889; demolished 1953); Walker Retail Store (1890; demolished 1926); and Auditorium's site. Drawing by author.

others. To cover operating costs and provide at least a nominal return on investment, Peck concluded that "a grand auditorium must be built on ground obtainable
from private owners, being *so located and having sufficient area to produce adequate
rentals out of improvements attached to and surrounding the auditorium.*"[10] He cited
two successful local models: the Central Music Hall and the Chicago Opera House.

From the beginning Peck reportedly wanted no site other than one on the west
side of Michigan Avenue. The avenue then had row houses and other residences
south of Congress Street, while hotels stood to the north. From Van Buren to Jackson, these included the Victoria (1875), Richelieu (1885), and Leland (1872) (fig. 54).
Michigan Avenue's popularity as a carriage drive had attracted the Studebaker Carriage Works, which housed its manufacturing and sales in a building of 1885 just
north of the Auditorium's eventual site. Its architect, Solon S. Beman, also designed
the Pullman Building (combining stores, offices, and apartments) on the southwest
corner of Adams and Michigan. Musicians and artists rented offices in the Studebaker Building, which eventually contained two theaters, called the Studebaker and
the Playhouse.[11] In 1885, just north of the Studebaker, the Art Institute began its
building, designed by Burnham and Root. In that year Peck led a group that secured
options on properties for an opera house farther north on Michigan at Monroe
Street. Legal complications obstructed this plan, yet Peck was "determined to have
an opera-house in some locality equally good if not there."[12]

By January 1886 Peck's activities had prompted the rumor that a hotel would
rise on the northwest corner of Michigan and Congress, where the Auditorium was
built. This was the southernmost property that Peck had considered and was at best
his third choice, after Dearborn Park and Monroe Street. By that time, although
substantial private houses with fenced lots still stood on Michigan Avenue south of
Congress Street, the avenue had lost its earlier status as a prime residential street. It
was this status that Peck wished to revive. As one of his contemporaries recalled:
"When I came here in 1883 Michigan Avenue was not the most prominent street in
Chicago; in fact it was inferior to Wabash Avenue where the buildings were more of
a business character than those on Michigan Avenue" and no horsecar lines ran.[13]
At that time Wabash Avenue had no elevated train. The northwest corner of Michigan and Congress was then largely occupied by the Princess Skating Rink, while the
Brunswick Hotel was on the southwest corner of the Auditorium's site. Other small
houses and commercial structures also stood on the property (fig. 55b). One of
Peck's contemporaries recalled that before the Auditorium was built, from Congress
"down to the next street there was a row of houses formerly occupied as residences,
but turned into boarding houses . . . . There was a famous beer garden just south of
the corner of Wabash and Congress, and on Congress Street west of Wabash Avenue
there were residences which had degenerated into a red light district where there were
well known disorderly houses. In both directions from the beer garden there were
cheap transient hotels, more or less disreputable."[14] In short, the area was then a marginal location for the kind of building Peck imagined. Yet the site had special meaning for him as that of his boyhood home among the houses of Michigan Terrace. A

Figure 55

Auditorium Building: (a) preliminary plan showing opera house wholly encased in hotel, without office block, from *Chicago Tribune*, 1 August 1886; and (b) properties the building would cover, adapted from *Chicago Tribune*, 28 March 1886.

(a)

(b)

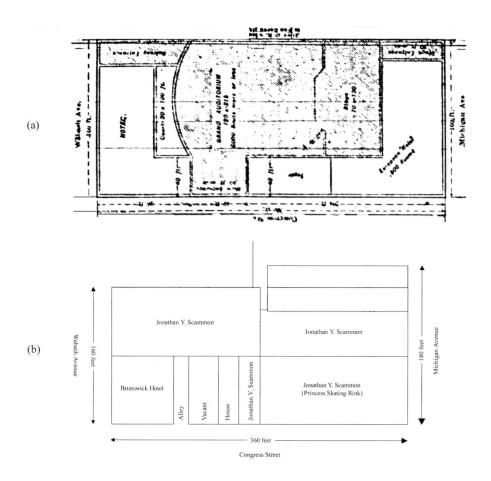

monumental building there would reclaim this area as the southeast corner of central Chicago, making an anchor for high capital and high culture.

In March 1886 one of Peck's allies, Wirt D. Walker, also heir to extensive holdings of Chicago properties, acquired an option on a set of contiguous plots on the north side of Congress from Michigan west toward Wabash Avenue. In May Peck informed the Commercial Club that Walker had transferred this option to the Chicago Grand Opera Festival Association at a moderate valuation, with a lease of ninety-nine years. Most important, the lease specified no increased valuation of the property for the first twenty years and hence provided a fixed annual rental for that time, with revaluation and increased rents every ten years thereafter. The southwest corner of the Auditorium's eventual site, then occupied by the Brunswick Hotel and two dwellings to its east facing Congress Street, was not among Walker's holdings. The Pecks sought local investors who would buy it and then lease it to the Auditorium Association. Yet at that time "Chicago capital was not a firm believer in the Auditorium project, and capitalist after capitalist declined to invest. The Peck brothers . . . despairing of finding a purchaser, finally decided to buy the property themselves, and did so, paying $193,000 for it."[15] The Auditorium site's proximity to the streetcar lines from the North, South, and West Sides, and its large area (362 feet east-west on Congress and 187 feet north-south on Michigan) prompted Peck to describe it to the Commercial Club as "the only place available" for an auditorium "which will fulfill all the requirements."[16]

To the Commercial Club, Peck stressed the future profitability of the site's proposed improvements, which he envisioned as including a large hotel conjoined with the opera house. Investment in the project would thus be "no donation, but one that will bring direct returns."[17] Peck proposed to cover half the costs of land rental and construction with an issue of bonds, paying their holders a fixed annual return of 5 percent and due at maturity in twenty or thirty years. The other half would be covered by an issue of closely held stock, whose value would be expected to increase, with dividends varying annually. If the venture was to be nominally profit making, then the nonprofit Chicago Grand Opera Festival Association could no longer serve as its organizational framework. In July 1886 Peck, with Fairbank, Walker, and others, applied to the state of Illinois to organize a corporation known as the Chicago Grand Auditorium Association, which was chartered to own real estate, build an auditorium, and organize musical and operatic events. The association then rented offices in the Chicago Opera House building, whose site the Pecks owned.[18]

In November 1886 the association issued stock of $750,000, in shares of $100, with blocks of shares to be paid for in installments as funds were needed for building. Initial pledges were commitments to buy quantities of this stock. Peck led the effort by pledging $100,000, by far the largest amount, with the Peck estate (represented by Peck and his older brothers Walter and Clarence) pledging an additional $30,000. Adler and Sullivan, presumably on Peck's assurance that they would receive the commission, pledged $25,000 as the only architects among the stockholders. Other initial supporters were Marshall Field ($30,000); Charles Cummings, Martin Ryerson, and the Chicago City Railway ($25,000 each); and Nathaniel K. Fairbank, Edson Keith, and Charles Hutchinson ($10,000 each). Formed in the early 1880s by downtown merchants, the Chicago City Railway operated the cable streetcar lines that converged near the Auditorium site. Hutchinson and Ryerson were chief benefactors of the Art Institute, which Peck also supported. In addition to these large contributions, totaling $260,000, there were twenty-five early pledges of $5,000 each and twenty-five of $2,500 each, for a total sum of almost $450,000. As one contemporary later wrote: "Night and day, year after year, in his offices at the south[west] corner of Clark and Washington streets . . . Peck measured, argued, pleaded, solicited, ordered, invested, and at last was in a position to erect his huge monument."[19] By late January 1887, when building started, the association had increased its capital stock issued to $1,500,000, of which $1,000,000 had been subscribed. As a building meant to unify the city, Peck's initiative drew a remarkable range of stockholders, so that "there was, perhaps, never a more representative list of subscribers to any project," with contributors "to the enterprise from the prominent German, Jewish and English circles."[20] Toward the end of 1888, as the building neared completion, Peck sought to broaden the project's base of financial support to include the relatively nonempowered that its cultural programs were to serve. He then wrote to the stockholders that "it is desired and expected that other citizens not now identified with the project will unite with us, thus continuing the policy originally adopted of distributing the ownership widely among our people."[21]

Unlike the Metropolitan's stockholders, the Auditorium's supporters did not receive boxes in the completed theater. The few boxes were auctioned separately for single seasons of opera. Nor did the Auditorium's shares increase much in value, as Peck had envisioned. Stockholders received annual dividends only once, in 1893, the year of the World's Columbian Exposition. Throughout his involvement with the project, Peck conveyed a double message: the building was to be profitable for stockholders yet of civic, charitable, and cultural benefit. Although his annual reports as the Auditorium Association's president stressed potential returns on investment, Peck's public statements presented the project as philanthropy, which it ultimately was for investors. Later it was reported that Peck "used to say that the only grudge he ever had against the Auditorium was that it once paid a dividend. It was and is an educational institution."[22]

Certainly its stockholders could have received a higher rate of return had they invested the same funds in a central office building. For example, while Peck was selling shares in the Auditorium, real estate agent Owen Aldis was managing sales of stock in what was then Chicago's largest office building, Burnham and Root's Rookery, on the southeast corner of LaSalle and Adams Streets. The site had been owned by Philip Peck, who sold it to the city in 1852. A huge cylindrical water tank of solid masonry was completed there the following year. This structure was incorporated into a city hall built on the site after the Great Fire of 1871. Once the municipal government moved into its new city hall in 1885, the site again became available for development. The city then leased it to the consortium of capitalists who began to build the Rookery in late 1885. These investors agreed to pay a fixed rent of $35,000 per year on the land. No taxes were to be paid on the city-owned land, but investors would pay an annual tax to the city on the building. The structure's cost of $1,600,000 was paid with $1,000,000 in stock and $600,000 in bonds, the latter maturing in ten or twenty years and paying 5 percent per year. On the building's completion early in 1888, annual gross returns from rents on its offices and stores were $290,000. After payment of the ground rent and bond interest (not including payments for tax, utilities, insurance, and maintenance), annual net return was $225,000, equivalent to a 22.5 percent return on the stockholders' investment of $1,000,000.[23]

For the Auditorium, Peck and his cosupporters forwent such high levels of direct return. Citizens subscribed to the project without "any financial inducement being held out."[24] Peck wrote that the aim was "the benefit and elevation of the public, and to add to the glory of our city—the public spirit and liberality of its citizens being necessary here to produce what governments build and support in other countries." His purpose was "*not to create a commercial enterprise.*"[25] For Peck the paradigm of a state effort was the Paris Opera, which he disliked. He did not refer to Parisian municipal theaters built, like the Auditorium, for popular audiences and encased within rented shops and apartments.[26] Instead he compared the Auditorium to European state opera houses. Even though the Auditorium would be privately and locally funded, this Chicago project would, Peck believed, attain the status of a national monument. As one local observer wrote early in 1888, "The enterprise is very different from any other ever started in the city, the idea being more like that which stands behind many of the great works of Europe."[27]

Purchases of stock in the Auditorium were to pay only for construction, so additional funding had to be found for maintaining the theater and staging opera. As Adler wrote in 1887, without public support, private capital for construction of such a building had to be supplemented by commercial facilities so that "revenue sufficient for the maintenance of stage and auditorium during the unavoidable periods of disuse may be obtained."[28] Since hotels had proliferated profitably nearby, Peck first proposed that the theater be encased entirely in a hotel. As built, the Auditorium Theater would be surrounded by a hotel east of the main tower and by rentable shops and offices to its west.[29] These facilities were to be the opera house's guarantors against loss in the way that boxholders were the primary support for the Metropolitan's productions, which were never expected to be profitable. The Met's building did have income-producing stores along the street and rentable second-floor ballrooms and dining rooms in its corner blocks below the bachelor apartments above.[30] Yet in Chicago's Auditorium Building, the analogous ancillary spaces for rent were to assume a much larger financial role. Peck elected not to follow the Met's financial plan of boxholders as guarantors, not only because he was ideologically opposed to it but also because it had not worked well in the Met's initial season (1883–1884). Boxholders had agreed to guarantee the theater's manager against a loss of $60,000. But after that first season of sixty-one performances, the Met amassed a loss of at least $250,000, owing in part to high initial costs of scenery and costumes. Also, seats other than boxes were priced too high to fill the house and, as noted, many seats had deficient sight lines. Adler later wrote: "The desire that the Auditorium be made self-sustaining, and not like the Metropolitan Opera House, a perpetual financial burden to its owners, rendered necessary the exterior subordination of the Auditorium itself to the business building and hotel, which, together with it, form the Auditorium Building."[31]

Peck derived the financing and program of his "Public Auditorium" from its civic purpose, and no feature of Peck's project conveyed such aims more than the building's name, which contrasted with that of the Metropolitan Opera House. New York's Academy of Music had been so named as a theater that was chartered by the state as an educational institution but that had served as a prime venue for opera since its opening. The Metropolitan Opera House Company not only openly declared its theatrical purpose but adopted the term *metropolitan*, connoting cultural centrality.[32] Sullivan later recalled that Peck chose the name Auditorium, preferring it to Grand Opera House.[33] The term *auditorium*, which properly refers to the space of the audience in a theater, had associations with ancient Rome. In its ancient Latin usage, *auditorium* could mean both a place for listening and the assembled audience itself. The term could also refer to a place where poets gave readings of works or legal proceedings were heard. The ancient word had civic and political connotations as well as cultural ones, just as Chicago's Auditorium would host musical and political gatherings. In antiquity, an auditorium as a public space was distinct from a ruler's private palace or *palatium*.[34] Chicago's Auditorium was likewise to contrast with palatial opera houses as a building type with origins in feudal courts. Within its walls, music and drama would be interpreted "not, as in the capitals of modern empires, to a favored few, but, as in the ancient republics, to the people of the city and Nation."[35]

Adler and Sullivan's Preliminary Designs for the Auditorium

Although they were not officially appointed as the Auditorium Building's architects until 22 December 1886, the month before construction began, Adler and Sullivan had made studies since early 1886 for a structure to cover only a portion of the final site. No record of these studies is known, and the earliest known plan, published in August 1886, was for the whole final site, shown here with a map indicating the multiple properties the building would cover (fig. 55a,b). The city had passed an ordinance permitting a north-south alley bisecting the site, but such an alley was never created, and the city council repealed the ordinance to give Peck's association control of this entire half city block.[36] This early plan shows the theater with its stage to the east and an entrance on the south near the theater's rear. The plan shows a light court (not built) behind the theater and a foyer adjacent to the entrance on the south. As built, the theater's foyer was moved to the house's rear, where the light court is shown on this plan. There is no indication of offices, even though office buildings had higher rental returns than hotels, which had large salaried staffs. At this early stage Peck presumably did not think that office space would be a good investment at what was then the central city's south edge. Instead, the theater is here shown surrounded by what was to be the world's largest "European hotel," meaning a hotel whose rates included only room charges, excluding the cost of meals. Earlier there had been notable American attempts to combine a hotel and theater in one structure, but Peck's Auditorium provided a new model for the idea on a large scale. As one observer of national hotel developments wrote when the building neared completion, "To build a theatre in the centre of a block and surround it wholly or in part with an outer building is to insure perfect freedom from any of the noises of the street; while to build a hotel on the outer edges of a block gives it the great length of street frontage and large proportion of front rooms that every hotel architect strives for. The incidental advantages to bar and restaurant business that proximity to an opera house gives are worth taking into consideration, and still more important is the access of hotel trade proper that an opera season brings."[37]

This preliminary plan helps clarify the logic behind the earliest known design for the Auditorium Building's exterior (fig. 56), prepared by September 1886, soon

after Peck had obtained control of all the site's parcels of land. A hand-colored rendering of the new opera house building, "nine stories high, with massive arches, minarets, and bays," was hung in a mammoth oak frame in Adler and Sullivan's office. By September the architects had completed transverse sections and other details, yet "these drawings are to a certain extent experimental and may be changed entirely before the foundations are laid."[38] The architectural renderer Paul C. Lautrup prepared this watercolor, as he would others of the building as its design changed. He also did at least one smaller rendering that Peck carried around the city in his pocket to help with fund-raising. At this time the project was still described as "the opera-house and hotel building."[39] The exterior was almost entirely that for a hotel, punctuated by the tower marking the theater's entrance. The design thus combined the image of a freestanding, monumental theater, associated with civic or state patronage, with the idea of the urban commercial theater entered along a street facade. The rendering shows the building from the southeast, across Lake Front Park, approximating the view of travelers arriving from the eastern United States on lakefront trains. The Auditorium would be the first monument that announced Chicago to arriving visitors.[40]

Both the construction and style of the Auditorium in this rendering were quite different from the exterior as it was built. This earliest known project may represent Sullivan's initial preferences more than the later designs, which were influenced by

Figure 56

Adler and Sullivan, earliest extant design for Auditorium Building's exterior, prepared by 26 September 1886. Rendering by Paul C. Lautrup. Auditorium Collection, Roosevelt University Archives.

his patrons and others. Celebrating his thirtieth birthday in September 1886, Sullivan presumably saw the Auditorium's form as an extraordinary opportunity and a formidable challenge. He had never designed such a large urban monument before and would never do so again. While the lower two floors were to be of stone, the upper floors were to be framed in iron and clad in "pressed brick, with stone and iron ornamentation."[41] Frank Lloyd Wright recalled that the "first designs for the Auditorium were made just before I came to the office [in 1887]. The first studies were brick and efflorescent terra cotta—a pointed tile roof on the tower."[42] Paul Mueller, Adler and Sullivan's office chief and an engineer, also recalled that by January 1887 there was one set of drawings "very ornate, made for terra cotta, very light, projecting bay windows, with iron columns from the second floor. It was all designed in detail."[43] Mueller later recalled that Sullivan had worked out this innovative exterior design in terra cotta, developing a system of cladding that was subsequently applied to Holabird and Roche's Tacoma Building of 1887–1889.

Stylistically Sullivan's design showed a five-story arcade above the base, its brick piers rising to ornate capitals and a continuously ornamented spandrel area. The arcade framed occasional projecting bay windows. Sullivan's elevation adapted the round-arched Romanesque style then emerging as characteristic of Chicago's monumental commercial buildings. Derived from Richardson's work, this style was seen as a distinctly American development, locally evident in such recent works as the Studebaker Building and the Chicago Opera House, where the Auditorium Association had its offices. The principal architect then working in this mode was John Wellborn Root, whose firm of Burnham and Root was Adler and Sullivan's principal competitor for the Auditorium commission. After Root's death in January 1891, the architect and critic Henry Van Brunt wrote that Root took the Romanesque style "still further [than Richardson] toward the point of its establishment as the characteristic architectural expression of American civilization." Root and others had proved that this stylistic movement was "the introduction and probable acclimatization of a *basis of design,* established upon Romanesque round-arched elements, which elements had never been carried to perfection here, and were, consequently, capable of progression." Sullivan admired Root, whose works by then included the Insurance Exchange Building finished in summer 1885 on the southwest corner of LaSalle and Adams Streets (fig. 57). Its principal rental agent, who had his office in the building, was William Penn Nixon, among Peck's close allies in projecting the Chicago Grand Opera Festival and the Auditorium Building. Van Brunt wrote that among Root's early works in the Romanesque

Figure 57

Daniel H. Burnham and John Wellborn Root, Insurance Exchange Building, southwest corner of LaSalle and Adams Streets, Chicago (1884–1885; demolished 1912). From *Inland Architect and News Record* 5 (July 1885). Architecture Photograph Collection, Courtesy of the Art Institute of Chicago.

style, this building "had the most extensive influence over architectural thought in the West."[44] Its strong cherry red color derived from its brickwork, then one of the finest examples of this craft in Chicago. Root's upper arcade had brick piers and ornamental spandrels of hand-carved brick (also found in Richardson's work), here extended to corner tourelles like those on the nearby Board of Trade's tower.

If Sullivan's style for the Auditorium was rooted in such contemporaneous local experiments, then its details bespoke the building's external identity as a hotel. The topmost floor had a colonnade below a gabled roof with dormers and chimneys and had tourelles capping rounded corner bays. Such motifs recurred in designs for hotels and apartment houses of the period in New York City, like Carl Pfeiffer's unbuilt design published in 1884 for the Plaza Apartments on Fifth Avenue between Fifty-eighth and Fifty-ninth Streets, facing the Grand Army Plaza south of Central Park (fig. 58).[45] Visitors to Chicago by train would have recognized the Auditorium as related to the type of the Victorian railway hotel, which had its roots in Great Britain. In Chicago the most prominent local adaptation of such motifs appeared in William Vigeant's design for McCoy's European Hotel (later the Victoria Hotel), opened 1 June 1885 on the northwest corner of Clark and Van Buren Streets (fig. 59), four blocks west of the Auditorium site. One Chicago guidebook of 1887 stated that McCoy's "is the best appointed and most elegant hotel west of New York, conducted exclusively on the European plan; and it is the only strictly first-class

Figure 58

Carl Pfeiffer, unbuilt design for Plaza Apartment House, on the west side of Fifth Avenue between Fifty-eighth and Fifty-ninth Streets, facing Grand Army Plaza south of Central Park, New York City (1883). From *American Architect and Building News* 16 (5 July 1884). This rendering, looking southwest, was by the English-born architect E. Eldon Deane. McKim, Mead and White designed the Plaza Hotel of 1890 on this site.

Figure 59

William Vigeant, McCoy's European Hotel (later the Victoria Hotel), northwest corner of Clark and Van Buren Streets, Chicago (opened 1 June 1885; demolished). From Marquis, *Marquis' Hand-Book of Chicago* (1887).

European hotel in Chicago."[46] Like Sullivan's design, McCoy's featured a cut stone base below an upper wall of red pressed brick piers encasing an iron skeleton of columns and girders. The towers, mansard roof, and gables were also of iron. This hotel, known for its excellent café on the main floor, perhaps had special meaning for Sullivan because it was "celebrated in Irish circles as the rendezvous of prominent Hibernians."[47]

On Michigan Avenue, the first monumental work of commercial architecture had been Beman's Pullman Building on the southwest corner of Michigan and Adams Street (fig. 60). This structure's innovations set a standard that was likely on the minds of Peck and his architects. Like the Auditorium's combination of hotel and office building, the Pullman Building housed a street level of shops below three stories of offices for the Pullman Company, while the higher floors were given over to apartments. These distinctions of internal use were marked in the exterior treatment of these different levels. Second, the building covered a large corner lot facing 169 feet on Adams Street and 120 feet on Michigan Avenue. This characteristic distinguished Chicago office buildings from those of Manhattan in this period. Finally, the exterior of pressed brick and ornamental terra cotta above a base of rusticated stone with carved columns made "this model building . . . peculiarly a landmark for Chicago—grand, massive and substantial." As one of the city's highest structures, Beman's building "shows how well terra-cotta, if properly made and set, is adapted for even the heaviest fronts."[48] Like the iron and steel for the internal structural skeleton, its exterior terra cotta cladding was manufactured in Chicago. For local capitalists, the Pullman Building represented the city's new tall commercial blocks as a focus for major investment. One contemporary wrote of their design, "The word 'permanent' seems best to express the character of this new era; permanence, substantial and for all time rather than to accommodate merely the present wants. There is an abundance of capital in the country, and a growing confidence that Chicago is the great center of the growing country."[49] The demand for enduring materials was aiding new local industries, so that buildings like the Pullman marked the converging interests of Chicago capital and labor in a new architecture, a central theme in building the Auditorium.

Sullivan undoubtedly approached the Auditorium's design not only in terms of its site, construction, and function, but with an awareness of its intended role as a civic symbol. This issue focused on the design of the tower, which Sullivan initially imagined with a hipped roof below a gable and crowning cupola. The tall hipped roof with the central frontal gable recalls Richardson's motifs for his town and city hall designs, such as those for Albany, New York, and North Easton, Massachusetts, and his unbuilt project for Brookline, Massachusetts.[50] The

Figure 60

Solon S. Beman, Pullman Building, southwest corner of Michigan Avenue and Adams Street, Chicago (1882–1883; demolished); photograph before 1889. Courtesy of the Chicago Historical Society, ICHi-19460.

projected crowning open cupola or lantern perhaps had sources in early sixteenth-century French Renaissance architecture, stemming from the period of Francis I, a favorite of Sullivan's. The major civic building of this period was Paris's original Hôtel de Ville, begun in 1532 but not completed until the time of Henry IV in the early 1600s. One of Sullivan's biographers noted that the Auditorium's preliminary design resembled Paris's Hôtel de Ville (fig. 61), shown here as rebuilt and expanded in the late nineteenth century.[51] It had been a focal point for revolutionary political activity in 1789, 1830, and 1848, and it occupied a strategic position in Georges-Eugène Haussmann's urbanism of the 1850s, when its northern front had been revealed along a broad newly cut avenue. In September 1870, after defeat in the Franco-Prussian War, the French launched their new government from the Hôtel de Ville. After the city's capitulation to a Prussian siege in January 1871, however, the Paris Commune replaced this government in March. In May, during the intense urban fighting that resulted in the Commune's overthrow, the Hôtel de Ville, where the Commune held its last meeting, was set afire by retreating communards and largely destroyed. Under the post-Commune Third Republic, the structure was rebuilt starting in 1874 (when Sullivan arrived in Paris for his year at the École des Beaux-Arts) and completed in 1882.[52]

The Auditorium design's possible reference to Paris's Hôtel de Ville would have been especially meaningful in the context of Chicago's struggles between capital and labor in the 1880s. As noted earlier, in keeping with international leftist custom, American workers staged their most prominent protests in mid-March near the anniversary of the Paris Commune's founding. These events included processions along Michigan Avenue past the Auditorium's site. On 18 March 1886, to commemorate the fifteenth anniversary of the Commune's founding, 1,500 people rallied at

Figure 61

Théodore Ballu, Hôtel de Ville, Paris, from the southwest (as rebuilt 1874–1882). From Ballu, *Reconstruction de l'Hôtel de Ville de Paris* (Paris, 1884), plate 60. Courtesy of the Library of Congress.

Vorwärts Turner Hall on West Twelfth Street. The program included speeches, a theatrical performance, music, and dancing. Parsons's *Alarm* asserted: "Vive la Commune! is a cry which condemns the state, the state which in all its forms seeks but one object, the oppression of the many by the few. Vive la Commune! is a protest against private property which kills all progress." Parsons proclaimed the need for an American Commune, as the "revolt of labor against the domination of capital."[53] If the Auditorium Tower's imagined crown referred to that of Paris's Hôtel de Ville, by then renewed as a symbol of bourgeois authority in the French Third Republic, then Sullivan's design asserted a civic order under the patronage of Chicago's capitalists. Their building was to be the city's center for workers' access to cultural traditions valued by those patrons, who created the Auditorium Theater in part to counter local labor's cultural self-definition in socialist theater, music, and dance.

According to Peck's original timetable, it was on Adler and Sullivan's first design "that work would have been begun on the 1st [of January 1887] . . . . This probably would have been the case had it not been for the fact that several new Directors coming into the councils of the corporation caused a temporary suspension of matters."[54] The initial design for the Auditorium's exterior drew the attention of its stockholders, who expressed "the utmost anxiety that the design for the building shall be scrutinized with great care." On 1 November 1886, Peck, Fairbank, and Hutchinson, whom the stockholders had elected as an informal executive committee, met to study plans for the building, now projected to cost $1,500,000. The next day it was reported that "several elevations have been submitted by architects [Adler and Sullivan], some of which come very near to the ideas of Mr. Peck and others deeply interested in the scheme."[55] Yet soon afterward, "some of the subscribers have expressed dissatisfaction with the front of the building" and made their suggestions known at the Auditorium Association's first organizational meeting on 4 December, where Peck was named the association's president.[56] That meeting was chaired by Marshall Field, whose name was consistently listed first among the stockholders. Nominated to be one of the association's directors, Field declined, but his brother and partner, Henry Field, also a major stockholder, was elected to the board. The board gave Peck authority to name an executive committee of four directors, which would oversee the project's financial and architectural development once construction began.[57]

Sullivan later recalled that Burnham and Root had been disappointed at not receiving the Auditorium commission. Three of their clients—Charles Hutchinson, the grain broker Charles Counselman, and the elevator manufacturer William E. Hale—were board members, and the last of these, according to Sullivan, opposed Adler and Sullivan's appointment.[58] It was presumably these directors who raised "the matter of allowing architects to enter into a competition." Yet this idea was "strenuously opposed by the President, Mr. Ferd. W. Peck, who stated that these architects [Adler and Sullivan] had really from the first been a part and parcel of the enterprise, and without whose assistance nothing would have come out of the idea."

This disagreement resulted in a compromise whereby Adler and Sullivan produced "an amended plan, supplementary to the first."[59]

Before the board's meeting of 11 December, its members received a photograph of Adler and Sullivan's revised design for the exterior (fig. 62).[60] The front's basic subdivisions of a two-story base, five-story arcade, and eighth-story attic remained from the first design, yet its pitched roof with gables had become a flat crown above full ninth and tenth stories. Four-story projecting bays through the arcade's height remained on both fronts and at the southeast corner. As in the first design, there were three arched doors along Congress Street, apart from the theater's triple-arched entrance at the tower's base, and a similar entrance to the hotel on Michigan Avenue. Mueller recalled that this second design had exterior masonry bearing walls instead of iron columns encased in masonry. After consulting many professionals, Adler and Sullivan considered that the first design "was too frivolous or ornate" and "should be more of a monumental character."[61] Yet this second design still called for extensive ornament. Upper stories were to be of brick and terra cotta, while on the two-story base "a vast amount of carved work will make the ornamentation in detail." These floors most visible along the sidewalk were "elaborately designed with facades and entrances carved and decorated in a manner not heretofore attempted in the city

Figure 62

Adler and Sullivan, revised design for Auditorium Building, prepared by 11 December 1886. Rendering by Paul C. Lautrup. Auditorium Collection, Roosevelt University Archives.

outside of the Pullman Building." The cornice was to have "a carved capstone and frieze," with ornament along the tenth-story frieze around rondel-like windows, and with a "perfectly flat and unornamented roof" as shown in the rendering.[62]

The most vivid change in the second design was the tower's transformation, following from changes in the roof. Now five stories above the main ten-story block, the tower became a rising foursquare mass free of the roofline below. Tall arches framed the tower's fenestration through three of its floors, with a columnar loggia on the fourth, round windows on a fifth level beneath its squared cornice, and an open balustrade for a viewing platform. The squared tower's base was to be "decorated with carved facsimiles of the pyramids."[63] Another Chicagoan of the period wrote of the whole building: "Stability and massiveness are apparent in all its parts, as if intended to be carried down the centuries like an Egyptian pyramid." In his view "the tower, with its attic colonnade, [is] more Egyptian than Doric, carrying out the idea expressed in the tenth story of the main building."[64] This allusion to Egyptian monumentality recurred at a large scale in the vertically accentuated pyramid atop the tower's foursquare mass, to rise to a locally salient height of 300 feet. At the building's dedication, one local writer said: "In a democracy Ferdinand W. Peck has been a Pharaoh, building like Cheops; if you entered Chicago from the south you saw the spike among the nails."[65] Although Sullivan had adopted Egyptian ornamental motifs in earlier designs of the 1880s, nowhere had he explicitly revived the form of a large-scale pyramid. Yet in this second design for the Auditorium the tower's crowning pyramid does not replicate the equilateral triangular shapes of canonical Egyptian pyramids at Gizeh. Instead, the isosceles triangular shape proposed for the Auditorium Tower approximates the crown of an obelisk, like that of the Washington Monument. This masonry tower had been dedicated on 21 February 1885 as the tallest structure in the United States. Its height made it the standard of comparison for the tower of Chicago's Board of Trade, dedicated on 28 April 1885, whose height the Auditorium was to match.[66]

The Auditorium's allusion to Egyptian monumentality had both local and national meaning. Locally Chicagoans compared their monumental commercial blocks of the 1880s to Egyptian hypostyle halls, whose architecture had advanced "to a high degree of perfection."[67] Root drew on the inwardly splayed bases and outwardly flaring capitals of Egyptian columns in such works as the Monadnock Building, built in 1889–1891 but designed from 1884. Sullivan saw the Monadnock and the Auditorium's tower, as built, as the last major masonry structures of the period.[68] Nationally, as the country's largest edifice built by private capital, the Auditorium Theater was to "be the only permanent hall in the United States large enough for a national political convention." Peck's aim was "to have the Republicans and Democrats meet in Chicago every time they nominate a candidate for President and Vice-President."[69] More generally, as one Chicago congressman said of Peck and his colleagues at the Auditorium Theater's dedication in 1889: "It was his and their hope to make it national in character . . . . Let the home of the Auditorium be in Chicago, but let its benefits be bounded by the seas." Claiming that "we have in this country few monuments of a national character," he noted that "Washington has one from whose lofty height the perpetual benediction of the father of his country descends upon its capital. The prairies of Illinois have another, blessed forever because it commemorates [Lincoln] the great liberator. But national temples we have none. It is the pride of those who have built the Auditorium that, from this night forward, there shall be a hall—a place of meeting—of proportions to convene, of beauty to please, of symmetry to invite the largest assemblages which the amusement, the instruction, the politics, or the business of the country may require."[70] Soaring above the entrance to Peck's theater-cum-convention hall, Sullivan's pyramid-crowned tower, if built, would have alluded to the first president's monument in the nation's capital and conveyed the Auditorium's much avowed national purpose.

Adler and Sullivan gave much time and thought to the Auditorium's design through 1886, yet by December they had neither been hired nor been paid by the association. On 11 December, with the second design in hand, the board met in part to decide the question of the architects. As late as 19 December it was reported that "while the architects and plans for the new structure were about decided upon, there was yet a chance that there would be a radical change in both."[71] Though Adler and Sullivan had not yet designed a hotel or a tall office building, Peck stayed with them because of their preeminence in theater design, a field where Burnham and Root had as yet done nothing. By 1885 Adler and Sullivan's "work upon the Grand Opera-House, Central Music Hall, in the reconstructions of Hooley's and the Columbia, lastly the perfect remodeling of McVicker's, has placed this firm far beyond all competitors."[72] Sullivan recalled that throughout the Auditorium's design, "Adler was Peck's man," and Peck had support from board members earlier associated with Adler and Sullivan's Central Music Hall and Chicago Grand Opera Festival. These included Martin Ryerson (himself an Adler and Sullivan client) and Nathaniel Fairbank, who were major Auditorium stockholders. These men trusted Adler, but Sullivan was barely thirty years old. He recalled: "As to Louis [Peck] was rather dubious, but gradually came around—conceding a superior aesthetic judgment—which for him was in the nature of a miracle."[73]

At a meeting of 15 December, Peck proposed to the board that if it was acceptable to Adler, outside experts would review his and Sullivan's design. After Adler accepted this proposal, Ryerson moved that he and Sullivan be confirmed as architects at the board's next weekly meeting on 22 December, though they were still not being paid.[74] Reports noted that "the drawings of Adler & Sullivan have recently been supervised by eastern experts."[75] Yet the sole authority invited to examine the design was Professor William Ware (1832–1915), founder and head of Columbia University's School of Architecture and former head of the first academic school of architecture in the United States at Massachusetts Institute of Technology. Ware had been Sullivan's principal teacher during the latter's single year at MIT in 1872–1873.[76] It is not known whether Peck knew of Ware's relation to Sullivan or whether Sullivan suggested Ware, but Ware's opinion would determine the design's final form.

In January 1887 the board summoned Ware. Mueller recalled that he critiqued the first and second designs, concentrating on the latter's exterior. Ware "criticized the proportions of the tower and added two stories to the tower after the bottom course of the tower foundations was already in."[77] He also recommended that the tower's pyramidal crown be removed and that the main block's walls below be re-composed into three stories at the base, four at the midsection, and three at the top, to heighten the design's unity. On 17 January, Ware read his written report to Adler and Sullivan before presenting it to the board that same afternoon. Sullivan recalled it to be a strong and sound endorsement, wherein Ware noted Adler and Sullivan's approval of his proposed minor changes. Yet Sullivan wrote to his brother Albert that "the opposition, as you will see had built up fond hopes, upon this forthcoming report." One opponent on the board was Eugene S. Pike (a future Burnham and Root client), who, as Sullivan recalled, queried Ware as follows:

> *Mr. Pike:* Professor Ware, I judge from the tenor of what you have just said, that you
>   have confined your effort solely to estimating the artistic quality of the present
>   designs, and to a search for means to improve them in detail, —assuming always
>   that these designs are a finality in the eyes of this board.
>
> *Professor:* Certainly. I understood it was for that purpose that I was called here.
>
> *Mr. Pike:* Very good. Now let me ask you this question. Assuming that you yourself,
>   instead of Messrs. [Adler and Sullivan] had from the inception of this project
>   been engaged to design this building. Would you, in your opinion, have arrived
>   at a result substantially similar to theirs, or do you believe that you would have
>   produced a result somewhat or a great deal better?
>
> *Professor:* Had I been entrusted with the designing of this building, I do not believe
>   I should have reached the same result. But had I reached such a result, I should
>   consider it *the inspiration of my life!*

The board were electrified, and stared at each other, at the professor, and at Pike who was completely knocked out. A & S stock rose into the hundreds.

To the question next put (to be exhaustive) as to whether there was any reasonable probability that by calling in the services of other prominent architects, a sufficiently better design could be secured, to justify the board in such action, the professor replied,—that while there was no telling *what might* be done, he thought it extremely problematical, and that in his judgment the board would not be justified in waiting a couple of months for such purpose.[78]

With this endorsement, Ware hugely aided the career of his former student Sullivan, whose national reputation began with the Auditorium's design. On 29 January, Fairbank moved that Adler and Sullivan "complete the drawings of the exterior of the building in substantial accordance with the recommendation of Prof. Ware."[79] Ware's report inspired the board to authorize a first payment to Adler and Sullivan of $10,000, or 20 percent of their initially contracted fee of $50,000, and to call for a first assessment on stock subscriptions to pay for construction. The episode highlights how far Chicago architects and patrons were willing to cede aesthetic judgment to eastern authorities. Peck did not call on Nathan Clifford Ricker, the renowned head of the University of Illinois's School of Architecture, the country's second oldest, founded in 1867. Instead he chose to solicit and defer to the New York–based dean of United States architectural education about a building that, ironically, would come to be seen as a pivotal monument of Chicago's regionally independent tradition of early modern architecture. Mueller later said he was "sorry to say that Adler and Sullivan were so solicitous of the opinions of others," presumably Ware's.[80] Yet Ware's review had been a condition of these architects' continuing with the project, and Ware's endorsement shifted the perception of Peck and his fellow directors in their favor, though the design was still not fixed. Before leaving Chicago, Ware said "it was his opinion that the new Auditorium would command more of a national attention and reputation than any building ever built in this country."[81]

Even as the site was cleared and excavated and the foundations were being set, the exterior continued to evolve in drawings and discussion until spring 1887. On 29 January, Peck called the board to a meeting in Adler and Sullivan's office to examine revised designs that still featured the tower's pyramidal roof. Some details were approved, but the next day it was reported that "changes . . . will be made in the elevations as the structure progresses, and it cannot be told definitely what the building will look like until the roof is on. The alterations so far run in the direction of

Figure 63

Auditorium Building, penultimate design corresponding to that documented in working drawings of April 1887. From *Inland Architect and News Record* 9 (April 1887), photogravure edition. Architecture Photograph Collection, Courtesy of the Art Institute of Chicago.

severe treatment, and the elevations finally agreed upon will be," to quote Peck, "'very dignified and majestic.'"[82] On 12 February Sullivan and Peck were in New York consulting further with Ware about revisions in the design.[83] Construction aboveground began based on this revised exterior, fixed in the working drawings of April 1887 and published as a perspective that same month (fig. 63).[84] The lower stories were still of stone, with those above of brick. Yet bay or oriel windows were removed, and the tenth floor had lost its round windows and ornamental frieze in favor of triple rectangular windows in each bay framed by pairs of inset columns. The second design's continuous projecting horizontal moldings below the eighth and ninth floors were also reduced to projecting lintels below the arched pairs of windows rising through the eighth and ninth floors. The tower lost its pyramidal roof and, perhaps to compensate for this decreased height, its squared mass was increased from fourteen to sixteen stories, which Mueller later recalled to have been Ware's recommendation.[85]

There were various accounts of how Sullivan arrived at the final design for the Auditorium's exterior. The Chicago architect Thomas Tallmadge recorded Mueller's recollection that "a remark of John Root was repeated to Sullivan, to the effect that 'Louis couldn't build an honest wall without covering it with ornament.' Sullivan was furious and, in order to show Root that he could, the nearly finished plans were discarded and what we now see resulted."[86] Sullivan and Root were both professional friends and artistic rivals, yet there were many factors that informed the Auditorium's direction. In October 1887, at the American Institute of Architects' annual meeting in Chicago, Adler and Cady were invited to give papers on the design of a large opera house. Much as Cady concluded, Adler stated that "the general proportions and materials of construction of such a building as this justify a general simplicity of treatment. This simplicity should, however, not become baldness, nor should the poetic element be excluded from the design."[87] Wright recalled that "under the Adler influence the design had become more the severe fenestration crowned by the nobly frowning tower we now see."[88] After the Auditorium's completion, Adler described its exteriors as "dignified, impressive, simple and straightforward." The theater was not visible from outside, and the hotel and offices determined the fenestration, so that "every square foot of street exposure serves commercial purposes, and serves them well. Utilitarian interests have nowhere been sacrificed." In this context, he attributed the built exterior's simplicity partly to "the financial policy of the earlier days of the enterprise."[89]

Above all, Adler attributed the final design to "the deep impression made by Richardson's 'Marshall Field Building' upon the Directory of the Auditorium Association," combined with a "reaction from a course of indulgence in the creation of highly decorative effects on the part of its architects."[90] As Sullivan was revising the Auditorium's exterior design through spring 1887, Richardson's Marshall Field Wholesale Store was the city's most prominent new commercial monument (fig. 64). Commissioned early in 1885, the building had been designed through that year,

Figure 64

Henry Hobson Richardson, Marshall Field and Company Wholesale Store, Chicago (1885–1887; demolished 1930), showing ratio of frontal width to height of 2.5:1. Courtesy of the Chicago Historical Society, ICHi-23209. Graphic notations by author.

with construction beginning in spring 1886 and the crowning stones set in place by early November. The exterior was wholly complete by January 1887, and the interior opened for business in June. For Peck, this structure was among the recent works that typified Chicago. Echoing Sullivan's ideas on architecture as a revelation of its society, Peck asked, "What is more typical of the artistic taste of any people than the architecture of their community? Look at the art in architecture of our city. Where can our great business buildings be equaled? Study the Field Mercantile Building; the beautiful Pullman Building; the Rookery; the Home Insurance Building . . . . In no city on this continent will be found so much art in modern architecture."[91]

Richardson's building for Field was thoroughly adapted to its mercantile function as a wholesale store for midwestern retail merchants visiting Chicago to select their inventories from the world's largest wholesale merchant and main supplier of goods and credit for a vast regional distribution. Yet to Marshall Field's building Richardson brought a range of architectural ideas, knowing it would be among his last major works before his premature death in April 1886. It was probably when visiting Chicago in October 1885 to work on this and other local projects that Richardson had written to his son: "There are no public buildings in Chicago worth seeing."[92] Presumably through this commission from Field, even though it was not for a government building, Richardson sought to create a monument that would provide a high standard for local public architecture. If this was his intention, then it bore immediate fruit in the Auditorium's exterior design. Yet why did Peck and his colleagues look to Richardson's monument as a model?

One answer is that it was then one of only two recently built local structures covering a comparable half-block site. Field's store was 325 feet long east-west on Adams Street and 190 feet north-south on Franklin Street and Fifth Avenue. The Auditorium front is 362 feet long east-west along Congress and 187 feet on its east front along Michigan Avenue. The seven-story Field block stood 130 feet high, while the Auditorium's ten-story main block is 145 feet high, so that both buildings showed the same ratio of frontal width to height of just over 2.5 to 1.[93] Sullivan's second design for the Auditorium's exterior of December 1886 (fig. 62), with its change to a block of this proportion with a flat roof, presumably reflected the influence of Field's building. Yet within that overall proportion, the two buildings' elevations differed. With its major arcade rising through four of its ten stories and across twenty bays along Congress Street, the Auditorium has a more vertical proportion than the Field Store, whose main arcade rose through three of its seven stories and extended thirteen bays along its main front on Adams Street. The Field Store thus embodied Richardson's general architectural ideal of a "quiet and massive treatment of wall surfaces."[94] The Auditorium's definitive composition of April 1887 (fig. 63), with its paired arched windows through the eighth and ninth floors and its rectangular windows in the tenth story, closely approximated Richardson's solutions for the comparable parts of the Field Store, which was by then completed. In its internal construction, Richardson's building was related to New England textile mills, and one observer termed its exterior that of "a glorified cotton factory."[95] In spring 1887 Peck's Auditorium Association received an anonymous letter critical of Adler and Sullivan's recently published exterior, which the authors claimed to "look very much like a Factory building."[96] As late as 9 April, when the Auditorium's foundations were being placed, "the material for the front [was] not decided upon."[97] In May, in part to enhance the Auditorium's image as a civic monument, its directors decided to replace the pressed brick and terra cotta in the upper walls with a facing of Indiana limestone, bringing Adler and Sullivan's fronts closer to Richardson's, which were granite through the first-story belt course and brick faced with brownstone above.[98]

In pragmatic terms, Richardson's choice of minimally ornamented stone walls for the Marshall Field Wholesale Store was consistent with those of local architects for buildings in central Chicago, whose air was notoriously polluted by soot and moisture. Pollution was generated from many buildings whose boilers were fueled by inexpensive soft bituminous coal. The result was a perpetually darkened atmosphere downtown, which necessitated use of streetlights all day in winter, with artificial interior light all through office workdays. The soot and moisture expelled from the smokestacks of heating plants limited visibility, choked pedestrians, and soiled surfaces of all descriptions, from clothes to building fronts. Control over the "smoke nuisance" through legal pressure was a continuing project of the Citizens' Association from its founding in 1874 through the 1880s, when Peck was active. Richardson had addressed this issue in his design for the Allegheny County Court

House in Pittsburgh, a city whose atmosphere was comparably polluted. In his description of his competition project of January 1884, Richardson wrote:

> As to architectural effect, with the atmospheric difficulties of the locality in view, the design has been to provide a building the character of which should depend on its outlines, on the massing and accentuation of the main features representing its leading purposes, and on the relation of the openings to the solid parts . . . the intention has been to produce that sense of solidity requisite in dignified, monumental work, by a careful study of the piers and by a quiet and massive treatment of the wall surfaces. In accordance with this policy, projecting string-courses and cornices, and elaborate capitals and carvings, are as much as possible avoided, and no dependence for architectural effect is placed upon features liable to be distorted by soot.[99]

Partly in response to such limitations of atmospheric pollution, Chicago architects had similarly developed unornamented smooth masonry walling as one of their period's signatures.

In symbolic terms, Sullivan and others saw Richardson's Chicago building as a monument to its patron, Marshall Field. As built, its upper walls alluded to Field's origins. Field had insisted that Richardson change his initial design for the upper walls from brick to a red sandstone that was quarried at Springfield, Massachusetts, less than thirty miles south of Field's birthplace near Conway. In its style, this wholesale store was "an independent idea of the owner and his architect . . . showing the heavy Romanesque of the Florentine School."[100] Both Field, in 1875, and Richardson, in 1882, had visited Florence, and their building was repeatedly compared to Florentine mercantile palaces of the fifteenth century, such as those of the Medici and their contemporaries. Adler admired this Chicago monument in the same terms, noting "How American is Richardson's reproduction of the somberness and dignity of the Palazzo Strozzi in the Marshall Field Building."[101]

Though cited by modernist historians as a protofunctionalist work, Richardson's building for Field had a representational, historically monumental exterior. The truly minimal solution to a block for wholesaling had appeared the year before in John Van Osdel's building for John V. Farwell (fig. 65), Field's former partner, whose firm was Field's chief wholesale competitor and whose building was sited one block northwest of Richardson's (fig. 87b). This structure replaced Farwell's earlier one on the same site, destroyed by fire in 1885. Occupying a similar block-length frontage, the Farwell Block had simple elevations of repeated rectangular windows through its six stories of cut stone and brick, with a slight emphasis on its central and corner sections. The comparison reveals the difference between Van Osdel and Richardson as architects a generation apart in age, as well as the personal symbolism of Field's structure. Farwell built his block on rented ground and rented out its interior floors to wholesalers of clothing, hats and caps, and other dry goods in an effort to compete with Field's facility without making the same investment. By

Figure 65

John Van Osdel, John V. Farwell and Company Wholesale Store Block, including rental space for tenant wholesalers, facing South Market Street between West Monroe and West Adams Streets, Chicago (1886; demolished). From Marquis, *Marquis' Hand-Book of Chicago*.

1883 Field personally owned the site of his future building, which consisted of fifty-two separately acquired parcels. He also owned the completed structure, whose floors were devoted to his company alone and not rented to other wholesalers.[102]

Richardson's wholesale store for Field had "an appearance of strength and endurance symbolic of the business carried on within it."[103] On one level, the audience for such a message included Field's customers, the retail merchants who traveled to Chicago to select goods and who depended on Field to extend credit for their purchases of inventories for their own stores year after year. Many regional merchants were long-term residents in the city's hotels, and the Auditorium's directors hoped to attract such men to suites in the Auditorium Hotel, perhaps another rationale for its external resemblance to the Marshall Field Wholesale Store. As a business whose size of operations could define a national standard, Field's store resembled its owner's other buildings as a projection of his conservative persona and values, which pervaded all aspects of his firm. As one of his colleagues later stated, "In what some might consider the trivial matter of architecture, [Field] wished no misrepresentation, no false impression conveyed . . . . It is not enough to say that his architecture was largely chosen to meet the requirements of Chicago. There was more to it than that. It met the moral requirements of Mr. Field himself and is a lasting monument to his character."[104] Much the same was said of Richardson's structure at the time of its opening in June 1887. One observer described it as "solid, substantial, well-proportioned—a building among buildings. Like, yet unlike others. Unostentatious, yet commanding attention; built for service, yet with a view to architectural detail." As one man told that writer, "'It's just like Marshall Field, and it will remain another monument to him when the present generation have passed away!'"[105]

Contemporaneous responses like these were echoed in Louis Sullivan's often cited commentary on Richardson's building in *Kindergarten Chats* (1901). Consistent with the traditional theory of architectural types taught at the École des Beaux-Arts,

Sullivan saw the Marshall Field Wholesale Store as conveying the general character of its historical period, the type character of its commercial function, and the specific character of its client and architect. Sullivan called it "a monument to trade, to the organized commercial spirit, to the power and progress of the age, to the strength and resource of individuality and force of character" of Marshall Field. Yet Sullivan also saw in this building testimony to Richardson's powers; it was "the index of a mind, large enough, courageous enough to cope with these things, master them, absorb them and give them back again."[106]

The Auditorium's directors presumably identified with Marshall Field in that they were patrons of an urban monument that would be a defining civic presence. After Peck and his family, Marshall Field was the Auditorium's largest stockholder. He declined to serve as a director, but since his brother and partner, Henry Field, was on the board, its response to Richardson's building was predictable. As architectural statements of an empowered elite in a contested urban social situation, both Richardson's Marshall Field Wholesale Store and Adler and Sullivan's Auditorium recalled Roman monuments. Scholars of Richardson's work have pointed out that his building for Field recalled the form of Roman aqueducts that Richardson saw on his trip to Europe in 1882, photographs of which he acquired. While the Field Wholesale Store and the Auditorium exhibited Romanesque forms, their contemporaries saw the medieval Romanesque as having evolved seamlessly from ancient Roman architecture. Such a Roman-inspired style contrasted with the ornate Second Empire style of postfire Chicago. In 1890 one local observer wrote: "There is no arbitrary line separating Roman architecture from its descendant Romanesque, as the evolution was gradual after the time of the Christian era." Speaking of Chicago's revival of Romanesque forms, he concluded: "It may be truthfully said in general of the styles used in Chicago . . . that the principal complex features came from the Romans."[107]

For Edward Garczynski, author of the commemorative book on the Auditorium of 1890, its exterior recalled the forms of Roman construction. The tall arched bays compared with those of the Aqua Claudia (A.D. 38–52) near Rome (fig. 66), the monumental ruin that had been a favorite subject of earlier American painters who traveled to the Roman Campagna in the nineteenth century. Garczynski wrote of Adler and Sullivan's edifice: "Here all is simplicity, stateliness, strength. There is in its granite pile a quality that strongly reminds the traveled spectator of those grand engineering constructions which the Romans raised in every part of their vast empire." Peck presumably saw such

Figure 66

Aqua Claudia, Via Appia, near Rome (A.D. 38–52). Courtesy of Alinari/Art Resource, New York City.

monuments during his European travels, and Garczynski wrote that their influence on the Auditorium "was an inspiration" from Peck, to whom "it is most probable we must look for its Roman character."[108] This classical association was consistent with Peck's choice of the name Auditorium for his building, with its origins in the ancient Latin term. Like surviving Roman monuments, the Auditorium was, in Peck's words, "built for all time."[109]

The Field Store's and the Auditorium's allusion to Roman forms also expressed the then prevalent idea of Chicago as the capital of its midwestern region that was a modern inland empire. Field's store signified the firm's predominance in the national wholesale trade, while the Auditorium was to be the national center for musical culture and political conventions. Both buildings could assume this role because of Chicago's central position in the country's rail network. Of the Auditorium, one of the city's historians wrote: "As all roads led to Rome in days of old, in the same way all roads lead to Chicago to-day by water and by rail, so that on the map she looks like the center of a huge web."[110] This mental image of Chicago as an imperial central city appeared in locally produced maps of the North American continent, such as one included in a guidebook for visitors to the World's Columbian Exposition (fig. 67). There lines indicated mileage between Chicago and not only a selection of major United States cities, but also those in other parts of the world. Field and Peck shared this vision at a time when their city's regional dominance was first assured. Thus their buildings, linked to this idea of centrality, adopted a Roman monumentality. As one New York observer wrote, the Auditorium "is less expressive of progress in architecture than of the march of empire" to the midwestern United States.[111]

Figure 67

Map of the United States, showing distances between Chicago and other major world cities. From Flinn, *Chicago, the Marvelous City of the West*.

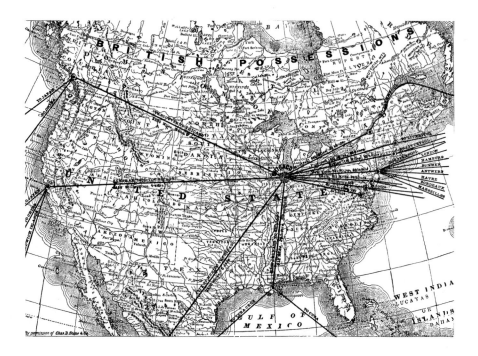

Adler's Construction Plan for the Auditorium

By the time construction began on the Auditorium's site on 28 January 1887, Adler had developed a structural plan for the building accommodating a wide range of spaces with different soil-loading conditions. A variety of foundational piers and walls for different sections had to be calculated and fabricated to ensure minimal, even settlement. These feats of construction had to succeed within one hundred yards of Lake Michigan and at depths below the lake's water level. The Auditorium Building's total weight exceeded 110,000 tons, making it enormously heavy for its ground area. To design the building's footings, Adler and local specialists adapted a body of theory and practice in the art of foundations developed in Chicago from the 1870s. This advance in the building art proceeded with knowledge of developments in New York City. Yet in Manhattan, proximity to bedrock meant that tall buildings of the period before 1890 were built mostly on pile foundations. Chicago's more treacherous clay soils were the impetus for devising a regionally specific technology of shallow pier foundations, which culminated in the design of the Auditorium Building, before the adoption of deep caisson foundations in the 1890s.[112]

For Peck, the issue of the building's foundations and their resistance to settlement was not only technically central but also civically symbolic, especially in view of the fact that three comparably large recent structures (the United States Post Office and Custom House, finally completed 1880, the Chicago City Hall and Cook County Courthouse of 1877–1885, and the Chicago Board of Trade, finished in 1885) all had problems with uneven settlement and consequent internal structural damage. When the Auditorium Hotel opened in 1890, Peck claimed at a meeting of the Chicago Real Estate Board that the Auditorium was an answer to a "frequent criticism of Chicago . . . that, having built upon what was once a swamp, there is lack of stability or sustaining power in the soil that underlies our improvements. Let me inform you, gentlemen, and through the real-estate men we reach the entire outside world, that the tower reared above this structure with its twenty floors rests upon an area of 70 by 40 feet, and the weight covering that area exceeds 15,000 tons."[113] Clearly Peck saw the Auditorium's stable weight, epitomized in its tower, as an announcement that Chicago properties were good investments for tall buildings. If the local architects had solved the foundation problem, their achievement would attract capital to the central city, where Peck and other Auditorium supporters owned multiple properties.

As Adler and his colleagues consistently acknowledged, the pioneering local theorist of foundations was the German-trained architect Frederick Baumann (1826–1921), who in 1873 published a seminal pamphlet, *The Art of Preparing Foundations for All Kinds of Buildings with Particular Illustrations of the "Method of Isolated Piers," as Followed in Chicago*. There he wrote that central Chicago was built on soils that were not close to bedrock. Instead, from five to twenty-five feet below the surface one found the top of a thick bed of clay, known as hardpan for its bearing capacity when dry. Though permeated with veins of water, when dry the hardpan would support loads with tolerably minimal compression or settlement (less than two inches). Pier foundations were set on top of the clay bed and were not to descend below its dry, hard upper layer, for beneath was a loose, watery soil of uncertain capacity. Bedrock below was encountered only at depths of fifty to seventy-five feet, and it was prohibitively expensive to excavate that far down.[114]

In order to construct any heavy building on this compressible clay soil, foundations had to conform to a basic principle: the ratio of building weight per unit area of foundation had to be uniform throughout the structure. Equal pressure (meaning equal ratios of weight or force per unit area of foundation) meant equal settlement, assuming that all sections of a building site had soils of equal bearing capacity. The design of foundations thus required two basic operations. First the soil's bearing capacity was determined through test loadings. Then, once this capacity was empirically established, the size of each foundation pier was calculated based on the portion of the building's weight it carried. Dividing the foundation into isolated piers, instead of continuous linear masonry walls or areal pads of concrete covering the whole site, enabled relatively exact calculation of the load each pier carried. For example, if soil was found to have a bearing capacity of 3,000 pounds per square foot (a figure commonly used by Chicago architects of the period) and a pier was to carry a load of 60,000 pounds, then the pier's foundational footing spread the load over a base area of twenty square feet. To ensure even settlement, all other foundations were to hold to this pressure of 3,000 pounds per square foot. Although simple in theory, this approach proved technically challenging to implement. First, any given site's soils were usually not uniform in compressibility or bearing capacity. Second, loads on parts of buildings, especially movable or live loads on floors not anticipated when a building was designed, were not easy to estimate accurately.[115]

Baumann conceded that his approach was not new, in that many premodern buildings had used isolated pier foundations. But he maintained that their historical use had not been based on exact calculation of loads. Also, premodern buildings tended to have mixed foundational systems of isolated piers combined with continuous walls. In his view, rigorously consistent use of isolated piers was new in its scientific precision, having evolved as "the result of modern wants as to the construction of mercantile buildings."[116] Adherence to Baumann's method had major implications for the aboveground architectural form of postfire Chicago commercial buildings. Paul Mueller claimed that the first local structure whose foundations were designed according to Baumann's method had been Adler and Sullivan's Borden Block (1880–1881), on the northwest corner of Dearborn and Randolph (fig. 14). Sullivan also recalled that the Borden Block "actually had solid stone piers on isolated foundations, which was a great innovation."[117] Adler and Sullivan had their offices on this building's top floor. The Borden Block's walls consisted of regular bays, partly to facilitate calculation of near equal loads on the foundation piers. The exterior's weight-bearing brick piers were the dominant verticals, their width reduced to ensure maximal daylight for offices inside. The top-floor arches were not structural but decorative, as suggested by their ornamental surfaces of terra cotta. Horizontal lintels over windows were cast iron I-beams spanning between vertical brick piers. The Borden Block exhibited the basic constructive and stylistic grammar, based on the logic of foundations, that Adler and Sullivan and their colleagues used for buildings through the 1880s.

William Le Baron Jenney's Home Insurance Building (1883–1885), on the northeast corner of LaSalle and Adams Streets, and Burnham and Root's Rookery (1885–1887), on the southeast corner of the same intersection, contained developments of Baumann's system that were integrated into the Auditorium's foundations. In his accounts of the Home Insurance Building, Jenney stressed its use of isolated pier foundations, designed as pyramidal footings of stone set on hardpan (fig. 68a). The pyramids were made of alternating courses of expensive squared dimension stone and cheaper irregular rubble. Aboveground, these footings continued as the tapering solid granite piers that formed the exterior's base, much as Adler and Sullivan's Auditorium had a periphery of solid granite piers emerging aboveground atop its foundations. In describing the Home Insurance Building, Jenney cautioned that "as settlements must take place, and although every care is taken to make settlements uniform, there will be more or less inequality, and to counteract these there must be elasticity in the construction."[118] By this he meant that all parts of the building must be tied together by iron beams and rods running horizontally between piers to ensure that settlement under any one pier would be transferred to adjacent parts of the building. This would avoid fractures between sections caused by uneven settlement of any one section. Adler adopted this idea in his design for the Auditorium Tower's foundations.

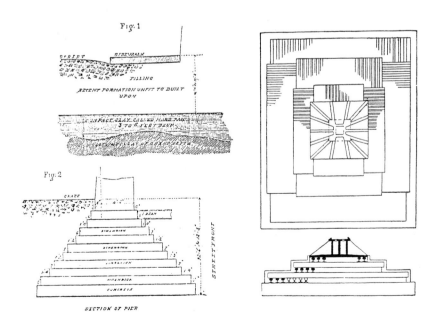

a   b

Figure 68

(a) William Le Baron Jenney, Home Insurance Building, northeast corner of LaSalle and Adams Streets, Chicago (1883–1885; demolished 1931). Sections through (above) Chicago soils from street, down through filling, to hardpan or compact clay, then soft wet clay of greater depth; and (below) pyramidal footings as isolated pier foundations, made of dimension or squarely cut stone courses alternating with rubble stone courses, all above a concrete base. From *Sanitary Engineer* 13 (10 December 1885). (b) Burnham and Root, Rookery, southeast corner of LaSalle and Adams Streets, Chicago (1885–1887). Section through rail grillage footings (steel rails encased in concrete) for an isolated pier foundations, with cast iron shoe set atop footing to receive base of steel column. From *Inland Architect and News Record* 15 (June 1890).

Isolated piers gave maximum strength with minimal expenditure, since they reduced the cost of dimension stone well below that of continuous wall foundations. In the Rookery, Root refined a form of isolated pier that eliminated expensive dimension stone altogether and further reduced dependence on the unionized masons who set the stone. As in Burnham and Root's earlier Montauk Block, completed in 1882, Root replaced Jenney's pyramids of stone with a minimally stepped flatter footing consisting of layers of steel rails laid crosswise and embedded in concrete (fig. 68b). This type of footing became known as a rail grillage foundation; by concentrating strength in thin beds of steel rails, it eliminated the cost and the bulk of stone pyramids. In discussing foundations with Baumann and Adler in 1886, Root said: "We have used steel rails for [foundation] piers because they have been forced on us. In large mercantile buildings, the sub-basement is quite as valuable as the first story and, with dimension stone, the piers are so large that no space is available."[119] Doing away with dimension stone, and with the large cranes in the open air needed to handle these stone blocks, meant that foundations could be set in winter weather under tarpaulins, decreasing construction time in buildings on valuable sites.

In designing the Auditorium Building's foundations, Adler adapted several ideas from local technical culture. The first problem was to accurately determine the site soil's bearing capacity. The Board of Trade had settled unevenly in part because the allowable pressure had been overestimated to be 9,000 pounds per square foot. Careful testing for the Home Insurance had yielded an estimate of 4,000 pounds per square foot as that site's uniform carrying capacity, but Adler thought even this number might be too high to ensure acceptably minimal settlement. As did his fellow architects, Adler worked with Gen. William Sooy Smith (1830–1916), a nationally known expert in foundation engineering. Smith developed a technique for determining a soil's allowable bearing pressure by driving wood shafts or piles deep into the ground, then loading them with tanks into which water was pumped. As the water's weight increased, gauges showed how far the piles sank under the loads. Adler wrote that Smith's "borings and tests made to determine the character of the soil underlying [the Auditorium's] foundations were unusually thorough."[120] Excavations went down to a uniform depth of twelve feet below the sidewalk, while trenches for wall and column footings were dug to a depth of from seventeen to twenty-five feet. Smith made borings twenty feet apart over the building's entire half-block site area. These borings went down in increments to depths of sixty feet through the hardpan into softer clays below. At several depths, Smith set shafts into the borings and weighted them with water to determine precisely the soil's bearing capacity at these different levels. Smith reported to Mueller that the capacity of 4,500 pounds per square foot varied little over the whole lakeside site. As Sullivan recalled, Smith thus recommended that the design loads on the foundations be 4,250 pounds per square foot.[121]

The Auditorium's site had special constraints that shaped Adler's design for the foundation's footings. He published illustrations of the footings, and they appear in a later isometric drawing of the basement structure (fig. 69). Unlike the Home

Insurance Building, commercial uses for the Auditorium's first floor dictated that it be kept as close to the sidewalk as possible, which meant sinking the basement and foundations completely below grade. To align the Auditorium's foundations on a level with those of the adjacent Studebaker Building, Adler set the bases of their footings at a datum of seventeen feet below grade. Since Lake Michigan's water level was from twelve to fifteen feet below grade, Adler set all footings in courses of heavy timbers (fig. 70, 1–1'a) continuously immersed in water to prevent rotting caused by exposing wood alternately to dryness and water. On these timber courses Adler then set a grillage of steel rails encased in concrete (fig. 70, 1–1'b). On these pads he set pyramids of rubble and dimension stone (fig. 70, 1–1'c) as the footings for isolated piers and segments of walling. For this extraordinarily heavy building on the least propitious of soils, these precautions proved inadequate, and the edifice began to sink shortly after construction began. Its total settlement under full load was eighteen inches. By 1890 "many of the floors in the building are already out of plumb and there are other plain evidences that the big building is settling, and not all over alike, either." The reason lay not in either Adler's or Smith's calculations, but in the fact "that the foundations were put in originally for a brick and not for a stone building," a stone that the Auditorium's directors chose in May 1887 after the foundations were in, which made the exterior walls one-third heavier than they were designed to

Figure 69

Auditorium Building, isometric drawing of basement structure, showing both continuous wall and isolated pier foundations. Sections 1-1', 2-2', and 3-3' along Congress Street refer to figure 70. Historic American Buildings Survey, IL-1007, 1980. Drawing by Laura Hochuli. Courtesy of the Library of Congress. Graphic notations by author.

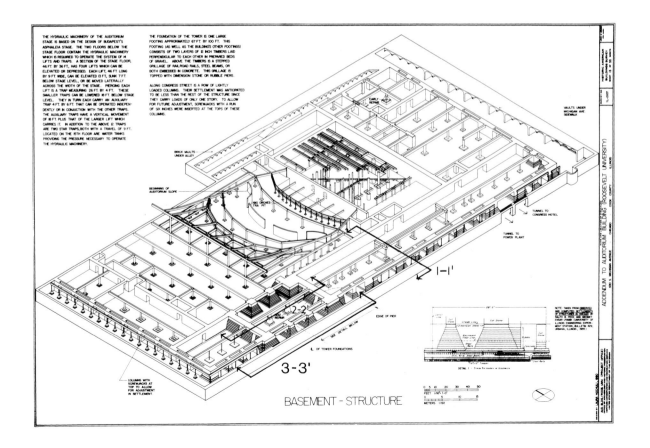

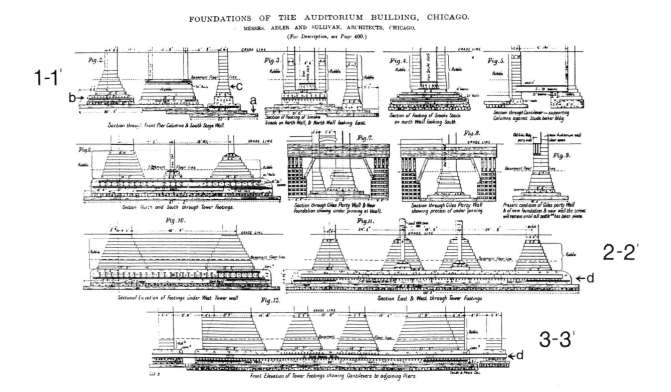

FOUNDATIONS OF THE AUDITORIUM BUILDING, CHICAGO.

MESSRS. ADLER AND SULLIVAN, ARCHITECTS, CHICAGO.

(For Description, see Page 400.)

Figure 70

Auditorium Building, foundation construction. (1-1') north-south section of hotel block on Congress Street looking west, cut through a south front pier, a pair of iron columns, and stone wall on north side of hotel block, showing (a) courses of heavy timbers; (b) grillage of steel rails encased in concrete; and (c) pyramids of rubble; (2-2') east-west section looking north through pyramidal tower footings of rubble courses, resting on beds of steel rails encased in concrete, with (d) fifteen-inch steel beams running between footings to resist shear; and (3-3') south front of tower footings looking north, with (d) steel beams extending to frontal piers on either side of tower as cantilevers, both for pier support and to equalize settlement with tower. From "The Auditorium Building, Chicago," *Engineering* (London) 51 (3 April 1891): 395. Graphic notations by author.

be.[122] This accentuated the unequal distribution of loads over the site, since the weight of the ten-story perimeter block's stone walls was much greater than that of the theater inside. Ultimately this led to the canted floors that one sees along the south and north sides of the theater today, with outer walls lower than the central theater. Having calculated the foundations to receive the lighter brick outer walls, Adler must have been dismayed at the directors' decision. The Auditorium's settlement concerned him to near the end of his life, when he contemplated lowering the theater's central floor to make it level again with the settled outer walls.

The tower's great weight (designed to be 14,800 tons) meant that its load had to be spread over the entire area of its base, so as to keep the bearing pressure on the soil uniform with the building's adjacent ten-story blocks. An east-west section through the tower's footings (fig. 70, 2–2') shows the tower's aboveground brick piers bearing on huge pyramids of rubble courses, presumably encased in concrete. The separate pier footings in turn rest on a common platform nearly seven feet thick, consisting of multiple layers of crisscrossed steel rails encased in courses of concrete. To avoid breakage due to shearing between segments of this platform, Adler joined together lines of steel rails running east-west (fig. 70, 2–2'd) and north-south. The east-west beams extended to frontal piers on either side of the tower (fig. 70, 3–3'd), partly supporting these piers as cantilevers, so helping to ensure their equal settling with the tower. Setting of the building's foundations is shown in figure

71, looking southeast across the site from west of Wabash Avenue. This view shows the following structures raised to the sidewalk level: (a) pier foundations for west and south street walls; (b) south side and west rear theater walls; and (c) pyramidal pier foundations at the base of the tower. By March 1888 these foundations were complete, yet the greatest challenge lay in building the tower above.

Adler designed a larger foundational area for the tower's greater weight to ensure that the ratio of building weight to foundational area (or bearing pressure on the soil) was the same as in the Auditorium's adjacent ten-story sections. These were lighter in weight and consequently had smaller foundational areas. By this means the *finished* sixteen-story tower would not stress the ground area more than the *finished* adjacent ten-story block (fig. 72a). Yet there remained the problem of differential settlement between the tower and adjacent sections during their construction. As Baumann and others had cautioned, all buildings sink initially when they first compress the soil beneath them. In the Auditorium, the lower tower's partial ten-story weight would be the same as that of the building's adjacent ten-story sections. Yet if no precautions were taken, the partial tower's weight would be spread over a foundational area designed for the heavier finished tower, yielding a lower bearing pressure on the soil (building weight per unit of foundational area) than that beneath the building's adjacent ten-story sections with their smaller foundations.

Figure 71

Auditorium Building, foundation construction looking southeast across the site from west of Wabash Avenue, showing the following structures raised to the sidewalk level: (a) pier foundations for west and south street walls; (b) south side and west rear theater walls; and (c) pyramidal pier foundations at base of tower. *Inland Architect and News Record* 11 (March 1888), photogravure edition. Architecture Photograph Collection, Courtesy of the Art Institute of Chicago. Graphic notations by author.

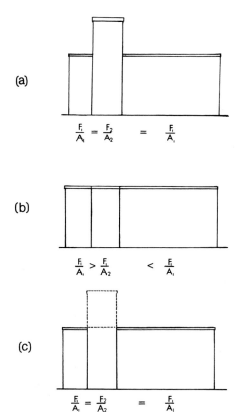

(a)

$$\frac{F_1}{A_1} = \frac{F_2}{A_2} \qquad = \qquad \frac{F_1}{A_1}$$

(b)

$$\frac{F_1}{A_1} > \frac{F_1}{A_2} \qquad < \qquad \frac{F_1}{A_1}$$

(c)

$$\frac{F_1}{A_1} = \frac{F_2}{A_2} \qquad = \qquad \frac{F_1}{A_1}$$

Figure 72

Auditorium Building, foundation diagrams of tower and adjacent sections of south front along Congress Street. F_1 = weight of ten stories; A_1= foundational area sized for ten stories; F_2 = weight of sixteen stories; A_2 = foundational area sized for sixteen stories. (Diagram a) bearing pressure on soil under finished ten-story block equals bearing pressure of finished sixteen-story tower (F_1/A_1 = F_2/A_2). (Diagram b) bearing pressure under ten-story block is greater than bearing pressure under ten-story base of tower (F_1/A_1 ˃ F_1/A_2), causing differential settlement between tower base and adjacent blocks. (Diagram c) bearing pressure under finished ten-story block equals bearing pressure of ten-story base of tower artificially loaded to equal weight of sixteen stories (F_1/A_1 = F_2/A_2). Drawing by author.

Before the tower was complete, this would cause the tower to settle less than these flanking sections (fig. 72b). As Sullivan later wrote, "If the foundation were made [small enough] under the tower for it to settle with the rest of the building, the foundation would be made too small when the tower was completed."[123]

To avoid this problem, Adler adapted Baumann's suggestion that the soil be prestressed with artificial loads to compact it before the permanent building's weight was placed on it. Adler had the tower's footing incrementally loaded with piles of brick and pig iron "at such a rate that when the entire building reached a height of ten stories, the full weight of the [sixteen-story] tower rested upon its footing."[124] This artificial loading compressed the soil by an amount equal to the compression caused by the weight of the adjacent ten-story sections on their smaller foundations (fig. 72c). This would prevent initial differential settlement of the tower relative to the flanking sections. When the time came to continue the tower above the adjacent sections, artificial loads in the tower's lower stories were removed in proportion to the increase in its permanent load. By this method, the tower's sixteen stories would not compress the soil more than did the adjacent ten-story sections (fig. 72a). To further minimize differential settlement, Adler and Sooy Smith tied the tower footings to the footings of adjacent sections with fifteen-inch I-beams (fig. 70, 3–3'd).

Sullivan recalled that Adler's ingenious solution was closely watched by other Chicago architects. At that time the Board of Trade's tower had begun to sink without apparent end, causing internal problems owing to differential settlement between the tower and the building's adjacent sections. Burnham and Root waited to see what would happen to the Auditorium's tower before they began the sixteen-story masonry mass of their Monadnock Building in 1889.[125] Unfortunately the Auditorium's tower did settle more than expected, and the settlement was differential relative to the adjacent sections, causing uneven floor levels at their junctures inside that still exist today. But again the problem derived from a change in design. Following Ware's advice and Peck's desire, after the foundations were already in, Adler and Sullivan added two stories totaling eighteen feet to the tower and changed its internal arrangements, increasing its weight to about 16,000 tons on its foundational area of about 100 by 71 feet (7,100 square feet). This increased the bearing pressure underneath to 4,480 pounds per square foot, greater than the designed load of 4,250 used for the adjacent sections. Thus, from Adler's perspective, the tower's resulting settlement was not mysterious. Rather, "the action of the tower was simply another demonstration of the correctness of the theory upon which Chicago constructors work, i.e., that equal loads per unit of soil area in different adjacent foundations produce equal settlements, and unequal loads per unit of soil area produce unequal settlements."[126] Ironically, at the Auditorium, failure in practice had demonstrated success in reasoning.

As Peck had said, the Auditorium Tower's foundations were meant to demonstrate that Chicago's soils could sustain the tallest structures and that Chicago's architects could design their foundation systems. Hence capital from beyond the city would be encouraged to invest in large structures in the Loop. In this spirit, the most daring proposal of the period was for a freestanding tower at the World's Columbian Exposition that would overtop Paris's Eiffel Tower of 1889. The Auditorium's mostly masonry tower of nearly 16,000 tons weighed over twice as much as the Eiffel Tower, whose skeletal iron and steel totaled about 7,000 tons. Yet the Eiffel Tower's height of 984 feet (300 meters) was over 3.6 times the Auditorium Tower's 271 feet, so that the stresses of lateral wind loading on the Parisian monument were much greater and did much to determine its form.[127]

Adler and Sullivan took up the challenge of much greater height in Chicago skyscrapers with their unbuilt project for an office building designed for the Illinois branch of the Independent Order of Odd Fellows, a fraternal organization rivaling the Masons. Announced in September 1891, by which time plans were completed, this project had an area whose perimeter would be fully occupied by fourteen-story blocks. At the centers of the street fronts would rise structures of twenty-one stories, about the height of Burnham and Root's twenty-two-story Masonic Temple, then the world's tallest building, completed in 1892 on the northeast corner of State and Randolph Streets. Crowning the center of the Odd Fellows' building would be a tower of thirty-six stories or 556 feet, just inches taller than the Washington Monument, whose nearly pyramidal cap Adler and Sullivan again recalled in their design (fig. 73). Construction of the Odd Fellows Temple would have been feasible only by abandoning the Auditorium's system of weight-bearing masonry piers and replacing it with newly conventional methods of iron and steel framing. In addition, "special arrangements will have to be made for a foundation for the central portion of the building."[128] This meant abandoning isolated pier foundations set on hardpan and replacing them with a system of either piles or caissons that would "carry the weight of the building down [through the soft earth below the hardpan] to the underlying bed rock."[129] Thus, only new techniques for foundations and framing could extend the architectural idea of the Auditorium's tower into the realm of modern skyscraper construction.

As in other local works of the period, the Auditorium Building's foundation system underlay the visual rhythm of its street elevations. Comparing the first floor's isometric

Figure 73

Adler and Sullivan, unbuilt design for Odd Fellows Temple, Chicago (1890–1891). From *Industrial Chicago*, vol. 2. Courtesy of the Chicago Historical Society, ICHi-31472.

PROPOSED ODD FELLOWS' TEMPLE.

diagram (fig. 74) with an elevation of the building's south front (fig. 75) reveals the relation between internal structure and exterior form. Adler stressed that in the architectural planning of commercial buildings there should be a consistent unit of subdivision for space and structure. As he wrote: "The unit of subdivision will also be the unit of construction and the unit of design."[130] Economy in metal-framed buildings meant adopting unit dimensions to simplify fabrication of iron and steel elements. This was a major cost concern in the Auditorium Building because of its enormous size and thus the large quantities of metal ordered. As Sullivan recalled, "The material required taxed the capacity of the Carnegie works at Pittsburgh, and then overtaxed their capacity so that we were delayed for months and months. They would wire us that work had been shipped when it had not been rolled, and the Carnegie Company staggered under the contract for the iron work in the Auditorium Building."[131] The delays Sullivan recalled may have been related to labor troubles. Mueller recalled that the Auditorium had its steel supplied by Carnegie's Homestead Mill, which had just been converted from manufacture of wrought iron to the Bessemer process for fabricating steel.[132] This plant was then the focus of intense labor conflicts including a major strike in 1888, a forerunner of the more violent and protracted Homestead strike of 1892. Ironically, when sailing to Europe in August 1888, Adler met Capt. William R. Jones, the superintendent of Carnegie's Braddock and Homestead Mills, who was "aboard to take a rest from fighting the big strike."[133]

Figure 74

Auditorium Building, isometric view of first-floor plan, showing (a) girders, set sixteen feet apart, spanning thirty-six feet between north and south walls of hotel block on Congress Street; (b) girders spanning between outer and inner walls of hotel lobby on Michigan Avenue; and (c) freestanding columns in lobby. Historic American Buildings Survey, IL-1007, 1980. Drawing by Michael Palmer. Courtesy of the Library of Congress. Graphic notations by author.

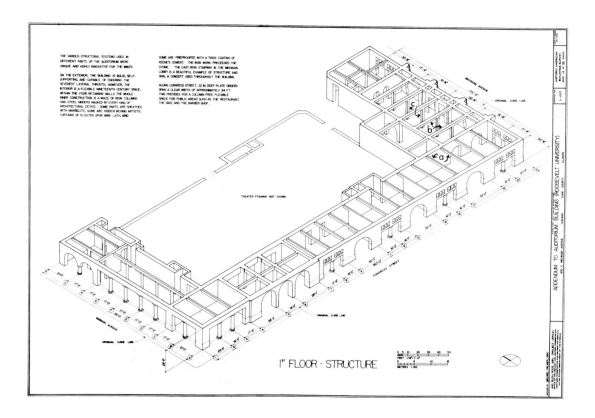

1ST FLOOR · STRUCTURE

As a consumer of large quantities of structural metalwork, the Auditorium Building exemplified Adler's dictum that economy of construction led to adopting large units of subdivision because of the greater strength of longer and deeper beams and to reducing the number of columns, yielding greater freedom in utilizing space.[134] For the Auditorium Hotel's public rooms along Congress Street, many pillars would have been objectionable. Thus the floors from the first story upward rest on riveted girders that span thirty-six feet between the north and south walls of the hotel block along Congress Street (fig. 74a). These girders were set sixteen feet apart atop the first floor's walls, so that their loads were evenly distributed over the foundation piers, most of which followed this modular rhythm. On Congress Street, the dimension between supports doubles to thirty-two feet around the arches on the sidewalk. The same module of sixteen feet recurs in the second and third floors of the granite base, marked by pairs of windows, and in the upper elevations as the spacing between the piers of the main four-story arcade (fig. 75a).

The Auditorium Building's construction is documented in two photographs: one from late 1887 showing the framing of the first five floors (fig. 76) and another from late 1888 showing the outer walls raised to the eighth floor (fig. 77). The earlier view shows the thirty-six-foot steel girders as they project from the hotel block's rear wall. The free ends of the girders are supported on temporary wood posts and beams, with temporary diagonal cross bracing (fig. 76a). As the south wall rose, these girders would anchor into its masonry piers, and the temporary wood supports

Figure 75

Auditorium Building, south elevation, working drawing of April 1887, showing (a) repeated module of sixteen feet between piers of main four-story arcade, doubling to thirty-two feet between supports on either side of arches at the sidewalk; ratio of height to width of 3.06:1 in (b) tower, (b') four-story arcade bay of fourth through seventh floors, and (b") two-story arches of eighth and ninth floors. Architecture Photograph Collection, Courtesy of the Art Institute of Chicago. Graphic notations by author.

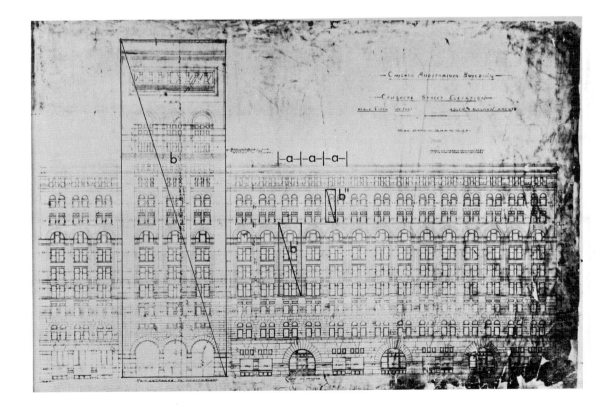

would be removed. A similar system of temporary wood posts and beams, joined by diagonal knee braces, upholds the free ends of the lighter steel beams on the west side. These beams would subsequently anchor into the permanent west wall. As Adler noted, the result around the block encasing the theater was a flexible space, without columns between its inner and outer masonry bearing walls.[135] In its combination of masonry walls, iron columns, and steel girders, the Auditorium's construction was not a consistently modern iron and steel skeleton, hence Sullivan recalled that it "may be considered the last of the old style buildings."[136]

Figure 76

Auditorium Building, construction photograph, from the southwest, probably from late 1887, showing initial framing of first five floors on south and west sides, with (a) free ends of permanent steel girders supported on temporary wood posts and beams, with diagonal knee and cross bracing. From *Engineering Magazine* 4 (November 1892). Courtesy of Watkinson Library, Trinity College, Hartford, Connecticut.

Figure 77

Auditorium Building, in construction, from the southeast, late 1888, showing base with outer bearing walls of granite, upper floors of brick faced with limestone, and steel cantilevers with bolts for midspan columns of second-story loggia on Michigan Avenue front. Auditorium Collection, Roosevelt University Archives.

Perhaps as important, the Auditorium was not innovative in the management of its construction. By the time the process began early in 1887, an increasing proportion of Chicago's tall office buildings were built by a general contractor, who organized most of the separate building trades as subcontractors and offered a single bid to complete a structure within a given time. The outstanding general contractor of the period was the George A. Fuller Company, whose emphasis on quality and speed recommended it to capitalists concerned with maximizing and expediting return on capital invested in large buildings.[137] By contrast, the Auditorium had no general contractor. Instead it was built under the older divided contract system, whereby the building owners (via the Auditorium Association's executive committee) contracted separately with each trade, including masons, iron and steel setters, and over forty others, all of whom reported ultimately to the architects, Adler and Sullivan, through their two superintendents of construction. As the agents of the owners, the architects worked with their consulting engineers, negotiated independent contracts, oversaw their execution, and coordinated the work of the different trades.

Adler attended most of the Auditorium Association's executive committee meetings alone, worked with consulting engineers for foundations, plumbing, and heating, and supervised contractors for the building's structural and mechanical systems. Sullivan, who came to committee meetings related to interior design, dealt with contractors and artists for the decorative arts. The architects' responsibilities were vast, especially near the end of the project in 1889, when over a thousand workers were on the site. Sullivan recalled that both his and Adler's health was strained. Yet Wright later remembered: "We used to call Dankmar Adler 'Chief' in those busy days when the Auditorium was building, and he stood squarely in the midst of the great turmoil, solidly dominating the whole building process, from the trenches where the footings were going into a floating foundation, to the great trusses that later spanned the greatest room for opera the world has ever seen." Contractors "who knew him feared and respected him mightily. He was master of their craft and they knew it. His bushy brows at that time almost hid a pair of piercing gray eyes. His square gray beard and squarish head seemed square with the building, and his personal solidity was a guarantee that out of all that confusion would issue the beauty of order."[138]

Construction photographs reveal the true structural roles of masonry and metal, yet the Auditorium's finished fronts were not about the literal expression of construction. Instead, Adler and Sullivan borrowed from Richardson the partly fictive representational character of the round-arched Romanesque style. Both architects reserved this vocabulary for their buildings' publicly visible, symbolically charged street fronts. Rear light courts in Richardson's Field Wholesale Store and in Adler and Sullivan's Auditorium were plain brick walls, unlike their outward urban facades of expensively quarried and crafted stone. In this sense Sullivan emulated Richardson as the architect whom Wright later called "the grand exteriorist," meaning a designer who thought in terms of exterior massing and detail rather than the three-dimensional interweaving of structure and space that Wright saw as a central virtue of his own works within the tradition of modern architecture after 1890.[139]

In the Field Wholesale Store there was a disjunction between outward appearance and internal structure. Inside the building's open floors, wrought iron ceiling beams spanned between structural columns, as seen in a view of the first floor (fig. 78). These beams extended to the outer walls, where they connected at right angles to box girders embedded in the walls, as seen in a section drawn through a window head on the first floor (fig. 79). The box girders spanned each window opening, on either side of which the girders rested on masonry piers. Thus, in reality, the Field Store's structure was one of internal columns and exterior piers upholding horizontal beams, or a post-and-lintel system. But all the exterior windows except those in the top story were spanned by arches. The arches bore their own weight and that of the exterior facing directly above them, but they did not support the floors behind. These were upheld by the girders in the outer walls spanning between vertical masonry piers. In fact, as the view inside the first floor shows, the low curved profile of the windows' segmental arches along the outer walls actually reduced interior daylight, whose adequacy was essential for inspection of the types of goods on display, especially fabrics.[140] The exterior arches, central to the building's urban image, were neither structurally nor functionally helpful, adding weight and blocking light. Nor were they constructionally truthful. As James O'Gorman has written: "Richardson took pains in the main facades to mask new materials [iron] with traditional ones [stone]."[141]

Figure 78

Richardson, Marshall Field Wholesale Store, interior view of first floor looking toward northwest corner, showing wrought iron ceiling beams spanning between structural columns. From Samuel H. Ditchett, *Marshall Field and Company: The Life Story of a Great Concern* (New York: Dry Goods Economist, 1922).

Figure 79

Richardson, Marshall Field Wholesale Store, section through first-floor window head showing iron box girder embedded in wall behind brownstone facing. Drawing MF-E1 from the H. H. Richardson Collection. Courtesy of the Department of Printing and Graphic Arts, the Houghton Library, Harvard College Library.

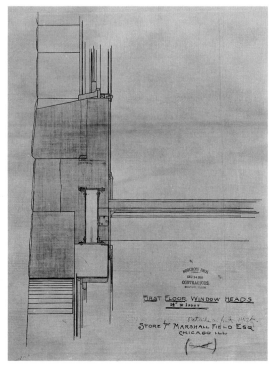

Similarly, above the two-story base the Auditorium's external allusions to arched Roman construction are only mural motifs crafted in facing stones. As in Richardson's Field Store, the Auditorium's exterior effect depended on Adler and Sullivan's selection and treatment of the stone for different levels. For the Field Store, Richardson selected a red Missouri granite for the base, with brownstone for the upper walls, which he initially envisioned in brick.[142] Though Sullivan apparently admired the Field Store's rich earthen colors, the Auditorium's civic purpose and lakefront site presumably influenced his and Adler's selection of a dark gray granite for the Auditorium's two lower floors and a lighter-toned Maine granite for the third story (fig. 80; plates 1 and 2). On the lower two floors, the exterior walls are solid granite. On the third story, the light-colored granite is a facing sixteen inches thick backed by twenty inches of brick, except for the tower, where the third story's outer wall is of solid granite. These distinctions between solid and facing granite are not externally apparent, since both types of stone were rock faced and were given a rough hammered finish on all three base stories outside, so that the lower walls present an image of massive indestructibility. As Garczynski stressed, the Auditorium's encasing block was "not a mere shell of masonry supported by iron columns and beams, but is solid, self-supporting, and capable of enduring the severest lateral thrusts."[143] This emphasis on an encasing mass of masonry corresponded to the period's debates about optimal construction of the new generation of tall buildings (meaning ten to twelve stories). Engineers and others then often voiced preference for the more conservative system of load-bearing outer walls as an unquestionably reliable method of resisting the lateral thrusts of wind loads and thus a more desirable alternative than the novelty of fully skeletal iron and steel frames with an exterior cladding of brick or stone.

Figure 80

Auditorium Building, recent view of base from southwest along Congress Street, after destruction of south interior of ground floor in the 1950s to create an outdoor covered sidewalk, showing oblique view of shadowed archways with original metal-framed windows removed. Photograph by Oliver Radford.

The Auditorium's Construction and the Labor Movement in Chicago's Building Trades

The Auditorium Building's exterior bearing walls were structurally traditional, yet their constructive methods and their symbolic intentions were also keyed to the intense conflict between capital and labor that continued in spring 1887, when Adler and Sullivan developed the Auditorium's final exterior design. As in 1883, the city's largest and most radical union associated with the construction trades, the United Order of American Bricklayers and Stonemasons of Chicago, was the leading power in the protest. This union's name signaled its local independence from national labor groups. To work as a bricklayer or stonemason in Chicago in this period, one had to belong to this union. The union was powerful enough to dictate the terms of contracts to the master masons who employed union members. It was the only union among Chicago's building trades with such collective bargaining power. Carpenters had their separate union, as did the bricklayers' assistants, the hod carriers, and the laborers. By winter 1887 the carpenters had revived their efforts to achieve collective power over their builder-employers. Their activist leadership in this period came largely from formerly independent German and Czech anarchist carpenters, who had rejoined the union in the wake of antiradical pressure following the Haymarket clash. In April 1887, just before the beginning of the prime building season on 1 May, when old leases on sites expired and new leases permitting construction began, all these groups presented demands to the building companies (or contractors for particular trades) that employed tradesmen. These demands included an eight-hour day, a standard minimum wage, exclusive use of unionized carpenters, and control over the day of the week when carpenters were paid, preferably Saturday.[144]

Chicago's other building workers looked on the carpenters' stand as representative of labor's cause. Before Sunday, 1 May, the laborers in Chicago's stone yards succeeded in forcing their employers, the stonecutting companies, to accede to their demand for an eight-hour rather than a ten-hour day. This action ended the threat of a strike in the stone yards, though the bricklayers did not reach an agreement with their employing contractors, the master masons, about their weekly payday. The bricklayers had presented their demands for a Saturday payday on Friday, 29 April, and the master masons refused it on Thursday, 5 May. The end of labor trouble in the stone yards, versus the probability of its continuing among the bricklayers' union, may have prompted the Auditorium Association's executive committee to adopt a resolution at their meeting of 6 May, to change the building's upper walls from a cladding of pressed brick to an exterior facing of Indiana limestone. On Tuesday, 10 May, the bricklayers presented a series of demands to the master masons' association. These included a demand for "the recognition of their union," which meant that the master masons would "pledge themselves to employ henceforth none but laborers belonging to their union, to grant to it the practical control of the labor market."[145] The master masons resolved to resist this demand, and 2,000 bricklayers promptly struck on 11 May. In retaliation, the master masons sought the cooperation of local suppliers to agree not to sell or deliver building materials to anyone pending settlement of the strike. The builders reasoned that the more complete the cessation of building, the shorter the strike would be, since bricklayers would be unable to find work anywhere. The suppliers, who had long resented the tyranny of the bricklayers' union, readily agreed to support the builders, and deliveries of stone, brick, lime, cement, sand, architectural iron, tile, and other materials soon stopped all over Chicago. The master masons agreed to a general shutting down of all work on which bricklayers and stonemasons were engaged, thereby turning the strike into a lockout. Soon after, construction around the city all but ceased, idling about 30,000 workers, including carpenters and other trades.[146]

As an architect of four buildings under construction and of nine more for which plans were ready, Dankmar Adler had much at stake in this strike. In his writings of that time, and in later essays, Adler described his professional role as representing his clients, the building owners. Like Peck, Adler was politically not a socialist, though he did sympathize with the plight of workingmen, writing that "there is much that is great and noble even in the trade unionism of our day."[147] Yet as the bricklayers' strike continued through mid-June, Adler saw this labor action as causing workers to lose income. One estimate was that the lockout caused a direct loss of $5,000,000 to all involved, both striking workers and idle builders. Adler noted that his clients waiting to build were "all agreed not to have a stroke of work done until this strike is ended by the giving in of the workmen. The [bricklayers'] union is what stands in the way of the erection of these buildings." Yet the Auditorium's construction then continued with workers who had left their union to return to work and who were sometimes subjected to intimidation. This building's size offered steady work for many over a long period, and Adler stated that some men had returned to work on the Auditorium because they had "become so destitute during the strike that they have sold their tools, and we have had to supply them."[148]

Adler's concerns about the strike's consequences went beyond the costs of stopping work. One of the issues that divided employing builders and unionized workers was the system of training and apprenticeship in skilled trades. Traditionally workers sought to limit the supply of well-schooled younger men in order to keep demand for skills (and thus wages) high. But builders and architects wanted a uniform system of apprenticeship and a consistently ample supply of well-trained craftsmen. They pushed for manual training in public schools and a system of night schools organized by local trade organizations. On 4 June Adler addressed this issue as president of the Illinois State Association of Architects, which had supported the builders' efforts to break the strike by shutting down deliveries of materials citywide. In opening the association's meeting, Adler "said that those present knew the demoralized condition of the building trades and the low character that they were drifting to in regard to the workmanship of mechanics engaged therein. It was becoming almost impossible to replace good men, because the trade-unions arbitrarily prevented the education of a sufficient number of apprentices to replace the good and competent mechanics, who appeared to be rapidly dying out. The difficulty was staring them in the face that soon they would not be able to secure competent me-chanical skill at all."[149] Presumably Adler was then facing this issue at the Auditorium as the city's largest building project, with its unprecedented demand for quantity and variety of skilled labor.

Citywide, the lockout continued until 11 July, after the builders' association and trade organizations agreed to submit future disputes to a new board of arbitration. This effectively limited the power of the bricklayers' union, which was forced to withdraw its key demand for a Saturday payday. The new arbiters were "also given power to determine what number of apprentices should be enrolled so as to afford all boys desiring to learn the trade an opportunity to do so without overcrowding, so as not to cause the coming workman to be unskilled in his art or the supply of labor to grossly exceed the demand therefor."[150] Public sympathy had grown on the side of the builders, who presented themselves as standing up to a union that trampled the individual's right to work outside the union's dicta. The two-month shutdown meant a loss to Chicagoans of about $20,000,000, "for the uncertainty of labor and its exorbitant demands deterred the would-be investors of that amount of capital from investing it here that year."[151] Perhaps to counter national perception of a local shortage of building craftsmen and thereby induce the continuing flow of distant capital to the city's prime building sites, the Auditorium's directors' public-ity about the construction consistently presented the huge monument as an impres-sive display of Chicago's workmanship in a wide range of architectural materials.

The strike of 1887 brought the issues of Haymarket into the building trades once again and into the history of the Auditorium, a structure that was intended to alle-viate social tensions. Democrat Grover Cleveland was then in power as his party's first president after the Civil War. As part of Peck's effort to promote the Audito-rium as a national political center, he had tried to have Cleveland participate in lay-ing the structure's cornerstone in October 1887 during the president's first visit to Chicago. The politics surrounding the building surfaced in planning for this event, which was to take place just over a month before the scheduled execution of the Haymarket anarchists in November. Their fate dominated discussions of class con-flict, locally and nationally, as Chicago socialists and capitalists battled for control over workers' minds and sympathies. For example, on 21 September police shad-owed an agent of New York City's Federation of Trade Unions who was distributing circulars to Chicago workers calling for public uprising against the Haymarket ver-dict. Handed out to those boarding morning cable cars on the West Side, the circu-lars read in part: "The aims and purposes of Anarchism have been blackguarded and vilified by the fiends of humanity, who feast upon your servitude . . . . Anarchy is not a frightful chaos, as pictured by the hired press; it aims, on the contrary, at the fraternal harmony of mankind."[152] That evening there were anarchist rallies at the usual halls along West Lake Street, where German and English orators decried the coming executions.

Meanwhile, on the same day, at the Palmer House, Peck tried to persuade the executive committee in charge of the presidential reception that Cleveland should lay the cornerstone of the Auditorium as a building "designed for National purposes, such as the holding of political conventions and all other National gatherings." He wanted the reviewing stand for the reception's civic procession (planned to be set up at the Palmer House, where the president would be staying) erected instead on Michigan Avenue in front of the Auditorium, so that "from 50,000 to 100,000 persons could get to see the President from the Lake-Front Park." Peck argued that "the soft pavement and comparative quiet of Michigan avenue would permit the numerous bands of music to be heard by the people." In this period, as in others, the public visibility and vicarious accessibility of the United States president was seen as a key symbol of American democracy, a symbol Peck wanted associated with his building and not with the elitist Palmer House, where "there would be a terrible crush and the number of persons to see the President limited."[153] If held in Lake Front Park, the review would achieve its maximum potential for rallying local support to the country's apparently democratic order, at a public space known for recent anarchist conclaves.

Peck's plan to unite site and ceremony as a counterweight to the mounting angst over the fate of the Haymarket prisoners did not come off quite as he had hoped. Just a week before Cleveland's visit, Peck's chances for success looked good. He had gone to Washington to call on the president and explain the Auditorium Building's purposes to him. Cleveland initially agreed to help lay the cornerstone, a three-ton block of blue gray granite that was to serve as the first course of the pier on the building's southeast corner. But Chicago's carpenters' union, which had been a central player in the building trades strike the previous spring, almost immediately opposed Cleveland's decision and planned to use it to put the president's friendship with labor to the test. Having failed to gain either recognition of their union or their demanded hourly wage of thirty-five cents, since the summer the carpenters had targeted their protests on the Auditorium Building, where fifty nonunion carpenters were steadily employed. The union informed Cleveland that it would take no part in the cornerstone-laying ceremony if he participated, and that it would regard his participation as hostile to labor's interests nationwide, implicitly threatening to withdraw crucial support for his reelection in 1888. Cleveland nominally backed down, rescinding his agreement with Peck to help set the great stone, which was placed on Thursday, 6 October, the day after the president's visit. Yet on 5 October the president, not wishing to alienate the Auditorium's supporters, did review a parade with Peck and others, including the contractors, from a temporary elevated stand at the Auditorium's site, as Peck wished. The parade "together called out immense crowds in procession," so that Peck effectively drew Cleveland "not unwillingly" into public perception of the laying of the building's cornerstone. The Auditorium, in turn, became a temporary national symbol as the backdrop for the presidential party seen by many people from across Michigan Avenue.[154]

The United Carpenters' Council of Chicago continued to battle Peck through the period of the Auditorium's construction. Their contest soon focused on the national conventions of Republicans and Democrats, both of which had been held at Chicago's Inter-state Industrial Exposition Building in 1884. Peck and others worked hard to convince the national committees of both parties to return to the city in 1888 and meet at the Auditorium.[155] Although they prevailed with the Republicans, the Democrats were more vulnerable to pressure from labor, at a time when the Socialist Labor Party did not seek to draw its members away from voting Democratic. At first the Democrats' national committee was favorably disposed toward returning to Chicago, where their victorious presidential candidate had been nominated in 1884. Local Democratic leaders formed a large lobby to persuade the national committee. However, the United Carpenters' Council also lobbied this committee, which was "given to understand that the consolidated building trades of the United States would refuse to support any man who was nominated in the Auditorium Building," whose contractors had refused to employ union men or pay union wages. Although the Auditorium Association did not control its contractors' policies on unions, labor identified these policies with the association as the building's owner. Carpenters warned Democrats that "a political boycott would be declared that would cost the offending party 250,000 votes [over ten times Cleveland's margin of victory in 1884]. That argument prevailed, and as a consequence the National Committee turned their backs upon Chicago and chose St. Louis."[156]

It was later claimed that "in all of Mr. Peck's building operations he has never himself had any difficulties with men in the working trades. Disturbances have now and then occurred as his buildings were going up, but in every case misunderstandings with individual contractors have been the cause, and in every case he has exerted himself in the most liberal manner to adjust any matters in dispute between the contractors and the men employed by them."[157] Yet in January 1888 the *Building Trades Journal,* published in St. Louis, claimed that the Auditorium Building "promises to become an important factor in national politics. This building is being erected independently of union mechanics. The stone was quarried and cut by Illinois convicts, and was hauled to Chicago by a railroad the president of which, as a state legislator, introduced a bill making a boycott [of this building project by trade unions] a criminal conspiracy. All this has raised the ire of the labor unions of Chicago, and their next gun will be pointed towards all political aspirants nominated at conventions held in the notorious auditorium."[158] In protest, on Labor Day, 3 September 1888, "the thousands of trade unionists marched past this hated pile to the doleful strains of the 'Dead March.'" Banners declared that they were "opposed to prison labor" and that there would be "no votes for a candidate who was nominated in a scab building," since Republicans had nominated Harrison there in June. By Labor Day 1888, over two years after Haymarket, local unions had declined in numbers and had divided between radical and moderate leadership. Bricklayers and stonecutters remained among the more militant, with the bricklayers marching that day to lay the cornerstone of their new monumental hall, the Bricklayers' Temple, on the West Side at Peoria and Monroe Streets. Later that fall, antipathy toward the Auditorium and its backers helped realize "to a large extent, the democratic majority in Cook County for Cleveland" in the presidential election of November 1888. Dispute with the Auditorium's directors "was also the potent factor" that helped pro-labor candidates win municipal elections of March 1889.[159]

The atmosphere of conflict between high capital and labor in the building trades also underlay the construction of the Marshall Field Wholesale Store, which was a commercial rather than a civic monument. Field's conservative views were well known, and his building had been a prime target of labor agitation that had slowed its construction. Its massive stonework may also have recalled the prefire armory building that had stood at this intersection of Franklin and Adams Streets and for a time had been used as headquarters for Chicago's first police precinct. Inside Field's store, each department was provided with a separate fireproof vault, where "funds and securities are beyond the reach of burglars, mobs, or dynamite bombs."[160] In this period it was not unusual to rhetorically link criminality and leftist political activity. Thus, to a working-class audience, Richardson's monument, and the language of its publicity, spoke assertively about Field's uncompromising resistance to labor's demands on the city's commercial establishment.

The procurement and treatment of the base's granites show how the Auditorium's construction represented Chicago capital's command of regional resources and how the process was enmeshed in labor issues that were then shaping much of the city's economic life. As William Le Baron Jenney said in 1884, "Our great system of railroads brings to Chicago every known building-stone in the country that is worth the transportation."[161] The Minnesota granite was obtained from the Mesabi Heights Quarries eighty miles north of Duluth and fifty miles west of Lake Superior, meaning that the stone had to be shipped to Chicago by rail and then by water. Its selection contrasted with the city's earlier preference for Lemont limestones (euphemistically called "Athens marble"), quarried about twenty miles southwest of Chicago, and other limestones quarried nearby in southern Illinois. By 1885 the Lemont quarries had become the site of fierce struggles between unionized stonecutters and their employers, as an extension of labor protests within Chicago's industries. Varied granites were preferred for the lower stories of the city's major new office buildings of the 1880s, but Adler and Sullivan were quite pleased with the architectural qualities of the Minnesota granite, which had a fine gray tone and a rose-colored tint. It was a compact, coarse-grained stone that cut well and was capable of receiving a high degree of polish.[162] The Auditorium's directors let the contract with the quarrying company in May 1887, yet by January 1888 it was clear that the company could not fulfill its agreement, partially owing to labor troubles. Under the contract's terms, the Auditorium Association then took possession of the quarries, arranging with a Chicago stonecutting firm to take over the beds and equipment and extract the stone.[163] Freight rates for its transport by rail were kept moderate because of the potential competition of shipment by water. Pressed by a deadline for completing the base before the Republican convention in June 1888, Adler went to the Minnesota quarries to help settle the labor disputes that had delayed the work there.[164]

Yet all was not resolved, for on this trip Adler found that the Minnesota quarries could not furnish stone blocks large enough for the round columns for the Auditorium's base. These columns' prime structural role at the building's base had demanded they be granite monoliths. The polished plate glass and metal frames in the large windows adjacent to these columns may have prompted Adler and Sullivan's specification that these columns be polished, unlike the stone of the wall. Polished granite columns had been conventional for earlier postfire monuments, such as Adler's Central Music Hall. North of the Auditorium, the neighboring Studebaker Building's main entrance was flanked by two large cylindrical shafts of red Syenite granite, like those set in its upper stories, including the columns rising through the third and fourth floors. At three feet eight inches thick and twenty-one feet tall, these were "the largest single polished stone shafts in the United States."[165] For the Auditorium's monoliths along the street level, Adler, after returning from Minnesota, conferred with the Hallowell Granite Company of Maine, the same firm that had supplied granite for the Board of Trade Building. This company owned quarries that contained a gray granite remarkably similar to that quarried in Minnesota. Adler then journeyed to these Maine quarries, where he arranged for production of the monoliths.

These columns were not carved and polished at the quarries. Instead they were brought to Chicago and polished with equipment then new to local stone yards. Up to that time Chicago architects had depended on eastern polishing companies to polish stones with their machines. This had meant extra expense and frequent delays. But the city's new polishing mills, with their own lays, meant that "the cutting, polishing, and other preparations are to be done in Chicago by Chicago workmen."[166] Mechanized cutting appears not only in the columns' capitals and bases but also in the projecting moldings running horizontally between the first three stories (fig. 80; plate 2). Like the columns, the moldings' smoothness and precision contrast sharply with the artificial irregularity of the rock-faced surfaces, proclaiming the new local capability to fashion stone. These facets of the Auditorium's progress exemplified the project's benefits to local workers, just as in 1885 it was said that on Richardson's Marshall Field Wholesale Store "the work will all be performed by Chicago artisans."[167] Such publicity asserted the city's emerging economic independence from the East. This independence had its cultural parallel in the formation of distinct regional traditions of music and architecture, which had been among Peck's central goals. In this way the processes of material fabrication that produced Adler and Sullivan's building reinforced their patron's vision of the structure's civic meaning.

At least in the eyes of militant union leaders, that Peck and his fellow directors had pressed ahead with building by using nonunion labor undercut their repeated public claims that the Auditorium was being built for the benefit of Chicago's working class. The project's large size, central location, and democratic ideology made it a flash point for workers' grievances and the translation of these grievances into local political action. Labor's opposition to the project peaked in May 1889 in response to the Auditorium Association's effort to secure the city council's permission to widen Congress Street, which was then thirty-eight feet from curb to curb, with a sidewalk of fourteen feet on each side for a total width of sixty-six feet between building fronts. In February 1884 Peck and his allies succeeded in getting the council to pass an ordinance that would permit widening the street to one hundred feet between building fronts, with the extra thirty-four feet to be taken from the street's south side and the cost of widening to be assessed upon nearby properties benefited, including mainly the Auditorium Association itself. Given the Auditorium Theater's enormous capacity, the widening would allow the projected large number of carriages to pass in multiple lanes along Congress Street to the theater's entrance. Yet in March, after elections strengthened labor's support in the city council, leaders of the local Trades Assembly persuaded the council to veto this ordinance. They then attempted to convince Chicago's new mayor, De Witt C. Cregier, to uphold the veto. The Trades Assembly delivered to him a long communication that read in part:

> The Auditorium Company is a private corporation organized for profit. The scheme is not a public necessity and is remarkable only for its size and not its character. Therefore we hold that this private speculation is entitled to no more municipal indulgence or privileges than is enjoyed by any other public place where physical or mental entertainment is sold for a money profit. The claim made by the directors of this corporation that their scheme is entitled to special privileges because the motive and object is to benefit the general public, even at the risk and sacrifice of the almighty dollar, is false, as proved by their operations thus far . . . .
>
> The foundation of the public welfare is the general welfare, is the general comfort and content of the laboring classes; hence the wants, desires, and the discontent of this class, expressed in the requests of organized labor through strikes, petitions, political action, and legislation, should receive the most favorable consideration of all public-spirited citizens. Instead of receiving this consideration from the directors of the Auditorium, who now ostentatiously parade themselves as public benefactors, all the prayers and petitions of labor asking them to respect the eight-hour law of the state and pay union wages for competent work have been treated by these modern Pharisees with contempt and scorn, and the power of unlimited wealth in their hands has been used to so humiliate, outrage and injure the interests of the organized workers that themselves and their money-making scheme will be the object of the everlasting hate of the organized labor of this city. On every visable [sic] portion of this vast building the trade unionist reads the words: "Erected by scab labor . . . ."
>
> In conclusion we desire to impress upon you that instead of this building and its ultimate purposes being a source of local pride, it stands forth as a disgraceful

illustration of the social and industrial gulf that has been created in this republic between the laboring poor and the idle rich, a banquet and a dinner-pail, grand opera and a dime museum.[168]

Mayor Cregier was ultimately unmoved by this statement and vetoed the ordinance repealing the widening. He disagreed with the Trades Assembly and their supporters on the city council, maintaining, like Peck, that the Auditorium, "although technically a private enterprise . . . has become of a quasi-public nature." The mayor said that the building would afford "unsurpassed opportunities for free or inexpensive musical and other entertainments on a grand scale for the masses of a refining and educational character."[169] In Cregier's view, promoting the new theater's success furthered the city's best interests. Earlier Peck had assured the Auditorium's stockholders that their investment would be profitable, even while he declared the project to be a gift to the city and hence unlike conventional commercial structures. The calculated ambiguity created by these twin ideas left the project open to labor's attacks, yet as long as local political power rested ultimately with capital, Peck's rhetoric of civic benefit could be invoked to fend off labor's criticisms.

Sullivan's Design for the Auditorium Building's Exterior

To some extent the Auditorium's ideological fate in the context of disputes among the building trades was beyond Peck's control, yet he sought a finished work of architecture whose exterior form would leave little doubt as to its patrons' motivations. As a statement to an audience of Chicago's visitors and citizens, the Auditorium Building's persona began with its entrances, which included the triple-arched entrance to the theater at the tower's base, single arches framing doorways to special rooms on Congress Street, and the hotel's triple-arched main portal and loggia on Michigan Avenue. The arches on Congress Street are rock faced, like the surrounding wall from which the voussoirs spring directly and with which the crowning cluster of keystone blocks merges. These represent Sullivan's first use of such massive Richardsonian Romanesque arches. From an oblique angle across Congress Street, a viewpoint that emphasizes the shadowed voids of the arches and the smaller, shallower openings between them, the arches (now devoid of their original glass and metal infill) look almost like portals in a city wall (fig. 80). When built, they did mark the southern edge of the commercial city along Congress Street. North of this street the Great Fire of 1871 had raged. As one local observer wrote in 1890, the Auditorium's "owners had witnessed the destruction of a city, and, like Justinian of Byzantium, in the restoration of the dome of St. Sophia, they resolved to have an indestructible building. The Romanesque idea was in consonance with this resolve, and hence it is the predominating feature of the great house."[170]

The individual arches along Congress Street are shaped differently from the tall, slender Romanesque-inspired arches of the upper walls. These mammoth stony voids along the southern base were described as "primordial," as if to evoke the image of cave entrances. The surrounding rusticated courses may call to mind the natural strata of ancient stone beds, much as Richardson's cyclopean stonework evokes geological associations.[171] If seen as cavelike, the base's arches convey the etymological origin of the name Chicago that Garczynski detailed, based on one strand of local lore. Among several contested sources for the city's name that had been traced to regional Indian languages, Garczynski rejected the most widely accepted origin of the city's name in the Chippewa word *She-gang*, meaning "place of the wild onion," or skunk weed. Instead he argued that the Miami Indians of the Northwest were Chichmecs, ultimately descended from the Toltec tribes of pre-Columbian Mexico. Garczynski concluded that the term *chicago* meant "the place or region of cave dwellers." This was not because the local Miami Indians who had lived there when Europeans came had dwelt in caves nearby, but because these Indians traced their ancestry to the distant Toltecs, who were said to have inhabited caves. Spanish colonial accounts had described Toltec civilization as wondrous. From this perspective, the cavelike entrances to the Auditorium conveyed its creators' aim that the building be "a sign and a token that a civilization shall arise here beside which the boasted marvels of the Toltec shall be as moonshine in winter compared with the radiance of the midday sun."[172]

The boast that modern Chicago had risen to dwarf the achievements of Native American settlements had a specific meaning given the Auditorium's exact site and the spot's relation to the most traumatic event in Chicago's early nineteenth-century history. The city had begun as a trading post guarded by Fort Dearborn, built in 1803 at the mouth of the Chicago River. Those Europeans who settled there bought furs from local Indians, on whose goodwill and fur hunting the European settlement depended. During the War of 1812, the British in Canada incited Wisconsin Miamis to attack Fort Dearborn. The United States government ordered its evacuation, and after some hesitation the fort's soldiers and settlers left its gates and began to move south along the lakeshore. Thus exposed, the evacuation party of 102 was attacked by some 500 Wisconsin Miamis. Friendly local Miamis intervened to prevent a total slaughter, so that, while 67 settlers and soldiers were killed, others were spared and taken to Canada as prisoners. Survivors, some of whom escaped to a boat offshore on Lake Michigan, recalled that the massacre had occurred about half a mile or 880 yards south of the fort, making "the scene of the fighting very close to the site of the Auditorium"—or so Garczynski claimed.[173]

The Fort Dearborn massacre had a powerful resonance in Chicago's collective memory, with variations of the story in many local histories and guides published for the World's Columbian Exposition in 1893. In that year George M. Pullman donated to the Chicago Historical Society a bronze statue commemorating the site of the massacre, which was then thought to have taken place near his own house at Eighteenth Street and Prairie Avenue, far south of the Auditorium. Unveiled in June 1893, just after the exposition had opened in May, this monument provided a kind of psychological closure on the Fort Dearborn massacre as an event that stood for the earliest phase of the city's history, now so clearly superseded by the fair. The statue's built surroundings made "most vivid the tremendous contrast between the Chicago of 1812 and the Chicago of 1893."[174] The guest of honor at the dedication was former president Benjamin Harrison, whose grandfather, William Henry Harrison, had defeated the Miamis at their siege of Fort Wayne in 1813.

Even after Ferdinand Peck's father, Philip, came to Chicago in 1830, the settlement was still a combined community of Europeans and Indians living near the rebuilt Fort Dearborn. One of Peck's fellow pioneers recalled how the village was set on "the long shores along which were clustered the picturesque lodges of the natives; the small, one storied dwellings, mostly constructed of logs."[175] When Philip Peck built a two-story frame store in 1832, its size and construction stood out in this context, just as his sons' Auditorium rose above its surroundings sixty years later. In 1832 Philip Peck had enrolled in the Chicago volunteer military company that took part in the Black Hawk War. Thus in 1889, at the Auditorium Theater's opening, Benjamin Harrison and Ferdinand Peck represented living connections to their forebears from the era of Chicago's founding. In this context the Auditorium's lithic monumentality signified the city's permanence and development after both the massacre of 1812 and the fire of 1871.

There was another implicit message in invoking the city's early conflict with Indians. Throughout the 1870s and 1880s, rebellious urban workers nationally were compared to Native Americans resisting the federal government's authority on the Great Plains. As Richard Slotkin has noted, a prevalent metaphor in upper-class discourse was that of "strikers as savages."[176] In July 1877 it had been United States Army units fighting Indians in the Dakotas that had been ordered to Chicago to help suppress the railroad and general strike throughout the city. In the wake of Haymarket, Theodore Roosevelt (among others) rhetorically proposed that cowboys from the plains, who habitually confronted Indians, be given "a chance with rifles at one of the mobs" that roamed the streets of industrial cities.[177] Thus descriptions of the Auditorium in 1890 as a monumental marker of triumph over Native Americans in Chicago's early history, or Pullman's gift in 1893 of the statue commemorating the Fort Dearborn massacre, conveyed associations with more recent clashes between the city's capitalists and its workers.

Ferdinand Peck had proposed an analogous monument near the Auditorium Building. In November 1891, at a meeting of the World's Columbian Exposition's board of directors, he introduced a resolution that "a permanent memorial monument of Columbus be erected in connection with the contemplated improvement of the Lake Front," earlier considered as a site for the exposition. Such a monument would be "a suitable and lasting memorial of the Exposition which would stand for ages after the buildings had been razed to the ground." In January 1892 Chicago's city council granted permission for such a monument to stand east of Michigan Avenue and south of Jackson Street. Peck then chaired a committee that oversaw a competition and selected the design of Chicago sculptor Howard Kretschmar over those of Lorado Taft, Johannes Gelert, and others. The twenty-foot-high bronze figure, cast in Chicago, showed Columbus facing west, "startled and surprised at the first site of land." This figure, then said to be the largest bronze statue in the United States, was set on a thirty-foot pedestal of the same Maine granite used in the Auditorium's base. The statue's unveiling on 25 April 1893, six days before the fair opened, marked the third anniversary of congressional passage of the act locating the World's Columbian Exposition in Chicago. The fifty-foot-high monument was the sculptural pendant to Adler and Sullivan's building, and both certified the rise of their city as a symbol of European settlement across North America.[178]

The emphasis on the Auditorium Building's massiveness and indestructibility also corresponded to post-Haymarket concerns about anarchist violence. Throughout this period, radical rhetoric and upper- and middle-class anxiety centered on what one scholar has called "the cult of dynamite."[179] Anarchist publications such as the *Alarm* not only advocated using this newly invented explosive for political agitation but printed detailed instructions for making bombs under such headlines as "a practical lesson in popular chemistry."[180] Innumerable speeches at workers' rallies around the city before 1886 advocated violent overthrow of the capitalist order, with dynamite as the radical weapon of choice. It had been this combination of politicized rhetoric and an underground culture of technical self-education in bomb making that led to the Haymarket explosion. The trial of the Haymarket conspirators in 1886 featured testimony of workers and police informants about the cult of dynamite as well as exhibits of weapons and photographs of dynamite bombs made from lengths of pipe and other metal casings. As a veteran socialist leader, Thomas Morgan, told an audience of reform-minded capitalists after the trial: "If this crime of silence, this infernal desire of the well-to-do to crush out of sight this awful suffering [of the masses] is persisted in, do not think that you will rest in security. If you well-to-do people do not listen—do not wake up . . . . And if the pleadings of Editor [William T.] Stead in the name of Christ or justice cannot shake you out of your false security may somebody use dynamite to blow you out."[181]

In the immediate wake of Haymarket, rumors of radical violence had focused on the capacity of dynamite to destroy Chicago's buildings as the visible symbols of capitalist control. As Robert Herrick recalled, the morning after the tragedy, citizens were so affected by these rumors that "the men on the street seemed to rub their eyes and stare up at the buildings in surprise to find them standing . . . . At the Yards, men were standing about in little groups discussing the rumors; they seemed really afraid to go into the buildings."[182] Perhaps no part of the city was so directly enervated by the anarchist cult of dynamite as the small residential enclave of wealthy businessmen on the South Side bounded by Prairie, Michigan, and Calumet Avenues. It was here that Pullman had endowed the monument to the Indian massacre of 1812. In the Auditorium's era, forty out of the sixty members of the Commercial Club had their houses in this district within a radius of five blocks.[183]

Among these was the club's historian, John J. Glessner, whose renowned house by H. H. Richardson on the southwest corner of Eighteenth Street and Prairie Avenue was designed and built in 1886–1887. The house stood diagonally opposite that of George M. Pullman on the intersection's northeast corner. In fact, on 4 May 1886, when the Glessners were reviewing their new house's plans in their earlier house on Washington Street in the near West Side, their conversation was interrupted by the sound of shots from the Haymarket clash a few blocks away.[184] Historians have often commented on the fortresslike form of the Glessner House (fig. 81), and contemporaries saw the building in these terms. One account of the design on 5 June 1886, just over a month after Haymarket, noted that "there will be no windows on the street fronts except in the second story," and "no one will be able to get in from the outside unless he forces the stout iron gate." In conclusion, "It is jokingly said that this castle is to be built in anticipation of the day when the rich will have to keep out of the way of Anarchists and other bloodthirsty individuals who believe in a division of property, but the real object of the designer was not only to get greater privacy but also to have a novelty in the way of a house."[185]

Glessner was among the Auditorium's stockholders, as he had earlier been a supporter of the Reverend David Swing's Central Church. In his Richardson-designed house, Glessner was also a neighbor of Ferdinand Peck, who, early in 1887, commissioned William Le Baron Jenney and William A. Otis to design a palatial residence for his family at 1826 South Michigan Avenue (fig. 82). The Auditorium provided a partial model for Peck's house. Its rock-faced stonework culminated in a

Figure 81

Richardson, house for Mr. and Mrs. John J. Glessner, southwest corner of Eighteenth Street and Prairie Avenue, Chicago (1886–1887). Photograph by John J. Glessner, 1923. Historic American Buildings Survey, ILL, 16-CHIG, 17-2. Courtesy of the Library of Congress.

Figure 82

William Le Baron Jenney and William A. Otis, Ferdinand Peck house, 1826 South Michigan Avenue, Chicago (1887; demolished). From *Architectural Reviewer* (Chicago) 1 (February 1897). Architecture Photograph Collection, Courtesy of the Art Institute of Chicago.

tower, with a round-arched porte cochere below. The tower featured a shadowed loggia below a foursquare crown, so that the house read in part as a miniature version of the Auditorium. When President Harrison was entertained at Peck's residence on the day of the Auditorium Theater's opening, he remarked that Peck's house was "the Auditorium, Jr." Peck responded that "the same spirit prevailed in both buildings."[186] The house reminded all that the Auditorium was Peck's project. The two buildings, by different architects, imaged one patron and were linked by Michigan Avenue. Both were monuments whose lithic architecture signaled the durability of capitalist interests.

The vividness of local class consciousness that prevailed in the Auditorium's era gave Adler and Sullivan's exterior forms a meaning that was legible to their contemporaries but not perceptible within the frame of reference provided by the later historiography of modern architecture. Historians from Sigfried Giedion had emphasized Chicago's development in the 1890s of light, open forms based on steel-frame construction as a precursor to the Modern Movement of the twentieth century. Yet what counted for Peck's generation was the Auditorium Building's massiveness. In their eyes it was a Gibraltar, whose lower walls had a rough-hammered finish. They saw its stone base as a built narrative of the city's persona. Sullivan had criticized Charles Atwood's slightly later Marshall Field Annex (1892–1893) because, although in Chicago, it "lacks, utterly, western frankness, directness, crudity if you will."[187] The Auditorium's base had conveyed precisely these values, through the very "uncouthness" of its cyclopean arches along Congress Street.[188] Chicagoans saw this lithic vocabulary as an architectural virtue that reinforced their city's self-image. One local critic wrote that Beman's Studebaker Building on Michigan Avenue adjacent to the Auditorium "is in the Romanesque style, with Chicagoesque improvements. The feature of this school is great, solid, rock-faced arches, and this is now by far the most popular architectural feature for big buildings in the city."[189] In adapting Richardson's Romanesque vocabulary to the Auditorium's base, Sullivan was not just exercising his individual preference but was appealing to local collective taste. In June 1888, at the time of the Republican national convention, when only the Auditorium's rock-faced granite base was visible, one reporter noted that temporary arc lamps and the "broad belt of red, white, and blue [bunting] about thirty feet from the ground were the only outer decorations, but they were in keeping with the rugged grandeur of the structure."[190] At that time the public assumed that the whole exterior would be of the base's darker granite. By August, as there appeared the lighter granite of the third story and the smooth limestone facing the floors above, the change from a heavy, dark, rough base to light, bright, smooth stone was "criticized by many people as weakening the impressive effect of the massive walls."[191]

Within the lithic ruggedness of the base, Sullivan set the Auditorium Hotel's entrance of three arched doorways on Michigan Avenue (fig. 83). In his larger public buildings, Richardson adapted the three-arched entrance motif from sources in

Romanesque religious architecture. Yet its presence on the Auditorium Building's east front might have also reminded travelers of the south front of Chicago's original Central Depot, on the north end of Lake Front Park at the east foot of South Water Street. Opened in 1856 by the Illinois Central Railroad and designed by architect Otto M. Matz, this terminal had been the largest gateway to the prefire city, serving several rail companies. The station's manager was William A. Spalding (Ferdinand Peck's father-in-law), who served in that position until his death in 1892, the same year the Central Depot was torn down. The building was unusual for railway stations of its period, whose sheds were often of light iron and glass construction, abutting a head house of masonry. By contrast, the Central Depot's shed and head house to the north were encased in massive walls of rusticated stone masonry. The shed's south wall of rock-faced granite contained three enormous semicircular arches as portals for multiple train tracks (fig. 84). Damaged in the fire of 1871, this terminal remained in service afterward, when a temporary structure to accommodate travelers was built inside the remaining granite walls of the original building. From the outside, these walls were prominently visible as "the only ruin of the Great Fire."[192] From 1871 to 1892 the Illinois Central Railroad unsuccessfully petitioned the city to permit the railroad to construct a new terminal in Lake Front Park at the foot of Washington Street. Sullivan's incorporation of three arched portals in the Auditorium Hotel's base, similar to those of the ruined station, would have reinforced the reading of Peck's monument as an architectural renewal of the lakefront intended to counter the memory of the fire's destruction.

Figure 83

Auditorium Hotel, three-arched entrance on Michigan Avenue, below second-story loggia supported on projecting granite brackets, showing (a) horizontal lintels with keystones below loggia columns. At midspans between brackets, iron beams project from wall to support columns and granite lintels. Loggia's midspan columns are also supported from above with steel cantilevers. Glass panels between columns date from after Roosevelt University's acquisition of the building. Photograph by Bart Harris, Chicago. Auditorium Collection, Roosevelt University Archives. Graphic notations by author.

ILLINOIS CENTRAL FREIGHT DEPOT & GRAIN ELEVATORS - 1858

Sullivan's treatment of the hotel's entrance portals and the projecting columnar loggia above differed from the continuous rock-faced base along Congress Street. The hotel entrance's arches were crafted of regularly sized, smoothly finished granite "that shows conspicuously against the rock-faced ashlars of the three lower stories." Between the arches, huge granite consoles with "a curve as graceful as the neck of a swan" uphold the projecting second-story loggia.[193] The second-story loggia's base and entablature have sharp, simple horizontal moldings that continue those of the main wall behind. The loggia's square end piers frame six bays marked by monolithic round columns like those along the sidewalk below. These uphold monolithic lintels each spanning about seventeen feet, the modular dimension for structural bays on the building's east side.

From Sullivan's perspective, the Auditorium was among the best and last works of his "masonry period," before he began to develop the expressive potential of the steel frame in his tall office buildings of the 1890s.[194] His sculptural handling of the Auditorium's outer stonework would be a mark of his sensibility as an architect in dialogue with his art's past lithic styles. The columns were described as "archaic," as if they represented an elemental type of column.[195] Their stout proportions, polished surface, and structural position beneath massive lintels of stone recall columns found in works of Sullivan's first employer-mentor in Philadelphia, Frank Furness. These include his Pennsylvania Academy of the Fine Arts (1872–1876), whose period of design encompassed Sullivan's apprenticeship in summer 1873. Here, as in other works, Furness fashioned highly personal, diminutive variations on classical and medieval columns, with molded bases, richly colored shafts, and carved foliate capitals. He often created visually dramatic contrasts of great loads apparently crushing columnar supports, giving vitality to his lithic architecture.

Figure 84

Otto M. Matz, Central Depot, north end of Lake Front Park at east foot of South Water Street, Chicago (built 1856 for Illinois Central Railroad; demolished 1892). Photograph of 1858, showing rock-faced granite arches on depot's south side and grain elevators to the northeast (right). Courtesy of the Chicago Historical Society, ICHi-05211.

Columns along the Auditorium's loggia had appeared in Sullivan's first and second recorded designs for the exterior, where they were shown with foliate capitals (figs. 56, 62). Yet in the base as built, all the base's granite monoliths had capitals that were as "simple as Tuscan columns," or "original in fact, being neither Tuscan nor Doric."[196] They became Sullivan's personal variation on these most rudimentary of the orders, originally meant to stand between bay windows along Congress Street's sidewalk.

For Sullivan, the columnar loggia above the arched portals presumably represented architecture's two elemental languages of expression: trabeated and arcuated stone. The Tuscan column and semicircular arch were the simplest versions of these elements. In his later reflections on architecture's history, Sullivan identified the pier and lintel as the essential beginnings of architecture. These constructive forms were "the basic origins of our art—elements and origins independent of time, of period, epoch, style, or styles." In his view, the perennial challenge of the architect, ancient or modern, was "to breathe into the simplest elements, lintel and pier, the breath of life."[197] Here as elsewhere, Sullivan identified the soul of the individual artist-architect as the source of inspiration for inventive treatment of these elemental forms, which gave any period's architecture its vitality.

Sullivan's treatment of basic constructive elements was not structurally rational but rather poetically expressive. At first glance the hotel's entrance does not read wholly as logical structural expression. As Montgomery Schuyler wrote, "The three low arches of the lake front are of a Roman largeness—true vomitoria—and their effectiveness is increased by the simplicity of their treatment, by the ample lateral abutment provided for them, and by the long shallow balcony that overhangs them." Yet Schuyler pointed out that if read as stone construction, the balcony contains a glaring inconsistency. The two end piers and the two interior columns directly over the four consoles logically transfer the weight of their lintels above down to the building through the consoles. Yet the three columns over the arches' crowns, at midspans between the consoles, appear to carry the same granite lintels but to rest only on the unsupported balcony's shelflike base. He wrote that this inconsistency "suggests that the construction so exhibited is not the true construction at all."[198]

The head-on view of the balcony suggests that Schuyler was correct, for the balcony's long granite horizontal lintels below the columns are, on close inspection, really like flat arches, with keystones beneath all the columns (fig. 83a). At the midspans between the consoles there are iron beams that cantilever out from the building's main east wall to support the midspan granite columns and the granite lintels below the columns. Paul Mueller recalled that "the granite lintels in the second floor were, of course, considered too long," so "they are hung on the iron and do not support themselves. These [midspan] granite columns are supported on a keystone." Yet the midspan columns are also supported from above. According to Mueller, "Mr. Sullivan did not want to have any chance of that stone being cracked, so the columns were drilled and a bolt put in and those columns are hanging on steel cantilevers."[199] The cantilevered beams and hanging bolts for the loggia's midspan columns appear in figure 77. Thus, what the balcony exhibits is not the ancient language of trabeation but rather the modern capacity of cantilevered metal to carry heavy loads.

As an extension of the Auditorium Hotel's main reception hall, this loggia was used for open air dining through the 1930s. When the loggia was built, with the shore less than one hundred yards to the east, one had a commanding gaze over the lakefront (fig. 85). The loggia was not only to serve guests of the hotel but also to function as a reviewing stand for Michigan Avenue parades. As the novelist Theodore Dreiser wrote: "I remember, as I hung about this chamber or general reception hall where a few guest tables and chairs were scattered about, looking out through great arched windows over the blue lake where white sails were to be seen and thinking how pagan and Roman it all was. To begin with, the Auditorium, because of its massive architecture suggested both Egypt and Rome. These heavy arched windows opening to the sky and giving out on a grey granite balcony permitted such an enchanting view of the lake and of the glittering sunshine outside."[200] As an architectural framing of this vista, Sullivan's loggia was unique among buildings along Michigan Avenue. Contemporaries debated the merits of Adler and Sullivan's severe exterior, epitomized by the elemental simplicity of the loggia's columns and lintels. One local observer wrote: "If a building may present a magnificent exterior and yet be wanting in beauty, that one is the Auditorium, varying in this respect from the work of Garnier of the *Ecole des beaux Arts*, who combined both."[201] In 1893 a French visitor wrote that Chicagoans considered their Auditorium Building a rival to Paris's Opera, yet on the Auditorium's exterior, "the

Figure 85

Auditorium Hotel, second-floor loggia looking northeast, c. 1890, before installation of outer glass panels. Photograph by J. W. Taylor. Avery Architectural and Fine Arts Library, Columbia University in the City of New York.

decorative element, painting, and sculpture, so abundant, too abundant even in our [Opera], is here totaling lacking."[202] Yet another voice of the period praised the exterior in much the same terms as would later modernist historians: "There is a hint of a nobler future for art in the severe aspect of the Auditorium Building. The effect of its massive grandeur is nowhere impaired by pointless ornamentation."[203]

The same simplicity appears in Adler and Sullivan's treatment of the upper walls, which are internally of brick but faced externally with a limestone from the quarries in Bedford, Indiana, first opened in 1879. Like the granites of the base, this limestone, used for many of Chicago's public buildings, was nationally renowned for its purity and durability. Whereas Lemont stone quarried near Chicago contained 60 percent lime, Bedford stone contained 97 percent lime and only 3 percent impurities. Solon Beman had used it for the upper stories of the adjacent Studebaker Building, above its red granite base. In the Auditorium's upper walls of Bedford stone, the main four-story arcade piers have stepped profiles that continue through their crowning arches. The plane of the stone steps back four times, each transition articulated by linear moldings running vertically through the full height of the arches (fig. 86). On one level these stepped profiles enhance passage of light into the windows between the piers, the same reason that Root had rounded the corners of his brick piers on the Rookery's upper-story arcades. Yet Sullivan's choice of a stepped profile to achieve this functional aim recalled the multiple jambs of a Romanesque church portal, as if this detail were a distended abstraction of such a historic motif. The profiles' verticality also visually lifts the building's mass upward, in contrast to the arcade on the Studebaker Building, whose piers are piled blocks of stone. As an English critic wrote of Chicago's architecture, the Auditorium was not designed in a purely utilitarian manner like local commercial office buildings, but rather "impresses by its mass, not only because of its size, but because, notwithstanding its utilitarian and business uses, it has a monumental aspect, dependent not only upon the sobriety of the design, but upon the dark grey granite and Bedford stone of which it is built."[204]

Although externally impressive as monumental form, the Auditorium's massive stone-faced walls, designed at the request of Peck and the Auditorium's directors, were neither structurally nor functionally helpful. Not only did they burden the foundations with their unanticipated extra weight, causing uneven settlement throughout the building, but they also made the hotel rooms and offices darker and more cramped. As a later director of the Auditorium Association testified: "The width of the massive exterior walls makes the rooms of the office and hotel building very dark . . . . These walls are so thick and massive that they take up a great deal of space in the rooms and also obscure the view from the rooms. The wall is so thick that the window must be located at the outside or the inside or somewhere between so as to affect [sic] entrance of the light and the possibility of inmates approaching the window itself. The thickness of the wall makes a sort of alcove in the room in order to get at the window, and takes that much more of the renting space of the

Figure 86

Auditorium Building, upper walls on Congress Street, May 1986, showing moldings of piers and arches in main four-story
arcade made of Bedford limestone facing. Gary Sigman Photography. Auditorium Collection, Roosevelt University Archives.

room."[205] This effect was a particular problem in the offices, whose rental value depended on maximal square footage and optimal daylight. Ironically, although conceived as symbols of capitalist power, the massive outer walls hindered the Auditorium Building's capacity to generate return on its investors' capital.

The lighter limestone recalls Sullivan's intention of making the upper walls distinct from the base, yet in a way unlike his earlier designs of pressed brick and terra cotta. The effect he originally envisioned for the Auditorium was realized in Adler and Sullivan's subsequent Wainwright Building in St. Louis of 1890–1892 (plate 4). As a cladding for its steel frame, the Wainwright's pressed brick was a precise, industrially fabricated material. The same was true of the ornamental terra cotta fired in small blocks and then assembled to create the large-scale pattern of foliate relief repeated across the frieze.[206] By contrast, the Auditorium block's top floor (plate 3) represented an alternative mechanization, that of stonecutting, which enabled its large walls to be raised quickly and precisely. The frames for the uppermost rectangular windows, the paired Tuscan columns forming miniature loggias in each bay, and the brackets like a dentil course above are all limestone, simply and cleanly cut with a repetitive precision. The distinct treatments of the Auditorium's and the Wainwright's crowns reveal a sensitivity to the expressive potential of different materials. Such details in turn convey these structures' different characters. The Auditorium presented itself as its association's philanthropic civic monument, whereas the Wainwright was its patron's individual commercial venture.

Figure 87

Bird's-eye view looking west on Adams Street, Chicago, showing (a) Marshall Field Wholesale Store, (b) Farwell Block, (c) Ryerson Building (Walker Wholesale Store), and (d) Union Station. From Rand McNally, *Bird's-Eye Views and Guide to Chicago*. Graphic notations by author.

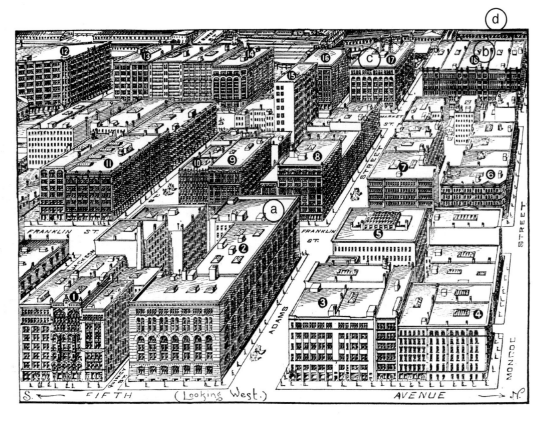

In Adler and Sullivan's oeuvre, the building that fell technically and stylistically between the Auditorium (designed 1886–1887) and the Wainwright (designed 1890–1891) is the wholesale store designed from March 1886 for Martin Ryerson Sr. before his death in late 1887 and built for Martin Ryerson Jr. from July 1888 to October 1889 on the southwest corner of Market and Adams Streets (fig. 87c). Demolished in 1953, this was the last and the most expensive ($325,942) of five buildings Adler and Sullivan designed for the Ryerson family. The senior Martin Ryerson had been one of their principal clients, as well as a member of the Auditorium Association's executive committee. The construction permit for this last Ryerson Building had been issued on 23 December 1886, the day after Martin Ryerson had moved that Adler and Sullivan be appointed architects of the Auditorium, for which the building permit had not yet been issued. Sited two blocks west of the Marshall Field Wholesale Store, the Ryerson wholesale store's "Norman arches of granite are the first architectural exhibit of Chicago to be seen by the visitor who arrives at the Union Passenger Station and comes over the Adams Street bridge near by."[207]

The Ryerson Building was historically known by the name of its major tenant, James H. Walker and Company. This firm, which specialized in home furnishings, subsequently built a six-story retail store in 1890 on the southwest corner of Wabash Avenue and Adams Street (fig. 88). This building, described as "one of the handsomest of the ante-steel era," was known for its window displays along the sidewalk as an invitation to its interior sales floors. These "are in themselves a fair, where nearly everything useful and ornamental pertaining to an American home may be seen or purchased," including carpets, upholstery, glassware, and art goods.[208] Externally, the building's elaborate Italianate style, with columnar arcades, keystones, and projecting cornices and balconies all in carved stone, recalled the postfire commercial palazzi of the 1870s, such as that of Field, Leiter, and Company (fig. 28). The sharp contrast in style between the Walker wholesale and retail stores underscored their differences as building types set in different urban districts and meant for different audiences. The wholesale store was for mainly male out-of-town buyers, like Richardson's nearby Marshall Field Wholesale Store, whereas the retail store was meant to appeal to local women shoppers, like other department stores nearby on State Street.

As Adler and Sullivan's building most closely related in type and locale to Richardson's monument, the Walker Wholesale Store represented Sullivan's response to the older master's Romanesque style (fig. 89). One local observer described the Walker Wholesale Store as "the Romanesque of Romanesque," continuing ideas developed in the Marshall Field Wholesale Store and

Figure 88

James H. Walker and Company Retail Store, southwest corner of Wabash Avenue and Adams Street, Chicago (1890; demolished 1936). From *Chicago Tribune* (6 August 1893).

Figure 89

Adler and Sullivan, Ryerson Building
(Walker Wholesale Store), southwest
corner of South Market (now Wacker
Drive) and Adams Streets, Chicago
(1888–1889; demolished 1953). View
showing carved botanical ornament at
crowning corner and on impost blocks
of arches facing north on Adams Street,
with carving in progress on impost
blocks of arches facing east on South
Market Street. Courtesy of the Chicago
Historical Society, ICHi-01647.

the Auditorium Building.[209] Wright recalled that Sullivan described the design to
him as "the last word in the Romanesque."[210] Technically the Walker Wholesale
Store resembled the Field Store, with an internal skeleton of "mill construction,"
meaning timber columns and girders externally encased in masonry bearing walls.
Richardson's block was faced in rusticated granite and brownstone, and Adler and
Sullivan's was originally designed in granite as well. As built, however, the Walker
Wholesale Store's outer walls were made of heavy blocks of the same smooth Bed-
ford limestone used for the Auditorium's upper walls.[211] Also, the Walker Wholesale
Store was more cubic, being 98 feet high above the sidewalk and 150 feet wide along
Adams Street, so that its proportion of width to height was about 3:2, unlike the
Field block's proportion of 2.5:1.

Sullivan composed each of the Walker store's street fronts into four major bays
each 36 feet (on the east facade) or 40 feet (on the north facade) wide, or twice the
size of the internal structural bays of 18 feet north-south by 20 feet east-west. Each
bay contained a pair of windows in the two-story base, which met the ground
through splayed granite foundation piers. Above the base, vertical piers rose unbroken from projecting sills through four central stories to arches below a crowning
story with four squared windows per bay. As in the Auditorium, the four-story piers
had recessed profiles through their height, while the arches above read more as flat
geometric shapes and less as historical forms. The wide corner piers and their
change from thicker to thinner courses of facing stone above the base anticipated

the treatment of the Wainwright's base and corners, underscoring the Walker store's role as a transitional work in Sullivan's development. Atop the Walker block there was a flat, outwardly stepping cornice with a dentil course and a nearly blank frieze, below a carved bead-and-reel molding enlarged in scale (like the Wainwright's crowning ornament) for visibility from the street level below.

Unlike its simple rectangularly framed entrances near the corners, the Walker building's central bays on each street front were marked by a pair of semicircular arches, each arch being two structural bays (36 or 40 feet) wide, hence scaled to the whole building. There were no such large, representational arches on the less visible south and west fronts. These arches originally framed not doorways but rather show windows for displaying products of wholesale tenants inside. At the base of these arches were impost blocks with Sullivan's richly carved ornamental designs at just above eye level, and above the raised first floor inside. Those on the east facade (fig. 90) differed from those on the north facade (fig. 91). Both read as enlarged ornamental capitals for the piers upholding the arches. As carved relief, the foliate motifs on the impost blocks exemplified Sullivan's dictum that "an ornamental design will be more beautiful if it seems a part of the surface or substance that receives it . . . . it should appear, when completed as though by the outworking of some beneficent agency it had come forth from the very substance of the material and was there by the same right that a flower appears amid the leaves of its parent plant."[212]

Like Sullivan's ornamental motifs on other buildings, the possible intended meaning of these impost blocks is elusive. Their foliate forms may be read contextually, alluding to the rich botanical growth originally bordering the Chicago River just to the west, which Sullivan had studied from his early days in the city. The north impost blocks' interlinked circular motifs perhaps alluded to the wheels and shafts of locomotives like those at the nearby Union Passenger Station, from which many of those passing along the Walker Wholesale Store's north side would be

Figure 90

Ryerson Building (Walker Wholesale Store), ornamental impost block of carved limestone on east facade. Architecture Photograph Collection, Courtesy of the Art Institute of Chicago.

Figure 91

Ryerson Building (Walker Wholesale Store), ornamental impost block of carved limestone on north facade. Architecture Photograph Collection, Courtesy of the Art Institute of Chicago.

coming. Alternatively, the impost blocks could have alluded to the vitality of internal structural pressures in the arches above or, in the north block, to forces in the raised first floor's beams. Interlinked ornamental rings rendered in terra cotta had marked junctures of columns and beams on the interior court of Burnham and Root's Rookery Building. The idea of using exterior ornament to represent internal structural forces recurred in Sullivan's writings and later appeared in Adler and Sullivan's Guaranty Building of 1894–1896 in Buffalo. The Walker Wholesale Store's decorative impost blocks were answered above in the ornamental corners of the otherwise blank frieze, where the building's terminal profiles were marked with swirling spirals and plant forms carved in relief (fig. 89). Sullivan's signature forms thus recurred at base and crown. These passages of ornament together conveyed his architectural ideal of "the true nature of the building as an organism or whole," like a living form in nature.[213]

Writing in the 1930s from a modernist perspective, Sullivan's first biographer, Hugh Morrison, praised the Walker Wholesale Store's precise cubic geometry, lack of ornament, and clean-cut silhouette. Morrison concluded that in this structure's "every detail, Sullivan develops toward an abstract architecture. The individual elements are both more clearly stated and more simply organized than in Richardson's building."[214] Yet less than a decade after Morrison's account, the Chicago architect Thomas Tallmadge, who also knew both the Field and Walker buildings firsthand, disagreed with Morrison's assessment of their relative merits. To Tallmadge, the Walker building "looks hard, gaunt and bony," while "the masterwork of Richardson left you uplifted with its majesty."[215] Perhaps Tallmadge's pleasurable impression came from precisely those historical forms of Roman architecture that Richardson's block more closely approximated. These forms represented Field as the building's owner and occupant, whereas Adler and Sullivan's Walker Wholesale Store was a shell for rental space, hence less a symbol of the Ryersons as patrons of architecture.

The Auditorium's expressive effect from afar depended on the relation of its tower to its long south elevation, whose rhythms Adler and Sullivan carefully calculated. The tower continues the vertical lines of the larger and smaller arcades in the block below. These elements share a common proportion of height to width (fig. 75b). The tower's overall proportion of height (236 feet from base to crown) to width (77 feet across the base) yields a ratio of about 3.06:1. This is the same ratio as that found in one bay of the main four-story arcade below (49 feet high by 16 feet wide) and as found in each of the two-story arches in the eighth and ninth floors (24.5 feet tall by 8 feet wide). Sullivan thus created a family of shapes at different scales that resonate with each other to give the major front a proportional consistency and visual unity, much as he did in the Wainwright Building, where a height-to-width ratio of 1.01:1 recurred at different scales on the street fronts.

As Wright recalled, the tower was "the best feature of the outside, the one causing most trouble and receiving most careful study from both men."[216] Intended to

Figure 92

Auditorium Building from southwest, showing corbeled moldings of tower above main block as possible inversions of tower's foundations underground. Courtesy of the Chicago Historical Society, ICHi-18768.

mark the theater's entrance, the tower housed the lobby in its ground floor and the men's smoking lounge on the second floor. The tower's next eight floors contained hotel rooms, while the top seven stories above the surrounding block housed offices. Elevators serving the upper office floors passed through but did not serve the hotel floors, which were instead served by the pair of elevators just to the east of the tower. Atop the tower were the water tanks that served the hydraulically powered elevators throughout the building. Unlike Chicago's other prominent towers of the period, the Auditorium's was wholly of masonry up to its coping (fig. 92). Its main local rival, the Board of Trade Building's tower, had a roof of galvanized sheet metal. By contrast, the Auditorium's limestone cladding gave the tower "an admirable solidity and massiveness of air."[217] Chicago's leading music critic of the period, George Upton, implied that it was Peck's idea to have the tower standing square "to the four winds."[218] Although part of the block below, the tower is subtly differentiated from it by its slight projection forward from the adjacent walls along Congress Street. Also, above the block's cornice, the freestanding tower's base has outwardly corbeled moldings that set off its mass above. These moldings, which project outward over each vertical pier, look like inversions of the tower's foundational footings underground (fig. 70), perhaps alluding to these unseen elements. Corbeling recurs at the tower's crown, where the projecting carved cornice below the topmost coping completes the outwardly flaring silhouette against the sky. As Sullivan wrote, the Auditorium's "tower holds its head in the air, as a tower should. It was the culmination of Louis's masonry 'period.'"[219]

Figure 93

George B. Post, Produce Exchange, with front in foreground on east side of Bowling Green and tower behind overlooking southwestern tip of Manhattan Island, New York City (1881–1884; demolished). From *A History of Real Estate, Building and Architecture in New York City during the Last Quarter of a Century* (New York, 1898).

As a vertical mass, the Auditorium's tower recalls the later medieval Italian campaniles that John Ruskin had reintroduced to architectural thought in the mid-nineteenth century. Ruskin particularly praised Florence's Palazzo Vecchio for its simple cubic mass from which its tall tower rose as a continuous vertical shaft, creating a vivid civic landmark. Such structures had partially inspired Richardson's towers for urban monuments like the Albany City Hall and Boston's Brattle Square Church, which Sullivan admired. The great tower of Richardson's Allegheny County Courthouse in Pittsburgh was a plausible recent model as well. But the closest source for the Auditorium's tower was the campanile-like tower of George B. Post's Produce Exchange in New York (1881–1884), facing Bowling Green to the west near the southern tip of Manhattan Island (fig. 93). Post's Produce Exchange was among the best-known, most conspicuous, and most critically discussed commercial monuments of the period. Adler admired the building, perhaps because it had dealt successfully with the problem of packing rentable shops into the ground floor and offices around and above the large central trading room, much as the Auditorium Building contained a hotel and offices and shops around the central theater's huge volume. One account of Adler and Sullivan's second design for the Auditorium in December 1886 noted that "in general appearance the building reminds one of the huge [Produce] Exchange in New York, although it is more novel and less simple in style."[220] Post's grandly arcuated elevations had also been a probable point of departure for the street fronts of Richardson's Field Wholesale Store.

Standing physically separate from its block, Post's 224-foot tower was described by one critic as "utterly superfluous and disturbing."[221] Yet its form was a major landmark at the tip of Manhattan. The tower's electrical illumination made it a beacon for the harbor, with the blazing lights visible miles away. The Produce Exchange was the main monument seen from afar when one approached New York City by water, just as the Auditorium and its tower announced Chicago to those arriving by ship or rail along the lakefront. Both buildings' towers were elevated observatories with panoramic views of their cities. Post's had projecting balconies for this purpose, while the spacious loggia of the Auditorium Tower's sixteenth floor (later Adler and Sullivan's offices) was originally to be a public observatory. Instead, as built, the Auditorium Tower upheld a small two-story wood structure with a balcony (later dismantled) that served as the public observation platform. It would "command an extensive view and the public will have what has never before existed in Chicago, a convenient point from which to observe the city and surrounding country."[222] This crowning wood superstructure atop the masonry tower made the whole composition look even more like the late medieval campaniles with belfries crowning the city halls of Siena or Florence, as if the Auditorium were a civic monument. The platform's height of 260 feet, among the highest artificial observation altitudes in the United States, "ought to enable the visitor to see the whole of the great city of Chicago, spread before him like a map."[223]

From 1 May 1890, Adler and Sullivan rented the tower's loggia-like sixteenth floor for their own offices. Peck granted them a rental rate of half what the building's other tenants paid per square foot, presumably in recognition of their contribution and in keeping with his desire to make the Auditorium Building a center for art.[224] On all four sides of this sixteenth floor, Sullivan designed screens of freestanding archaic Tuscan columns, here intended to define this floor's observation hall as the building's crowning public space. This motif echoed the columnar screen of the loggia above the hotel's arched entrance on Michigan Avenue. As Sullivan's assistant, George Elmslie, recalled: "The upper reaches of the Tower is where the real Sullivan began to appear."[225] A plan of the sixteenth-floor offices published in 1890 shows Adler's personal office on the south side, and Sullivan's in the southeast corner (fig. 94). Wright claimed to have made this plan, which shows his own room in the northeast corner adjoining Sullivan's, both of which "had the best of the wide 'guillotine' windows to the east overlooking the lake: Lake Michigan." There Wright and Sullivan worked together for about three years before Wright left by May 1893. Since so much of Sullivan's life was his work, the tower office became a kind of home for him until he could no longer pay its rent and left in 1918. Indeed, in 1900, in a deposition recalling his witnessing of Adler's will in August 1895, Sullivan, when queried as to his residential address, stated instead that his place of business was 1600 Auditorium Tower.[226]

Though Sullivan and Wright shared the same vista from the tower, they focused on different facets of what they saw. In his later autobiography, Sullivan recalled that from his arrival in Chicago, "his eye was ever on the boundless prairie and the mighty lake." He described the prairie "stretching like a floor to the far horizon . . . . Here was power—power greater than the mountains." So too the "great lake, spreading also like a floor to the far horizon, superbly beautiful in color, under a lucent sky. Here again was power, naked power, naked as the prairies, greater than the

Figure 94

Auditorium Tower, plan of sixteenth- and
seventeenth-floor offices of Adler and
Sullivan. From *Engineering and Building
Record* 22 (7 June 1890).

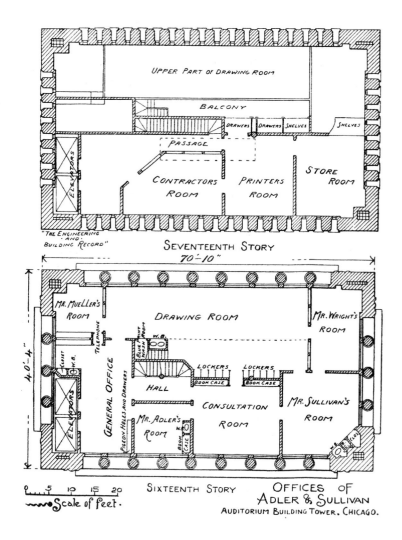

mountains. And over all spanned the dome of the sky, resting on the rim of the
horizon far away on all sides, eternally calm overhead, holding an atmosphere pel-
lucid and serene."[227] By contrast, in his address of 1901, "The Art and Craft of the
Machine," Wright invited his audience to imagine the view at nightfall of the electrically lit cityscape from the top of a great downtown office building, a view he
knew well from his many late evenings in the Auditorium Tower. Surveying the
panorama of an industrial metropolis, Wright wrote: "You may see how the image
of material man, at once his glory and his menace, is this thing we call a city . . . the
monster leviathan, stretching acre upon acre into the far distance. High overhead
hangs the stagnant pall of its fetid breath, reddened with the light from its myriad
eyes endlessly everywhere blinking. Ten thousand acres of cellular tissue, layer upon
layer, the city's flesh, outspreads enmeshed by intricate network of veins and arteries, radiating into the gloom." In this period Chicago writers similarly invoked their
city's horizontal spread over the landscape as an image of uncontrolled industrial

expansion, even while they saw the vertical rise of towers like the Auditorium's as heroic symbols of human ambition.[228]

From the same vantage point, Sullivan saw raw nature, whereas Wright imaged the raw city. Neither wrote of Chicago and its environs as a repository of tradition or history. Both felt themselves to be in a new place, whose great message was its present vitality and future potential. They shared an awareness of Chicago's regional and modern character with Peck, for whom the Auditorium Building spoke of its own place and time. If from one perspective the Auditorium's exterior displayed a Roman-inspired monumentality, then from another the building's relative planar simplicity and crispness of detail made it stand out against Chicago's ornate postfire blocks, whose surfaces carried Renaissance ornament modeled after the style of the French Second Empire. Wright saw Adler and Sullivan's buildings of the 1880s in this way, as fresh contrasts to the prevailing norm of Chicago's decorative commercial palazzi of the 1870s, the most prominent of which were also hotels. As Garczynski wrote, between such postfire structures and the Auditorium, "the progress has been a mighty leap forward . . . making this building the commencement of a new era."[229] Sullivan too saw the Auditorium as innovative and not historicizing, similar in spirit to his and Adler's Kehilath Anshe Ma'ariv synagogue (1890–1891). When this structure was built, one local observer described it as "the most noted departure in church architecture in [Chicago], or anywhere else." When asked about this structure's style, Sullivan said: "It is the nineteenth century school. That is all I can say for it. It has no historical style. It is the present. We have got to get away from schools in architecture. As long as we adhere to schools of anything there is no progress; nothing gained; no advancement. Look at the Auditorium. What school does that represent. None."[230]

Adler and Sullivan's desire to surpass historical types in order to serve modern functions also pervaded their design for the Auditorium Theater's interior, which, like the building's outward form, responded closely to Peck's priorities.

The Auditorium Theater 4

The Auditorium's exterior emerged as a major urban landmark, yet the great building's success depended on Adler and Sullivan's design for the theater's interior. While closely related to their earlier successful experiments with theater design, the Auditorium's interior would be different in several key respects. First, it was much larger than any permanent hall Adler and Sullivan had previously designed or remodeled. Its mammoth size raised new questions of acoustics, circulation, and ornamentation that demanded innovative responses from both its architects. Second, the Auditorium was designed to be more spatially flexible than their earlier halls. Its unique adaptability to multiple uses shaped its interior structure and ornament. Third, as the lithic exteriors powerfully suggested, the Auditorium was treated not as a commercial playhouse or music hall but as a civic and even a national monument. Its interior was to serve a different order of functions and to fulfill a broader spatial agenda than those of Adler and Sullivan's previous theaters. Finally, above all, the Auditorium was to be the prime symbol of Chicago's aspiration to a regionally distinctive cultural life that professed a socially inclusive, democratic character. This ideological aim compelled Adler and Sullivan to rethink conventions of nineteenth-century European and American opera houses and to create a room that was a critique of this type.

Peck's and Adler's Collaboration in Planning the Theater

Though Adler and Sullivan had done earlier studies of such a theater for Peck's friend Nathaniel Fairbank and had prepared preliminary plans and sections for the Auditorium Theater by September 1886, the earliest known designs for the theater are those recorded in their initial set of working drawings dated April 1887. Although we do not know their conversations, we do know that Peck and Adler developed a close working relationship. Paul Mueller, then working in Adler and Sullivan's office as its foreman and as Adler's chief assistant in structural design, recalled that he "knew Ferdinand Peck by sight. He was very often in the office . . . . He was constantly in touch with Mr. Adler."[1] Peck and his allies did everything possible to ensure that no financial constraints would compromise the hall's quality. Writing in November 1886, after the first phases of the Auditorium's design, Adler presumably alluded to his relationship with clients like Peck when he stated that in private commissions, as opposed to government building projects, "the architect becomes imbued with the enthusiasm of the client, and the client receives the benefit of his enthusiastic devotion."[2] Sullivan saw this issue in much the same way. In his later remarks on architect Solon Beman's long relationship with his client George Pullman, Sullivan said: "I always agree that it takes two to make a building. An architect alone cannot make a building. An architect is generally the instrument whereby a building is made, and, from the surface of things he appears to be creator of it. That is only, however, the surface of things—beneath that surface comes the impulse for the creation of things, and that impulse comes through the client. The client is interested in the character of the building. It is the client's thought that goes into the building, it is the client's thought that leads to the selection of the architect and it is this impulse and selection that brings men together and produces the result."[3]

Although the completed Auditorium Building launched Adler and Sullivan's national and international reputation, their engagement with Peck's project was neither simple nor profitable. Two years after the structure's completion, Adler wrote that the building as built was much larger and more costly than originally projected. After many months he and his colleagues had produced a carefully integrated initial design, documented in almost two hundred plans and diagrams. But as the financial horizon of the enterprise widened, his office had to rethink the design of this complex building twenty times, with major changes after construction began.[4] Such extensive redesign meant there was no net financial return to the architects. Adler and Sullivan were eventually paid $50,000 in cash and $25,000 in stock, for a total compensation of $75,000, yet this was less than 2.5 percent of the total construction costs of $3,100,000, or less than half the then conventional architects' fee of 5 percent of construction costs. Mueller later confirmed that Adler and Sullivan "spent nearly all their commissions [*sic*] making drawings. They spent nearly $60,000 making plans for the Auditorium."[5] Given the uncertain future value of their stock, the architects made essentially no money on what was by far the largest built project in their firm's history. Yet Peck knew the value of Adler's contributions, writing to him in June 1888 when the unfinished Auditorium Theater hosted the Republican national convention: "While you doubtless have received many congratulations as well as myself arising from the success of our Hall, yet I must personally send you this tribute of my personal recognition of your genius and services in the designing and construction of the Auditorium . . . . Your part in the achievement will never be forgotten by me."[6] In 1893 Peck gave Adler and Sullivan the commission for the Chicago Stock Exchange Building, which proved to be the largest project the firm received before or after the Auditorium Building.

Peck's and Adler's shared assumptions about theater design can be compared from their statements in various contexts during and after their collaboration. As a permanent building intended to replicate many effects of Chicago's Grand Opera Festival of 1885, the Auditorium's mandate was to provide "music for the people." This meant first a hall of large capacity, one whose great number of seats, combined with revenues from commercial spaces encasing the theater, financially permitted productions of grand opera with low prices for tickets. Peck and his supporters had good reason to believe that lower prices would attract enough people to support first-class entertainment. For example, in winter 1887 Chicago's Columbia Theater (formerly Haverly's) led a local movement to cut ticket prices for an evening's performance to a uniform $1 per seat throughout the house. Its managers believed that the "lowering of rates had a benevolent appearance. There was a large class of those who desired to go to the theater who could not afford the habit of theater-going where rates were as formerly, and they would draw from this class a large following." The experiment proved so successful that the Columbia, which seated over 2,500 after its renovation in summer 1884, not only sold every ticket for its performances but turned away over 500 people each night.[7]

In 1886–1887, before the Auditorium's design crystallized, early announcements of the theater's capacity repeatedly projected that it would contain about 5,000 fixed seats for most occasions, with an expanded maximum of 8,000 for special events.[8] A permanent theater that large had no precedent among European opera houses. According to the Auditorium Theater's manager, Milward Adams, the room as built had 4,237 seats, making it "the largest opera house in the world." He cited the second largest as Milan's La Scala, seating about 3,600.[9] Paris's Opera had 2,156 permanent seats, New York's Metropolitan had just over 3,000, and Cincinnati's Music Hall had 3,632. Moreover, none of these models had any significant capacity for occasional expansion. By contrast, the Auditorium's originally projected capacity of 5,000 approximated that of temporary auditoriums built inside exhibition halls, like that for Chicago's Grand Opera Festival or that for the Nord-Amerikanisches Sängerbund's festival in Cincinnati's exposition hall, built by that city in 1870 on the site of the later permanent Music Hall of 1878. When fully occupied, the theater, with tiered seats on the stage and the boxes reseated to maximize capacity, "will accommodate more people than the famous Albert Hall in London."[10]

Among permanent American theaters, the only house whose permanent seating capacity approached that of the projected Auditorium was New York's Academy of Music, which originally seated 4,550, though renovations after a fire of 1866 reduced its capacity to 2,700, including several sets of private boxes. Architect Thomas R. Jackson increased the number of proscenium boxes from eighteen to twenty-eight, adding a fourth uppermost tier of boxes atop the three original ones (fig. 9).

The boxes held a total of about 150, only 3 percent of the hall's capacity. To complement these privileged seats, thirty-one boxes were added on the main balcony and twenty more on the mezzanine above.[11] Yet even the renovated Academy of Music did not have enough prestigiously positioned boxes to obviate the need for the Metropolitan Opera House begun thirteen years later. After the Met opened in 1883, the Academy of Music represented a less hierarchical idea of audience than the Met. The Academy may also have served as a partial model for Peck's and Adler's project because of its association with its longtime impresario, Col. James H. Mapleson. It was his traveling company that had brought Italian grand opera on the English model to Chicago from 1879 to 1884, and it was with Mapleson that Peck had contracted to produce the Grand Opera Festival in 1885.[12] For Peck and Chicagoans who patronized opera, Mapleson's more affordable productions were identified with the architectural arrangement of the New York Academy, still its city's largest theater in 1890, whose capacity enabled lower ticket prices than those at the Met.

As the Auditorium Theater was being readied for its first major event, the Republican national convention held in June 1888, Peck, seated in one corner of the empty parquet and contemplating a large engraving of the completed theater, remarked that "the thing had been in my mind a long time."[13] Peck's earlier travels had presumably taken him to the main opera houses of Europe, which he visited again with Dankmar Adler during late summer 1888. As Roula Geraniotis has shown, Adler's itinerary reflected his familiarity with the most technically advanced German theaters of the period. The trip also included a visit to Bayreuth's Festspielhaus. Peck stated in 1888: "We've had the plans of all the leading opera houses and theaters of Europe in our architects' offices from the beginning of the [Auditorium] enterprise."[14] It was not unusual for Chicago architects in this period to study major European examples of building types commissioned for Chicago. Before the city's Grand Central Station was begun in October 1887, its architect, Solon S. Beman, "made a special trip to Europe and visited all the large railroad stations of Great Britain and the Continent to get ideas for his architectural plans."[15]

Yet as they repeatedly stated, Peck and his architects, in seeking to realize an ideal of public access to opera, chose to devise a theater different from the tradition of the large state-supported opera house as it had developed in Europe. Peck was adamantly opposed to the concept of an opera house primarily for the privileged classes, with its audience hall dominated by private boxes. On 7 December 1889, two days before the Auditorium's theater opened, he wrote to the 180 stockholders (who constituted Chicago's capitalist elite) that the great opera houses of Europe, those of Paris, Vienna, Frankfurt, Dresden, Berlin, and Milan, "are all smaller in capacity, exclusive boxes occupying much of the space. They are built rather for the few than for the masses—the titled and the wealthy rather than for the people—lacking the broad democratic policy of providing for all which prevails in the arrangement of your Auditorium, thereby lessening the gulf between the classes."[16]

Peck had also consistently opposed boxes as a symbol of those differences in social class that had been so sharply drawn in Chicago and that the Auditorium was intended to lessen. Its lack of boxes "was [Peck's] idea, for he has no belief in privi-leged classes, and regards the Metropolitan Opera House of New York, where the whole structure is sacrificed to the boxes, with infinite scorn and patriotic dislike. This was a repetition of effete European ideas, and if there was one thing he im-pressed upon the architects, it was that he wanted the Auditorium to represent the present and the future and not the corrupted past."[17] Although Peck had initially preferred no boxes, by late 1886 the Auditorium Theater was projected to contain "fifty-one elegantly fashioned boxes" arranged "about the proscenium openings."[18] This approximated the position and design of boxes in the Grand Opera Festival's hall of 1885. As in New York, such seats were social attractions to Chicago's wealthy, who did not necessarily share Peck's singularly democratic vision of the theater's social purpose. Boxes eventually seated some of the project's stockholders, even though their investments did not entitle them to boxes, which were auctioned sepa-rately.

There were forty boxes in the Auditorium Theater as initially built. These were set to the sides of the theater in two tiers above the parquet, and even the most frontal boxes were set well back from the proscenium. Unlike the Met's boxes as closed rooms separated by partitions, the Auditorium's upper boxes were like open dress boxes in older theaters, with only posts between them and curtains behind, while the lower boxes, screened on all four sides with arches, had only curtains between and behind each box, which could be open or closed depending on the size of the seated party (figs. 95, 114, and 116).[19] In all, the Auditorium's boxes, which well-known

Figure 95

Auditorium Theater, interior looking northwest from stage, showing rising floor of parquet with *vomitorium*-like tunnels from west foyer, north boxes, main balcony, lower and upper galleries. Albert Fleury's mural of autumn on north wall is faintly visible in bright daylight from skylight over main balcony behind ceiling arches. Photograph by J. W. Taylor. Architecture Photograph Collection, Courtesy of the Art Institute of Chicago.

individual Chicagoans bid to possess for a season, accommodated about 200 people, fewer than 5 percent of the theater's total seating. This was much less than at the Met, where boxes accommodated almost one-fourth of the audience.[20] The Auditorium's boxes, set conspicuously above the main parquet and parquet circle and most highly visible from the balconies above the box tiers, were clearly intended as prime locations for social display of the city's leading families. Yet unlike those at the Met or its European models, the Auditorium's boxes were not so numerous or centrally positioned as to dominate the theater. Nor were they optimally positioned for seeing and hearing performances on the stage, since they were set to the sides of the house. As Sullivan said, "We are democratic in America and the masses demand the best seats. The boxes, you see, are on the sides and do not furnish the best possible view. In the imperial theaters the boxes are closed and take up all the best part of the house. Those occupying boxes in America desire to be seen, probably, more than they desire to see."[21]

Such a position corresponded closely to Adler's, whose views appeared in an essay on the theater probably written shortly before his death in 1900. There Adler argued for a progressive view of architecture, meaning that older building types like theaters would adapt to modern social changes by omitting nonfunctional historical conventions. He wrote that in 1800 just one kind of theater had been "common to the civilized world. The typical characteristics of its auditorium were: level or nearly level pit; high surrounding walls masked by many balconies and galleries; a ceiling raised high above these high walls by the interposition of an entablature or cove, or of both; within the ceiling a dome rising high enough to allow the main central chandelier to be hung above the line of vision of the greater part of the audience;

Figure 96

Auditorium Theater, main entry level plan, showing (a) exits to west behind foyer leading to Wabash Avenue, and (b) shaft for fresh air intake south of stage front. From *Engineering Magazine* 7 (August 1894). Courtesy of Watkinson Library, Trinity College, Hartford, Connecticut. Graphic additions by author.

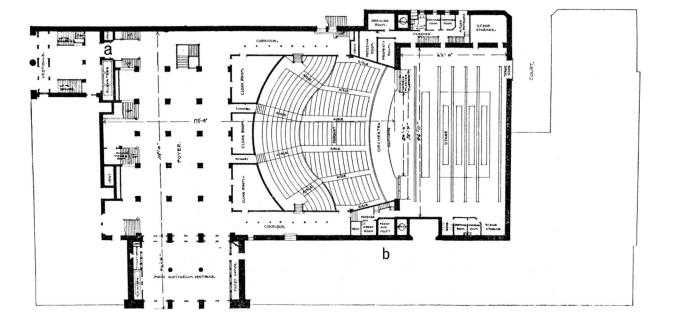

and a proscenium fashioned and decorated according to the rules conventionally accepted for the proportions of a doorway in a palace of the period of the Renaissance. Almost the entire nineteenth century has lapsed, and theater design is still dominated by reverence for this historically transmitted type."[22] Adler advocated "non-historical theater design," for "neither historical nor conventionally aesthetic considerations justify the use of forms and types which do not adapt to practical requirements."[23]

In Chicago's Auditorium, Adler sought to provide views and acoustics of similar quality for all patrons in a room of 4,237 fixed seats. His design focused not on the boxes but on the main mass of the audience. Plans were originally described as "arranged after the most modern way, and have, besides a main floor seating 3,000, two extensive balconies with chairs for 2,000."[24] The provision of individual fixed chairs for all theatergoers, no matter where they sat, adapted an innovation of the Central Music Hall. This design reflected New York's Academy of Music, as renovated in 1867–1868, whose upper gallery was then fitted with individual seats. The Academy's renovated auditorium, 70 feet wide by 102 feet deep, seated 2,700. The Auditorium Theater was a larger rectangular volume, measuring 118 feet wide between side walls by 178 feet deep from the stage's proscenium front to the foyer's rear wall (fig. 96). An interior perspective based on a longitudinal section looking south (fig. 97) clarifies that to include 4,237 seats, and to minimize overhang of the main balcony above the parquet's rear, the main balcony was set back, as Adler had

Figure 97

Auditorium Theater, interior perspective based on a longitudinal section looking south, showing raised hinged ceiling panels that could otherwise close off lower and upper galleries, Recital Hall above upper gallery, trusses spanning auditorium's width above stepped ceiling, and reducing curtain raised at front of stage, which is equipped with counterweights to move scenery vertically and hydraulic lifts for sections of stage floor. George C. Izenour Archive, Department of Special Collections, the Pennsylvania State University Library, accession no. 1998-0342R.

done in his theaters since the Central Music Hall. This limited the main balcony's seating capacity, which in turn necessitated including the two upper galleries at the theater's rear. As built, the main floor seated 1,400 and the main balcony 1,600, which together constituted the 3,000 seats originally projected for the main floor alone. The two upper galleries included in the original scheme, and not characteristic of Adler and Sullivan's earlier theaters, each seated just over 500. The result was a vertically segmented audience rising toward the house's rear. The Auditorium reworked the capacious volume of temporary music halls into its permanent plan's rectangular shape and dimensional limits. The combination of parquet, parquet circle, main balcony, and two upper galleries also approximated the tiered seating in the original New York Academy of Music of 1854, which had held 4,550, including benches in its top gallery seating 1,850.

What was most extraordinary about the Auditorium Theater's seating was that its large capacity had been compactly set in a room 92 feet wide between the boxes and 110 feet from the orchestra pit to the last row of seats on the main floor. As Milward Adams explained, "This space being nearly square, brings the main body of the audience within easy reach of the stage and does away with all disagreeable features of a long and narrow room. You perceive that the architectural features have been handled in such a manner as to rob the theatre of any appearance of being a vast and empty space. This is usually the trouble in very large interiors," such as in the Inter-state Industrial Exposition Hall and several of the European theaters that Adams had seen on his tour with Peck and Adler in September 1888. As the Auditorium neared completion, Adams said, "We have studied all the great playhouses of the world, and have sought to avoid their defects and combine all their merits."[25] Today, as one stands at almost any point in the theater's main floor, one can converse in a normal speaking voice with someone in the diagonally opposite corner of the hall. The resulting feeling of intimacy across the house testifies to Adler and Sullivan's skill in compacting the capacious seating within the room's floor area.

Adler devised a system of circulation for moving the Auditorium Theater's large audiences from streets to seats and out again efficiently, especially in case of fire. In this respect, the Auditorium's design responded to local concerns about fire safety in reports to the city council of the Committee on Public Buildings in the early 1880s.[26] The site permitted a main entrance only on the south side near the rear (fig. 96), like the entrances to the rear west side of the Grand Opera Festival Hall of 1885 (fig. 50). Like the Metropolitan, the Auditorium did not have sufficient space for a large multilevel, open stair hall as a central rendezvous on the model of the Paris Opera. Instead, most patrons entered through the theater lobby. Those going to the least expensive seats in the two galleries above the balcony entered most conveniently through the building's west lobby on Wabash Avenue and took elevators to their seating levels. To enable circulation of large audiences, the Auditorium had stairways between rear (western) foyers on different seating levels, seen in the section (fig. 97). From the foyers, aisles led patrons to their seats.

Ease of movement to and between boxes had shaped circulation inside the Metropolitan, but the Auditorium Theater's passageways were keyed to its large general audience. As he had in the Grand Opera Festival Hall, Adler used tunnel-like passageways leading from the rear foyer beneath the raised tiers of the parquet circle and into the multiple aisles of the parquet. Similar passageways provided access to the main balcony from its rear foyer. These multiple aisles and tunnel-like passageways recalled *vomitoria,* a term Adler used, which referred to the vaulted entrances in Roman amphitheaters (fig. 95).[27] In badly arranged theaters, "crowds block a common center, awaiting the tardy motions of overworked ushers."[28] Instead Adler advocated a maximum number of narrow aisles (rather than fewer wide aisles) for ease of egress in case of fire. A maximum number of aisles also produced a larger number of aisle seats, which were the most desirable. On the Auditorium's main floor and balcony, no seat was more than seven seats from an aisle.

Theater fire safety was partly a matter of fire prevention and control, but it also meant reassuring an audience that people could get out in case of fire. As the Citizens' Association's Committee on Theatres and Public Halls had concluded: "It may be assumed as a fact that no building can be constructed so carefully that a panic-stricken audience may get out with safety to all or without great loss of life. The most that can be done is to provide such resources for emptying a house that by giving audiences confidence in them panics themselves may be prevented. And this brings us to the consideration that the safety of audiences in theaters must be always regarded from two points of view. First, the prevention of fire, which is the general cause of panics, and second, the proper provision for escape in case of fire."[29] For practical and psychological reasons, exit doors are set on both sides of the Auditorium Theater toward its front, clearly visible to audience members, who would walk down to them in sight ahead rather than having to turn around, find the locations of exits, and then walk up to them. On the main floor, exit paths originally led directly to Congress Street (south), to an outdoor alley (north), and to Wabash Avenue (west) behind the foyer's rear (fig. 96a).

Adler's Ideas on Acoustics and Their Application to the Auditorium

The design of the Auditorium's seating was part of the larger issue of perfecting the experience of the theater for all members of the audience. In keeping with his own and Peck's ethos, Adler sought to provide optimal conditions for seeing and hearing for all patrons in a room for opera whose dimensions and capacity were among the world's largest. To achieve this result, he could have drawn on a European and American tradition of writings on architectural acoustics since the late eighteenth century. While Sullivan's library as of 1909 is known in detail, however, we know very little of Adler's collection of books on architecture and building technology. In his autobiography, Adler wrote that he read avidly in high school, when he kept a list of books read, and that he subsequently gathered books on architecture and engineering from southern homes during his service in the Civil War. When the Auditorium opened in 1890, his office was "chiefly noticeable from the number of works on architectural engineering in the bookcase, and from the large table, generally overflowed by a tide of technical publications."[30] By the time he died in 1900, Adler's library included some two hundred books; he willed the scientific and technical titles to his eldest son, architect and engineer Abraham K. Adler (1872–1914).[31]

Dankmar Adler's writings noted names of American authors on building construction, fire prevention, and technical fields other than acoustics, so that his understanding of these arts of building presumably represented his integration and extension of existing thought.[32] Among the many treatises on theater acoustics since the late eighteenth century, John Scott Russell's paper (noted earlier as a source for Adler's design for the Central Music Hall) was widely cited and was the only one Adler referred to in his own writings.[33] Yet the issue of acoustics held a personal significance for Adler that prompted him to develop an expertise in this area beyond that found in existing technical literature. Sullivan recalled that in the period of the Auditorium's design, Adler was "the only man living, at the time, who had had the intelligence to discern that the matter of acoustics is not a science but an art."[34] Elsewhere Sullivan recalled that with Adler acoustics "was not a matter of mathematics, nor a matter of science. There is a feeling, perception, instinct—and that Mr. Adler had. Mr. Adler had a grasp of the subject of acoustics which he could not have gained from study, for it was not in books. He must have gotten it by feeling."[35]

There is a family tradition that Dankmar Adler first became interested in the problem of architectural acoustics while listening to the voice of his father, Liebman Adler, long the rabbi and cantor of Chicago's Kehilath Anshe Ma'ariv, seeking to improve its audibility in the synagogue.[36] Before his marriage in 1872 Adler lived with his father, and he later remained close to him and Kehilath Anshe Ma'ariv, Chicago's oldest synagogue, which developed into one of the city's most prominent early Reform congregations. From Liebman Adler's arrival in 1861, this congregation had worshiped in several locations. Its early homes included three structures originally built as churches but converted by the congregation into synagogues, until Adler and Sullivan's building for KAM was completed in 1891. Thus for about thirty years Dankmar Adler worshiped in structures whose interiors had to be adapted, acoustically and otherwise, to his father's ministry and to this congregation's rituals. What part Dankmar Adler as an architect may have played in these adaptations is not known. Yet it is likely that Liebman Adler's career influenced his son Dankmar's view of acoustics as an important component of religious architecture.[37]

Before the Auditorium's design, the one structure outside Chicago that Adler was said to have studied for its acoustic properties was the Mormon Tabernacle in Salt Lake City, Utah. He supposedly first visited this building in 1885, the year he and Sullivan remodeled the Exposition Building's interior for Ferdinand Peck's Grand Opera Festival. Adler may have been directed to the Mormon hall by James Mapleson, the festival's impresario, who had produced two operas there in 1884, when

Figure 98

William H. Folsom, Henry Grow, and Truman O. Angell, Mormon Tabernacle, Salt Lake City, Utah (begun 1863; dedicated 1867; gallery added 1870). Courtesy of the Historical Department, Archives Division, the Church of Jesus Christ of Latter-day Saints, Salt Lake City, Utah, negative no. P500/14, 6.

Adelina Patti had desired to sing at the Mormon Tabernacle because of its acoustics.[38] Dedicated in 1867, the Large Tabernacle, as it was originally called, had a great domed ceiling (240 by 150 feet) in the shape of a turtleback shell. This ceiling was suspended below timber trusses that spanned the space, resting on exterior sandstone piers along its sides. The audience floor, which seated 7,000, sloped down from east to west, where there was a four-tier rostrum and choir, whose floor was 65 feet below the ceiling (fig. 98). Initially inadequate acoustics prompted the construction of a 30-foot-wide gallery around the interior, with a 30-inch gap left between the gallery's rear and the outer walls. This gap diffused sound waves from the rostrum, thereby eliminating echoes of such sound, which otherwise would have been reflected directly off the walls and back into the central space. Completed in 1870, this gallery perfected the tabernacle's acoustics and provided an additional 3,000 seats. The interior's overall design with its organ was a remarkable frontier adaptation of such buildings as the Boston Music Hall, also known for its choral events.[39] Adler visited the tabernacle during crowded services, observing the acoustic advantages of the gallery with its open back. This he adapted in the Auditorium, whose rear foyers had open stairwells that allowed sound to move vertically through their volume, diffusing the sound rather than having rear walls reflect it back into the theater as echoes.

As Charles Gregersen has shown, Adler's design for the Auditorium Theater developed ideas pioneered in his earlier Central Music Hall. Yet the Auditorium Theater's large size demanded Adler's ingenuity in adapting Scott Russell's principles and inventing additional techniques to optimize the huge room. Horizontally, the Auditorium's deep rectangular plan let him include a large number of seats in two sections of seating on the main floor: the parquet near the stage and the parquet circle farther back. The seating in both directions was set in "generous sweeping

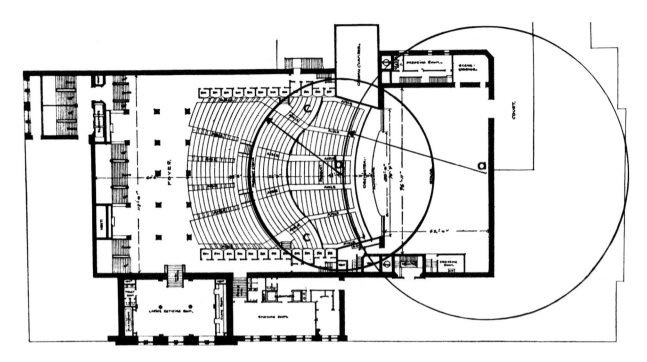

Figure 99

Auditorium Theater, second-story plan
showing (a) central point of circle
defining curvature of seating rows in
lower parquet, (b) central point of circle
defining curvature of seating rows in
upper parquet, and (c) seating rows at
sides of upper parquet with rows of
convex curvature toward stage. From
Engineering Magazine 7 (August 1894).
Courtesy of Watkinson Library, Trinity
College, Hartford, Connecticut. Graphic
additions by author.

Figure 100

Auditorium Theater, main balcony plan
showing elliptical curvature of seating
rows. From E. L. Lomax, *Diagrams:
Chicago Theatres*, 2d ed. (Chicago, 1890).
Courtesy of the Chicago Historical Society.

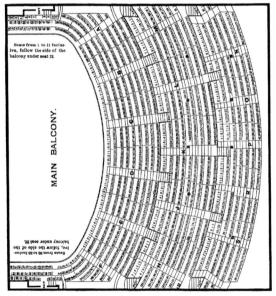

curves."[40] Adler did not specify these curvatures, but figure 99 shows that they are segments of circles. He did not center these seating rows at the stage's front, so that the rows would not reflect sound back to its source on the stage front, thus avoiding echoes there.[41] In the theater, the central point of the circle from which the arcs of the parquet rows are swung is at the stage's rear center (fig. 99a), while the central point of the circle from which the arcs of the parquet circle rows are swung is behind the first parquet row (fig. 99b). This corresponded to the front of the orchestra pit, whose space for ninety musicians, it was said, could have accommodated at once the orchestras from all Chicago's downtown theaters of the period. At the parquet circle's frontal sides, the curvature of the seating rows reverses, becoming convex rather than concave relative to the stage to ensure optimal views of the stage from these lateral seats (fig. 99c). As Adler wrote, the main balcony (fig. 100) was elliptical in plan, reducing the number of side seats with awkwardly angled views. This broad, shallow curve yielded superb frontal views of the stage from seats on this level.

Vertically, as Gregersen showed, Adler adapted Scott Russell's ideas in order to calculate the steep rise in seating rows of the main floor (seventeen feet from front to rear). Because so many seats had to be included within a room whose total height above the stage had to be limited, Adler elevated seats by about fifteen inches over every two rows instead of over every row, as Scott Russell had proposed, so that the total rise of the parquet seating was less than in Scott Russell's models. As in the Central Music Hall, ascending rows let observers see and hear above the heads of others directly in front, as shown in the section (fig. 97).[42] Also, as in his earlier works, throughout the theater Adler set seats in successive rows between those in front, "so that each spectator sees between and not over the heads of those immediately before him."[43] The resulting banked tiers of seating rise impressively from the stage up through the main floor, continuing into the balcony and galleries, the topmost having an extreme slope of forty-one degrees.[44] From the uppermost row of this topmost gallery, one clearly hears an unamplified singing voice from the stage. As Adler said, "The acoustic properties of the house are such as to permit the easy and distinct transmission of articulated sound to its remotest parts."[45] Tickets for this topmost gallery were initially priced at $1, the same as the least expensive tickets for the Chicago Grand Opera Festival, which Peck and Adler also designed so singers could be heard by patrons seated in this distant loft.[46]

The Auditorium's design contains a number of features that reflect Adler's interest in ancient Roman and Greek theaters as functionally viable models for modern theaters. In referring to the Auditorium's tunnel-like passageways as *vomitoria*, Adler implicitly recalled the prototype of the Roman Colosseum, the only ancient theater he referred to in his writings. Another report noted that the Auditorium "will be the modern rival in regard to perfect arrangement, of the historic arena of the Roman Colosseum."[47] Known for its efficiency of circulation and its steeply tiered seating, the Colosseum was also elliptical. Adler's use of the ellipse in designing the balcony floor and ceiling arches of the Auditorium recalled a preference for this form for theaters by European architectural writers since the late eighteenth century. Gottfried Semper, whose studies of theater design with Richard Wagner provided one basis for the latter's Festspielhaus at Bayreuth, had also believed in the advantages of the ellipse for sound projection.[48]

Adler's essays on theater design echoed ideas from the Roman architectural writer Vitruvius, whose analysis of the acoustically optimal design of theaters remained a standard reference before the problem received sustained scientific inquiry starting in the late eighteenth century. Based on his knowledge of Greek theaters, Vitruvius had endorsed the idea of ascending tiers of seating to optimize acoustics. To avoid spectators' blocking sound from those behind them, he advised that "it should be so contrived that a line drawn from the lowest to the highest seat will touch the top edges and angles of all the seats. Thus the voice will meet with no obstruction."[49] Adler cited Vitruvius's writings on acoustics and, like Vitruvius, wrote that sound waves travel outward from a source until they are obstructed by an object.[50] Adler described the phenomenon of concentric waves of sound that emanate from a source just as Vitruvius had described transmission of sound in ancient theaters, where seating rows were set in concentric rings around a stage. Vitruvius observed that to enable sound to flow unobstructed, "ancient architects, following in the footsteps of nature, perfected the ascending rows of seats in theatres from their investigations of the ascending voice," endeavoring "to make every voice uttered on the stage come with greater clearness and sweetness to the ears of the audience."[51] Thus, in adapting Scott Russell's isacoustic curve, Adler reworked a principle of design that he, like Scott Russell earlier, presumably knew from Vitruvius's description of classical theaters.

Adler's contemporary, architect John A. Fox of Boston, had articulated the rationale for modern American adaptation of ancient classical theater design. In a lecture of 1879, Fox noted that the term *theatre* was derived from the Greek word signifying "to see." He cited James Fergusson, then perhaps the most widely read English architectural historian, who wrote that the Greeks "hit on the very best form in plan for the transmission of the greatest quantity of sound, with the greatest clearness, to the greatest possible number."[52] Fox proposed a modern adaptation of a Greek theater plan (fig. 101) that anticipated Adler's Auditorium plan. In a modern theater, the need to see into the stage's depth some distance back from the proscenium called for abandoning the extreme side seats found in a Greek semicircular plan. The result was "the fan-shape; or more accurately, a portion of the sector of a circle, the centre for the radius of which shall be behind the proscenium, instead of in front of it as in the Greek form." Just as Adler would, Fox argued for multiplying the points of egress to subdivide the audience for rapid exit in case of fire. During performances, the Greek idea of rising tiers of seats gave the opportunity "for every one in the hall to see almost everybody else . . . . There is no more valuable adjunct to noble architecture than this sea of interested and sympathetic faces, supplemented by the bloom of color in varied costumes."[53] This social effect anticipated descriptions of the Auditorium Theater's opening, when the full house became a metaphor for civic unity.[54]

As an American adaptation of classical theaters, the Auditorium both resembled and differed from the adaptation of ancient models at Bayreuth's Festspielhaus, which was an extension of Semper's ideas. Both buildings abandoned the primacy of the loges or tiers of boxes in favor of seating that appeared more equal, democratic, and unified. The dramatic upward rise of the seating at Bayreuth was also modeled on Scott Russell's idea of ensuring acoustic and visual access to the

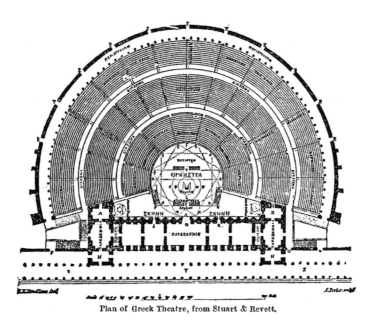

Plan of Greek Theatre, from Stuart & Revett.

Figure 101

Plan of an ancient Greek theater, from James Stuart and Nicholas Revett, *The Antiquities of Athens* (London, 1762–1816), and modern adaptation of the Greek form, with longitudinal section at right, from John A. Fox, "American Dramatic Theatres," part 3, *American Architect and Building News* 6 (2 August 1879): 36.

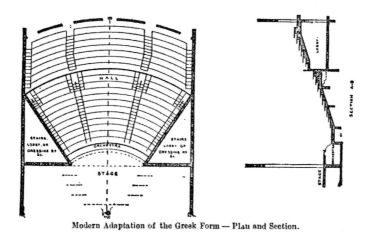

Modern Adaptation of the Greek Form — Plan and Section.

stage.[55] Unlike the Auditorium Theater, however, Bayreuth's Festspielhaus had no single main public foyer in the theater's rear. As noted earlier, no aisles ran to the stage between seating groups, leaving an unbroken curvature of seating as a direct evocation of an ancient Greek theater. Bayreuth's rear gallery was small relative to the Auditorium's balcony plus two galleries, which together had well over half the seating.

Apart from the rise and curvature of seating on parquet and balcony, the most important element in the Auditorium's acoustic design was the containment of sound as it emerged from the stage. Like Scott Russell, Adler cited the analogy of the trumpet or the speaking tube, which concentrated sound near its source and ensured its powerful projection.[56] In the Auditorium this meant eliminating seats with extreme lateral positions on each side of the parquet so that no spectators were so far to the side that they could not see the sides as well as the center of the stage. All audience members had good sight lines on the diagonal across the stage and frontally through the stage's full depth. If spectators could see the stage's sides, they could also hear sound emanating from there.

Adler reasoned that in the vertical dimension there was no practical way to control sound within the volume of the stage, so its control depended on the shaping of the theater's architectural volumes forward of the stage. Earlier studies of acoustics had shown that the human ear cannot distinguish between sounds that are less than about one-tenth of a second apart. Hence, if an initial sound and a reflection of it off the ceiling or other surface strike a listener's ear within one-tenth of a second of each other, they are heard as uniting and reinforcing. But if an initial sound and its reflection off a surface strike the ear more than one-tenth of a second apart, the two are heard as separate. This results "in a reverberatory effect which makes for unintelligibility and confusion of sound."[57] Such unwanted reverberation was directly proportional to an auditorium's total volume. So the larger such a room's total volume, the more the unwanted reverberation, meaning reflected sounds were dissipated and confused with initial sounds. Adler proposed that sound-reflecting surfaces be placed as near to a source of sound as possible in order to retain the strength of the reflected sound before it dissipated at a distance from its source and to ensure that "the difference in time required by original and reflected sound waves to travel to the ear of the auditor shall be less than one-tenth of a second."[58]

In practice this meant that the auditorium's ceiling should be as low as possible from the proscenium of the stage outward. In an operatic theater, the proscenium had to be high enough to allow those in the uppermost rear seats to see the full depth of the stage and its scenic effects. Conventional prosceniums were rectangular and classically proportioned like doorways or windows, hence taller than desirable, with attached columns or pilasters to each side. Adler lowered the Auditorium's proscenium to reduce the room's volume, conserve sound produced on stage, and direct it outward to the audience. This principle implied the fan-shaped seating on raised levels, "but the effort to conserve the sound waves influences to a still greater extent the vertical dimensions of the auditorium. The proscenium must be low, not a foot higher than is necessary to permit full view of any possible grouping at the back of the stage from the last and highest seat in the house."[59] Adler objected to theater design inspired by European court opera houses, "whose strongest manifestation is found in efforts to fashion with historical correctness and academic accuracy the proportions of the proscenium opening."[60]

Adler's acoustic strategy produced the Auditorium's most inventive feature: its arched ceiling. This was unlike the shallow domes of such theaters as the Metropolitan or the low, canopylike ceiling of the Bayreuth Festspielhaus, which was meant to recall a classical velarium. Bayreuth had a triple proscenium, providing multiple rectangular frames for the stage. The Chicago Auditorium's arched proscenium expanded into a multiarched ceiling that had no precedent in European or American

opera houses. One account claimed: "The design is unique in that it is the first theater ever built with the interior shaped like a cone or speaking trumpet. The stage
being taken as the apex of a hollow cone, the arched roof, and diverging walls retreat in a series of constantly widening circles, being the acme of acoustic achievement."[61] As noted, the Metropolitan's acoustic difficulties came from the high
proscenium and ceiling needed to accommodate tiered boxes. By contrast, Adler
complemented the low proscenium of the Auditorium Theater with "a gradual increase in height of ceiling from the proscenium outward." He modulated the rising
ceiling planes "into a profile which deflects the sound waves downward toward the
rear of the lower portion of the house."[62] The Auditorium's ceiling was designed as
four elliptically arched segments that share a common long or horizontal axis.
These repeat the proscenium arch at progressively larger scales overhead (fig. 3;
plates 5 and 6). The four arches contain the sound emanating from the stage and reflect it back down into the theater quickly enough to prevent confusing reverberation or a discernible echo of direct sound from the stage. Both the direct and reflected sound arrived at the listener's ear at about the same time, hence producing
no distinct echo. As Wright recalled, "The receding elliptical arches spanning the
great room were a development by Sullivan of Adler's invention of the sounding
board of sloping ceiling above the proscenium."[63] Sullivan thus took an acoustically
functional ceiling shape as the basis for the room's aesthetic, exemplifying his later
dictum that in architecture "form follows function." Adler wrote: "The architectural
and decorative forms found in the auditorium are unconventional in the extreme
and are determined to a great extent by the acoustic effects to be obtained."[64]

The Auditorium Theater's arched proscenium contrasted with the squared
frame of the Metropolitan's stage (fig. 40) and Wagner's Festspielhaus (fig. 47). As
an ellipse, the proscenium conjoined the architectural spaces of stage and audience.
One observer wrote that the four great arches, with their very low crowns, "repeat
the proscenium arch, and blend together most beautifully the two portions of the
building, so that they have a unity of which architects never before dreamed."[65] The
Auditorium's ceiling arches embrace the collective totality of the audience in the
main floor and balcony below. This balcony's horizontal elliptical curves echo the
ceiling arches' vertical elliptical curves. These curves recall the seating's rising slope
below, so that lines in all three dimensions convey a functional ideal of acoustic and
visual linkage between audience and stage.

This effect was even more evident in Adler and Sullivan's original design, as
shown in the cross-section working drawing dated April 1887 (fig. 102), in which
multiple arched frames surround the proscenium opening. At their sides the arches
spring from splayed jambs with multiple colonnettes, like the exterior portal of a
Romanesque church. This drawing also shows that there was to be a fifth arched
segment nearest the stage, but this arch was omitted during construction to place
the organ to the stage's left.[66] This change also set the theater's boxes well back from
the proscenium, thus distinguishing them from traditional, highly privileged proscenium boxes near the stage. As seen in this section and in the longitudinal section

Figure 102

Auditorium Theater, cross-section
drawing looking east, April 1887, showing
(a) elliptical arched iron trusses below
(b) horizontal iron trusses above ceiling.
Architecture Photograph Collection,
Courtesy of the Art Institute of Chicago.
Graphic notations by author.

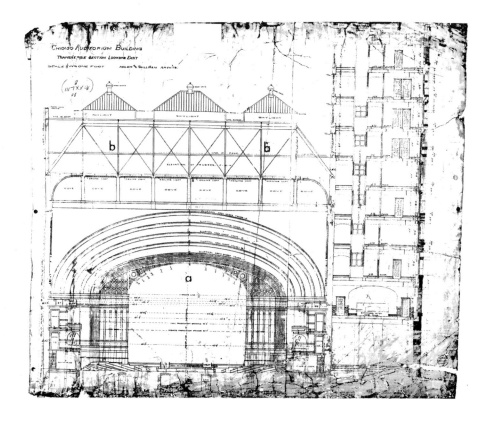

(fig. 97), the Auditorium's five elliptical arches (including the proscenium) are set fourteen feet apart and were made of arched iron trusses (fig. 102a). These were in turn set beneath six much deeper horizontal iron trusses above (fig. 102b) each spanning 118 feet north-south across the room.

In addition to the position of seats and the shaping of space above, an acoustic logic also informed the choice of materials for walls and ceilings. These were not to be so soft (such as plush upholstery or drapery) as to absorb sound to the point of deadening it or so hard (such as brick or marble) as to reflect sound too harshly. The intermediate ideal was a material environment that was both moderately resonant and reflective. In practice this meant surfaces either of wood or of thick plaster set on metal lath. The latter predominated throughout the Auditorium because of plaster's superiority in terms of fireproofing. The plaster surfaces were to be broken up (as in the stepped ceiling arches and, on a smaller scale, in their ornamental relief) so that reflections of sound striking the ear at intervals greater than one-tenth of a second would not be "sufficiently cumulative" to cause echoes.[67]

According to earlier nineteenth-century writers on architectural acoustics, the method of ventilation was an important means of enhancing the quality of sound in auditoriums as well as ensuring the comfort of audiences. Yet in the Metropolitan and the Auditorium, different concepts of audience led to selecting different ventilating systems. Both Cady and Adler adopted a forced-air system modeled on

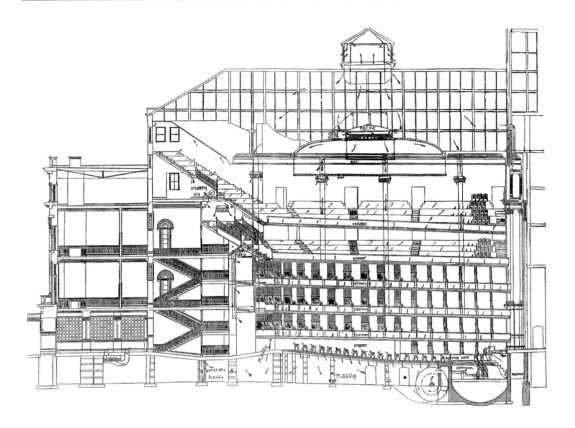

that of the Royal and Imperial Opera House in Vienna, opened in 1869, yet they made different use of mechanisms for moving air. Cady wrote that the comfort of the audience through long performances was achieved "mainly by powerful machinery forcing large volumes of fresh and suitably tempered air into all parts of the house."[68] The theater's gas lighting created exhaust that had to be expelled upward and outward. The Met's first-story plan shows the air intake shaft to the north of the stage front, west of the Green Room (fig. 38). As shown by the arrows in the section (fig. 103), the Metropolitan's air came from the basement and rose upward through plenums, passing through grilles in the risers of the seating tiers. One steam-powered fan forced the air up through the theater, creating a positive pressure that forced the air through the grilles. Each part of the house was supplied through a different set of ducts. Air supplied to the upper balconies was cooler than air supplied to the lower seating sections, so that there would be a relatively even temperature throughout the house. Gas lamps near the upper exhaust vents above also created heat to draw the vitiated air out by convection. The most generous supplies of warmed air were directed toward the boxes, each of which had its own duct. Thus "a fresh atmosphere is continually forced into the auditorium, the box-holders being particularly well cared for in this respect."[69]

Unlike the Met's, the Auditorium's ventilation also included a system for cooling summer air. The Met's operatic season ran from October through April, but Chicago's Auditorium had a broader range of projected functions, including hosting

Figure 103

Cady, Berg, and See, Metropolitan Opera House, longitudinal section looking south with arrows showing scheme of ventilation from basement up through seating risers into auditorium and out through ventilating lantern in roof above domed ceiling. From *Sanitary Engineer* 9 (6 December 1883). Courtesy of the Library of Congress.

national political conventions, which were always held in summer. To minimize the need to clean intake air, Adler and his consultants may have considered drawing it in through the top of the Auditorium Tower, as far as possible above the city's smoke-filled atmosphere. This method of air intake was used in Richardson's Allegheny County Courthouse in Pittsburgh, whose tall frontal tower had "nostrils" or openings for drawing relatively pure air into the tower's crown and down into the building's basement. For the Auditorium Theater, a shaft for taking in fresh air was south of the stage front (fig. 96b), with an outlet at the sixth floor. In winter the air was washed clean with a water spray in the basement, then heated by passing over a bank of steam radiator coils, and finally humidified before it was mechanically forced into circulation through the structure's many levels and chambers. In summer the bank of radiators was bypassed and the air was forced through a spray of water cooled by beds of crushed ice. The basement had enormous storage bins for blocks of ice delivered through the sidewalk. The vast hall's topmost levels thus were unlike the notoriously sweltering galleries of some Chicago theaters. In this era lack of comfortable ventilation in the galleries marked a theater as socially elitist. As a modern mechanism for cooling a mass audience, the Auditorium's ventilation system brought a then advanced technology into the service of Peck's democratic ideal for the theater.[70]

In the Metropolitan, the direction of air supply up and toward the stage was opposite the direction of the sound waves. Yet for the Auditorium, Adler later wrote: "It is desirable for acoustic effect, to have all air currents tending from the stage outward. It will be easiest to attain these ends if the fresh air is chiefly introduced at and from the top and in greatest volume on or near the stage."[71] Adler implied that the direction of airflow out from the stage enhanced the projection of sound. Later he and other acoustic theorists reasoned that since the velocity of sound waves (1,100 feet per second) is much greater than that of forced air, transmission of sound to an audience would not be appreciably affected by the direction and speed of ventilation. Yet Adler's early acoustic assumption was one basis for the Auditorium Theater's remarkable system of ventilation. On the west vertical face of each of the three main ceiling arches, there are nineteen circular supply vents, whose domed ornamental wrought iron covers are perforated to supply air to the main mass of the audience above their heads, mechanically forcing the air outward from the frontal stage (figs. 3 and 113). The novel electric lighting enabled this system of downward ventilation, since the exhaust from gas lighting did not have to be expelled upward as in the Met. Unlike the Met's varied ducts for different seating sections, all parts of the Auditorium Theater were supplied from the ceiling vents.

For cooling, the downward flow of air in the Auditorium Theater avoided the cold drafts around people's feet that would have come had the air been supplied beneath each seat. Instead, the downward-falling cooled air picks up the heat rising from the audience so that the air reaches seated people at an agreeable temperature. Exhaust vents are set in floor-level risers of the steppings of the seating throughout the house, except for the boxes, which have no exhaust vents. Electrical power permitted the multiplicity and dispersion of fans connected by wires to distant dynamos, rather than steam-powered fans connected by belts to nearby engines. Thus, in the Auditorium Theater four electrically powered fans drew air to these exhaust vents, which increase in size toward the rear of the theater. If all the vents were the same size, too much air would be drawn through the exhaust vents near the supply vents, depriving the rear upper levels of a generous supply. But the larger rear vents exhaust more air than the smaller near ones, thereby compensating for their greater distance from the supply vents, to ensure a uniform air flow to the rear galleries and hence the comfort of the less wealthy patrons farthest from the stage.

One of the most important ways Chicago's Auditorium compared with the Metropolitan Opera House was in its spatial flexibility. The Met was largely fixed in its seating and stage, but like the Auditorium's, its parquet could be overlaid with a temporary floor to transform the opera house into a ballroom. In the Chicago Auditorium the parquet floor was equipped throughout with cast iron shoes (still visible today) to hold a forest of vertical rods that supported the temporary floor on a level with the stage. This idea's many precedents included Barry's Covent Garden and the Versailles Opera House completed by Ange-Jacques Gabriel in 1770. After its opening, Chicago's Auditorium often served as a venue for banquets and charity balls, which made use of the temporary flooring over the parquet. For charity balls, funds were raised from auction sales of boxes for spectators. In these ways, like the Metropolitan, Adler and Sullivan's theater adapted a European courtly device to the social uses of an American public hall.[72]

The varied program of events the Auditorium Theater was to house meant that the desired size and character of audiences would also vary considerably. To accommodate these, its interior did have a degree of spatial flexibility not possible in the smaller Met with its arrangement of box tiers. In general, Adler recommended reduced seating and smaller spatial volume in theaters designed for events other than grand opera, which required a large stage.[73] In a large opera house, closing off sections of seating helped make less spectacular and less voluble nonoperatic events visible and audible. The reduced spatial volume also lowered costs for heating and cooling the house. Finally, closing off the balcony's rear and galleries for certain events made their less expensive seats unavailable, limiting the audience to the usually higher-priced seats in the parquet and the balcony's front.

Optional closure of the uppermost sections of a large theater's seating was socially motivated. Through the nineteenth century, the uppermost galleries had been the lair of the most raucous male theatergoers, known as the "gallery gods," who issued jeering decrees from their spatially lofty but socially lowly benches. Additionally, the uppermost rear level of seating in theaters was often shunned as "that guilty third tier" because of its association with prostitution in a period when some lower-class theaters relied financially on prostitutes as regular patrons.[74] To counter these widely held perceptions, the topmost gallery in the Auditorium Theater, as in the New York Academy of Music and other theaters, was named the "family circle." The leader in efforts to "purify" audiences was the New York theatrical manager Augustin Daly, whom Adler consulted in designing the Auditorium Theater. In his own theaters in New York City, Daly prohibited prostitutes and raucous customers in the galleries. He perfected these policies in his own Daly Theater on Broadway and Thirty-ninth Street, opened in 1879 just south of the site of the future Metropolitan Opera House. As he wrote in 1886, "From the topmost gallery down, respectability reigns . . . . There is no attraction for the vicious. The constant patrons of the drama belong to the class of people who are strictest in the performance of every duty."[75]

In Chicago's Auditorium, it was planned from the start that patrons in the two topmost galleries would not enter the building through the theater's main doors on Congress Street, which led to the vestibule and foyers for boxholders and those who sat on the parquet and balcony. Instead, gallery patrons would enter through the office building's lobby off Wabash Avenue and ascend to and descend from the gallery-level foyers by separate staircases and elevators. A separate system of access and seating for the least wealthy in the audience was built into the design, although these audience members were provided with the same individual folding opera chairs, and cloakrooms and retiring rooms, as patrons on lower levels. Gallery patrons were to observe the same behavioral standards as those with higher incomes seated below. As one account described the uppermost "family circle" on the Auditorium's opening night, "It was not occupied by 'the gods,' to use theatrical vernacular, but a refined, intellectual and cultivated gathering, people who would grace the parquet at any theatre or the parlor of any home . . . . The same decorum and dignity that marked the atmosphere of the lower portions of the temple were prevalent there as well."[76]

To accommodate smaller events and control their audiences in the Auditorium Theater, Adler adopted Augustin Daly's suggestion to provide hinged ceilings for the upper and lower galleries. These could be lowered to close off the fronts of these spaces, as shown in figures 97 and 104, eliminating sections of seating traditionally associated with less wealthy patrons. As Adler wrote, "The lowered portions of the ceiling then form part of the general ceiling treatment of the hall, and the galleries are entirely shut off without impairment of the general architecture or decorative effect."[77] Curtains lowered between pillars on the main balcony could close off the rear section of that level, further reducing the theater's spatial volume and seating capacity to 2,500. By contrast, for conventions and mass meetings of very large size, stepped rows of seating could be added at the parquet circle's rear and on the stage. These changes, together with reseating the boxes and the corridors behind boxes, created a total maximum capacity of 7,000.[78]

To control the size of the opening around the stage, the Auditorium had an iron reducing curtain, covered with ornamental plaster, that could be raised or lowered. This reducing curtain framed the central heavy silk drop curtain behind it. When

Figure 104
Auditorium Theater, interior looking
south across parquet and balcony toward
Fleury's mural of spring, showing (a)
movable ceiling partitions lowered to
close off lower and upper balcony, and
skylights above coved, stenciled ceiling
vaults. A central ornamental panel of
one theater skylight bay is shown in
plate 7. Photograph by J. W. Taylor.
Architecture Photograph Collection,
Courtesy of the Art Institute of Chicago.
Graphic notations by author.

lowered, the reducing curtain framed an opening 47 feet wide and 35 feet high for opera, drama, lectures, and concerts with no chorus (figs. 3, 105). Alternatively, to accommodate large choral performances, the reducing curtain was raised and the stage's entire width of 75 feet was made spatially continuous with the rest of the auditorium. In Sullivan's design of April 1887 (fig. 102), the reducing curtain was to be elliptically arched with circular motifs in its spandrels, unlike the squared frame and motifs of the curtain as built. Adler wrote: "The success of the room is greatest when used as a hall for mass concerts. The chorus seems thus to blend with the audience, and the house is so open that one can see at a glance almost the entire audience and the whole chorus."[79] This effect appeared on the Auditorium's opening night, when the reducing curtain was raised to bring the whole stage into view from the house, including a chorus in banked seating on the stage (figs. 97, 106).

Combined lectures and choral performances were a part of Peck's social vision of the Auditorium. He proposed that the room house a series of Sunday night lectures by eminent orators of the English-speaking world. These were "not to be the star performances of mere oratory, but real speeches upon important questions of the day—philanthropic, economic, educational, artistic, social." The lectures were to be accompanied by great choral performances of five hundred voices drawn from the Chicago public and eliciting choral responses from the audience filling the house. Wealthy guarantors, such as Peck, would underwrite the cost of these events to ensure that seats could be sold at nominal prices to intelligent workers "upon whom the existing inequalities of social conditions weigh most heavily." Men would

Figure 105

Auditorium Theater, stage set for scene from *Lohengrin*, showing panoramic sky in background, stage framed by reducing curtain, and Charles Holloway's mural along proscenium arch. Architecture Photograph Collection, Courtesy of the Art Institute of Chicago.

Figure 106

Auditorium Theater, opening night, 9 December 1889, showing reducing curtain raised and seating added to stage flanking chorus. From *Frank Leslie's Illustrated Newspaper* (New York), 21 December 1889. Courtesy of the Chicago Historical Society, ICHi-00609.

be "brought into a higher range of ideas and more stimulating and self-rewarding thought than that possible for them to pick up in assembly-rooms or in the little reading their daily fatigue permits them."[80] In April 1890 the Chicago Bureau of Popular and Scientific Lectures, which had formerly organized events in the Central Music Hall, arranged for the first lecture to be held in the Auditorium. The speaker was the Reverend T. De Witt Talmage, whose address on political corruption was titled "The School of Scandal," a play on the title of Sheridan's famous play.[81] Through such events, the Auditorium Theater fulfilled Peck's aim of housing nominally democratic yet nonthreatening political activity, an ideal first realized when the room hosted the Republican national convention of 1888.

The Auditorium Theater as a Convention Hall, 1888

To Peck and his allies, it was important that the Auditorium be selected as the site of the first political conventions for which it could be readied, to enhance its claim to national standing. In this role Peck's hall would prove itself to be the local successor to the Inter-state Industrial Exposition Building, which had hosted the Democrats and Republicans in 1884, while the Auditorium Hotel was to succeed to the role of the Grand Pacific and the Palmer House as the headquarters for convention delegates. Peck hoped to repeat this unprecedented meeting of both parties in Chicago in 1888. The Democrats, under pressure from the building trades not to meet in the Auditorium, chose to meet in St. Louis's much larger exposition building. In December 1887 the Republicans, then the party out of power, announced their decision to convene in Chicago the following June.[82] The Auditorium's granite outer walls had barely begun to be laid, and the theater's brick inner walls were less than halfway up. From December on, the plan for construction was to complete the theater alone as "a building within a building," meaning the completion of its encasing walls and the trusses across the theater that would support its roof. This roof, with its skylights, was finished in late March 1888. At that time a temporary roof was also closed above the stage, where no tall fly tower for opera was yet needed. Further interior work on the hall followed until early June, when attention returned to the outer walls just before the Republicans convened. By then one observer was "surprised at the rapidity with which course upon course of dressed stone has been added, until now the rough inner structure of brick was almost concealed from view."[83]

The rushed effort to face the lower exterior with granite in time for the Auditorium's first national convention fit with Peck's strategy to make the building enhance perceptions of Chicago. An engraving of the exterior in June 1888 shows its three-story granite base complete, with derricks for lifting stone and the theater's inner brick walls above (fig. 107). Peck told reporters that though construction was then hurried, "no work or material of a temporary character was permitted to go into the framework of the Auditorium. This is now exactly as it was originally designed to be—of the most enduring and massive description. The entire structure is

THE CITY OF CHICAGO.

SUPPLEMENT TO HARPER'S WEEKLY, JUNE 23, 1888.

THE AUDITORIUM BUILDING—THE PLACE OF MEETING OF THE NATIONAL REPUBLICAN CONVENTION.
DRAWN BY CHARLES GRAHAM FROM SKETCHES BY WALTER BURRIDGE.

Figure 107

Auditorium Building, view from southeast, June 1888, showing outer three-story granite base, theater's inner brick walls, and temporary roof covering. Drawing by Charles Graham, based on sketches by Walter Burridge. From Supplement to *Harper's Weekly*, 23 June 1888. Courtesy of Watkinson Library, Trinity College, Hartford, Connecticut.

as nearly fireproof as modern means can provide."[84] Such remarks countered memories of Chicago's earlier temporary wooden convention halls, which Peck wanted his building to supersede. His emphasis on the Auditorium's solidity also helped counter the disappointment of arriving delegates on seeing the building's unfinished state. One wrote that the Auditorium's exterior then looked like "an irregular heap of massive granite blocks averaging three stories in height, derrick poles here and there like the dismantled masts of ships," from the center of which rose "four walls of rough brick [surrounding the theater itself] towering far above everything else."[85]

The theater inside, though designed primarily to house evening performances, had to function as a daylit space for the convention. In a paper of 1887 on the design of opera houses, Adler proposed to secure "partial sunlight illumination of the house, and thus avoid the expense of artificial illumination for daily cleaning, rehearsals, and for daylight assemblies, such as conventions, mass meetings, concerts, etc., when scenic effects are not to be produced."[86] A view of the Auditorium as prepared for the Republican convention shows the elliptical arched trusses above the hall, which is bathed in daylight entering through the roof's skylights (fig. 108). Accounts described rays of summer sunlight passing into the hall from the highest reaches of the room and falling directly on the speakers' platform. The skylights also helped ventilate the hall, then holding 9,000 in warm weather, before the theater's permanent mechanical system for moving and cooling air was installed. Terra cotta–colored muslin was stretched beneath the skylights to soften and color the sunlight coming from above. This was only one element in an elaborate scheme of temporary decorations throughout the hall, which covered the walls, trusses, and railings with bunting, giant flags, and other ephemera. These decorations were in the colors of the American flag, partly in contrast to the socialist and anarchist use of the red flag. As one account of the convention hall noted: "No red bandana humbug is brought into competition here with the glorious 'red, white and blue.'" The convention's temporary interior was the work of a decorator, not of Sullivan, who was then designing the permanent ornamental scheme for the finished theater. The brick and metal shell was described at the convention as denuded, to the point that some accounts confused the hall with the Inter-state Industrial Exposition Building.[87]

Figure 108

Auditorium Theater as Republican
national convention hall, June 1888,
looking west from stage. Architecture
Photograph Collection, Courtesy of
the Art Institute of Chicago.

The most spectacular aspect of the hall's lighting was its system of electric incandescent bulbs installed for the convention's evening sessions. The Metropolitan
Opera House relied on gaslights when it opened in 1883. In that year the Chicago
Citizens' Association recommended that local theater owners switch to incandescent electric light because "the use of gas for illumination has always been a fruitful
cause of theatre disasters."[88] By 1888 almost all of Chicago's theaters were lighted
by electricity, yet none had a system as large as the Auditorium's. For the convention, its scheme of 3,500 bulbs included sets running along the ceiling arches and
along the balcony and gallery fronts, enveloping the general audience. This system,
with its own generator, was retained for the permanent theater but was first tested
during the convention. Sullivan, who had been intrigued with the decorative potential of electric lights since his renovation of McVicker's Theater in 1885, provided
"an original design" for the convention hall's distribution of bulbs. This included
"the arrangement of electric lamps, in great stars, suspended from the roof and
walls of the house" as "one of the most effective and beautiful features of the
scene."[89] Below were giant electrically framed portraits of the deceased Lincoln and
Grant on either side of the hall, where Albert Fleury's murals appeared in the permanent theater. Above the speakers' platform was a large national shield of 750 red,
white, and blue globes. The Chicago Edison Electric Light Company developed
these circuits of bulbs, but the interior's display was so technically novel that Peck
took the precaution of fitting the hall with gas jets in case the electrical machinery
gave way. In this period before urban power systems, only the most up-to-date

commercial buildings had electricity, generated from their own power plants. As in McVicker's Theater, the convention hall's illumination underscored the fact that electrification was not yet a public utility but a rare commodity that bespoke financial or political power.[90]

In 1895 Adler detailed the specific requirements for a large convention hall of the period. By then he not only had been the architect in charge of preparing the Inter-state Industrial Exposition Building for both parties in 1884 and the Auditorium in 1888 but had been an associate architect for preparation of the 1892 Democratic national convention's hall in Minneapolis.[91] The organization of these meetings guided planning for their built settings. In those years each party had about nine hundred delegates, with additional officers. Their meetings drew about fifty reporters and fifty telegraph operators and required about fifty pages. These modest numbers meant that every sizable city in the United States had at least one hall that could accommodate such a convention. Before state primaries and caucuses began to shape national presidential campaigns after 1912, nineteenth-century conventions decided party nominees for president and vice president, often through multiple ballots.[92] In both parties there were advocates for limiting the scope of conventions to delegates and the press, which would report proceedings to the nation. But, Adler wrote, "the American people will have none of this. From East and West, from North and South they come, intent upon seeing and hearing the great and honored leaders of their parties, eager to shout and to cheer as their political idols give utterance to their campaign cries and watchwords."[93] Given such popular enthusiasm, the size of a convention, including supporters from all over the country, was of great symbolic significance, vividly conveying the national breadth of each political party.

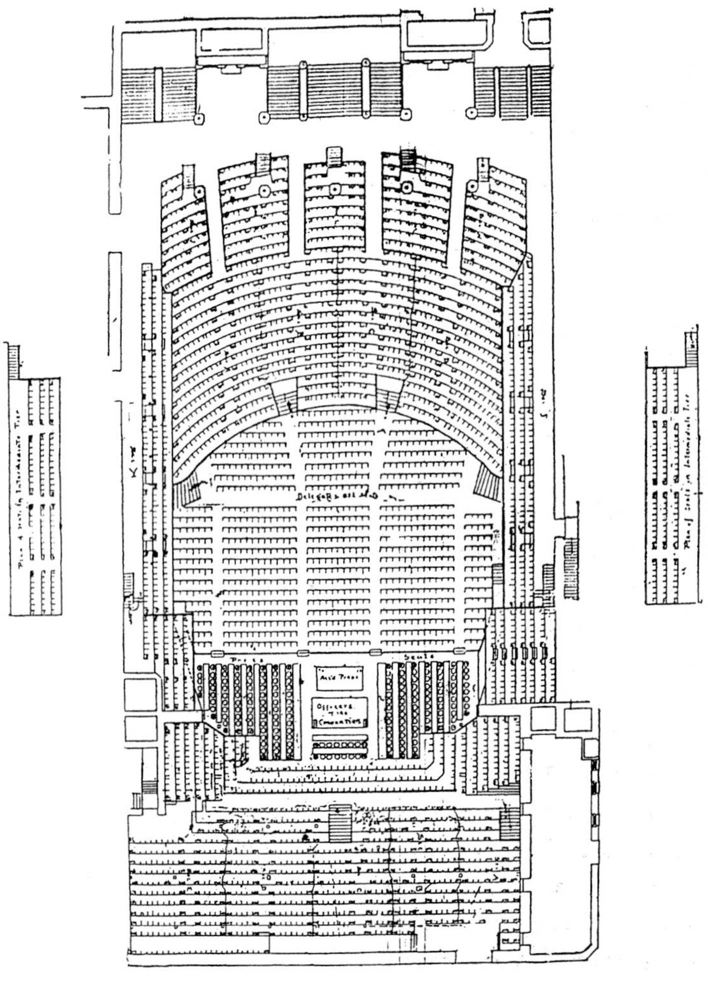

The host city's local party committee met the convention's expenses, but the national party committee directed architectural arrangements, acting as Adler and Sullivan's clients for fitting up the Auditorium in 1888. The event's priorities determined the convention hall's plan (fig. 109). There was minimal distinction between areas that would become the stage and the audience hall of the finished theater. Instead, seats

Figure 109

Auditorium Theater as Republican national convention hall, June 1888, main floor plan showing officers' platform on central stage, flanked by press seats, with seating for state delegates in parquet area in front of stage and for alternates behind in the parquet circle area. Ticketed visitors sat in the rear balcony and galleries (not shown on this plan). From *Chicago Tribune*, 20 June 1888.

surrounded a series of platforms for officers of the convention near the room's front center at the foot of the stage. Flanking these platforms to left and right were the press seats, also on the raised stage. These platforms had to be high enough for party officials to see the face of every delegate. In front of the stage, in the floor area that became the finished theater's parquet, there were seats for delegates grouped by states, with broad aisles for constant intercommunication. Pneumatic tubes conveyed messages from the central platform to offices of the telegraph companies on either side of the hall.

Seats in the theater's parquet circle area were for the alternates to the state delegations, while ticketed visitors occupied seats in the rear balcony and galleries. There were also seats on the stage and a stage gallery behind the speakers' platform. There sat the national committee and "distinguished guests," meaning the party's current or former governors, congressmen, judges, military officers, and their families. Those viewing the stage saw the entire leadership of the party displayed together. There were also extensions of parquet and parquet circle seating around the sides of the hall, so that 9,000 seats were brought as close together as possible. In St. Louis's exposition building in 1888, the Democrats met in a room 400 feet long, with delegates unable to hear distinctly through its length. In the Auditorium the spatial core of the delegates' seating was only 80 by 90 feet, within the hall's dimensions of 120 by 260 feet including the stage. No delegate's seat was more than 175 feet from the speakers' platform. Of the plan one observer wrote: "Without crowding it makes the audience compact and brings everyone within hearing distance." Moreover, the sight lines were "so perfect that the space for the delegates may be seen from any seat in the building," equalizing the desirability of seats for different state groups near and far from the stage.[94]

When used as a convention hall, the Auditorium Theater had to enable vocal and visual communication, especially when a presidential nomination was being decided. As Adler wrote, "Every member wants to see every delegate and all the officers and to hear every word." Over the convention floor of about 7,000 square feet, "a speaker in whom the entire audience is interested may stand up anywhere within that area and may face in almost any direction."[95] Since walls could not be placed near all delegates to contain and help project their voices, "it becomes necessary as far as this can be done, to utilize the audience itself as a sound conserver and deflector."[96] With this principle in mind, Adler steeply banked seating rows in accord with Scott Russell's isacoustic curve. Adler noted that isacoustic lines of seating tiers are almost identical with good sight lines. Yet these needed to be checked in drawings, studying at least three sight lines from different individual seats in a given seating section to ensure good views, as Scott Russell had recommended.[97]

Adler tested the convention hall's acoustic properties by going to the remotest seat of the highest gallery, 180 feet from the stage, and talking with others near the chairman's desk on the stage. With their voices pitched just above conversational tone, they could hear each other distinctly. Yet the real test came after the convention started, when the hall was filled with voices and spectators, whose collective

Figure 110

Auditorium Theater as Republican national convention hall, June 1888, at demonstration following announcement of Benjamin Harrison's unanimous nomination. From Lew Wallace, *Life of Gen. Benjamin Harrison* (Hartford, Conn.: S. S. Scranton, 1888).

presence also cut reverberation time, deadening sound (fig. 110). Shaped as a compact amphitheater rather than as a long rectangle, the horseshoe tiers of seating rose on all sides, "from every point of which the spectator looks down upon the delegates and speakers' stand, focused at the bottom of this human crater." Responsive shouts of approbation or condemnation bespoke the universal audibility of remarks and exchange. As one account of the proceedings noted, "The spectacle of this building completely filled is an inspiring one. There is always a peculiar magnetism in great bodies of people when moved by a common purpose, but in this building, where the difficulties of distance are obviated, this magnetism is all the more contagious. Enthusiasm does not break out at a certain point and travel by slow contagion, but seems to be spontaneous. Applause, laughter, and all expressions of popular sentiment follow the occasion as quickly and sharply as a thunder clap follows lightning overhead."[98]

In this way the Auditorium Theater's architecture contributed to the sense of cohesion and unity that was, then as now, one of the principal purposes of a national convention. In 1888 the issue of party unity was paramount for the Republicans, who in 1884 had lost the presidency for the first time in twenty-four years and whose constituencies supported nineteen candidates for president going into the convention of 1888. Only on the convention's sixth day, and on its eighth ballot, was Benjamin Harrison finally nominated. Immediately the nomination was made unanimous, and the convention broke into an enthusiastic demonstration (fig. 110). Adler and Sullivan's interior helped to reunify a party previously divided on platform and personalities. The visitors also identified the Auditorium Building with Chicago. Of the 100,000 who sought admission to the convention's day sessions, 9,000 were admitted. One visiting editor concluded that each of them "will never forget the impression wrought upon him, while the scene at night, under the flood of brilliance that filled it, is simply defiant of description. To say that the city distinguished itself in the arrangements, the finish and the decorations is saying much in little. Her matchless audacity of enterprise was probably never better illustrated."[99]

The unfinished convention hall, with its massive walls encasing huge spans, recalled both a modern structure like a railroad bridge and a traditional monument like a cathedral. Both metaphors were operative for Peck and his architects. Sullivan waxed eloquent in his accounts of his own enthusiasm for the major railroad bridges of his time, especially the Eads Bridge (1868–1874) at St. Louis, whose three segmental steel-arched spans of 520 feet epitomized the modern structural ideal of the later nineteenth century. The Auditorium Theater's uncovered elliptical trusses spanned only 118 feet, but their sweeping arched shape echoed that of a bridge, so that some critics "compared the body of the hall to a railway arch."[100] Yet Peck and his allies envisioned the Auditorium Theater as an exalted communal and national gathering place, created as a civically philanthropic if not religious monument. Garczynski's commemorative book on the Auditorium invoked the cathedral metaphor for the whole building and for the theater. The idea of the medieval cathedral as a historical model for a modern tall building recurred in the description of Adler and Sullivan's unbuilt project for the Odd Fellows Temple of 1891.[101] To later observers, the finished Auditorium Theater, as an interior designed by Sullivan, conveyed these dual associations of structural modernity and spiritual monumentality.

The Auditorium Theater and Sullivan's Theory of Architecture

The Auditorium Theater took its final form between June 1888 and December 1889. Sullivan, together with a group of collaborating artists and craftsmen, designed its system of ornamental, coloristic, and pictorial surfaces. Although he had not been to Europe since his return from the École des Beaux-Arts in May 1875, Sullivan, like Adler, was well informed about major European theaters. Sullivan greatly admired Wagner, in an era when many traveling Americans were among the non-Germans who went to see performances at Bayreuth. Yet he also knew the Paris Opera from his period of study at the École in 1874–1875. Its exterior had been visible from 1867, near the rue de la Paix, where he recalled his pleasure in strolling and window shopping. The Paris Opera's opening as a theater on 5 January 1875, before Sullivan sailed back to the United States, was a national event. He owned Charles Garnier's two-volume folio monograph on the building, published in 1880, and similar publications on the opera houses of Vienna (1883) and Frankfurt (1885). Yet there is no indication that Peck wished Sullivan to imitate these famous halls in ornamental display. Instead, the Auditorium Theater was to be relatively simple in its decorative treatment, just as its exterior eschewed the ornamental elaboration of a European state opera house. Peck contrasted the private Auditorium with such European halls, most of which had "grand approaches and splendid vestibules, embellished with costly frescoes and statuary which governments have paid for."[102] He reminded his stockholders that the Paris Opera cost more than twice as much as the Auditorium and took thirteen years to build, yet its seating capacity was only half that of the Auditorium Theater, which rose in three years. Peck stressed his building's economy and functionality, much as Sullivan later advocated that form follow function. As one local observer wrote, "Compared with the greatest European auditoriums [Chicago's] will fall below many of them in costly ornamental display, but will excel any edifice in the world used for like purpose in seating capacity and utility."[103]

As Peck and Adler saw the Auditorium Theater's planning to be different from major European models, so Sullivan saw the theater's interior as departing from such precedents. This idea was consistent with his theoretical position in architecture, which he first articulated about the time he and Adler received the Auditorium commission. The huge project undoubtedly stimulated Sullivan to publicly define his own artistic credo. He announced his ideas in a reading of his extended prose poem "Inspiration" at the annual meeting of the Western Association of Architects in Chicago in November 1886. Sullivan was then revising the Auditorium's exterior design, the month before he and Adler were confirmed as the building's architects. As president of the Illinois Association of Architects, Adler gave the welcoming address to the Western Association. He said that he "felt grateful for the privilege of being part, not of a renaissance, but of a naissance in architecture, for he recognized the birth of an American style of architecture, developed by the wants, conditions and limitations of the nineteenth century."[104]

What Adler saw as an original development, later histories characterize more as the creative adaptation of the European Romanesque style to meet new American needs. Adler referred to the work of architects born and trained in Europe who had made their home in the United States, bringing their methods and styles with them. Their work he found admirable and influential, though not American in character. As noted earlier, Adler saw this quality in buildings by United States architects, such as Richardson's Marshall Field Wholesale Store, where "this European influence has been thoroughly Americanized. How thoroughly American is Post's Italian of the Produce Exchange . . . . How American is the application of Indian motifs in Root's ornamentation of the Rookery Building. How American are Sullivan's reminiscences of the training of the École des Beaux Arts. This growth of a quarter of a century has called out unstinted praise from European critics."[105] Adler's reference to his partner Sullivan's position was the only one in which he did not mention a specific building. Adler and Sullivan's Auditorium was to be their contribution to this development. As the decorator for the Republican national convention had said, "Nearly all the Auditorium decorations are a novelty. The building itself is a novelty."[106]

The period of the Auditorium's design and construction (1886–1890) corresponded to Sullivan's initial development as an architectural theorist. His essay "Inspiration" was the first of three major statements of these years. It preceded his essays "Style" (1888) and "The Artistic Use of the Imagination" (1889). All were closely related in their themes. Earlier Sullivan had published a shorter statement titled

"Characteristics and Tendencies of American Architecture" (1885), in which his main emphasis was on the idea of a national style of architecture emerging as a slow growth.[107] Yet, more distinctly than Adler, who framed the issue as one of American architects' adapting historical European types, Sullivan was committed to an architecture that would be an original expression of United States national character, arising "in sympathy with the emotions latent or conspicuous in our people."[108]

In the essay "Inspiration," Sullivan proposed that the art of a nation emerges from a widespread desire for such expression interpreted by a sympathetic artist. Rather than adapting historical styles, Sullivan proposed "that a spontaneous and vital art must come fresh from nature, and can only thus come."[109] In his discussions of nature, Sullivan referred to nonhuman botanical life and humanity's collective life as deriving from the same creative force. Thus he wrote: "And so the living present, firm-rooted in the past, grows within its atmosphere, takes on local coloring of identity, fulfills its ordained rhythm of growth, condenses its results, and, waning hour by hour in all that marks its physical, mesmeric presence, fading into the inevitable twilight, it too becomes in turn a stratum of the fertile past."[110] Seeing human society as a part of the natural living world, Sullivan concluded that "to typify in materials harmoniously interblended rhythms of nature and humanity . . . indicates the deepest inspiration and the most exalted reach of art."[111] For him the most profound rhythm found in human and nonhuman nature was that of growth and decay, an eternal cycle of life and death, signified by the annual rotation of the seasons.

In "Style," Sullivan defined this term not with respect to historical styles of architecture but as a general idea of style as the essence of any living thing, whether human or nonhuman. Sullivan's view recalled that of Hippolyte Taine (1828–1893), professor of aesthetics and history of art at the École des Beaux-Arts when Sullivan studied there. In his keynote lecture "The Nature of a Work of Art," Taine had proposed that the imitative arts of painting and sculpture represented the essential character of living and inanimate objects as their subjects. The artist's creativity centered on his power to perceive the essential character of an object and to accentuate that essence in its representation. As Taine argued, "In nature, this essential character is simply dominant; it is the aim of art to render it predominant."[112] Taine's idea of an object's essential identity corresponded to Sullivan's idea of its style. Sullivan concluded: "It is the function of intuition, the eye of identity, the soul, to discern the identity of truth inherent in all things."[113] For Taine, the artist's ability to perceive such essential identity depended on his capacity not for analytical reasoning but for emotional response: "There is one gift indispensable to all artists . . . . In confronting objects the artist must experience *original sensation;* the character of an object strikes him, and the effect of this sensation is a strong peculiar sensation."[114] In his essay "Style," Sullivan similarly wrote that an artist's emotional instinct was the faculty that enabled him to sympathetically comprehend a living object's essential identity, or its style.

In the last of his early cycle of theoretical essays, "The Artistic Use of the Imagination," Sullivan exchanged his idea of the artist for that of the poet, whom he distinguished from the artist by the quality of reflection. The poet's reflection on experience, as distinct from the artist's response to objects, enabled the poet to arouse the sympathetic thoughts of the reader. He wrote that "it is this capacity to excite responsive imagination that characterizes a poet."[115] For Sullivan, the model individual poet of his period was Walt Whitman, whose poem "There Was a Child Went Forth" Sullivan read in his talk as an example of his essay's thesis.[116] In this light the aesthetic intuition of the artist and the social function of the poet became Sullivan's twin aspirations as an architect. The first had to do with shaping buildings as living objects whose style conveyed their essential identity. The second concerned the prophetic and cultural function of architecture for society, as both its source and its audience. By 1889, as his work on the Auditorium interiors was being completed, Sullivan developed this dual view of his role as an architect, one that combined an artist's responsiveness to nature with a poet's capacity for conveying his reflections on the collective experience of his American contemporaries.

Though Sullivan usually addressed his talks and essays to other architects, nowhere in his writings of 1886–1889 on inspiration, style, or imagination did he speak explicitly of the architect or of architecture. These theoretical statements articulated his approach to architecture metaphorically, speaking of the complementary roles of the artist and the poet, as if Sullivan's most fundamental ideas about his work were independent of the possibilities and limitations of his own medium. Only in his writings of the 1890s, when his professional and creative life had developed further, did he explicitly connect his ideas of the later 1880s to architecture. He did so in general terms in a statement of 1899 to younger architects, titled "The Modern Phase of Architecture." There Sullivan stressed the concept of the architect as "a poet and an interpreter of the national life of his time." He advised younger colleagues:

> If you take the pains truly to understand your country, your people, your day, your generation; the time, the place in which you live; if you seek to understand, absorb, and sympathize with the life around you, you will be understood and sympathetically received in return . . . .
>
> The greatest poet will be he who shall grasp and deify the commonplaces of our life—those simple, normal feelings which the people of his day will be helpless, otherwise, to express—and here you have the key with which, individually, you may unlock, in time, the portal of your art.[117]

This idea likely represented Sullivan's approach to the Auditorium's design, his first major commission to engage the period's broad social ideals. In this credo Sullivan recalled the thought of Taine, who argued that the arts of the past had emerged within the context of their era's social and intellectual conditions. Along these lines, Taine offered extended analyses of art in ancient Greece, Renaissance

Italy, and the Netherlands in the seventeenth century. According to him, in each of these eras the artist had first perceived the period's essential characteristics, then offered vivid interpretations of them in a body of work that was authentic and unique to its place and time. As Sullivan wrote in 1901, "The Parthenon was, in fact, the Greek nature, mind, heart, soul, beliefs, hopes, aspirations, known, felt and interpreted by a great Greek artist, and translated by him into an objective symbol of Greek civilization."[118] Sullivan aspired to create a comparably compelling interpretation of American civilization in the Auditorium.

Yet Sullivan went beyond Taine in one important respect that had a direct bearing on his approach to socially signifying works such as the Auditorium. For Sullivan, the role of the architect was not simply to characterize or reflect a society's existing conditions; he was to interpret those conditions to which his people aspired as a desirable cultural ideal. The architect was first to discern such aspirations in the life of his times, even if they were not fully apparent, and then to make these ideals visible in built form. In 1901, writing "What Is an Architect?", one of his Kindergarten Chats, Sullivan concluded that the architect was "a poet who uses not words but building materials as his medium of expression." He wrote, "To vitalize building materials, to animate them collectively with a thought, a state of feeling, to charge them with a subjective significance and value, to make them a visible part of the genuine social fabric, to infuse into them the true life of the people, to impart to them the best that is in the people, as the eye of the poet, looking below the surface of life, sees the best that is in the people—such is the real function of the architect."[119]

The collective, civic, and even national character of the Auditorium made it the first building where Sullivan had the opportunity to realize art as an expression of a people's identity. Indeed, this project likely shaped his credo. Sullivan's program as an artist-poet paralleled Peck's as a client who saw the Auditorium as a statement of regional cultural achievement and social goals. In June 1888, during the Republican national convention, one account noted that the Auditorium's "main object and function was to be that of affording a meeting ground for the people, where the working masses could experience the influence of the finest music."[120] As the embodiment of Peck's ideal for the city, the Auditorium was the epitome of Sullivan's concept of architecture as the interpretation of a people's identity, defined in terms of high capitalist philanthropy. Like the Parthenon, the Auditorium's eloquence as the interpretation of a culture gave it significance as a work of art. It was this level of aspiration that Sullivan brought to this work of architecture, one that Chicagoans compared to major monuments of earlier Western civilization.[121]

Opera as Spectacle and the Auditorium's Stage

What enabled the Auditorium Theater to fulfill its distinctive function as a civic cultural center was not only the form of its audience hall, but also the design of its stage. The stage's dimensions and equipment were crucial to the building's success as a theater for grand opera. In the late nineteenth century, opera came to distinguish itself from other types of music and drama in the size of its choral casts and the splendor of its stage settings. The Metropolitan's first season of performances in 1883–1884 initiated a national taste for operatic spectacle. The Met's scenery had done more than its singers to differentiate its productions from those of the New York Academy of Music. To present such performances, the Met's stage had to be among the largest in the world. When Henry Abbey first brought the Met's company to Haverly's Theater in Chicago in January 1884, he opened with a performance of Gounod's *Faust,* the opera that had opened the Met's inaugural season in October 1883. Yet Abbey found that Haverly's stage was not large enough to accommodate the complete corps de ballet or the full chorus employed at the Met. As a result, "the great ballet scene was entirely omitted"[122] and "the chorus was dreadfully crowded upon the stage." Abbey was also unable to use any of the large scenery created for the opera when he had staged it at the Met three months earlier.[123]

Taste for elaborate scenic effect in opera developed in the 1880s partly in response to performances of Wagner's works at Bayreuth. His Festspielhaus was inaugurated in August 1876 with a spectacular presentation of *Der Ring des Nibelungen.* One of Wagner's most controversial innovations was lowering the orchestra pit below the audience's view into a deep well in front of the stage. As shown in figure 47, the purpose of this device was to bring audience and action close together and so heighten the emotional experience of musical drama. The music itself arose from the orchestra's hidden pit as from a "mystical abyss," creating an illusion heightened by the extensive naturalistic and architectural scenery on stage.[124] The costs of such staging made the total expense of the inaugural production of the Ring cycle at Bayreuth so great that the Festspielhaus had to close, reopening six years later in 1882.

The example of Bayreuth's Wagnerian productions shaped the Metropolitan's operatic program from 1884 to 1891, when Wagner's operas and others in German became the new norm. This program distinguished the Met from the Academy of Music, which continued to feature Italian opera. During the Met's seven German seasons, Wagner's operas made up over half the performances. They were presented with sets, costumes, and staging faithfully copied from performances at Bayreuth. When Anton Seidl, Wagner's protégé at Bayreuth, became conductor at the Met in 1885, he exercised enormous influence on American expectations for opera. Because it did not feature high-priced star performers, German opera was less expensive to produce, so ticket prices could be lowered to fill the house and please the Met's then largely German-speaking, immigrant audience.[125]

Chicago Germans similarly supported a large number of musical events, including the Metropolitan's first Wagnerian tour of the city in January 1885. Chicago audiences had heard Wagner's music before, largely because of the efforts of Theodore Thomas, who did more than anyone else to popularize Wagner for American audiences beginning in the 1870s. Wagner was a particular favorite in Cincinnati, with its large and musically active German population, and Thomas had included Wagnerian selections on festival programs there and at Chicago in 1882 and 1884. Yet, as noted, these pieces were not full operas but orchestral segments. The Met's tour of 1885 presented the full operas of which Thomas's selections were only a part, further educating Chicagoans' tastes for Wagnerian integration of music, drama, and stage spectacle. In summer 1889 Chicago organist Clarence Eddy, who designed and played the Auditorium Theater's instrument, toured European opera houses, churches, and concert halls for four months and stayed a week in Bayreuth. There Eddy, in the words of a friend, was able to "drink from the pure source of unadulterated Wagner music in its most aesthetical form, and with all the purifying surroundings, the High Church of pure music."[126]

In this context Sullivan's own exposure to Wagner and enthusiasm for his music was not untypical of the 1870s, just as Walt Whitman's enthusiasm for opera in New York had been characteristic of the 1850s. In his autobiography, Sullivan recalled that he had first heard Wagner's music at a Theodore Thomas concert in Philadelphia in summer 1873. Sullivan wrote of his own reactions to that concert: "During the course of the program he had become listless, when of a sudden came the first bars of a piece so fiery, that, startled, all alert, he listened in amazement to the end. What was this? It was new—brand new. The program now consulted, said: *Vorspiel*, Third Act, Lohengrin—Richard Wagner. Who was Richard Wagner? Why had he never heard of him? He must look him up; for one could see at a glance that this piece was a work of genius."[127] In Chicago the following year (1873–1874), Sullivan wrote that he attended the concerts of Hans Balatka at Turner Hall on the city's North Side. In these Sunday afternoon events Balatka introduced Wagner to Chicago. Sullivan soon became a devotee of the Wagnerian canon: *Die Meistersinger von Nürnberg, Tristan und Isolde, Der Fliegende Holländer,* and musical episodes of the Ring cycle—all then new to Sullivan. He wrote: "As piece after piece was deployed, before his open mind, he saw arise a Mighty Personality—a great Free Spirit, a Poet, a Master Craftsman, striding in power through a vast domain that was his own, that imagination and will had bodied forth out of himself. Suffice it—as useless to say—Louis became an ardent Wagnerite."[128] Wright recalled of Sullivan in the era of the Auditorium, "He was absorbed in what seemed extravagant worship of Wagner at the time . . . . He would often try to sing the leitmotifs for me and describe the scenes to which they belong as he sat at my drawing board."[129]

To Sullivan and his contemporaries, Wagner was a revolutionary figure in musical art and thus a model for Sullivan's own aims in architecture. As a New York editor wrote of Bayreuth's opening in 1876, earlier operatic composers had added incrementally to the Italian tradition. Yet with such works as his Ring cycle, Wagner "has scattered the old theories to the winds, and initiated a system so new that, saving the fact that the notes of the diatonic scale are the same to all, he seems to have but little else in common with them. Away have gone recitatives, arias, cavatinas, nicely adjusted trios, quartets and concerted pieces, and all the other ordinary machinery of operatic representation. In their place is a new and strange musical language. If this is accepted by the world, then farewell to Italian opera, for its day is done."[130] Wagner's break with operatic conventions made him an archetype of the modern artist in the nineteenth century. Yet his contemporaries also saw his oeuvre as providing a vantage point for estimates of music's previous achievement. As Walter Damrosch wrote: "Not to say that our appreciation of the olden masters suffers thereby; on the contrary, looking backward on the line from Wagner's position, we first arrive at a real sense of the logical sequence with which all the arts, music, in especial, have developed."[131] Sullivan may have seen Wagner in this way: as an artist who both transformed and summarized his medium's history. From the time of his youthful visit to the Sistine Chapel, probably early in 1875, Sullivan saw Michelangelo in similarly heroic terms, as a master who was both revolutionary in style and encompassing of history. The work of Michelangelo and Wagner came to represent Sullivan's high standard for his own achievements in architecture. The Auditorium Theater gave him his first opportunity to realize such aspirations on a grand public scale.

More specifically, Wagner's writings on musical drama as a kind of *Gesamtkunstwerk* or total artwork, where music, drama, poetry, and spectacle created a unified effect on the psyche of the audience, provided Sullivan and his contemporaries with a model for comparable possibilities in architecture. In his paper of 1883 titled "The Art of Pure Color," John Wellborn Root imagined the artist-architect of the future who would combine a love for and knowledge of the properties of color in visual art, the science of color perception, and the analogy of color to music, where different colors corresponded to the range of musical effects or orchestral instruments. Root envisioned that such a color artist could accomplish "the complete unification of the arts for which Wagner labored."[132] When the Auditorium Theater was completed, it not only exhibited a coloristic unity but brought architectural effects together with mural painting, poetic inscriptions, and musical drama performed on its stage. In introducing Sullivan's own description of the theater, one of his contemporaries praised the room as a "total artwork," invoking the Wagnerian ideal.[133]

The new Wagnerian canon did not ultimately displace the popularity of Italian opera with American audiences, who delighted in the latter's tradition of vocal display. Although Wagner's works had been included among the thirteen productions of the Chicago Grand Opera Festival of 1885, Peck refused to imitate the Metropolitan's conversion to an all-German program highlighting Wagner. In September 1888, as the Auditorium's Theater was being completed, Peck was asked whether the new facility would confine itself to any particular type of opera or drama. He replied, "No, sir. This enterprise is a broad one from the foundation to the tower. All classes and all languages—English, German and Italian opera—will receive equal recognition and will find a home on the Auditorium stage."[134] At the project's beginning, the Auditorium's stage had been announced as second in size only to that of Milan's La Scala. The stage (originally planned as 120 feet wide and 70 feet deep) was to be larger than the Metropolitan's; but as Peck's building developed, the adjacent hotel's public rooms expanded so that the stage shrank in area below announced estimates. It was reduced to minimally acceptable dimensions of 98 feet wide between the side walls and 62.5 feet deep from the curtain line to the rear wall (fig. 99). In 1888, during building, Peck thought that "the stage of the Metropolitan Opera House in New York [101 feet wide by 86 feet deep] is slightly deeper but not so wide." The Auditorium had "room on the stage for an ensemble of over six hundred if necessary, a number which was presented during the opera festival three years ago."[135]

The different social intentions of Cady's and Adler's theaters underlay their approaches to designing the stage and its equipment. Although opera's hallmark in the late nineteenth century was its elaboration of spectacle through lavish scenery and costumes, spatial and technical provision for such productions developed slowly. Neither the Met nor the Auditorium originally had a permanent opera company that would need more storage space than the traveling companies for which both theaters had been planned. The Met staged a different opera every night, but because of a tight site Cady's stage was less deep than those in European theaters. There had been little room for storing scenery, which had to be moved outdoors onto Seventh Avenue through the tall door backstage or taken to warehouses around the city, thus increasing costs.[136] In the Auditorium, Adler provided storage spaces above, below, and beside the stage to hold the theater's initial complement of 150 drops (made in Vienna) and full scenery for thirty famous operas, with over 300 set pieces. This set of scenery was "after the plan of that of the Grand Opera House, Paris."[137]

In opera houses, one key question for stage design was how to ease multiple scenic transformations during and between acts of a production. In the Metropolitan this had been accomplished with a stage whose 86-foot depth was sufficient for ten backdrops that could be raised from or lowered into a sinkage of 30 feet below the stage, which Cady had planned as the main storage for drops. Movement of scenery and stage setting was done manually by stagehands, without any counterweights or powered machinery. These operations took time, especially between acts. Soprano Lilli Lehmann recalled that "every change turned into a trial of patience."[138] Yet lengthy intervals allowed for extended social visits among boxholders. On opening night, Gounod's *Faust* was performed in five acts, with four long intermissions to enable visiting between boxes.[139]

Since social visiting among the elite in boxes was not to be as crucial in Chicago's Auditorium Theater, the time interval between acts was regarded as more a delay than an occasion. Adler wrote: "Nothing is more annoying to American audiences than the excessively long waits between acts so characteristic of operatic performances on a large scale as we know them on the American stage."[140] To speed handling scenery within the Auditorium stage's area, Adler proposed "as far as possible to make transformations by upward and downward movement of stage paraphernalia, by which means the horizontal dimensions of the stage can be minimized, although great depth below and height above the stage floor would become

Figure 111

Kautsky brothers, Asphaleia Gesellschaft, Vienna, hydraulic system for raising and lowering sections of stage and canvas roll for varied painted panoramas as backdrops, adapted to the Auditorium Theater in 1888. From *Engineering* (London), 25 September 1896. Courtesy of the Watkinson Library, Trinity College, Hartford, Connecticut.

essentials."[141] He devised a set of counterweights to help raise drops above the stage into a rigging loft 95 feet high, reducing the time and number of stagehands for these operations. All the sheaves, pulleys, and bearings were iron, and the twelve miles of cable were flexible steel. Adler also adapted a hydraulic system for raising and lowering sections of the stage to simulate varied terrain or moving on water. This system, developed by the Asphaleia Gesellschaft of Vienna after the Ring Theater fire of 1881, both reduced the hand labor of stage setting and lessened the danger of fire by being made of iron (fig. 111).[142] Adler, Peck, and John Bairstow, the theater's stage carpenter, toured European opera houses in the late summer of 1888 to inspect stage mechanisms and contracted for manufacture of an Asphaleia system like that in the Budapest Opera House.

In the Auditorium, twenty-six of these hydraulic lifts could raise varied sections of scenery from below the stage (fig. 97). Modification of the Asphaleia system enabled the Auditorium's lifts to be quicker acting than those in Budapest, further reducing the time needed for stage setting between acts. The stage could be raised or lowered, in whole or in part, so that "all the improvements of the celebrated double stage of the Madison Square Theatre in New York will be incorporated . . . . One complete 'set' can be arranged while another is in use, and will be raised into position at the instant when wanted. A feature of the stage mechanism will be that when the curtain rises no stage will be displayed, but the 'set' will be elevated entire in full view of the audience, with the artists upon it."[143] The Kautsky brothers of Vienna, who had created the Asphaleia system, also built and painted the Auditorium Theater's original scenery to work with the stage's mechanical equipment. After three years of its operation, Adler wrote of the Auditorium's modified Asphaleia system: "With stage hands one third in number those required for similar work at the Metropolitan Opera House all changes and transformations are made quickly and smoothly and there has never yet been a case where the actors have waited for the stage."[144]

Adler's statement reminds us that there were labor issues not only in the construction trades but also in the theaters of the period. In Chicago the trade group that included the stagehands and stage carpenters was the Theatrical Mechanics' Association, sometimes called the Theatrical Mechanical Association, which began publishing its local newsletter in 1881. The Auditorium's adoption of the Asphaleia system meant a high initial cost for this equipment yet greatly decreased costs for stage labor over time, much as mechanized techniques had reduced dependence on hand labor in the building trades. Such changes drew resistance from an organized workforce in the theaters, just as they had done in the realm of construction. At the Auditorium this issue surfaced over the question of the sets used as backdrops for operatic scenes. Traditionally, to portray different weather and different times of day, many "sky borders" were built by stage carpenters and changed by stagehands. These were so named because they were skirts of canvas that hung above and behind other stage scenery, completing the stage picture visible to the audience with their image of outdoor conditions. Unfortunately, these "sky borders" had long been seen as ineffectual in conveying the intended illusions of nature. To enhance the impression of realism, the Auditorium's adaptation of the Asphaleia stage included a horseshoe-shaped canvas roll (300 feet long by 75 feet high) curving around the rear and sides, painted by the Kautsky brothers, showing panoramas of the sky in various seasons and weathers. As seen in figure 111, this horizonlike backdrop was "to produce the illusion of the immensity of the heavens."[145] It required only stage carpenters for installation and a few stagehands for rolling the canvas to change the backdrop, in open scene, either gradually or quickly as the action of the play demanded. One account of the Auditorium's "modern stage setting" noted that "this reform was attempted many years ago at Booth's Theatre in New York, but through the opposition of stage carpenters and other mechanics who clung to the old customs it proved abortive."[146] Thus, through hydraulic floor lifts and a rolling backdrop canvas, the Asphaleia system enabled the Auditorium Association to minimize dependence on a unionized workforce in the operation of the completed theater, much as Peck had done in his building's external construction.

Sullivan's Design for the Theater's Interior

The panoramic Asphaleia backdrop created a naturalistic illusion of open nature around the stage, a theme Sullivan pursued in designing the Auditorium Theater's interior. In this huge public hall he had an opportunity to develop a system of decorative forms on a scale that would not recur in his lifetime. As Frank Lloyd Wright recalled, Chicago's Auditorium "was entirely Adler's commission and more largely Adler's own building than Sullivan's—where its constitution and plan were concerned. The dramatic expression of the interior was Sullivan's."[147] George Elmslie, another of Sullivan's principal assistants, asserted: "The interior is pure Sullivan in decorative form allied with shapes devised for best acoustic results and how superb they are! Sullivan was aided in the working out of these forms by Adler who was, much more than Sullivan ever pretended to be, an expert on acoustics. The two men had the give and take process most amiably adjusted."[148] Given the space's acoustically innovative shape, Sullivan chose to modify the conventions of ornament and iconography then prevailing in such opera houses as the Metropolitan. His design may have been a kind of corrective rethinking of interiors like the Met's, whose decorative program had been criticized at its opening. Sullivan's forms asserted a new character for a major civic theater that conveyed Peck's programmatic aims.

In the Metropolitan and the Auditorium, the chief decorative effect derived from the overall color treatment, which depended on the house's lighting scheme. In a theater for opera, house lights had to be dim enough to focus attention on the stage yet bright enough for display and observation among the audience. During the Metropolitan's German seasons, wealthy boxholders insisted that the house lights be kept up throughout performances so that women's costumes and jewelry would be visible throughout the house. Yet those not seated in boxes, including many German immigrants who were more keyed on the performances, wanted the lights dimmed so they could see stage effects better.[149] In the Auditorium, Adler equipped the stage with powerful electric illumination to ensure the drama's visibility. It was the more subtle scheme of lighting in the house beyond the stage that was most closely related to Sullivan's architecture.

As Adler described, light-colored surfaces reflected light while dark colors set off evening wear, so the theater architect had to strike a mean between these effects. Sullivan wrote that throughout the Auditorium Building, in each public room, "a single idea or principle is taken as a basis of the color scheme, that is to say, use is made of but one color in each instance, and that color is associated with gold."[150] Sullivan's choice of gold as the building's thematic color took advantage of the innovations of its lighting system. Under the flicker and glare of gaslights, the Met's original interior had been yellow white with gold relief. In the Auditorium, Adler had sought a "uniform and general illumination, a lighting up of shadows under galleries."[151] This theater's softer, more even electric light came from clear glass carbon-filament bulbs each radiating twenty-five watts and eight candlepower. The ratio of electric power (wattage) to luminous intensity (candlepower) was thus higher than in later frosted tungsten-filament bulbs. The Auditorium had the world's largest lighting plant, with 3,500 incandescent bulbs running along the theater's ceiling arches and along the fronts of the balcony and galleries (plates 5 and 6). The light along the arches was "so even, so white and free from shadows, that it resembles a mild sunlight."[152] The scheme of lighting did away with the conventional chandelier in the center of a domed ceiling; instead, arcs of light enveloped the audience as a whole. When dimmed to pinpoints of light, these bulbs resembled jewels. Their effect recalled the renovated McVicker's Theater of 1885, where electric lighting enabled "the fullest appreciation of the most delicate tints and the most subtile gradations."[153]

Like McVicker's, the Auditorium Theater's surfaces were painted an old ivory in subtly graded tones. Over the ivory-toned surfaces, there were areas of twenty-three-karat gold leaf, a substance Peck valued for its permanence and purity, apart from its identification with wealth. Gold leaf and oil colors were used, "thus insuring pure tone and avoiding the frequent renovations which are so costly and so inferior."[154] Working with George L. Healy and Louis J. Millet, Sullivan varied tones on different surfaces, with those nearer the front of the house tinted a bit lighter than those toward the rear. Also, one account noted, "In order to enhance the effect the decorators have painted the left [north] side of the hall a slightly darker tone [than the south side]. The difference is so slight that the average observer would not detect it."[155] Some surfaces had old ivory graded from dark to light; others, ivory and gold intermingled; elsewhere the ivory and gold were kept separate. In crevices of plaster relief such as on the ceiling, a brown stain was used to recall the tone of old ivory.

In describing the Auditorium Theater, Sullivan wrote that "the first principle is that the decoration is architectural, and not a thing in fragments and independent of structural mass and relation."[156] Sullivan's idea appeared most prominently in the ceiling's coloring. As one report noted, "The elliptical arches are treated in a scientific manner. They are dark at the base and light at the springing of the arch. This gives atmosphere and lightness to the arch."[157] One observer wrote on the night of the theater's opening: "Instead of rafters the hall was roofed with ivory and gold and starred with electricity." Under the white-and-gold ribbed vault, "you were not satiated or overpowered by the decorations. In light there is no satiety; and richness was kept from being overpowering because it was expressed in white and gold. It was sumptuous and chaste." In its choice of colors, the Auditorium Theater omitted the deep red surfaces and upholstery often found in opera houses, as if the great hall's interior were to be a symbol of purity within a civic temple of high culture. The prevalence of white also contrasted with red as the color then associated with working-class radicalism. Rather than having a fixed architectural polychromy, the Auditorium's color variation came from the variety of women's costumes, set off against the uniform black of menswear, so that "there sloped back from the parquet a stretch like a flower garden."[158]

As Sullivan's collaborators in the theater's color and ornamental design, Healy and Millet contracted for designing its stained glass in July 1888 and for decorating its surfaces in March 1889, nine months before the theater opened. On Sullivan's recommendation, Peck and his fellow directors gave them full charge of hiring workers, purchasing materials, and executing the interior design. Their principal task was designing the flat ornamental stencils on the ceiling vaults and box faces and the skylights' art glass, through which filtered "a dim and mildly religious light."[159] The skylights were set above and behind the major ceiling arches atop richly stenciled coved vaults of plaster (fig. 104). For each major bay of these skylights, Healy and Millet designed a nine-panel motif, with the center rectangular panel featuring a green brown foliate motif set in a design of interlaced russet, ocher, and yellow tendrils (plate 7). Healy and Millet presumably collaborated with Sullivan on selecting the precise colors for the interior. Flat stenciled ornament of gold leaf (not yet restored) ran along the ceiling arch soffits (fig. 112). Small sections of Healy and Millet's gilded stenciled ornament have been uncovered in recent restoration, as on the rear soffit of the main balcony above the parquet circle toward the hall's south side.

Along the vertical faces of these ceiling arches, Sullivan also designed scores of foliate motifs in cast plaster relief as settings for the projecting lightbulbs. Decorative plasterwork was considered optimal fireproofing for structural elements in

Figure 112

Auditorium Theater as originally completed in 1890, looking south toward frontal boxes and organ screen, showing ornamental gold leaf stenciling on ceiling arches and relief busts of Demosthenes and Shakespeare in arch spandrels at left. Photograph by J. W. Taylor. Courtesy of the Library of Congress.

theaters. When Sullivan helped lead a tour of the building for Chicago's mayor and other notables, they viewed "the work of making the plaster-of-Paris decorations, every bit of which is designed and made right in the building. The process is a very interesting one, and excited much interest and admiration."[160] The ornamental plastering was carried out by the firm of James Legge, who had done the work on McVicker's Theater. Sullivan selected the individual modelers who developed his two-dimensional ornamental drawings into three-dimensional sculpted forms for casting. Legge supervised as many as nine modelers, who created the clay models and casts, working on the second floor of the uncompleted building. Among Legge's modelers Sullivan discovered the Norwegian-born Kristian Schneider, whom Sullivan later employed on other buildings to model his ornament in terra cotta and cast iron. In the Auditorium Theater the restored plasterwork is now visible. The plaster motifs were fashioned by fastening the ornamental casts to a plain plaster rough coat applied to a metal lath. Framed by the cast plaster decoration, the bulbs' light springs from the surrounding ornamental relief. When the room is illuminated the elliptical ceiling arches, with their combination of light, ornament, and color, present an almost magical vista, as if they transcend their material form as planes to become an encompassing luminous vault in space. This effect cannot be grasped from photographs alone but is experienced in the room. As Adler wrote, "The use of richly-modulated plastic surface ornament is an important aid to successful color decoration. It gives a rare interest to even the simplest scheme of color distribution by the introduction of modulations of light and shade, by the constant variation of perspective effects, and by the brilliancy of the protuberant points and edges as they catch and reflect the light."[161]

The Auditorium Theater eschewed the elaborate classical and political iconography of the Paris Opera. The Auditorium's great scale, and its purported ideological distance from such models, warranted an alternative decorative program, equally unlike that found in Chicago's existing theaters. As one account of Sullivan's art noted, "All of the petty ornamentation and excess of pretentious gingerbread work common to the minor theatres are lacking, and in place thereof there is breadth and dignity of treatment that harmonizes with the massive characteristics of the structure."[162] With Peck's approval, Sullivan created a distinct symbolic program for the room that embodied his ideal of architecture as nature. This program appears in many ornamental motifs, such as the plaster relief that framed the light-bulbs and ventilating rondels on the ceiling arches (fig. 113). These Garczynski likened to sunflowers, signifying the theater's locale as a prairie metropolis. On the main balcony Sullivan also repeated interpretations of pods of the milkweed, a plant native to Chicago's region, thereby creating a botanically specific reference to place rather than a variation on a historical style of ornament. As Garczynski wrote, "It is indubitable that there is within these walls an architecture and a decorative art that are truly American, and that owe nothing to any other country or any other time."[163]

Figure 113

Auditorium Theater, after restoration completed in 1967, showing ornamental cast plaster relief on west face of ceiling arches with circular ventilating screens alternating with groups of incandescent bulbs. Photograph by Hedrich-Blessing, 1967. Courtesy of the Chicago Historical Society, HB-31105-K.

Accounts of the opening in 1889 focused on the boxes and their occupants, drawn from many of Chicago's most prominent families. The most elaborate stencils were those on the cast iron faces of the two levels of boxes along the house's sides (figs. 114 and 116). These surfaces were keyed to the idea of boxes as feminine space, in which the front chairs were occupied by women, whose ornate dress and jewelry were described in minute detail in newspaper accounts of the period.[164] The fabrics and gems chosen by individual women in all forty boxes came under the audience's scrutiny as a representative measure of local taste and wealth. In American theaters earlier in the nineteenth century, women hardly ever sat in what was then called the pit, later termed the parquet. Rather, they occupied the boxes around the edge of the house, at once privileged and confined. In this period, Mapleson recalled, every American opera house had a "young ladies' box," subscribed to only by younger women, whose male visitors supplied them with bouquets so that "the front of the young ladies' box is kept constantly furnished with the most beautiful flowers."[165] On the Auditorium's opening night, "the place was pervaded with the fragrance of violets and roses. The flowers of themselves were something wonderful, and the boxes blossomed with them—roses, pink, white, and yellow; priceless orchids, and violets in profusion."[166]

Figure 114

Auditorium Theater, upper north boxes looking east, 1890, showing ornamental stencils on cast iron railing faces and ornamental cast iron pillars and brackets between boxes. From Garczynski, *Auditorium*. Courtesy of the Library of Congress.

Figure 115

Palazzo Fava, Bologna, detail of corbeled loggia in cortile. From John Kinross, *Details from Italian Buildings, Chiefly Renaissance* (Edinburgh, 1882), plate 8. Sullivan had this volume in his library when it was auctioned in 1909.

Boxes Executed in Cast Iron by
THE SNEAD & CO. IRON WORKS,
Louisville, Ky., and Chicago, Ill.

Bologna.
Cortile of Palazzo Fava.

The association of boxes with flowers was consistent with the floral forms of stenciled ornament on the box faces. The upper-level boxes were open to each other, like dress boxes in other opera houses. The decorative cast iron brackets upholding the balcony over these upper boxes recalled brackets or corbels supporting outdoor balconies of Italian villas, as illustrated in a volume in Sullivan's library (fig. 115). He adapted the older architectural form of the corbel in a wholly different context. The role of the upper boxes as a balcony from which to see and be seen opened views of boxholders to each other and to the house. Sullivan treated the lower tiers of boxes differently, with each box framed by a bowed semicircular arch like a private box in other opera houses. As shown in figure 116, the lower boxes had heavy curtains between them and behind them, rather than fixed side and rear walls like traditional private boxes, so that each box could be temporarily enclosed or several boxes could be opened to each other for parties of theatergoers. The columns between all boxes, the spandrels of the lower arcade, and the brackets of the upper boxes were all of ornamental cast iron. Arch spandrels of the lower arcade, where the more prestigious and expensive boxes were, had ornamental relief, echoed in the chair upholstery. Their forms brought to mind "Irish spirals and palmetto leaves

Figure 116

Auditorium Theater, lower north boxes, showing ornamental cast iron spandrels fabricated by Snead and Company Iron Works. Photograph by J. W. Taylor. Avery Architectural and Fine Arts Library, Columbia University in the City of New York.

Figure 117

Joseph P. Birren, drawing of Auditorium Theater looking from lower south boxes toward stage, with scene from Gounod's *Faust* at opening of grand opera season. From *Graphic* (Chicago), n.s., 10 (17 March 1894). Courtesy of the Chicago Historical Society, ICHi-31478.

that spread themselves over the surface as if they were exuberantly happy. Indeed, the spirals seem to be dancing jigs."[167] These forms' allusions to the dance could have been associated with grand operatic ballet or with the use of the theater for balls. Yet their Celtic intricacy also perhaps conveyed Sullivan's ideal of a personal style, since his father, Patrick Sullivan, had taught dancing.[168]

The view up into these arched boxes may be contrasted with the view out from them (fig. 117), published shortly after the Auditorium opened, which shows a series of boxes opened to each other. As Sullivan wrote, the arches partially obstructed views of the stage from these boxes' lateral position within the theater. Yet the arcade also functioned as a screen that somewhat secluded the boxes' occupants from general view. This period image confirms diaries of the time that conveyed the importance of social visiting between boxes within the Auditorium during performances. The screening arches meant that this interaction, important to boxholders, took place in shadowed recesses. One observer of the Auditorium's opening wrote of its boxes: "The dainty nooks were so many settings for elegant displays in the way of unrivaled costumes, jewels, bright eyes, and beaming faces. In their semi-privacy the happy possessors of the boxes were a center of attraction."[169] In their highly visible location, costumes of women boxholders near the stage became the scene "at which formidable batteries of opera glasses were leveled from all parts of the house." This was why lower, more private boxes, screened with arches, drew higher prices when Chicago's wealthy bid for them before the Auditorium's opening opera season in 1889. As a frame for these boxes, Sullivan's ornament had powerful class and gender associations for his contemporaries, just as did boxes in Parisian theaters depicted in paintings of the period. Yet figure 117 shows a freedom of male-female interaction in the Auditorium's relatively open lower boxes not usually found in images of boxholders in Parisian opera houses.[170]

Sullivan had chosen stenciling of gold leaf applied over the ivory tones of the boxes' walls behind the seats. As with Cady's original interior for the Metropolitan Opera House, however, these light colors were soon replaced because they did not adequately set off the costumes of the women in the boxes. In February 1896 Chicagoans learned that in the six years the Auditorium had been open, "there has been but one complaint made regarding the color scheme of the theater as originally designed by Architect Sullivan. This was that the background of the boxes had a tendency to kill the effect of the elaborate costumes worn by those seated in them at every fashionable event. This background is now ivory, but after the house cleaners have finished their labors, decorators are likely to invade the place and change it to one of the lighter shades of red. This had been practically agreed to by Ferdinand Peck, Manager Adams and Architect Sullivan." Adams noted: "A shade of red will be selected as best harmonizing with the gold and ivory tints used in the main body of the house."[171] In this change there was a conflict between Peck's and Sullivan's ideals for the theater as a democratically inclusive hall and the demands of elite social conventions.

Sullivan's interior design culminated in his treatment of the theater's frontal frame for the stage. The ceiling's multiple arches telescope inward to the proscenium, drawing the eye to the reducing curtain, whose decorative plaster facing was set over an iron structure. Elmslie recalled that, in the theater, Wright "did none of the interior decoration except that part framing in the space between the grand opera proscenium and the minor opening."[172] On the reducing curtain's sides are inscribed the names of ten composers: Rossini, Haydn, Schubert, and Berlioz were added to the six named above the Metropolitan's proscenium (Gluck, Mozart, Beethoven, Verdi, Wagner, and Gounod), with one exception: Bach's name replaced Wagner's. A greater variety of names conveyed the Auditorium's broad musical program, which began in December 1889 with a first season of Italian opera. Wagner's portrait, along with Haydn's, does appear in gold relief in the arch spandrels of the organ screen to the stage's left. Sullivan's arched ornamental filigree screened an elaborate instrument, intended to be among the world's finest, built in New York to the specifications of its Chicago organist Clarence Eddy. The corresponding screen to the stage's right masked multistory dressing rooms. The portrait medallions to the stage's right are those of Shakespeare (representing drama) and Demosthenes (representing oratory), the latter perhaps signaling the public lecture program Peck envisioned. The four portrait medallions in the main theater, and two others in the spandrels of the smaller Recital Hall's proscenium, were all designed and modeled by Johannes Gelert (1852–1923), a Danish-born sculptor who immigrated permanently to the United States, coming to Chicago in 1887, where Healy and Millet chose him to work on the Auditorium. Gelert was also known in Chicago as the sculptor of the police force's Haymarket Monument, dedicated on 31 May 1889 at the site where the clash had occurred three years earlier.[173]

Sullivan's scheme of ornament for the reducing curtain is a richly plastic evocation of natural forms. These reliefs recall representations of nature found in operatic sets of the period, as in a scene from Wagner's *Lohengrin* on the Auditorium's stage (fig. 105). Sullivan identified this opera as having a great impact on his appreciation of Wagner.[174] In this view of 1890, the canopy of trees forms an arched frame that reiterates the proscenium's elliptical arch above. At the rear is a distant expanse of landscape receding in perspective toward the painted backdrop showing horizon and sky. The foliage on stage continues the foliate plaster ornament in the reducing curtain framing the stage, linking representation of nature in operatic scenery to the theater's permanent architecture. The naturalistic spatial illusion of an expanse of landscape behind the stage was meant to be convincing. As Adler wrote, "On this stage there are no 'sky borders,' and in fact no 'borders' or 'flies' of any kind. The entire stage is surrounded by the 'horizon,' which is a panoramic representation of the sky in every gradation from clear to extreme cloudiness."[175]

Sullivan's idea that nature provided the common source of inspiration for musical drama and architecture became the unifying symbolic theme for the Auditorium Theater's mural paintings. It was an extraordinary case of an architect's shaping a

PROSCENIUM ARCH DECORATION—AUDITORIUM.

Figure 118

Charles Holloway, mural over proscenium, Auditorium Theater (1889). From *Chicago Daily Inter Ocean*, 11 December 1889.

program of meaning for a major public interior. Sullivan developed these themes from those of his prose poem "Inspiration." In his description of the interior published in the Auditorium Theater's inaugural program, he wrote that the room's murals were to express growth and decadence as the two great cyclic rhythms of nature.[176] Above the proscenium arch, this idea inspired the continuous processional mural of life-size figures on a gold background (plate 5; fig. 118). Perhaps the closest precedent for a proscenium mural of such composition was Charles Lameire's allegorical image "France Welcoming the Nations" at the Palais du Trocadéro, the 5,000-seat concert hall opened for the Paris international exposition of 1878 (fig. 119). In keeping with the theme of the exposition, the first mounted by the nascent Third Republic after the Franco-Prussian War and the Paris Commune, Lameire's mural featured a central enthroned feminine personification of France at the apex, toward which there ascended figures identified with the countries of Europe and their colonies. Though no such overt nationalistic or imperial themes appeared in the Auditorium Theater's mural, the model of the Trocadéro's mural would have been ideologically consistent with Peck's aims because the Trocadéro was intended for a large, popular audience as opposed to the more socially stratified Paris Opera, by then identified with the discredited Second Empire.[177]

The Auditorium Theater's mural was largely the work of the young American artist Charles Holloway (1859–1941), who later recalled that his symbolic theme and compositional plan were selected from a competition administered by Healy and

Millet. Raised and educated in St. Louis, Holloway had come to Chicago in 1879. Though trained as a painter, he learned the art and craft of stained glass and was working as a designer of stained glass for Healy and Millet when he won the Auditorium competition over hundreds of other entrants, including Louis C. Tiffany of New York City. The choice of a midwestern artist underscored Peck's ideal of regional cultural independence. As with the ornamental scheme elsewhere in the building, Peck and the Auditorium's directors approved the choice of Holloway and his program. Holloway painted the original mural in 1889 at age twenty-nine and returned to it forty-four years later in 1932 to restore the oil painting's faded colors. The original mural took several months to paint. To reach Holloway's work station at the level of the proscenium arch, "one climbs high ladders, walks skittishly and timidly along narrow boards over wide reaches of scaffolding, with a terrifying drop staring up from below." Yet there the artist worked "as calmly as if he were in his studio with his canvas on an easel. He is perfectly oblivious to the swaying boards and dizzy heights."[178] Such an implicit comparison to Michelangelo at work on the Sistine Chapel was consistent with Holloway's preference for anatomically heroic seminude figures like those on the Sistine's ceiling, whose overall creation Sullivan had so admired.

As the statement of his mural's theme, Holloway identified the inscription set over the central crowning figure of the Present: "The utterance of life is a song, the symphony of nature." The phrase is thought to have been associated with Sullivan's

Figure 119

Gabriel Davioud (1824–1881), Palais du Trocadéro, built for the Paris international exposition (1878; demolished 1937). Cross section showing mural over proscenium arch by Charles Lameire, titled "La France sous les traits de l'Harmonie accueille les Nations." From *Monographie des palais et constructions diverses de l'exposition universelle de 1878* (Paris, 1882). Courtesy of the Library of Congress.

1886 poem "Inspiration." Unlike paintings over the prosceniums of the Metropolitan and other opera houses, Holloway's mural did not depict Muses signifying inspiration for the production of musical and dramatic art. Instead his composition sought to express "the manifold influence of music on the human mind—the dance, the serenade, the dirge."[179] To Sullivan these effects took their inspiration from deeper rhythms of life and death as constantly cyclical in nature. The idea is represented by a series of human figures depicted through the full curvature of the arch. Years later Holloway described a threefold development of his theme to include the past, or the "Song of Sorrow"; the present, the "Song of Joy"; and the future, the "Song of Hope." Descriptions of the mural as completed in 1889 listed its human figures, to be viewed from right (or south) as one faces the stage, over to the left (north). These begin with the winged figure before a bright fire, at the mural's south end. This image, typifying youth and inspiration, signified the dawn of life or springtime, like an allegro tempo in music or the scherzo movement of a typical symphony. Above this image of youth, on the mural's right arch, from base to crown, there is first a trio of figures signifying music and its inspirations, poetry and the dance. Above this trio are groups of dancers, followed by an allegory of love and its power, showing a male hero receiving a garland from a woman; a mother with a baby at her breast greeting a father returned home from the harvest; a tiger playing with gleeful children; and youthful lovers recumbent on a green near the arch's crown like the brow of a hill. The premodern gender roles thus presented were consistent with the conventions of older musical dramas.

To the left or north side of the mural there is a series of images of decline, beginning near the top with an aged philosopher with one hand on a skull and the other on the head of a disciple at his feet and a martyr bearing a palm branch. Then come typifications of agonized grief and sorrow, with a bereaved wife kneeling by her dead husband and a young man holding a dying companion in his arms. These are followed down the arch's curvature by remorse, represented by a repentant daughter at the feet of her aging mother, then the image of the cross, followed by a group of monks chanting, presumably a dirge. Below these monks, four female figures personify the seasons from spring down to winter, who is sitting apart, with worn face and silver hair. Below winter, the angel-like winged figure at the north (left) end represents twilight and memory. She reaches down to a low fire, whose feeble flame flickers toward its demise like autumn, the season Sullivan likened to an adagio effect in music, or the andante movement of a symphony.

At the proscenium mural's central crown are three figures (fig. 120). Although she holds a lyre, the central figure is not an ancient deity like the Apollo who presided over the Met's proscenium, but a personification of the present, just as Peck believed that the Auditorium would represent "the present and the future, not the corrupted past."[180] Below and to the left of the enthroned crowning figure of the present is the past, holding in her hands a distaff from which the thread of life passes between the strings of the present's lyre and is severed by the shears in the hand of the future, to the right. As he declared in the poem, Sullivan's ideal for the

Figure 120

Holloway, detail of proscenium mural showing figures representing past on right (south), present in center, and future on left (north). Courtesy of the Art Institute of Chicago.

present was a spontaneous and vital art coming fresh from nature rather than from inherited styles. In this spirit, all forty-five figures were painted by Holloway, "who made the sketches from living models posing for each separate figure" so that "everything is true to nature."[181] Unlike the larger-than-life figures over the Met's proscenium, the Auditorium's mural figures are life-size. Hence in one sense their scale makes them plausible intermediaries between human actors on the stage and audience members in the house. Yet in another sense Holloway's procession, with its timeless gold background, represents an archetypal spectrum of music's effects, so that his idealized figural types belong to neither stage nor house. They are literally above diurnal or theatrical realities. Clearly the mural was meant to be seen as a major statement of the theater's goals, yet it does not stand out in its architectural setting. As one observer wrote, "Thousands of the spectators who enter the Auditorium will look admiringly on that work of art, but few will stop to reason out the subject treated there."[182]

The two murals toward the rear sides of the house were to continue the theme of that over the proscenium. The side murals were designed and painted by the French-trained artist Albert Francis Fleury (1848–1924). Originally educated as an architect, Fleury entered the École des Beaux-Arts after the Franco-Prussian War to study painting. His time there overlapped with that of Sullivan and also of Healy and Millet, under whose guidance Fleury worked at the Auditorium. Fleury came to the United States in 1888 to assist his former teacher, Émile Renouf, in making a large commissioned painting of the Brooklyn Bridge. Offers were made to Renouf and Fleury to assist in the Chicago Auditorium's decoration, and Fleury accepted. Like Holloway's mural, Fleury's images were approved by the Auditorium Association's executive committee, headed by Peck.[183]

As an architect, Fleury specialized not only in murals but also in enhancing such paintings' relations to built interiors. Consequently the side murals he made in

Figure 121

Albert Fleury, south mural (Spring Song),
Auditorium (1889). Courtesy of the Art
Institute of Chicago.

Figure 122

Fleury, north mural (Autumn Reverie),
Auditorium (1889). From Garczynski,
Auditorium. Courtesy of the Library of
Congress.

the Auditorium are large (24 feet wide and 20 feet high) and have a perspectival depth of landscape that appears to extend the interior space of the adjacent balconies. They thus recall the illusionistic natural expanse created by scenic backdrops for opera on the frontal stage. Fleury's images of nature were originally illuminated by natural daylight from the art glass skylights over the balcony. As in the proscenium's mural, the south mural depicts spring (fig. 121), while the north shows an autumnal scene (fig. 122). From his youth, Fleury "was always a lover and a close student of nature, and besides he always followed the practice of painting his figures in the open air."[184] He sketched the north mural's scene "from a Wisconsin dell" like the wooded Wisconsin landscapes that Peck enjoyed. The south mural depicts "a scene near Highland Park," a suburb on Chicago's North Shore, emphasizing the Auditorium's regional character.[185]

Each side mural shows a single creative figure or poet who is communing with the season for inspiration. In spring's portrayal a gentle stream winds through a meadow where the trees are newly leafed out and the grass is a fresh, soft green. Above, the sky is suffused with the bright tint of early morning and the awakened birds are flitting about. The season corresponds to the allegretto of a symphony, inspiring the poet to respond with the words inscribed at the painting's base: "O, soft, melodious spring time! First-born of life and love." The north mural shows the pathless wilds in dreary autumn, when the horizon is tinged with the fading light of departed day and overhead the sky is gray and cold. The trees have lost their foliage, and brown, withered leaves lie thick over the ground. Descending into this valley, the poet is moved to utter the refrain inscribed below: "A great life has passed into the tomb and there awaits the requiem of winter's snows."

As Sullivan wrote, "By their symbolism do these mural poems suggest the compensating phases of nature and of human life in all their varied manifestations. Naturally are suggested the light and the grave in music, the joyous and the tragic in drama."[186] Through these murals and their inscriptions, Sullivan stated his personal belief in nature's emotional effects on the individual artist, which he considered analogous to the emotional effect of musical drama on its audiences. In "Inspiration," he referred repeatedly to the sun's daily course across the sky and its repetition through the seasons as a visible measure of nature's cyclic rhythm of growth and decay. Spring and summer, associated with southern sunlight, represented growth, whereas autumn and winter, identified with northern light, embodied decay. Sullivan's poem read: "Through lesser springtime expanding, merging, completing, courses mysterious life, unfolding toward greater, ever greater, ever broadening spring times, successively through these."[187] In his travels by railroad around the United States, Sullivan recalled having "visualized [the country's] main rhythms as south to north, and north to south."[188] Fleury's murals suggested such a meaning for the arches that spanned the Auditorium's ceiling between south (spring) and north (autumn), as if these elliptical forms represented the solar cycle of seasons and years in expanded repetition. The subtle gradation of color over the walls, from lighter on the south to darker on the north, would have reinforced this reading.

Thus, out of the ceiling's functional form as Adler's solution to optimal acoustics for a mass audience, Sullivan developed a program of ornament and images that made the Auditorium's arches into an expansive cosmic allegory comprehensible to such an audience, different from the conventional shallow domes at the Metropolitan and many European theaters. In this way the Auditorium Theater's architecture generated social and cultural meanings of its own, which Sullivan intended to help structure the meaning of the entire theater experience.

The Auditorium Theater's Opening and Critical Reception

The social, political, and cultural agenda that underlay the Auditorium Theater's creation converged in the event of its opening on Monday, 9 December 1889. The arrangements for seating and ceremonies inside the hall itself were carefully orchestrated by Peck as a statement of the building's intentions. For months the theater's interior appearance had been kept a mystery. Peck allowed no one inside, partly to avoid disrupting the work, but also to heighten popular anticipation about the great room's form. His goal was to make the opening a national event of the first importance. The auction of boxes for the inaugural opera season had been so profitable that Peck could lower prices for the thousands of nonbox seats, fulfilling his ideal of first-class music for the people at low prices. Tickets for the opening dedication night were priced far above those for subsequent evenings. however. The least expensive seat for the occasion cost $50, normally the price of a season ticket for a balcony seat. This excluded all but the city's wealthiest, yet many classes converged on the building for the event. As one account noted: "All routes centered at the Auditorium last night. From ten thousand homes came little groups. The rills of the populace poured into the cross-streets. The smaller streams emptied into the great rivers that surged down-town. The rivers plunged into the ocean of people that roared about the massive granite walls. The tide beat against the great structure and crowded beneath its lofty arches."[189]

The opening drew ticket holders from beyond Chicago, accommodated in special trains that ran from outlying communities to the city's multiple railway stations. Specially scheduled trains to the suburbs made commuting to the Auditorium Theater easy on later evenings. Most of the urban audience arrived by carriages, which packed Congress Street and Michigan Avenue through the early evening. Horse-drawn vehicles stood two and even five abreast waiting to deposit their passengers, with onlookers on both sides of the narrow street passage that police had cleared for the carriages. The crowd, estimated at 20,000 to 30,000, included hundreds of frustrated ticket seekers, and many with tickets had to elbow their way from the curb to the great arched entrances. As one observer wrote, "Almost every imaginable phase of life was represented on the sidewalks and in the streets."[190] As seen from atop a house on the south side of Congress Street, the crowd, lit by dim electric arc lights hung above the sidewalk for the occasion, presented "a sea of heads. And the heads moved and swayed like a field of wheat in the wind."[191] Bystanders occasionally hurled jests at the coachmen of the arriving wealthy, many of whom they recognized by sight and greeted loudly by name. Yet most of those on the street were not hostile, and there were no organized political protests. The absence of violent confrontation or leftist demonstration was a measure of relative capitalist control over Chicago in the years after Haymarket. Those outside included a high proportion of poor women who commented on the dress and jewelry of the well-off women alighting from carriages. The spectacle of the Chicago elite's mass arrival had no precedent in local memory. The onlooking mob temporarily possessed the sidewalk along the building, so that the carriage-borne wealthy were not free of jostling until they were inside the main vestibule.

At the opening of his 1903 novel *The Pit*, Frank Norris described such a scene of contrasts on a wintry day at the Auditorium Theater's entrance. Inside the steam-heated vestibule, "the women were, almost without exception, in light-coloured gowns, white, pale blue, Nile green, and pink, while over these costumes were thrown opera cloaks and capes of astonishing complexity and elaborateness. Nearly all were bareheaded, and nearly all wore aigrettes; a score of these, a hundred of them, nodded and vibrated with an incessant agitation over the heads of the crowd and flashed like mica flakes as the wearers moved. Everywhere the eye was arrested by the luxury of stuffs, the brilliance and delicacy of fabrics, laces as white and soft as froth, crisp, shining silks, suave satins, heavy gleaming velvets, and brocades and plushes, nearly all of them white—violently so—dazzling and splendid under the blaze of the electrics." Meanwhile, outside on a bitterly cold day, with a freezing wind blowing in off the lake, "the coachmen on the boxes of the carriages that succeeded one another in an interminable line before the entrance of the theatre, were swathed to the eyes in furs. The spume and froth froze on the bits of the horses." There "a crowd had collected about the awning on the sidewalk, and even upon the opposite side of the street, peeping and peering from behind the broad shoulders of policemen—a crowd of miserables, shivering in rags and tattered comforters, who found, nevertheless, an unexplainable satisfaction in this prolonged defile of millionaires."[192]

As the architectural setting for this process of arrival, the vestibule was directly beneath the great tower, whose entire weight was supported on the room's walls and two massive freestanding columns inside (fig. 123). Spectators were thus introduced to the theater by passing through structural evidence of the tower as a spectacular feat of engineering. These columns were of steel, yet they were clad in scagliola to resemble marble monoliths. Their round shape eased passage around them, while their bases were

Figure 123
Auditorium Theater, vestibule looking northwest before destruction of this room's south half in the 1950s, showing iron columns clad in scagliola with plaster capitals and heating and ventilating grilles around column bases. Floors are marble mosaic, and walls are clad in Numidian marble. Small arched transoms directly above six inner doors are art glass designed and fabricated by George L. Healy and Louis J. Millet. Photograph by J. W. Taylor. Avery Architectural and Fine Arts Library, Columbia University in the City of New York.

fitted with heating and ventilating grilles. These provisions were important because the Auditorium's vestibule was the rendezvous for theatergoers, and parties sometimes waited a long time before their friends arrived. The space was thus not purely to be passed through but was to be experienced and observed, as by those who queued before the ticket window on the lobby's east side. The week before the theater opened, "three hundred patient people stood hugging the cold marble wainscoting of the Auditorium lobby Monday morning until the box office opened for the sale of opera season tickets." Numidian (Algerian) marble was used for the floor's mosaic and the walls' veneer. Six doors led from this high vestibule into the lower foyer. Over the doors were arched lunettes of colored art glass designed by Healy and Millet, showing allegorical figures of Wisdom, Oratory, Drama, Music, Poetry, and the Dance, announcing the theater's varied purposes.[193]

Once in the lower foyer past the main vestibule, ticket holders could deposit their wraps and congregate before entering the theater. As a network of piers supporting elliptical arches between them, this space repeated on a small scale the theater's main ceiling arches (fig. 124). These arches were not structural but were hung from horizontal iron beams between the piers, which were of iron encased in fireproofing and externally squared to look like stone piers. With its marble mosaic floor, the lower vestibule had a cavernlike appearance, resembling "not a little the crypt of some old cathedral of the Middle Ages."[194] This broad, low hall served as a prefatory contrast to the immense clear span of the theater, whose parquet was accessible through the tunnel-like passageways on the foyer's east or right side. People going to seats in the upper parquet circle, or in one of the main balcony levels, ascended one of the three main staircases on the lower foyer's west or left side. These were open flights that connected all the upper foyers at the theater's rear. As noted, there was no single unifying grand stair hall as in the Paris Opera, whose seating

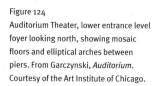

Figure 124
Auditorium Theater, lower entrance level foyer looking north, showing mosaic floors and elliptical arches between piers. From Garczynski, *Auditorium*. Courtesy of the Art Institute of Chicago.

capacity was about one-half the Auditorium's. Yet the social use of Adler and Sullivan's foyers was much like that of the Auditorium's European counterparts. One observer wrote of the opening: "The early arrivals filled the lobby, foyer and grand staircases to have a glance at the late comers. The foyer, much doubted and not a little smiled about at first as a Frenchified institution unknown or unnecessary to an American theatre audience, turned out to be a real necessity last night. It became at once what the management intended it should be, the social feature of the season. People took to it as naturally as if they had been habitués of the Imperial Opera or the Théâtre Français in Paris for years."[195]

The Auditorium's main upper or grand foyer shows that it continued the theme of piers and elliptical arches found below, but that the treatment of surfaces changed (fig. 125). Here floors were not of cream mosaic but were covered by maroon wool Wilton carpets whose thickness, weave, color, and ornamental pattern were specified by Sullivan and supplied through Marshall Field and Company, which arranged for their manufacture by W. and J. Sloan Company of New York.[196] The carpet's motifs of interlaced tendrils, flowers, and leaves recurred in richly colored stenciled designs on flat wall surfaces, in the shapes of wrought iron on the stair railings nearby, and on the plaster relief and flat stencils on the stairway's soffits, so that the eye encountered Sullivan's consistent visual language in varied materials (fig. 126). These architectural choices were not meant to be seen only in an empty hall. As one observer of the opening wrote: "Art could not have invented a

Figure 125

Auditorium Theater, main upper foyer looking north, showing steel columns clad in scagliola, ornamental wrought iron railings, and wool carpets with patterns specified by Sullivan. Photograph by J. W. Taylor. Avery Architectural and Fine Arts Library, Columbia University in the City of New York.

Figure 126

Auditorium Theater, main upper foyer, stairs leading to main balcony level, showing scagliola-clad iron column, Sullivan's ornamental designs on iron railings, stenciled panels and plaster light fixtures on stair soffit, and stenciled wall on landing between main foyer and main balcony. Photograph by Hedrich-Blessing, 1967. Courtesy of the Chicago Historical Society, HB-31105-L.

finer background for the display of works of the milliner than that afforded by the non-committal decorations, if one may say so, of the foyer and the interior of the auditorium. It suits alike well the warm crimson, the deep blue and the rich green of velvets and silks in opera cloaks, as well as the delicate shades of creamy white, canary color and all the paler tints in robes. The foyer must be seen, under the magic effect of the incandescent light, filled with elegantly attired people, to comprehend the genius of the artist who decided upon what at first appears a risky combination for a background for the display of gorgeous costumes."[197]

The most distinctive spaces in the grand foyer were the inglenook seating areas around working fireplaces, set off from the main promenade by oak railings (fig. 127). Over their mantels Peck later had excerpts carved from President Harrison's and Chauncey Depew's brief addresses praising the theater's purpose and design. Domestic in character, these inglenooks were richly surfaced with fireplaces of Numidian marble and furnished with sofas below foliate mosaic friezes. Their frontal railings created the aura of a semiprivate setting, an accessible alternative to a private box, for conversation within the foyer as a public social space. Like the foyer itself, the inglenooks were used by both genders, whereas there were a separate ladies'

Figure 127

Auditorium Theater, main upper foyer, inglenook seating below mosaic frieze and ornamental plaster board flanking working marble-fronted fireplaces, set off from foyer by oak railings. Photograph by J. W. Taylor. Avery Architectural and Fine Arts Library, Columbia University in the City of New York.

retiring room (in the tower) and men's smoking room (east of the tower) raised a few steps off the main second-floor foyer's south side (fig. 99). Overall these ancillary spaces around the upper foyer provided a range of options for interaction between the vast majority of theatergoers who were not boxholders. In 1889–1890 the Auditorium Theater's management included a special notice in programs of events held there, desiring "that each entertainment at the Auditorium should be made a social occasion, for which ample facilities have been provided, and the audience, especially the ladies, are requested to leave their seats during the intermission." Presumably this notice was to inhibit prostitutes from meeting potential clients in the relative privacy of theater seats during intermissions. Manager Milward Adams sought to counter this familiar practice with ample provision for foyers where such contacts were discouraged by being more easily observed.[198]

If ticket holders were divided into groups by seating level in the rear foyers, they came together as a collective presence in the theater, which was seen and filled for the first time on opening night. Extra seats swelled the audience to over 7,000, rising through all seating levels to the uppermost gallery (fig. 128). The reducing curtain was raised to reveal rising tiers of seated choristers on the stage (fig. 106). One observer wrote of the scene:

> You could not feel the sense of immensity till you turned from the footlights and looked back under the white and gold-ribbed vault of the body of the Auditorium to the balconies, which flattered the eye and then bewildered it; for, first, there sloped

back from the parquet a stretch like a flower garden; then came the curving balcony, black with thousands, as if more people were there than anywhere else; above it the straight line of the second balcony, with banks of sightseers; and last and highest of all the gallery, whose occupants looked like dots. Now came the triumph of architecture— for, while you felt the largeness, you also felt the compactness of the whole. Despite the distance, you knew these dots in the gallery were near you, and could hear every word or note uttered on the stage.[199]

Other accounts attested to the rapport the audience felt with those who spoke or sang on stage, so that the room's acoustic clarity powerfully reinforced the ideal of civic unity Peck had envisioned. That night the Auditorium recalled the old English definition of a theater as a town in itself. Adler and Sullivan's space enabled bourgeois Chicago to present itself to itself in a way unlike any other interior in the city's history.

If the audience represented the Auditorium's civic purpose, then the honored guests on stage conveyed Peck's goal of shaping perception of the building as a national monument. He stated that "it is the wish of the projectors that the Auditorium shall eventually come to be the great art center of America."[200] Even though they were criticized for attending the dedication of a nongovernment building, President Benjamin Harrison and Vice President Levi Morton came from Washington for the ceremony, both returning to the hall where they had been nominated

Figure 128

Auditorium Theater looking west from stage into house, including main floor, main balcony, lower gallery, and upper gallery or family circle. From Garczynski, *Auditorium*. Courtesy of the Library of Congress.

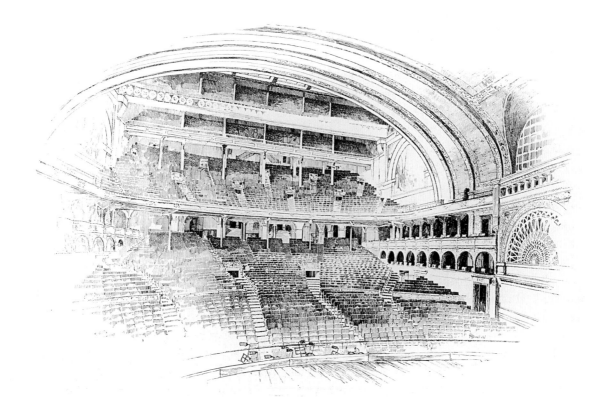

eighteen months before. Peck met Harrison's train and hosted him in his own home on Michigan Avenue. For the theater's opening, Peck and Harrison occupied temporary boxes set up on the stage's left side. This arrangement revived an older custom of forestage boxes for honored members of the audience, approximating such boxes in European court opera houses. Other special stage boxes contained the governors of several nearby states and prominent Canadian officials. Peck felt that the "Auditorium will be in a sense nationalized by the presence of distinguished men of the country."[201] By December 1889 Chicago was in intense competition with other major United States cities for congressional authorization to host what became the World's Columbian Exposition. Peck headed the local finance committee for the exposition, and the Auditorium Association contributed to its funding. The presence of national and international political figures at the Auditorium Theater's opening projected the image of Chicago as an urban center worthy of the coming world's fair. That night Adler and Sullivan's building itself was on display "to show the people of this continent," and "to insure the world's exposition in Chicago in 1892."[202]

Although Harrison, Peck, Mayor De Witt Cregier, and others gave brief, well-received speeches from the stage, the audience's anticipation focused on the appearance of Adelina Patti, the prima donna whose performances drew immense and enthusiastic audiences from New York to San Francisco. Even at this late stage in her career, Patti's voice and persona retained a remarkable hold on the American public, as evinced by Chicago's response to her evenings at the Grand Opera Festival of 1885. Patti was a master at sustaining her career, musically and financially, through artful cultivation of her public image. By 1889 Mapleson had retired from his career as an impresario, and Peck negotiated with Henry Abbey and conductor Maurice Grau (son of Jacob, whose company had opened Crosby's Opera House in 1865) to manage the Auditorium Theater's inaugural four-week opera season featuring Patti, which began the night after the opening. Abbey had originally thought of creating only a concert company, with Patti as the main singer, but Peck persuaded him to organize a full Italian opera company. Peck's arrangements with Abbey, combined with Milward Adams's efforts abroad, resulted "in the importation direct from Europe of one of the largest and most effective opera troupes ever organized. Thus, while other American cities are still dependent upon New York, Chicago has emancipated herself and no longer takes her music second-hand from that city."[203]

Patti's appearance climaxed the great hall's opening. She would receive $4,200 for singing on the occasion, whose paid admissions totaled $10,235.47. One account noted: "The audience had been stringing up to a high pitch. A general appearance of nervousness was noticeable. The ladies fidgeted and the men rolled and unrolled their programs. The chorus cast expectant glances toward the north entrance to the stage. The fiddlers grated their bows. The house shuddered in a brief spasm of applause" when Patti finally appeared. Unaccompanied, she sang the American composer John Howard Payne's "Home, Sweet Home," which had enjoyed great national popularity since the 1820s and had been a favorite of Patti's concert repertoire in London from the 1860s. Focusing her gaze on Peck through this number, Patti rendered the melody "so well that President Benjamin Harrison rose from his seat and smote his right hand with his left as everybody else was doing."[204] In response, Mme Patti turned to the audience and sang an encore, Eckert's "Echo in Walde" (Echo in the woods), or "Swiss Echo Song," which had first been made popular by Jenny Lind and which Patti had sung at her first public concert in 1850. This song's intricate melody made its rendition "an important episode, for it established beyond any doubt the acoustic properties of the great Auditorium. Not a note of the marvelous pianissimo in the echo figurations of the song was lost to any listener in the top gallery, almost three hundred feet distant from the stage."[205] After performing in Gounod's *Roméo et Juliette* the next evening, Patti, whose voice was not powerful, praised the theater. There, she said, "even the lowest note goes out freely and is perfectly audible. The acoustics are perfect." There was "no comparison at all" between the Auditorium and the Metropolitan, and there was "nothing in Europe to compare [the Auditorium] with."[206]

Patti's renown as an honored stage artist was not a new phenomenon in the nineteenth-century United States. Its prototype had been Lind's career as a singer and an actress. Her national fame and her impact on the crowds who came to see and hear her were legendary. In their later careers, Lind and Patti attracted audiences in part because of their fame alone. Yet their renown as artists originated in their capacity to appeal to emotional and even spiritual feelings that resisted verbal characterization. As one of Lind's contemporaries wrote of her performances, "We feel only the presence of the beautiful, the advent of a new creation, the irresistible appeal of the highest instincts of the soul."[207] It was this capacity to shape the responses of a mass audience that gave artists like Patti their prime place in Peck's view of opera as a force for social pacification. As those at the Auditorium's dedication knew, despite the evening's appearance of civic unity, Chicago was bitterly divided along class lines. Yet in the new Auditorium, opera was to have an ennobling effect on the broadest range of listeners, an outcome ensured by its seating capacity and pricing policies. As patron of the whole effort, Peck perhaps viewed Patti in 1889 as Ralph Waldo Emerson had described her American antetype in 1850: "Jenny Lind needs no police. Her voice is worth a hundred constables, and instantly silenced the uproar of the mob."[208]

The presence of Harrison and Patti constituted a key component of Peck's orchestration of the dedication, yet in his mind the event's central ideological theme was what the building represented for Chicago's workers. While the structure was compared to the monuments of past civilizations, it was also differentiated from them as having been built not for personal power or material aggrandizement but, as the mayor said, for "the city and the culture of our people." As such, the building embodied a "wealth that is used and devoted for the best end, for the greatest number." Within its walls were "ample facilities for the masses of people to enjoy the display and portrayal of art, science, literature, poetry, music, and drama. Here Shakespeare, Milton, Webster, Clay, a Forrest, a Cushman, a Lind may metaphorically speak again."[209] Repeatedly praised on this occasion, Peck was asked to speak. He lauded the architects, who "are entitled to a large share of credit. [Applause.] These men have faced successfully unprecedented problems. These men should never be forgotten." Perhaps alluding to labor troubles in the building trades, he praised the workers who had fashioned the structure, implying that, since the Auditorium was not financed or built to be profitable, the theater represented something different for them than the construction of other commercial blocks. Since the project had by then been supported by both large and small stockholders, Peck said, "This has been done out of a desire to educate and entertain the masses. This has been done out of the rich man's largesse and the poor man's mite for the benefit of all." He concluded, to repeated applause: "We must not forget the army of workingmen who have labored with their hands day and night, and have shown a zeal which is without precedent. They knew that they were erecting an edifice for themselves and their associates as much as for any class. They knew that the Auditorium stood for all."[210] If the Metropolitan's boxes had held Manhattan's high society, then the Auditorium's tiers held a much larger public. As one observer wrote, "New York, with its 400, will have to give way to the Chicago 4,000."[211]

Peck's ideological intention for the Auditorium Theater as a nonelite public hall had a parallel in Montgomery Schuyler's critique of its architecture, which was the first informed response to its design. As Schuyler had recognized in his earlier essay on the Metropolitan Opera House, that building did serve as a cultural resource for a broad urban audience. Yet its interior architecture, because of the primacy of its boxes, privileged its city's financial and social elite, recalling the typological tradition of European court and state opera houses. As an intended contrast meant to surpass the Metropolitan, Chicago's Auditorium shaped a different relationship between stage and audience because of its patron Peck's democratic ideal. In this spirit, Garczynski wrote: "To the performers on the stage the sight of the public on crowded nights must be to the last degree impressive. The ascent of the seats is very gradual for a long time and there is an immense mass of spectators without a break . . . . The performers can neither sing to the boxes nor play to them, but must address themselves to the public."[212] Schuyler saw the Auditorium's contrast with the Metropolitan as a sign of Chicago architecture's regional distinction. He wrote of Adler and Sullivan's interior: "The type of an opera-house, which the auditorium essentially is, is so well settled and so universally accepted that the variations ordinarily attempted upon it, even by architects of original force, are comparatively slight. While the component parts of the accepted type are retained in this interior, they are transmuted into an entirely new result."[213]

For Schuyler the significance of this result paralleled what Paul Bourget, a student of Taine, had seen in Chicago's tall office buildings of the same period. Bourget wrote: "The simple force of need is such a principle of beauty, and these buildings so conspicuously manifest that need that in contemplating them you experience a singular emotion. The sketch appears here of a new kind of art, an art of democracy, made by the crowd and for the crowd, an art of science in which the certainty of natural laws gives to audacities in appearance the most unbridled the tranquillity of geometric figures."[214] Bourget here referred to structural engineering as the form-giving logic in the design of the city's tall office buildings. In the Auditorium Theater, acoustic principles found expression in the precise geometric form of the stepped elliptical ceiling. Schuyler concluded that the theater, in "extending and proclaiming a hospitality as nearly as may be equal and undistinguishing, illustrates, as plainly as the exterior of the many-storied office buildings, and in contrast with the 'royal' and 'imperial' opera-houses, M. Bourget's conception of 'a new kind of art, an art of democracy.'"[215] Whether knowingly or not, Schuyler here returned to Peck's original intention for this space, as if Adler and Sullivan's interior had elicited from this prominent eastern critic, as it had from Patti, precisely the reading its patron would have wished.

The Apollo Club's Workingmen's Concerts at the Auditorium, 1889–1894

Schuyler, Peck, and his architects were not alone in perceiving the democratic cultural potential of the Auditorium Theater. In January 1889 William Tomlins, musical director of the Apollo Club, wrote to its members about the coming hall's potential. Born and trained in England, Tomlins was presumably aware of debates in London about providing orchestral and choral concerts for mass audiences, such as those occasionally held at Albert Hall and the Crystal Palace at Sydenham. In 1885 George Bernard Shaw wrote that "there is practically no regular provision made at any time throughout the year for the mass of people who like good orchestral music, but who cannot afford more than a couple of shillings a week on gratifying their taste."[216] Four years later, following on the methods of English and Continental cities, where the best oratorios were performed for the poor almost without cost, Tomlins wrote of the Auditorium's approaching completion:

> In this favored land, the time should speedily come, when, through the economy of scientific discoveries and inventions, and a general distribution of the advantages accruing therefrom, a comfortable living should reward all intelligent industry, when none need want, when the helpless are all cared for, when all may work who wish, and none need slave. Then, work of every kind will be honorable, and only drones dishonored. The advancement of the real man will be more important than his physical sustenance. The arts and sciences, as we understand them, will be greatly advanced, and new arts and new sciences will be unfolded. Then every man's increase will be his neighbor's profit. And to share with another will multiply our own treasure.[217]

Tomlins noted that the club worked for months preparing one of its musical programs, the most frequently performed being Handel's *Messiah*. A single concert of such a work would then be given to elite subscribers to season tickets for the

club's performances. Tomlins argued that this tradition of giving a single performance of such a work should be supplemented by "a repetition performance to a hall
full of respectable music lovers who are unable to pay for it, and yet are appreciative
of the performance." He suggested that the club "may be able to tender its gratu-
itous services in a season's repetition performances, each to be given the night following the regular subscription concert, the local cost of each repetition (much less
than the original cost) to be defrayed by subscription amongst public-spirited citizens. And the five-thousand tickets to each concert to be distributed through the influence of large employers of labor to the families of respectable working men.
Thus harnessing music to the yoke as a working factor in civilization, and evidenc-
ing good will from affluence and art to those who toil."[218]

Tomlins's message, simultaneously idealistic and patronizing, was unevenly received by elite and democratic leaders. In May 1889 the club passed a resolution in
support of his basic idea of repetition concerts for working people, with 5,000 tickets sold at prices of five, ten, and twenty-five cents each, in a period when some estimates placed the average skilled worker's wages at about $15 a week. After Tomlins
had arranged a conference with representatives of the local Trades and Labor Assembly early in 1889, it was agreed that these tickets would be supplied on application to labor assemblies and through large employers. The intention was "to reach
out in courtesy to a large self-respecting and charity-repudiating class who have so
little in common with the moneyed strata of society."[219] One local critic stated that
some of the local wealthy thought that Tomlins was overstating the difference between classes in the United States, "that the classes here were not sufficiently separated from each other and that a few seats at low prices would meet the demand."[220]
Another editor took an opposite view, stating that the Apollo Club was too elitist in
its membership and repertoire for its appearances and programs to appeal to a
broad audience. This observer advocated that the club "abolish the aristocratic, exclusive, close-corporation subscription concerts altogether. Secure, either among its
own active members or its friends, a sufficient guarantee subscription to assure the
management against loss, independent of concerts, and then give the concert programmes such as they propose at the prices named above, open to everybody."[221]

On 28 December 1889, nineteen days after the Auditorium Theater had opened
on 9 December, the Apollo Club gave its first Workingmen's Concert, repeating a
Christmas Day production of Handel's *Messiah* given for the club's wealthy season
ticket holders. Applications for tickets numbered 22,000, and the Apollo Club sold
tickets in workshops and stores, not to "the ragamuffin, hooting, tough rabble," but
to "wage-earners, working by the day or piece or else drawing a salary not exceeding
$15 a week." The house was filled to its capacity with a seated audience of 4,250 sup-
plemented by 200 standees. Although the performance itself was precisely the same
as that given three nights earlier, the audience was entirely different in its lack of social pretensions. A prominent socialist, Thomas J. Morgan, and his wife sat in one of
the boxes normally occupied by a leading capitalist. In the other boxes, "where the
décolleté dresses of Parisian design and make, bold and beautiful in their colors,

had been, were high-necked gray and black gowns designed and made [in workers' homes] on Milwaukee Avenue. Old fashioned shawls were thrown over the backs of chairs which had known only the touch of swan's down wraps. There was not an evening costume in the building except those worn on the stage." The only men in dress suits were three who had repurchased tickets from workers who had sold them at a high profit. The only elite invited were Lyman Gage and two other capitalists known to working people for their participation in economic conferences and arbitrations.[222]

The behavior as well as the dress of this audience differed from the one that had heard the earlier performance. Virtually none of the workers had come to the building by hired horse cabs—they had either walked or taken streetcars. Once inside, they had no servants to assist them with their wraps or check them outside the theater. Instead, they carried their overcoats to and from their seats. Once seated, the workers, unlike privileged patrons, had few opera glasses to gaze at boxholders as well as the stage. Although the subscribers' reception of the earlier version of the concert had been generous, the workers' response "was heartfelt and deeply expressive. The auditors did not turn to right or left to look at their neighbors or even scan the boxes; there were no costumes to look at. But they kept them riveted on the stage. They drank in the music as a thirsty man in the desert drinks water. Many had never heard such music before. Many had heard it only in dreams prompted by an old score-book. Many had never dreamed there could be such music." Orchestral and vocal numbers were enthusiastically received, "but it must not be imagined that the applause was indiscriminate. On the contrary, it was often technically pointed." One observer present saw "Germans and Scandinavians here who are as familiar with this music as with their tools." Among these were four bearded older men seated in the orchestra circle who "held their heads down and poured over two thumbed and worn librettos. They were brothers." When asked about their behavior, one answered: "We used to hear the 'Messiah' at Bayreuth when we were boys, and these are the same books with which we followed the music then."[223] In such instances, the Anglo-American elite who staged these concerts successfully invoked a high culture of music and religion that they shared with German-speaking workers, then sometimes seen as a political threat.

Coming after a first two-week season of opera featuring Adelina Patti and other stars, this Workingmen's Concert was a fulfillment of Peck's vision. The *Tribune* concluded: "From its broad human significance last night's entertainment at the Auditorium was the most notable the great hall has yet witnessed. The opening night was a tribute to people of place and power. At the Patti opera the following night incense was burned at the altar of society and the nights since have been devoted to keeping it aglow. But last night the triumphs of public spirit, architecture, art, and music represented by the Auditorium were dedicated anew to the people." Peck himself, who was there, said: "I feel that the Auditorium has been put to a noble use tonight—one in keeping with its own greatness."[224]

Three additional repetition concerts were given during the 1889–1890 season, all attracting far more applicants than there were tickets. The same pattern was repeated in the season of 1890–1891, when 13,000 applied to hear Handel's *Messiah*. Ferdinand Peck was among the local elite who subscribed to a guaranty fund to cover any financial losses. For the wageworkers' concerts, the two galleries above the Auditorium's main balcony were thrown open. Instead of the fashionable, in Adler and Sullivan's foyers several Apollo Club members greeted and talked informally with the audience. The club members "came into other relationship to the attendant working men and women—that of a reception committee, or of semi-official ushers, in which capacity we have become acquainted with some of the faces, and can see that ours are becoming familiar to many of them."[225] At these events the Auditorium's importance lay in its capacity to provide a common ground for social and cultural interaction between classes, yet in a building mainly created by, and with a musical program defined by, Chicago's most empowered citizens.

During Theodore Thomas's first season as a resident orchestral conductor in Chicago (October 1891 to April 1892), he led a series of twenty concerts at the Auditorium featuring classical music (mainly works by Bach, Beethoven, Berlioz, and Brahms) and accompanied William Tomlins's Apollo Club for several choral concerts. These programs drew such meager audiences that by April 1892 one local observer wrote: "If it be desirable to educate the 'masses' to a liking for any certain style of music, sound policy dictates that some effective means must be adopted for bringing 'the masses' aforesaid within the reach of educative influences, and that the uniform and exclusive offering of what they will not tolerate is hardly to be reckoned among effective means." In his second season at the Auditorium (1892–1893), Thomas gave a series of "popular concerts," still emphasizing classical works. In December 1892 he offered a Beethoven program including the Ninth Symphony, with two hundred voices of the Apollo Club. One chorister recalled: "What an audience it was, as seen from the stage! The vast Auditorium filled with 'the plain people,' 'the masses,' eager to enjoy the feast of glorious music." One critic praised "the steadily increasing patronage which is being bestowed upon these truly superb concerts."[226]

From January to March 1893, Thomas gave three such "workingmen's" or "people's" concerts, for which he led the orchestra in programs of Beethoven, Wagner, Liszt, and Tchaikovsky. These concerts were meant to "not only give evenings of enjoyment to many who have but few such evenings, but also afford them an opportunity to become familiar with the playing of an orchestra and acquainted with some of the standard modern and classical works of orchestral literature." As Peck envisioned, audiences of 6,000 filled the hall, including workers' families with children, described as delighted, showing quiet, rapt attention to the music. One reporter wrote of Thomas's program on 30 January 1893: "The audience last night left not a vacant place in boxes, parquet and balcony. A more appreciative company of listeners the great Conductor and his men may have had, but certainly none that ever followed their work more closely or evinced a keener desire to understand and appreciate their work."[227] Clearly the capitalist press, like the Apollo Club and its supporters, wanted to see these events as evidence of broad social rapprochement.

Despite their popular success, the Workingmen's Concerts ended after the 1893–1894 season, reportedly because of the widespread resale of tickets by workers who found they could profitably sell their inexpensive tickets to those the concerts were not intended for. The capitalists who underwrote the guaranty fund presumably felt their philanthropy was being misdirected. Yet the concerts provoked other responses. George W. James was among those religious reformers who were familiar with working-class entertainments elsewhere around the city, including the theaters and music halls that he saw as tied to alcohol and prostitution. Unlike earlier clerical critics of local amusements, James had no quarrel with "the managers of the better class of theaters, concert halls and museums [who] are striving to entertain and elevate their patrons." He praised the Apollo Club's wageworkers' concerts, which briefly fulfilled Peck's vision for the Auditorium, even though these events separate from the club's regular concerts for moneyed audiences reinforced the city's social segmentation. Yet James observed that because most workers lived in outlying districts, "it takes too long and costs too much for many of the poor laboring men to get to the Auditorium. The cost of car fare would be sufficient to pay for an entertainment in the very heart of the district in which workers live." He proposed that philanthropists "establish in every quarter of the city a number of large public halls, dotted here and there—more than there are theaters—where, for a very small fee, people may attend good concerts, entertainments, lectures, exhibitions and the like."[228]

Perhaps unknowingly, James was describing a distribution of popular entertainments already developed in Chicago. By 1889 there had been "a tendency to carry the smaller places of amusement nearer the homes of the people . . . . As the city spreads the wisdom of the managers of these theatres becomes more apparent year by year. There has been a tendency during the year to get the better class of plays in the minor theatres at popular prices."[229] The rapid growth of the city's German population enabled establishment of commercial popular theater companies that performed in halls with affordable rent. These halls were often the gymnasiums of the local *Turnvereine*. Since almost all the managers of these companies had been actors or managers with the prefire troupe of the Deutsches Haus, they staged light plays and sometimes serious drama, often before full houses. The popular postfire German companies performing in outlying *Turnhalle* reached those audiences in German neighborhoods that had neither the means nor the desire to take a streetcar trip to central Chicago's theaters. Indeed, the city's cable and elevated lines were not even extended into some peripheral workers' neighborhoods until the 1890s. To respond to this situation, the larger German companies founded theaters in various neighborhoods, controlled by the same management and running the same plays in different halls around the city, much as George Carpenter had done just after the fire. In 1896–1897, when the popularity of these German theaters peaked, there were nine companies operating on the North and Northwest Sides and five on the South and Southwest Sides. All of them staged programs comprising comedies, farces, and musical vignettes based on everyday life, after which the halls were cleared of their movable chairs so the audience could dance to music provided by small orchestras. Since weekday performances drew too small an audience, plays were staged on Sunday evenings, with tickets costing from twenty-five to fifty cents, the latter the price of the least expensive tickets in regular theaters downtown. Although the rented halls were often poorly ventilated and cramped, "tickets are so cheap that even [male] workers with large families and not so much money can afford to attend performances, frequently with 'Mother and all the little children.'"[230] German theatrical entrepreneurs created their own cultural system, defying the dominance of the Loop's houses, whose productions were linguistically as well as transportationally inaccessible to many Chicago workers. Peck surely knew of the outlying theaters, but he had created the Auditorium as an alternative civic center of entertainment, whose elevated cultural fare would draw a public away from the usual working-class amusements, and away from politics.

The Auditorium Offices and Recital Hall

For the Auditorium Building's patrons the issue had been their control of their city's center, both physically and culturally. This idea had also shaped the original program for the structure's office block and its Recital Hall. Although Peck and his board initially envisioned the building's street fronts entirely as a hotel, by July 1888, long after Adler and Sullivan had fixed their exterior design, the directors decided to complete the business block west of the hotel as rentable stores and offices. The hotel's interiors would include the tower's lower stories above the second, while the upper tower and the block to its west would become rentable spaces. These, especially the storefronts, were quickly leased at high rentals, the Auditorium Building having elevated the prospects for Wabash Avenue on the structure's west side. By autumn 1888, enhancements of the architecture meant the Auditorium Association had almost exhausted its capital stock of $1,500,000, and the directors were compelled to pay for further construction with a new bond issue of $900,000. Although the association had not been bound to pay dividends to stockholders, it now had to pay the 5 percent annual interest on these forty-year bonds, whose principal would become due in February 1929. The interest was now added to the building's annual carrying costs of operating expenses, ground rent, and taxes.[231]

To start the flow of income, the directors decided in September 1888 to push completion of the offices so tenants could move in by 1 May 1889. Many were like those who had rented space in the Central Music Hall—involved with the music trade and hence "of a class that cannot afford to pay high rents. It is not like an office building on La Salle street."[232] The first tenant was the Chicago Conservatory of Music and Dramatic Art, in which Peck was a major stockholder. Healy and Millet decorated the school's main eighteen-room suite on the ninth floor, yet its growth was such that it was expected to occupy half the building's rental space. Peck also authorized the Illinois Humane Society, of which he had been vice president, to rent rooms on the fourth floor. One account noted: "Apart from the hotel and auditorium, almost one-third of the entire building will be devoted as far as practical to *Art,* both useful and fine, to *Music,* to Art Studies, Artistic Merchandising, and to Education in its various branches. Many institutions of a more or less public character will find a home in the vast structure."[233]

The most significant public space within the office block on the Auditorium Building's west side was the seventh-floor Recital Hall, opened on 12 October 1889, about two months before the main theater (fig. 129). Perhaps no other interior in the structure better embodied Peck's ideal of the Auditorium's democratic social and cultural goals. He called this room a "little gem . . . the mouthpiece of the mighty pile."[234] Accessible by three special elevators from the street level, the Recital Hall was set above and behind the main theater's gallery, as shown in the longitudinal section (fig. 97). Linked to the office wing on the Auditorium Building's west side, the Recital Hall and its parlors were later annexed by the rapidly growing Chicago Conservatory. The hall's five hundred seats in semicircular rows "rise from the center toward all sides except that occupied by the stage, somewhat after the fashion of the ancient amphitheaters."[235] The ceiling had a central multipanel skylight of stained glass (which still exists) to light the hall by day, supplemented by electric bulbs set in decorative plaster rosettes for evening events. At the hall's rear, the east-west ceiling beams rested on three tall freestanding columns. From floor to ceiling the hall, like the main theater, was "beaming and gleaming and glittering in the decorative ivory and gold of its walls." Because the Recital Hall had to accommodate no changes of scenery, the stage's rear wall could be "a novelty in construction—a side

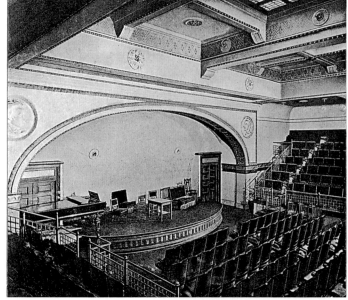

Figure 129

Auditorium Building, Recital Hall looking northwest toward stage, showing Johannes Gelert's medallions of Beethoven and Mendelssohn in arch spandrels and coved rear wall of stage, with central skylight over audience room. The early tenant of this room was the Chicago Conservatory of Music and Drama. From Garczynski, *Auditorium.* Courtesy of the Library of Congress.

section of a dome slanting toward the main room, from which its upper part is separated by a wide-extending arch, whose down-looking surface [intrados] is one spread of gold leaf from side to side to where it rests on either hand on capitals in gold leaf, all this gold-leaf surface being worked out in delicately figured designs."[236] Together, the stage wall's curvatures and the proscenium's arch contained sound near its source on stage to better project it outward, so that "the room is exceedingly sensitive as regards its acoustical qualities, and a moderate expenditure of power is sufficient to more than fill it satisfactorily."[237]

Johannes Gelert's plaster medallions of Beethoven and Mendelssohn in the spandrels of the arches above the stage identified the Recital Hall's principal purpose as the rented space for performances of the Chicago Conservatory. Yet its relatively small size meant it could also accommodate other civic groups to enable "good deeds done by the mighty lifting hand of united action in conference, convention, and scientific gatherings."[238] To make this point, the Recital Hall was dedicated on Columbus Day, 12 October 1889, two months after Peck and other powerful Chicagoans began formal efforts to bring the World's Columbian Exposition to their city. The dedicatory event was not a concert but the twentieth anniversary meeting of the Illinois Humane Society, founded in 1869 on the model of New York City's Humane Society. In its efforts to take legal action against abuse of children and animals, the Illinois Humane Society enjoyed wide local support. For the society's president, its work and the Auditorium Building were measures of civic patriotism in action. Peck compared the society to the building, which "stands for the entertainment and elevation of the masses . . . . The Humane Society and this great edifice are standing together to promote humanity, culture, and education among our people."[239] The Reverend David Swing observed that Peck had sought compassionate treatment of horses long before he began the Auditorium project. For Swing, the society's and the Auditorium's missions were intertwined humanitarian ventures. In his view the goal of the fine arts represented in the building was not to divide social classes but to unify them through appeal to common humane impulses. As he said, "The arts did not engender the vanity that separates souls, but rather the humility which makes rich and poor to be as one."[240] Rabbi Emil Hirsch, leader of Sinai Temple, one of Chicago's leading Reform Jewish congregations, sounded a similar theme, arguing that modern society should unite the artistic achievements of Greco-Roman antiquity with the concern for the poor and the weak that "rose on the heights of Palestine."[241] In sum, the Recital Hall that evening was the focus for attempts to articulate values that animated the whole Auditorium. To fulfill its social aim, in its first season the hall was the setting for monthly Sunday evening meetings between local leaders of capital and labor for sharing ideas and resolving differences. Jane Addams, who had founded Hull House earlier in 1889, recalled that these meetings across class divides were then unique in Chicago. They were led by banker Lyman Gage, an Auditorium stockholder and a Peck ally.[242] Yet like the concerts, the Recital Hall's meetings aimed at bridging between classes did not last long, as the Auditorium Building became a centerpiece for urban development under the control of large capital interests. In this project, Peck intended that the Auditorium Hotel play an important role.

Plate 1

Dankmar Adler and Louis Sullivan, Auditorium Building, Chicago (1886–1890) looking northwest, showing fire escapes on east face of tower added in 1901, hotel entrance marked as Roosevelt University from 1946, and Congress Drive in foreground east of Michigan Avenue opened in 1955. Photograph © Cervin Robinson.

Plate 2

Auditorium Building, lower east end of south front, showing solid walls of rock-faced Minnesota granite on first two floors, with polished monolithic columns of matching Maine granite on sidewalk, below facing of lighter-toned Maine granite on third story. Machine-cut projecting horizontal moldings run above first, second, and third stories. Smooth Indiana limestone facing for brick walls above. Photograph © Cervin Robinson.

Plate 3

Auditorium Building, crowning tenth story of south front along Congress Street, showing Tuscan columns and bracketed cornice of Indiana limestone. Photograph by Brad Bellows, Tektonica.

Plate 4

Adler and Sullivan, Wainwright Building, northwest corner of Seventh and Chestnut Streets, St. Louis (1890–1892), showing upper walls with pressed brick and column capitals, attic story, and cornice of ornamental terra cotta cladding for iron and steel frame. E. Teitelman, Photography 143-E.

Plate 5

Auditorium Theater, after partial restoration completed in 1967, looking northeast toward stage, showing incandescent lights on ceiling arches, whose original ornamental gold stenciling is not yet replaced. Photograph by Hedrich-Blessing, HB-31105-C. Courtesy of the Chicago Historical Society.

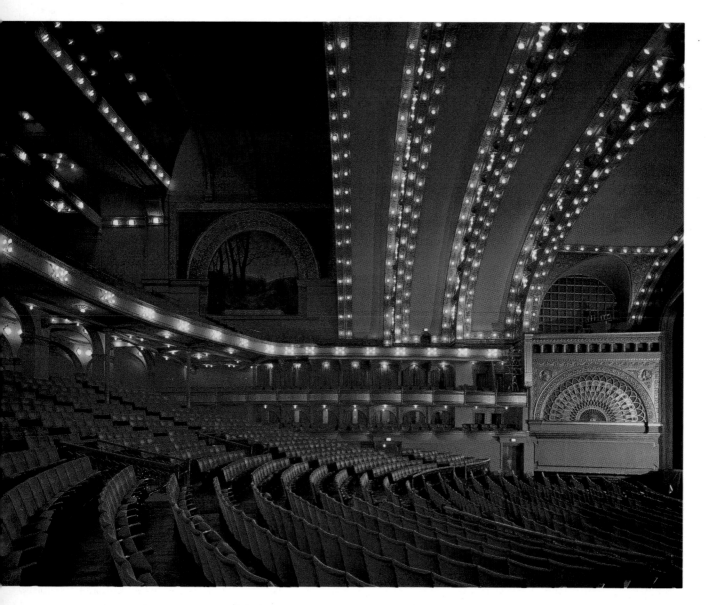

Plate 6

Auditorium Theater, after partial restoration completed in 1967, looking north, showing incandescent lights on ceiling arches and balcony and gallery railings. Vertical elliptical curvature of ceiling arches matches horizontal elliptical curvature of balcony railing. North mural, *Autumn Reverie*, by Albert Fleury. Photograph © Cervin Robinson.

Plate 7

Auditorium Theater, central art glass panel from one original nine-panel skylight bay atop coved vault over main balcony, as shown in figure 104, designed and fabricated by George L. Healy and Louis J. Millet for Adler and Sullivan. Central foliate pattern of opalescent glass (meaning colors chemically mixed in molten glass) with background of translucent cathedral glass. Photograph by Susan Reich/Richard Thomas.

Plate 8

Auditorium Hotel, dining room, central four art glass panels from one original sixteen-panel skylight bay, as shown in figures 155 and 156, designed and fabricated by Healy and Millet for Adler and Sullivan. Background of opalescent glass, combined with details of jewel-like cut or molded glass. Photograph by Susan Reich/Richard Thomas.

Plate 9

Auditorium Hotel lobby looking south, in 2000, showing tessellated marble floor, Mexican onyx marble wainscoting, scagliola-clad columns with gilded plaster capitals, and stenciled ceiling. Photograph by Jeffrey Millies © Hedrich-Blessing, negative no. 58500-A.

Plate 10

Auditorium Hotel, main stairway, landing between first and second floors looking north, in 2000, showing gold-painted wrought iron railings and bronze-plated cast iron newel posts, Mexican marble onyx wainscoting, and decorative plasterwork framing light fixtures. Ornamental tessellated marble floor of landing shown in figure 149 does not survive. Photograph by Jeffrey Millies © Hedrich-Blessing, negative no. 58500-B.

Plate 11

Auditorium Hotel, banquet hall (first restored and reopened in 1957; now Rudolf Ganz Memorial Hall, Roosevelt University) looking southeast, showing birchwood columns and capitals carved by Robert W. Bates, murals along side walls originally painted by Albert Fleury and repainted in the 1950s, original stencil panels restored by Crombie Taylor in the 1950s, and original arched art glass transom lights designed and fabricated by Healy and Millet for Adler and Sullivan. Photograph © Cervin Robinson.

Plate 12

Auditorium Hotel, banquet hall (now Rudolf Ganz Memorial Hall) looking south, showing central bay with birchwood columns and capitals carved by Robert W. Bates, restored stencil panels, and original art glass transom lights by Healy and Millet. Photograph © Cervin Robinson.

Plate 13

Adler and Sullivan, Chicago Stock Exchange Building, trading room looking northwest (1893–1894; demolished 1972); as reconstructed in the Art Institute of Chicago, 1974, showing scagliola-clad columns, gilded plaster capitals, terra cotta moldings and perforated ceiling screens, stained glass skylight panels and stenciled wall and ceiling surfaces. Reconstruction and reinstallation of the trading room was made possible through a grant from the Walter E. Heller Foundation and its president, Mrs. Edwin J. DeCosta, with additional gifts from the city of Chicago, Mrs. Eugene A. Davidson, the Graham Foundation for Advanced Studies in the Fine Arts, and Three Oaks Wrecking. Reconstruction by Vinci-Kenny, Architects. © 2000, the Art Institute of Chicago. All rights reserved.

Plate 14

Adler and Sullivan, Chicago Stock Exchange Building, reconstructed trading room looking northeast, showing scagliola-clad columns, gilded plaster capitals, terra cotta moldings and perforated ceiling screens, stained glass skylight panels, and stenciled wall and ceiling surfaces. Reconstruction and reinstallation of the trading room was made possible through a grant from the Walter E. Heller Foundation and its president, Mrs. Edwin J. DeCosta, with additional gifts from the city of Chicago, Mrs. Eugene A. Davidson, the Graham Foundation for Advanced Studies in the Fine Arts, and Three Oaks Wrecking. Reconstruction by Vinci-Kenny, Architects. © 2000, the Art Institute of Chicago. All rights reserved.

Plate 15

Chicago Stock Exchange Building, trading room, stencil on soffit of main trusses, showing application of twenty-one colors, by Healy and Millet. Photograph by Bob Shimer, Hedrich-Blessing, August 1977, HB-40799-D.

Plate 16

Chicago Stock Exchange Building, trading room, stencil on vertical face of main trusses, showing application of fifty-two colors, by Healy and Millet. Photograph by Bob Shimer, Hedrich-Blessing, August 1977, HB-40799-C.

The Auditorium Hotel: 5
Architecture and Urban Life

I f the Auditorium Theater was to be the civic locus for culture and politics, then the Auditorium Hotel was its necessary adjunct, not only as a financial support but also as a complementary architectural statement and social setting. To understand what Peck and Adler and Sullivan sought to accomplish in the hotel, one needs to examine earlier hotels in and beyond Chicago. Visitors to the Auditorium Hotel would likely be familiar with these structures, which provided functional and aesthetic standards that the Auditorium Hotel sought to surpass. Such visitors constituted a well-informed audience for Adler and Sullivan's interiors, which were keyed to the building's larger purpose as a symbol of regional identity. The hotel's facilities were to make it a civic, and occasionally national, meeting place, in the tradition of other major Chicago hotels. In this role the Auditorium Hotel's architectural interiors invited the empowered and accommodated many events central to Chicago's social history. The hotel, like elite local private clubs, housed the life of a class from which broad segments of the city's population were implicitly excluded. Yet from Peck's perspective, the Auditorium Hotel was to be inclusive and welcoming to a range of local users, reinforcing urban cohesion among different upper- and middle-class groups. Like the theater, the hotel's architecture was a statement of Chicago's capabilities in the art and craft of building. These issues underlay Adler and Sullivan's solutions, which were an inspired response to the conventions of the hotel as a modern building type.

Chicago's Hotels before and after the Great Fire

More than any other commercial building type, Chicago's hotels developed in tandem with the city's identity as a national center for railway traffic. They were the places where travelers met other travelers, travelers met local people, and locals mingled. Of the city's 125 hotels in 1876, there were 16 leading ones whose registration totals were published weekly and that collectively hosted 355,100 transient guests in that year, estimated as half Chicago's total. The major central hotels were highly self-conscious about how they compared with each other and with hotels elsewhere. Each major hotel had its own persona. Collectively they constituted a powerful interest group shaping urban life. Architecturally the hotels' scale and splendor made them the city's dominant central monuments in the era just before and after the Great Fire. One Chicago architect recalled that the hotels of the 1870s "with their legitimate architectural display exerted the controlling influences in commercial architecture."[1] More than theaters, department stores, or office buildings, the hotels were the structures by which Chicago measured its progress and visitors gauged the city's national and world standing. Yet as structures that asserted the interests of a traveling class, the hotels also prompted critique and resistance.

What gave Chicago's hotels their prominent urban role was the central city's compact commercial geography. Throughout the nineteenth century, hotels as an architectural type in Europe and the United States developed in close conjunction with railway networks. In London, where railroads first developed, the type of the railway hotel evolved as the fusion of a railway station and a hotel in one composite building. London had multiple terminals around its large periphery. In Chicago, when rail lines first connected to the eastern United States in the 1850s, railway hotels on the English model were not built. Instead, because the central city was only about one square mile in area, a ring of railroad terminals emerged around this small core, which contained a high concentration of hotel buildings as structures separate from the terminals. In the 1850s horse-drawn buses first connected the city's four major hotels and its three original stations. By 1898 this system had grown to include ten stations, accommodating twenty-five separate railway companies. Within this area, and extending into the Near West and Near North Sides, sixty-three hotels were situated in or near the elevated Loop finished in 1897. The Auditorium Hotel was inserted into one of the densest clusters of these hotels along Michigan Avenue south of the river.[2]

Before the Civil War, Chicago's two largest, most architecturally prominent hotels initiated the tradition of serving as social centers for local citizens who were prominent in business and politics. These were the third Tremont House (1850; cost, $75,000), designed by John Van Osdel as the city's first brick hotel, on the southeast corner of Lake and Dearborn, and the second Sherman House (1861; cost, $350,000), designed by William Boyington as Chicago's first marble hotel, one block to the west on the northwest corner of Clark and Randolph (fig. 130). Their locations reflected the primacy of Lake Street as the city's main commercial axis close to the Chicago River docks, the Board of Trade before it moved southward in the 1880s, the City Hall and Cook County Courthouse, and the Illinois Central Railroad's lakefront terminal. Standing five to six stories, these hotels were the first to claim artistic distinction for their interior arrangements, ornamentation, and furnishings.

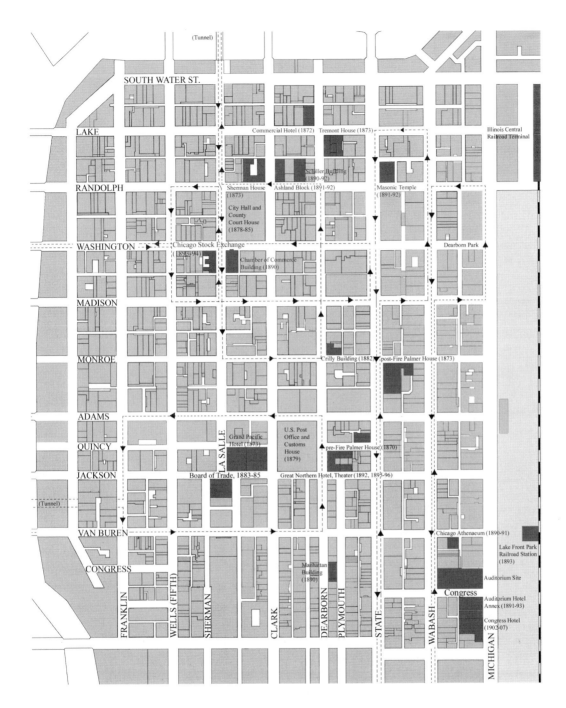

Figure 130

Chicago's Loop, c. 1896; showing major hotels, Adler and Sullivan's works, and related buildings of the 1890s, including: Tremont House (1873; demolished 1937); Sherman House (1873; rebuilt 1911); original prefire Palmer House (1870); Commercial Hotel (1872; demolished); Grand Pacific Hotel (1873; demolished 1921); postfire Palmer House (1873); Crilly Building (old Chicago Stock Exchange) (1882; demolished); Chicago City Hall and Cook County Building (1882–1885; rebuilt 1906–1911); Lake Front Park station for local trains to the World's Columbian Exposition at Jackson Park; Chicago Athenaeum, south side of Van Buren Street west of Michigan Avenue (1890–1891); Manhattan Building (1890); Chamber of Commerce Building (1890; demolished 1928); Schiller Building (1890–1892; demolished 1961); Masonic Temple (1891–1892; demolished 1939); Ashland Block (1891–1892; demolished 1929); Auditorium Hotel Annex (1891–1893) and Congress Hotel (1902–1907); Chicago Stock Exchange Building (1893–1894; demolished 1972); Great Northern Hotel and Theater (1892, 1895–1896; demolished 1961). Drawing by author.

Amenities included large public rooms, such as the Tremont House's dining room, which hosted banquets of political parties as early as 1856.[3]

During the Civil War, Chicago's economic growth as a center for railroad-dependent manufacturing, and for processing commodities like grain, meat, and timber, increased the demand for hotels, especially with completion of the first transcontinental rail link in 1869. By the 1870s Chicago and New York led other American cities in the development of the hotel building type. Hotels built after 1865 had many more private rooms, with elaborate service and grand public rooms that accommodated commercial, political, and social gatherings. Their exteriors were the first to adopt a monumental style of architecture. The redefinition of the type appeared in two prime examples before the Great Fire of 1871: the original Palmer House, designed by Van Osdel on the northwest corner of State and Quincy and opened in 1870, and the first Grand Pacific Hotel, designed by Boyington to face south on Jackson Boulevard between Clark and LaSalle Streets, and near completion when the fire destroyed it (fig. 130). These buildings set architectural standards for hotels that were not redefined until the Auditorium Hotel opened.

Begun in 1869, the original Palmer House was Chicago's first hotel designed as part of a larger vision for urban development. The prefire Palmer House was the southern anchor for the development of State Street as Chicago's leading retail street, a project initiated in the late 1860s by the hotel's owner and manager, Potter Palmer, whose real estate wealth matched the value of the Peck holdings. Having made his original fortune as a merchant during the Civil War, Palmer in 1867 took an extended vacation in Europe, where he observed the later phase of Georges-Eugène Haussmann's rebuilding of Paris under Napoleon III. When Palmer returned to Chicago, he began what one contemporary called "the Haussmannizing of State Street."[4] Assuming that Chicago would grow along the lines of its new horsecar railways, Palmer bought three-fourths of a mile of frontage along State Street, where the first horsecar line had been inaugurated in 1859. He then gave a frontal strip of his holdings to the city so the street could be widened. Palmer commissioned and encouraged others to construct new marble-fronted buildings in ornate classical styles to approximate the unified streetscape of a Parisian boulevard. By 1870 State Street had "taken the precedence over all others in point of substantial improvements, and is now the fashionable retail street—the Rue de Rivoli—of Chicago."[5] It "is Chicago concentrated. Its crowds depict the hurry of the Western metropolis. It is the artery of the city's life."[6]

Along this new urban axis, the defining stylistic ideal was that of the Renaissance as developed in such recent Parisian monuments as the Grand Hôtel de la Paix, designed by Alfred Armand on the boulevard des Capucines near the Paris Opera and opened for the international exposition of 1862 (fig. 131). Palmer thought the Grand Hôtel was the best in Europe. He had stayed there, as had Dankmar Adler when he visited Paris in 1888 during his tour of European theaters. The Grand Hôtel's street fronts displayed a commercial adaptation of the modern French classicism of the Second Empire, whose major sources in public architecture included

Figure 131

Alfred Armand, Grand Hôtel de la Paix looking southwest along the boulevard des Capucines, near the Paris Opera, opened for the international exposition of 1862. © Cliché Bibliothèque Nationale de France, Paris.

Napoleon III's New Louvre (1852–1857). This hotel had a base of shopfronts and a mezzanine below a midsection with fluted Corinthian pilasters rising from this base through two upper floors to a pronounced cornice, an attic floor, and a two-story mansard roof. These fronts screened a large glass-covered carriage court within the block, among this district's prime public interiors.[7]

American accounts described such classicism as the "modern French" style or "the modern Italian style," and its adaptation in the United States was a national trend in the 1860s and 1870s. The architect Gridley J. F. Bryant, who with Arthur Gilman adapted this style for Boston's City Hall (1861–1865), wrote of this building, "The particular style chosen is the modern style of Renaissance architecture, a style which, from its own inherent beauties, not less than from its almost universal susceptibility of adoption to structures of a dignified and monumental character, stands confessedly at the head of all the forms of modern secular architecture in the chief capitals of the world."[8] From this perspective, the Second Empire style was valued not because it was distinctly American, but because it would mark major United States cities as continuations of cosmopolitan norms.

The first major American hotel to exhibit this Second Empire style was New York's Grand Hotel, built in 1868 at 1232–1238 Broadway by architect Henry Englebert for Elias S. Higgins. Standing on the acutely angled southeast corner of Thirty-first Street, this marble-faced seven-story building had corner and central pavilions below a high-dormered mansard roof. Such transplantations of Parisian styles to Broadway were Palmer's most direct sources for his original, prefire Palmer House, begun the next year. Containing 225 rooms and costing $225,000, this first Palmer House was created to be the finest hotel in the country. Yet by the time it opened in October 1870 this distinction went to New York's Grand Central Hotel, originally known as the Broadway Central, at 667–677 Broadway, on the street's west side,

Figure 132

Henry Engelbert, architect, for Elias Higgins, Grand Central Hotel (originally Broadway Central Hotel), 667–677 Broadway, between Bleecker and West Third Streets, New York City (opened August 1870). Museum of the City of New York.

between Bleecker and West Third Streets (fig. 132), also designed by Henry Englebert for Elias Higgins. Opened in August 1870, the Broadway Central was built on the five-story marble front of the LaFarge House, an earlier hotel on the site that had survived a fire of 1867. The Broadway Central added a new sixth story and two additional floors within a mansard roof featuring a central and two end pavilions. Costing $2,000,000, with a capacity of 1,500 guests in 650 rooms, and with six dining rooms and six parlors, the Broadway Central remained New York's largest hotel as late as 1893. Palmer knew its environs, for while engaged in transforming Chicago's State Street in 1868, he said that he intended to reshape it as "the Broadway of Chicago."[9]

Completed almost simultaneously with the Broadway Central, the original Palmer House was intended to ensure that Palmer's "State street real estate has been enhanced in value, and its locality redeemed from the small class of buildings which formerly stood on the site."[10] This hotel's high cost per room, and its ornate interiors and exterior, enabled it to surpass its major local competitors and in turn inspired others to overtake Palmer. His peers included Philip F. W. Peck, Ferdinand's father and Palmer's equal as an owner of central properties. The elder Peck owned the eastern half of what became the site of the Grand Pacific Hotel. The site's value derived from its location a block north of the LaSalle Street Station, then a combined facility for two major railways. Since the Grand Pacific's leading stockholders were identified with these companies, the hotel's name alluded to Chicago's then new rail connections to the West Coast. Philip Peck had helped advance the project by agreeing to a long, thirty-year lease for his ground from 1 January 1870, for which the hotel company initially paid him $12,000 a year in rent. Peck must have assumed that improving the site with a major hotel would hugely enhance the property's value for his heirs, which it did.[11]

Boyington's design for the Grand Pacific began with a study of the country's most completely appointed hotels, and he reportedly incorporated the advice of their proprietors. His plans called for a building that "will equal the great hotels of London and Paris, and be the largest on this continent."[12] Covering a half-block site almost exactly the size of the later Marshall Field Wholesale Store's lot, the Grand Pacific's original plan featured a first floor of rentable stores and offices along its street fronts. These took advantage of the site's size to secure a large amount of rental income, which would be greater than the hotel's own ground rent. The lack of comparable rental spaces in the Auditorium Hotel proved a financial problem. In the Grand Pacific, there was a carriage entrance from Jackson Boulevard and a

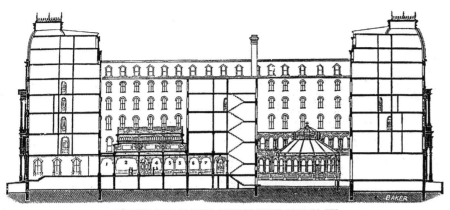

SECTIONAL VIEW OF HOTEL, SHOWING OFFICE, ROTUNDA. ETC.

1—Quincy Street Entrance. 2—News and Cigar Stands. 3—Billiards. 4—Cashier. 5—5—Office. 6—Keys. 7—Packages.

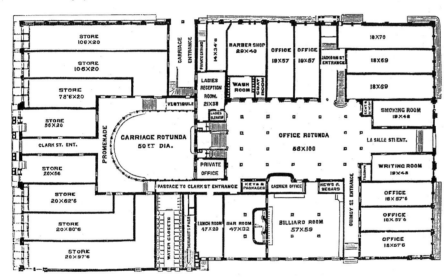

Figure 133

William Boyington, Grand Pacific Hotel, Chicago, main floor plan and east-west section looking north, showing carriage entrance off Jackson Boulevard leading to carriage rotunda and pedestrian entrance off LaSalle and Clark Streets leading to office rotunda. Rental stores and offices open onto LaSalle, Jackson, and Clark. From *Land Owner* 3 (March 1871). Courtesy of the Chicago Historical Society.

pedestrian entrance off LaSalle, both leading to rotundas roofed in glass and iron (fig. 133). The glass-roofed carriage court recalled that of Paris's Grand Hôtel de la Paix. The Grand Pacific Hotel's lobby rotunda off LaSalle Street had its roof supported on twenty Composite columns, forming a daylit hypostyle hall of 58 by 100 feet leading to a grand marble staircase at its east end. This space was perhaps a source for the famous interior glass-roofed court of Burnham and Root's Rookery one block to the north.[13]

Above the Grand Pacific's entrance level, the marble stairway led to a second floor with large reception and dining rooms. These became the informal headquarters of the local Republican Party, where many national figures were received. It was the first Chicago hotel whose interiors featured distant styles to stimulate exotic fantasies, including an India room, an Egyptian room, and an Oriental parlor for ladies. Within the main five-story block there were 550 separate guest rooms around the building's two open inner light courts above the glazed rotundas. For such special events as political conventions, there was capacity for 300 more guests in large communal wards beneath the sixth-floor mansard roofs. Dormitories in the seventh or attic floor housed guests' servants and hotel staff. On the exterior, Boyington shaped the stone in tiers of pilastered stories in the "modern French" style, with projecting columnar porticoes two stories high marking the major entrances on Clark and LaSalle Streets.[14] As the plan indicates, one could walk through promenades across the whole site between these entrances, making the hotel's lower public interiors into a variation on an urban arcade. The Grand Pacific was to serve as Chicago's central rendezvous, completely overshadowing the original Palmer House. The Grand Pacific's anticipated completion in late 1871 was to be a triumph for Philip Peck and his collaborators, yet he did not live to see the event. The Great Fire in October of that year destroyed the building just as its roof was being finished, and the elder Peck died two weeks later. Rebuilt after the fire according to the same plans, the new Grand Pacific Hotel opened in June 1873.

Even as the Grand Pacific's foundations were being laid in fall 1870, when the first Palmer House opened, Potter Palmer was planning to regain his lead by building a second Palmer House. There was a political dimension to this hotel rivalry, because Palmer was one of Chicago's leading Democrats while Peck and other supporters of the Grand Pacific were Republicans. Designed and begun before the Great Fire but not completed until 1874, the much larger postfire Palmer House was the hotel that Ferdinand Peck sought to outdo in creating the Auditorium Hotel. Adler and Sullivan's building was to succeed to the role of Chicago's leading civic gathering place. As one local observer concluded, "The Auditorium is to the city of 1891 what the Palmer House was to that of 1874."[15] Before the fire, Palmer had identified the southeast corner of State and Monroe Streets as his new site, and his architect Van Osdel drew several versions of a plan for a mammoth hotel there. Construction began before the fire of 1871, but immediately afterward Van Osdel's design was developed into its final form by the architect Charles M. Palmer (no known relation to Potter Palmer). Client and architect traveled across Europe, gathering ideas from architects and hotels in London, Paris, and Geneva, from which Potter Palmer reportedly returned with a "determination to eclipse them all" by erecting the costliest hotel in the world.[16] Palmer was compelled by local competition as the Tremont House and Sherman House rose after the fire at their old locations, on a grander scale and in Second Empire style. From 1871 to 1874 Chicagoans had invested over $20,000,000 in postfire hotel construction to provide accommodations for 5,000 guests. In 1876 one English visitor to America concluded: "More than any other city I have seen, Chicago is the city of great hotels."[17]

Like the Auditorium fifteen years later, the postfire Palmer House was the most expensive of Chicago's buildings funded by private capital, costing $2,000,000 to build and $500,000 to furnish. Palmer acquired the land, valued at $1,500,000. The postfire structure had over 700 guest rooms, which could accommodate 2,400 guests in its upper stories. Opened in November 1873, the Palmer House soon housed more guests annually than any other first-class hotel in the United States. In

1876 it registered 37,616, compared with the Grand Pacific's 32,002 and the Sherman House's 31,172, though the less expensive Commercial Hotel was the city's most popular, with 40,796 registrants. Palmer lived at his hotel with his wife, personally hosting well-known guests before building his own mansion north of the downtown on Lake Shore Drive in 1882. In the 1850s he had been among the most prominent residents of the Sherman House, along with Marshall Field's partner Levi Leiter, representing a tradition of hotel residence by leading Chicago citizens that continued in the 1880s. The Palmer House's vast ground area of 75,000 square feet made it the world's largest, fronting on three streets: State, Monroe, and Wabash Avenue. A large European palace such as the Louvre in Paris was "the work of different builders, and while some parts of it are grand and imposing, others are gloomy, dark and almost untenable."[18] By contrast, the new Palmer House was designed and built as a uniform whole, its plan brought to rapid completion to ensure architectural consistency. To guarantee fireproofing and daylight for all rooms, the ground plan was divided into open courts, the largest of which was the central carriage court (90 by 120 feet) entered by porte cocheres from all three streets. The most imposing of these on State Street had paired banded columns and a broken segmental pediment framing its arched passage, while a ladies' entrance on Monroe had a glass and iron canopy projecting over the sidewalk. The main pedestrian entrance was at the round corner's base (fig. 134). As in the Grand Pacific, distinct systems of access and movement for men and women continued inside, with separate reception rooms and elevators. Analogous public interiors meant to serve different genders recurred in Adler and Sullivan's Auditorium Hotel.

Figure 134

John Van Osdel succeeded by Charles M. Palmer, Palmer House, southeast corner of State and Monroe, Chicago (1872–1874). Photograph c. 1905. Courtesy of the Chicago Historical Society, ICHi-19225.

As Chicago's chief postfire monument, designed to house guests whose image of the city had been shaped by the Great Fire, the Palmer House was to confront visitors and citizens alike with an image of massiveness and solidity. Many of its materials were imported from Europe, their cost reduced by congressional legislation of April 1872 that allowed a rebate of import duties on materials "actually used in buildings erected on the site of buildings burned" by the Great Fire within a year of the act's passage. Over six hundred tons of wrought iron I-beams imported from Belgium supported the floors, while all bearing walls and even nonbearing partitions were of brick. To convince guests of his hotel's fireproofing, Palmer claimed that more brick was used than in any two hotels in the country and more iron than in any other United States hotel except A. T. Stewart's Working Women's Hotel in New York City. His employees made six trips to Europe to order and supervise the iron and marble work. By March 1873 crews of 350 rushed construction at night to meet the rebate deadline. Calcium lights and lanterns illuminated the "huge structure, that stood out in the artificial light like a great skeleton."[19]

The exteriors above the base were faced with a gray granite, rendered with carved detail in "the French Renaissance style."[20] One contemporary compared the exterior not to that of the Louvre but to that of the Paris Hôtel de Ville, whose crowning roofs and central lantern may have inspired Sullivan's preliminary design of the Auditorium Tower. Among private buildings, the Palmer House was considered Chicago's finest specimen of this French style. In 1890 one local observer wrote: "The center of the State street facade and the corner tower are the prime parts of the whole exterior. For almost twenty years they have claimed the worship of sightseers."[21] Like the Grand Pacific, the Palmer House's base had sixteen rental shops, whose specialties (jewelry, tailoring, confectionery, etc.) catered to the hotel's class of trade, which included long-term residents. Sixty offices occupied not only the street level but also an entresol or mezzanine story below the full second floor, long a custom in European commercial fronts, but then an innovation for Chicago. Both street level and entresol had plate glass windows framed in huge castings of locally cast ornamental iron, which cost $100,000. Later it was "advertised that patrons of the Palmer House, Chicago, can buy any conceivable article without leaving the building. The hotel is surrounded with stores and crowded with drummers," or traveling salesmen.[22]

The postfire Palmer House's interiors carried through the palatial Continental image established outside. They set a local standard that Adler and Sullivan presumably had in mind when designing the comparable spaces of the Auditorium Hotel. A visitor to the Palmer House first came into its immense lobby, 64 by 106 feet and 36 feet high (fig. 135). There Corinthian columns of yellow marble from Catalonia had gilded capitals and extraordinary spiraling brackets beneath the ceiling beams, while the surrounding counters had wainscoting of white Carrara marble with inset panels of rose brocatelle, a richly patterned marble mosaic. These were only three of the thirty-four kinds of marble imported from as many quarries. The columns gave "a grand and palatial effect to the rooms, which reminds one of the state apartments of the Tuileries in the palmy days of the [Second] Empire."[23] A grand staircase rose from this level (fig. 136). Its steps were also of Carrara marble blocks weighing 1,200 pounds, each cantilevered out from the walls, while stones at landings through all nine stories weighed 5,200 pounds each. The cantilevered staircase was modeled on that leading to the whispering gallery in the dome of Saint Paul's Cathedral, London. Bronze griffins crowned the lower newel posts, and a massive mirror of Venetian glass on the landing reflected the lobby. In 1885 Ferdinand Peck's Grand Opera Festival Association leased space for its headquarters in the Palmer House just off the lobby, near rooms where Mapleson and his performers stayed.

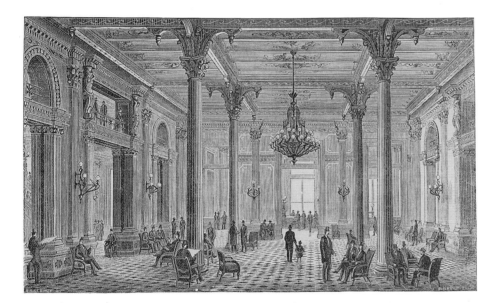

Figure 135

Palmer House, main lobby, called the grand rotunda, with Corinthian columns of yellow Catalonian marble and gilded capitals, and counters of white Carrara marble with inset panels of rose brocatelle mosaic. From Wing, *Palmer House, Chicago, Illustrated.* Courtesy of the Chicago Historical Society, ICHi-31506.

Figure 136

Palmer House, grand staircase and balcony, of white Carrara marble. From Wing, *Palmer House, Chicago, Illustrated.* Courtesy of the Chicago Historical Society, ICHi-31460.

Palmer's allusions to multiple styles of European architecture were not simply provincial eclecticism, because even by the early 1870s those who traveled to Chicago came from many countries. The style of architecture, then prevalent across Europe, was partly keyed to encouraging mercantile exchange between foreign visitors and local agents of American companies. The Palmer House claimed to be "the world in miniature, for Chicago is a cosmopolitan city, and hither come the people of all nations to traffic with our merchants; to buy our grain, lumber, live stock, and to sell us the products of the looms and forges of the old world, as well as the fruits of the tropics and the furs of the polar zone. It is not alone the English tongue or the German that one hears in the saloons of the Palmer House. The volatile Frenchman, the strange retiring Austrian, the astute Russian, the Neapolitan, the merchant of India, the restless Savoyard are there, a motley gathering of Europeans." There were several period rooms, called parlors, on the Palmer House's second floor, representing the old Egyptian and Roman styles as well as the modern French and English, so that "the parlors, halls and dining saloons are a museum of art, taking the visitor back through the ages, and recalling to mind his knowledge of history." The most famous of these was the Egyptian parlor, whose "artists studied carefully the history of that ancient civilization to enable them to depict it so perfectly and truly in the decoration."[24] It was precisely such a retrospective, Eurocentric attitude that Sullivan sought to counter in his original ornamentation for the major public interiors of the later Auditorium Hotel.

The postfire Palmer House had five dining rooms, two of them architecturally unrivaled for the period. As elsewhere, the prevailing impression was palatial and European. One was a circular room set in a rectangular hall of 48 by 56 feet built into the building's northeastern light court and entered through a hall from Monroe Street. The lack of upper floors above this dining room permitted a central

Figure 137

Palmer House, restaurant, with Corinthian columns and central skylight, surrounded by Ionic columns and mirrored wall. From Wing, *Palmer House, Chicago, Illustrated*. Courtesy of the Chicago Historical Society, ICHi-31461.

domed skylight, supported on a ring of freestanding Corinthian columns made from different-colored marbles. Around the room's outer wall, engaged Ionic columns marked bays of immense mirrors between windows (fig. 137). The mirrored outer walls created a series of reflections of the curved interior and of the outdoors seen through the windows, so that the whole restaurant was "arranged to suggest an open Italian court."[25] Artists brought from Italy and working under Potter Palmer's personal supervision fashioned this room's frescoes, marble wainscoting, and tessellated marble floor. In its function as a restaurant, and in its unique spatial shape and skylighting, this interior set an architectural standard that Adler and Sullivan sought to surpass in the Auditorium Hotel's dining room.

Given its occasional function as a rented banquet hall, the grand dining room was a larger space (64 by 76 feet and 27.5 feet high), capable of seating 1,000. It also was to serve as a ballroom (fig. 138). The room featured massive gilded fluted Corinthian columns supporting beams defining ceiling panels with frescoes, again by Italian artists. Set beneath the hotel's upper floors, the grand dining room was lighted by tall windows set between pilasters on two sides. Doors in these side walls could be thrown open to connect to three other smaller dining rooms. At each end of the room were monumental doorways, while overhead were frescoes, the central one showing "a Roman charioteer, after the style of the ancient frescoes in the ceiling of the grand hall of the [once papal] Quirinal Palace." Allusions to a papal residence were consistent with the idea of the room as "a princely *salon*," compared to the palace of the Prussian crown prince at Potsdam. In the grand dining room, "on every hand is a wealth of artistic ornamentation that astonishes and pleases the beholder . . . . The rich, variegated marble floor, the rare marbles interwoven deftly in the wainscoting, the rich paneling, the massive gilded columns, and the curiously wrought bronze chandeliers, all unite to form a scene of wonderful effect."[26] Among

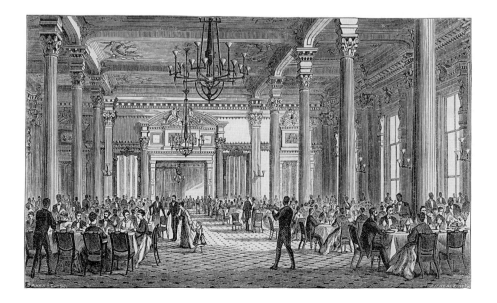

Figure 138

Palmer House, grand dining room, with gilded fluted Corinthian columns and ceiling with frescoes by Italian artists. From Wing, *Palmer House, Chicago, Illustrated*. Courtesy of the Chicago Historical Society, ICHi-31459.

the Palmer House's public interiors, it was presumably this room's architecture that Adler and Sullivan later sought to surpass in designing the Auditorium Hotel's banquet hall.

The Palmer House's grand dining room was the setting for spectacular civic banquets. Whereas local Republicans met frequently at the Grand Pacific, Potter Palmer's leadership among Chicago's Democrats made his new hotel their gathering place. Yet among the famous events in this room was a grand banquet in November 1879 for seven hundred veterans and locals honoring Ulysses S. Grant on his return from a trip around the world. Ferdinand Peck was a guest that evening and was on the reception committee at the Palmer House the day before. In November 1886 local and national Democrats dined in this room for the annual banquet of Chicago's Iroquois Club, the city's social and political group for leading party members. The club's quarters were then in the Columbia Theater building, but it leased the Palmer House's grand dining room for this fete honoring the party's national leaders. Only the city's wealthiest commercial and political groups could afford to rent such hotel facilities for special events. By contrast, Chicago's trade unions, most of which remained politically moderate and emulated the ways of the wealthy rather than revolting against them, held their dinners and dances in less central and less opulent rented spaces. In December 1887 the local Stonecutters' Union held its annual banquet in a less prestigious hotel and then repaired for its evening ball to Vorwärts Turner Hall on the West Side.[27]

Events at the Palmer House and similar hotels had more elaborate decorative settings than those for workers' festivities. An evening's decor signified a group's temporary possession of a rented space as the permanent interior architecture could not. At the Iroquois Club's banquet, American flags were draped around the room to reinforce the speakers' theme that the party's presidential victory in 1884 had reunited the country politically after the Civil War. They then discussed a range of policy issues that defined their national agenda, just two weeks after the midterm congressional elections. Palmer was always concerned with the lighting systems for his hotel's interiors, and on that evening the dining room was ablaze: "One hundred incandescent electric lights and eighty gas jets shed a strong mellow light which was brightly reflected from the huge mirrors on the walls and from the profusion of glass and silverware on the tables as well as the dazzlingly white table linen and the polished marble floor."[28] The room's eight Corinthian columns were festooned with wreaths of smilax vines and cut flowers. Similar floral centerpieces sat on twenty-four tables, each seating ten diners. Every detail of the tableware, the menu cards, and the fare bespoke Chicago's wealth as the host city, both for this evening of party solidarity and hopefully for the national convention of 1888.

One of the most characteristic features of Chicago banquets in this era was a preference for exotic game. Though the architecture was European, the meats, like the flowers, were representatively American. All manner of fish, fowl, and beast from remote regions of North America was prepared and served in multiple courses reported in local accounts of these affairs. Victual-rich menus pervaded special banquets for clubs, associations, and individuals held at hotels. The most famous social event was the Grand Pacific Hotel's annual invitation-only game banquet for over 450 of the city's leaders in business and politics. An invitation to this dinner was a prized symbol of social acceptance. Held shortly before Thanksgiving, the Grand Pacific's game banquets were designed by the proprietor, John B. Drake, who had begun the tradition in 1858 while comanaging the Tremont House. Drake employed every device to introduce nature into this urbane setting. For the banquet of 1876, the hotel's dining room "blazed with splendid appointments, flowers and center pieces of ornamental birds and wild animals perched on trees," while every place setting had an individual bouquet—larger ones for women and smaller ones for men. In the room's center "a pretty artificial mound of earth and moss was arrayed with a fountain playing in the middle, and wild fowl apparently disporting themselves under the falling spray. The top of the mound was decorated with the loveliest exotics and evergreens."[29] In 1884 the banquet's announced bill of fare featured roasted and broiled meats including buffalo, antelope, mountain sheep, and smoke-cured bear ham, while ornamental dishes were described as boned quail in plumage, partridge in nest prairie, blackbird, and sandhill crane. These repasts recalled the city's distinction as then the world's leading meatpacking center and the regional focus for consumption of rare viands from frontier lands.

The extremes of display and dining exhibited in postfire palatial hotels like the Palmer House drew criticism and protest. In Rudyard Kipling's account of his American travels in 1889, he focused on the Palmer House, "which is a gilded and mirrored rabbit warren, and there I found a huge hall of tessellated marble, crammed with people talking about money."[30] Such a critical view recurred in Frank Norris's novel *The Pit,* where he portrayed the Grand Pacific's rooms as the spatial adjunct to the ruthless struggle for wealth that dominated the Board of Trade's exchange room across Jackson Boulevard.[31] While the buildings themselves could be condemned for vulgar ostentation, it was the banquets in these hotels that most aroused the ire of local workers, whose families often were hungry. They made their protest on Thanksgiving Day, 27 November 1884, five days after the Grand Pacific's well-publicized annual game banquet for the elite. Albert Parsons's *Alarm* proclaimed: "When our Lords and Masters are feasting on Turkey and Champagne, and offering prayers of gratitude for the bounties they enjoy, the wage-slaves of Chicago, the unemployed, the enforced idle, the tramps—and the homeless and destitute will assemble in Market Square, between Randolph and Madison Sts., to mutter their curses loud and deep against the 'Lords' who have deprived them of every blessing during the past year."[32] Carrying the red flag of revolution and the black flag as a symbol of death from hunger, some 3,000 protesters assembled on that day, when sleet, rain, and snow fell continuously. After Parsons and others had spoken, the crowd proceeded south on Market Street to Monroe, where they turned east to march straight at the Palmer House's round corner before turning north on State Street. As the marchers passed this hotel, "the band struck up the 'Marseillaise' and the procession cheered and groaned alternately. One gentleman who evidently 'puts up' at the Palmer and had had his full supply of 'turkey and champaign' was heard to say: 'Oh, this is only intended to scare us. It's only a bluff.' A bystander replied, 'Well, my friend, before two years roll round, this thing will be serious enough to suit you or anybody else.'"[33] This anonymous prophecy proved accurate, for the Haymarket tragedy was then less than eighteen months away.

Peck's Program for the Auditorium Hotel, Michigan Avenue, and the Lakefront

Chicago's postfire efforts at hotel building yielded accommodations for 5,000 guests; by the opening of the World's Columbian Exposition twenty years later, the city's hotel capacity had grown to accommodate 500,000 visitors. By 1890 it was estimated that Chicago's population included about 200,000 transients, in a city by then geographically expanded to include 1,900,000 permanent residents. In the 1880s the prime location for new hotels was Michigan Avenue opposite Lake Front Park (fig. 54). On the southwest corner of Michigan and Jackson was the Leland Hotel (later known as the Stratford). First designed by Boyington in 1872 as the Gardner Hotel, it was Michigan Avenue's first successful luxury hotel.[34] Built in 1875, the Victoria Hotel (earlier known as the Beaurivage Bachelor Apartments) stood on the northwest corner of Michigan and Van Buren. The Brunswick Hotel eventually had the six-story building designed by Burnham and Root and completed in 1883 on the northwest corner of Michigan and Adams. Like the Auditorium Hotel, these structures functioned partly as residential hotels for the wealthy in addition to accommodating traveling guests. Peck envisioned that the Auditorium Hotel would both surpass these neighboring predecessors in size and contrast with them in style.

The most recent and prestigious of the Auditorium Hotel's competitors was the Hotel Richelieu, opened in 1885 as the remodeling of a six-story postfire apartment building on Michigan Avenue between Jackson and Van Buren. Created by H. V. Bemis, a local entrepreneur, the Richelieu was designed to attract European visitors. Its name was similar to those of the period's first-class New York hotels, over half of which had British or French names designed to appeal to a "class, especially among the newly rich, for whom the 'imported' alone has charms."[35] Chicago's Richelieu Hotel was the most Francophile establishment in the city. Over its arched entrance stood a white marble statue of Cardinal Richelieu by a French sculptor. Interiors ornamented in papier-mâché included the clubroom, where Bemis had assembled a collection of glass and china that included the dining plates of the Napoleonic family. Bemis also created the Richelieu Art Gallery, stocked with a collection of paintings he acquired while traveling abroad. The hotel's most notable room was a café whose cuisine was "the first and only example of high-class French cooking in a Chicago hotel," enhanced by a nationally reputed wine collection.[36] In 1893 a local guide reported that the Richelieu's interiors, service, "and the indefinable thing called 'tone' are such as to attract guests of great reputation and large wealth."[37] Among these were opera personalities, including Adelina Patti, who stayed at the Richelieu when she came to Chicago to inaugurate the Auditorium Theater in December 1889.

It was into this context that Peck sought to introduce a different kind of hotel within the Auditorium Building. More than most prominent hotels, the Auditorium's would link to the theatrical world. Yet unlike its local predecessors, it was not designed to imitate European architecture. Instead its material language proclaimed its original, American, and distinctly regional character. By 1890 the Grand Pacific and the Palmer House were the favorite hotels for well-heeled commercial travelers, whereas the Auditorium Hotel was more often the choice of first-time visitors to Chicago, who came not on business but as tourists. Whereas the Richelieu specialized in catering to European visitors, the Auditorium Hotel was meant to attract "those very sensible Americans who believe in traveling in their own country."[38] As Sullivan later recalled, the Auditorium Hotel "at that time was considered the most magnificent in the country."[39] After it opened in winter 1890, Peck wrote that the Auditorium Association had "done more and proposed a more liberal policy in building this hotel and gone further in fixtures, appliances, fittings, etc. than any other case in this country in the history of hotel construction so far as we are able to ascertain."[40]

As in Chicago's other hotels, some suites of the Auditorium Hotel were meant to house long-term residents. A number of Chicago's leading citizens, including Mayor John Wentworth and Gen. Philip Sheridan, were permanent hotel residents. Sullivan himself lived in residential hotels among his many addresses from his return to Chicago from Paris in 1875 until he moved into his own house in 1892, and again from 1896 until his death in 1924. To accommodate such people, the Auditorium Hotel's most fully equipped guest suites were "designed as flats with private halls leading into them."[41] From the beginning it was planned to "serve a double purpose—a public and a private institution—catering particularly, however, to the very large class to be found in every city that prefers hotel life to the trouble and expense of a home . . . . The management of the new hotel will also make a special effort to obtain the patronage of the representatives of various commercial lines—milliners, dressmakers, and dry-goods men—who come from the neighboring towns and cities to remain for some time, and who do not like the noise and bustle of the average hotel devoted to the entertainment of transients who come for a day."[42] The Auditorium Hotel, like its rivals, combined the functions of commercial hotel, apartment house, and downtown club.

With over four hundred rooms, the Auditorium Hotel's capacity was twice that of its neighbors along Michigan Avenue. In Peck's view, the building's monumental scale served to hasten the lakefront's improvement, which was the most contested urban design issue in Chicago. Part of the controversy lay in the alternative futures projected for Michigan Avenue. On one hand, the presence of five major hotels within several blocks implied that it would become a central tourist axis, as it eventually did. In this scenario, the Auditorium would do for Michigan Avenue what the Palmer House had done for State Street. Yet having grown up on Michigan Avenue when its frontage was residential, Peck did not wish to see it go the way of New York City's Fifth Avenue, where by 1890 commercial functions were supplanting fine residences. Although he anticipated that the World's Columbian Exposition would mean an increase in the number of Michigan Avenue's stores and restaurants, he imagined that such commercial development would be only temporary. He hoped that after the exposition, Chicago's wealthy citizens would build a new generation of villa-like residences on Michigan Avenue. Peck wanted them to relocate there from Prairie Avenue on the South Side, where he, Marshall Field, and their peers lived, and from Lake Shore Drive on the North Side, whose development for the rich began with Potter Palmer's castellated mansion there, built in 1882. Peck wanted such residences to become characteristic of Michigan Avenue downtown, "so that it would again be what it was in the old days when [Chicago's] first citizens resided here."[43] The city's elite would repossess the central lakefront's axial street, while the park to the east and shoreline would be publicly accessible.

Peck and others foresaw that the fair's long-term effect would be the improvement of Lake Front Park. In April 1893, when unveiling the bronze statue of Columbus in Lake Front Park, Peck told Mayor Carter Harrison: "Our metropolis needs more monuments, and what more fitting place for them than this beautiful Lake- Front, which, lying at the very doors of our business center, should forever be the people's park, enlarged if possible, and embellished with statues, fountains, and walks—a great open lawn upon the shores of Lake Michigan."[44] Peck's vision was rooted in his boyhood memory of the lakefront when his family lived on the site of what became the Grand Pacific Hotel. In 1889 he remembered "distinctly that in his day he could look across an almost unbroken distance of nearly half a mile to the shore of Lake Michigan, where the waves dashed upon the very spot [where the Richelieu Hotel stood]. Hardly a house or improvement of any kind to obscure the view, and no railroad trestle, breakwater, or government pier to break the surf on this shore."[45] In this context, Peck's call for an unobstructed lakefront corresponded to his aim of reshaping Michigan Avenue into a residential boulevard, as if he wished to return to a time when the wealthy lived near the lake's natural shoreline.

The restoration of Michigan Avenue as Chicago's prime residential street along an enhanced Lake Front Park depended on changes in the permanent tracks of the Illinois Central Railroad. In the late 1880s this company, the Michigan Central, and their connections ran more than sixty trains a day past the Auditorium's site. A local observer wrote of the lakefront's adjacent recreational landscape: "The beauty of this park is sadly marred by the continual passing along its front of the trains."[46] In February 1886, just as his allies were negotiating acquisition of the Auditorium's site, Peck and other civic leaders met in the Grand Pacific Hotel to protest the prolonged

inactivity of federal, state, and municipal governments in planning for public reclamation of the lakefront. Earlier state and city actions had given the railroad a 300-
foot right-of-way, but ownership of the land east of Michigan Avenue was not clear.
The United States, the state of Illinois, the city of Chicago, and the Illinois Central
all cited evidence of their rights to these properties, by then worth millions.[47] Peck
read a resolution that "some organized movement should be made to bring the
controversy between the public authorities in behalf of the people and the Illinois
Central Railroad company in behalf of the stockholders to the speediest possible
conclusion."[48] Peck was appointed to a committee to pursue this issue with the governor, the mayor, and Illinois congressmen and senators.

Controversy between public interest and the Illinois Central over the lakefront's fate was not resolved while the Auditorium was being built, but there was no
doubt about Peck's vision of his building as a monumental backdrop for Chicago's
central shoreline park. His intentions for the lakefront contained the mix of elite
and democratic attitudes that informed his ideas for the theater. What held these
contradictions together in his mind was the ideal of building and lakefront as non-
commercial urban places. Peck was not alone in this view. In 1887 a friend sought to
build a for-profit toboggan slide on the lakefront. Hotel owner Warren Leland, who
feared his guests would be disturbed by rowdiness, sought an injunction to stop the
project. He argued "that it has no right there; that the city owes its good health to
the open front; and that if the city cannot afford to develop the ground and make a
good park or common of it for the sake of the enjoyment of its poor who haven't
their carriages, then the ground should be put in the hands of the Park Commissioners." In 1890 Leland pushed for closure and demolition of the Exposition Building, nearly opposite his hotel, as a commercial blot on the lakefront that obstructed
views of the water. He was also among those Michigan Avenue property owners
who took legal steps to stop the downtown lakefront from being used as the site for
the World's Columbian Exposition.[49]

Such anticommercial attitudes toward the lakefront derived from the special
character of Michigan Avenue (officially called Michigan Boulevard south of Jackson Street), which was reserved for horseback riding and pleasure driving in carriages. Like other avenues connected to Chicago's park system, Michigan was not
under the care of the city but was controlled by the park commissioners, to whom
"almost despotic powers have been entrusted in order to secure first-class streets."[50]
Michigan Avenue's conversion into a driving boulevard began in spring 1881 with
the improvement of paving, sidewalks, and curbing extending south from Lake
Front Park to Twenty-seventh Street. No heavy commercial traffic was permitted on
its macadamized pavement to preserve its surface of pulverized white granite in superb condition for horseback riding, carriage driving, and later bicycling, socially
privileged modes of recreation. The cost of such paving was $200,000 a mile, met by
a tax assessed on nearby properties.

Michigan Avenue's paving differed dramatically from that of Chicago's downtown streets. One account of the city's typical pavements in 1880 recalled that a man

Figure 139

Michigan Avenue, c. 1890, looking north, with Auditorium Hotel at left, Studebaker Building and Art Institute to the north, and the Victoria, Richelieu, and Leland hotels in the distance. East of Michigan Avenue, the Inter-state Industrial Exposition Building was taken down from May 1891. Auditorium Collection, Roosevelt University Archives.

who walked "would make his way over wooden sidewalks of various levels, his footsteps resounding with the planks. If he drove, his carriage would roll over wooden blocks in which the wheels of traffic had often made deep ruts."[51] An eastern observer noted that "the solid-looking, well-filled business blocks seem to demand a paving of nothing less substantial than Belgian stone, instead of the round pieces of wood placed on end that are to be found in a large number of the bustling thoroughfares, even including some of the busiest streets of the business district." This writer noted that "from ten o'clock in the morning until late in the afternoon, the curbstones are well nigh monopolized by rows of horses and light buggies."[52] By contrast, an observer of 1888 wrote: "The whole length of Michigan Avenue you will never see a loaded team." The lack of such vehicles and the quality of the paving meant that when a pleasure driver "has entered Michigan Avenue he need not pull rein for twenty or thirty miles."[53] A varied throng of light vehicles paraded daily past the Studebaker Building, where many were built and sold (fig. 139).

Sunday drives were an urban social ritual in many European and American cities, especially in New York City's Central Park. Visitors to Chicago remarked on the great extent of the paved drives and the uninhibited speed of the teams there.

As one easterner observed, the city "does everything that it puts its hand to with tremendous energy." On a Sunday in January, when the sleigh riding was good, someone estimated that there were as many as "ten thousand teams flying up and down Michigan Avenue and the Grand Boulevard," another avenue of Chicago's park system.[54] Sporting use of public drives was not a male prerogative, since women also sped by with fast horses pulling sleighs. In summer the sleighs were replaced by bicycles, whose riders organized cycling clubs that made the Auditorium their rendezvous before construction of the Chicago Athletic Association's building farther north on Michigan Avenue in 1892. As a national center for bicycle manufacture by 1895, Chicago then had no fewer than five hundred cyclists' clubs for a range of social classes.[55] These activities distinguished Michigan Avenue from the city's commercial streets, just as the Auditorium Building was the civic counterweight to the Board of Trade. Recreational use of Michigan Avenue claimed this prime axis for privileged owners of pleasure horses and vehicles, effacing the memory of the avenue's use as a parade route and meeting place for Chicago's anarchists before Haymarket.

Peck's proposals for the lakefront improvement reached to the water's edge and beyond. He imagined that the broad ribbon of railroad tracks between the avenue and the shore would be sunk and terraced over, so that the eastern edge of Lake Front Park would become a stone breakwater. In addition to the railroads, however, shipping companies like those that handled the city's enormous lumber trade pushed for permits to build docks along the lakeshore south of the Chicago River. In this period some Chicagoans asserted that their city was the country's leading port, with annual statistics of ship arrivals and departures (though not tonnage) greater than even New York's. On 1 July 1889, lumber interests petitioned the city council to improve the river's outer harbor, including "the sale of the lake front property, and the use of the proceeds for the construction of wharves and docks." If this petition had been accepted, the city would have lost this defining civic lakefront to docks that would be privately controlled for commercial purposes.[56]

From 1833 to 1839, Ferdinand Peck's father had petitioned the city council to grant him wharfing privileges on the Chicago River near his Lake Street store to handle goods and build a wharf. These wharfing lots along both sides of the river inland from its mouth at the lakefront still existed in the 1880s. It was presumably this kind of private control of the shoreline that Ferdinand Peck, the philanthropic son of his entrepreneurial father, wanted to ban from the lakefront. In the meeting of February 1886, Ferdinand Peck advanced a resolution that "no corporation or individual should be permitted to build docks within the limits of the harbor, and that we believe it to be vital to the interests of the City of Chicago that the municipality should own and control all such docks."[57] Peck wanted the lakefront to have purely recreational dockage, like the summer resort at Oconomowoc, Wisconsin, where he sailed Lake Michigan for pleasure and led a boating club. In Chicago the variety of commercial boats on the lake included tugs and steamboats that burned soft coal and expelled greasy black smoke like railway steam engines. Many sailboats offshore rented out their mainsails for advertising, so that even looking out onto the lake one saw the city's commercial impulse in black lettering on white sails announcing to those on shore the virtues of local products and attractions. After 1885, introduction of a new type of gasoline-powered launch, combined with new ordinances banning commercial vessels from the lakefront, was to rid Chicago's shore of chemical and visual pollution south of the river. Peck envisioned that sails hired for advertising would be replaced by the unmarked canvas of recreational boats, complementing the cleanliness of the modern launches.[58] The public lakefront would be the antithesis of the river's private wharves, just as recreational Michigan Avenue contrasted with the Loop's commercially clogged streets.

The Auditorium Hotel as Regional Statement and Public Club

Given Peck's aims for the Auditorium Building's urban environs, the hotel's public rooms had to convey a clear civic dimension. With the theater in the center of the site, these rooms had to be arranged around the periphery on the east and south sides. This sacrificed the possibility of placing revenue-generating stores around these areas on the first floor, spaces important to the solvency of the Grand Pacific and the Palmer House. The theater's volume filled most of the Auditorium Building's central court, blocking daylight around the court's inner walls. Therefore the hotel's lower floors had rooms with windows only along the outside walls. Even with these drawbacks, the Auditorium Hotel was a crucial source of income for Peck's project, given the large bond issue required to finance its construction and the consequent annual interest payments.

The hotel was to be managed by a separate company that would pay an annual rental to the Auditorium Association. In October 1888 the directors recommended that the hotel's annual rental be fixed at $100,000 for its first five years of operation.[59] In January 1889 Peck and his colleagues met with several local prospective hotel proprietors. To the association's dismay, they estimated that, given its architectural configuration, the hotel would reliably generate an annual rental income of only $50,000.[60] Peck then traveled to New York to interview other prospective proprietors who had approached him about leasing what was to be "the finest of all hotels in America."[61] On his return he recommended that the board approve a lease with a company to be created and headed by James H. Breslin, manager of the Gilsey House on Broadway and Twenty-ninth Street from its opening in 1871, and Richard Southgate, managing proprietor of New York's Brunswick Hotel at 225 Fifth Avenue, which had closed in 1885. Both men had made their reputations as creators of Saratoga's Congress Hall, built in 1868 as one of the country's premier Victorian resort hotels. After meeting with the Auditorium's directors, Breslin and Southgate agreed to operate the hotel for an annual rental of $100,000.[62] The Auditorium Association agreed to share expenses of the hotel's operation in return for receiving a share of its gross earnings to help finance the theater. As a condition of this agreement, Breslin and Southgate demanded that a banquet hall be added to the building. Adler and Sullivan were then instructed to insert this large hall and its ancillary rooms into the structure, whose hotel was to open in January 1890. By then the Auditorium was "the chief topic of conversation among the hotel fraternity for months past," since the national hotel managers' association had toured the building during their Chicago convention in May 1889.[63]

Peck's engaging New Yorkers to manage Chicago's Auditorium Hotel hints at the continuing interaction between the two cities as a powerful motive underlying Adler and Sullivan's design not only of the theater but also of the hotel. Just as the Auditorium Hotel was the first of Chicago's larger new hotels of the 1890s, so this decade saw the emergence of the large luxury hotel in Manhattan. When the Auditorium Hotel opened, it was, as Peck had intended, larger and more elaborate than hotels built in New York in the 1880s. In 1889, just after the opening of London's Savoy Hotel, a Manhattan editor lamented the city's lack of "a really great hotel," concluding that "there is nothing distinctive, nothing Metropolitan," about any of the existing ones.[64] The next year that situation changed with the opening of the original Plaza Hotel, on the west side of Fifth Avenue between Fifty-eighth and Fifty-ninth Streets, and the Imperial Hotel on the southeast corner of Broadway and Thirty-second Street. The first as built was largely designed by McKim, Mead and White, who wholly designed the second. Both structures illuminate by contrast Adler and Sullivan's intentions for the Auditorium Hotel.

In both cities, the hotels of 1890 set new standards of decorative splendor in their public interiors; yet in contrast to Sullivan's ideal of distinct American character in architecture, Stanford White designed his hotels' major rooms as emulations of European settings. The Plaza's ground-floor reception rooms were hung with Gobelin tapestries, while above, its enormous main dining room had a ceiling decorated with frescoes and walls hung with large paintings executed in Paris, representing the five senses. Second-floor parlors facing Fifth Avenue were furnished in eighteenth-century French styles. At the Imperial, White went a step further, reproducing whole rooms from illustrious European buildings.[65] In his Kindergarten Chats of 1901, Sullivan criticized the Imperial (fig. 140) and those Chicago buildings that imitated it, such as the Marshall Field Annex (1892–1893), designed by Charles Atwood of D. H. Burnham and Company. For Sullivan such works typified "a large class of structures fortunately for us more rampant in the East than in the West," whose historical motifs failed to clearly convey their use type or function.[66] Sullivan saw these buildings as representing a commercial appropriation or commodification of older styles, without the expressive power as architecture that he felt must be deeply rooted in the culture of their modern period and American location. For Sullivan such buildings contrasted with Richardson's Marshall Field Wholesale Store, whose forms did powerfully convey the character of its society. Similarly, as

Figure 140

McKim, Mead and White, Imperial Hotel, southeast corner of Broadway and Thirty-second Street, New York City (1889–1891). From *American Architect and Building News* 30 (25 October 1890). Photograph courtesy of Leland M. Roth.

Peck intended, the Auditorium Building was to represent the present as an American monument of the nineteenth century. Though informed by historical styles, it would, as Adler said of Richardson's and Root's buildings, transform these sources into an architecture that signified its own country and time.

Beyond this, the Auditorium was also to represent the persona of its city as a culturally independent region. In January 1890, at one of the hotel's dedicatory events, Peck said that the building was an answer to "criticisms that have been made of our beloved city," one being "that we lack an appreciation of art. The art which is represented in the architecture and within the interior of the Auditorium Building, and the musical art which it fosters, all made possible by the liberality of our cultured citizens, are the most tangible evidences of Chicago's love and appreciation of the artistic."[67] Rudyard Kipling's negative response to Chicago epitomized the kind of criticism Peck referred to, where the city was seen as barbaric in its rampant materialism. Kipling's critique was well known locally, but the Auditorium's supporters also noted that Kipling wrote that Chicago "was the one great American city having a civilization of its own, a sense of the beautiful in nature belonging to itself, and ideas of applied art based upon its own wants, its own ideas, its own appreciations."[68] The Auditorium would not only offer proof of Chicago's aesthetic appreciation but present that sensibility as distinctive in the nation, especially relative to New York's dependence on European models of architecture.

From Sullivan's perspective, the ideal of an American architecture merged with Chicago's efforts to find its voice through this medium. In this spirit, Garczynski wrote of the Auditorium: "Chicagoans are as exacting as their climate, and will not long endure the presence of that which lives among them without becoming of them. And this explains the passionate attachment that all feel for the Auditorium, which is of Chicago to the smallest detail. The architecture, the decoration, the engineering, the metal work, the wood carving, the mosaic floor, the scagliola, all owe their being and their inception to Chicago men."[69] Very little of this art and craft was imported from the East or from Europe, unlike that in the Palmer House. Of the Auditorium Building's forty-five contractors and manufacturers, at least thirty-five were Chicago firms, five had offices in both Chicago and another city, and five were from outside Chicago. The Auditorium thus signified local technical and artistic independence and originality. This message merged with Peck's social agenda for the project because it demonstrated Chicago's capabilities in the building arts, which would draw contracts to the city's firms and improve the economic condition of skilled workers in these trades. Peck believed that Chicago's future hinged on the opinions of such skilled workers, long solicited by the anarchists. The Auditorium's construction and programs would provide a compelling alternative to such radical doctrines. The architecture of its hotel was to be a display of formal imagination and craftsmanly skill unique to the city, whose contractors were eager "to show the world what could be done in Chicago."[70]

While the project's goal was to display local artistry and workmanship, the interiors of the Auditorium Hotel were for patrons who would enjoy there an approximation of an elite gentlemen's club. As an English visitor in 1887 wrote of the Palmer House, "the word 'hotel' in its broadest sense in the States includes much more than merely food and lodging. It means, in addition, a sort of public club. There are extensive parlours, reception, reading, writing, and smoking rooms, lifts constantly running, electric call bells and lights, with complete attendance and messenger service; . . . [a] most gorgeous bar and barber's shop, each having a fortune invested in their decoration; the eating rooms that keep going from before daylight till past midnight without interruption; the restaurant, wine, and coffee rooms."[71] The Auditorium Hotel was to surpass not only the Palmer House but Chicago's private men's clubs, which had developed their own architecture.

Peck was a member of several clubs. The most politically and architecturally important was the Union League Club, whose monumental headquarters on the southwest corner of Jackson Boulevard and Fourth Street had opened on Monday, 10 May 1886, six days after Haymarket (fig. 141). Designed by William Le Baron Jenney, who was also a member, this five-story building was expanded in 1889 with a twenty-five-foot addition to the west on Jackson Boulevard. By then Chicago's Union League Club was the largest building in the country devoted to club purposes, including the Union League Club in New York. Jenney's exterior of brick, trimmed with red sandstone and Bedford limestone, was said to be modeled on fourteenth-century Lombard and Florentine sources. Healy and Millet decorated its interiors, the most celebrated being the two-story banquet hall on the fourth floor, seating four hundred and crowned by a circular skylight of stained glass. This room could be thrown open to an adjacent art gallery in the annex to double the available seating. The art gallery was canopied with a skylight for nearly its full length of seventy-five feet, with wall space tall enough for hanging pictures twenty-five feet high. Members acquired over one hundred paintings from Europe and the United States for this room, opened as part of the annex on 7 December 1889, two days before the Auditorium Theater's dedication, when President Harrison was Peck's guest at the club.

Figure 141

William Le Baron Jenney, Union League Club, 65 West Jackson Boulevard, southwest corner of Custom House Place (later Federal Street), Chicago (opened May 1886, with annex of 1889 as last bay at right, on Jackson; demolished 1927). The original north half of the Monadnock Building (1891) by Burnham and Root stood across Custom House Place to the east (left) beyond this view. From a drawing by William B. Mundie, then Jenney's assistant and later partner from 1891. From *Graphic* (Chicago), o.s., 12 (22 March 1890). Courtesy of the Chicago Historical Society.

"Commanding a fine outlook on Lake Michigan," the dining room's panorama spatially certified its members' disproportionate power over their city. From the windows of the semicircular room for private dinner parties in the corner tower, "one can gaze in every direction."[72] While it was a source of pride to members, the Union League Club building's fusion of capital and culture made it a symbol of those disparities decried by the period's radical labor leaders. During the IWPA's protest march on Thanksgiving Day 1884, "As the procession moved through the boulevards and avenues, which were lined with aristocratic palaces on either side, the men in line would cheer. At one fashionable club house [the Union Club] of the high toned on the corner of Washington Park and Dearborn Ave., the demonstrators groaned, hissed and hooted at the old and young sprigs of aristocracy who filled the windows and were beholding their future executioners."[73] In the face of such threats, one symbol of the Union League Club's political stance appeared in its annex's art gallery. Among the pictures hung there, "the most noticeable . . . was the immense painting of 'Custer's Last Rally,' which occupied the entire south wall."[74] In the late nineteenth century the image of "the last stand" was frequently invoked as a metaphor for defense of high capitalist views against real or imagined opponents of the established economic order.

Although politically conservative, the Union League Club was the first in Chicago to admit women as guests, if not as members. Women had had a voice in the development of Jenney's design, which, at their request, included a separate entrance, elevator, reception room, and private dining room for wives of members. The building's opening marked Chicago women's entry into the city's club life, and those who came that night "were grateful for the hospitality with which they were received into the club, and expressed their gratitude openly. The Union League Club is the only club in the country which extends to the ladies of the members the same privileges which it does to the members themselves. For the present there is virtually no difference."[75] Adler and Sullivan engaged the same issue in their design for the Standard Club's new building of 1887–1888, on the southwest corner of Michigan Avenue and Twenty-fourth Street. Founded in 1869, the Standard Club was created by and for prominent Jewish men, with Adler being a member. Like the Union League Club's quarters, the Standard Club's new building included a suite of rooms for wives of members, who were part of the club's life.[76] These interior arrangements for both men and women in club buildings had their counterparts in the public rooms that Adler and Sullivan designed in the Auditorium Hotel.

Adler and Sullivan's Designs for the Lower Public Rooms

In describing the Auditorium Building's foundations, Adler noted that the goal for the hotel's structural design was to create flexible interiors for the public rooms on its street level and second floor. To achieve this aim, Adler minimized fixed interior bearing walls and structural columns between the inner and outer masonry bearing walls of the hotel block on Michigan Avenue and Congress Street. The structural plan of the first floor reveals that along Congress Street, deep steel girders created a column-free, clear span of about thirty-six feet between inner and outer walls (fig. 74a). Deep girders also span between the hotel lobby's inner and outer walls on Michigan Avenue (fig. 74b), yet this east space's greater depth below the hotel's nine upper floors necessitated a row of five columns in the first-floor lobby (fig. 74c) and in the second-floor reception hall.[77]

The original spaces on the hotel's first floor are shown in its plan of 1887 (fig. 142). These spaces were the lobby or office off Michigan Avenue, which still exists in a partially restored form, and the reading room and porter's den north of the lobby and also extant, but not in their original condition. In a special doorway set in the southernmost of the three main arched entrances off Michigan Avenue, there was an entrance to the hotel for ladies, which led directly to the paired elevators. Accessible from this hall was the ladies' restaurant in the southeast corner. Heading west, one passed from the lobby through a long corridor to the men's café and bar and the barbershop, which served both men and women, also along the hotel's south side. The men's cafe and ladies' restaurant shared a serving room linked to the basement kitchens. Originally the three individual arched doors from Congress Street led directly into the ladies' restaurant, men's café, and barbershop. West of the barbershop, just east of the tower, was another entrance to the hotel for ladies, which also served as the theater's main south exit to Congress Street. This entrance led to

Figure 142

Auditorium Building, first-floor plan, 1887, showing (a) lobby or office off Michigan Avenue; (b) reading room and (c) porter's den north of lobby; (d) ladies' entrance south of lobby, leading to (e) elevators and (f) ladies' restaurant in southeast corner, with its own separate entrance from Congress Street; (g) corridor leading from lobby west to (h) men's café and bar and (i) barber shop; (j) serving room between men's café and ladies' restaurant, with stairs to basement kitchen; and (k) ladies' entrance to hotel on Congress Street, with elevators (l) serving banquet hall on seventh floor. This entrance also served as the theater's exit south to Congress Street. Architecture Photograph Collection, Courtesy of the Art Institute of Chicago.

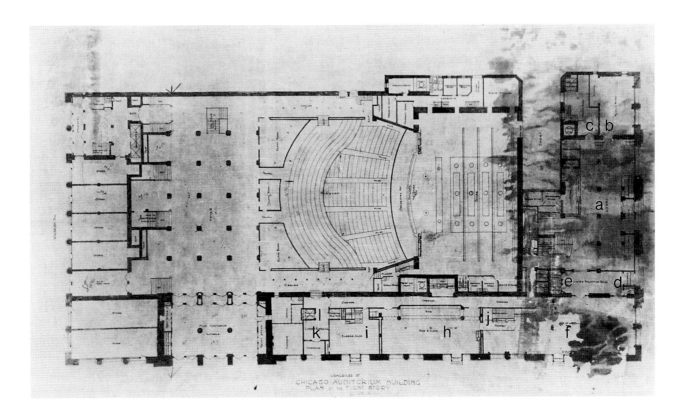

elevators that rose to the hotel's seventh-floor banquet hall. In the 1950s the street's widening and the creation of an outdoor sidewalk within the Auditorium's granite arcade there destroyed the hotel's interiors along Congress, the outer half of the theater's lobby, and the office block's southwestern corner bay.[78]

As in the theater, so in the hotel one does not see the structure of brick walls, iron columns, and trussed ceilings. Instead these skeletal elements are covered by a system of ornamental surfaces. The Auditorium's interiors were not about the literal expression of structure that preoccupied the later Modern Movement. Rather, Sullivan, like most architects of the period, clad iron construction with decoratively rendered materials. As Garczynski wrote, "Within the four retaining walls, the whole inner construction is a maze of iron columns and steel girders, masked by every kind of architectural device."[79] Sullivan and his collaborators developed cladding to address "the imperative necessity for some substance of a decorative character that would hide the iron in fireproof structures."[80]

The original hotel's lobby or office was to be the showpiece of Chicago's building arts for out-of-town guests (fig. 143; plate 9). In 1887 an English visitor wrote of the Palmer House: "The capacious hall in front of the office is a news exchange for the busy town, who bustle and talk, and give, in the swarming crowd who throng there, an active business air."[81] Like the Palmer House, the Auditorium Hotel's lobby (75 by 90 feet) had freestanding columns supporting a beamed ceiling and arched motifs recurring around the walls. But Sullivan treated these elements differently than had Palmer's architect. His highly original foliate ornament provided a consistent visual theme overlaid onto capitals, arches, cornices, balusters, and corbels, architecturally unifying this space of many disparate elements. The surfaces were fabricated mostly by local firms, who reportedly responded to Peck's enthusiasm for making the Auditorium's architecture outstanding in every detail so "that they turned out the very best work that was possible."[82]

Around the lobby, walls and counters were clad not in European marbles, as in the Palmer House, but in a wainscoting of Mexican onyx ten feet high. The onyx did not exhibit a pure white surface like the Carrara marble in the Palmer House's counter. Instead, "the variations of color and veining are apparently endless in these exquisite specimens" of Mexican onyx, including "mixed translucent, opalescent, and opaque passages."[83] The colors range from dark brown, yellow and green to aquamarine, purple, and white. Mexican onyx was thought to be equal to Algerian onyx, one of the most celebrated ornamental marbles for ancient Roman architecture. In the Auditorium Hotel, the interior onyx wainscoting, like the granite base outside, provided a geologic display of nature's variety analogous to what Sullivan admired in plant life. One of his contemporaries wrote: "Limestones are, in one sense, a link between the mineral and the animal kingdoms, since most of them have an organic origin and possess, on that account, an interest above that of most other rocks . . . . They contain more organic remains than any other rock and by their general distribution afford proof that the waters of the earth, in past eras, as they are now, were inhabited by an unlimited number and diversity of organized

Figure 143

Auditorium Hotel lobby looking south, showing tessellated marble floor, wainscoting of Mexican onyx, iron columns clad in scagliola with gilded plaster capitals, and stenciled ceiling. At right is hotel desk with main staircase beyond framed by arch with clear span of thirty-four feet. At south end of lobby is onyx partition wall screening ladies' entrance corridor from southernmost doors off Michigan Avenue (out of view at left) to elevators at right (framed by farthest foreshortened arch). Arch beyond opening in onyx wall frames entrance to ladies' restaurant. Compare with contemporary view of this space in plate 9. Photograph by J. W. Taylor. Avery Architectural and Fine Arts Library, Columbia University in the City of New York.

beings."[84] The allusion to marine life implicit in this choice of stone would relate to the Auditorium Building's proximity to Lake Michigan as an inland sea.

On another level, the onyx panels displayed modern means of stonecutting. Because their especially rich veining was not expected to be available in generations to come, the blocks themselves had been taken years earlier from nearly exhausted quarries. When the Auditorium was built, these quarries could no longer provide comparable stone for other buildings, so the onyx in Adler and Sullivan's interiors was unique. Sawing the quarried blocks into thin plates of wainscoting and polishing these plates were by then fully mechanized processes. In 1901 Frank Lloyd Wright, who helped design the Auditorium's interiors, wrote that new gang saws "made it possible to cut a block of marble ten feet long, six feet deep and two feet thick, into slabs of the size ⅛" in thickness in eight hours, making it possible as an exquisite wall covering in which the slabs as a veneer may be turned and matched at the edges to develop pattern, emancipating hundreds of superficial feet of color and marking that formerly were wasted in the heart of the block, making possible a distinctly new use to bring out the beauty of this material."[85] The Auditorium lobby's onyx walls demonstrated how such modern mechanized stonecutting revealed the natural richness of surfaces, thus exemplifying the ideal of "the art and craft of the machine" that Wright developed in part from Adler and Sullivan's work and thought.

The massive cast iron columns in the Auditorium lobby supported the weight of nine floors above. These columns and the beams they supported were encased in terra cotta blocks as a fireproofing. For the columns' visible surfaces, Sullivan worked with the Chicago Art Marble Company to develop a superior type of scagliola known as marbelite. Throughout Europe scagliola had long been used to imitate marble in public buildings of many kinds, including churches and palaces, since it was about half the price of real marble cladding. Scagliola was a hard polished plaster, prepared from gypsum, isinglass, alum, and varied coloring to imitate rare and expensive marbles. These included ancient Roman marbles, many original quarries for which were unknown through the nineteenth century. In the columns of the Auditorium Hotel's lobby, the scagliola recalled a variegated Sienese marble, its colors keyed to those of the onyx. As a superficial cladding for the iron columns encased in terra cotta, scagliola had no joint lines like those between marble panels. It thus looked like an unbroken monolithic surface and was laboriously hand polished to yield the color, mottling, and luster of old natural marbles.[86]

For the columns' crowns, Sullivan devised faceted foliate capitals of gilded plasterwork, and across the ceiling planes he designed multicolored fields of stenciled ornaments. He developed a language of decorative surfaces consistent with prevailing ideas of a hotel's character. Yet while observing the conventions of this building type, Sullivan's ornament is highly inventive. As Garczynski wrote, Sullivan "lavished upon this building a wealth of original decoration, that astonishes by its unceasing variety."[87] A prime example is the plasterwork of the dual arches framing the entrances to what were originally the porter's den and reading room at the lobby's north end (fig. 144). Unlike the tectonic granite arches of the exterior entrance,

these plaster archivolts do not express weight and
mass through individuated stone voussoirs. Instead, fields of foliate relief spring from the
arches' common central base. The motifs form a
wreath, traditionally a symbol of welcome, with
fantastic pointed leaves that roll over the impost
molding of the arches near their base, like ivy or
wisteria, and then rise through the arches to their
crowns. At the crowns, rather than a structural
keystone, there is a congeries of spirals. Sullivan
transformed the arch into a field of ornament
that conveyed his thesis of nature's vitality as the
source for living architecture. The extreme originality of his forms contrasted with the conventional classical pilasters below molded arches
lining the Palmer House's lobby (fig. 135), as if
Sullivan's innovations were in dialogue with local
predecessors. Though ornamented, his interiors
were viewed as modern. The hotel's lobby was "all
the more pleasing in that it is unique, no other
hotel rotunda in the country being at all like it."[88]

Nowhere was the implicit comparison with
the Palmer House more prominent than in the
Auditorium Hotel's main staircase (fig. 143; plate
10). In keeping with the theater, Sullivan specified
a broad arch framing the base of the main stairway, flanked by two smaller arches.
He requested that Adler design an enormous steel transfer beam to carry the loads
of the nine floors above, providing a clear span of at least two structural bays or
thirty-four feet over the stairway.[89] Beneath this hidden beam is Sullivan's great
rounded arch, unlike the columns supporting the entresol-level floor and framing
the base of the Palmer House's grand staircase (fig. 136). Both hotels' ceremonial
staircases had wide lower flights of marble steps with an outward-flaring base. Since
both staircases were places of social display for large numbers of ascending and descending guests, they featured a low ratio of riser to tread to ease passage going up
and to slow movement coming down. But instead of the classical stone balustrade
and winged griffins that crowned the anchoring newel posts of the Palmer House's
staircase, the Auditorium's had a balustrade of curving gilded iron and ornamentally enriched cast iron for the visible undersides of the upper flights, all made by
Winslow Brothers. Electric lights were installed for certain rooms in the Palmer
House in 1882, a year after they had appeared in the Grand Pacific, but from the
start the Auditorium Hotel was designed for electric lighting. Initially, atop the
bronzed newel posts there were brass electroliers "from which electric lights burst
forth like blossoms."[90]

Figure 144
Auditorium Hotel lobby looking north
to doorways leading to porter's den
(left) and reading room (right) with
ornamental plasterwork over the dual
arches. Photograph by J. W. Taylor.
Avery Architectural and Fine Arts Library,
Columbia University in the City of New
York.

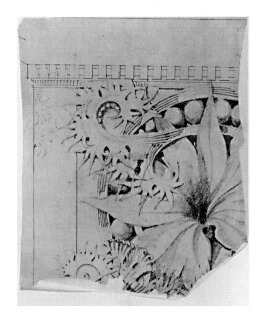

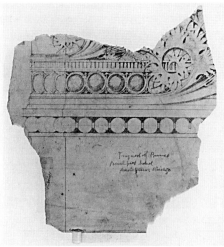

Figure 145

Auditorium Hotel, newel post at base of grand staircase, showing motif of milkweed pod in bronze-plated cast iron. Copyright © Donald Rocker. Auditorium Collection, Roosevelt University Archives.

Figure 146

Pencil drawing for bronze-plated cast iron newel post head at base of grand staircase, Auditorium Hotel. Handwritten notation by Frank Lloyd Wright. (Top) Frank Lloyd Wright Collection of Drawings by Louis Henry Sullivan. Avery Architectural and Fine Arts Library, Columbia University in the City of New York. (Bottom) Frank Lloyd Wright Archives, drawing no. 8801.001. © 2001 the Frank Lloyd Wright Foundation.

It was under such softer, more even incandescent light that the newel posts' relief was to be seen. Like the newel posts at the base of the theater's grand staircase, those in the hotel have their upper block faces rendered as an open pod of milkweed, a regionally characteristic plant (fig. 145). One small pencil study for this newel post survives, though the drawing is not attributed to Sullivan (fig. 146). Frank Lloyd Wright later claimed that the designs of the newel posts in the theater and hotel were among his first assignments when he began working for Adler and Sullivan.[91] The extant pencil study anticipates many details of the newel post as cast by Winslow Brothers, yet the post includes rich foliate forms at the corners not shown in the drawing. This discrepancy is consistent with Wright's recollection that Sullivan criticized Wright's own ornamental drawings for their relative stiffness and lack of vitality. He recalled that in one instance Sullivan worked over one of his

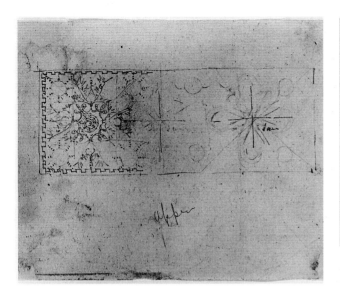

drawings, urging Wright, "Make it live, man! Make it live!"[92] The difference between the newel post as drawn and as cast shows a similar revision toward more richly botanical forms typical of Sullivan's ornament after 1885.[93]

On the stair landings throughout the Auditorium Hotel and Theater were Sullivan's designs for ornamental motifs in floors of tessellated marble. As the semicircular arches of the hotel and theater entrances were Roman in style, so the floors throughout these public interiors were Roman mosaic in an ancient Pompeian style, unlike the geometrically repetitive tessellated marble floor of the Palmer House's lobby (fig. 135). The mosaic floors carried many original foliate motifs, like Sullivan's ornamental vocabulary in other materials around the surfaces of these rooms. His sketch for the pattern on the landing of the hotel's main staircase between the second and third floors (fig. 147) compares with the executed mosaic there (fig. 148). The sketch shows the basic lines of a two-dimensional design that Italian mosaicists rendered in varied colors and elaborated detail. Discovered in quantity at Pompeii in the eighteenth century and revived for major European public buildings in the mid-nineteenth century, including the Paris Opera, Roman traditions of marble mosaic were introduced in Chicago by John Wellborn Root after his trip to Europe in 1886. The next year he incorporated them into the lobby floors of the Rookery Building. These were executed by the English firm of William Henry Burke, whose workers also executed the Auditorium's 50,000 square feet of mosaic floors.[94]

To save time and money, the old technique of laying a floor design's tiny marble cubes one at a time on site was replaced by gumming whole sections of the design to sheets of paper. This was done by women workers in France and Italy. Once transported to Chicago, these paper-gummed sections were laid into the floor's cement bed with the paper on top. The paper was saturated with water and pressed under a granite roller until it loosened and was removed. Ramming the mosaic

Figure 147

Sullivan, drawing for tessellated marble mosaic floor on landing between second and third floors of main hotel staircase. Frank Lloyd Wright Collection of Drawings by Louis Henry Sullivan. Avery Architectural and Fine Arts Library, Columbia University in the City of New York.

Figure 148

Auditorium Hotel, tessellated marble mosaic on landing between second and third floors of main staircase. Sullivan's design executed by Burke and Company. From *Industrial Chicago*, vol. 2. Courtesy of the Chicago Historical Society, ICHi-31473.

pavement forced cement to ooze up around the marble pieces to form a solid, homogeneous pavement, resilient enough for years of wear in heavily trafficked public interiors like a hotel or theater. The firmness of such pavement recommended it to Chicago's architects, whom Burke described as "trying to outvie the Romans in building, not for an age but for all time." He wrote that Sullivan, "fully alive to the opportunity offered by mosaic to his fertile pencil, specially designed the landings of the hotel and theater. They are different from any designs ever before translated into mosaic, and are as beautiful as they are unique."[95] Sullivan's designs differed from conventional classicizing patterns of marble mosaic, as if he intended to create a modern American variation on this ancient art.

The Auditorium Hotel's staircase exhibited the work of many artisans in its varied surfaces: floor mosaic, balustrade, plaster, and stair soffits (fig. 149; plate 10). Sullivan bounded these ornamental fields with straight constructional lines that defined these areas of different materials, each exhibiting the skill of a different firm of craftsmen. Though Wright later wrote of Sullivan's ornament as consistent across different materials, Garczynski claimed that Sullivan took care to vary his ornamental designs according to their location and their suitability for a specific material. The architect thereby kept to "the first law of decoration . . . that the design must be made expressly for the material which is its vehicle." Given the Auditorium Hotel's location at the edge of Lake Michigan, its interior surfaces are replete with allusions to living forms found in the sea. The decorative plaster frieze on the staircase's main landing demonstrates the potential for such reinterpretation. As modeled by the local firm of James Legge, who had done the theater's cast plaster motifs, this frieze was in deep relief as a setting for groups of incandescent lights, whose sockets are still visible. The plaster was rendered as "a series of circles of sea weed arranged around burner attachments," including "whorls that look like coils made of the weed that grows in the Sargasso sea."[96] To enhance a subaqueous reading, this frieze was originally painted a light green, and the wall above was coated with a deeper tone of the same color. Such direct allusion to natural forms complemented the richly geologic pattern of the onyx below, whose top course included slabs with a greenish translucence. Atop these stairs, visitors face east toward the lake through the second floor's parlor, whose surfaces were originally decorated in gold and peacock blue, with blue art glass facing the water beyond. Sullivan's motifs did not allude to Europe but spoke of the hotel's regional place.

Sullivan's interiors for the ladies' restaurant and the men's bar and café were innovative variations on similar spaces found in earlier local hotels. In each, his personal decorative language and its crafted realization were keyed to assumptions about gender. The Grand Pacific and the postfire Palmer House had set the precedent of providing a separate ladies' entrance and public interiors, both so that women would not be subjected to unwanted contact with men in these hotels and so that women prostitutes would be discouraged from mixing with potential male clients there. This logic had led to the provision for separate women's and men's retiring

Figure 149

Auditorium Hotel, main staircase looking north at landing between first and second floors, showing Mexican marble onyx wainscoting, tessellated marble mosaic (no longer extant), wrought iron balustrade, bronze-plated cast iron newel posts and stair soffits, and plaster frieze with incandescent bulbs. Compare with contemporary view in plate 10. Photograph by J. W. Taylor. Avery Architectural and Fine Arts Library, Columbia University in the City of New York.

rooms off the Auditorium Theater's grand foyer. Spatial constraints had limited implementation of this idea in the Auditorium Hotel to a main ladies' entrance as the southernmost of the three arched portals on Michigan Avenue. This led to a screened corridor with an arched doorway to the ladies' restaurant on its south side and the hotel's pair of passenger elevators directly ahead, used by both men and women (fig. 142). The ladies' restaurant could also be entered directly from outside on Congress Street through the vestibule in the easternmost arch. There was also a separate ladies' entrance to the hotel from Congress Street near elevators east of the tower, but there was no common entrance to both the ladies' restaurant and the men's bar either from inside or from outside the hotel. As one local reformer said of ladies' entrances to Chicago's saloons: "Why the need of a separate entrance for ladies? Is this not a tacit acknowledgment, and yet openly flaunted in the face of the world, that the saloon is not a fit place for men and women to meet together?"[97]

Public opinion of the time focused on the separation of women from bars frequented by men, in a city where such saloons were often associated with prostitution. For the same reason, in Boston the period's segregation-of-sexes laws aimed to forbid women to drink in public places, except hotels, and to ban unaccompanied men in places where alcohol was served to women. In that city the visibility of bars' interiors from the street was also legally limited. In the Auditorium Hotel's ladies' restaurant, where alcohol was served, the entrances from both Congress Street and the hotel's lobby were veiled with translucent colored glass, so that the interior was not visible until entered. The idea was to create a socially acceptable place for women, separate from casual associations with men. As Garczynski wrote, this room "the ladies of Chicago have consecrated to their use. Bold, indeed, is the man who, unaccompanied by fair companions, ventures to take a seat at one of the numerous small tables. He sees ladies to the right of him, ladies to the left of him, ladies on every hand and in every direction, with male escort, and without."[98]

These social issues shaped Sullivan's architecture for both the ladies' restaurant and the men's bar and café. First, not only were the rooms separate spheres for men and women, they were also entirely open, with no closed compartments adjacent to the main spaces, such as were then notorious in local saloons as rooms of private drinking and debauchery. Second, unlike the city's saloons, there was no suggestive figurative art on the walls. As a reformer of the period asked, "How is it that in most of the saloons the walls are decorated (?) with lascivious pictures? . . . Call them works of art if you will, they provoke comments from the drinking bystanders that must make devils chuckle with delight."[99] In this era Sullivan's florally inspired ornament would be seen as a "chaste" alternative, just as that word had been invoked to describe his ornamental scheme for the theater. At the ladies' restaurant, Sullivan's ornamental treatment of the entrances evoked associations of delicacy and fantasy. On Congress Street, the arch framing the entrance vestibule was "filled with colored glass of the softest and most velvety effect," while the plasterwork over the arches framing entrance from the hotel lobby "have the maddest, merriest, most whimsical, most exquisite design" as "a series of leaves turning into spirals, of spirals turning into leaves, of blossoms bursting out of the whirling leaves."[100] Both the ornament itself and the language used to characterize it bore connotations of gender as then socially constructed.

Inside the restaurant there were only small tables, which allowed diners to face each other and encouraged them to tarry (fig. 150). Envisioning its use for evening theater parties and women's receptions, Sullivan designed freestanding candelabra-style electroliers of silver along the room's ninety-six-foot central axis. From these electroliers "there is a branching out of incandescent electric lights hid snugly in glass holders made like the corolla of a convolvulus with ivory edges and with threads of opalescent color running spirally through their transparent cups." The form of these light fixtures alluded to convolvulus as twining vines with large, showy trumpet-shaped flowers. The design resembled contemporaneous glasswork of the French art nouveau designer Émile Gallé. Around the ceiling's cornice and along its beams were rows of incandescent burners set in whorls of decorative plaster. Shining on the ceiling's recessed planes between the beams, these lights revealed colored stenciling whose patterns had "the charm of a delicate textile fabric."[101]

Figure 150
Auditorium Hotel, ladies' restaurant, southeast corner of first floor: (above) looking northwest, showing freestanding electroliers of silver and opalescent glass, wall friezes of decorative plaster-work with incandescent bulbs above maple wainscoting; (below) arched entrance to restaurant from inside ladies' entrance to hotel. From Garczynski, *Auditorium*. Courtesy of the Library of Congress.

While the plasterwork and stenciling echoed the hotel lobby, inside the ladies' restaurant the high wainscoting was not onyx but elaborate paneling of bird's-eye maple, whose carving was under the care of local artist Robert W. Bates. The wainscoting's subdued tone served as a visual backdrop and foil for the richly colored costumes seen throughout the room. Sullivan keyed this interior to its prescribed feminine persona.

Sullivan's interior for the ladies' restaurant differed in style and materials from architect Charles M. Palmer's design for the soda fountain of Charles F. Gunther's six-story confectionery store at 212 State Street, opened in May 1887 and also done under Bates's supervision (fig. 151).[102] As a showcase for candies, pastries, ices, ice creams, and soda water made in the building, this room for nonalcoholic consumption conveyed different associations. Its architecture was "of the Italian Renaissance style," with an arched canopylike ceiling modeled on the Vatican Palace. The ornamental motif of the ceiling panels and cornices was the acanthus leaf, with surfaces tinted a lemon color relieved by glazed blue. Instead of stained maple panels, woodwork was polished and enameled holly. The soda fountain, among the largest then built, had a counter of rose-colored onyx and jasper marble, inlaid with gold leaf. Decorative vases intentionally evoked French models, with mirror plates of crystal glass manufactured in Paris. Ceiling lights shined through chains of cut glass resembling the glazed fruits and candies displayed below. In short, all the resources of decorative art served a promotional ideal for a particular business and its local clientele. When Sullivan worked with Bates on the Auditorium Hotel's interiors three years later, rather than emulating historical European sources, architect and artist created original forms that conveyed Chicago's regional distinction.

The men's bar and café in the Auditorium Hotel reworked a well-known spatial type. Smaller than the ladies' restaurant, the men's bar and café was not intended

Figure 151

Charles M. Palmer, Charles F. Gunther's Confectionery, 212 State Street, c. 1888, showing soda fountain on street level. Interior by Robert W. Bates and Company (1887). Courtesy of the Chicago Historical Society, ICHi-31697.

for public receptions, and its interior was screened from public view along Congress Street by generous passages of stained glass (fig. 152). The café's woodwork was not of light maple but of dark oak, carved in the shops of Brunswick, Balke, Collender and Company, known mainly as manufacturers of billiard tables, a staple of hotel furnishings.[103] In the men's café, the bar's wainscoting and its counter featured right-angled patterns of solid layered veneers. These were cut across the oak's grain with a whipsaw, a difficult way of crafting this hardwood. Atop the wainscoting around the room, and along the oak-paneled beams over the bar there were precisely cut dentil courses and classical moldings (egg and dart or bead and reel). This carving's excellence exemplified the Auditorium's capacity to inspire new standards of local workmanship. Unlike the proliferation of small tables in the ladies' restaurant, the café's stand-up bar and foot rail were to accommodate with relative efficiency large numbers of male drinkers, mostly paired or alone. One account of the period noted that, at both nonalcoholic restaurants and saloons, "the lunch counter is a Chicago institution, and abundant though they are and affording facilities for feeding large numbers they are invariably crowded at the noon hour. The long counters are supplied with stools, and each of these is preempted by a hungry man. Dozens of busy waiters are engaged in passing out coffee, sandwiches, pieces of pie, and other light refreshments."[104]

Figure 152

Auditorium Hotel, men's bar and café looking west, showing stout oak columns, thin bronze-plated cast iron columns with circlets of incandescent bulbs, oak wainscoting along bar, and plaster ceiling with hand-modeled foliate relief. Mezzanine billiard room above bar. Photograph by J. W. Taylor. Avery Architectural and Fine Arts Library, Columbia University in the City of New York.

Figure 153

Auditorium Hotel, men's bar and café, detail of oak column with carved foliate ornament continuing molding atop bar, oak wainscoting, and bronze-plated cast iron column. From Garczynski, *Auditorium*. Courtesy of the Library of Congress.

At each end of Sullivan's forty-five-foot bar stood a stout column described as "the trunk of a mammoth oak tree, richly carved and rising to the ceiling."[105] These two unusually proportioned and ornamented oak columns supported the café's low ceiling near the bar. Above this low ceiling was a mezzanine for billiards. The end columns had exaggerated entasis in their shafts, on which foliate relief swirled, continuing from the bar's straight top molding (fig. 153). These spiraling swirls were a tour de force for both designer and carver. Above, twisted fluting defined each column's neck, beneath a broadly spread capital "curving like a market basket." These capitals supported a nearly plain frieze and cornice, also of oak. Out from the bar were three taller freestanding tapering octagonal columns of bronze-plated cast iron, "slender and graceful like young birch trees, with capitals square and flat, precisely like a Doric abacus, only enriched with tracery."[106] Winslow Brothers cast these columns, which also helped hold up the billiard room on the mezzanine above. Such hollow columns doubled as electroliers, each having a circlet of eight bulbs below its neck. Between these and the bar ran a plaster ceiling with foliate relief whose rich modeling was variably tinted in browns, again as a decorative setting for incandescent bulbs in this ceiling. Sullivan created these slender ("young") iron and stout ("older") oak columns as extreme variations on the canonically proportioned classical orders, which he had drawn as a student. Like the woodwork, the café's columns, with their possible anthropomorphic analogies, conveyed this room's gender associations.

The Auditorium Hotel Dining Room and Banquet Hall

Like the no longer extant ladies' restaurant and men's café and bar, the Auditorium Hotel's surviving and partially restored dining room and banquet hall were to convey Chicago's distinct regional persona through their interior architecture. As elsewhere in the building, the effect of Adler and Sullivan's designs for these rooms depended on their ability to inventively integrate structure, lighting, and ornament. Compared with earlier hotels, one of the Auditorium's major innovations was the location of its dining room on the top (tenth) floor. Its kitchen to the west was carried over the Auditorium Theater's stage and its multistoried rigging loft. This location for dining room and kitchen was not in the plans of April 1887 but rather followed the executive committee's instructions to Adler of 6 July 1888, just after the Republican convention in the theater. This change demanded rethinking the hotel's planning and its structure. The new arrangement allowed the dining room to take advantage of an elevated view over the lakefront and helped sustain the analogy of the hotel with a public club, because elevated dining rooms were then found in private clubs. The trend began in London clubs of the earlier nineteenth century and was first adapted in the United States by architects Peabody and Stearns in New York City's Union League Club, opened in 1881.[107] Clubs elevated their dining rooms to eliminate cooking odors coming from their kitchens, before the invention of powerful electric fans as part of mechanical systems of ventilation. In hotels, the feasibility of large top-floor dining rooms depended on the speed and capacity of elevators to carry many guests from stories below.

As shown in an isometric drawing of the tenth floor's structure, Adler designed arched iron trusses between inner and outer masonry walls. These trusses spanned 45 feet and rose to an apex of 24 feet, creating a raised vaulted ceiling over half the dining room's total length of 172 feet (fig. 154). The arches' overall spatial effect recalls that of the theater ceiling and clarifies the room's constructive modernity relative to the classical column-and-beam structure found in such local prototypes as

Figure 154

Auditorium Building, structural isometric drawing of tenth floor, showing (a) arched trusses spanning dining room. Drawing by August Ventura. Historic American Buildings Survey, IL-1007 (1980). Courtesy of the Library of Congress. Graphic addition by author.

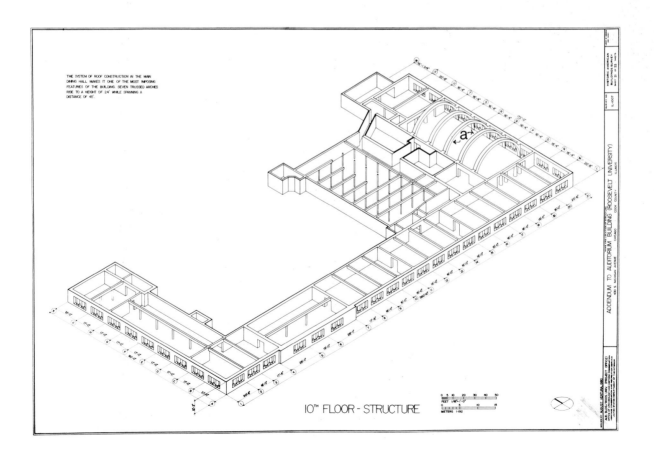

THE SYSTEM OF ROOF CONSTRUCTION IN THE MAIN DINING HALL MAKES IT ONE OF THE MOST IMPOSING FEATURES OF THE BUILDING. SEVEN TRUSSED ARCHES RISE TO A HEIGHT OF 24' WHILE SPANNING A DISTANCE OF 45'.

10TH FLOOR - STRUCTURE

ADDENDUM TO AUDITORIUM BUILDING (ROOSEVELT UNIVERSITY)
430 S. MICHIGAN AVENUE CHICAGO COOK COUNTY ILLINOIS

the Palmer House's dining room (fig. 138). Such a column-filled hall was the norm for older hotels. As one observer of the type wrote in 1887: "You enter the huge dining-room of [London's] Hotel Metropole and find a series of pillars in the middle of the room. These pillars are all useless and unnecessary, and they separate people who eat from other people who eat."[108] By contrast, the Auditorium Hotel's dining room was free of columns, so that its large central floor area could be rearranged for different ceremonial functions to intensify the diners' experience of group unity. Sized for such occasions, the dining room could seat four hundred (fig. 155). Garczynski wrote that the "trussed arches rise from either side with a majestic sweep, and give to the room immense loftiness, airiness, and lightness."[109] As Hugh Morrison noted, this room's structure resembled that of a glass-and-iron shed for steam-powered railway trains. These sheds were then quintessentially modern types of spaces that visitors to hotels like the Auditorium's would have passed through when arriving at and leaving Chicago.

The dining room's top-floor position let it receive light not only from its east and south peripheral windows, with their views of the lake, but also from six squared skylights in the ceiling bays between the trusses. As seen in figures 155 and 156, each

Figure 155

Auditorium Hotel, dining room looking north, with tables arranged for a group banquet, showing ornamental stenciling on ceiling, colored glass skylights, and incandescent bulbs set in ornamental plasterwork illuminating arches. The central four art glass panels in a skylight bay are shown in plate 8. Photograph by J. W. Taylor. Avery Architectural and Fine Arts Library, Columbia University in the City of New York.

of these skylights had sixteen glass panels, the center four framing a design with four foliate clusters extending out into a circle of interlaced tendrils and an outer triplet of blossoms in each quadrant (plate 8). These skylights had borders of Sullivan's plaster ornament, their relief modeled by daylight, and at night the skylights glowed with incandescent bulbs above panes of "cathedral" glass. Bulbs were also set in ornamental plaster coffers along the arches' soffits. Before completing the dining room's design, Sullivan traveled to Florida in 1888 "on hotel business." Although his itinerary is not known, he may have gone to St. Augustine to see Carrère and Hastings's Hotel Ponce de León, opened in 1887 as the first in the United States to be almost wholly lighted by electricity.[110] Peck also frequented Florida's Atlantic coast for deep-sea fishing, and he presumably knew of its nascent culture of resort hotels. In the Auditorium Hotel's dining room, the modern structure would correspond to the novelty of brilliant electric lighting, powered by what was then the world's largest electrical plant for a single building. At night the rings of bulbs across the arches cast reflective light onto tablecloths, cut glass, and silverware, giving the room a theatrical aspect completed by well-dressed diners, just as audiences in evening wear completed the theater's interior scene.

Figure 156

Auditorium Hotel, dining room looking north, showing arched tympanum with ornamental plaster frieze below mural of trout fishing by Oliver D. Grover. Ceiling stenciling and oak paneling in north alcove no longer extant. Photograph by J. W. Taylor. Avery Architectural and Fine Arts Library, Columbia University in the City of New York.

The dining room's day and evening lighting also reflected off the curved ceiling vault, originally richly stenciled (fig. 156). For these surfaces Sullivan designed interlaced arabesque patterns of sand-colored gold leaf on an old ivory ground, recalling the theater's tonalities. The colors for the vaulted ceiling were to complement those of the floor's marble mosaic and the room's mahogany wainscoting, pillars, and furniture. Given the room's dimensions, the stencil patterns were large in scale, with each design measuring five feet by five. Their thin layer of gold leaf was applied by hand. As repeated over the vaults, these nonextant flat stencil patterns had a geometric abstraction appropriate to the medium. They differed from the literally naturalistic relief of the plaster friezes below the tympana at the central space's south and north ends. These friezes were initially stained a light brown, like the borders of ornamental plaster around the skylights. In the coloring of this and other public rooms, "the artists followed no known style but created one of their own, for which a name is yet to be given . . . . It is a combination of some light color (according to taste) and gold, the gold finding its place principally in stencil work and beading and occasionally in broad bands."[111]

As in the Auditorium Theater, geometrically abstract flat stenciling and naturalistic foliate plaster relief were complemented by figurative paintings. In the dining room's south and north tympana, originally daylit from above by the skylights, there were paired murals on canvas over thirty feet wide and ten feet high at their centers. In the scene on the north, "an angler standing knee-deep in a mountain stream appears engrossed heart and soul in his fascinating pursuit," endeavoring to capture a brook trout. The painting on the south "represents the hunter standing in a skiff half-concealed among the reeds, his gun at his shoulder, with a flock of mallards in easy range."[112] These images evoked the game-laden menus of the period and reminded visitors that "Chicago is the *entrepôt* of a vast country from which all the most desirable edibles flow."[113] Though not portraits, the murals' figures call to mind accounts of Peck's delight in hunting and fishing in Wisconsin's woodlands north of Chicago, reinforcing the hotel's regional persona just as Fleury's theater murals were based directly on observation of nearby landscape.

The painter of these murals, Oliver D. Grover (1861–1927), like Sullivan, personified the Chicago ideal of a highly proficient local artist whose training included time in Europe yet whose career focused on shaping a midwestern identity in public imagery. Born in the small town of Earlville, Illinois, Grover studied briefly at the University of Chicago and the Chicago Academy of Design before going to Europe in 1879. There he studied for a year at the Royal Academy of Art in Munich, followed by three years in Italy, with winters in Florence and summers in Venice. During this period, in 1881–1883, he produced pictures from his own studio in Florence, where he also taught painting. After a year's further study in Paris, he returned briefly to Chicago, but the city was then too great a contrast to his European venues, and he returned to Venice to paint scenes of that city, several of which were acquired by Chicago collectors. Grover claimed the distinction of never having had a picture rejected from an exhibition, including Munich's International Exhibition, Paris's

Salon, London's National Academy, and exhibitions in Florence, New York, and Chicago, to which he returned in May 1887. He continued his studio work, painted "cycloramas," and taught drawing and painting at the Art Institute from 1888. For Chicagoans, Grover's wide recognition rebutted "the feeling abroad that only in the older portions of our land can we look for artists and men of letters."[114]

Nowhere was a regional theme more fully developed than in the banquet hall, the most civic of all the Auditorium Hotel's public interiors and the last major room that Adler and Sullivan created for the building. The Auditorium Association instructed the architects to prepare this room's design in April 1889. The banquet hall was not opened until October 1890, ten months after the dining room hosted its first major event on 30 January. Unlike the dining room, which served the hotel's guests, the banquet hall was a rentable facility for special events. To avoid traversing hotel spaces, those going to the banquet hall took elevators that led directly to the seventh floor from the ladies' entrance off Congress Street. For banquets the room could seat 300, and for balls its floor could hold 100 couples. This limited capacity marked the room as socially exclusive in a period when local halls rented for workers' balls had to accommodate 500 to 600 couples on the dance floor. The Auditorium Hotel's Banquet Hall would be Chicago's stylistic variation on the type of room represented in New York City by Louis Sherry's first white-and-gold ballroom of 1889 on Fifth Avenue, designed by Stanford White, where the "Four Hundred" of the metropolis gathered for their most exclusive social functions. This space was the prototype for Adler and Sullivan's seventh-floor banquet hall and ballroom in their later St. Nicholas Hotel in St. Louis of 1892–1893. Local business associations, like those of Chicago's realtors and jewelers, dined in the Auditorium Hotel's banquet hall. In this room were entertained groups of out-of-town visitors, "for whom an evening reception at the Auditorium is a matter of course."[115] The banquet hall functioned like a municipal reception room in a European town hall, such as Brussels's Hôtel de Ville, whose interiors Adler admired on his trip to Europe in 1888.

As shown in a structural isometric of the seventh floor, Adler decided to carry the banquet hall above the theater on giant iron trusses spanning north-south and bearing on the brick walls flanking the theater's north and south sides (fig. 157).[116] These walls already bore the weight of the theater's ceiling, and the south wall additionally bore part of the hotel's weight on Congress Street. Figure 158, looking north with the rigging loft's west wall at right, shows these enormous trusses in place (a), each spanning 120 feet and carrying a load of 660 tons. Between these trusses open-web floor beams (b) spanned 40 feet east-west. Atop these floor beams, Adler set lightweight latticework steel columns (c), which in turn supported rolled beams (d) spanning east-west above the hall. To minimize additional weight on the brick walls and their foundations, all these structural elements were as light as possible. So pressing was the need to conserve weight that none of these metal members were encased in terra cotta fireproofing. Instead they were completely covered with plaster on metal lath inside, and metal siding raised to a parapet ringing the hall outside.

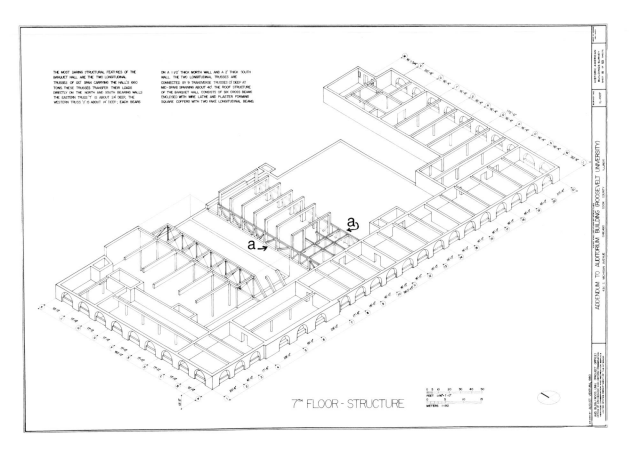

THE MOST DARING STRUCTURAL FEATURES OF THE BANQUET HALL ARE THE TWO LONGITUDINAL TRUSSES OF 120' SPAN CARRYING THE HALL'S 660 TONS. THESE TRUSSES TRANSFER THEIR LOADS DIRECTLY ON THE NORTH AND SOUTH BEARING WALLS. THE EASTERN TRUSS 'T' IS ABOUT 24' DEEP, THE WESTERN TRUSS 'U' IS ABOUT 14' DEEP; EACH BEARS

ON A 1 1/2' THICK NORTH WALL AND A 2' THICK SOUTH WALL. THE TWO LONGITUDINAL TRUSSES ARE CONNECTED BY 9 TRANSVERSE TRUSSES 1.5' DEEP AT MID-SPAN SPANNING ABOUT 40'. THE ROOF STRUCTURE OF THE BANQUET HALL CONSISTS OF SIX CROSS BEAMS ENCLOSED WITH WIRE LATHE AND PLASTER FORMING SQUARE COFFERS WITH TWO FAKE LONGITUDINAL BEAMS.

7ᵀᴴ FLOOR - STRUCTURE

Figure 157

Auditorium Building, structural isometric drawing of seventh floor showing (a) banquet hall's trusses spanning 120 feet north-south between brick walls along north and south sides of theater. Drawing by August Ventura. Historic American Buildings Survey, IL-1007 (1980). Courtesy of the Library of Congress. Graphic additions by author.

Figure 158

Auditorium Building, view of banquet hall in construction looking north, showing (a) main trusses spanning 120 feet; (b) open-web floor beams spanning east-west between trusses; (c) latticework steel columns resting on open-web beams; and (d) rolled steel beams spanning east-west above banquet hall ceiling. From Garczynski, *Auditorium*. Courtesy of the Chicago Historical Society, ICHi-31474. Graphic additions by author.

Floors were of hollow clay tile, weighing one-third less than brick and superior to brick in insulating and acoustic properties. Calculating the weight and size of the banquet hall's iron- and steelwork, the location of all bolts and rivets, and the total cost of its structure's materials and labor took a month's time for two experts, a publicly announced statistic that certified the hall's safety as a work of modern scientific engineering. Adler later recalled that for the whole Auditorium Building, the structural calculations had "required the equal of one man's time for five years."[117]

The experience of the banquet hall begins with the low ceiling in its southern vestibule, to which the hall's height of 25 feet and its area of 86 by 36 feet form a powerful contrast. The banquet hall's greater height gives it a large scale and civic dignity that distinguish it from the dining room, which was used both day and evening, whereas Sullivan designed the banquet hall to be seen mainly in the late afternoon and after dark. Thus the room lacks skylights, although its arched clerestory windows admit daylight around the west, south, and east sides. Those on the east and south are open to ambient daylight, but there the building's mass outside the hall blocks direct sunlight, whereas those on the west admit late afternoon sunlight. The corresponding arched level on the north side originally served as a musicians' gallery. The art glass of the semicircular tympanumlike windows set within the arches varies around the three sides of the room (fig. 159). As with the arched colored glass panels over the doors to the theater's lobby, Healy and Millet designed these glass patterns, but the ornamental plaster soffits of their framing arches were Sullivan's work. The hall's ceiling had six deep low crossbeams and two

Figure 159

Auditorium Hotel, banquet hall (now Rudolf Ganz Memorial Hall) looking north, showing arched clerestory art glass windows with gilded plaster reveals on west wall (above mural stencils shortly thereafter replaced by Fleury paintings), musicians' gallery at north end, birchwood columns and carved capitals, gilded electroliers hanging from ceiling beams, and ornamental stenciling of beams and of coved north wall below musicians' gallery. From Garczynski, *Auditorium*. Courtesy of the Library of Congress.

Figure 160

Auditorium Hotel, banquet hall, detail
of bay on east wall, showing birch
wainscoting and columns, Fleury's mural
paintings, and art glass tympana above.
Door in central bay led to corridor to
banquet hall kitchen. Compare with
plate 11. From Garczynski, *Auditorium*.
Courtesy of the Library of Congress.

Figure 161

Auditorium Hotel, banquet hall, floor
plan showing locations of Fleury's mural
paintings. Adapted from a drawing by
Tobin Kendrick and Cathy Berlow.
Historic American Buildings Survey,
IL-1007 (1980). Notations of paintings
by author.

high shallow longitudinal beams carrying stenciled ornament with gilded edging.
Where these beams crossed, huge gilded electroliers hung like enormous pendants as
Sullivan's interpretation of conventional chandeliers, their foliate surfaces reflecting
light from clusters of incandescent bulbs (fig. 159). In this evening room, Garczynski
wrote, "in the night, the time of joy, they seem like inverted fountains of solid
beaten silver spouting out light," whose evenness "seems like the prolongation of
summer days."[118]

On 8 July 1890 the Auditorium's directors approved Peck's ordering "twelve
paintings for the Banquet Hall at a cost of [$3,600], the work to be executed by Healy
and Millet," who also did the room's stenciling.[119] The paintings replaced stenciled
wall areas of dark green paint on solid gold leaf (visible in figure 159), which architect Crombie Taylor restored in the hall's north and south ends in the 1950s (plates
11 and 12). For the murals, Healy and Millet presumably subcontracted with painter
Albert Fleury, whose canvases were to represent the arts and industries of America.

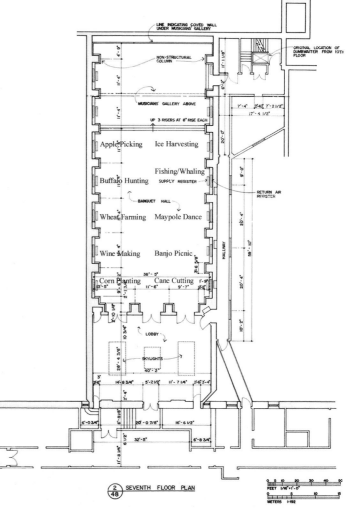

The subjects were "chosen from periods of historic interest, and the themes illustrate the feast, music and the dance."[120] As completed, this program included ten scenes, each about 9 feet wide and 4.5 feet high. The canvases were cleaned and largely repainted in the 1950s. Beginning in 2000, these murals are being restored one by one to approximate their original condition. Several of the paintings appear in figure 160 and plate 11, and the location and apparent subjects of all ten are noted on the banquet hall's floor plan in figure 161. On the east wall, scenes representing the eastern United States are, north to south: (1) ice harvesting and (2) fishing or whaling, as in New England; (3) a Maypole dance, with a colonial cemetery nearby, as in Virginia; (4) a picnic with banjo music, as in the southern states; and (5) cutting sugar cane, with a steamboat in the background, as in Louisiana. All these scenes are not only eastern but antebellum. The west wall's scenes portray territories whose settlement largely postdated the Civil War. They show, north to south, (6) apple picking, as in Washington; (7) buffalo hunting, as on the Great Plains; (8) wheat farming, as in Kansas; (9) wine making, as in California; and (10) corn planting, as in Iowa.

The scenes represent regional life in natural environs, with no portrayal of cities or nonagricultural industries. These images were keyed to audiences that would include visitors from all over the country, as at the national political conventions the Auditorium Theater was to host. Their geographic and chronological range presented scenes that guests from almost any region of the United States could identify with, as if Chicago were implicitly portrayed as the central metropolis of the continental nation. Most of the west wall's paintings show sunlight emanating from the rear of the fictive scene, as if to complement the actual daylight that passes through the arched glass windows above. As in the dining room's murals and skylight overhead, there is a play between Fleury's literal representation of nature in the paintings and the conventionalized nature of the daylit art glass. In several murals treetops are cut off, as if to imply that the art glass above is a decorative analogy to the foliate crown of the painted trees (fig. 160). As with Fleury's larger theater murals, the banquet hall's continue the naturalistic themes of Sullivan's ornament, presenting the scenes as conceptual extensions of the room's architecture.

The most distinctive decorative feature of the banquet hall was its woodwork, which culminated in the twenty individually carved capitals atop the wall columns (figs. 160 and 163; plates 11 and 12). These capitals epitomized Adler's assessment of the banquet hall's "peculiar artistic conception and treatment, at once aggressively unconventional and original and still extremely delicate and refined."[121] Designed by Sullivan, these were executed by Bates, who also assembled the red birch veneer strips that formed the column shafts and the wainscoting below the paintings. Sullivan's idea was to show that a regional wood could be as architecturally effective as a European wood. Two years were spent collecting curly heartwood red birch in Michigan and two more years in cutting, fashioning, and checking it for matching grains. In this lower wainscoting there were also panels of fretwork cut with a whipsaw to allow heated air to pass into the room from its mechanical system's ducts below the floor. In designing this series of different foliate capitals to be executed by Bates,

Sullivan was reinterpreting an idea of architecturally expressive craft earlier celebrated by John Ruskin in his account of the series of marble capitals along the loggias of the Venetian Doge's Palace (1309–1424). These capitals, with their varied flora and fauna, were a key example for Ruskin's well-known argument that medieval craftsmen were free to design and execute varied motifs of their choice, unlike identically repetitive classical capitals. Sullivan owned Ruskin's writings on architecture where this argument was developed, and Garczynski hinted at a Ruskinian ideal when he wrote that in the banquet hall "there is all the engineering knowledge of the 19th century as well as a return to the ideally creative art of the Middle Ages."[122]

Unlike Ruskin's vision of medieval craftsmen's freedom, Sullivan's method as an architect was to design motifs, such as the column capitals, that were executed rather than invented by his artisan-collaborators. Yet in these capitals Sullivan clearly

Figure 162

Sullivan, drawing for capital on east wall of banquet hall, Auditorium Hotel, 15 April 1890, showing ornamental pattern on capital face, soffit, and neck as guide for carving. Frank Lloyd Wright Collection of Drawings by Louis Henry Sullivan at the Avery Architectural and Fine Arts Library, Columbia University, New York.

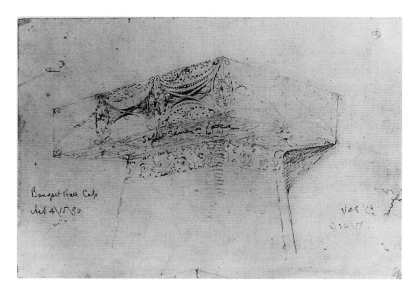

Figure 163

Auditorium Hotel, banquet hall, same birchwood capital as carved by Robert W. Bates. Compare with plate 12. Photograph by Paul Sprague.

responded to Ruskin's stylistic ideal of naturalistic variety. Each capital's design gave the carver an opportunity to display his technical abilities. Sullivan drew the motifs to be carved in dimensioned pencil drawings that showed each capital's outer face, its soffit, and its neck. One of these drawings, made for a capital on the east wall and dated 15 April 1890 (fig. 162), may be compared with the capital carved by Bates (fig. 163). The drawing shows the capital's width of six feet two inches and its height of two feet two inches. The capital's face and soffit were both to be carved with the same repeated interlaced motif. The drawing's shading hints at the relief Sullivan sought for these linear and foliate forms, which Bates interpreted closely in the finished capital. Like Sullivan's ornament throughout the Auditorium, these capitals' carved surfaces were "to show not the form merely of plants, but their vitality, and this quality can be rendered only by a constant fluctuation of relief, a change in the plane of thickness . . . . Here there is a crescendo of projection, here there is a recession, and it is in this movement that the real force of Sullivan's decoration lies."[123]

Perhaps more than any other single detail in the Auditorium Building, these capitals were meant to display an original school of decorative art that would serve as a model for future local architecture. The carver Bates was one of many artists and craftsmen attracted to the Auditorium project, which Peck envisioned as an inaugural effort to create a new regional tradition of monumental public buildings. Sullivan's prolific inventiveness as a designer of ornamental forms in different materials was the wellspring of this initiative. At the Auditorium Theater's dedication in December 1889, both Peck and Mayor Cregier praised the architects. Yet neither Adler, Sullivan, nor any of those who made the building was mentioned by name. In response, one of their supervising contractors for the project wrote: "Workmen employed upon the building know that Mr. Sullivan was the guiding spirit, everywhere and all over, attending to the smallest details . . . . Had such an event as the opening of this building occurred in Paris or any large city in England the architects would have been among the first called before the people and publically thanked upon the stage. It is their due, and I am surprised that the citizens of Chicago should neglect to give the full measure of praise to whom it belongs."[124]

In the banquet hall, Adler and Sullivan's technical and artistic skills created an interior that was an original interpretation of its type, like the Auditorium Theater. As a reception room for out-of-town visitors, the banquet hall was intended to help attract outside capital to the city. In this sense its architecture served the economic agenda of local capitalists since the 1840s, when Rice's Theater had opened coincidentally with Chicago's hosting the national River and Harbor Convention. By 1890 the city's transportation infrastructure had developed to the point where business leaders promoted its excellence as a means of drawing investment to Chicago's manufacturing enterprises. This was the idea behind the inaugural event of the Auditorium banquet hall in October 1890: a reception held by Chicagoans as part of the city's two-day effort to host members of the British Iron and Steel Institute and the similar Verein Deutscher Eisenhüttenleute. These delegates to the International

Iron and Steel Congress came to Chicago from Pittsburgh as a westward extension of their United States tour. The hundred-man local committee for this hospitality included architects Adler, Sullivan, Burnham, and Jenney and Auditorium stockholders Ferdinand Peck, Marshall Field, Lyman Gage, and Nathaniel Fairbank, among others. By then these men were among many committed to bringing the next world's fair to Chicago.

From 1865, when a local mill had rolled the first steel rail in the United States, the city's mills had grown to account for one-third of total American rail production, an output second only to Pittsburgh's. Other concerns included the McCormick works, whose production of over 100,000 reaping machines a year was then one-third of the world's total. The evening reception tendered to foreign industrialists in Adler and Sullivan's banquet hall was a statement about Chicago's new prominence in the international economy. The room's structure, where huge iron trusses carried all columns and beams, would have been particularly significant to this audience of iron and steel magnates. Writing in a booklet prepared for these visitors, Peck and his fellow committeemen felt "justified in believing that [Chicago's] manifest destiny is ultimately to occupy the proud position of first American city."[125] The novelty of Chicago's industrial prominence had its parallel in the novelty of Sullivan's individual style. Days before the English and German visitors came, one editor wrote: "Of this beautiful chamber we can truly say that no sign of the times points more significantly towards a splendid future for American architecture."[126]

The Auditorium Building, the Auditorium Annex, and Chicago's Urban Image

The Auditorium Hotel's public interiors were special opportunities for Peck, his architects, and their craftsmen collaborators to advance their program for a relatively privileged audience of visitors and empowered locals. Yet their building's primary impact came from its exterior seen at a distance. On its completion in 1890, visitors saw the Auditorium's enormous mass and high tower at the northerly end of a series of large grain elevators along the lakeshore. Since the 1850s, these structures had lined the railroads along the lakefront southeast of the central city and along the banks of the Chicago River to the southwest. Recalling his own early explorations of Chicago's environs in the 1870s, Sullivan wrote: "From a distance one saw many a steeple, rising from the green, as landmarks, and in the distances the gray bulk of the grain elevators."[127] By 1885 the city had twenty-eight grain elevators. Among the most monumental was Armour's Elevator E near Sixteenth Street (fig. 164). Early in his career, Adler and other architects, such as Edward Burling and Frederick Baumann, had designed grain elevators before their construction passed to specialists. Adler admired these structures for their sturdy deep-pile foundations, which sustained large, unevenly distributed loads of grain filling their different bins and

Figure 164

Armour Elevator E, on south branch of
Chicago River, near Sixteenth Street,
with the *Arthur Orr* docked alongside.
Photograph by Barnes and Crosby,
BC-120. Courtesy of the Chicago
Historical Society, ICHi-19120.

heavy vibrations of steam-powered conveyors that brought the grain shipments to
the top for distribution into the bins below. Fast movement of upward of 200,000
bushels a day into and out of these structures also stressed them. Citing the role of
pile foundations in grain elevators, Adler revived the use of piles in foundations for
such tall office buildings as the Schiller Theater of 1890–1892. As large geometric
forms in the landscape, and as resilient constructions, Chicago's grain elevators
were the most locally compelling works of modern industrial architecture.

In designing the Auditorium as a monument for Chicago's skyline, Adler and
Sullivan presumably appreciated that it was comparable to these structures that,
perhaps more than any others, signified their city's regional economic identity and
its process of capital formation. The grain elevators epitomized the local ideal of
utility in built form on a large scale, as did Chicago's new steel-frame buildings. As
one local observer wrote in 1891 of structures like Armour's Elevator E, "Those immense grainhouses are purely Chicagoan, originating their massive forms here like
the Chicago construction of later days."[128] The next year, local author Franklin Head
wrote: "In approaching the city of Chicago, the conspicuous objects are the massive
temples of trade and commerce, the vast warehouses for the storage of grain, the
lofty buildings, or the great Auditorium, where even the most superb temple of the
Muses and Graces which the world has seen, in its hotel and office annex, is made to
subserve the purposes of commerce."[129] The building fit ideologically within an
urban environment ordered by capital; its cultural functions were inextricable from
the local economic order. Yet as a monument created for public benefit, Adler and
Sullivan's building represented the redirection of local capital toward cultural ends.
The Reverend David Swing said after the Auditorium Theater's opening: "The new

temple of song has brought to an end the empire of elevators and stock yards. All those old dethroned kings can do henceforth is to make money for the arts to consume . . . . The inquiry about the price of cattle on foot in Texas and of wheat in Dakota next June has been overwhelmed by the 'encores' offered Patti, [Lillian] Nordica, and similar children of art."[130]

As an architectural response to Chicago's urban class strife in the era of Haymarket, the Auditorium's exterior may also be compared with other buildings that represented response to labor unrest. One of the most prominent of these was a new armory for the First Regiment of the Illinois National Guard, a project proposed in 1885. Organized in 1874, the First Regiment came to enroll about six hundred local men from the city's middle and upper classes, who "represent, in many instances, the oldest and best families of Chicago."[131] Their number included at least one of Adler and Sullivan's draftsmen. All volunteers, the regiment's members prided themselves on their social standing and training. Having made its first appearance in 1875 during riotous demonstrations against the Chicago Relief and Aid Society, the regiment had twice dispersed crowds without firing during the railroad strikes of 1877 and also confronted labor protests around the city in November 1886. The regiment had great popularity among Chicago's propertied classes, but to radical socialist leaders this military unit epitomized armed force in the service of powerful capitalists.

When the First Regiment sought to build a new armory, Marshall Field offered a site he owned on the northwest corner of Michigan Avenue and Sixteenth Street, not far from his own home. Field, who was closely identified with this regiment and other efforts to support armed force against civil disturbances, agreed to lease the site to the unit for $4,000 per year (then only half its value) for ninety-nine years with no revaluation of the site or annual rent increase. His offer to the regiment was virtually a gift of $400,000 at a time when the Illinois legislature gave the unit little money. For this site Burnham and Root designed the First Regiment Armory from March 1889. Its cornerstone was laid in July 1890, and the building was dedicated in September 1891 (fig. 165). One contemporary described it as "perhaps the most massive structure in Chicago."[132]

Burnham and Root wrote that the First Regiment Armory was to "be the perfect embodiment of the spirit of regimental life in peace or in war." The result was a "building which should be held against any mob,

Figure 165

Daniel Burnham and John Wellborn Root, First Regiment Armory, northwest corner of South Michigan Avenue and Sixteenth Street, Chicago (1889–1891; largely rebuilt after fire of 1894; demolished 1929). From Gilbert and Bryson, *Chicago and Its Makers*. Courtesy of the Library of Congress.

unless it rise to the dignity of a revolutionary force, and be possessed of heavy ordnance. The conditions are practically identical to those which caused the building of medieval castles, and the design being thus caused by analogous conditions, is strongly suggestive of a fortress." Its heavy brownstone walls rose unbroken to a height of thirty-five feet on all four sides. The randomly laid stone walls were open only in the front, with a wide sally port for troops marching abreast in ranks of thirty. Set back of the embrasures in these thick walls, the arch's massive oak and steel portcullis epitomized a design that "is to the last degree business-like in a military sense, and cannot fail to impress a passer-by with the full extent of its purpose, and its ability to carry it out."[133] Above the rusticated base were brick walls with arched openings and round corner bartizans for raking fire along the walls. Atop all four walls ran a projecting machicolated cornice crowned with gun slits. Within there was a large drill hall that Adler and Sullivan redesigned in 1893 as a temporary theater known as the Trocadero Music Hall, after the Parisian theater by Gabriel Davioud opened in 1878. Adler and Sullivan's client was Dr. Florenz Ziegfeld, founding president of the Chicago Musical College, which had its quarters in Adler's Central Music Hall and for a time contemplated leasing space in the new Auditorium Building. The armory theater's performances were to raise funds for the regiment. Yet in April 1893, fire destroyed this last theater by Adler and Sullivan five days before it was to open. Ironically, firemen were unable to break through the armory's massive portcullis, designed to resist armed assault, to quench the blaze and rescue the building's caretakers, who died inside its great door.[134]

This regiment's treasurer was Charles Hutchinson, a leading trustee of the Art Institute and treasurer of the Chicago Auditorium Association. In 1885 the committee in charge of the regiment's new armory had proposed to Peck that the armory and the Auditorium project be combined in the same structure. In January 1890 Dr. Ziegfeld directed a musical festival at the Auditorium Theater to raise funds for the construction of the First Regiment's new armory. Early Auditorium board members were leaders of Chicago's Citizens' Association, which supported the militia against labor agitation in 1877 and 1885. Peck and Fairbank were also among the directors of the Chicago Citizens' Law and Order League founded in 1877, just after the city's railroad strikes, to prevent sale of alcohol to minors, since the strikers were believed to have included a large number of half-drunken boys. In this context, the First Regiment Armory and the Auditorium were facets of a broad range of elite responses to threats of social unrest.[135]

The Auditorium was neither an armory nor a fortress, yet it did have as its social aim the pacification of urban workers, not through armed control but through cultural suasion. As a capitalist monument, the Auditorium presented an image of indestructibility, as in its eye-level granite base. Moreover, the tower, in addition to the rectangular slotlike windows within its stylized machicolated cornice, had windows within its arches below that Garczynski described as "square and deeply recessed, like embrasures in a fortification."[136] In these ways the Auditorium conveyed many messages simultaneously. On one level it was a civic and cultural monument.

On another it projected the city's power and enterprise. On yet a third it stood for an elite's will to direct Chicago's social, economic, and political future. The building's outer architecture stood figuratively against socialism and anarchism, while the theater inside offered alternatives to local workers' own theatrical culture keyed to labor politics and to nonpoliticized but less elevated urban entertainment.

Interpretation of the Auditorium as a heavy lithic mass contrasts with its place in the conventional historiography of the Chicago school of architecture, which stressed local efforts to lighten or open up walls of the city's commercial buildings from about 1880 to 1900. From this viewpoint, what was valued about the Auditorium's exterior was not its solid piers of walling but its arched voids of windows. From this perspective the Auditorium compares not with Burnham and Root's armory but with the building closest to Peck's own attitude toward urban workers: the new quarters for Chicago's Athenaeum, opened in May 1891 (fig. 166). Originally planned to be incorporated into the Auditorium Building, the Athenaeum's new quarters stood on the same block as the Auditorium on the south side of Van Buren Street. They adjoined the earlier home of the Art Institute of Chicago on the southwest corner of Van Buren and Michigan Avenue, opened in 1887. Peck and other Auditorium patrons also supported the Art Institute. In December 1889 the Athenaeum's head, the Reverend Edward I. Galvin, a Unitarian minister, congratulated Peck on the new Auditorium, asserting that "such a building for the public good in culture and wholesome recreation . . . must find universal endorsement." He wrote, "The next crowning glory of your life will be the completion and opening of the Athenaeum Building."[137]

As the Athenaeum's president in the same years when he was directing the Auditorium project's realization, Peck bought the Van Buren Street building for the Athenaeum and oversaw its expansion from four to seven stories. As designed by Thomas Wing, the new structure had classrooms, a large lecture hall, recreational rooms, a library, and a gymnasium, all accessible to members for a nominal annual fee. Facing north, the Athenaeum's street front had an abundance of windows with minimal piers and columns between, approaching the image of a typical Chicago loft building of the period. The Athenaeum's appearance was determined almost wholly by utilitarian needs to light interior spaces and limit construction costs. The Roman associations of the Auditorium's exterior were lacking in this building, which was meant for the education of workers but did not have the Auditorium's monumental scale, lakefront site, and representational purpose.

From the beginning of his project, Peck wanted the Auditorium to enhance its urban environs. While the building was being built, it elevated nearby land values,

Figure 166

Thomas Wing, Chicago Athenaeum, south side of Van Buren Street west of Michigan Avenue, as expanded and remodeled into a seven-story building (1890–1891; demolished 1929). From *Chicago Tribune*, 10 May 1891.

especially along Wabash Avenue, where commercial development accelerated. Prospects in the vicinity were so good that Ferdinand Peck's brothers invested in previously depressed commercial properties on this avenue. Yet the Auditorium's biggest impact was on the properties directly to its south on Michigan Avenue across Congress Street. In February 1889 Chicago's City Council passed an ordinance to widen Congress from sixty-four feet to one hundred by condemning privately held residential properties on its south side. As one report noted: "It has long been considered unfortunate that so magnificent a structure as the Auditorium should face on so narrow a street as Congress, which afforded little room for display of the great facade, particularly if high buildings were erected on that side of the street. But the promoters have long had in contemplation the widening of that street."[138]

Though the ordinance was passed, some property owners on the south side of Congress Street were not pleased. Among them, William Fitzgerald, who had led the fight to block the ordinance widening Congress Street, announced by December 1891 that he had secured options on properties that together constituted a large site on the southwest corner of Michigan and Congress. There he planned to build "the imperial hotel of the city," desiring "to make it the finest hotel of the kind in the country," with its four hundred rooms to equal the Auditorium's capacity. Fitzgerald gave the commission to architect Clinton J. Warren, who had designed four earlier successful Chicago hotels.[139] To prevent such competition, Peck and the Auditorium's directors soon responded by forming a new corporation, the Congress Hotel Company, to buy out Fitzgerald and his proposed hotel. Since the Auditorium Hotel had opened, its success had been phenomenal, and accommodations had been insufficient to meet the demand. Yet Peck and others "held consistently to the idea that the Auditorium Building is and must continue to be a center of Art and Education, and they do not intend to surrender any more rooms for hotel purposes."[140] They first sought more hotel space in the Studebaker Building to the north, and they also contemplated adding two stories to Adler and Sullivan's block. Knowing the Auditorium Hotel's need for expansion, Fitzgerald perhaps anticipated that Peck's association would buy him out.

Known as the Auditorium Annex, the hotel across Congress came under the Auditorium Hotel's management. Although the new building followed Warren's plans inside, Adler and Sullivan were retained as consultants. Warren had projected its exterior of pressed brick and terra cotta in "the modern classic" style. Yet as Peck wrote, "The design was greatly changed so as to have a stone exterior and conform in a measure in other respects to the Auditorium building."[141] To signify the two buildings' common ownership, the Auditorium Annex's exterior was built to the same height as Adler and Sullivan's block, was "Romanesque" in style, and was entirely of Bedford limestone (fig. 167). The principal difference in Warren's street fronts were their columns of bay windows and the rooms behind, which all had open fireplaces and private bathrooms. Since expenses for utilities in the Auditorium Hotel had been somewhat large in proportion to its number of rooms, Adler designed a new, more efficient power plant underneath a plot of land south of the

Figure 167

Clinton J. Warren, Auditorium Hotel Annex, southwest corner of Michigan Avenue and Congress Street, Chicago (1891–1893), with John Holabird and Martin Roche's Congress Hotel (1902–1907) at left. Interstitial four-story section served as light well for taller hotels to north and south. Photograph by Detroit Publishing Company. Architecture Photograph Collection, Courtesy of the Art Institute of Chicago.

Auditorium Annex to serve both hotels. He and Sullivan designed a marble-finished pedestrian tunnel under Congress Street to link the two hotels internally, just as their exterior blocks above formed an anchoring gateway into the city from the lakefront.

Timely completion of the Auditorium Annex by 1 May 1893 enabled both hotels to accommodate visitors to the World's Columbian Exposition, which opened that day. Many visitors boarded trains at Lake Front Park almost directly across Michigan Avenue for excursions to the fair in Jackson Park. From a distance these buildings' matching heights and similar elevations merged with those of the Studebaker Building to the north and, later, Holabird and Roche's Congress Hotel (1902–1907) to the south, whose first section appeared on the letterhead of the Auditorium Hotel's stationery in 1902 (fig. 168). The four-story building between the Auditorium Annex and the Congress Hotel had been planned by Warren to ensure daylight for the Auditorium Annex's south side. Before the Auditorium Hotel and Auditorium Annex were built, Wabash Avenue, served by street railways, was more important than Michigan Avenue. Yet as one Chicagoan who arrived in 1883 later observed, "The development of Michigan Avenue started after the Auditorium was built and after the Congress Hotel Annex on the opposite side of Congress Street was built a year or two later, and from then on the whole character of Michigan Avenue changed so that it is now [in 1925] the most prominent street in the City and becoming more so every day for shops, hotels and office buildings."[142]

The Auditorium Hotel, Auditorium Annex, and Congress Hotel had a collective urban presence that anticipated the emphasis on common cornice heights and uniform exteriors for major structures on Michigan Avenue and elsewhere downtown

Figure 168

Auditorium Hotel stationery, 1902, showing north to south: Studebaker Building after remodeling of upper floors in 1896; Auditorium Building, Congress Street; Auditorium Hotel Annex; interstitial four-story building; and first section of Congress Hotel, all facing Lake Front Park. Auditorium Collection, Roosevelt University Archives.

as proposed in Burnham and Bennett's plan for Chicago of 1909. The model for this plan's regulation of building heights and fronts was ultimately Second Empire Paris. Such a Continental image of broad streets lined with consistently designed stone buildings perhaps underlay Peck's plan to widen Congress Street, just as Haussmann's Paris had served as the model for Potter Palmer's program for a widened and embellished State Street in the late 1860s. As one Chicagoan wrote of the widening of Congress Street in 1889, "The extraordinary improvements in this locality form a nucleus about which will cluster the grandest buildings of modern times, as in Paris they centre at the Grand Opera House."[143]

The Paris Opera had not been the model for the Auditorium Theater. Yet Garnier's great monument served as the focal point for extensive surrounding urban development, including the Grand Hôtel de la Paix and buildings with externally similar frontages. Peck, who knew Paris, presumably envisioned that the Auditorium Building would have a comparable effect on nearby architecture for the Chicago of the 1890s. In both cities, a monumental uniformity in large buildings and wide streets would help to constitute an urban society ordered by capital, symbolically subduing the radical labor politics that threatened it. Yet the Auditorium's influence on Chicago's architecture before 1900 was clearest in Adler and Sullivan's later works, in which they advanced technical, aesthetic, and cultural aims that they first explored on a large scale in Peck's lakefront monument.

Adler and Sullivan's Later Architecture in Chicago, 1890–1894 $\quad$ 6

As the Auditorium Hotel was completed and opened in stages during 1890, the national and international response established Adler and Sullivan's reputation as among Chicago's most innovative architects. Their subsequent major buildings marked the culmination of their careers both technically and aesthetically. Adler and Sullivan's Chicago buildings of the early 1890s also reshaped the identities of their clients, who took the Auditorium as their point of departure but responded to its example in different ways. These local clients looked to Adler and Sullivan to create monumental exteriors and public interiors that announced their institutional aims. Peck commissioned the last of the firm's large local projects, the Chicago Stock Exchange Building of 1893–1894, Adler and Sullivan's largest work after the Auditorium. In all these projects, these designers pursued their constructive and formal ideas in the midst of a city that sought to project its stature through architecture.

Adler and Sullivan's solutions emerged not only from their own architectural agenda but in relation to comparable projects by other Chicago architects. On one level this relationship was competitive. On another it was cooperative, in that collectively these designers created a professional culture wherein sharing information and exchanging ideas enhanced the quality of all their efforts. As in the 1880s, Chicago architects developed their work with an eye to parallel developments in New York City. Yet their clients were also responding to Chicago's own difficult economic, social, and cultural history through the early 1890s. Adler and Sullivan's contemporaries saw their buildings as part of this broader urban situation, frequently defined by competing interests. These included struggles between empowered capital and less empowered labor and, just as important, competition between leading groups whose agendas shaped their architecture.

Ferdinand Peck and Planning for the World's Columbian Exposition

In the early 1890s the civic keynote for Adler and Sullivan's major Chicago projects was the level of expectation and aspiration surrounding the World's Columbian Exposition. While this fair as constructed has been extensively studied, the impact of its announcement in 1890 on Chicago's urban architecture up to 1893 has not been systematically analyzed. Nor has the fair's contested role for different groups in the socially segmented city after Haymarket. In the early 1890s most Chicago architects and clients for large structures worked with the exposition in mind, even if their buildings looked very different from those of the White City. Chicago's successful bid to become the site of the fair engaged many of the same leaders and methods that led to the Auditorium Building's realization. Both projects demonstrated the ability of local capitalists to organize effectively to realize common economic and cultural goals. Ferdinand Peck's efforts were a key link between the Auditorium and the exposition, whose histories overlapped from 1889.

Between 1885 and 1888, as the Auditorium was being conceived and built, there had been several failed efforts to promote the idea of a world's fair in Chicago. In July 1889 local private initiatives succeeded in prompting the city's newly elected Democratic mayor, De Witt Cregier, to obtain the city council's permission to name "a committee of one hundred citizens to take preliminary steps toward securing the location of the World's Fair to Chicago."[1] An expanded version of this committee chose an executive committee, which, in August, established a corporation called "the World's Exposition of 1892," later changed to "the World's Columbian Exposition." Initially a member of this executive committee of thirty, Peck was soon among the exposition's seven original incorporators, who were licensed to sell shares of the corporation's initial issue of $5,000,000 in stock. This was to be sold in shares each costing $10, "so as to enable persons of limited means to contribute toward the success of the fair and share in the financial profits, if there should be any."[2] This approach was to ensure the same broad participation that Peck sought for the Auditorium Association. Sales proceeded, with Peck among those soliciting contributions from both wealthy and working citizens. The latter were canvassed by members of their own professions, trades, or unions. This process meant that "the project is a project of the people and not of any one class," modeled on democratic shareholding for such world's fairs going back to London's Great Exposition in 1851.[3] Peck convinced the Auditorium Association's board to purchase a sizable block of shares in the exposition, and when the theater opened in December 1889, Mayor Cregier invited the assembled governors, national figures, and Canadian guests to visit Chicago for a world's fair then projected for 1892.[4] The theater's dedication was one of a series of events designed to demonstrate the city's potential for hosting the exposition. The effort exhibited what one scholar has called the "civic patriotism" that created the Auditorium, where success depended on unity of purpose. Intraurban social divisions based on class, ethnicity, and district had hampered New York City's drive to attract the fair, whereas Chicagoans were unified in their efforts. As speakers at the first meeting of the mayor's committee in August 1889 emphasized, "Chicago must have the World's Fair, and we are all Chicagoans."[5]

By January 1890, when the Auditorium Hotel opened, Chicagoans realized that continuing competition from New York as the leading contender for the fair necessitated raising more money. After an intense battle against Manhattan in the United States Congress, Chicago, with support from the South and West, was named the host city on 24 February 1890. Congress required that Chicago raise another $5,000,000 before final presidential approval for the fair's location would be granted. In April the corporation's stockholders held a mass meeting to elect directors to realize the exposition. Peck was first vice president and a director of this corporation. The directors then appointed a standing committee on finance to find ways to raise the additional $5,000,000. Peck was named chair of this committee, on whose success the fate of the whole project then depended. In June the city council agreed to increase the municipally bonded debt by $5,000,000 to help fund the fair, after the state of Illinois had authorized it. This yielded combined resources of corporation stock and municipal bonds totaling just over $10,000,000. Once congressional conditions had been complied with, Peck missed a board of trustees meeting at the University of Chicago to hurry to Washington. There, on Christmas Eve 1890, he personally secured an official proclamation from President Harrison, nominated in the Auditorium, for the exposition to be held in Chicago.[6]

Peck's motivation to lead the fund-raising for the exposition grew out of the same ideological vision that motivated him to create the Auditorium. The audience he most sought to reach with the theater's programs of lectures and concerts was the city's skilled industrial workmen and mechanics. It was this group that he thought would benefit most from the fair. This concern animated his later efforts as commissioner general for the United States at the Paris exposition of 1900, a position to which Peck was appointed by President McKinley, partly because of his success as financial overseer of the World's Columbian Exposition. In his view these workers "form the sinew of this country as a nation," and their economic well-being depended on boosting exports.[7] Peck argued that the United States was then the world's leading country in industry but that it had not yet won for itself the place it should hold in commerce. He recounted that while American production in agriculture, manufacturing, machinery, mining, railroads, forestry, and fisheries far exceeded that of any other nation, its foreign trade did not match that of other major countries. Great Britain, much less wealthy than the United States and with just over half its population, then enjoyed double the American overseas trade. American consuls throughout Europe wrote that demand for American-made goods was great but that United States firms had not cultivated these markets to build up the country's exports.

The World's Columbian Exposition played a key role in reversing this trend, as foreign buyers at the fair were convinced of the superiority of many American products, some of them made in the Chicago factories that had been the targets of anarchist agitation through the 1880s. Buyers followed up their visits to the fair by contacting these and other United States manufacturers to arrange exports of goods overseas. As an example, Peck cited the manufacture of agricultural implements, an industry that "gives employment to over 500,000 of America's best mechanics and brightest laboring men." Loss of any foreign trade in this line "would throw many of these mechanics and workmen out of employment, and inflict a corresponding injury upon the prosperity of the country."[8] The national center for this industry was Chicago's McCormick Reaper Plant, the site of the confrontations between striking workers and armed authorities in 1885–1886 that had fueled the anarchist cause. At that time, overproduction in many of Chicago's industries had led to price deflation, wage cuts, and worker unrest. Peck's aim of increasing exports from such local plants as McCormick's ideally would have the effect of relieving these economic pressures and related political violence in the city.[9] As with the Auditorium Building, the exposition's economic and festive dimensions were intertwined. Similar links between Chicago's social order and cultural life shaped Adler and Sullivan's major urban buildings in the early 1890s, which were variously keyed to the coming exposition.

The Rebuilding of McVicker's Theater, 1890–1891

After the Auditorium Theater's opening in December 1889, and as Chicago completed its successful effort to become the site of the exposition, Adler and Sullivan's first major local commission was the reconstruction of McVicker's Theater after a fire of August 1890 destroyed its interior, five years after Adler and Sullivan had remodeled the house in 1885. To sustain his theater financially during the intervening years, McVicker booked traveling companies to play contemporary comedies or melodramas, which remained for long runs of up to twelve weeks. A single production would be repeated for as long as it could draw an audience. Yet McVicker had continued to cultivate his house's reputation as Chicago's home for traditional English drama by presenting historical plays for at least part of each season. From June to August 1889 he staged a production of *The Tempest,* one of Shakespeare's works rarely performed in Chicago. Early in its run, one critic proclaimed: "So beautiful an entertainment is above the taste of the multitude, and manager McVicker therefore deserves the more credit that with little or no hope of profit he had honored his art and rendered a service to the cause of culture."[10] McVicker's adherence to an older standard of productions for a limited audience animated Adler and Sullivan's reconstruction of his house, as it had their design of 1885.

The fire prompted a major organizational change in McVicker's financial management. Insurance had not covered the property's losses, leaving McVicker with inadequate funds for rebuilding. He then chose to create a joint stock company with a stock issue of $500,000, of which he bought a controlling interest of $300,000 while other theatrical professionals and Chicago capitalists backed him by buying the remaining shares. In effect, McVicker traded on his theater's social reputation

Figure 169

Adler and Sullivan, McVicker's Theater, Chicago, as renovated 1890–1891, interior looking north from stage (interior demolished 1922). From *Observanda: McVicker's New Theatre, Chicago.* Courtesy of the Chicago Historical Society, ICHi-31466.

and long-term profitability to reinvent it as a semipublic institution, much like the Auditorium, whose theater served as the interim home for McVicker's productions. In his theater as remodeled in 1890–1891, McVicker wanted no change in seating, sight lines, and balcony pitches, since the room had worked so well since its remodeling in 1885.[11] In place of the gradually stepped ceiling of 1885, which expanded upward and outward from the proscenium, Adler created a level coffered ceiling raised to a new height over the topmost rear gallery (fig. 169). The new ceiling followed in part from Adler's structural decision to span the auditorium with six steel trusses set above this ceiling, much like those of the Auditorium Theater. These horizontal trusses were supported on latticed wrought steel columns rising from new footings inside the old walls, seen as the projecting vertical piers along the new interior's side walls. This new structural system supported two new office floors above the theater, connected to the upper levels of the front office block, which had survived the fire thanks to the brick fire wall between it and the gutted theater. Like the front offices, office floors newly built over the theater provided rental income to supplement the theater's receipts.[12]

The ceiling's elevation also had a specific social rationale in serving a broad audience, which would exclude prostitutes and raucous male patrons from the upper galleries. As in 1885, McVicker's solution to this issue in his newly rebuilt theater was to improve the architectural quality of the galleries, thereby "making that part of the theatre a place where people of humble means may procure wholesome amusement amid equally wholesome surroundings."[13] He maintained that "the 25 and 50-cent customers are just as worthy of managerial consideration as those who prefer seats at $1.50 . . . . In a thoroughly well-managed theater the purchaser of a low-priced ticket has a good seat in a clean and comfortable part of the theater, from which the sight and hearing are as good (in *a properly built theater*) as that of any other part of the house."[14] In this light, the most important change was the raised ceiling over the balcony and main gallery above (both furnished with individual chairs), below a smaller topmost gallery of benches. The increased ceiling height added greatly to the desirability of seats in these upper levels, so that more civil, if not more wealthy, patrons would buy tickets on these levels, driving down the proportion of rowdies. McVicker observed that those sections of the house that for generations had heard loud rants would know such behavior no more. Like the Auditorium Theater's upper galleries, McVicker's galleries as renovated in 1891 accommodated less wealthy patrons, who were to conform to standards of respectability defined by the patrons with higher incomes who constituted the core of the theatergoing public. Emphasis on the audience's propriety corresponded to use of the rebuilt McVicker's for weekly Sunday religious services of the People's Church, a theologically liberal congregation led by the Reverend Hiram W. Thomas, whose urban ministry resembled that of the Reverend David Swing.[15]

To distinguish McVicker's from the poorly ventilated theaters that staged less culturally elevated productions, the rebuilt house had a system of ventilation modeled on that of the Auditorium, with lighter fresh air supplied through ornamental grilles in the ceiling and heavier vitiated air exhausted through plenums under the seats. The system provided double the estimated amount of twelve cubic feet of fresh air per minute required by each adult. As in the Auditorium, ventilation was to equalize climatic effects in all parts of the house, so that "there is no appreciable difference in this respect between the gallery and the dress circle or the boxes." To equalize comfort "without distinction of place or price," galleries, like the parquet and boxes below, had cushioned seats, carpeted aisles, and retiring rooms for both men and women. McVicker was particularly proud of his treatment of the galleries.

Figure 170

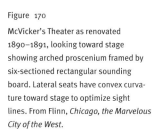

McVicker's Theater as renovated 1890–1891, looking toward stage showing arched proscenium framed by six-sectioned rectangular sounding board. Lateral seats have convex curvature toward stage to optimize sight lines. From Flinn, *Chicago, the Marvelous City of the West.*

The result was that "the poor man need not be driven to patronize the low dives on the plea that he cannot afford to pay fancy prices for his evening's entertainment. He can secure for twenty-five cents, precisely the same privilege as the man who can afford to pay for the private box. He can sit in a comfortable seat, breathe a pure, wholesome atmosphere, and command a perfect view and hearing of the performance on the stage."[16]

More so than in the larger Auditorium Theater, where the huge ceiling arches shaped the space overhead, Adler and Sullivan's ornamental treatment of the proscenium defined the public image of the remodeled McVicker's interior (fig. 170). Consistent with Adler's acoustic theory, the arched proscenium (with its embossed ornament) was small, with rectangular ornamental borders stepped outward and upward to meet the new high ceiling. The six sections of the rectangular border came forward to form a canopylike sounding board over the orchestra and the parquet's front, containing and directing sound from the stage toward the audience. As in the 1885 remodeling, the 1891 interior had electric lights set behind this perforated rectangular frame, so that "the incandescent burners are so masked and placed that the light falls over the assembly in diffused, soft glow, and in such way as to offer no interference with the view of people."[17] Instead of chandeliers, the ceiling coffers had central hanging perforated cones of Sullivan's design, "through which a mellow radiance comes like the reflection of burnished gold."[18]

The ornamental surfaces of proscenium and ceiling were of cast plaster filigree modeled by Kristian Schneider, for whom Sullivan sketched different patterns for each band.[19] The perforated ornament along the east (left) wall served as a screen for the theater's new organ behind, manufactured by the same New York firm that had built the Auditorium's organ (fig. 171). The ornament's chromatic scheme, which Sullivan developed with Healy and Millet, was described as subdued and unified, calling to mind the colors of nature. Most shades were like "the surface of freshly baked brown earth," with decorative highlights picked out in bands of gold leaf.[20] Such artistry would make the theater unique:

The entire surface of the proscenium is covered with the most exquisitely wrought plastic ornamentation, graceful, yet vigorous, with a charming play of surface light and shade. The superb effect of this original and fine proscenium is heightened by the extreme beauty of the color scheme which seems to play over the house, so skillfully worked out has been the symphony of tints and shades. The basis is a deep salmon brown, that gradually diminishes into a delicate pink as it ascends to the ceiling. The eye is at once captivated and soothed, so perfectly in harmony are all the striking effects of this art treasury. Gold and bronze enter sparingly into the ornamentation, and a dark wood wainscoting serves as a strong basic contrast to the whole color scheme that is preserved in the rich carpets, draperies and red plush of the unique opera chairs. An auditorium more beautiful, balancing charm with dignity and grace with solidity, is hardly to be imagined.[21]

Figure 171

McVicker's Theater as renovated 1890–1891, looking southeast toward stage showing arched proscenium framed by six-sectioned rectangular sounding board. Perforated cast plaster segments of sounding board were for emission of organ sounds from behind. From *Observanda: McVicker's New Theatre, Chicago.* Courtesy of the Chicago Historical Society, ICHi-31463.

As in the Auditorium, within these ornamental fields there were representational works of sculpture and painting. These images identified McVicker's with the history of Chicago, some of whose leading citizens were now shareholders, so that this theater was presented as "one of the most splendid monuments" of the city's progress.[22] This historicizing tone anticipated themes of Chicago's self-presentation in the World's Columbian Exposition. Rather than two tiers of boxes flanking the proscenium as in the 1885 interior, there were now only lower boxes in sets of three on each side. Where the upper second tier of boxes had formerly been, there were now two panels in low relief with life-size figures flanking the stage. Sculpted by Johannes Gelert, the panels represented (at right facing the stage) the initial march of the French explorer La Salle into Illinois in 1682 and (at left) the Fort Dearborn massacre of 1812 (fig. 171). Between these reliefs hung the stage's asbestos fire curtain painted by scenic artist Walter Burridge (b. 1857), who had done stage designs at McVicker's and the Chicago Opera House. His curtain was a view of Chicago in 1833, the year of the city's incorporation, showing Potawatomi Indians ceding territory to the United States on the site soon to be occupied by Chicago (fig. 172). Behind this was a drop curtain painted by Ernest Albert (1858–1946), Burridge's partner, which showed an idyll of a Greek landscape, suggested by a line from the poet Sappho: "To sit and muse by thee in twilight realms." Two figures seated on a circular marble bench in the foreground gazed out on Athens, with its fallen temple and ancient dwellings, and the blue Mediterranean in the foreground (fig. 173). Though this image alluded to the origins of European theater, it was titled *A Reverie of the Future,* implying a coming cultural golden age, centered on Chicago and McVicker's. The two curtains' presentation of locale and of fictive past and future realms recalled the Auditorium Theater's side and proscenium murals, where Albert had worked as a scenic artist in its first season of 1889–1890.[23]

The historicizing images corresponded to the description of Sullivan's ornamental style. Although its motifs were in his personal idiom, the ornament was not described as Sullivanesque, a term used to characterize it in other buildings. Rather, McVicker's booklet on the remodeled theater noted "the striking Egyptian character of the proscenium environments," while the boxes had "massive dividing columns modeled after the Egyptian and finely sculptured."[24] This historical naming of Sullivan's style contrasts with the terms found in accounts of his 1885 remodeling of the

Figure 172

Walter Burridge, McVicker's Theater as
renovated 1890–1891, principal or fire
curtain, showing *Chicago, Sept. 26 1833.
Pottawatomies Ceding Territory to United
States*. From *Observanda: McVicker's
New Theatre, Chicago*. Courtesy of the
Chicago Historical Society, ICHi-31464.

Figure 173

Ernest Albert, McVicker's Theater as
renovated 1890–1891, act drop curtain,
showing *A Reverie of the Future*. From
*Observanda: McVicker's New Theatre,
Chicago*. Courtesy of the Chicago
Historical Society, ICHi-31465.

same space, whose ornaments were identified as Moorish. By 1891 Sullivan's ornament was interpreted to allude to the Egyptian as the most archaic of Western architectural styles, to which observers had compared the Auditorium's exterior
columns and its tower's crowning profile. In both buildings, invoking Egypt conveyed ideas of the city's monumental permanence and stability over a long history,
in contrast to contemporaneous perceptions of its rapid rise.

The main foyers largely escaped the fire and so retained much of their original
decor from 1885, which "equals, if not surpasses, the parlor and drawing room appointments of the most costly residences."[25] For Sullivan, the theater's remodeled
vestibule and main foyer (fig. 174), with their walls and ceilings stenciled in repeated
foliate patterns, perhaps had a link to the Egyptian tradition of conventionalized

Figure 174

McVicker's Theater as renovated 1890–1891, main foyer and promenade, showing stenciled ornament with likeness of James McVicker (circled) standing left of center. From *Observanda: McVicker's New Theatre, Chicago*. Courtesy of the Chicago Historical Society, ICHi-31462. Graphic addition by author.

ornamental forms derived from the lotus, papyrus, and other river plants. One historian has suggested that Egyptian motifs in Chicago's architecture of this period referred to the city's own low-lying terrain on Lake Michigan, with its plethora of plant species in the shoreline's soils. If so, their appearance in McVicker's foyer was consistent with this theater's publicly promoted image as a civic institution, whose fortunes historically had been tied to those of Chicago. In this way Sullivan's decorative aesthetic framed perceptions of McVicker as a cultural leader, and McVicker's likeness appeared among those of his patrons in one view of the newly remodeled foyer, as circled in figure 174. In the Central Music Hall a bust of its founder, George B. Carpenter, was installed in the foyer after his death in 1881. In 1890 the Auditorium's directors authorized placing a bust of that theater's creator, Ferdinand Peck, in its foyer. Until his death in 1896, McVicker greeted guests in his theater's foyer as the living symbol of his enterprise, surrounded by Sullivan's ornamental surfaces. McVicker bemoaned the tendency in theater, as in national affairs, "toward organization and away from individualism."[26] This outlook predisposed McVicker to Sullivan's art, which embodied an ideal of individual expression.

Chicago's German Bourgeoisie and the Schiller Building, 1886–1892

If McVicker's was Chicago's home for the English dramatic tradition, its development paralleled that of the city's German theatrical organizations after 1871. Like the choral singing of the German *Männerchor,* German theater was an alternative tradition of an ethnic minority, independent from local theater in English. As there were German elite and socialist singing societies in the postfire decades, so German theatrical culture was multifaceted, corresponding to the segmentation of social classes within the immigrant community. In addition to popular theatricals in dispersed locations, acting companies featured plays of Schiller, Goethe, Lessing, and other classic authors performed for a German upper- and middle-class audience in commercial theaters through the central city, which the companies owned rather than rented. Repertoires were steady, and seasons were planned as a whole. In the 1870s a new local tradition of German working-class theater (*Arbeitertheater*) emerged. This was ideologically developed within the labor movement, with openly propagandistic performances at socialist picnics, festivals, and rallies. By the late 1880s and early 1890s, nonpoliticized comedies and farces imported from Germany also became part of the *Arbeitertheater* repertoire.[27]

Within this spectrum, successful German capitalists supported classic dramas for an educated audience, just as their Anglo-American counterparts patronized McVicker's more serious plays. Even before Haymarket, Chicago's upper- and middle-class German community wanted to dissociate itself from the labor movement then so strongly identified with German agitators and workers. As early as 1885, one leader of Chicago's German bourgeois community wrote a text in English aimed partly at an Anglo-American audience. Opening with the claim that "the radical beer-drinkers and opponents of Sunday laws do not fitly represent their countrymen in America," he concluded that "the 200,000 Germans of Chicago should establish in Chicago an Institute for the collection of German literature, painting and music, and for the cultivation of the higher order of German talents; the German opera, the Sängerfest, distinguished German musicians, artists and scholars to be introduced through its medium to Americans; encouragement extended to German youth seeking to perfect themselves in the fine arts, and receptions and concerts given for the advancement of German culture in America."[28]

In this spirit, in 1886 the bourgeois German community erected a bronze statue of Schiller, the hero of German high culture, close to the east end of Webster Avenue at its entrance to Lincoln Park on the Near North Side. Created by Ernst B. Rau, the Schiller figure was a copy of one at Schiller's birthplace in Marbach. The Chicago sculpture's dedication was originally set for Saturday, 8 May, but it was postponed a week owing to the ban on large assemblies that the city issued just after the Haymarket clash on Tuesday, 4 May. When held, the dedication attracted 8,000. The Schiller figure preceded two other statues erected by the German community in Humboldt Park on the West Side and a memorial to Goethe in Lincoln Park unveiled in June 1914. These images represented German intellectual ideals amid commemorative statues erected by other ethnic groups in Chicago's parks as public places then dominated by the city's propertied classes.[29]

By the later 1880s, the Germania Männerchor had become more of an elite social club than a performing musical organization. In 1888 this group commissioned

Figure 175

August Fiedler and John Addison,
Germania Club, 1536 North Clark Street,
on northwest corner of Germania Place,
Chicago (1888–1889; renovated as
Germania Place in 1992–1993 by Harold
D. Rider and Nidata, Inc.). Photograph
of 1904 by Barnes and Crosby, BC-260.
Courtesy of the Chicago Historical
Society, ICHi-19260.

the architects John Addison and August Fiedler to design a monumental meeting hall, known as the Germania Club, which still stands at 1536 North Clark Street on the northwest corner of Germania Place (fig. 175). Opened in 1889, the Germania Club stood as a monumental anchor at the entrance to what was then the premier German neighborhood, whose origins as an ethnic enclave dated back to 1848–1849. To signify the new club's association with the Germania Männerchor, the exterior terra cotta ornament included lyres centered on the Ionic capitals of the second floor's columns. This monumental building perhaps responded to the new quarters of the predominantly Anglo-American Union League Club, opened in 1886. The Germania Club was also an upper-class counterweight to the worker-dominated North Side Turner Hall, also on Clark Street nine blocks to the south, which had become publicly if not accurately identified with the labor agitation surrounding Haymarket.[30]

Within the German community, class conflict through the 1880s informed the editorial positions of two of the city's principal German-language newspapers, the capitalist *Illinois Staats-Zeitung,* founded in 1848 and owned from 1867 by Anton C. Hesing (1823–1895), and the socialist *Chicagoer Arbeiter-Zeitung,* revived after its temporary suppression in the wake of Haymarket. These two papers had carried on a running feud since the *Arbeiter-Zeitung*'s founding in 1876, waging an editorial battle that corresponded to the antipathy between the English-language papers, especially Joseph Medill's capitalist *Chicago Tribune* and Albert Parsons's anarchist *Alarm.* As an extension of their politics, both German papers regularly reviewed theatrical productions aimed at their readerships. The *Arbeiter-Zeitung* encouraged attendance at politically charged shows and comic productions if the latter were thought to educate popular tastes.[31]

As with McVicker's, the national depression of the 1870s put severe financial pressure on the German theaters with stock companies that performed classic plays. In Chicago, Deutsches Haus had operated continuously as a center of serious drama for fourteen years, from its opening in 1856 through 1870. After the fire, the most important serious troupe was the Globe Theater Company, sometimes known as the German Theater Company, active before the Great Fire. This company inaugurated the New Chicago Theater (later the Grand Opera House) in 1875, playing there until 1879 and then at Hooley's Theater until 1882. Both interiors had been remodeled by Adler and Sullivan. The Globe Theater Company, whose standards were praised by the local English-language press, retained a focus on Schiller in local German theaters that went back to the 1850s, when staging his works had been part of the immigrant community's response to harassment by native-born Americans. By 1888 commercial pressures had led the German Theater Company to adopt more profitable popular plays, to the point where a reviewer in the *Staats-Zeitung* complained: "Today's drama director seems only to be a speculator who counts heads in the theater and dollars in the box."[32] To counter this trend, in November 1889, the month before the Auditorium Theater opened, the German Theater Company staged a series of outstanding performances in honor of Schiller's 130th birthday, 10 November, which was the occasion for other local German celebrations each year.

The enthusiastic public reception of the Schiller festival, combined with the opening of the Auditorium Theater and Hotel and congressional approval of Chicago as the host city for the World's Columbian Exposition, stimulated a group of leading German Americans to organize the German Theater Association. This corporation was legally chartered in 1891 as the German Opera-House Company, on the model of the Auditorium Association. The company, headed by Anton C. Hesing of the *Staats-Zeitung*, Franz Amberg, long the president of the Germans' Orpheus Singing Club, and the realtor Charles Wacker, sought to realize "the idea of a 'German' theater," meaning a permanent home for year-round German drama and opera in Chicago, the role Deutsches Haus had pioneered to 1870. By 1890 over one-third of the city's people were German immigrants, making Chicago's one of the largest German urban populations in the world after Berlin's and New York's.[33] Yet "notwithstanding the various turner halls and the homes of the various German singing societies, there has been felt among the Germans the need for a general gathering place and a home for the German theater. The present halls are comparatively small and the lines of admission so closely drawn that they cannot be said to belong to the Germans at large. With the view of supplying this want has the Chicago German Opera-House Company been formed and chartered" for "a building which shall be for the German element of Chicago what the Auditorium is to the citizens at large."[34]

These Chicagoans presumably modeled their project after the major German theaters of New York City, all of which had surged with the large influx of German immigrants in the 1880s. The leading producer of German plays in Manhattan was Augustin Daly, who had consulted with Adler on the Auditorium Theater. Daly successfully specialized in adapting newly written German farces and musical comedies, known not for their polish and sophistication but for their innocence and respectability. This made them widely popular with audiences of women. In New York, one principal company staging these plays in the 1890s was the Germania Theater, housed in a converted Roman Catholic church. As in Manhattan, Chicago's German theater companies played to smaller audiences than their English-speaking counterparts, so the Schiller Theater was among the smallest of Adler and Sullivan's theaters in the city, seating just 1,270. When completed, its auditorium was described as "an ideal theater for comedy."[35]

By April 1890, Chicago's German Opera-House Company issued capital stock of $500,000 and leased a property 80 feet wide by 180 feet deep on the north side of Randolph Street west of State, adjacent to Adler and Sullivan's Borden Block. As Peck did for the Auditorium, Hesing emphasized that a central site was critical to ensure access from around the city.[36] The initial project called for a theater seating 1,300 and a set of new clubrooms for the Germania Männerchor, which also sought a more central urban position.[37] Presumably in anticipation of the World's Columbian Exposition, the building's upper floors were to contain a hotel, "first class and equal to the Auditorium in every respect and distinctively German in its character. It is urged that there is not a really first-class German hotel in the country and that such an institution would assuredly be both popular and profitable. The large number of wealthy German-Americans who visit and pass through the city, with all others who through European travel or associations have a liking for German cuisine, would, it is argued, insure such a project's success."[38]

Adler and Sullivan were selected as architects "on general reputation, but principally on account of their success in the designing and construction of theaters."[39] Earlier in 1890 they had been selected to remodel Milwaukee's Grand Opera House into the Deutsches Stadt Theater, a project that paralleled Chicago's German Opera-House Company but was not carried out according to Adler and Sullivan's designs.[40] By February 1891 these architects had drawn plans for a German Opera House structure fourteen stories high in front, with its central tower rising 230 feet from the street. Behind the front block was a midsection of eight stories containing the theater and a rear block of twelve stories. As in the Auditorium, the rental income from commercial spaces was meant to sustain the theater as a cultural center. After plans were drawn, the decision was taken to replace the hotel interiors with rentable offices, which would require less of an investment. The clubrooms, including banquet, dancing, and rehearsal halls, were moved from their original position on the front second floor to the rear block's upper floors (fig. 176).

Hesing and his colleagues on the German Opera-House Company's board estimated that the building's eighty offices would bring in $44,000 annually, while the theater's receipts would be $22,500, as part of the building's anticipated annual income of $85,000. Given its estimated annual operating expenses of $52,800, this would leave a yearly surplus of $32,200, or a return of just over 6 percent on the project's projected investment of $500,000.[41] To command high rentals, all offices had to be well supplied with daylight. Thus the front tower above the eighth story was

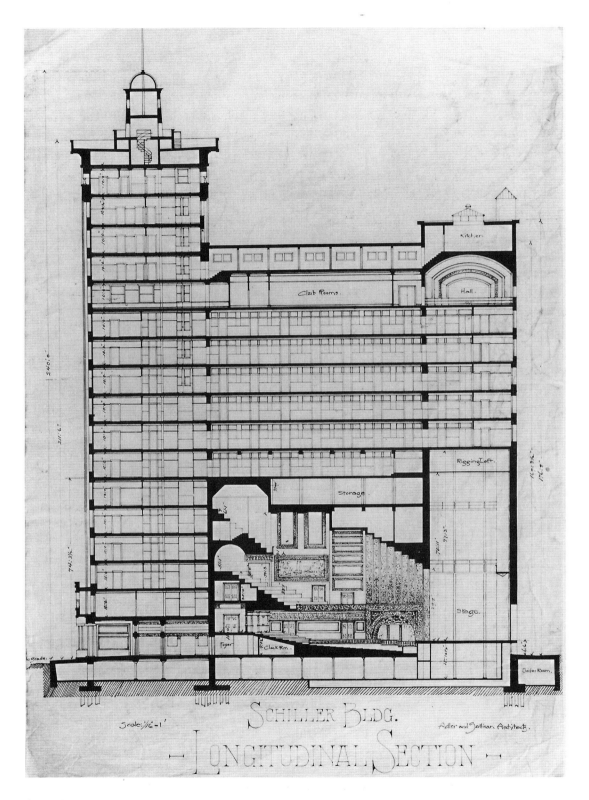

Figure 176

Adler and Sullivan, Schiller Theater Building (later the Garrick Theater), 64 Randolph Street (north side), west of State, Chicago (1890–1892; demolished 1961). Longitudinal section looking west, showing theater in lower floors and clubrooms mainly on thirteenth floor. Courtesy of the Richard Nickel Committee Archive, Chicago, Illinois.

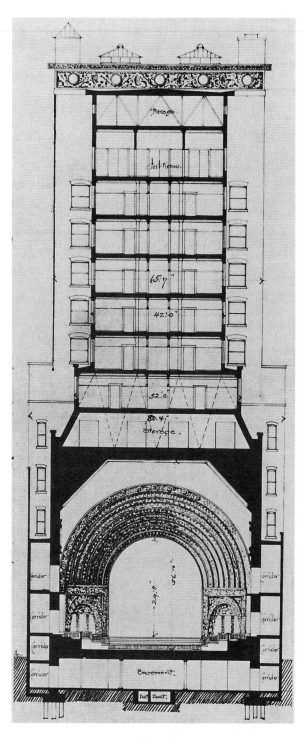

forty feet wide, leaving twenty feet on each side for light and air to reach the site's core. The midsection was also set in twenty feet from the side lot lines, creating a pair of light courts (fig. 177). As Adler wrote, the configuration ensured adequate daylight to all interiors through the site's depth, making the Schiller Building a forerunner of later taller setback skyscrapers.[42]

As shown in the sections and floor plans, Adler set the theater compactly within the overall built volume. The theater proper was surrounded by brick bearing walls, which supported steel trusses spanning its ceiling above the sixth floor (fig. 177). These trusses carried eight upper office floors, which, like the front tower, were framed in steel and clad externally in terra cotta. The

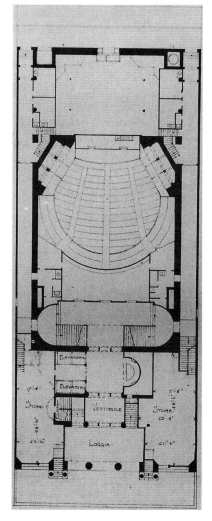

Figure 177

Schiller Theater Building, cross section looking north, showing inset of theater on either side, two-story trusses spanning theater, and corridors for fire exits flanking theater. Courtesy of the Richard Nickel Committee Archive, Chicago, Illinois.

a

Schiller Theater was only sixty feet wide, making it smaller in capacity and narrower than McVicker's, which seated 1,865. In both halls, Adler replaced the parquet's extreme lateral seats with walls splayed out from the proscenium to direct sound to the audience (fig. 178). As in the Auditorium Theater, the parquet's seating rows had a circular curvature centered on the stage's rear, while rows in the parquet circle and the balcony had their circular curvature centered within the parquet.

To gain access to the theater, patrons entered through the front open loggia on Randolph Street, coming into the lobby with the elevators to the office floors on the left and the theater ticket office on the right (fig. 178a). Passing through the theater's brick fire wall on this level, they entered a lower foyer with a cloakroom straight ahead. From this first-floor foyer, stairs led to the theater's second-floor main foyer, from which they could see the whole theater from the parquet's high rear before moving down aisles into the parquet seating (fig. 178b). At the main foyer's sides, stairs led to foyers at the balcony's lower and upper levels, seen in the longitudinal section (fig. 176) and floor plans (fig. 178c, d). In these ways the Schiller Theater's system of rear foyers and staircases followed "somewhat after the manner of the

Figure 178

Schiller Theater Building, plans of (a) first or entry story; (b) second story showing frontal loggia and theater's parquet and parquet circle; (c) third story showing theater's main balcony; and (d) fourth story, showing upper part of main balcony. Sullivaniana Collection, gift of Gordon D. Orr. Courtesy of the Art Institute of Chicago.

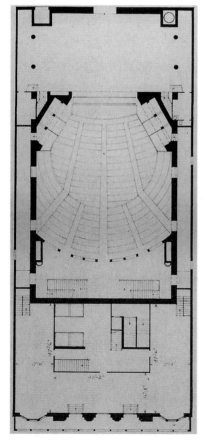

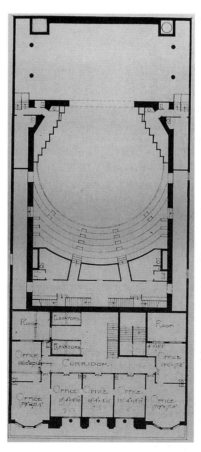

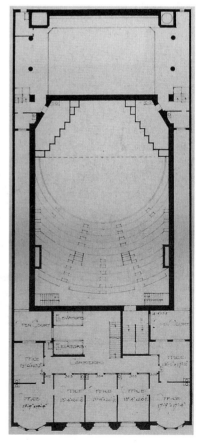

b

c

d

entrance to the Auditorium."[43] In both theaters, the high upper galleries above the main balcony served as less expensive seating for socially lower classes. From any level, in case of fire, one exited the theater through side doors into corridors with stairways leading down into the alley north of the building, as seen in the cross section (fig. 177). McVicker's Theater had similar fire stairs along the sides, but its stairs were outside in alleys rather than enclosed.

One major difference between the Schiller and the Auditorium was that the latter hall's great width (118 feet between its north and south fire walls) necessitated rows of columns to support the main balcony and upper galleries (figs. 95 and 104). By contrast, in the sixty-foot-wide Schiller Theater, "no columns will be used to support the balcony, the cantilever principle being applied instead."[44] This meant that the balcony and gallery would be carried by continuous steel beams that spanned their width, with the balcony's front sections cantilevered forward from the beams toward the stage (fig. 179). In the theater there would be "not a single pillar to obstruct the view of any one, either on the main floor or in the balcony or gallery."[45] Adler and Sullivan modeled this structural solution on their earlier Grand Opera House in Pueblo, Colorado, "the only other house in the country without pillars," designed from June 1888 and opened in October 1890.[46]

The Schiller Theater's columnless interior, made possible by the new technology of structural steel, increased the impression of spatial freedom and constructive modernity. As Anton Hesing's *Staats-Zeitung* described the resulting space, "With the final abolition of many tiers, parterres, little angles, and little corners of all

Figure 179

Schiller Theater Building, interior view toward balcony and upper gallery, 1950s, without columnar supports. Photograph by Richard Nickel. Courtesy of the Richard Nickel Committee, Chicago, Illinois.

kinds, modern theater architecture has taken a powerful step forward. For the chief advantage of simplification and spatial expansion lies in the increase in the audience's security. The modern architect thus transforms the theater into a free space, and therewith sets himself the new task, to create an artistic and majestic wall covering."[47] Hesing raised this theme at the theater's dedication, stating that "no post or column hems the view nor disturbs those moments in which we often wish to forget that we are in a confined space or inclosure."[48]

Inside the theater, eight concentric arches acting as a sound container stepped up and out from the stage toward the semicircular vault over the central parquet (fig. 180). Beyond this vault, the cross section shows a three-sided ceiling (originally stenciled in intertwined tracery of gold on a background of beige relief) to reduce spatial volume over the parquet's rear, thereby decreasing dissonant reverberation. The longitudinal section shows similar volumetric economies in the coved ceilings above the balcony and gallery, whose seats were more steeply banked than those of the parquet to ensure that their elevated distant patrons could see and hear to the stage's full depth. One contemporary wrote that this theater "is to the taste of many the most beautiful in the city. Representatives from the leading old theaters of the city pronounced the place a gem, and gazed about with envy. The lines of the Auditorium have been reproduced in miniature . . . . The Schiller is the Auditorium on a small scale, but even more striking in magnificence of decorative detail."[49]

Sullivan, again collaborating with Healy and Millet, developed surfaces of decorative plasterwork for the proscenium arches and frieze at their base on either side,

Figure 180

Schiller Theater Building, interior view toward stage, 1950s, showing semicircular arches in perforated cast plaster for ventilation. Ornamental patterns of plaster vary in successive arches. Photograph by Richard Nickel. Courtesy of the Richard Nickel Committee, Chicago, Illinois.

the soffit of the main vault beyond the proscenium, the facings of the balcony and gallery railings, and other surfaces. The theater's ornamental program dated from the spring of 1892, about the same time Sullivan designed the Golden Doorway for the Transportation Building of the World's Columbian Exposition. Observers compared this building to the Schiller's completed interior when it opened in September 1892, by which time the Transportation Building was also visible on the fairgrounds. Inside the Schiller, "a curious feature is the shape of the proscenium arch, which is in the form of concentric semicircular Romanesque arches, each with a deep reveal."[50] The Schiller's proscenium thus revived the multiarched treatment that Sullivan originally planned for the Auditorium Theater and that he used to great effect surrounding the Transportation Building's entrance. Inside the Schiller, Sullivan designed different motifs for the proscenium's nine concentric arch faces. Through these motifs of perforated plaster glowed the house's electric lights. The filigree arches also served as grilles through which fresh air was supplied to the house, again showing Adler and Sullivan's integration of technical and ornamental ideas.

Whereas the Auditorium Theater's interior displayed gradations of ivory accented with gold stenciling, the Schiller Theater's "color scheme is particularly beautiful, the prevailing shades being a sea-green and a delicate pink."[51] As in McVicker's, Sullivan and his collaborators developed a richly varied, subtly graded system of interior color. One account of the original interior similarly described it as "extremely successful, being a most pleasing mingling of green, gold and red, green being the body-color used . . . . The finish of the lower floor is in mahogany, which harmonizes with the red in the decoration. The pale-green, being approached by this red through the gold, makes an especially charming effect."[52] Lighter colors toward the ceiling harmonized with the yellow white glow of the incandescent light shining through the perforated decorative plasterwork overhead. The *Staats-Zeitung* described the view from the main balcony: "Here, in increasing admiration for all the shimmering gold, dashes of color, and ornamental pictures, one soon finds an idea that the construction of the whole joins into a unity."[53]

As in the Auditorium and the remodeled McVicker's, the Schiller Theater's interior focused on figural images set into Sullivan's surfaces of ornament and color. At the theater's dedication, Anton Hesing asserted: "Art has no native land, it belongs to the entire world; but in order that it may be grasped by the soul it must find expression in its mother tongue. There are thousands of Germans here who never enjoy dramatic art from the bottom of their hearts and never learn to honor it when it is presented in a foreign language."[54] In January 1892 the Schiller Theater was leased to theatrical manager A. S. Temple, then the Auditorium Theater's treasurer, who would present non-German productions through most of the year except for Sunday evenings and a period of six weeks annually, when the impresarios Friedrich Welb and Albert Wachsner would stage German-language drama.[55] The ethnically limited audience for such drama made it insufficiently remunerative to justify longer runs, much as McVicker's stock productions of classic plays were confined to the summer season. Yet Hesing still looked forward to the day when "only the sounds of the mother tongue, only German sounds will penetrate this space," to become "a pilgrims' resort in which the Germans, who will fill it nightly, will manifest their love for German life, for German art, in order that their children may gain by it."[56]

Given this cultural nationalism, German artists worked with Sullivan on a series of images to clarify the theater's cultural meaning. In the entrance foyer, Milwaukee painter Hermann Michalowski created an allegorical mural showing the Genius of Rhetoric standing between busts of Schiller and Shakespeare, at whose feet sat Clio, the muse of history, writing the names of these titans in the annals of world history. Inside the theater, painter Arthur Feudel created two murals in rectangular panels on the high lateral walls to each side of the main balcony, analogous to Fleury's murals in the Auditorium Theater. One of Feudel's images showed the scene of Mary Stuart meeting Queen Elizabeth, from Schiller's drama *Maria Stuart*. The other showed the market square at Nürnberg, where Gretchen encountered Faust, from Goethe's *Faust*. The German-born sculptor Richard Bock created two large elaborate ivory-toned plaster reliefs for the arched tympana over the proscenium boxes. The image on the left as one faced the stage showed Homer, depicted as a seated Zeus, reading his verse in a condensed, romanticized setting with a Greek Doric temple in the background. The relief on the right (fig. 181) depicted Schiller riding the winged horse Pegasus, led by the figure of Genius, who held the torch of enlightenment. In the spandrels were figures of Hercules (strength) and Diana (beauty). Bock's reliefs invoked the Enlightenment ideal of Greece as the source of German culture, which had been a major theme in the construction of German national identity through the earlier nineteenth century and an idea that Wagner had reinterpreted.[57]

Figure 181

Richard Bock, plaster relief depicting Schiller riding Pegasus led by Genius holding torch of enlightenment, with Hercules and Diana in spandrels. Photograph by J. W. Taylor. Architecture Photograph Collection, Courtesy of the Art Institute of Chicago.

Figure 182

Schiller Theater Building looking east along Randolph Street, showing Adler and Sullivan's Borden Block (1880–1881) at Dearborn Street and, in the distance, Burnham and Root's Masonic Temple Building (1891–1892) at State Street. The Schiller Building's arched loggia in the upper tower had spandrel busts of German folklore heroes sculpted by Frederick Almenröder beneath an ornamental terra cotta cornice. Photograph by J. W. Taylor. Architecture Photograph Collection, Courtesy of the Art Institute of Chicago.

The Schiller Building's exterior ornament carried through the culturally specific iconography of the theater. Overall, the steel frame was externally clad in plain blocks of light brown terra cotta set in red mortar. Along the second story, above the entrance, there was a bowed eleven-arch loggia covered with foliate ornamental relief in terra cotta (figs. 182 and 183). This loggia recalled the one Sullivan had projected earlier over the Auditorium Theater's entrance, shown in his preliminary designs (figs. 56 and 62) but not built. For the spandrels of the Schiller's arcade, sculptor Frederick Almenröder (1832–1900) modeled portraits of the most esteemed German composers and poets, including Beethoven, Wagner, and Goethe. With these figures, the loggia marked the whole building's cultural impetus. In a period when local German immigrants staged frequent and elaborate parades, the loggia served as "a covered balcony in front from which street parades may be advantageously viewed."[58] The spandrel figures' heads turned in different directions, looking down and along the street, as if simulating the act of viewing such a parade. As one critic wrote, "The balcony would be an anomaly in a strictly commercial building, but here it has a natural function in setting the building apart, as it were, from strictly commercial buildings."[59] The Schiller Theater was similarly enriched at its tower's crowning frieze, where Almenröder sculpted busts of heroes of German folklore in the top loggia's arch spandrels. Below, on each face of the tower, three

Figure 183

Schiller Theater Building, showing second-story loggia with portrait busts of German composers and poets in spandrels, sculpted by Frederick Almenröder. Photograph by Richard Nickel. Courtesy of the Richard Nickel Committee, Chicago, Illinois.

larger theatrical masks adorned the lintels of the windows below the main arches (fig. 182). Almenröder's figures both served as symbols of the theater's programmatic ideals and enriched Sullivan's ornamental treatment of the structure's crown, so that the whole building conveyed specific character. The Schiller exemplified Sullivan's emphasis on the necessity of ornament in architecture, distinct from minimal office buildings for which Chicago was then renowned.

Sullivan designed the Schiller Building's tower with aesthetic aims in mind that transcended its function as a container of rentable offices. Though different in plan, one local precursor of the Schiller's massing was William Le Baron Jenney's Manhattan Building of 1890 (fig. 184), financed by the German-born Charles C. Heisen. Situated on a midblock site facing west on Dearborn Street below Jackson, the Manhattan's higher central mass is flanked by two lower sections of nine stories. Originally the central block was twelve stories, but four more were added above a provisional cornice to make the Manhattan the world's first sixteen-story building.[60] Composing a symmetrical design, Jenney set higher columns of bay windows on the central section than on the sides. Sullivan shaped the Schiller's much narrower high central mass as a distinct squared tower. Avoiding the multistory pilasters, horizontal cornices, and ornamental stringcourses of Jenney's work, the Schiller Building's tower displayed the insistent verticality that Sullivan advocated to give formal unity to the tall office building as a modern type.

Figure 184
William Le Baron Jenney, Manhattan Building, east side, 431 South Dearborn Street below Jackson Boulevard, Chicago (1890). From *Inland Architect and News Record* 13 (July 1889). Courtesy of the Art Institute of Chicago.

Given Hesing's concept of his building as the Germanic response to the Auditorium, Sullivan's treatment of the Schiller Building's tower (236 feet) can be compared with his design for the Auditorium Tower (238 feet). The lower part of the Auditorium Tower continues the fenestration of the flanking block, whereas the Schiller Tower's uninterrupted vertical piers and windows from loggia to roof make it appear as a separate form. The Schiller Tower's piers align with the steel columns of its frame (fig. 182), whose soaring lightness Sullivan admired as a modern constructive ideal. The stepped profiles in the piers and arches of the Schiller's terra cotta front recall those in the main arcade of the Auditorium's stone fronts. As similar forms rendered in different materials, the stepped arch profiles of both buildings helped admit daylight. The Schiller's enriched and concentrated terra cotta ornament contrasted with the simple, severe molding profiles and carved details in the Auditorium's stone tower. The Schiller Tower had a broadly projecting lidlike cornice, built out on overhanging steel beams, unlike the Auditorium Tower's incrementally corbeled profile of stone courses. Both towers

Figure 185

Ernest Fuchs, drawing of Schiller Theater Building, with medallion of Friedrich Schiller suspended from Composite column. From *Graphic* (Chicago), n.s., 7 (1 October 1892). Courtesy of the Chicago Historical Society, ICHi-31477.

were originally crowned with observation platforms. The Schiller's was capped by "a dome-shaped spire with lookout windows."[61] This octagonal cupola had a dome clad in ornamental terra cotta, completing the program of decorative relief begun at the sidewalk and second-story loggia and taken up again in the tower's crowning stories and projecting cornice (fig. 185). Sullivan considered "terra-cotta to be a superior material" through which imagination and handwork could be reasserted in modern steel building. The decorative effect that he initially proposed for the Auditorium's elevations appears in the Schiller's crown. The terra cotta on the Auditorium's exterior was to have been fabricated by the Northwestern Terra-Cotta Company, which manufactured the Schiller's ornamental and plain cladding blocks.[62]

The Schiller Theater opened on 29 September 1892, three weeks before the dedication of the World's Columbian Exposition on 21 October. Among the thousands of foreign visitors attracted to the fair was the English architectural historian Sir Bannister Fletcher, whose monumental book *A History of Architecture on the Comparative Method* was published in 1896. He wrote that the Schiller "appeals at once to me as being the best designed tall structure, not only in Chicago, but in the

States."[63] French and German critics who visited the United States also praised the Schiller's design as aesthetically outstanding compared with other tall buildings in the Loop. This was indeed high praise, considering that Burnham and Root's 326-foot Masonic Temple, then the world's tallest building, stood just half a block away on the northeast corner of State and Randolph (fig. 182). Fletcher spoke well of this structure, whose promoters also responded to the Auditorium, but he felt that the Schiller's tower had a superior formal unity from base to crown. He asserted that such unity was the fundamental aesthetic principle of all architecture, first embodied in the Western tradition by the Greek temple. Fletcher compared the Schiller's design to a classical column, with a distinct base, shaft, and capital, concluding that "the Schiller Theater is in the same relation to the new style of tall building as the Parthenon bears to the architecture of Greece."[64] The Schiller's classicizing exterior corresponded to iconography of the theater's interior, which asserted that modern German drama had its model in ancient Greece. Classical drama had served as a model for Schiller and other modern German playwrights.[65] Ernest Fuchs's commemorative drawing of the opening of the Schiller Theater in 1892 adopted this classicizing theme, showing a medallion of Schiller suspended from a Composite capital, with a curtain parted to reveal the Schiller Building's front (fig. 185). Adler and Sullivan's design was here linked to a renewal of classicism that was the dominant theme of the World's Columbian Exposition.

Yet the Schiller Building's identification with German neoclassical culture of the Enlightenment perhaps responded to earlier German working-class efforts to identify their own cause with this literary tradition. As in nineteenth-century Germany, so in German Chicago, workers' literature represented the bourgeoisie as corrupt, in contrast to the cause of labor, which represented the virtues of reason celebrated in the revolutionary eighteenth century. For example, the German American labor writer Gustav Lyser adapted the poetic style of Schiller, and quoted from several of Schiller's classic plays, in one of Lyser's own dramas satirizing United States congressional mishandling of the labor issue after the great railroad strike of 1877. In 1888 the *Chicagoer Arbeiter-Zeitung* claimed that the city's middle-class Germans favored a shallow culture of comedy and thus neglected the theater as a force for moral education of the people, as a concept strongly identified with Schiller's work and politics. This editorial concluded that Chicago's German workers, with their politically motivated theatrical presentations, had been the true sustainers of Germany's cultural heritage. German theater should be "an enterprise which is not only one of the strongest bases for the preservation of the German language and literature in this country, but, if conducted properly, moreover a powerful instrument for educating the masses."[66]

In this light, Adler and Sullivan's Schiller Building signified the attempts of its middle- and upper-class German patrons to wrest back the cultural tradition epitomized by Schiller as a resource to serve propertied interests rather than anarchism. This message was not lost on German workers, who made their feelings known by attending en masse the 1894 presentation of Karl Böttcher's play *Ausgewiesen* (Exiled) at the Schiller Theater. This play, whose performance was banned in Germany, dealt with the antisocialist law enacted under Bismarck in 1878, which drove many German radicals to New York and Chicago. Though the law had been repealed by 1894, the play's theme resonated with working-class viewers, who packed Adler and Sullivan's galleries to applaud this drama, which drew negative reactions from more privileged patrons seated below and from the *Illinois Staats-Zeitung.* By their mass presence and strong reaction, German workers on this occasion claimed for their own cause this architectural interior intended for cultural privilege.

Unfortunately, Hesing's vision of German drama flourishing in Adler and Sullivan's theater did not succeed financially, and the Schiller closed in spring 1894 after its second season. Serious German drama again lacked a home in Chicago. The Schiller Theater's failure in 1894 contrasted with the rapid growth of outlying German commercial theater companies playing mostly in the *Turnhalle,* whose popularity peaked with the season of 1896–1897. In that year the Chicago Stadttheater opened on the North Side, neither a direct successor to the Schiller Theater nor a home for *Arbeitertheater,* but a playhouse for German middle-class spectators who had shown their strong interest in original plays about German American urban life rather than canonical German drama.[67]

The innovative style of Adler and Sullivan's McVicker's and Schiller Theater interiors was not the norm for Chicago in the later 1890s, when historical motifs became more explicit in all public architecture after the fair. Before Root's death in January 1891, he and Burnham designed the first phase of a building they hoped would rival the Auditorium, for which they had sought the commission. Initiated in November 1889 and finished by summer 1891, Burnham and Root's Chicago Hotel (later the Great Northern Hotel) rose on the northeast corner of Dearborn Street and Jackson Boulevard two blocks west of the Board of Trade. The client was Eugene S. Pike, the Auditorium board member who had skeptically queried William Ware about Adler and Sullivan's design. Created for the fair's guests, Pike's initial project expanded in 1895 to include the Great Northern Office and Theater Building to the west. Opened in November 1896, the theater interior returned to the Moorish style found in theaters of the 1880s, with a wealth of stenciled ornament across its elevated box fronts flanking the stage (fig. 186). Such explicit historicizing appeared in architects H. R. Wilson and Benjamin Marshall's remodeling of Hooley's Theater under a new manager in 1897–1898. Probably to stay abreast of nearby competition, Hooley's "inartistic boxes," perhaps referring to Sullivan's of 1882, were now among the "evils to be remedied." In their place, around the new proscenium and boxes appeared a decorative scheme of "dainty Rococo traceries that speak of a

Figure 186

Daniel H. Burnham and Company, Great Northern Theater, 20 West Jackson Boulevard, west of Dearborn, Chicago (opened November 1896; demolished 1961); interior showing Moorish motifs and elevated boxes with stenciled fronts. Photograph by J. W. Taylor. Architecture Photograph Collection, Courtesy of the Art Institute of Chicago.

well remembered period of French art." These rococo panels framed a drop curtain depicting the courtship of Louis XIV. In short, Adler and Sullivan's style signifying regional cultural independence, which animated the Auditorium and other theater interiors, did not survive the combined effects of the World's Columbian Exposition and the Panic of 1893. Sullivan later recalled that these twin events diminished appreciation and patronage of Adler's and his innovative architecture.[68]

The Auditorium, Ferdinand Peck, and the Columbian Exposition's Musical Programs

The dedication of the Schiller Theater in September 1892 anticipated the week of ceremonies that culminated in the exposition's Dedication Day. Had the exposition been sited at Chicago's central lakefront, as had long been proposed, rather than at Jackson Park several miles to the south, the Auditorium Building would have been almost an extension of the fair across Michigan Avenue. Instead, the Auditorium acted as an adjunct to the distant fair in many ceremonies, so that Peck's monument performed the functions of local civic center and national cultural center that he envisioned for it. Over the next year, until the exposition's closing in October 1893, both the Auditorium and Peck played central roles in events that defined Chicago to the world. On Wednesday, 19 October 1892, the Auditorium Theater hosted a reception and ball organized by the fair's leading local organizers, including Peck. On Thursday the twentieth the Auditorium Tower served as the chief vantage point for surveying the civic parade down Michigan Avenue. The huge crowds observing this event on the ground concentrated at the building's base to witness a procession of scores of local organizations that formed a column ten miles long and took three hours to pass any given point along its route. The parade had representations from all the city's ethnic groups, creating a staged display of social unity that temporarily effaced class divisions along the same line of march where Parsons had led May Day processions before Haymarket. On Thursday evening the Auditorium Theater was the setting for the dedication of the World's Congress Auxiliary, which organized meetings in almost every branch of learning through the period of the fair. On 21 October the Auditorium Hotel was the starting point for the grand procession of locals and invited guests toward the fairgrounds at Jackson Park where the exposition would be dedicated. First in this procession was the exposition's Special Committee on Ceremonies, which included Ferdinand Peck, who was also first vice president of the executive committee of the exposition's board of directors and still chair of the all-important finance committee.[69]

From April through November 1893, the Auditorium Theater offered 253 performances of the grand historical spectacle *America*, produced by Imre Kirafly. Neither an opera nor a drama, this large production was created for the fair's national audience as well as for Chicagoans. The patriotic spectacle consisted of a prologue and two acts comprising twenty-five scenes and as many tableaux or stage pictures, fetes, processions, and ballets recounting what were interpreted as the leading incidents of American history in the four hundred years since Columbus, echoing the main commemorative theme of the World's Columbian Exposition. Parts of the show reappropriated the theatrical device of the tableau vivant from its local use in workers' theaters. *America* featured allegorical characters such as Bigotry, Education, Invention, Liberty, and the piece's central figure, Progress, all played by American and European vocal artists. The succession of patriotic tableaux was "built on massive lines and constructed to occupy the extreme width of the great stage."[70] For this show, the theater's reducing curtain was raised and replaced by a temporary frame that increased the stage's width to seventy-five feet to accommodate ballet scenes containing two hundred dancers. The production was repeated almost every afternoon and evening of its seven-month run, "and for the last twenty weeks of that time the throng of would-be spectators [occupied] every available inch of space of the Auditorium, and thousands were turned away from the box office without seats."[71]

The exposition opened in Jackson Park on 1 May 1893, effectively countering the local tradition of May Day demonstrations. By this time the cost of its construction had soared to over $18,000,000, while the fair's staffing and other expenses raised the local exposition corporation's total costs to over $27,000,000. To meet expenses, the corporation had sold stock of $5,600,000, on which a return was expected, and the city of Chicago had issued $5,500,000 in bonds, which had to be repaid. By September 1892, before the fair opened and generated income, its directors were so pressed for funds that they issued $4,000,000 in debenture bonds to be taken by the city's various banks.[72] Beyond this capital, the corporation relied for income on the fair's gate receipts, supplemented by concessions, exhibitor receipts, and sales of an issue of congressionally authorized souvenir coins. As with the Auditorium Theater, the exposition's financial and cultural success depended on a mass audience. The standard admission price of fifty cents restricted attendance by many local workers. Yet railroads, which were major investors in the exposition, developed numerous plans that enabled distant individuals and groups of limited means to travel to Chicago, so that the exposition approximated "a World's Fair for the rich and the poor."[73]

In his role as chair of the finance committee, Peck watched the situation closely. He was managing a capital flow whose mix of stocks and bonds resembled the Auditorium's, though on a much larger scale. The onset of the most severe depression in national history held attendance down through the initial month of May, so that Peck and his colleagues decided to cut some of the fair's programs to save expenses. Yet monthly attendance grew steadily from June through October. In this last month over 6,800,000 people attended, more than had come to the Paris International Exposition of 1889 during its best month. On 9 October, the twenty-second anniversary of the Great Fire, the exposition climaxed with "Chicago Day," when more than 700,000 came to Jackson Park. This surge enabled Peck and the exposition's treasurer, Anthony Seeberger, to carry a check for $1.5 million to the Illinois Trust and Savings

Bank the next day, therewith paying off the last debenture bonds held by any party against the exposition's corporation. Peck's committee had also succeeded in collecting 93 percent of funds subscribed by the fair's stockholders, and the fair's total receipts of over $28,000,000 from all sources enabled the corporation to pay a small dividend to investors. This made the 1893 fair into a financial triumph that distinguished Chicago from other host cities of expositions, which had almost always lost money, often repaid by national governments. No fair official rejoiced more than Peck, who "had been enthusiastic over the Exposition company paying all its obligations" and who, with his finance committee, "conceived the plan of liquidating the indebtedness on Chicago Day."[74] This well-publicized act symbolically recalled Chicago's paying off its debts on outside capital lent for rebuilding after the Great Fire of 1871, a blaze reprised in a grand display of fireworks on the fairgrounds on the fire's anniversary. Like the Auditorium Building's solidity, the exposition's festivity that evening exorcised the memory of the fire, so that blaze would no longer define Chicago to the world.

Initially Peck also had a voice in one of the corporation's other powerful standing committees, buildings and grounds, whose members approved Jackson Park as the fair's site in November 1890.[75] This committee then directed Burnham and Root, who were jointly the exposition's architectural consultants before Root's premature death in January 1891, to select the architects for the fair's principal buildings. In December 1890 Burnham, named chief of construction, proposed that the buildings around the exposition's central Court of Honor be given to five non-Chicago firms, whose principals were all easterners by training. On 27 December, Burnham set before the committee a list of Chicago architects to design the five other major buildings north of the court. First on his list was Adler and Sullivan, to whom Burnham proposed the design of the music building, which he envisioned as a temporary recreation of the Auditorium Theater's acoustics and ornamentation as a setting for the fair's orchestral and choral programs.[76]

When the Committee on Buildings and Grounds met in Burnham and Root's office in the Rookery Building to consider these suggestions, Peck and Potter Palmer were invited to attend. They both "objected to the employment of men from out of town to do the work around the grand court," the Court of Honor. Peck "wished to have those invited from outside and those from Chicago mixed up in the work throughout the Park," so that Chicago architects would do buildings both on and away from the Court of Honor, "and Mr. Palmer expressed the opinion that there were plenty of architects in Chicago to do the work without going outside at all."[77] Citing superior aesthetic judgment as a professional architect, Burnham resisted these protests and eventually agreed with the committee on a list of ten architects, including five Chicago firms, who would constitute the fair's board of architects and design its major buildings. Adler and Sullivan were on this list, and Sullivan served as secretary of this board. Yet Adler and Sullivan delayed assenting to participate, demurring over the value of a temporary music building. At the board's meeting on 10 January 1891, Sullivan suggested that the transportation exhibits, heretofore envisioned among others in the Machinery Hall, be given their own separate structure, known as the Transportation Building. The board then assigned this building to Adler and Sullivan.[78]

Equally characteristic of the exposition's cultural purposes, and closer to the social issues that had been the impetus for Peck's Auditorium, were the fair's musical programs and their architectural settings. Theodore Thomas, whose orchestra had permanently relocated to Chicago in 1891–1892 to play at the Auditorium Theater, directed the exposition's Bureau of Music. His patrons included Nathaniel Fairbank, Peck's colleague on the Auditorium's board and president of the Chicago Orchestral Association, which financially backed Thomas's coming as a major cultural coup for the city. When approached by the association's founders, Peck had urged that the initial guaranty fund for the orchestra be broadened to include $1,000 apiece from fifty local sponsors, going back to the Central Church's more democratic model of financial support of sixteen years earlier.[79]

The idea of providing symphonic music for a mass audience merged powerfully with the aims of the World's Columbian Exposition, whose dedication ceremony on 21 October 1892 exhibited the concept on a grand scale. The proceedings were led by Vice President Levi Morton, President Harrison's wife being near death. The event took place in the vast interior of the Manufactures and Liberal Arts Building (fig. 187). There Milward Adams, the Auditorium Theater's manager, planned the

Figure 187

World's Columbian Exposition, Dedication Day, 21 October 1892, in Manufactures and Liberal Arts Building, ceremony orchestrated by Milward Adams, manager, Auditorium Theater. Courtesy of the Chicago Historical Society, ICHi-02204.

ceremonies witnessed by a gathering of 150,000. Thomas led an orchestra of 300 instrumentalists, while Tomlins conducted Chicago's combined Apollo, Children's, German, Swedish, and Welsh choral societies, along with many church choirs, totaling 3,500 voices. The theme was civic unity across ethnic and religious lines. The program included Handel's "Hallelujah Chorus" and choral numbers sung while the director general presented medals to the exposition's master artists and architects.[80] As a member of the exposition's Special Committee on Ceremonies, Peck had a hand in planning this keynote event, held in a hall whose exterior featured vast colonnades and main entrances shaped like triumphal arches. Though later modernist historiography drew a sharp distinction between Adler and Sullivan's Auditorium and the exposition's classical architecture, contemporaries saw both as having Roman sources. Perhaps in this spirit, Peck praised the temporary buildings of the White City of 1893 as a model for the later expositional architecture at Paris in 1900.[81]

Among the structures were two buildings for the Bureau of Music: a Music Hall seating 2,000 for orchestra performances with an attached Recital Hall seating 600 for chamber concerts, and a choral Festival Hall equipped with an organ and seating 4,000, with standing room for 2,000 more. Had the exposition been sited on the downtown lakefront instead of at Jackson Park, then the Auditorium Theater likely would have served the purposes of both these buildings. Of the two, the more frequently used was the Music Hall, sited at the north end of the Court of Honor's lakefront peristyle and designed by Charles Atwood, who was chief designer for D. H. Burnham and Company after Root's death in January 1891. Done in a Roman Renaissance style with the giant Corinthian columns prevailing throughout the fair,

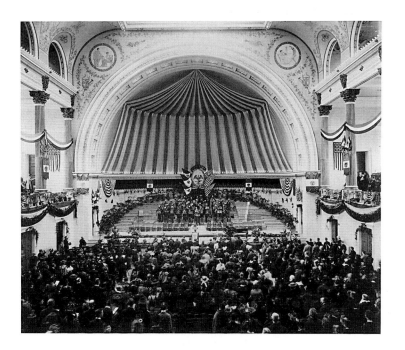

Figure 188

Francis M. Whitehouse, Festival Hall, World's Columbian Exposition, Chicago (1893). World's Columbian Exposition Photographs by C. D. Arnold. Courtesy of the Art Institute of Chicago.

the Music Hall had the stage at its east end overlooking Lake Michigan. The larger Festival Hall, designed by Chicago architect Francis M. Whitehouse, stood just north of Adler and Sullivan's Transportation Building facing the lagoon and its wooded isle, north of the Court of Honor. This circular choral hall was 250 feet in diameter with Doric porticoes skirting half-domes on three sides. Inside its huge amphitheater was a decorative program tracing the progress of music (fig. 188). The classical architecture of such buildings was intended to familiarize the fair's millions of visitors with what organizers regarded as established cultural standards. This intention extended into the musical programs that Thomas held in the Music Hall and Festival Hall.[82]

For these spaces, Thomas envisioned fourteen varieties of concerts, including daily free programs presented by his and visiting orchestras, as well as choral, children's, amateur, chamber, and symphony concerts. Silas G. Pratt, Peck's ally in the Chicago Grand Opera Festival of 1885, proposed a national choral union made up of groups from cities and states all over the country, which would stage inaugural performances at the World's Columbian Exposition. As held, the Festival Hall's concerts included local German and Bohemian groups as well as many American and foreign artists from beyond Chicago. As in the Auditorium's Workingmen's Concerts, in the Music Hall Thomas held to an elevated repertoire. Yet this hall proved acoustically disastrous, with constant reverberations off its walls and floors that hastily installed draperies and rugs could not dampen. The Festival Hall was acoustically better, yet serious musical programs in both buildings failed to draw audiences. The Music Hall filled only for the free daily noontime concerts of light music. Total income from thirty-two paid admission concerts in the two buildings was just over $15,000, whereas the Bureau of Music had expected ten times that much in receipts.[83]

Difficulties in drawing a popular audience for symphonic and chamber music at the fair mirrored Thomas's relative lack of success with his Chicago Symphony Orchestra playing at the Auditorium in its first two seasons in 1891–1892 and 1892–1893. A consensus formed that neither the fair's visitors nor Chicago's citizens were sufficiently inclined toward nonpopular musical programs. As Thomas's wife wrote, "Mr. Thomas is here to establish a great art work, and to make Chicago one of the first musical centers of the world—and not to provide a series of cheap musical entertainments for the riff-raff of the public." Unlike Peck as a building patron or Tomlins as a choral master, Thomas as an orchestral leader did not believe that the highest forms of art, whether in music or in other media, were within the comprehension of the masses. His wife echoed this view that "it is a useless task to attempt to produce the highest form in any art, in such a way that it can be appreciated by the ignorant."[84] Yet there were other cultural initiatives in tandem with the fair that took a more inclusive view of the potential audience for musical drama.

Although Thomas's musical programs and their exposition halls had been ambitious and costly, the cultural debate between elevated and popular entertainment for Chicago's public inspired an even more gargantuan and elaborate building that, if realized, would have taken the Auditorium Theater's premises to their extreme limits. This project, known as the Spectatorium, was the idea of New York theatrical producer James Steele MacKaye, who had built the Madison Square Theater with its two-tiered stage in 1880. Several months before the exposition, MacKaye came to Chicago to solicit support for "a vast theatre only second in dimension to the Roman amphitheatre."[85] The term *spectatorium,* with its emphasis on visual stage display, perhaps countered Chicago's Auditorium, with its acoustics perfected for musical drama. In his novel structure MacKaye proposed to produce a spectacle titled "The

World Finder," narrating the epic voyage of Columbus. MacKaye commissioned Antonín Dvořák to compose the music, and the Bohemian composer produced the symphony *From the New World* to accompany the spectacle. After MacKaye presented his ideas to the Union League Club in late 1891, a number of members helped to incorporate the Columbian Celebration Company. Over $550,000 in bonds were subscribed, in addition to stock sold at $1,000 per share. Ferdinand and Clarence Peck were two of the nine Chicago investors who bought ten shares each in the enterprise.[86]

Designed by club member William Le Baron Jenney and his partner William B. Mundie, the Spectatorium was planned and partially built on the lakeshore at Fifty-sixth Street, just north of the fairgrounds. MacKaye wanted the building in the grounds, but his plans were too late for this. The Spectatorium was designed as a structure of iron and wood, with an exterior rendered in a variety of Renaissance and Romanesque motifs (fig. 189). As monumental and fantastic as it appeared from the outside, the building's novelty lay in its hall designed to seat 8,000 in a huge semicircular amphitheater with a balcony. The result was to be "the largest building ever erected in the world for amusement purposes."[87] MacKaye described the Spectatorium as "an entirely new species of building, invented and devised for the production of a new order of entertainment entitled a spectatorio."[88] The audience would face a stage whose proscenium opening would be 170 feet wide and whose semicircular perimeter behind would be 600 feet. Formed as a watertight concrete pad, this vast stage would serve as a base for parallel railroad tracks on which different scenes

Figure 189

William Le Baron Jenney and William B. Mundie, Spectatorium, for James Steele MacKaye, Fifty-sixth Street at Lake Michigan, north of World's Columbian Exposition, Chicago (1891–1893; unfinished). Watercolor signed by Childe Hassam. From MacKaye, *Epoch*, vol. 2.

mounted on railway cars would be transported into view from a point of conceal-ment. Unlike smaller conventional theater backdrops of painted canvas or papier-mâché, the Spectatorium's rail-borne scenery would be of real building materials, deployed in combinations to form multilayered settings through the stage's depth.

Since most of the production's episodes would be marine scenes, there would be a pool of water six feet deep over the entire stage forming a miniature ocean on which Columbus's fleet would make its voyage (fig. 190). Three full-scale "exact fac-similes" of the *Santa Maria, the Pinta,* and the *Niña,* replicating period details down to masts, spars and ropes and manned by bona fide sailors, would cross the stage on their tracks, buffeted by simulations of wind and wave created by powerful electric cyclone fans and water agitators. Overhead newly designed arc lights would repre-sent the moon and the sun to replicate any phase of sky and weather, "not only the effulgent light of the meridian sun at noontide and the mellow, silvery light of the moon in a clear light, but also the hazy, murky atmosphere of the approaching hur-ricane."[89] Accompanying Dvořák's symphonic score would be musical narration by vast choruses, one visible and another unseen by the audience, representing earthly and heavenly choirs, which would celebrate each major event in the story. In sum, MacKaye adapted Wagnerian techniques of staging to an American historical epic to be staged as a commercial spectacle at Chicago's exposition of 1893. The project epitomized what one scholar has traced as the craving for simulated reality among American middle-class audiences of the period, a taste soon to be developed by the productions of New York impresario David Belasco.[90]

MacKaye's Spectatorium reached only a skeletal stage of construction before the financial panic of May 1893 halted all further work. The result was that "all sum-mer long the towering, incomplete structure has glowered down upon the dainty

Figure 190

Spectatorium, imagined view of stage and proscenium, showing full-sized replica of Columbus's flagship the *Santa Maria*. Drawing by Robert Edmond Jones. From MacKaye, *Epoch*, vol. 2.

State and foreign pavilions at the north end of Jackson Park," so that visitors "wondered why, among all the massive and beautiful buildings of the Dream City, this unsightly colossus should have been left incomplete."[91] Although the project had consumed over $550,000 in capital, its steel was sold for $2,250 at forced sale and dismantled in October 1893, just as Peck paid off the last debts of the fair. As Peck had sought to do in the Auditorium, MacKaye conceived the Spectatorium as a medium through which an entertainment, "whose aim should be to uplift as much as to amuse, might secure the patronage of the multitude essential to its financial maintenance.—*How to make the lofty and the refined popular is an aim which seemed to me to be worthy the devotion of a lifetime.*"[92] Driven by MacKaye's theatrical imagination and vast ambition, the project was to result in a permanent hall that would continue to serve its public purpose after the fair closed. A similar cultural ideal and its monumental setting had been central to Peck's vision for the Auditorium, where MacKaye had his office while in Chicago from October 1891 until his death in February 1894.[93] Just before MacKaye's death, a smaller version of the Spectatorium project, known as the Scenitorium, was constructed as a new theater built inside the shell of the twelve-sided Chicago Fire Cyclorama building, erected in 1892 on the west side of Michigan Avenue north of Monroe, four blocks north of the Auditorium. Although the Scenitorium soon failed financially, it too drew support from those capitalists who had backed the Auditorium and who saw both of these projects as means to raise the tone of local popular culture.[94]

The Chicago Stock Exchange and Its Building of 1893–1894

From the time of the Auditorium, Peck had been engaged in other building projects on his family's city properties, leasing a number of lots on which his long-term tenants erected important structures. The Peck estate also built on many of its own lots, so that by 1898 it owned no unimproved properties in the Loop. Among these large projects, Peck's aspirations focused on the Chicago Stock Exchange Building, built on the site of his family's earliest brick house of 1837 on the southwest corner of LaSalle and Washington Streets. Conceived from late 1892 and opened in April 1894, the Chicago Stock Exchange Building was Adler and Sullivan's last major structure in Chicago. It epitomized the issue of regional identity in commerce and architecture that had informed the Auditorium. As the leader in the effort to build a new facility for the Chicago Stock Exchange, Peck implicitly competed against the institution that more than any other represented the power of eastern capital—the New York Stock Exchange. In their design of a trading room for the Chicago Stock Exchange within Peck's building, Adler and Sullivan created an architecture that was as structurally and aesthetically different from the New York Stock Exchange as the earlier Auditorium Theater was from Manhattan's Metropolitan Opera House.

The Met had been built largely with wealth tied to New York's Stock Exchange, as if the city's financial capital had created a setting for opera as part of its cultural

Figure 191

James Renwick Jr., New York Stock Exchange, board room looking southeast, as expanded to 1887. From Eames, *New York Stock Exchange.*

capital.[95] Founded in 1792, the New York Stock Exchange, after its itinerant early decades in rented halls, had met in its own building at 10–12 Broad Street from 1865. Designed by the architect John Kellum in a modern French style, this structure was owned by the New York Stock Exchange Building Company, whose stock had been subscribed by members of the exchange to fund construction. Soon organizational changes resulted in enlarging the trading hall or board room into a two-story space in 1869. As its volume of business grew, the exchange decided to expand by buying additional properties on Broad Street, and on New Street behind to the west, paid for by sale of new exchange memberships. Architect James Renwick Jr. designed alterations and an addition to the 1865 building, which were completed late in 1881. Changes included a new second-floor board room, which was expanded in 1887 to occupy all the ground area owned by the exchange (fig. 191).[96]

A view of the New York Stock Exchange's board room in 1894, the year Adler and Sullivan's trading room for the Chicago Stock Exchange opened, shows the interior as one looked southeast toward Broad Street. Hours for trading were 10 A.M. to 3 P.M., so the T-shaped room was exclusively a daytime space, measuring 138 feet wide north-south and 128 feet deep east-west. Members who sought to deal in a certain stock gathered at the recognized place for that stock on the trading floor, making their bids and offers publicly. Atop the circular stands set at intervals across the floor, an indicator was set on a post near the place allotted for trading a stock, showing the price at which the last sale was made.[97] Trussed iron beams concealed within the 55-foot-high ceiling spanned the three-story hall. Cast iron columns clad as layered Corinthian pilasters on the first story supported the beams. Between the columns and the main ceiling were suspended coved plaster vaults with pointed arches. Like the walls below and ceiling above, the coved vaults were elaborately stenciled. The interior combined references to classical and Gothic architecture in one eclectic design. Ringing the walls was a visitors' gallery upheld on brackets. To the east, interior windows of upper office floors looked down into the board room. These offices borrowed natural light from the coffered skylit ceiling that rose 80 feet above the room's floor. In this hall, exchange members met daily until the building was demolished in 1901 to make room for George B. Post's new exchange building, opened in 1903.[98]

The New York Stock Exchange set standards for operation of the many other smaller exchanges that appeared through the United States in the nineteenth century. Preceded by earlier, short-lived local organizations, the Chicago Stock Exchange was founded in 1882 as a mutual association of local brokers for trading stocks and bonds. To the surprise of its organizers, the new exchange quickly won the New York Stock Exchange's support as a midwestern outlet for trading of stocks hitherto listed only in Manhattan.[99] The Chicago Stock Exchange emerged as a democratic alternative to memberships in the New York Stock Exchange and the Chicago Board of Trade. With its business strong, Wall Street saw the price of individual membership advance from $5,000 in 1879 to $35,000 in 1882, while membership in Chicago's Board of Trade increased from $250 to $4,000 in these same years. By contrast, the Chicago Stock Exchange's initial memberships in 1882 sold for $50 to $250 each, "enough to induce applications from financial men from all over the country. Out of the thousands of applications made, 750 were selected as desirable members."[100] By 1893, after the exchange had bought back memberships unwanted in the recession of the mid-1880s, there remained 450 members, including Ferdinand Peck.[101]

Through the 1880s, the Chicago Stock Exchange came to specialize in the market for newly issued stocks of local gas, street railway, and industrial companies, including meatpackers, brewers, grain elevators, and manufacturers of mining machinery. Promotion of purchases of local industrial stocks began in 1889, and soon Chicago became "a favorite place for the exploitation of these enterprises."[102] In addition to the region's rapidly expanding population, the World's Columbian Exposition created a boom in local stocks, particularly those of rail companies whose trains would move millions of visitors around the city. With these expectations, the number of shares traded on the exchange jumped from 145,725 in 1889 to 1,097,663 in 1890, so that it "made greater progress in 1890 toward becoming an institution of prime importance in the financial situation of Chicago and the West than it had made in all the previous years of its existence."[103]

By the early 1890s, Chicago-based companies drew investors from the East and from England, with the Chicago Stock Exchange as the authorized place for brokers to clear daily business. The advantage of trading stocks in regional companies on the Chicago Stock Exchange was its physical proximity to these businesses. As one observer of Chicago's exchange wrote in 1892, "Many investors prefer to buy and sell the leading speculative stocks of Chicago in this exchange, as they are surer of finding quotations near actual values than if they sent orders to the East, where the nature of Chicago properties are comparatively unknown."[104] Trading of non-Chicago stocks was still mainly done in New York, so that the Chicago Stock Exchange was almost exclusively identified with local industries. This exchange's limited (if regionally important) role meant that its trading volume was minute compared with New York's. In 1890 over 70,000,000 shares were traded on the New York Stock Exchange, where the value of bonds traded was almost $410,000,000. In that same year, as noted, Chicago's exchange counted just over 1,000,000 shares traded and $18,000,000 worth of bonds sold. Even so, a local guide claimed that "the immensity of these operations is only second to those of Wall Street."[105]

From its founding, the Chicago Stock Exchange had rented space in a variety of buildings, including attics, basements, and rooms in the Board of Trade and in the Chicago Opera House after its completion in 1885. The boom of 1890 triggered by the coming World's Columbian Exposition prompted the exchange's members to call for larger quarters. From November 1889, the exchange had met on the top floor of the Crilly Building on the northeast corner of Dearborn and Monroe Streets. Then renamed the Stock Exchange Building in honor of its prime tenant, this structure, built in 1882, had been expanded from five to seven stories (fig. 192). It was this business block that Adler and Sullivan's subsequent building of the same name was to surpass as the urban symbol of the exchange.[106] The exchange's membership had been limited to preserve its volume of business for existing member brokers. After transactions increased markedly in 1890, more memberships were sold, putting spatial pressure on existing quarters and giving rise to speculation that the exchange would soon move. This possibility created competition among Chicago realtors through 1891–1892 to attract the newly prominent exchange into a building they either owned or planned to build, "because it is believed that wherever that body locates an important financial center will be permanently established."[107]

In this situation, Ferdinand Peck and his brothers saw an opportunity to provide a building for the exchange that would improve their own position and enhance the exchange as a representative institution of Chicago. Their attention focused on one of their estate's most valuable central properties, a plot one hundred feet square on the southwest corner of LaSalle and Washington Streets, which their father had bought in 1836.[108] After the fire this site

Figure 192

Crilly Building (old Chicago Stock Exchange Building), northeast corner of Dearborn and Monroe Streets (built 1882; shown here as it appeared after being remodeled and expanded to seven stories in 1889; demolished). From *Chicago and Its Resources Twenty Years After, 1871–1891*. Chicago Historical Society, ICHi-31638.

STOCK EXCHANGE BUILDING
Dearborn & Monroe Sts. Chicago.

held the second five-story Union Building (1873), most of which was occupied by the Chicago offices of the Western Union Telegraph Company. The Pecks had leased the property for this building's construction with provision for revaluation of the land every five years. By the revaluation of 1892, the land's value had risen to the point where it was "impossible for an old style building to earn what a building on that corner should earn."[109] The Pecks canceled the lease and offered the building's lessees a larger sum for the structure, which would "soon give place to a lofty building of modern design."[110] To provide spatially adequate quarters for itself, the Chicago Stock Exchange had contemplated creating its own tall office building, but when its directors heard of Ferdinand Peck's project, they queried him about new quarters in his future structure.

Initially the Pecks demanded a heavy rental, thinking that their new building's location would make its offices "rent readily if anything in Chicago will rent."[111] Yet nearby offices had been vacated and land values declined after 1880, when the Board of Trade moved to the southern end of LaSalle Street's financial corridor. Thus the exchange's building committee returned to the Pecks with a counteroffer to accept space in their building if it was at least twelve stories tall to provide many brokers' offices, was named for the Chicago Stock Exchange, and provided free quarters for the exchange for fifteen years. The committee further required that the building site be expanded to provide adequate ground for such a building, leading the Pecks to negotiate a long-term lease on an adjoining property with 80 feet of frontage immediately south of theirs, creating a site 180 feet long on LaSalle Street.[112] The exchange also asked the Pecks to call on neighboring property owners to raise a guaranty fund that would ensure the building's profitability to the Pecks even if the exchange itself did not pay rent. Nearby owners readily raised the guaranty fund, believing that with the exchange's relocation in their midst, property on LaSalle from Washington south to Jackson "will, within a few years, be worth more per front foot than any other real estate in the world."[113] With its conditions met, on 1 January 1893 the exchange signed a lease with the Pecks for fifteen years at one dollar per year.

The expense of acquiring the old building, leasing additional land, demolishing the postfire structures on both sites, and constructing the new building brought the project's total costs to $2,500,000. To realize their plans, the Pecks secured a loan of $600,000 from the New York Life Insurance Company in April 1893, negotiated by its local agent, Edward C. Waller, earlier a major investor in the Rookery Building to the south on LaSalle Street. After they had secured this sum and a loan of $160,000 against another of their properties, demolition of the old buildings began on 3 May 1893, two days after the world's fair opened.[114] Early that year they commissioned Adler and Sullivan to prepare designs for the new Chicago Stock Exchange Building, instructing them to design its lower floors to meet the exchange's needs, including a separate room for bankers "who have made a specialty of handling securities and documentary loans that represent corporations of great wealth."[115] The major spaces for the exchange and bank would be on the south and north sides of the second floor (fig. 193), above ten shops opening to the sidewalk on the first level.

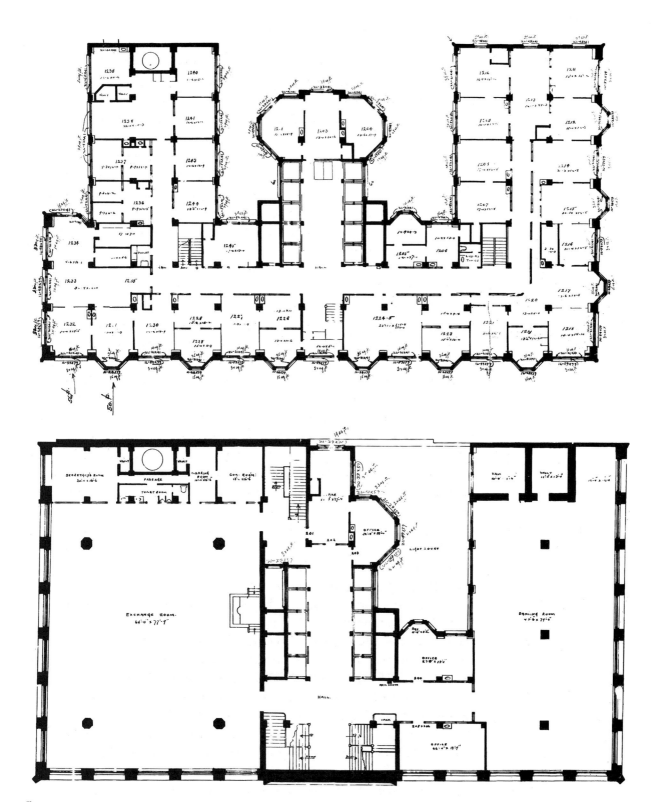

Figure 193

Adler and Sullivan, Chicago Stock Exchange Building: (below) second-floor plan, and (above) twelfth-floor plan. Original penciled notations show square footages of offices, bay windows, and window areas, the last perhaps included in calculating rents charged to office tenants. Sullivaniana Collection, Courtesy of the Art Institute of Chicago.

The upper floors would contain offices arranged along the east front and along double-loaded corridors in the north and south wings. Offices were for brokers and other tenants who congregated as in the exchange's old building, where "the arrangement of offices [was] peculiarly adapted to the quick despatch of business,"[116] a criterion Adler identified as basic to the design of modern tall office buildings.[117] Since rental values of office space depended on ample daylight, alternate offices on the east and north street fronts had projecting bays (fig. 193). On the south side, the office floors were set back to ensure access to daylight if another tall building was built south of the alley. On all office floors, light entered offices from adjacent corridors through translucent glass walls. There was a western outdoor court for light and ventilation. This open space, together with the light court of the Chicago Herald Building to the west, formed the largest outdoor court of any local office building, with daylight for offices to be enhanced by facing the Chicago Stock Exchange Building's west court walls with reflective white enameled brick.[118]

Adler and Sullivan planned the floors above the exchange's hall as an efficient spatial machine for renting its over four hundred offices. When the building opened, one observer wrote: "It will take its place as one of the most remarkable examples of Chicago steel-skeleton construction. Utility and esthetics have been conserved to an

Figure 194

LaSalle Street looking southeast, showing John M. Van Osdel's Chicago City Hall, northeast corner of Washington Street (completed 1885), and Edward Baumann and Harris Huehl's Chamber of Commerce Building, southeast corner of Washington Street (1890; demolished 1928) across LaSalle Street from Adler and Sullivan's Chicago Stock Exchange Building later built out of view at right. The Board of Trade Building's tower is visible in the distance at the south end of LaSalle Street. From Flinn, *Chicago, the Marvelous City of the West*. Courtesy of the Chicago Historical Society, ICHi-31458.

unusual degree. In fact, the designers hope that it will serve to disarm the criticism which has been laid at the door of the system—that it precluded the possibility of artistic effects without extravagant sacrifice of the income-earning capacity of tall buildings."[119] Years later one of Sullivan's associates, William Purcell, wrote that to understand the Chicago Stock Exchange and similar buildings, one had "to realize the war against architects, at the turn of the century, by building owners who sought rentable space, light in every office, and plenty of glass."[120] Adler stressed this point in his essays on tall office buildings. The Chicago Stock Exchange Building fulfilled this and other functional criteria, for it was one of only two or three Chicago office buildings that had a 95 percent occupancy rate during the Great Depression of the 1930s. In its rental history it fulfilled Sullivan's theoretical ideal of the functional imperative that shaped living forms in nature. In Purcell's view, this idea was a "mechanical functionalism which [Sullivan] thought should be part of the creation of every building." He recalled that Sullivan saw buildings embodying "the idea of the perfect machine," a concept of "absolute mechanical perfection expressing itself like a bird in flight," a metaphor for functionality that Sullivan used in his own writings.[121]

Figure 195

Chicago Stock Exchange Building, 30 North LaSalle Street, southwest corner of Washington Street (1893–1894; demolished 1972). Photograph by Barnes and Crosby, BC-8, c. 1905. Courtesy of the Chicago Historical Society, ICHi-19456.

The Chicago Stock Exchange's structure was an iron and steel frame throughout, with cast iron columns marking thirteen-foot bays as the unit dimension of both the plans and the elevations. This relatively narrow column spacing meant there was a one-to-one correspondence between structural steel bays and exterior office windows. In this period, when the chief structural uncertainty of tall office buildings was their resistance to wind loads, Adler wrote: "The most effective opposition to wind pressure is in mere weight of structure and in base area."[122] The Chicago Stock Exchange's 180-foot frontage and 100-foot depth gave it a greater base area than Adler and Sullivan's other tall office buildings of the 1890s, so that it was the only one of these without an internal system of wind bracing.

Because of its foursquare shape and relatively unornamented terra cotta cladding, the Chicago Stock Exchange's exterior realized Sullivan's ideal of a modern structure whose mass alone had a powerful architectural quality, much like the foursquare block of the Auditorium Building. The Stock Exchange's northeast corner projected into the streetscape when viewed from the north down LaSalle (fig. 195). In this way Adler and Sullivan's building, together with Baumann and Huehl's Chamber of Commerce Building of 1890 directly across LaSalle Street, performed an urbanistic function, marking the northern end of the financial corridor, whose distant southern terminus was the tower of William Boyington's Board of Trade Building. It was then "the general opinion that the move of the Stock Exchange from Dearborn street to LaSalle will make the latter thoroughfare the 'Wall street' of Chicago."[123] Sullivan's fronts stood diagonally opposite the Chicago City Hall and Cook County Courthouse on the northwest corner of LaSalle and Washington. The Chicago Stock Exchange's clean-cut elevations contrasted with this municipal monument, the city's most ornamentally elaborate classical pile (fig. 194). As Sullivan wrote in 1892, "I take it as self-evident that a building, quite devoid of ornament, may convey a noble and dignified sentiment by virtue of mass and proportion."[124] Two years later, one critic wrote that Adler and Sullivan's works recognized "the possibilities of impressiveness which these office buildings contain in their mere mass, their logical subdivision, their simplicity of outline so consistently emphasized through the buildings by use of nothing but the simplest forms and the subordination of everything to a simple unity of effect."[125]

Sullivan perhaps developed the Chicago Stock Exchange Building's exterior from that of D. H. Burnham and Company's Ashland Block, designed in late 1891 and early 1892 (after John Wellborn Root had died on 15 January 1891) and built through 1892 on the northeast corner of Dearborn and Randolph Streets (fig. 196), one-half block west of Adler and Sullivan's Schiller Building. Developed as an office building by Robert A. Waller (brother of Edward C.), the Ashland was taller (sixteen stories) and narrower (140 by 100 feet) than the Stock Exchange, with mostly brick rather than terra cotta cladding for its steel frame.[126] Both structures had a street level of glass shop windows between columns and an arched main entrance set in a projecting rectangular panel. This entrance arch and the Ashland's crowning cornice were rendered in terra cotta. In both buildings, the second and third floors

Figure 196

Daniel H. Burnham and Company, Ashland Block, northeast corner of Dearborn and Randolph Streets, Chicago (1891–1892; demolished 1949). Upper west flank of Adler and Sullivan's Schiller Theater Building is visible at right, showing terra cotta–clad cupola over observation platform. Photograph by J. W. Taylor. Architecture Photograph Collection, Courtesy of the Art Institute of Chicago.

were treated as round-arched arcades. Those on the Stock Exchange had "thirteen Roman arches of ten-foot spring, and the piers are so slender as to give the effect of Gothic mullions."[127] Above, the Ashland's upper office floors on its main front had alternating flat and round bay windows, like the Stock Exchange's polygonal bays. The angularity of Sullivan's bays created sharply folded planes in light, making the stacks of bays or oriels into vertical accents for a building that was slightly wider in its main front (180 feet) than it was tall (172 feet). The Ashland also had round corner bays, unlike the Stock Exchange's squared corners, which enhanced the latter's precise profile. The Ashland's crowning story was a row of squared windows, while the Stock Exchange's was a rectangular frame for a loggia-like colonnade set forward of plate glass windows that abutted the rear of the columns. Both buildings had large overhanging cornices, though the Stock Exchange's cornice displayed Sullivan's individual ornamental style in terra cotta.

If Sullivan developed the Chicago Stock Exchange's exterior from Burnham and Root, then he adapted its upper-floor "Chicago windows" from the nearby new office buildings of Holabird and Roche, the architects who most frequently employed this fenestration after its introduction about 1892.[128] As a horizontal rectangular opening across a full structural bay, the Chicago window featured a large central pane of plate glass, which rotated on center pins to open out (as is visible in fig. 195), flanked by two operable double-hung windows for ventilation. Sullivan's Chicago windows between projecting bays on the Stock Exchange's fronts corresponded to his dictum that windows on a tall office building's upper floors should be alike because the spaces behind them were functionally alike.[129] Although praised in later modernist historiography, the Chicago window was criticized by one of Sullivan's contemporaries, George Twose. He agreed that Chicago windows satisfied the reasoning that similar functions should have similar forms, but he decried the repeated form as "the repression of all character in the windows." Claiming that "the history of windows is the history of civilization," Twose recalled the richness of treatment accorded windows in medieval and Renaissance architecture, whereas "in the Stock Exchange Building these beautiful traditions receive no recognition whatever."[130] Finding fault with Holabird and Roche's works, he saw the Chicago window as regressing to a more primitive idea of windows as mere openings or incidents in a wall.

Twose did acknowledge that in the Chicago Stock Exchange, Sullivan's "desire to use the decoration so that its entire absence would not affect the mass of the building is everywhere the guiding idea behind its disposition."[131] As in the Schiller Building, the Chicago Stock Exchange's cladding comprised mostly plain surfaces, with concentrations of ornament around the entrance and atop the cornice. Originally, Adler and Sullivan had planned to clad their building's exterior in terra cotta or in Bedford limestone, the same material used on the Auditorium's upper walls. If stone had been used for the Stock Exchange, then both buildings for Peck would have had a lithic monumentality. Perhaps to recall limestone, the Chicago Stock Exchange's terra cotta blocks had a warm yellow gray color. In December 1893 one local observer wrote that Chicago's "new office buildings are running decidedly in light colors . . . the Champlain, the Stock Exchange, the Christian Association and the New York Life are all light. It used to be thought that the walls of our buildings should be dark, so they would not show the soot, but they can be kept in presentable condition by frequent cleaning."[132]

Around the Chicago Stock Exchange's entrance arch, the plain voussoirs provided a foil for the decorative interlaced lines of their extrados and the spandrels' foliate relief, within which were set rondels (fig. 197). This view shows that the left rondel contained an image of the Peck brick house of 1837. An earlier view showed that the right rondel originally framed an inscription that read: "The first brick building in Chicago was built upon this site." These plaques evinced Peck's intention of making the Chicago Stock Exchange "a memorial building . . . in memory of his father."[133] When the claim that the Peck house was Chicago's earliest brick building was later disproved, the right rondel was replaced to show the year of the exchange's construction (1893), also the year of the World's Columbian Exposition. The rondels' dates marked the city's infancy and maturity, both of which involved initiatives of the Peck family. As specified in the exchange's agreement with the Peck estate, the arch's frieze carried the name "Chicago Stock Exchange Building." The name implied that the exchange was the structure's patron, when in fact the exchange was Peck's tenant. The owners of the exchange's previous headquarters, heretofore known as the Chicago Stock Exchange Building, tried to get an injunction to stop the placing of that name on Adler and Sullivan's building. The injunction was denied and the lettering went on, transferring this institutional cachet to the Pecks' property.[134]

Figure 197

Chicago Stock Exchange Building, detail of original entrance arch with left rondel showing the Philip F. W. Peck House built on site in 1837. Right rondel initially framed an inscription inaccurately identifying the Peck House as Chicago's first brick building. Courtesy of the Art Institute of Chicago.

The two-story arcade of the exchange's second and third floors marked the trading and banking rooms (fig. 195). Unlike the Ashland Block's arcade, Sullivan's showed no hint of tectonic pilasters with capitals. Instead, his piers and arches had continuous linear profiles, with the whole arcade set in a rectangular terra cotta frame that projected diagonally at the building's corners. Sullivan celebrated the cladding's plasticity in the interlaced linear relief of the arcade spandrels. The intricacy of the entrance arch's cornice recurs in the crowning cornice above the attic story's colonnade. Although fabricated in terra cotta, the Ashland Block's cornice recalled an overhanging classical cornice of stone, whereas Sullivan gave the Chicago Stock Exchange an ornamentally original terra cotta cornice. Its frieze, framed by variations on classical moldings above and below, contained a lush pattern of inventive foliate forms, culminating in the leaflike corner motifs (fig. 198). The outward flare of the cornice complemented the inward splay of the piers at the sidewalk. Drawings show that the cornice's terra cotta blocks were anchored into steel channels within the wall behind, enabling the cornice to tilt outward and downward to enhance its visibility from the street (fig. 195). As he did with crowning ornamental passages atop his other tall steel and terra cotta buildings, Sullivan enlarged the scale of the cornice's decorative detail to enhance its legibility from the sidewalk, about 170 feet below. Looking up from the street, one saw the attic story's foliate column capitals and the ornamental terra cotta reveals framing the colonnade. As one account noted, "When viewed from near at hand the designs seem so fine and small as to suggest that at a distance they would become quite lost. But this

Figure 198

Chicago Stock Exchange Building, detail
of original thirteenth-floor colonnade
below ornamental terra cotta cornice.
From *Brickbuilder* 4 (June 1895). Courtesy
of the Art Institute of Chicago.

is not the case, for when viewed from a block away, as in the case of the upper stories it is possible to do, they come out clear and distinct and sharp, having a much
better carrying quality than designs of apparently a bolder and much coarser
kind."[135] In such ornament, set within crisp overall massing, Sullivan distinguished
his style from that of other architects working in the same building types.

Nowhere was the individuality of Sullivan's approach more apparent than in the
Stock Exchange's trading room, originally called "the exchange auditorium," on the
second floor's south side. One entered on the room's north side, through one of two
doorways on either side of the central rostrum. On the wall behind was a large
blackboard on which there were quotations from the Chicago and New York Stock
Exchanges. The room's two-story height was attributed to Peck, perhaps meant to
enhance visibility.[136] In this room brokers gathered every morning to exchange
views on local securities, make quotations, and give each other some idea of their
orders in various stocks and bonds. The quotations went to the banks, and the brokers transacted business on the floor during the rest of the day based on these quotations. As in the Schiller Building, Adler created this large space by using massive
overhead trusses (thirteen feet six inches deep) to carry the weight of the eleven office floors (fig. 199; plates 13 and 14). The two main trusses spanning east-west each
supported a weight of 1,200 tons, or that of twelve large railroad locomotives piled
atop each other. Four cast iron columns supported these trusses to form the room's
rectangular core, with each column bearing a weight of 750 tons.[137] Within this
core's ceiling, three trusses six feet deep spanned north-south between the deeper

Figure 199

Chicago Stock Exchange Building, trading room looking northwest shortly after its opening on 30 April 1894, showing exchange's membership. Architecture Photograph Collection, Courtesy of the Art Institute of Chicago.

long east-west trusses. This structure freed the space from the visual obstruction of multiple columns, to enhance views of the trading boards and floor locations for dealing in specific stocks.

Along the room's west side was a visitors' gallery, while the main floor's east side was set aside for the press and special members of the exchange. The trading room was to be used almost exclusively in the daytime, with calls on stocks and bonds at 10:30 A.M. and 2:15 P.M. Since Chicago's air was darkened by smoke from boilers fired by bituminous coal, artificial light was often needed through the workday, especially in winter. The trading room's lighting was important to the exchange, whose building committee had rejected new quarters in the rear of an existing building nearby on LaSalle Street because those spaces "could not be properly lighted." The trading room's south and east sides received direct daylight through tall wide windows. Light also entered the room through horizontal panels of art glass along its north and south ceilings. Skylights over these panels were made possible by insetting the office floors above (plates 13 and 14). Illumination of these art glass panels was enhanced by prismatic glass roofs for the skylights and by carbon-filament incandescent lamps set above the art glass as a secondary light source.[138]

A photograph of the Chicago Stock Exchange members shows the trading room after it opened on 30 April 1894 (fig. 199). The year-long process of demolition and new construction had continued during a severe economic depression, which had lowered prices for materials and labor, and "in the face of . . . two or three serious strikes that greatly delayed work for a time."[139] As in the New York Stock Exchange, the trading floor had designated places for dealing in particular stocks. Adler and Sullivan's new trading room was larger (79 by 64 feet), better lighted, and better ventilated than the exchange's old quarters. Like these, the new hall was also intended to accommodate a limited number of members. Individual memberships were sold as before, and any purchaser still had to be approved by election, as had been the procedure on the New York Stock Exchange from 1868. In December 1893, when Adler and Sullivan's building was under way, the Chicago Stock Exchange's 445 memberships could be transferred to others by their owners (with the exchange's approval) for variable sums, as much as $2,000 apiece. By then the exchange did not sell any new membership for less than $10,000.[140] Membership constituted peer recognition that helped to sustain organizational standards. The Pecks asserted that they would have gone ahead with the building "irrespective of the action of the Chicago Stock Exchange" to lease this space.[141] Yet as that part of the building set aside for the exchange, the trading room helped constitute this group's identity.

In the original building, the experience of the trading room began outside in the second-floor hall, as a publicly trafficked space whose light-filled aura was to convey the plenitude of daylight in the offices. This hall had white marble floors and wainscoting beneath a polished reflective ceiling, the whole lighted by the segmental window marking the crown of the entrance arch outside (fig. 200). Adler and Sullivan's interiors were distinct in that "for the first time in Chicago American marble was alone used for decorative and other purposes, every foot of the 100,000 feet of marble used in the building having come from American quarries."[142] Daylight was apparent through the stairwells and elevator shafts, the westernmost of

Figure 200

Chicago Stock Exchange Building, second-floor hallway looking east, showing white marble floors and wainscoting with elevator grilles of cast and wrought iron finished by Bower-Barff process. From *Ornamental Iron* 2 (July 1894). Courtesy of the Art Institute of Chicago.

which had rear outer walls of translucent glass opening onto the light court. Light shone through the stair and elevator grilles of cast and wrought iron, which were framed at their sides in tawny copper-plated cast iron lintels and pilasters. The iron grilles were not electroplated but were given a rust-resistant blue black hydrocarbon coating through the patented Bower-Barff process. Sullivan designed the metal ornamentation, fabricated by Winslow Brothers. As Purcell recalled of the building, "When the first of the cast and wrought iron work for the main stairs from basement to roof was delivered for erection it was found that through a draftsman's error the stairs were framed several inches too wide to go into the stairwell. How it came that the fabricator had failed to verify his shop drawings at the building, I do not know. Sullivan felt that the error was his and gave his personal check for $8,700 to cover the cost of rebuilding the iron work."[143]

In 1971 the Chicago Stock Exchange Building was torn down, and its trading room was reconstructed at the Art Institute of Chicago. The rebuilt room has the distinction of being one of Adler and Sullivan's only Chicago interiors to have survived. Of their total original oeuvre in the city, all the theaters except the Auditorium are gone. The firm's only other local public interior to have survived in a partially restored form is that of the Kehilath Anshe Ma'ariv synagogue of 1891. The reconstructed trading room affords a special opportunity to study Sullivan's aims and methods as a designer of interiors. Unlike the hall outside, the trading room's main floor was open only to members of the exchange. Visitors did not enter the room on this level; they gained access to the gallery on the third floor from stairs outside the trading room at the building's rear. Nonmembers could also pay a fee to use enclosed offices off the floor's west side. The room's character as privileged space was the social parameter within which Sullivan created its system of surfaces. As in the Auditorium, he designed fields of ornament that covered the structure even as they celebrated and revealed its major elements. The trading room's decorative program would epitomize the Chicago Stock Exchange Building, whose design its architects hoped "will serve to disarm the criticism which has been laid at the door of the system [of steel-frame construction]—that it precluded the possibility of artistic effects without extravagant sacrifice of the income-earning capacity of tall buildings."[144]

As in his interiors for McVicker's Theater and the Schiller Theater, Sullivan designed the trading room as a gradation of materials and colors from its floor through its multilevel ceiling. From the white marble hall, members came into a room with an oiled and polished red oak floor, like those of the building's private offices. The trading room's wainscoting was not marble but horizontal boards and battens of Honduran mahogany, the wood used for the rostrum or president's desk, which was described as "the finest piece of cabinet work in the city."[145] As in the Auditorium, each column was encased in scagliola imitating Sienese marble rendered in eight facets around the column. Atop each shaft was an eight-sided gilded plaster capital, expanding to a crown six feet six inches in diameter. As shown in a Sullivan sketch dated 1 February 1894, the capital has a profile like that of the whole building's exterior cornice. The capital's curvatures reflect light from incandescent bulbs in brass sconces mounted near the shaft's top. Gold leaf recurs in a number of Sullivan's works, yet the trading room's huge gilded capitals may have recalled the Stock Exchange's origins as Chicago's center for trading in gold after the Civil War.[146]

The capitals' gilding also reflects daylight from the surrounding art glass skylights, whose polychrome panels were designed by Healy and Millet, Sullivan's collaborators for the interior (plates 13 and 14). Along with John La Farge, they introduced a new way of making stained glass as panels of colored and textured opalescent glass, a method that became characteristic of American art glass.[147] Light colored by this art glass washes over the green-toned stenciling that forms a frieze above the mahogany wainscoting on the trading room's upper north, east, and south walls. This frieze is crowned by the cast plaster moldings running along the top of these walls. Hundreds of electric bulbs in both the plaster molding and the stenciled frieze below illuminate the ornament, as in the Auditorium Theater and Hotel. Accounts of the original room noted that the Chicago Stock Exchange's monogram was visually interwoven at intervals into this frieze.[148] Like the room's other stencils, this one contains a pattern eighteen inches wide repeated across the frieze's long surface. As duplicated for the room's restoration, stencils were made by cutting each different-colored part of the pattern into a separate sheet of heavy treated paper. Each sheet containing its one-color component of the pattern was then overlaid onto canvas laid out on a work table, and the single paint color was applied through the cut-out paper onto the canvas with a stiff, short-bristled brush. The main frieze's stenciling shows twenty-eight colors in each eighteen-inch segment, with each color applied separately before the canvas was set onto the wall.[149]

In addition to the frieze, there are six other stencil designs for different surfaces overhead, including the soffits and sides of the main and the smaller trusses, the ceiling itself between the trusses, and the beam soffit above the visitors' gallery. Sullivan is credited with the design of these stencils as patterns of shapes, though their precise color combinations may be attributed to Healy and Millet, who were also responsible for their execution.[150] In all, the seven patterns exhibit the interplay of fifty-seven distinct colors, which blend together when seen from below the ceiling, whose central area is thirty feet above the floor. Certain stencils, like that on the main trusses' soffit (plate 15), were seen as "thoroughly Mooresque in design," while others, such as those on these trusses' vertical faces (plate 16), appear almost wholly invented.[151] This last stencil was the richest in its polychromy, with fifty-two colors applied to create its lively visual rhythms. The vivid contrasts of many shades of orange, gold, brown, yellow, blue, ocher, and green combine to obscure the solidity of the planar surfaces they are stenciled on, dematerializing the ceiling into a field of ornament, illuminated by sunlight and electricity. Although the range of colors in the trading room is much greater than in the Auditorium Theater, the ultimate effect of Sullivan's art in these spaces is similar: architectural forms deriving from structure are overlaid with ornament, color, and light to become immaterial. Such a transcendent effect, more apparent in situ than in photographs, was presumably visible in the Schiller and McVicker's Theaters, whose interiors do not survive.

As the defining architectural statement of the trading room, these stencils convey several levels of meaning. First, their richness of pattern and color as decorative art suggest the wealth of the exchange, which "appropriated a large amount of money for decoration."[152] With green and gold as their predominant colors, these stencils conveyed the trading room's function as a theater for speculation in stocks and bonds. To Stock Exchange members, the trading room's columns, stencils, and art glass perhaps recalled those found in Boyington's trading room for the Chicago Board of Trade (fig. 53), thus alluding to ties between these institutions. From its founding, most Stock Exchange members were also members of the Board of Trade, whose building for a time had served as the quarters of the Chicago Stock Exchange. Boyington's vast room had historicizing architecture and allegorical images that impressed contemporaries but were conventional in their form and meaning. Yet Peck, Adler, and Sullivan surely saw the Stock Exchange's trading room as a modern alternative to the Board of Trade's older monumental style. Their smaller, light-filled, steel-framed, uniquely stenciled space had a different character than did the Board of Trade's legendary great hall. At least one contemporary perceived Sullivan's decorative surfaces as transcending the Stock Exchange's financial functions altogether. At its opening, which attracted the city's wealthiest citizens, this observer wrote: "Scores of men who could have gold chairs to sit on, if they cared to, stood up, marveling at the beauty of the tinted traceries and panels on ceiling and wall which seemed to make the assembly hall too poetic a place for money makers to buy and sell in."[153]

On another level, the trading room's allusion to nature is apparent on every side, from the wood wainscoting below, through the stenciling and art glass above. In one sense this room's overall evocation of nature suggests Chicago's regional identity as a city whose economic prosperity then derived from the richness of the vast cultivated landscape around the metropolis. Sullivan later wrote: "As we walk together in the heart of the Great City, is there aught greeting our eyes to suggest or even hint the nearby presence of a noble Lake, the teeming prairies, green and radiant, half-encircling the Great and gloomy City?"[154] In the trading room's conventionalization of nature's surrounding beauty, Sullivan created not an allegorical but an ornamental narrative of Chicago's distinct stature as an urban center of wealth commanding a prairie empire of natural resources. As he wrote to his patron Carl Bennett while he was designing the color stencils for the National Farmers' Bank in Owatonna, Minnesota, after returning to Chicago in late March 1908, Sullivan went out at about 5:00 A.M., "studying the color effects of the lovely grass, of very early skies, as seen along the valley of the Illinois River. My spring is wrapt up just now in the study of color and out of doors for the sake of your bank decorations—which I wish to make out of doors–indoors if I can. I am almost abnormally sensitive to color just now and every shade and nuance produces upon me an effect that is orchestral and patently sensitive to all the instruments."[155] In the earlier trading room, Sullivan's geometric patterns of interlaced stenciled colors were plausibly architectural condensations of his direct visual experience of nature's colors encountered outdoors near the city.

In Sullivan's mind, nature proved an abundant source for the invention of motifs, superseding dependence on historical styles of ornament. In this way his design for the trading room displayed his agenda to create a new architecture not dependent for its vocabulary on past styles. The trading room was not only "about" Chicago but about Sullivan's ideal of personal creativity. The stenciled forms were derived in part from literal foliate forms. Yet for Sullivan, the "flower is the [artist's] own sensitive nature."[156] Thus foliate ornamental patterns were also his representation of his own sensibility. In his essay of 1889, "The Artistic Use of the Imagination," he wrote: "He is an artist, who, gifted with a capacity to receive impressions, and to transmit them in a more or less permanent form, adds, to the body of his work, a certain quality or spirit characteristic of himself."[157] One observer wrote of the trading room shortly after the building opened: "The mural decoration is a symphony in color, a chromatic expression of the sentiment conveyed by the complex traceries in the outer walls—essentially Sullivanesque . . . . These compositions, inspired by the genius of an individual, are so original and so striking that precedents there are none to measure them by—the critical judgment stands in abeyance."[158]

Sullivan's views on art echoed those of John Ruskin in his essay "The Influence of Imagination in Architecture," given as an address to London's Architectural Association in December 1857. This essay was published in an authorized American edition of his essays in 1887, which Sullivan owned. Ruskin asserted that the qualities that chiefly distinguish great artists "are those of sympathy and imagination." He maintained that an architect must perforce be an expert builder, and an efficient administrator of construction, "but he must, somehow, tell us a fairy tale out of his head beside all this, else we cannot praise him for his imagination, nor speak of him . . . as being in any wise out of the common way, a rather remarkable architect."[159] For Ruskin, the younger architects of England in the 1850s were preoccupied with the development of imagination as a resource for creating a new style "worthy of modern civilization in general."[160] One later account of the new Chicago Stock Exchange Building quoted Ruskin's definition of imagination in architecture as part of an analysis of Sullivan's ornamental interior for the trading room: "Here, behold, is a fairy tale, told not only in iron but in terra cotta, in marble and color."[161]

In his later autobiography, Sullivan wrote that as a child in Boston he was greatly taken with the Irish fairy tales told to him by his grandparents' housekeeper. As oral expression, these represented to him the ideal of romance in a way not found in stories he read in books.[162] In this period, he also recalled his first sight of a man identified to him as an architect. He was someone who made buildings "'out of his head; and he had books besides.'" Sullivan wrote of himself, "Then and there Louis made up his mind to become an architect and make beautiful buildings 'out of his head.'"[163] For Sullivan, to create buildings from the imagination was the opposite of deriving them from books as the records of historical styles. His contemporary, the critic Montgomery Schuyler, wrote that "aesthetic scholarship is good, excellence of execution is good, but they are only helps to a real artist to express what is within himself. If he have no idea of his own to realize, it does not help him nor us to galvanize the corpses of a bygone world."[164] This ideal of imagination as opposed to imitation, analogous to the orality of poetry versus the textuality of prose, was central to Sullivan's architectural theory, where he posited a view of the creative architect that corresponded to Ruskin's.

In the Stock Exchange's trading room, Sullivan's personal vision of an imaginative architecture that was based in nature and individually expressive provided a symbolically appropriate setting for a space that announced Chicago's distinctive regional economy. The novelty of his ornamental forms conveyed the city's self-image as more modern and progressive than its eastern counterparts. This was the theme Peck announced in his assessment of the Chicago Stock Exchange as a civically representative monument, much like his view of the Auditorium Building. At the trading room's dedication on 30 April, just before May Day 1894, Peck told the exchange's members: "I believe that with exports and imports exceeding those of her rival in the Empire state, with a population which will soon equal it, this great city with the tributary wealth of the rapidly growing West pouring into her monetary institutions, must at some day be the leading financial center of the United States." Thus, while the exchange was still in its infancy, it was destined to grow to magnificent proportions, playing a key role "in the future development of our beloved city of Chicago."[165] The new architectural style created by Sullivan in the room where Peck spoke corresponded to this view of their city that represented the rise of its region relative to the eastern United States, as the World's Columbian Exposition had done when it had opened almost exactly a year earlier. Chicago had emerged entirely in the nineteenth century, largely within the lifetime of those assembled in the trading room. Like the Auditorium, the Chicago Stock Exchange Building marked a convergence of the city's urban narrative with Peck's family history, for both were situated on sites where his parents had lived.

Peck's narrative of progress under capitalist control was not shared by those opposed to the concentration of wealth epitomized in the trading room. On 11 May 1894, eleven days after the Chicago Stock Exchange's dedication, unionized employees of the Pullman Palace Car Company in Pullman began a strike in the face of layoffs, lowered wages, and other grievances. Their actions protested the company's changed policies following the economic slowdown brought on by the Panic of 1893. In June the American Railway Union, which had organized the workers at Pullman, plunged its national membership into a sympathetic strike, initially against those railways using Pullman cars. On 5 July, local clashes between strikers and police had preceded a fire that destroyed most of the remaining buildings of the World's Columbian Exposition, whose main classical structures had survived an earlier fire of January 1894 three months after the fair closed. The storm of labor unrest that spread out from Chicago came back to the city with a shutdown of its rail traffic, which triggered the use of federal troops. By late summer the strike was broken, locally and nationally, and Chicago's last major labor crisis before 1900 was ended.[166]

A year earlier, even while the Chicago Stock Exchange Building was rising, the Panic of 1893 had devastated the city's banking industry and halted financing for major new construction. In the face of the worst depression in national history, Adler and Sullivan, like other architects, received no new work through spring 1893, except for the project that eventually became the Guaranty Building in Buffalo. During the period of the Auditorium's creation and into the 1890s, they had built up an office staff of over fifty architects, engineers, and draftsmen. Yet on 12 June 1893, Charles H. Bebb, Adler and Sullivan's superintending architect for several of their major projects after the Auditorium, including the Schiller Building, wrote: "The condition of all lines of business in Chicago is deplorable. Adler & Sullivan are doing nothing and Mr. Adler told me he could not even make collections of moneys due him, and consequently he has had to reduce the office force to three men, and these have nothing to do. I have found that all architects and contractors are in the same or even worse shape."[167] By July, Adler was borrowing from friends to meet even this reduced weekly payroll. After the Guaranty Building's design was completed and construction on it began early in 1895, Adler, his office still lacking work as the depression continued, decided to leave the architectural profession in July. He took a well-paid position as consulting architect with the Crane Elevator Company, working for Richard T. Crane, whose firm had made the Auditorium Building's passenger elevators and the theater's hydraulic lifts. Ironically, Crane's factory stood astride Haymarket Square, where the clash had occurred in May 1886 that had prompted Peck to publicly appeal for the Auditorium's creation. The arrangement with Crane lasted only six months, and Adler returned to architecture in January 1896, in practice with his sons. He and Sullivan did not renew their partnership before Adler's death in April 1900.[168]

In their fifteen years together, Adler and Sullivan, working for Peck and clients with similar ambitions, had created an extraordinary series of buildings in Chicago. Their projects integrated Adler's functional and constructive planning with Sullivan's original ornamental and coloristic designs, especially for interiors. One marvels at how well these two architects' individual abilities complemented each other and how effective their working relationship must have been in all phases of design and construction. Each needed the other to create the works that achieved such high levels of distinction and in which their complementary efforts merged into wholly unified gems of architecture. Yet Adler and Sullivan's buildings stood for something more than their surpassing skills. It was the impulse and support of clients like Ferdinand Peck that provided the situational framework within which Adler and Sullivan could excel. What gave their architecture resonance was the link it forged between an innovative visual style and a democratic regional ideology, epitomized in the Auditorium. Such buildings did not merely mirror the conditions of their society, they helped constitute that society's identity, with all its contradictions of good intentions and conflicting interests. The buildings conveyed both the high aspirations of their institutional clients and their architects' vision for a renewal of their art in their time. Adler and Sullivan's works emerged from their specific cultural moment in Chicago's history, which their unique architecture in turn did much to define.

The Chicago Auditorium Building since 1890

The history of the Auditorium Building after Adler and Sullivan completed its interiors in 1890 sheds light on the condition of these spaces over a century later and illustrates how finances, uses, and public and private concerns interacted to preserve and restore a major work of architecture. Its diverse parts each have their own structural, mechanical, and programmatic histories. When a major section of the building was made new, reused, or refitted, this usually affected other components. The chronology of the building's early success, decline, survival, and stages of renewal reveals the perspectives and agenda that different groups have brought to the Auditorium. Their actions on behalf of the building reflect shifting priorities in the city's life and changing views on the historical significance of Chicago's architecture. The Auditorium Building's varied uses also show how it adhered to and departed from its creators' vision of its role as a cultural center.

Ferdinand Peck continued to head the Chicago Auditorium Association's board of directors for a decade after the hotel opened in 1890. In his annual reports to the association's stockholders, he was consistently optimistic. The project had been well timed to reap the benefits of the city's prosperity attendant on the World's Columbian Exposition. At the end of 1891 Peck reported that the main source of revenue, the hotel, had had a prosperous year, with public demand for its spaces frequently greater than their capacity. The office building was three-quarters filled, and the theater, though always financially uncertain, had successfully served its projected variety of purposes. Of the building's total cost of $3,400,000, almost 60 percent, or $1,760,000, had been paid for by purchased capital stock. The remaining 40 percent had been funded by a first mortgage bond issue of $900,000 and a second debenture (or unsecured) bond issue of $500,000. The floating debt (not funded by stocks or bonds) had been reduced to $185,000, which was less than the $240,000 worth of unsold stock in the Auditorium Association's treasury.[1]

In July 1891, to strengthen the building's financial situation, Peck renegotiated its ninety-nine-year ground leases. The largest plots the building stood on were owned by a sympathetic Chicago capitalist, Henry J. Willing, who agreed to extend the leases for another hundred years. More important, he conceded to abolishing the original leases' revaluation clause, which required reappraisal of the land value every ten years after the first twenty from the leases' original date of 1 August 1886. This fixed for nearly two hundred years, to A.D. 2085, the annual rent the Auditorium Association would pay, so that the association's stockholders would reap all future enhancement of the site's anticipated natural rise in value. The landowner, in turn, would have the security of a sure annual rental income, which would never be less than the original rate of 1886.[2] Peck reported that Willing had "made the liberal arrangement . . . in consideration of the public nature of the enterprise."[3] This agreement helped save the Auditorium Building.

To further enhance the project's financial base, in May 1892 the association adopted a refinancing plan that entailed an issue of $1,600,000 in first mortgage bonds redeemable in gold after fifty years. Holders of the earlier bond issues were induced to trade their old bonds for the new gold bonds, which could not be redeemed by the association for fifty years. Annual interest would thus be paid over this entire period, whereas the earlier first mortgage and debenture bonds were subject to redemption in the near future, at which time interest payments to their holders would stop. After the new gold bonds were placed, the Auditorium Association would save annually, since it would pay a lower rate of interest (5 percent) than on the debenture bonds (6 percent). These gold bond holdings, which would become due in 1942, were to be the new financial foundation for the building's life. Yet not all holders of the first mortgage and debenture bonds chose to relinquish them. If not redeemed earlier, these would be due for payment by the Auditorium Association in 1929.[4]

The Auditorium Association's acquisition in April 1892 of the hotel that became the Auditorium Annex was enormously helpful in nearly doubling the number of guest rooms. The earning capacity of much of the original Auditorium Hotel had been limited because of its configuration around the theater. As a later president of the Auditorium Association said, "When the Building was constructed every part was, so to speak, sacrificed for the benefit of the Auditorium Theater."[5] This had forced the hotel's public rooms to be placed along the street level, where there would ideally have been more rental spaces. Also, many rooms on each floor in the original hotel housed staff who maintained the guest rooms, yet the theater inside the outer building block had prevented double-loaded corridors along the floors. This meant that there was too high a proportion of staff's quarters to guest rooms along single-loaded corridors on each floor, so when the Auditorium Annex was built, most of the staff members occupying rooms in the original hotel were moved to the Annex, freeing up rooms for paying guests. The new electrical plant south of the Annex also freed space in the original hotel's basement for rental purposes. But the original hotel, as Sullivan recalled, had only one bath for every ten rooms. Only guest suites had full private baths; single rooms had just washstands. Although this arrangement had been competitive with other hotels built to 1890, it quickly fell behind standards of comfort in newer hotels like the Auditorium Annex, whose rooms were "arranged, singly or in suites, with baths."[6]

From 1893 to 1900 the Auditorium Building earned a small profit, but except for 1893, payment of interest on bonds and increasing property taxes had made it impossible to pay dividends to stockholders, of which there had been 280 at the close of 1891. Their criticism prompted Peck's resignation as president of the board of directors in 1900, though he remained on the board and retained most of his own shares. During the 1890s the building's outer walls had settled continuously. As noted in chapter 3, this was largely because their foundations had been designed for a lighter brick and terra cotta construction than the stone adopted, which had increased the walls' dead load by one-third. Meanwhile, the inner columns carried less live load than they were sized for, so there was a severe differential settlement between the overloaded outer walls and the underloaded inner columns. This caused the floors to deform, tilting downward toward the exterior walls, as is plainly seen within the theater's entrance lobby, along the boxes on the theater's south side, and in the staircases on its north side. The canted floors worried the Auditorium Association's directors, and in 1900 they recommended that the central columns be cut off to lower them and even the floor levels down to that of the exterior walls. Paul Mueller recalled that Adler, troubled by this situation, approached him about doing this work, but Adler died in April 1900 before anything was done. In 1901 the city ordered installation of exterior fire escapes, which are still in place, notably on the tower's east side. After the disastrous Iroquois Theater fire in 1903, further precautions were taken in the Auditorium Theater, notably the construction of walls separating the first- and second-floor foyers.[7]

During the theater's first two decades, it served its original purpose of being Chicago's home for the production of grand opera. From 1889 to 1899, New York City's Metropolitan Opera Company performed there at least once a year, and often twice. Thirteen other opera companies appeared between 1889 and 1910. Yet from its opening in 1889 to the formation of a resident opera company in 1910, musical recitals and concerts were consistently the most popular entertainment in the Auditorium Theater. The theater's large stage made it ideal for choral performances, such as those of the Apollo Club, and for much larger choral festivals with upward of a thousand singers. From October 1891 to 1904 the Auditorium was the permanent home of the Chicago Symphony Orchestra under Theodore Thomas, which performed over forty times each season. As a service to music teachers, students, and workers, the orchestra also gave public rehearsals before formal performances, charging small admission fees.[8] Although the Auditorium Theater was cleaned and refurbished in 1896, the room experienced its first major change only in summer 1902, when its first comprehensive redecoration replaced its original ivory and gold color scheme with a more conventional minimally saturated red.[9]

The Auditorium Theater's great size discouraged the sale of season tickets, which were the foundational revenue for Thomas's orchestra, since people felt they could always purchase a good seat for individual performances. Also, the theater's volume gave it a longer reverberation time than smaller concert halls, so that orchestral players could not hear the echoes that normally allowed them to gauge the quality of the sound they were producing. Frank Lloyd Wright recalled hearing Thomas once say to Sullivan: "Nothing comes back!"[10] Finally, since the resident orchestra had to share the theater with visiting companies, it did not have adequate storage space or rehearsal facilities of its own. Thus, in 1904 Thomas and his orchestra moved into the newly built Orchestra Hall on Michigan Avenue, two blocks north of the Auditorium. This 2,300-seat hall was designed by D. H. Burnham and Company; Burnham had been a staunch supporter of Thomas since they first met to plan the musical events and halls for the World's Columbian Exposition.[11] In 1904 Sullivan, who acted as consultant to the Auditorium Association after Adler's death and who was asked to consult on the acoustic design of Orchestra Hall, produced a design that may have been for Orchestra Hall's facade on Michigan Avenue. This drawing, which hung for years in Sullivan's office, was very different from Burnham's neo-Georgian front for the hall.[12]

In 1904 the Republican national convention was held in the new Chicago Coliseum, on South Wabash Avenue at Fourteenth Place, designed and built in 1900 as a castellated encasing of an existing building, the Libby Prison Museum. Much larger than the Auditorium, the Coliseum was the site of five successive Republican national conventions from 1904 through 1920, when the size of these gatherings also grew.[13] Before 1910 the Auditorium Theater still served as a prime venue for political and nonpolitical oratory, with memorable addresses by national figures, such as appeals for world peace in 1898 by both President McKinley and Booker T. Washington and early performances by Will Rogers. To counter the Republican convention of 1912 at the Coliseum, which renominated William Howard Taft, Theodore Roosevelt's Progressive Party held its conclave in the Auditorium Theater, from whose stage Roosevelt launched his Bull Moose campaign.[14] In this period vaudeville became a prime form of public amusement nationally, and Chicago had an impressive network of theaters devoted to such bookings. Yet the Auditorium's manager, Milward Adams, backed by the Auditorium Association's board of directors, did not favor vaudeville performances in the theater, feeling that this kind of popular entertainment was inconsistent with the building's purposes. Alternatively, such Protestant revivalists as the Reverend Frank Gunsaulus, Newell Dwight Hillis, and Dwight Moody did hold meetings in the Auditorium Theater. Seeking to use the room's acoustics to move his audiences, Moody "would install a little cottage organ in that topmost gallery and between whiles of prayer and preaching would have it waft faint, plaintive whisperings of old hymns to the people far below, and the people, catching every whisper and thinking of their age of innocence, would become tearful and penitent."[15] These Sunday events, which often drew full houses, contrasted with the Auditorium's programming, which tended toward more scenic spectacles such as renditions of *Ben Hur,* complete with chariots and horses, and *Uncle Tom's Cabin,* with Eliza crossing an ice-filled re-creation of the surging Ohio River on the stage. Such scenes made full use of the Auditorium stage's extraordinary mechanical equipment and the theater's seating capacity, which permitted minimal admission prices, even with the high costs of producing such shows. Before 1907 the Auditorium Association managed the theater through Milward Adams, but in that summer, after negotiations with other managers, it was leased for ten years to New York theater producers Mark Klaw and Abraham L. Erlanger. They booked a program of vaudeville, comparable to that in other older Chicago theaters, but the Auditorium Association successfully resisted this redirection of the theater toward popular culture.[16]

The loss of conventions to the Chicago Coliseum and the departure of the Chicago Symphony Orchestra as the Auditorium Theater's prime resident tenant precipitated the first major reconsideration of the building's future. In 1905, when Sullivan was still the Auditorium Association's architectural consultant, he was asked for ideas on how to make the building more profitable. Early in 1906 the board's executive committee considered a scheme to demolish the theater and replace it with a twenty-story hotel in the central part of the Auditorium's site to create a total capacity of nine hundred rooms. By February 1908 Sullivan had made tentative plans "for a remodeled hotel, twenty-two stories high, with the most magnificent rotunda in the world . . . . Upon this rotunda the most lavish creations of the decorator's art will be expended, with fountains, rich statuary, and rare paintings." The hotel's original entrance on Michigan Avenue was to be abandoned in favor of an elaborate new entrance on Congress Street, while a "new tower that will crown the hotel will occupy the entire portion now devoted to the theater."[17] With this project (ultimately unexecuted) Sullivan and the Auditorium Association presumably aimed to compete with Chicago's most recent large business hotels: Holabird and Roche's twenty-two-story Hotel LaSalle (1907–1909) and their new Sherman House, commissioned in 1906 but not finished until 1911.[18]

New York City felt directly challenged by the Auditorium's construction, just as Peck and his fellow Chicagoans had intended. Responses in Manhattan were varied, focusing not on one but on several building projects, including the new Madison Square Garden, a project for varied public amusements and civic events, which developed from 1887.[19] Late in 1889 Adler was retained as an architectural consultant for the design of New York City's Carnegie Hall, although the commission had gone to a New York architect, William B. Tuthill.[20] More broadly, Peck's original goal of making opera more accessible to a larger audience resonated in Manhattan, where an increasing immigrant population had been effectively barred from the Metropolitan Opera House because of its limited space and steep prices. By 1893 New York producer Oscar Hammerstein had begun to stage opera at more reasonable prices while maintaining the Metropolitan's production standards even as he broadened the repertoire to include innovative works and new singers. In December 1906 Hammerstein opened his Manhattan Opera House, relying neither on subscribers to its boxes nor guarantors of its finances but on revenues from ticket sales to the general public for individual performances.[21] Although it failed financially after four seasons, the Manhattan Opera Company broadened the popular audience for the medium, which in turn affected the Metropolitan's policies. The Met's transforming figure was financier Otto Kahn, who, partially in response to Hammerstein's efforts, proposed to build a new opera house for the Metropolitan that would seat 4,500, reducing the number of boxes and abolishing the tradition of box ownership, just as Peck had done at Chicago's Auditorium thirty years before. If it had been built, such a facility would have fulfilled the intention of Kahn as the Met's general manager to make opera "far more an entertainment of all the people than has been the case in the past."[22]

In fall 1909, twenty years after the Auditorium Theater had first opened, a group of wealthy Chicagoans were negotiating with the Metropolitan Opera House Company to bring a permanent opera company to Chicago. At that time the Metropolitan was engaged in its last season of spectacular competition with Oscar Hammerstein's Manhattan Opera Company. Both the Metropolitan and Manhattan companies had played traveling engagements at the Auditorium. At first Chicago supporters of opera had negotiated with Hammerstein, who offered to give Chicago a first-class opera company and build a new opera house, as he had done in New York, if Chicago would help finance it. But when Chicagoans accepted this offer on condition that there be local citizens on the new company's board of directors, Hammerstein, who had always managed his business alone, would not accept the arrangement. These negotiations prompted the Metropolitan's president, Otto Kahn, to cable Chicago that he would match Hammerstein's offer to provide that city with a resident company and build a new opera house to replace the Auditorium. But the Auditorium Theater's great size, its acoustics, and its stage equipment were still adequate for Kahn's purposes, and he agreed to rent Adler and Sullivan's hall.[23] Kahn's new Chicago Grand Opera Company was formed largely from Hammerstein's disbanded Manhattan Opera Company, whose scenery, costumes, and musical scores he purchased.[24]

To accommodate the new company, the Auditorium Association commissioned architect Benjamin Marshall to remodel the theater in summer 1910. It is unclear why Sullivan, who was then still renting an office in the Auditorium's tower, was not chosen for this assignment. Frank Lloyd Wright recalled that the wealthy of Chicago wanted a "golden horseshoe" of boxes like that found in the Metropolitan Opera House. Marshall did install a row of boxes across the rear of the main floor. This was later increased to two superimposed rows of boxes, added to the original theater's forty boxes along its side walls. This replacement of seating sections with boxes reduced the theater's overall seating capacity to 3,600.[25] On stage, the floor was realigned and raised, and the orchestra pit was expanded by removing the first two rows of seats. In this remodeled state, the Auditorium Theater reopened in November 1910 as the home of Chicago's first permanent resident opera company. The Chicago Grand Opera Company sought to support itself on ticket sales alone during its existence from 1910 to 1914. After its financial failure, the company was succeeded by the local Chicago Opera Association (1915–1922), with wealthy Chicagoans giving a guaranty to make up deficits. Yet this association's indebtedness mounted to the point where it was in turn succeeded by the Chicago Civic Opera Company, led by Samuel Insull, head of Commonwealth Edison Company, Chicago's giant electrical utility, and a leading director of the Auditorium Association. Insull favored a conservative operatic repertoire, which, with low ticket prices and small deficits, was relatively successful financially through the 1920s, when the company played to 84 percent of capacity houses. Its last performance, in January 1929, was a presentation of Gounod's *Roméo et Juliette,* the same opera in which Adelina Patti had sung to open the Auditorium's operatic career in 1889.[26] During this period both Sullivan and Peck had died, in 1924.

Through the 1920s, Insull took an active interest in the Auditorium Association as one of its substantial shareholders. He consistently tried to secure good tenants for the office building, at the same time that he was a major financial supporter of the theater's opera company. As it became clear that the Auditorium Association would not succeed in its legal campaign to rebuild the hotel and theater on their original site, Insull, to ensure a home for Chicago opera, began to promote the construction of a new building elsewhere. This became the Chicago Civic Opera House, designed by Graham, Anderson, Probst, and White and built in 1927–1929 at 20 Wacker Drive at the northern edge of the Loop. After leaving the Auditorium Theater in January 1929, the Chicago Civic Opera Company moved into the new opera house. Its design was modeled on the acoustic scientist Paul Sabine's analysis of the Auditorium's shape and materials, though the new theater was not as acoustically optimal as Adler and Sullivan's. Other features of the building's architecture were much admired, yet the new opera house and its company soon fell victim to the Great Depression, which also brought down Insull's empire.[27]

The Auditorium Hotel's future had also been reconsidered from the time of Sullivan's proposals for rebuilding in 1906. The hotel's managers held their original lease through 1909. After its expiration, the Auditorium Association took over the management of the hotel directly, and in 1910 the directors commissioned Marshall to remodel all guest rooms on the Michigan Avenue side to include new bathrooms. The hotel's basement was again rearranged, and one proposal called for rebuilding the hotel's entire first floor, moving the lobby to the Congress Street side, and turning Adler and Sullivan's original lobby into shops. These changes to the first floor were not made.[28] The renovations of 1910 to both the theater and the hotel did not effectively improve the building's financial state. Although Peck's negotiated lease had kept ground rent low, increased income from offices and the few retail tenants did not keep pace with taxes on the property, whose assessed value grew dramatically. Annual city taxes increased from about $3,500 in 1888 to over $145,000 in 1922. Moreover, depreciation ate up nominal annual profits, so it became clear that the Auditorium Building was being operated at a loss going into the 1920s. A portion of the first mortgage and debenture bond issues, amounting to a total of $843,000, would be due in 1929. By early 1923, inability to pay even the interest on the bonded debt led the Auditorium Association to file suit against the landowners to force changes in the leases to allow the association to demolish the Auditorium and build a profitable, much taller building on the site. The landowners resisted, claiming that the Auditorium Association's leases did not permit removing the original structure as the site's only sure source of rental income. These legal efforts, which continued from 1923 to 1928, did not lead to a decisive ruling, and the original leases remained in force up to the time when the first bonds came due on 1 February 1929. Since it could not pay the principal on these bonds, the Auditorium Association declared bankruptcy.[29]

With its opera company gone and its association in receivership, the Auditorium Building closed its theater. In 1932 the United States Supreme Court ruled that the original leases for the Auditorium Building's site were still binding. Since the association's last assets had gone for payment of its property taxes in 1928, it defaulted on payments of its annual ground rent to the landowners, dissolved itself as a corporation, and returned the building to the landowners.[30] As early as 1930–1931 these owners contemplated demolishing the building, but bids for wrecking Adler and Sullivan's monument were at least $400,000—prohibitively costly.

To avoid leaving the structure vacant, the owners managed it themselves through a newly created entity called the Auditorium Building Corporation. In 1932–1933, in order to profit from the expected visitors to Chicago's Century of Progress Exhibition, this corporation commissioned Holabird and Root to renovate the building. A major part of this project included repairs to the theater's roof trusses and to the tower's footings. The Auditorium Association had called their safety into question as part of its legal efforts to have the building taken down in the 1920s. The hotel was also redecorated, but bathrooms were still not put into all of its main block of rooms on Congress Street.

In the theater, a new color scheme recalled the original, and the sixty-two boxes (Adler and Sullivan's original forty on the sides plus Marshall's twenty-two across the parquet's back) were refurbished. For the rededication, some older operagoers requested the same seats they had had previously. Charles Holloway came out of retirement to restore his proscenium mural, and Fleury's murals, the marble and scagliola surfaces, and the mosaic floors were all cleaned. In the theater, the art glass was removed from the lunettes over the doors leading from the lobby into the main foyer, where crystal chandeliers were then hung. A new steel canopy was hung above the theater entrance on Congress Street. Also at this time, the stage's original lighting system was replaced. In December 1932 the remodeled theater opened and hosted major operatic and musical theatrical events through June 1941.[31]

Yet as the depression deepened and offices emptied of tenants, the Auditorium Building Corporation could no longer pay property taxes when the building's value was assessed as low as $2,000,000. By 1940 the corporation was $1,150,000 in debt, and its directors decided to close the building, including the theater, by 30 June 1941 except for some of its rent-paying first-floor stores.[32]

With the Auditorium's failure as a private venture, the building immediately drew philanthropic and municipal efforts to save it. These began in 1941 with Mayor Edward Kelly's chartering of the nonprofit Auditorium Music Foundation, which raised money to operate the building as a musical center. One of Ferdinand Peck's sons was among its founders, yet at the start of American involvement in World War II, the foundation's initial fund-raising fell short of its goals, and the building's movable contents were placed at auction to help pay its back taxes. Contents sold included furnishings of the four hundred bedroom suites, paintings from the theater and hotel lobbies, carpets, silverware, and the theater's scenery, pianos, 3,665 of its seats, and its organ. Some who had attended the Auditorium's opening in 1889 bought mementos, and some long-term residents of the hotel bought the furnishings of their rooms. The city's efforts to foreclose on the Auditorium's owners led to a municipal takeover of the structure as a servicemen's center later in 1942. During the war, the theater's stage was floored over to become a bowling alley, the bar in the men's café was replaced by a lunch counter, and ornamental plasterwork, stenciling, and woodwork in several public interiors were painted over.[33]

In August 1946 the newly chartered Roosevelt University negotiated an agreement with the city to take over the building's operation. The new institution bought the structure from its owners, who had earlier formed the Auditorium Building Corporation. With the university's promise to eventually restore the theater, the Auditorium Music Foundation dissolved in 1946, and its benefactors were repaid. Early in its occupancy, Roosevelt University converted hotel rooms and offices to classrooms. But it gained clear title to the building only after the city waived back taxes in exchange for the right to cut an exterior sidewalk along the Auditorium Building's front facing Congress Street, which the city had decided to widen. As noted in chapter 5, this process carried out during the 1950s destroyed the ladies' restaurant, all of the men's café, the southern half of the theater lobby, and the original southwestern storefront, leaving an open arcade along Congress Street between Michigan and Wabash Avenues.[34]

In 1956 the centennial of Sullivan's birth prompted new interest in the Auditorium Building's condition, and in the next year Roosevelt commissioned architect Crombie Taylor to undertake restoration beginning with the banquet hall, which reopened in 1957 as the Rudolf Ganz Recital Hall (later Rudolf Ganz Memorial

Hall), named for the former head of the Chicago Music School, which became Roosevelt's Music Department. In 1958 the ladies' parlor of the hotel, set in the second floor's southeast corner, was restored as the Louis Sullivan Room. In 1962 the hotel's main second-floor reception hall was partially restored, also under Taylor. In 1960 Roosevelt University's trustees formed the Auditorium Theater Council to undertake "to restore, operate and manage the Auditorium Theater as a civic enterprise," with the restored theater to be operated as a nonprofit free public entity, meaning that it would not be taxed.[35] The council's chairwoman was Roosevelt trustee Beatrice Spachner, who was chief fund-raiser and organizer of the theater's restoration. A violinist, Spachner had attended concerts at the Auditorium as a child and wanted to re-create their combination of music and setting by restoring the theater for future generations. As she later said, "Because we are a not-for-profit institution, and because our money came from the whole community, we feel the theater should serve as many of the people of Chicago as possible."[36] The council then hired architects Crombie Taylor and Associates and Skidmore, Owings and Merrill to make initial studies of the building's condition and the work needed. Skidmore, Owings and Merrill concluded that the building's structure was in serious trouble, although this was later discovered not to be the case. Acting as an aesthetic consultant, Taylor devoted himself to an in-depth study of the stenciled ornament that Sullivan used to decorate the interior. In this era, Taylor recalled standing on the stage and watching rainwater pour into the theater through its yet to be repaired roof, whose drains no longer functioned properly. It was then not clear that the room would survive.[37]

In summer 1963 Chicago architect Harry Weese became the chair of the Auditorium Theater Council's building committee and undertook a new study. He offered his services free of charge. In early 1964 he advised that the structure was reasonably sound, with few elements in need of reinforcement. Under his direction, the theater was comprehensively restored, the aim being to re-create as far as possible the room's original appearance in 1889. The ceiling's ornamental plaster was cleaned, and missing or damaged pieces were replaced with new ones cast from latex molds made from the old surfaces. The variety of Sullivan's designs necessitated making hundreds of molds to cast new plaster pieces. These were painted gold to match the original gold leaf, sections of which were still in place and were cleaned. The lights in the ceiling were replaced with clear carbon-filament bulbs like those originally used. The rear boxes installed in 1932 were removed, and the original seats were washed and painted, then reupholstered in a fabric that duplicated the original. Missing seats were rebuilt from the original designs. Albert Fleury's side murals were cleaned and restored. In the foyers, new carpets based on Sullivan's three-color original design were woven and set in place. Healy and Millet's six original stained glass windows over the lobby doors were reinstalled. Throughout the theater and lobby, mural stencils that had been painted over were to be replaced, and Taylor made tracings of most designs after stripping away layers of paint. They were to be reapplied in metallic gold on the newly painted soft gold surfaces, initially only on the theater's box faces.[38] Original stencils that were never painted over still remain visible on the landings of the lobby's stairway. The partially restored theater was re-opened in December 1967, and work then continued with improvements in the stage and dressing rooms. The reducing curtain was again made operable, although the original silk drop curtain was not duplicated in the same material.[39]

With the theater's reopening, attention turned back to the hotel. In 1972 Roosevelt's trustees resolved to carry out all future restoration work through consultation with a single architectural firm known for its competence in adaptive reuse and for its knowledge of Adler and Sullivan's work. The firm selected was Brenner, Danforth, Rockwell (later Danforth, Rockwell, Carow), which then prepared an extensive master plan except for further restoration of the theater, which remained separate. Under its direction the hotel lobby was partly restored in 1973. This effort uncovered the original mosaic floor, although the room's wood trim and light fixtures were not then restored. In 1975 the art glass in the hotel's main stairway and banquet hall (by then Rudolf Ganz Memorial Hall) was restored.[40] In 1979–1980 the Historic American Buildings Survey and the Historic American Engineering Record undertook a comprehensive study of the building's structural and mechanical systems for heating and air conditioning.[41] In 1980 architect John Vinci carried out the restoration of the south alcove of the hotel's tenth-floor dining room, including refinishing its mahogany woodwork and restoring its art glass. At that time restorers remarked on the quality and substantiality of the original materials in these interiors.[42]

Unfortunately, the university's spatial needs have not always enabled restoration of Adler and Sullivan's original interiors. In 1963–1964, the office building's lobby on Wabash Avenue, which had survived from 1890, was refitted along with neighboring store interiors to provide space for Roosevelt's new bookstore. In 1973 the university's growth required adding office space and new classrooms over the light court on the building's north side. This new construction greatly altered the dining room's north alcove and limited the theater's ability to handle large opera sets. About this time the tower was remodeled to provide sixty faculty offices, including several on the sixteenth floor, where Adler and Sullivan had their offices after the building's completion.[43] In 2000 Roosevelt initiated further restoration planning for its parts of the building, with a conservation master plan produced by Booth Hansen Associates. The banquet hall's murals are being cleaned, and there are plans to replace the ornamental gilded electroliers. The Auditorium Theater Council is also continuing its efforts to further restore the theater. Plans include restoring the gold leaf finish to the ornamental plasterwork and putting back the borders of ornamental stenciling on the ceiling arches. All told, since 1946, the Auditorium Building has been the focus of an extraordinary effort for its preservation and renewal, sustained by the fund-raising and architectural skills of many Chicagoans. As Wright said when the building was imperiled in 1941,

By way of its citizens it was a great Chicago act that put Chicago on the cultural map of the world . . . . And it did this so well that wherever I have been about the world, Tokyo, Moscow, Zagreb, Warsaw, Vienna, Constantinople, Rio de Janeiro, Paris, London or Berlin, when Chicago would be mentioned it would be identified there with its great Auditorium. The great building is famous the world over today not only as a great public enterprise and public monument but as a superior building— a great building modern for its purpose—the greatest room for music and opera in the world today, bar none. Although Chicago did not know it when she built it, Chicago produced a building at least 50 years ahead of its time and only now coming into its own: A building not grown out of fashion but one that could never go out of fashion.[44]

Chicago Loop Properties of Philip F. W. Peck and His Sons, 1849–1896

As elsewhere, ownership records for Chicago properties are indexed by property location, not by property owner. Tax assessment and tax payment records of Chicago properties, also indexed by location and not by owner, are kept by the Cook County Tax Assessor's Office and the Tax Redemption Department of the Cook County Clerk's Office. Most records do not go back before the 1950s, however, so one must go to other sources for earlier lists of Chicago properties in an individual's possession and their assessed values. Fortunately there are at least three comprehensive lists of Chicago Loop properties owned by Philip Peck and his immediate descendants. The lists are:

1849 Chicago City Clerk. Assessment Roll, Real Estate, in South Division of Chicago, 1849. Manuscripts and Archives Collection, Chicago Historical Society. This lists Philip F. W. Peck as owner of the properties. His eldest son Ferdinand was born in 1848.

1872 "Inventory of the Real and Personal Estate of Philip F. W. Peck, late of the City of Chicago, in the County of Cook and State of Illinois, deceased," filed 7 February 1872. County Court of Cook County, docket A, page 5. Probate Records, Estate of Philip Ferdinand Peck (Clerk of the Circuit Court of Cook County Archives, Chicago, Illinois). Philip F. W. Peck had begun to transfer ownership of his properties to his sons (Ferdinand, Clarence, Walter, and Harold) before his death. Only some of his sons' properties are included in this list, which omits those properties acquired by the elder Peck after 1849 that had been sold by 1871.

1896 *Ninth Annual Report of the Bureau of Labor Statistics of Illinois, Subject: Franchises and Taxation, 1896.* This list notes properties owned by

Ferdinand, Clarence, and Walter Peck and by Annah B. Peck, the widow of Harold, who had died in 1884. Some properties that the Pecks owned in 1871 had been sold by 1896 and are not listed here. Others were sold later.

The accompanying table lists these properties according to numbers corresponding to those on figure 5. Each property's assessed value is listed in 1849, 1872, and 1896 unless the property was not listed in those years. Most properties listed below included only parts of the lots noted. Street addresses of all properties were according to the numbering system in place before the current system was adopted in 1911.

NUMBER	DESCRIPTION	LOCATION	1849	1872	1896
1	Wharfing Lot 12	West half northeast corner LaSalle and South Water (174–176 S. Water)	$2,750	$30,000	$75,700
2	Wharfing Lot 6	West quarter north side South Water, between Dearborn and Clark (128 S. Water)	1,250	12,000	35,890
3	Original Town, block 18, in lot 4	Southeast corner LaSalle and South Water (173–175 S. Water)	4,000	Not listed	131,360
4	Original Town, block 17, in lot 2	South side South Water, between Dearborn and Clark (127 S. Water)	4,500	20,000	61,320
5	Original Town, block 21, lot ?	North side Lake, between Franklin and Market (240 Lake)	Not listed	Not listed	38,210
5a	Original Town, block 21, lot ?	South side South Water, between Franklin and Lake (263 S. Water)	Not listed	Not listed	37,080
6	Original Town, block 20, lot 6	North side Lake, between Wells and Franklin (210–216 Lake)	12,000	64,000	131,400
7	Original Town, block 17, in lot 5	Southeast corner Clark and Haddock (15–17 Clark)	1,500	50,000	201,980
8	Fort Dearborn Addition, block 8, in lot 22	North side Lake, between State and Wabash (46 Lake)	1,200	Not listed	Not listed
9	Original Town, block 33, in lots 1–2	Southwest corner Lake and LaSalle (159–169 Lake)	11,300	190,000	Not listed
10	Original Town, block 34, in lot 4	Southeast corner Lake and LaSalle (155–157 Lake)	650	Not listed	Not listed
11	Fort Dearborn Addition, block 9, in lot 30	East side State, between Randolph and Benton (51 State)	700	Not listed	Not listed
12	Fort Dearborn Addition, block 12, lot 3	East side Wabash, between Washington and Randolph (72–74 Wabash)	Not listed	86,400	Not listed
13	Original Town, block 41, lot 4	Southeast corner Franklin and Randolph (216–222 Randolph)	6,500	80,000	Not listed
14	Original Town, block 55, in lots 1–2	Southwest corner LaSalle and Washington (Chicago Stock Exchange)	4,000	200,000	Not listed
15	Original Town, block 56, in lots 1–2	Southwest corner Clark and Washington (Chicago Opera House)	Not listed	331,200	881,440
16	Original Town, block 58, in lots 3–4	Southeast corner Dearborn and Washington (111–117 Dearborn)	1,750	90,000	Not listed
17	School Section Addition, block 116, lots 24–?	Southeast corner LaSalle and Adams (later Rookery Building)	9,000	Sold 1852 (for 8,750)	Not listed
18	School Section Addition, block 116, lots 1–4	Southwest corner Clark and Adams (Lakeside Press Building)	Not listed	100,000	Not listed
19	School Section Addition, block 116, lots 8–14	Northwest corner Jackson and Clark (Grand Pacific Hotel, east)	Not listed	186,250	Sold 1886 (for 377,530)
20	Fractional Section 15 Addition to Chicago, block 5, in lot 9	Northwest corner Michigan and Jackson	Not listed	30,600	Sold 1901 (for 250,000)
21	Fractional Section 15 Addition to Chicago, block 10, in lots 2–3	Southeast corner State and Van Buren	1,200	13,200	Not listed
22	Fractional Section 15 Addition to Chicago, block 9, in lot 4	203 Michigan Avenue (prefire Peck home in Michigan Terrace)	Not listed	16,000	Not listed

INTRODUCTION

1. Local newspaper accounts of the Chicago Auditorium Building at the time its theater opened included Editorial, "The Dedication of the Auditorium," *Chicago Tribune,* 8 December 1889; "The Pride of Chicago," *Chicago Daily News,* 9 December 1889; "Patti and the President," *Chicago Inter Ocean,* 9 December 1889; "A Temple of Song," *Chicago Globe,* 10 December 1889; "Pride of All Chicago," *Chicago Herald,* 10 December 1889; "A Hall for the People," *Chicago Inter Ocean,* 10 December 1889; "Dedicated to Music," *Chicago Morning News,* 10 December 1889; "In a Glare of Glory," *Chicago Times,* 10 December 1889; "Dedicated to Music and the People," *Chicago Tribune,* 10 December 1889; "Peerless Patti Sang," *Chicago Herald,* 11 December 1889; "Auditorium Supplement," *Chicago Inter Ocean,* 11 December 1889; "Patti in Grand Opera," *Chicago Morning News,* 11 December 1889; Editorial, "Auditorium Oratory," *Chicago Times,* 11 December 1889; "Some Future Uses of the Auditorium," *Chicago Tribune,* 11 December 1889; "The Auditorium Dedication," *Anchor and Shield,* 14 December 1889; "The Auditorium," *Chicago Evening Herald,* 14 December 1889; "The Auditorium Building" and "The Auditorium Dedication," *Graphic* (Chicago), o.s. 11 (14 December 1889); "The Dedication of the Auditorium," *Chicago Legal News,* 14 December 1889. The book on the building then published was Edward R. Garczynski, *The Auditorium* (New York: Exhibit, 1890). This book was the most ambitious among at least eight illustrated volumes on recent individual United States buildings published in 1889–1891 by the Exhibit Publishing Company, New York, headed by Ellwood S. Hand, who wrote the preface and dedication to Garczynski's Auditorium book. Ferdinand Peck kept a scrapbook titled "Auditorium Dedication Volume," which contained letters related to the Auditorium Theater's opening and clippings of stories about the event from newspapers in Chicago, other parts of the United States, and Western Europe. One of his sons, Ferdinand W. Peck Jr., donated this volume to the Newberry Library, Chicago, in 1941.

Accounts of the Auditorium in local histories and guidebooks of the period included Alfred T. Andreas, *History of Chicago,* 3 vols. (Chicago: Alfred T. Andreas, 1884–1886), 3:649–650, 652–653; George W. Orear, *Commerical and Architectural Chicago* (Chicago: G. W. Orear, 1887), 53–60; *Industrial Chicago,* 6 vols. (Chicago: Goodspeed, 1891–1896), vols. 1 and 2, *The Building Interests,* 1:194–196, 2:73–86, 466–488, 490–491; John J. Flinn, *Chicago, the Marvelous City of the West: A History, an Encyclopedia, and a Guide,* 2d ed. (Chicago: Standard Guide, 1892), 120–128; Joseph Kirkland and Caroline Kirkland, *The Story of*

Chicago, 2 vols. (Chicago: Dibble, 1894), 2:362–364; and Rand McNally, *Bird's-Eye Views and Guide to Chicago* (Chicago: Rand McNally, 1898), 78–92. European commentaries on the Auditorium are noted in Arnold Lewis, *An Early Encounter with Tomorrow: Europeans, Chicago's Loop, and the World's Columbian Exposition* (Urbana: University of Illinois Press, 1997), 213, 228 nn. 38, 39.

2. Adler's published writings related to the Auditorium include "The Paramount Requirements of a Large Opera House," *Inland Architect and News Record* 10 (October 1887): 45–46, also published as "Theatres," *American Architect and Building News* 22 (29 October 1887): 206–208; "Foundations of the Auditorium Building, Chicago," *Inland Architect and News Record* 11 (March 1888): 31–32 and plates; "Stage Mechanisms," *Inland Architect and News Record* 13 (March 1889): 42–43, also published in *Building Budget* 15 (February 1889): 21–22; "The Auditorium Tower," *American Architect and Building News* 32 (4 April 1891): 15–16; "On Inspection of Buildings," *Economist* 5 (30 May 1891): 946–947; "Foundations," *Economist* (27 June 1891): 1136–1138; "Engineering Supervision of Building Operations," *Economist* 33 (4 July 1891): 11–12; "The Chicago Auditorium," *Architectural Record* 1 (April–June 1892): 415–434; "Theater Building for American Cities: First Paper," *Engineering Magazine* 7 (August 1894): 717–730; Second Paper, September 1894, 815–829; "Convention Halls," *Inland Architect and News Record* 26 (September 1895): 13–14; (October 1895): 22–23; "Slow Burning and Fireproof Construction," *Inland Architect and News Record* 26 (January 1896): 60; and "The Theater," edited by Rachel Baron, *Prairie School Review* 2 (second quarter 1965): 21–27.

Sullivan's writings related to the Auditorium include "Plastic and Color Decoration of the Auditorium," originally published as "Harmony in Decoration," *Chicago Tribune*, 16 November 1889, 12, and reprinted in *Industrial Chicago*, 2:490–491; in Sherman Paul, *Louis Sullivan: An Architect in American Thought* (Englewood Cliffs, N.J.: Prentice-Hall, 1962), 143–146; and in Louis Sullivan, *Louis Sullivan: The Public Papers*, ed. Robert Twombly (Chicago: University of Chicago Press, 1988), 74–76; "Development of Construction, I," *Economist* 55 (24 June 1916): 1252, reprinted in *Louis Sullivan: The Public Papers*, ed. Twombly, 214–222; and Sullivan, *The Autobiography of an Idea* (1924; reprint, New York: Dover, 1971), 292–294, 303, 309. See also Sullivan's remarks quoted in "Church Spires Must Go," *Chicago Tribune*, 30 November 1890, 36, reprinted in *Louis Sullivan: The Public Papers*, ed. Twombly, 72–73.

Other accounts of the building include "The Chicago Auditorium," *Architect* (London) 43 (21 February 1890): 125–126; "The Auditorium Building, Chicago," *Engineering* (London) 51 (3 April 1891): 394, 395, 400; (24 April 1891): 488, 489, 490; Montgomery Schuyler, "Glimpses of Western Architecture: Chicago," *Harper's Magazine* 83 (August 1891): 395–406, reprinted in *"American Architecture" and Other Writings*, ed. William H. Jordy and Ralph Coe, 2 vols. (Cambridge: Harvard University Press, 1961), 1:246–291; and Schuyler, *A Critique of the Works of Adler and Sullivan, D. H. Burnham and Co., Henry Ives Cobb*, Great American Architects Series 2, Architecture in Chicago (New York: Architectural Record, 1896), 2–27, partly reprinted in *"American Architecture" and Other Writings*, ed. Jordy and Coe, 2:377–404; Leopold Gmelin, "Architektonisches aus Nordamerika: V. Die vielstöckigen Geschäftshäuser [Part 2]," *Deutsche Bauzeitung* 28 (27 October 1894): 532–534; Paul F. P. Mueller, Testimony, Chicago Auditorium Association vs. Mark Skinner Willing and the Northern Trust Co., as Trustees, etc., et al., in United States Circuit Court of Appeals for the Seventh Circuit, October [1925] Term, no. 3733, pp. 440–468, mostly reprinted in Edgar J. Kaufmann Jr., "Frank Lloyd Wright's 'Lieber Meister,'" in *Nine Commentaries on Frank Lloyd Wright*, ed. Edgar J. Kaufmann Jr. (New York: Architectural History Foundation and MIT Press, 1989): 42–62; Paul Sabine, "The Acoustics of the Chicago Civic Opera House," *Architectural Forum* 52 (April 1930): 599–604; Frank Lloyd Wright, *An Autobiography* (New York: Longmans, Green, 1932), 105–106; Hugh Morrison, *Louis Sullivan, Prophet of Modern Architecture* (1935; reprint, New York: W. W. Norton, 1962): 80–110; Wright, quoted in "Chicago's Auditorium Is Fifty Years Old," *Architectural Forum* 73 (September 1940): 11–12; Frank A. Randall, *History of the Development of Building Construction in Chicago* (Urbana: University of Illinois Press, 1949), 117; Frank Lloyd Wright, *Genius and the Mobocracy* (New York: Duell, Sloan and Pearce, 1949), 42–53; Carl W. Condit, "Sullivan's Skyscrapers as the Expression of Nineteenth Century Technology," *Technology and Culture* 1 (winter 1959): 78–93; Historic

American Buildings Survey, Survey ILL-1007: Auditorium Building (1960; Addendum, 1980); Albert Bush-Brown, *Louis Sullivan* (New York: George Braziller, 1960), 15–16; Willard Connely, *Louis Sullivan as He Lived: The Shaping of American Architecture* (New York: Horizon, 1960), 102–122; Carl W. Condit, *The Chicago School of Architecture: A History of Commercial and Public Building in the Chicago Area, 1875–1925* (Chicago: University of Chicago Press, 1964), 69–79; Paul E. Sprague, "The Architectural Ornament of Louis Sullivan and His Chief Draftsmen" (Ph.D. diss., Princeton University, 1968), 396–398; William H. Jordy, *American Buildings and Their Architects,* vol. 4, *Progressive and Academic Ideals at the Turn of the Twentieth Century* (1972; reprint, New York: Oxford University Press, 1986), 101–104, 118–119, 161–162; Simon Tidworth, *Theatres: An Architectural and Cultural History* (New York: Praeger, 1973), 177–180; Wilbur T. Denson, "A History of the Chicago Auditorium" (Ph.D. diss., University of Wisconsin, Madison, 1974); Daniel H. Perlman, *The Auditorium Building: Its History and Architectural Significance* (Chicago: Roosevelt University, 1976); George C. Izenour, *Theater Design* (New York: McGraw-Hill, 1977), 82–86; Paul E. Sprague, *The Drawings of Louis Henry Sullivan* (Princeton: Princeton University Press, 1979), 6–7, 33–37; Charles E. Gregersen, "History of the Auditorium Building" and "Architectural Description of the Auditorium Building," in Addendum, Historic American Buildings Survey, Survey ILL-1007 (1980); Narciso G. Menocal, *Architecture as Nature: The Transcendentalist Idea of Louis Sullivan* (Madison: University of Wisconsin Press, 1981), 18, 45–46; John A. Burns, "Structure and Mechanics Viewed as Sculpture," *American Institute of Architects Journal* 72 (April 1983): 44–49; Charles E. Grimsley, "A Study of the Contributions of Dankmar Adler to the Theatre Building Practice of the Late Nineteenth Century" (Ph.D. diss., Northwestern University, 1984), 215–304; David S. Andrew, *Louis Sullivan and the Polemics of Modern Architecture* (Urbana: University of Illinois Press, 1985), 82–92; Michael Forsyth, *Buildings for Music: The Architect, the Musician, and the Listener from the Seventeenth Century to the Present* (Cambridge: MIT Press, 1985), 236–243; Lauren S. Weingarden, "The Colors of Nature: Louis Sullivan's Architectural Polychromy and Nineteenth-Century Color Theory," *Winterthur Portfolio* 20 (1985): 250–252; David Van Zanten, "Sullivan to 1890," in *Louis Sullivan: The Function of Ornament,* ed. Wim de Wit (New York: W. W. Norton, 1986), 36–51; Jordy, "The Tall Buildings," in *Louis Sullivan: The Function of Ornament,* ed. de Wit, 65–71; Robert Twombly, *Louis Sullivan: His Life and Work* (New York: Viking/Penguin, 1986), 161–195; Joseph Rykwert, "Louis Sullivan and the Gospel of Height," *Art in America* 75 (November 1987): 162–165; David G. Lowe, "Monument of an Age," *American Craft* 48 (June–July 1988): 40–47, 104; Lauren S. Weingarden, "Naturalized Nationalism: A Ruskinian Discourse on the Search for an American Style of Architecture," *Winterthur Portfolio* 24 (spring 1989): 63–67; Carol Baldridge and Alan Willis, "The Business of Culture," *Chicago History* 19 (spring–summer 1990): 32–51; Charles E. Gregersen, *Dankmar Adler: His Theaters and Auditoriums* (Athens: Swallow Press and Ohio University Press, 1990), 4–6, 9–23, 65–70; Ross Miller, *American Apocalypse: Chicago and the Myth of the Great Fire* (Chicago: University of Chicago Press, 1990), 111–121; Roula M. Geraniotis, "German Design Influences in the Auditorium Theater," in *The Midwest in American Architecture,* ed. John S. Garner (Urbana: University of Illinois Press, 1991), 42–75; Miles L. Berger, *They Built Chicago: Entrepreneurs Who Shaped a Great City's Architecture* (Chicago: Bonus Books, 1992), 93–103; Hans Frei, *Louis Henry Sullivan* (Zurich: Verlag für Architektur, 1992), 68–75; John L. Dizikes, *Opera in America: A Cultural History* (New Haven: Yale University Press, 1993), 247–256; Donald L. Miller, *City of the Century: The Epic of Chicago and the Making of America* (New York: Simon and Schuster, 1996), 354–366; Mario Manieri Elia, *Louis Henry Sullivan* (New York: Princeton Architectural Press, 1996), 38–59; Joseph M. Siry, "Chicago's Auditorium Building: Opera or Anarchism," *Journal of the Society of Architectural Historians* 57 (June 1998): 2–33; Gilbert Herbert and Mark Donchin, *Speculations on a Black Hole: Adler and Sullivan, and the Planning of the Chicago Auditorium Building* (Haifa: Architectural Heritage Research Centre, 1998); David Van Zanten, *Sullivan's City: The Meaning of Ornament for Louis Sullivan* (New York: W. W. Norton, 2000), 27–32; and Robert Twombly and Narciso G. Menocal, *Louis Sullivan: The Poetry of Architecture* (New York: W. W. Norton, 2001), 46–47, 90–92, 231, 250–257.

3. Giuseppe Giacosa, "Chicago and Her Italian Colony," *Nuova Antologia* 128 (March 1893): 16–28, trans. L. B. Davis in *As Others See Chicago: Impressions of Visitors, 1673–1933,* ed. Bessie L. Pierce (Chicago: University of Chicago Press, 1933), 280.

4. On the Auditorium's observation tower and its views, see Garczynski, *Auditorium,* 143–144; Flinn, *Chicago, the Marvelous City of the West* (1892), 141; and Harold R. Vynne, *Chicago by Day and Night: The Pleasure Seeker's Guide to the Paris of America* (Chicago: Thomson and Zimmerman, 1892), 46.

5. Charles Dudley Warner, "Chicago," in *Studies in the South and West, with Comments on Canada,* by Charles Dudley Warner (New York: Harper, 1889), 190. In 1903 one German critic comparing these three buildings concluded that the Auditorium "is a proof of the artistic efforts of the architect to make as beautiful a building as possible while being restricted, on utilitarian grounds, to the montonous arrangement of design and details. A far more artistic result must be conceded to the middle and still higher building by the architect S. S. Beman and called the Studebaker building . . . . The architect has succeeded in avoiding the barracks-like appearance of most business houses and has happily achieved a satisfactory result." See *Die Architektur des XX. Jahrhunderts—Zeitschrift für moderne Baukunst* (Berlin: Ernst Wasmuth, 1903): 33, translated in Peter Haiko, *Architecture of the Early XX. Century* (New York: Rizzoli, 1989), 92. On the Studebaker Building, see "Real Estate: Plans for the Costly Studebaker Building on Michigan Avenue," *Chicago Tribune,* 16 August 1885, 20; "The Studebaker Building," *Chicago Tribune,* 26 March 1887, 7; Charles E. Jenkins, "A Review of the Works of S. S. Beman," *Architectural Reviewer* 1 (31 March 1897): 62–69; Thomas J. Schlereth, "Solon Spencer Beman: The Social History of a Midwest Architect," *Chicago Architectural Journal* 5 (1985): 20; Schlereth, "Solon Spencer Beman, Pullman, and the European Influence on and Interest in His Chicago Architecture," in *Chicago Architecture, 1872–1922: Birth of a Metropolis,* ed. John Zukowsky (Munich: Prestel-Verlag, 1987), 183–184; and Perry R. Duis, "'Where Is Athens Now?' The Fine Arts Building, 1898 to 1918," *Chicago History* 6 (summer 1977): 66–78. On the Art Institute's 1885 (or second) building, see "Art in Chicago," *Chicago Tribune,* 1 August 1886, 13; "Chicago," *American Architect and Building News* 23 (21 January 1888): 30; Donald Hoffmann, *The Architecture of John Wellborn Root* (Baltimore: Johns Hopkins University Press, 1973), 49–54; and "The Art Institute of Chicago Buildings, 1879–1988: A Chronology," *Art Institute of Chicago Museum Studies* 14 (1988): 7–27.

6. Chauncey Depew, quoted in "A Peep at the Auditorium," *Chicago Tribune,* 18 October 1888, 1, and "Depew Sees Wonders," *Chicago Herald,* 18 October 1888. A plaque above one of the fireplaces in the Auditorium Theater's upper foyer recorded Depew's statement: "I have stood in every great hall and sat in all the famous theaters and opera houses in the world, but in its unrivaled acoustics, both for oratory and music, in its unequaled capacity to comfortably accommodate vast audiences, and in the harmony and taste of its ornamentation, this Auditorium of Chicago is without a rival or a peer." See "Old Auditorium Is Restored to Former Glory," *Chicago Tribune,* 11 December 1932, pt. 1, p. 8.

7. Quoted in "Harrison and Morton," *Chicago Inter Ocean,* 10 December 1889, 1.

8. "The Auditorium Association," *Economist* 8 (10 December 1892): 825.

9. Garczynski, *Auditorium,* 11.

10. Kurt W. Forster and Richard J. Tuttle, "The Palazzo del Tè," *Journal of the Society of Architectural Historians* 30 (December 1974): 267.

11. Influential characterizations of the "Chicago school" include Sigfried Giedion, *Space, Time and Architecture,* 5th ed., rev. and enl. (Cambridge: Harvard University Press, 1982), 368–393; Carl W. Condit, "The Chicago School and the Modern Movement in Architecture," *Art in America* 36 (January 1948): 19–36; Condit, *The Rise of the Skyscraper* (Chicago: University of Chicago Press, 1952); and Condit, *Chicago School.* See H. Allen Brooks, "Chicago School: Metamorphosis of a Term," *Journal of the Society of Architectural Historians* 25 (May 1966): 115–118, and Robert Bruegmann, "The Marquette and the Myth of the Chicago School," *Threshold* 5–6 (fall 1991): 6–23. Revisions of Giedion's and Condit's ideas appear in Art Institute of Chicago, *Chicago and New York: Architectural Interactions* (Chicago: Art Institute of

Chicago, 1984); John Zukowsky, ed., *Chicago Architecture, 1872–1922: Birth of a Metropolis* (Munich: Prestel-Verlag, 1987); and Robert Bruegmann, *The Architects and the City: Holabird and Roche of Chicago, 1880–1918* (Chicago: University of Chicago Press, 1997). See also Sarah B. Landau and Carl Condit, *The Rise of the New York Skyscraper, 1865–1913* (New Haven: Yale University Press, 1996).

12. Recent studies of Chicago's labor history in the late 1800s include Kenneth L. Kann, "Working Class Culture and the Labor Movement in Nineteenth-Century Chicago" (Ph.D., diss., University of California at Berkeley, 1977); Hartmut Keil and John B. Jentz, eds., *German Workers in Industrial Chicago, 1850–1910: A Comparative Perspective* (De Kalb, Ill.: Northern Illinois University Press, 1983); Paul Avrich, *The Haymarket Tragedy* (Princeton: Princeton University Press, 1984); Hartmut Keil and John B. Jentz, eds., *German Workers in Chicago: A Documentary History of Working Class Culture from 1850 to World War I* (Urbana: University of Illinois Press, 1988); Bruce C. Nelson, *Beyond the Martyrs: A Social History of Chicago's Anarchists, 1870–1900* (New Brunswick, N.J.: Rutgers University Press, 1988); Richard Schneirov and Thomas J. Suhrbur, *Union Brotherhood, Union Town: The History of the Carpenters' Union of Chicago, 1863–1987* (Carbondale: Southern Illinois University Press, 1988); Eric L. Hirsch, *Urban Revolt: Ethnic Politics in the Nineteenth-Century Chicago Labor Movement* (Berkeley: University of California Press, 1990); Jentz, "Class and Politics in an Emerging Industrial City: Chicago in the 1860s and 1870s," *Journal of Urban History* 17 (May 1991): 227–263; Schneirov, "Political Cultures and the Role of the State in Labor's Republic: The View from Chicago, 1848–1877," *Labor History* 32 (summer 1991): 376–400; and Schneirov, *Labor and Urban Politics: Class Conflict and the Origins of Modern Liberalism in Chicago, 1864–97* (Urbana: University of Illinois Press, 1998). See also Bessie L. Pierce, *A History of Chicago*, 3 vols. (Chicago: University of Chicago Press, 1937–1957), 3:234–299. Steven Sopolsky at the University of Pittsburgh has studied in great detail the history of building trades workers in Chicago in the late 1800s and early 1900s. Future publication of his work is anticipated. For a comparative perspective, see Dorothee Schneider, *Trade Unions and Community: The German Working Class in New York City, 1870–1900* (Urbana: University of Illinois Press, 1994).

13. Christine M. Rosen, *The Limits of Power: Great Fires and the Process of City Growth in America* (New York: Cambridge University Press, 1987), 109–120; and Karen Sawislak, *Smoldering City: Chicagoans and the Great Fire, 1871–1874* (Chicago: University of Chicago Press, 1995), 121–216. On responses to class conflict in Chicago from 1871 to 1894, see also Carl Smith, *Urban Disorder and the Shape of Belief: The Great Fire, The Haymarket Bomb, and the Model Town of Pullman* (Chicago: University of Chicago Press, 1995).

14. Daniel Bluestone, *Constructing Chicago* (New Haven: Yale University Press, 1991), 104–151; Berger, *They Built Chicago;* and Bruegmann, *Architects and the City.*

15. See Helen L. Horowitz, *Culture and the City: Cultural Philanthropy in Chicago from the 1880s to 1917* (Lexington: University Press of Kentucky, 1976); Kathleen D. McCarthy, *Noblesse Oblige: Charity and Cultural Philanthropy in Chicago, 1849–1929* (Chicago: University of Chicago Press, 1982); and Frederic C. Jaher, *The Urban Establishment: Upper Strata in Boston, New York, Charleston, Chicago, and Los Angeles* (Urbana: University of Illinois Press, 1982). See also Calvin Tompkins, *Merchants and Masterpieces: The Story of the Metropolitan Museum of Art*, rev. ed. (New York: H. Holt, 1989); and Nathaniel Burt, *Palaces for the People: A Social History of American Art Museums* (Boston: Little, Brown, 1977).

16. Harmut Keil and Heinz Ickstadt, "Elements of German Working-Class Culture in Chicago, 1880 to 1890," in *German Workers' Culture in the United States, 1850 to 1920*, ed. Hartmut Keil (Washington, D.C.: Smithsonian Institution Press, 1988), 82–83. See Keil and Jentz, *German Workers in Chicago,* 276–99.

17. On amusement and class in late nineteenth-century America, see Lewis Erenberg, *Steppin' Out: New York Nightlife and the Transformation of American Culture, 1890–1930* (Westport, Conn.: Greenwood Press, 1981); Roy Rosenzweig, *Eight Hours for What We Will: Workers and Leisure in an Industrial City, 1870–1920* (New York: Cambridge University Press, 1983); Peter Buckley, "'To the Opera House': Culture and Society in New York City, 1820–1860" (Ph.D. diss., State University of New York

at Stony Brook, 1984); Bruce A. McConachie and Daniel Friedman, eds., *Theatre for Working-Class Audiences in the United States, 1830–1980* (Westport, Conn.: Greenwood Press, 1985); Kathy Peiss, *Cheap Amusements: Working Women and Leisure in Turn-of-the-Century New York* (Philadelphia: Temple University Press, 1986); Lawrence L. Levine, *Highbrow/Lowbrow: The Emergence of Cultural Hierarchy in America* (Cambridge: Harvard University Press, 1988); Robert W. Snyder, *The Voice of the City: Vaudeville and Popular Culture in New York* (New York: Oxford University Press, 1989); Richard Butsch, ed., *For Fun and Profit: The Transformation of Leisure into Consumption* (Philadelphia: Temple University Press, 1990); John F. Kasson, *Rudeness and Civility: Manners in Nineteenth-Century Urban America* (New York: Hill and Wang, 1990), 215–256; James Gilbert, *Perfect Cities: Chicago's Utopias of 1893* (Chicago: University of Chicago Press, 1991); David Nasaw, *Going Out: The Rise and Fall of Public Amusements* (New York: Basic Books, 1993); Karen Ahlquist, *Democracy at the Opera: Music, Theater, and Culture in New York City, 1815–60* (Urbana: University of Illinois Press, 1997); Perry Duis, *Challenging Chicago: Coping with Everyday Life, 1837–1920* (Urbana: University of Illinois Press, 1998), 204–239; and Richard Butsch, *The Making of American Audiences: from Stage to Television, 1750–1990* (New York: Cambridge University Press, 2000).

Recent literature on class, amusement, and urban sites in England and France from the seventeenth to the nineteenth century includes Michèle Root-Bernstein, *Boulevard Theater and Revolution in Eighteenth-Century Paris* (Ann Arbor: UMI Research Press, 1984); Robert M. Isherwood, *Farce and Fantasy: Popular Entertainment in Eighteenth-Century Paris* (New York: Oxford University Press, 1986); Peter Bailey, ed., *Music Hall: The Business of Pleasure* (Philadelphia: Open University Press, 1986); Marc Baer, *Theatre and Disorder in Late Georgian London* (Oxford: Clarendon Press, 1992); F. W. J. Hemmings, *The Theatre Industry in Nineteenth-Century France* (New York: Cambridge University Press, 1993); W. Scott Haine, *The World of the Paris Café: Sociability among the French Working Class, 1789–1914* (Baltimore: Johns Hopkins University Press, 1996); Emmet Kennedy, *Theatre, Opera, and Audiences in Revolutionary Paris: Analysis and Repertory* (Westport, Conn.: Greenwood Press, 1996); Dagmar Kift, *The Victorian Music Hall: Culture, Class, and Conflict,* trans. Roy Kift (New York: Cambridge University Press, 1996); Peter Bailey, *Popular Culture and Performance in the Victorian City* (New York: Cambridge University Press, 1998); Vanessa R. Schwartz, *Spectacular Realities: Early Mass Culture in Fin-de-Siècle Paris* (Berkeley: University of California Press, 1998); André Michael Spies, *Opera, State and Society in the Third Republic, 1875–1914* (New York: P. Lang, 1998); Jeffrey S. Ravel, *The Contested Parterre: Public Theater and French Political Culture, 1680–1791* (Ithaca: Cornell University Press, 1999); and Janette Dillon, *Theatre, Court and City, 1595–1610: Drama and Social Space In London* (New York: Cambridge University Press, 2000). See also Hugh Cunningham, *Leisure in the Industrial Revolution: c. 1780–c. 1880* (New York: St. Martin's Press, 1980); and Chris Rojek, *Capitalism and Leisure Theory* (New York: Tavistock, 1985).

CHAPTER 1

1. On Chicago's theaters in the era of the Auditorium, see Andreas, *History of Chicago,* 3:658–673; Orear, *Commercial and Architectural Chicago,* 53–60; Albert N. Marquis, *Marquis' Hand-Book of Chicago: A Complete History Reference Book and Guide to the City* (Chicago: A. N. Marquis, 1887); Flinn, *Chicago, the Marvelous City of the West,* 120–128; Vynne, *Chicago by Day and Night,* 34–68; Rand McNally, *Bird's-Eye Views and Guide to Chicago,* 78–92; and Paul T. Gilbert and Charles L. Bryson, *Chicago and Its Makers* (Chicago: F. Mendelsohn, 1929), 144–150, 429, 431. See also Sandy R. Mazzola, "When Music Is Labor: Chicago Bands and Orchestras and the Origins of the Chicago Federation of Musicians, 1880–1902" (Ph.D. diss., Northern Illinois University, 1984). On Adler and Sullivan's remodelings of Chicago's principal theaters in the 1880s before the Auditorium, see chapter 2, note 2.

2. "Chicagoan, Head to Heels: Ferdinand Wythe Peck Is in All Ways to the Manor Born," *Chicago Sunday Chronicle,* 28 August 1898.

3. See "Death of P. F. W. Peck—Another One of the Old Settlers Gone," *Chicago Tribune,* 26

October 1871, 2. On Philip Ferdinand Wheeler Peck, see also Henry H. Hurlburt, *Chicago Antiquities* (Chicago: Fergus, 1881), 93, 113, 288, 290, 493, 505, 605; Andreas, *History of Chicago,* 1:115, 116, 132, 222, 223, 289, 303, 561; 2:327, 328, 568, 733; Kirkland and Kirkland, *Story of Chicago,* 2:482–484; *Album of Genealogy and Biography, Cook County, Illinois,* 1st ed. (Chicago: Calumet Book and Engraving, 1895), 533–536; Arba N. Waterman, *Historical Review of Chicago and Cook County, and Selected Biography,* 3 vols. (Chicago: Lewis, 1908), 3:924–926; Josiah Seymour Currey, *Chicago: Its History and Its Builders, a Century of Marvelous Growth,* 5 vols. (Chicago: S. J. Clarke, 1912), 1:227–229, 269, 317, 5:352–357; Felix Mendelsohn, *Chicago Yesterday and Today* (Chicago: F. Mendelsohn, 1932), 1027; and Gilbert and Bryson, *Chicago and Its Makers,* 1037. On Philip Peck and his contemporaries, see Craig Buettinger, "The Concept of Jacksonian Aristocracy: Chicago as a Test Case, 1833–1857" (Ph.D. diss., Northwestern University, 1982). See also Erne R. Frueh, "Retail Merchandising in Chicago, 1833–1848," *Journal of the Illinois State Historical Society* 32 (June 1939): 149–172.

Adler and Sullivan's business block for Walter and Clarence Peck at 169–175 South Water Street on the southeast corner with LaSalle was noted in *Inland Architect and News Record* 7 (February 1886); *Building Budget,* February 1886, 24; *Building Budget,* March 1886; "The City," *Chicago Tribune,* 22 March 1886, 6; *Building Budget,* May 1886, 58; *Inland Architect and News Record* 7 (May 1886): 75; and Morrison, *Louis Sullivan,* 62. A photograph is in Gilbert and Bryson, *Chicago and Its Makers,* 229, which incorrectly identified the building as on the southwest (rather than the southeast) corner. On the LaSalle–Wacker Building, in which one of Philip Peck's grandsons played a major role, see "Begin Work on 37-Story Shaft at LaSalle and Wacker," *Chicago Tribune,* 2 September 1928, pt. 3, p. 1; "New Portal to Money Lane to Be Forty Stories," *Chicago Tribune,* 26 May 1929, pt. 3, p. 1; "City's Fastest Elevators for New Skyscraper," *Chicago Tribune,* 29 September 1929, pt. 3, p. 7; and Robert Bruegmann, *Holabird and Roche and Holabird and Root: An Illustrated Catalog of Works, 1880–1940,* 3 vols. (New York: Garland, 1991), vol. 2, entry 1093, pp. 364–368.

4. See James William Putnam, *The Illinois and Michigan Canal: A Study in Economic History* (Chicago: University of Chicago Press, 1918); George J. Fleming, "Canal at Chicago: A Study in Political and Social History" (Ph.D. diss., Catholic University of America, 1951); Homer N. Hoyt, *One Hundred Years of Land Values in Chicago: The Relationship of the Growth of Chicago to the Rise in Its Land Values, 1830–1930* (Chicago: University of Chicago Press, 1933), 10–13; James W. Piety, "The Illinois and Michigan Canal and the Early Historical Geography of Chicago," *Geographical Perspectives* 47 (1981): 30–37; Robin L. Einhorn, *Property Rules: Political Economy in Chicago, 1833–1872* (Chicago: University of Chicago Press, 1991), 30–39; and Robert G. Spinney, *City of Big Shoulders: A History of Chicago* (Dekalb: Northern Illinois University Press, 2000), 32–25.

5. "Chicagoan, Head to Heels," *Chicago Sunday Chronicle,* 28 August 1898, and Currey, *Chicago: Its History and Its Builders,* 5:356. On local effects of the Panic of 1837, see Andreas, *History of Chicago,* 1:168–171, and Hoyt, *Land Values in Chicago,* 37–44. See also Patrick E. McLear, "Land Speculators and Urban and Regional Development: Chicago in the 1830s," *Old Northwest* 6 (summer 1980): 137–151; and Edward W. Wolner, "The City Builder in Chicago, 1834–1871," *Old Northwest* 13 (1987): 3–22.

6. Kirkland and Kirkland, *Story of Chicago,* 2:484. Philip Peck's retirement from active trade was noted in Buettinger, "Concept of Jacksonian Aristocracy," 98. Assessment rolls for property taxes in 1849 and 1850 were handwritten by the Chicago city clerk in three ledger books, one each for the North, South, and West Divisions. These books survive in the Manuscripts and Archives Collection, Chicago Historical Society. The data they contain are cited and analyzed in Buettinger, "Concept of Jacksonian Aristocracy," 19–29. At his death, Philip Peck's real estate holdings (by then all in Chicago) and their assessed values were listed in "Inventory of the Real and Personal Estate of Philip F. W. Peck, late of the City of Chicago, in the County of Cook and State of Illinois, deceased," filed 7 February 1872, County Court of Cook County, docket A, p. 5, Probate Records, Estate of Philip Ferdinand Peck (Clerk of the Circuit Court of Cook County Archives, Chicago, Illinois). The document also details Peck's personal estate (stocks, bonds, loans, etc.) of $1,250,000.

7. Buettinger, "Concept of Jacksonian Aristocracy," 10.

8. John Van Osdel Account Books, Manuscripts and Archives, Chicago Historical Society, noted in vol. 1, 1856–1868, the P. F. W. Peck Store, South Water Street (1860); P. F. W. Peck Building, Wabash Avenue (1868); and in vol. 2, 1868–1886, a building for P. F. W. Peck, Wabash Avenue near Washington (1872). On Van Osdel's work for P. F. W. Peck, see Henry L. Ericsson, *Sixty Years a Builder: The Autobiography of Henry Ericsson* (Chicago: A Kroch, 1942; reprint, New York, 1972), 124, 176, 197, 197, 200. Buettinger, "Concept of Jacksonian Aristocracy," 92, notes Peck's key holdings and buildings to 1857 as 159–161 Lake Street (acquired 1841, built 1853), 167–169 Lake Street (acquired 1841, built 1855), and 105 South Water Street (acquired 1844, built 1844).

9. In 1890 the Peck estate was exceeded by only three private fortunes in Chicago: those of Marshall Field ($25,000,000), Philip D. Armour ($25,000,000), and George M. Pullman ($15,000,000). Potter Palmer and Mrs. Cyrus H. McCormick also had wealth estimated at $10,000,000. See "The Men of Millions," *Chicago Tribune*, 6 April 1890, 25–26. Central properties owned by Peck family members in the original town of Chicago were listed with valuations in [Illinois Bureau of Labor Statistics], *Ninth Annual Report of the Bureau of Labor Statistics of Illinois: Subject, Franchises and Taxation, 1896* (Springfield, Ill., 1897), part 2, Taxation.

10. On Mary Kent Wythe Peck, see "Mrs. P. F. W. Peck Dead," *Chicago Tribune*, 24 September 1899, 8. Her marriage was noted in *Chicago [Daily] American,* 27 June 1835, 3. See Pierce, *History of Chicago,* 1:281 n. 82. On the Peck House at LaSalle and Washington Streets, see Thomas E. Tallmadge, *Architecture in Old Chicago* (Chicago: University of Chicago Press, 1941), 49. Mrs. Ferdinand W. Peck Jr. recalled that the family tradition was that the brick for this house had been imported from England. See Edward Lee Michael, "Adler and Sullivan's Palace of Trade: The Chicago Stock Exchange Building," seminar paper for Professor Paul E. Sprague, University of Chicago, spring 1972, 35. A copy of this paper is in the Richard Nickel files, Office of John Vinci, AIA, Chicago. Another report noted that the bricks were brought into the city by ship, indicating that Chicago then had no brickyards. "Temple of Finance," *Chicago Evening Post,* 30 April 1894, 2. On the Chicago Stock Exchange Building, see chapter 6, ?-?. Accounts of Ferdinand Peck's life include "Ferdinand W. Peck," in *The Biographical Dictionary and Portrait Gallery of Representative Men of Chicago, Minnesota Cities and the World's Columbian Exposition* (Chicago: American Biographical Publishing, 1892), 106–109; C. Dean, *The World's Fair City and Her Enterprising Sons* (Chicago: United, 1892), 36–74; John J. Flinn, *Hand-Book of Chicago Biography* (Chicago: Standard Guide, 1893), 283–284; *Album of Genealogy and Biography, Cook County, Illinois,* 2d ed. (Chicago: Calumet Book and Engraving, 1895), 339–341; John Moses and Joseph Kirkland, eds., *History of Chicago, Illinois,* 2 vols. (Chicago: Munsell, 1895), 2:660–661; "Chicagoan, Head to Heels," *Chicago Sunday Chronicle,* 28 August 1898; Waterman, *Historical Review of Chicago and Cook County,* 3:926–930; Currey, *Chicago: Its History and Its Builders,* 3:4–8; "Ferdinand Peck, Widely Known Chicagoan, Dies," *Chicago Tribune,* 5 November 1924, 19; Gilbert and Bryson, *Chicago and Its Makers,* 625; and Berger, *They Built Chicago,* 93–104. Michael, "Adler and Sullivan's Palace of Trade," 43 n. 53, wrote that Mrs. Ferdinand Wythe Peck Jr. informed him that all of the Pecks' private and business papers were destroyed when the Peck estate vacated its offices in the (south) Monadnock Building. Ferdinand W. Peck Jr. died in 1960. "F. W. Peck Jr., Pioneer's Son, Dies at Age 88," *Chicago Tribune,* 19 January 1960, pt. 1, p. 25.

11. Ferdinand W. Peck, quoted in "Christmas Recollections of Noted Chicagoans," *Chicago Tribune,* 25 December 1892, 32. On the Peck estate's sale of its half of the Grand Pacific's site to Levi Z. Leiter, see "Chicago Real Estate," *Chicago Tribune,* 28 November 1886, 7. See also Waterman, *Chicago and Cook County,* 3:926. On Leiter's control of the property, see Harold M. Mayer and Richard C. Wade, *Chicago: Growth of a Metropolis* (Chicago: University of Chicago Press, 1969), 225.

12. Buettinger, "Concept of Jacksonian Aristocracy," 22, and Buettinger, "Economic Inequality in Early Chicago, 1849–1850," *Journal of Social History* 11 (spring 1978): 414, cited in Einhorn, *Property Rules,* 249. On Michigan Terrace, see Andreas, *History of Chicago,* 2:733, and Bluestone, *Constructing*

Chicago, 75–78. In 1891 one local observer recalled that in the 1850s "the corner of Michigan avenue and Congress street was occupied then as at present with one of the finest buildings in the city. Where the Auditorium now stands a four-story marble front residence block known as Terrace row was built. The public acknowledged its opinion of the owner's temerity in erecting such a building by calling it 'crazy row'" ("Advances Made in Thirty Years," *Chicago Tribune,* 12 July 1891, 14). On the lakefront, see Einhorn, "A Taxing Dilemma: Early Lake Shore Protection," *Chicago History* 18 (fall 1989): 34–51.

13. On the strike of 1853, see Buettinger, "Concept of Jacksonian Aristocracy," 14–15, referencing *Chicago Daily Democratic Press,* 9 August 1853, 2; and *Weekly Chicago Democrat,* 13 August 1853, 2. On Dearborn Park, see Perry R. Duis, "Yesterday's City: Dearborn Park," *Chicago History* 15 (winter 1986–1987): 66–69, and Bluestone, *Constructing Chicago,* 12–17. On Ferdinand Peck's effort to site the Auditorium at Dearborn Park, see chapter 3, 124.

14. Mabel McIlvaine, *Reminiscences of Chicago during the Forties and Fifties* (Chicago: Lakeside Press, 1913), xviii. On the Pecks and Chicago's earliest religious life, see Jeremiah Porter, *The Earliest Religious History of Chicago* (Chicago: Fergus, 1881), 55, 57–58, 67, 70; Philo Adams Otis, *First Presbyterian Church, 1833–1913: A History of the Oldest Organization in Chicago,* 2d ed. (Chicago: F. H. Revell, 1913), 29. See also Anthony F. C. Wallace, "Prelude to Disaster: The Course of Indian-White Relations Which Led to the Black Hawk War of 1832," *Wisconsin Magazine of History* 65 (1982): 247–88; Anselm J. Gerwing, "The Chicago Indian Treaty of 1833," *Journal of the Illinois State Historical Society* 57 (1964): 117–142; and James A. Clifford, "Chicago, September 14, 1833: The Last Great Indian Treaty in the Old Northwest," *Chicago History* 9 (summer 1980): 86–97.

15. Jaher, *Urban Establishment,* 463, and Donald S. Bradley and Mayer N. Zald, "From Commercial Elite to Political Administrator: The Recruitment of the Mayors of Chicago," *American Journal of Sociology* 71 (1966): 154–160.

16. John J. Flinn, *History of the Chicago Police from the Settlement of the Community to the Present Time* (1887; reprint, Montclair, N.J.: Patterson Smith, 1973), 73. See also Richard W. Renner, "In a Perfect Ferment: Chicago, the Know-Nothings, and the Riot for Lager Beer," *Chicago History* 5 (fall 1976): 161–179; Bruce C. Levine, "Free Soil, Free Labor, and Freimänner: German Chicago in the Civil War Era," in *German Workers in Industrial Chicago, 1850–1910: A Comparative Perspective,* ed. Hartmut Keil and John B. Jentz, 163–182 (De Kalb: Northern Illinois University Press, 1983), and Levine, *The Spirit of 1848: German Immigrants, Labor Conflict, and the Coming of the Civil War* (Urbana: University of Illinois Press, 1992).

17. Flinn, *History of the Chicago Police,* 73–79. See also Pierce, *History of Chicago,* 2:437–438. On the formation of early German communities in American cities, see Kathleen N. Conzen, "Immigrants, Immigrant Neighborhoods, and Ethnic Identity: Historical Issues," *Journal of American History* 66 (December 1979): 603–615; Harzig, "Chicago's German North Side, 1880–1900: The Structure of a Gilded Age Ethnic Neighborhood," in *German Workers in Industrial Chicago, 1850–1910: A Comparative Perspective,* ed. Hartmut Keil and John B. Jentz (De Kalb: Northern Illinois University Press, 1983), 127–144; and Harzig, "Creating a Community: German-American Women in Chicago," in *Peasant Maids, City Women: From the European Countryside to Urban America,* ed. Christiane Harzig (Ithaca: Cornell University Press, 1997), 185–222.

18. Isaac N. Arnold, quoted in Byron York, "The Pursuit of Culture: Founding the Chicago Historical Society, 1856," *Chicago History* 10 (fall 1981): 141. On Chicagoans' need to attract outside capital, see Rima L. Schultz, "The Businessman's Role in Western Settlement: The Entrepreneurial Frontier, Chicago, 1833–1872" (Ph.D. diss., Boston University, 1985), 184.

19. On Rice's Theater, see James H. McVicker, *The Theatre: Its Early Days in Chicago* (Chicago: Knight and Leonard, 1884); Andreas, *History of Chicago,* 1:484–494, 2:596–597; James N. Wilt, "The History of the Two Rice Theatres in Chicago from 1847 to 1857" (Ph.D. diss., University of Chicago, 1923); and Gilbert and Bryson, *Chicago and Its Makers,* 102–103. On the River and Harbor Convention, see

Robert Fergus, comp., *Chicago River-and-Harbor Convention*, Fergus Historical Series 18 (Chicago: Fergus, 1882); Pierce, *History of Chicago*, 1:394–397; Carl Abbott, *Boosters and Businessmen: Popular Economic Thought and Urban Growth in the Antebellum Middle West* (Westport, Conn.: Greenwood Press, 1981), 132–133; and Einhorn, *Property Rules*, 63–66.

20. Rudolf A. Hofmeister, *The Germans of Chicago* (Champaign, Ill.: Stipes, 1976), 239–240, citing Esther Marie Olson, "The German Theater in Chicago," *Deutsch-Amerikanische Geschichtsblätter* 33 (1937): 74–75. See also Heinrich Kenkel, "Der Bau des 'Deutschen Hauses' und die Gründung des 'Theaters' in Chicago," in *Deutsch-Amerikanische Geschichtsblätter* 3 (1901): 38–43. On Adler and Sullivan's Schiller Theater Building, see chapter 6, 340–358.

21. On McVicker's first theater, see Andreas, *History of Chicago*, 2:597–601; Lois M. Bergstrom, "The History of McVicker's Theatre, 1857–1861" (M.A. thesis, University of Chicago, 1930); and Jay F. Ludwig, "McVicker's Theatre, 1857–1896" (Ph.D. diss., University of Illinois, 1958), 22–28.

22. *Chicago Tribune*, 6 November 1857, quoted in William C. Young, *Documents of American Theater History*, vol. 1, *Famous American Playhouses, 1716–1899* (Chicago: American Library Association, 1973), 175.

23. On the Chicago Board of Trade's fundamental role in managing Chicago's grain trade, see William Cronon, *Nature's Metropolis: Chicago and the Great West* (New York: W. W. Norton, 1991), 114–119. On the Chicago, Rock Island, and Pacific Railway and its bridging of the Mississippi, see Andreas, *History of Chicago*, 2:148–151, and Pierce, *History of Chicago*, 2:40–41. See also Wyatt W. Belcher, *The Economic Rivalry between St. Louis and Chicago, 1850–1880* (New York: Columbia University Press, 1947), 55–71; John F. Stover, *History of the Illinois Central Railroad* (New York: Macmillan, 1975), 31–84; and Stover, "The Illinois Central and the Growth of Illinois and Chicago in the 1850s," *Railroad History* 159 (1988): 39–50.

24. On Edwin Booth in *Richard III* at McVicker's in spring 1858, see Andreas, *History of Chicago*, 2:599. *Richard III* was then one of Shakespeare's most frequently presented plays in the United States. Its antiroyalist political themes were highly appealing to antebellum American audiences, whose knowledge of the Shakespearean canon had impressed foreign visitors. See Levine, *Highbrow/Lowbrow*, 14, 18, 19. In addition to Bergstrom and Ludwig (see note 21 above), accounts of McVicker's life appeared in many obituaries, such as "J. H. McVicker Dead," *Chicago Inter Ocean*, 8 March 1896, 1–3. On the Booths, see most recently Gene Smith, *American Gothic: The Story of America's Legendary Theatrical Family—Junius, Edwin, and John Wilkes Booth* (New York: Simon and Schuster, 1992).

25. On Chicago's economic growth during and immediately after the Civil War, see Hoyt, *Land Values in Chicago*, 81–88. On growth of local manufacturing in this period, see Elmer Riley, "The Development of Chicago and Vicinity as a Manufacturing Center prior to 1880" (Ph.D. diss., University of Chicago, 1911); Pierce, *History of Chicago*, 2:112–117; David R. Meyer, "Midwestern Industrialization and the American Manufacturing Belt in the Nineteenth Century," *Journal of Economic History* 59 (December 1989): 921–935; and Theodore J. Karamanski, *Rally 'Round the Flag: Chicago and the Civil War* (Chicago: Nelson-Hall, 1993), 159–178. On prefire urban development related to this wartime boom, see also Elias Colbert, *Chicago and the Great Conflagration* (Cincinnati: C. F. Vent, 1872).

26. *Industrial Chicago*, 1:108. See also "The Opera Inauguration Night," *Chicago Tribune*, 21 April 1865, 4, reprinted in Young, *Documents of American Theater History*, 1:188–190; Andreas, *History of Chicago*, 2:601–607; Florence Ffrench, *Music and Musicians in Chicago* (Chicago: Florence Ffrench, 1899), 14–16; George P. Upton, *Musical Memories: My Recollections of Celebrities of the Half Century 1850–1900* (Chicago: A. C. McClurg, 1908), 237–252; Randall, *Building Construction in Chicago*, 48–49; Ronald L. Davis, *Opera in Chicago* (New York: Appleton-Century, 1965), 17–31; Dizikes, *Opera in America*, 247–248; Karyl L. Zietz, *The National Trust Guide to Great Opera Houses in America* (New York: Preservation Press/John Wiley, 1996), 31–32; and Eugene H. Cropsey, *Crosby's Opera House: Symbol of Chicago's Cultural Awakening* (Cranbury, N.J.: Fairleigh Dickinson University Press, 1999).

27. "What Old-Timers Will Think," *Chicago Tribune,* 10 December 1889, 3.

28. Andreas, *History of Chicago,* 2:601.

29. Ibid. In Italy, Crosby and Boyington visited the Teatro Reale di San Carlo in Naples, the Teatro Regio in Parma, the Teatro Regio in Turin, and the Teatro della Pergola in Florence, but not La Scala in Milan. See Cropsey, *Crosby's Opera House,* 51–52, whose account of this trip is based on notes from oral histories preserved in the Crosby family.

30. See Richard Moody, *The Astor Place Riot* (Bloomington: Indiana University Press, 1958); Buckley, "'To the Opera House'"; Bruce A. McConachie, "New York Operagoing, 1825–50: Creating an Elite Social Ritual," *American Music* 6 (summer 1988): 181–192; Kasson, *Rudeness and Civility,* 222–228; and Ahlquist, *Democracy at the Opera,* 133–42.

31. James V. Kavenaugh, "Three American Opera Houses: The Boston Theatre, the New York Academy of Music, the Philadelphia American Academy of Music" (Ph.D. diss., University of Delaware, 1967), 28–51; Dizikes, *Opera in America,* 166–167; Robert A. M. Stern, Thomas Mellins, and David Fishman, *New York 1880: Architecture and Urbanism in the Gilded Age* (New York: Monacelli Press, 1999), 678–681. On theatrical culture and architecture in New York City in the eighteenth and early nineteenth centuries, see Mary C. Henderson, *The City and the Theatre: New York Playhouses from Bowling Green to Times Square* (Clifton, N.J.: James T. White, 1973); Young, *Documents in American Theater History,* vol. 1; Buckley, "'To the Opera House'"; and Ahlquist, *Democracy at the Opera.* On operatic culture in New York, see Richard Grant White, "Opera in New York," *Century Magazine* 23 (March 1882): 686–703; 23 (April 1882): 865–882; 24 (May 1882): 31–43; 24 (June 1882): 193–210; George C. D. Odell, *Annals of the New York Stage, 1815–1925,* 15 vols. (New York: Columbia University Press, 1927–1949); and Levine, *Highbrow/Lowbrow,* 85–104. On moral concerns in New York City about operas of Verdi and Offenbach in the 1850s and 1860s, see Dizikes, *Opera in America,* 171–173, 193–194.

32. On the amusement district on Broadway near New York's Academy of Music, see M. Christine Boyer, *Manhattan Manners: Architecture and Style, 1850–1900* (New York: Rizzoli, 1985), 62–73. See also John Frick, "The Rialto: A Study of Union Square, the Center of New York's First Theatre District, 1870–1900" (Ph.D. diss., New York University, 1983). On New York City's amusement districts about 1900, see Snyder, *Voice of the City,* 82–103.

33. On European court and public theaters to the 1850s, the major source is Joseph de Filippi and Clément Contant, *Parallèle des principaux théâtres modernes de l'Europe et des machines théâtrales françaises, allemandes et anglaises* (1860; New York: B. Blom, 1968). On later nineteenth-century theaters, see Edwin O. Sachs and Ernest A. F. Woodrow, *Modern Opera Houses and Theatres,* 3 vols. (London: B. T. Batsford, 1896–1898). Recently, see Tidworth, *Theatres;* Sir Nikolaus Pevsner, *A History of Building Types* (Princeton: Princeton University Press, 1976); Izenour, *Theater Design;* and Marvin Carlson, *Places of Performance: The Semiotics of Theatre Architecture* (Ithaca: Cornell University Press, 1989). On La Scala's architecture, in addition to the sources above, see Giuseppe Piermarini, *Teatro della Scala in Milano* (Milan, 1789); James Fergusson, *History of the Modern Styles of Architecture,* 2 vols. (1862; 3d ed., New York: Dodd, Mead, 1891), 2:387–389; Gianni Mezzanotte, *L'architettura della Scala nell'età neoclassica* (Milan, 1982); and Forsyth, *Buildings for Music,* 96–100. On E. M. Barry's Covent Garden, see Harold D. Rosenthal, *Two Centuries of Opera at Covent Garden* (London: Putnam, 1958), 117–119, and Richard Leacroft, *The Development of the English Playhouse* (Ithaca: Cornell University Press, 1973), 221–230. On the Opéra National, see Jane Fulcher, *The Nation's Image: French Opera as Politics and Politicized Art* (Princeton: Princeton University Press, 1976), 113–121, 171, and T. J. Walsh, *Second Empire Opera: The Théâtre Lyrique, Paris, 1851–1870* (New York: Riverrun Press, 1981), 1–12, 149–162.

34. Alexander Sältzer, *A Treatise on Acoustics in Connection with Ventilation* (New York: D. Van Nostrand, 1872), 21–22. Carl Ferdinand Langhans (1782–1869) was the son of Carl Gotthard Langhans (1733–1808), who built the National Theater in Berlin of 1801–1802, replaced by Karl Friedrich Schinkel's theater of 1818–1821. Carl F. Langhans's earlier treatise cited by Sältzer was titled *Über Theater, oder*

Bemerkungen über Katacoustics (Berlin, 1810). On Carl F. Langhans's remodeling of Knobelsdorff's Opera House after a fire, see Louis Schneider, *Geschichte der Oper und des königlichen Opernhauses in Berlin, mit den architektonischen Plänen des 1740 vom Freiherrn von Knobelsdorf und des 1844 vom königlichen Ober-Bau-Rath Langhans neuerbauten Berliner Opernhauses* (Berlin, 1852).

35. Sältzer, *Treatise on Acoustics*, 19, 20, 34. Earlier European treatises on architectural acoustics included Pierre Patte, *Essai sur l'architecture théâtrale* (Paris, 1782); George Saunders, *A Treatise on Theatres* (London, 1790); Johann G. Rhode, *Theorie der Verbreitung des Schalles für Baukünstler* (Berlin, 1800); and Ernst F. Chladni, *Traité d'acoustique* (Paris, 1809). On Scott Russell's papers on acoustics, see note 128 below. American studies included Jabez B. Upham, *Acoustic Architecture* (New Haven, Conn.: B. L. Hamlen, 1853).

36. Levine, *Highbrow/Lowbrow*, 86.

37. Kavenaugh, "Three American Opera Houses," 46–47.

38. "The Great Fire," *New York Times*, 23 May 1866.

39. *Crosby Opera House Art Association: Its Plan and Objects* (n.p., [1866?]), 34 (Chicago Historical Society).

40. Andreas, *History of Chicago*, 2:557–559.

41. "What Old-Timers Will Think," *Chicago Tribune*, 10 December 1889, 3.

42. Ibid. On meetings of Chicago's public school teachers at Crosby's Opera House, see Katherine Morgan, "'We Do Have to Work Hard,'" *Chicago History* 26 (spring 1997): 34. On Grant's and Sherman's feted attendance at Crosby's Opera House on 12 June 1865, see Davis, *Opera in Chicago*, 23–24. On Grant's nomination there in 1868, see John Tweedy, *A History of the Republican National Conventions from 1856 to 1908* (Danbury, Conn.: J. Tweedy, 1910), 88–89, William Starr Myers, *The Republican Party: A History* (New York: Century, 1928), 180–185; and R. Craig Sautter and Edward M. Burke, *Inside the Wigwam: Chicago Presidential Conventions, 1860–1896* (Chicago: Wild Onion Books, 1996), 28–32.

43. Amasa McCoy, "Appeal for the Fine Arts in the Republic," an address delivered at the Artists' Reception, Crosby's Opera House, 26 March 1866, 20 (Chicago Historical Society).

44. *Crosby's Opera House, Inauguration Season of the Grand Italian Opera*, Director, J. Grau, 17 April 1865, 10 (Chicago Historical Society).

45. Arthur Meeker, *Chicago, with Love: A Polite and Personal History* (New York: Knopf, 1955), 223.

46. "The Opera: Inauguration Night," *Chicago Tribune*, 21 April 1865, 4.

47. *Crosby's Opera House, Inauguration Season of the Grand Italian Opera*, Director, J. Grau, 17 April 1865, 5 (Chicago Historical Society).

48. Quoted in Pierce, *History of Chicago*, 2:171. On the West Side labor hall of 1864, see "The New Hall of the West Side Social Workers Association," *Illinois Staats-Zeitung*, 13 October 1864, translated and quoted in Keil and Jentz, *German Workers in Chicago*, 237–238. On the formation of a multiethnic, politically contentious working class in Chicago from 1864 to the early 1870s, see Schneirov, *Labor and Urban Politics*, 17–40.

49. Andreas, *History of Chicago*, 2:603. See also Harry Hansen, "How to Give away an Opera House," *Journal of the Illinois State Historical Society* 39 (December 1946): 419–424, and Cropsey, *Crosby's Opera House*.

50. Andreas, *History of Chicago*, 2:607.

51. On Rice's mayoral support for propertied interests, and changes in local voting laws as of February 1865, see Pierce, *History of Chicago*, 2:175, and Einhorn, *Property Rules*, 1–2, 248. On Chicago's first period of unethical "ring" politics of 1863–1869, based on labor support, see Schneirov, *Labor and Urban Politics*, 46–49. See also Dick Simpson, *Rogues, Rebels, and Rubber Stamps: The Politics of the Chicago City Council from 1863 to the Present* (Boulder, Colo.: Westview Press, 2000).

52. *Illinois Staats-Zeitung*, 2 and 3 May 1867, translated in Keil and Jentz, *German Workers in Chicago*, 254. See also *Chicago Tribune*, 2 May 1867, quoted in Pierce, *History of Chicago*, 2:177. On the international May Day, see Lewis L. Lorwin, *Labor and Internationalism* (New York: Macmillan, 1929), 71, and Hubert Perrier and Michel Cordillot, "Aux origines du premier mai: Les événements de 1886 à Chicago et leur répercussions internationales," *Cahiers d'Histoire de l'Institute de Recherches Marxistes* 33 (1988): 85–116.

53. On Peck's education and brief law practice, see Flinn, *Hand-Book of Chicago Biography*, 283; *Album of Genealogy and Biography, Cook County, Illinois*, 2d ed., 339; and Gilbert and Bryson, *Chicago and Its Makers*, 625. On old Chicago University and its Union College of Law, see Andreas, *History of Chicago*, 2:460–461, and Kirkland and Moses, *History of Chicago*, 2:116–117. His wife, Mrs. Tilla C. Peck, had an obituary in *Chicago Tribune*, 22 April 1944, 8. On her social life, see also Berger, *They Built Chicago*, 102. On her adoptive father, William A. Spalding (1815–1892), see *Album of Genealogy and Biography, Cook County, Illinois*, 2d ed., 381–382.

54. "Death of P. F. W. Peck—Another One of the Old Settlers Gone," *Chicago Tribune*, 26 October 1871, 2. Andreas, *History of Chicago*, 2:733, quoted the fire narrative of H. W. S. Cleaveland: "The fire had already worked so far south and east as to attack the stables in the rear of Terrace Row, between Van Buren and Congress Streets. Many friends rushed into the houses in the block, and helped to carry out heavy furniture, such as pianos and bookcases. We succeeded in carrying the bulk of it to the shore. There I sat with a few others by our household goods, calmly awaiting the destruction of our property— one of the most splendid blocks in Chicago."

55. On changing percentages of non-native-born in Chicago, see Einhorn, *Property Rules*, 248.

56. On the local elite's withdrawal from urban politics, see Helen L. Horowitz, "The Art Institute of Chicago: The First Forty Years," *Chicago History* 8 (spring 1979): 5; Jaher, *Urban Establishment*, 505; Robin L. Einhorn, "The Civil War and Municipal Government in Chicago," in *Toward a Social History of the American Civil War: Exploratory Essays*, ed. Maris A. Vinovskis (New York: Cambridge University Press, 1990), 117–138; and John B. Jentz, "Class and Politics in an Emerging Industrial City: Chicago in the 1860s and 1870s," *Journal of Urban History* 17 (May 1991): 227–263. On elite efforts at local political reform after 1871, see Sidney I. Roberts, "Businessmen in Revolt: Chicago, 1874–1900" (Ph.D. diss., Northwestern University, 1960).

57. *Industrial Chicago*, 1:157.

58. On Chicago's Inter-state Industrial Exposition Building, see "Exposition," *Chicago Tribune*, 25 September 1873, 5–8; Everett Chamberlain, "The Chicago of the Visitor," *Lakeside Monthly* 10 (October 1873): 272–277; *The Inter-state Exposition Souvenir: Containing a Historical Sketch of Chicago and a Record of the Great Inter-state Exposition of 1873* (Chicago: Van Arsdale and Massie, 1873); Andreas, *History of Chicago*, 3:655–657; Pierce, *History of Chicago*, 3:18–19, 475; Horowitz, *Culture and the City*, 36–39; and Perry Duis, "Yesterday's City: The Lakefront: Chicago's Selling Point," *Chicago History* 17 (1988): 106–108.

59. "Exposition," *Chicago Tribune*, 25 September 1873, 5.

60. Ibid.

61. Chamberlain, "Chicago of the Visitor," 275.

62. Ibid., 274. On Union Hall, the Northwestern Sanitary Commission, and its fair of May 1865, see Karamanski, *Rally 'Round the Flag*, 93–132, 236, and Sarah E. Henshaw, *Our Branch and Its Tributaries: A History of the Work of the Northwestern Sanitary Commission* (Chicago, 1868).

63. Chamberlain, "Chicago of the Visitor," 276.

64. "Exposition," *Chicago Tribune*, 25 September 1873, 5.

65. Ibid., 7.

66. Ibid., 5.

67. D. A. Gage, quoted in ibid., 7.

68. "The Exposition," *Chicago Tribune,* 18 November 1877, 7. See John D. Kysela, S.J., "Sara Hallowell Brings 'Modern Art' to the Midwest," *Art Quarterly* 27 (1964): 150–155; Andreas, *History of Chicago,* 3:655; "Art at the Exposition," *Chicago Inter Ocean,* 30 August 1879, 3; "The Exposition," *Chicago Inter Ocean,* 4 September 1879, 8; *1883 Catalogue of the Art Hall of the InterState Industrial Exposition* (Chicago Historical Society); Horowitz, *Culture and the City,* 37–38; and Stefan Germer, "Pictures at an Exhibition," *Chicago History* 16 (1987): 4–21.

69. "Exposition," *Chicago Tribune,* 25 September 1873, 5.

70. See Chicago Relief and Aid Society, *Report of the Chicago Relief and Aid Society of Disbursements of Contributions for the Sufferers by the Chicago Fire* (Cambridge, Mass., 1874); Otto M. Nelson, "The Chicago Relief and Aid Society, 1850–1874," *Journal of the Illinois State Historical Society* 59 (1966): 48–66; and Sawislak, *Smoldering City,* 69–119.

71. *Chicago Tribune,* 23 December 1873, 1, quoted in Nelson, *Beyond the Martyrs,* 53. See also Smith, *Urban Disorder and the Shape of Belief,* 104; Pierce, *History of Chicago,* 3:239–42; and "The History of the Development of the Labor Movement in Chicago," *Vorbote,* 4 and 18 May 1887, excerpts translated in Keil and Jentz, *German Workers in Chicago,* 226–227.

72. Richard Schneirov, "Class Conflict, Municipal Politics, and Governmental Reform in Gilded Age Chicago, 1871–1875," in *German Workers in Industrial Chicago, 1850–1910: A Comparative Perspective,* ed. Hartmut Keil and John B. Jentz (De Kalb: Northern Illinois University Press, 1983), 187–188. On postfire urban rebuilding, see Pierce, *History of Chicago,* 3:308–309; Rosen, *Limits of Power,* 92–176; and Sawislak, *Smoldering City,* 121–162.

73. Schneirov, "Class Conflict, Municipal Politics, and Governmental Reform," 192–196, and Roberts, "Businessmen in Revolt," 1–11. See also Schneirov, *Labor and Urban Politics,* 53–63; Jonathan J. Keyes, "The Forgotten Fire," *Chicago History* 26 (fall 1997): 52–65; and Nelson, *Beyond the Martyrs,* 53–54.

74. President Franklin MacVeagh, Address, 11 September 1874, in *Addresses and Reports of the Citizens' Association of Chicago; 1874 to 1876* (Chicago, 1876), 5, quoted in Schneirov, "Class Conflict, Municipal Politics, and Governmental Reform," 194. See also "Citizens' Association," *Chicago Tribune,* 1 August 1874, 2.

75. "The Communists," *Chicago Tribune,* 24 February 1875, 7, quoted in Schneirov, "Class Conflict, Municipal Politics, and Governmental Reform," 194. See Holdridge O. Collins, *History of the Illinois National Guard, from the Organization of the First Regiment in September, 1874, to the Enactment of the Military Code, in May 1879* (Chicago, 1884), 17; Andreas, *History of Chicago,* 3:585; Henry L. Turner, *Souvenir Album and Sketchbook: First Infantry, Illinois National Guard of Chicago* (Chicago, 1890), 7; and Roy Turnbaugh, "Ethnicity, Civic Pride, and Commitment: The Evolution of the Chicago Militia," *Journal of the Illinois State Historical Society* 62 (May 1979): 111–112.

76. Charles H. Ham, "The Chicago Auditorium Building," *Harper's Weekly* 31 (2 July 1887): 471. On Peck and the Citizens' Association, see Jaher, *Urban Establishment,* 505. He was listed on the executive committee in *Annual Report of the Citizens' Association of Chicago, October 1877,* and *Annual Report of the Citizens' Association of Chicago, October 1879.*

77. Waterman, *Chicago and Cook County,* 3:929.

78. Gilbert and Bryson, *Chicago and Its Makers,* 625. See also Dean, *World's Fair City,* 71, and Sullivan, *Autobiography of an Idea,* 292, 293.

79. "Chicagoan, Head to Heels," *Chicago Sunday Chronicle,* 28 August 1898.

80. Sullivan, *Autobiography of an Idea,* 204–205. See Donald D. Egbert and Paul E. Sprague, "In Search of John Edelmann: Architect and Anarchist," *American Institute of Architects Journal* 45 (February 1966): 35–41.

81. "Chicagoan, Head to Heels," *Chicago Sunday Chronicle,* 28 August 1898.

82. *Nineteenth Annual Report of the Chicago Athenaeum, 1889-'90* (Chicago, 1890), 9, 13. The Athenaeum's *Annual Reports* (1873–1877, 1878–1879, 1881–1887, and 1888–1890) are in the Chicago Historical Society. See also Andreas, *History of Chicago,* 3:416–417; Marquis, *Marquis' Hand-Book of Chicago,* 215–216; Flinn, *Chicago, the Marvelous City of the West,* 265–266; and McCarthy, *Noblesse Oblige,* 82–84.

83. *Nineteenth Annual Report of the Chicago Athenaeum,1889–'90* (Chicago, 1890), 9, and "Warming Its New Home," *Chicago Tribune,* 10 May 1891, 1.

84. Rand McNally, *Bird's-Eye Views and Guide to Chicago* (Chicago: Rand McNally, 1898), 32; reprinted in Randall, *Building Construction in Chicago,* 160.

85. Edward I. Galvin, in *Nineteenth Annual Report of the Chicago Athenaeum, 1889–'90*. On the "Dime Course on Art Topics," see McCarthy, *Noblesse Oblige,* 82.

86. On the Central Church, see Andreas, *History of Chicago,* 3:827; Helen Swing Starring, comp., *David Swing: A Memorial Volume* (Chicago: F. T. Neely, 1894), 23–28; Joseph Fort Newton, *David Swing: Poet Preacher* (Chicago: Unity, 1909), 111–117; Pierce, *History of Chicago,* 3:431; William Hutchison, "Disapproval of Chicago: The Symbolic Trial of David Swing," *Journal of American History* 59 (June 1972): 30–47; Hutchison, *The Modernist Impulse in American Protestantism* (Cambridge: Harvard University Press, 1976), 48–75; and Bluestone, *Constructing Chicago,* 99–101. See also these works by David Swing: *David Swing's Sermons* (Chicago: Jansen, 1874); *Truths for Today: Second Series* (Chicago: Jansen, McClurg, 1876); *Motives of Life* (Chicago: Jansen, McClurg, 1882); *Sermons* (Chicago: Jansen, McClurg, 1884); *Address to the New Generation* (Rockford, Ill.: W. A. Talcott, 1888); *Club Essays,* new ed. (Chicago: A. C. McClurg, 1889); *Art, Music and Nature: Selections from the Writings of David Swing,* ed. Mary E. Pratt (Chicago: Seale and Gorton, 1893); *Echoes from Central Music Hall: Selections from the Recent Sermons of Professor David Swing,* ed. Thomas W. Handford (Chicago: Donohue, Henneberry, 1894); *Three Sermons, with Selections and Letters* (Chicago: W. A. Talcott, 1894); *Thoughts That Will Live: Choice Selections from the Popular Addresses of David Swing* (Chicago: J. C. Winship, 1900); *Truths Leaf by Leaf,* ed. Sophie Burt Kimball (Chicago: [Lakeside Press], 1905); and *The Message of David Swing to His Generation: Addresses and Papers* (New York: F. H. Revell, 1913). He edited the weekly *Chicago Alliance* (1873–1876) and *Alliance* (1876–1881).

87. Meeting, 4 December 1875, *The Central Church of Chicago, Illinois: Record, from December 4, 1875,* 3 (Department of Archives and Manuscripts, Chicago Historical Society). On the prefire relocation of churches away from Chicago's center, see Bluestone, *Constructing Chicago,* 68–85.

88. Quoted in Newton, *David Swing,* 115.

89. Swing, "The Reasons for a Central Church," in *David Swing: A Memorial Volume,* comp. Starring, 376.

90. Ibid.

91. *Central Church of Chicago, Record,* 9.

92. Ibid.

93. Newton, *David Swing,* 117; Bluestone, *Constructing Chicago,* 99–100.

94. On Carpenter and Sheldon's postfire activities, see *In Memory of George Benedict Carpenter, Died January 7, 1881,* Chicago Historical Society; George Upton, quoted in Andreas, *History of Chicago,* 3:641; and *Album of Genealogy and Biography,* 2d ed., 363–365.

95. On the Union Park Congregational Church and Chicago's auditorium churches, see Bluestone, *Constructing Chicago,* 85–90.

96. George B. Carpenter, quoted in "Music Has Charms," *Chicago Times,* 2 March 1879, 14. Before the fire, one of the major central auditoriums had been Farwell Hall (1867), on Madison Street between Clark and LaSalle Streets, built mainly for the YMCA under the leadership of the Reverend Dwight

Moody. See Andreas, *History of Chicago,* 3:511–512. After the fire, Carpenter and Sheldon at first had planned to lease the rebuilt Farwell Hall for lectures and concerts, but they concluded that it was architecturally inadequate.

97. See "[Kingsbury] Music Hall," *Land Owner* 5 (October 1873): 174; "McCormick Hall," *Land Owner* 5 (November 1873): 178; and Andreas, *History of Chicago,* 3:651–652. On the postfire Kingsbury Music Hall, see also Gregersen, *Dankmar Adler,* 41–42.

98. Andreas, *History of Chicago,* 3:300–301. On Fairbank, see also Flinn, *Hand-Book of Chicago Biography,* 142–143.

99. On Chicago's *Turnvereine,* see Flinn, *Chicago, the Marvelous City of the West,* 524; Marquis, *Marquis' Hand-Book of Chicago,* 143–144; Theodor Janssen, *Geschichte der Chicago Turn-gemeinde* (Chicago: M. Stern, 1897); Royal L. Melendy, "The Saloon in Chicago," *American Journal of Sociology* 6 (January 1901): 437; Adolph Georg, "Aus der Geschichte der Chicago Turngemeinde," *Deutsch-Amerikanische Geschichtsblätter* 5 (July 1905): 42–51; Hermann Schlüter, *Die Anfange der deutschen Arbeitbewegung in Amerika* (Stuttgart, 1907), 199–214; Andrew J. Townsend, "The Germans of Chicago" (Ph.D. diss., University of Chicago, 1927), 25, 43, 126–127; Pierce, *History of Chicago,* 3:23; Hofmeister, *Germans of Chicago,* 176–177; Keil and Jentz, *German Workers in Chicago,* 153–155, 160–169; Nelson, *Beyond the Martyrs,* 148; Hirsch, *Urban Revolt,* 158–166; Ralf Wagner, "Turner Societies and the Socialist Tradition," in *German Workers' Culture in the United States,* ed. Keil, 221–240; and Eric L. Pumroy and Katja Rampelmann, comps., *Research Guide to the Turner Movement in the United States* (Westport, Conn.: Greenwood Press, 1996), esp. 91–105. Among other German clubs in Manhattan, there were the New-York Turn-Verein (founded 1849), at 66–68 East Fourth Street, and the Central Turn-Vereine (founded 1886), at 205–217 East Sixty-seventh Street, both noted in Moses King, *King's Handbook of New York City* (Boston: Moses King, 1893), 566–567. On the Central Turn-Verein's building of 1887–1889, designed by Albert Wagner, see Stern, Mellins, and Fishman, *New York 1880,* 223–224.

100. Marquis, *Marquis' Hand-Book of Chicago,* 143–144. On the North Side Turner Hall and its programs, see Janssen, *Geschichte der Chicago Turn-gemeinde,* 41–50, 62–66. On August Bauer, see Andreas, *History of Chicago,* 2:565. On Adler's employment with Bauer, see Gregersen, *Dankmar Adler,* 2.

101. *Illinois Staats-Zeitung,* 11 October 1867, 55, quoted and translated in Hirsch, *Urban Revolt,* 163.

102. "City Matters: A Lesson from the Germans," *Workingman's Advocate,* 8 January 1876, 12, quoted in Hirsch, *Urban Revolt,* 160.

103. Sullivan, *Autobiography of an Idea,* 208. See Egbert and Sprague, "In Search of John Edelmann," 35–41. A member of the Socialist Labor Party, Edelmann hosted the Russian anarchist Peter Kropotkin on the latter's first visit to New York City in 1897. Edelmann also contributed to *Solidarity,* New York City's first anarchist communist newspaper in English. See George Woodcock and Ivan Avakumovic, *The Anarchist Prince* (New York: T. V. Boardman, 1950), 277. On Hans Balatka, see Andreas, *History of Chicago,* 2:593, 3:640; Upton, *Musical Memories,* 253–268; Ffrench, *Music and Musicians in Chicago,* 17–18; and Philo Adams Otis, *The Chicago Symphony Orchestra* (1924; reprint, Freeport, N.Y.: Books for Libraries Press, 1972), 9–11. A typical event at Turner Hall was "The First Anniversary Ball of the Chicago Tug Pilots' Association, at North Side Turner Hall, Friday evening, Nov. 19, 1875," whose program is at the Illinois State Historical Library.

104. "Among the Turners," *Chicago Herald,* 2 May 1886, 16.

105. Ibid. The *Turnvereine* led in efforts to introduce systematic physical education into Chicago's public schools in the 1880s, and the city hired many instructors from the *Turnvereine* to develop these programs. See Robin L. Chambers, "Chicago's Turners: Inspired Leadership in the Promotion of Public Physical Education, 1860–1900," *Yearbook of German-American Studies* 24 (1989): 105–114, and Steven A. Riess, *City Games: The Evolution of American Urban Society and the Rise of Sports* (Urbana: University of Illinois Press, 1989), 23, 96–99.

106. "In General: The Regulars: Their Triumphal Return," *Chicago Tribune*, 26 July 1877, 3, cited in Smith, *Urban Disorder and the Shape of Belief*, 106–107. On Chicago's railroad strike of 1877, see Flinn, *History of the Chicago Police*, 153–201; Pierce, *History of Chicago*, 3:244–252; Robert V. Bruce, *1877: Year of Violence* (1959; reprint, Chicago: Quadrangle Books, 1970), 233–253; Philip S. Foner, *The Great Labor Uprising of 1877* (New York: Monad Press, 1977), 138–156; Richard Schneirov, "Chicago's Great Upheaval of 1877," *Chicago History* 9 (spring 1980): 3–17; Avrich, *Haymarket Tragedy*, 26–38; and Schneirov, *Labor and Urban Politics*, 69–76. Compare with Dorothee Schneider, *Trade Unions and Community: The German Working Class in New York City, 1870–1900* (Urbana: University of Illinois Press, 1994), 74–88.

107. "Turner-Hall: The Opening Trouble of Yesterday," *Chicago Tribune*, 27 July 1877, 1; "The Great Strike," *Harper's Weekly* 21 (18 August 1877): 647; "The Aurora Turn Verein," *Der Westen: Frauen Zeitung*, 15 and 22 November 1896, translated in Keil and Jentz, *German Workers in Chicago*, 160–161; Flinn, *History of the Chicago Police*, 197–198; Pierce, *History of Chicago*, 3:253; and Foner, *Great Labor Uprising of 1877*, 152–153. See also "The History of the Development of the Labor Movement in Chicago," *Vorbote*, 4 and 18 May 1887, translated and excerpted in Keil and Jentz, *German Workers in Chicago*, 228–233. On the meeting of December 1873, see Townsend, "Germans of Chicago," 45–46.

108. On socialist candidates in the state elections of fall 1878 and the municipal elections of spring 1879, see Avrich, *Haymarket Tragedy*, 39, 44, and Schneirov, *Labor and Urban Politics*, 81–91. See also Edward B. Mittelman, "Chicago Labor in Politics 1877–96," *Journal of Political Economy* 28 (May 1920): 415.

109. On the socialist picnic at Ogden's Grove on 4 July 1879, see *Socialist*, 12 July 1879; Avrich, *Haymarket Tragedy*, 41, 42, 140; and Nelson, *Beyond the Martyrs*, 138. *Chicago Directory of Picnic Grounds and Public Halls* (Chicago, 1899) listed twenty-seven publicly usable outdoor sites like Ogden's Grove, most within forty miles of the city. Miller, *City of the Century*, 82, notes that Chicago's lack of park space enabled private cemeteries to do a large business in fees charged to picnickers.

110. "The Reds," *Chicago Tribune*, 23 March 1879, 7; "The Communist Demonstration," *Chicago Tribune*, 24 March 1879, 4; "The Red Rag," *Chicago Tribune*, 24 March 1879, 6.

111. Schneirov, "Class Conflict, Municipal Politics, and Governmental Reform," 198. On the First Regiment's actions in the Great Strike of 1877, see "The First Regiment," *Chicago Tribune*, 26 July 1877, 3; "The Militia," *Chicago Tribune*, 28 July 1877, 2; and Turner, *Souvenir Album and Sketchbook*, 9. On German *Lehr- und Wehr-Verein*, see Michael J. Schaack, *Anarchy and Anarchists* (Chicago: F. J. Schulte, 1889), 64; Christine Heiss "Der Lehr- und Wehr-Verein von Chicago, 1875–1887: Ein sozialgeschichtlicher Beitrag zur Radikalisierung deutscher Arbeiter in den U.S.A." (master's thesis, Ludwig-Maximilians-Universität, Munich, 1981); Heiss, "German Radicals in Industrial America: The Lehr- und Wehr-Verein in Gilded Age Chicago," in *German Workers in Industrial Chicago*, ed. Keil and Jentz, 206–223; Keil and Jentz, *German Workers in Chicago*, 238–241; Avrich, *Haymarket Tragedy*, 45–46, 160–162; and Hirsch, *Urban Revolt*, 22.

112. Collins, *History of the Illinois National Guard*, 86–96, and *Chicago Tribune*, 2 September 1879, 6. On efforts to raise funds and legislative support for militia, see the *Annual Report of the Citizens' Association of Chicago*, October 1877, 9; October 1878, 19; October 1879, 11; and October 1880, 6–7. The role of militia, both capitalist and socialist, stirred much legal and political debate in the city and at meetings of the Citizens' Association. See "The Conference: Militia Law," *Chicago Tribune*, 27 December 1878, 4–5, and "Militia Law," *Chicago Tribune*, 2 September 1879, 6.

113. Andreas, *History of Chicago*, 3:656.

114. Theodore Thomas, *A Musical Autobiography*, ed. George P. Upton, 2 vols. (Chicago: A. C. McClurg, 1905), 1:80. See Zane L. Miller and George F. Roth, *Cincinnati's Music Hall* (Virginia Beach, Va.: Jordan, 1978); Ezra Schabas, *Theodore Thomas: America's Conductor and Builder of Orchestras, 1835–1905* (Urbana: University of Illinois Press, 1989), 64–65; and John Clubbe, *Cincinnati Observed: Architecture*

and History (Columbus: Ohio State University Press, 1992), 246–254. See also Sylvia K. Sheblessy, *One Hundred Years of the Cincinnati May Festival* (Cincinnati, 1973), and Robert C. Vitz, *The Queen and the Arts: Cultural Life in Nineteenth-Century Cincinnati* (Kent, Ohio: Kent State University Press, 1989).

115. Dankmar Adler, letter, n.d. (Newberry Library, Chicago). Later Adler recalled that during the last nine months of his military career, he worked as a draftsman to the Topographic Engineers' Office of the Military Division of the Tennessee, spending much time in Chattanooga in company with Milo D. Burke, later an eminent civil engineer in Cincinnati. See Adler, Autobiography, in "Autobiography and Letters of Dankmar Adler," ed. Joan W. Saltzstein, *Inland Architect* 27 (September–October 1983): 19.

116. Peter B. Wight, "On the Present Condition of Architectural Art in the Western States," *American Art Review* (Boston) 1 (1880): 141.

117. William Penn Nixon, quoted in "Music for the People," *Chicago Inter Ocean,* 3 May 1885, 6.

118. Upton, quoted in Andreas, *History of Chicago,* 3:641. On Thomas's early visits to Chicago, see also Upton, *Musical Memories,* 180–182, and Ffrench, *Music and Musicians in Chicago,* 21.

119. "Chicago Real Estate," *Chicago Tribune,* 22 January 1888, 7. On the meeting of December 1878, see "New Music Hall: The Capitalists Getting Interested," *Chicago Tribune,* 24 December 1878, 8. On site ownership and financing, see *Industrial Chicago,* 1:172, 238, and Ericsson, *Sixty Years a Builder,* 220. Field, Leiter and Company bought the Singer Building at about the same time that Carpenter's Central Music Hall Company bought the site for its building. See "Real Estate," *Chicago Tribune,* 2 March 1879, 6.

120. Adler, Autobiography, in "Autobiography and Letters of Dankmar Adler," ed. Saltzstein, 19.

121. Carpenter, quoted in "Music Has Charms," *Chicago Times,* 2 March 1879, 14. Another account noted: "During the past five years Mr. Carpenter has visited every important amusement-place between Boston and San Francisco. As the result of his labors during the past three years, six complete sets of plans have been worked out by Mr. Adler (who was the architect of the Kingsbury Hall and New Chicago Theatre)." See "Real Estate," *Chicago Tribune,* 2 March 1879, 6.

122. Carpenter, quoted in "Music Has Charms," *Chicago Times,* 2 March 1879, 14. On Chickering Hall, see Boyer, *Manhattan Manners,* 72–73; Sarah Bradford Landau, *George B. Post, Architect: Picturesque Designer and Determined Realist* (New York: Monacelli Press, 1998), 31–33; and Stern, Mellins, and Fishman, *New York 1880,* 688–691. King, *King's Handbook of New York City,* 1:287, noted that the liberal religious Society for Ethical Culture, founded by Professor Felix Adler in 1888, held Sunday services in Chickering Hall before creating its own building. Carpenter may have known Berlin's halls, since his widow took their daughters to that city to study violin and painting. See *Album of Genealogy and Biography,* 2d ed., 364.

123. Adler, in "Autobiography and Letters of Dankmar Adler," ed. Saltzstein, 19. See also David Swing et al., *In Memory of George Benedict Carpenter, Died 7 January 1881* (Chicago Historical Society). Previously Carpenter edited the weekly religious periodicals *Interior* (begun 1870) and *Church Pulpit* (begun 1871), both of which published Swing's sermons. See "The New Central Music Hall," *American Architect and Building News* 6 (8 November 1879): 150; L. G. Hallberg, "The Central Music Hall," *American Architect and Building News* 6 (29 November 1879): 174–175; Alex Black, "Central Music Hall," *American Architect and Building News* 6 (20 December 1879): 199; "The Music Hall," *Chicago Tribune,* 4 December 1879, 8; and "The Music Hall," *Chicago Tribune,* 5 December 1879, 6; "Central Music Hall," *Chicago Inter Ocean,* 5 December 1879, 8; "Religious," *Chicago Tribune,* 5 January 1880, 2; "Social Events: Music Hall," *Chicago Inter Ocean,* 6 February 1880, 8; "Social Pleasures: Music-Hall," *Chicago Tribune,* 6 February 1880, 5; "A Day in Town," *Chicago Times,* 8 February 1880, 6; "Amusements: Central Music-Hall Organ," *Chicago Tribune,* 22 October 1880, 8. Views and seating plans appeared in a pamphlet, *Central Music Hall* (Chicago, c. 1880, Chicago Historical Society). Later accounts include Ffrench, *Music and Musicians in Chicago,* 91–94; Newton, *David Swing,* 34–35; Morrison, *Louis Sullivan,* 66, 286–289; Condit, *Chicago School,* 31–32; Twombly, *Louis Sullivan,* 98–99, 139–141; Grimsley, "Contributions of

Dankmar Adler," 80–130; Gregersen, *Dankmar Adler*, 47–49; Bluestone, *Constructing Chicago*, 101; and Frei, *Louis Henry Sullivan*, 50.

124. Carpenter, quoted in "Music Has Charms," *Chicago Times*, 2 March 1879, 14.

125. Horace Jay Mellum, "The Centennial Kid, or All in a Lifetime," 6 (Archives and Manuscripts Department, Chicago Historical Society).

126. L. D. Cleaveland, Report to the Hon. Monroe Heath, Mayor of the City of Chicago, quoted in *Report of the Committee on Theatres and Public Halls, of the Citizens' Association of Chicago, January, 1882* (Chicago: George K. Hazlitt, 1882), 6–7. On 5 December 1876, Mrs. Conway's Theatre in Brooklyn had burned during a performance, killing 283 persons and injuring many more. The fire started from a side light on the stage. See Sachs and Woodrow, *Modern Opera Houses and Theatres*, 3:100.

127. *Report of the Committee on Theatres and Public Halls, January, 1882*, 22.

128. Gregersen, *Dankmar Adler*, 11–19. On Scott Russell's methods for the banking of seating, see Izenour, *Theater Design*, 71 and appendix 3 (597–599), which is a republication of John Scott Russell, "Elementary Considerations of Some Principles in Construction of Buildings Designed to Accommodate Spectators and Auditors," from *Edinburgh New Philosophical Journal* 27 (April–October 1838): 131–136. See also Forsyth, *Buildings for Music*, 235–243. Scott Russell's two papers on theater acoustics read before the Royal Institute of British Architects in February and March 1847 were summarized in *Builder*, 1847, 82, 118, and in "On the Construction of Buildings with Reference to Sound," *Building News*, 26 November 1858, 1178; 3 December 1858, 1195–1196; and 10 December 1858, 1228. On Scott Russell's other pursuits, see George S. Emmerson, *John Scott Russell: A Great Victorian Engineer and Naval Architect* (London: Murray, 1977).

129. Scott Russell, "Elementary Considerations," 132–133, 135, 136.

130. Carpenter, quoted in "Music Has Charms," *Chicago Times*, 2 March 1879, 14.

131. "The Music Hall," *Chicago Tribune*, 5 December 1879, 6.

132. Mellum, "Centennial Kid," 6 (Chicago Historical Society).

133. The skylight's colors were noted in "The Music Hall," *Chicago Tribune*, 5 December 1879, 6. On Healy and Millet, see *Industrial Chicago*, 2:707–708, quoted in David Hanks, "Louis J. Millet and the Art Institute of Chicago," *Bulletin of The Art Institute of Chicago* 67 (1973): 13–19. See also Sharon S. Darling, *Chicago Ceramics and Glass: An Illustrated History from 1871 to 1933* (Chicago: Chicago Historical Society, 1979), 104–108. On Sullivan's earlier frescoes, see Twombly, *Louis Sullivan*, 87–92, and "Religious," *Chicago Tribune*, 2 June 1876, 8.

134. Dean, *World's Fair City*, 71.

135. Carpenter, quoted in "Music Has Charms," *Chicago Times*, 2 March 1879, 14.

136. "Real Estate," *Chicago Tribune*, 2 March 1879, 6.

137. Carpenter, quoted in "Music Has Charms," *Chicago Times*, 2 March 1879, 14.

138. "Religious," *Chicago Tribune*, 5 January 1880, 2.

139. "New Music-Hall," *Chicago Tribune*, 24 December 1878, 8.

140. Miller and Roth, *Cincinnati's Music Hall*, 83; Clubbe, *Cincinnati Observed*, 251–253.

141. "Amusements: Central Music-Hall Organ," *Chicago Tribune*, 22 October 1880, 8.

142. Ibid. On Sullivan as designer of the organ cases and ornament around the Central Music Hall's stage, see Twombly, *Louis Sullivan*, 98, and Gregersen, *Dankmar Adler*, 48. The Central Music Hall's organ was among the elaborate instruments built in the city in the postfire years. See "Noteworthy Great Organs in Chicago," *Presto* 8 (11 July 1891): 591.

143. Marquis, *Marquis' Hand-Book of Chicago*, 242.

144. Sullivan, quoted in *Chicago Inter Ocean,* 12 August 1882, 13, in *Louis Sullivan: The Public Papers,* ed. Twombly, 1–2. On Adler and Sullivan's 1882 remodeling of Hooley's Theater, see Twombly, *Louis Sullivan,* 144–145, and Gregersen, *Dankmar Adler,* 56.

145. "Real Estate," *Chicago Tribune,* 2 March 1879, 6.

146. "Social Events: Music-Hall," *Chicago Tribune,* 6 February 1880, 5. See also "Social Pleasures: Music Hall," *Chicago Inter Ocean,* 6 February 1880, 8.

147. Ffrench, *Music and Musicians in Chicago,* 52–53. On the Germania Männerchor and related musical societies, see also Marquis, *Marquis' Hand-Book of Chicago,* 259; Flinn, *Chicago, the Marvelous City of the West,* 214; Rand McNally, *Bird's-Eye Views and Guide to Chicago,* 99; Upton, *Musical Memories,* 270–293; and Hofmeister, *Germans of Chicago,* 221–223. The club's early document is *Grund- und Neben-Gesetze und Mitglieder-Liste des Germania Männer-chor* (Chicago, 1869), a copy of which is at the Newberry Library. See also the Germania Männerchor *Jahrbuch,* published from at least 1892, and *Germania Club, Year Book and Historical Review, 1940–1941* (Chicago, 1941). On Chicago workers' singing societies, see Keil and Jentz, *German Workers in Chicago,* 276–277, 284–291. Nationally, see Mary J. Corry, "The Role of German Singing Societies in Nineteenth-Century America," in *Germans in America: Aspects of German-American Relations in the Nineteenth Century,* ed. E. Allen McCormick (New York: Brooklyn College Press, 1983), 155–168.

148. On the Apollo Club, and William Tomlins, see Andreas, *History of Chicago,* 3:629–633; Upton, *Musical Memories,* 286–291; Ffrench, *Music and Musicians in Chicago,* 20–22, 172–175, 204–205; Lawrence L. Edlund, *The Apollo Musical Club of Chicago: A Historical Sketch* (Chicago: Apollo Musical Club, 1946); and Mary C. Helfrich, *Apollo Chorus of Chicago: Celebrating 125 Years, 1872–1997* (Chicago: Apollo Chorus of Chicago, 1997). A listing of the club's principal performances from its founding in 1873 appeared in "The Apollo Club Past and Present," *Indicator* 11 (14 December 1889): 13–14.

149. Sullivan, *Autobiography of an Idea,* 217.

150. Joseph Bennett, "An Englishman on Music in Chicago," *Indicator* 6 (18 July 1885): 590–591.

151. *Industrial Chicago,* 1:168.

152. John Wellborn Root, "Architects of Chicago," *Inland Architect and News Record* 16 (January 1891): 92. Carpenter, quoted in "Music Has Charms," *Chicago Times,* 2 March 1879, 14, said: "Mr. Adler has been very happy in his treatment of the exterior, which, owing to the broken construction required in a building to be used half for art and half for business purposes, presented unusual architectural difficulties." Another account of the completed Central Music Hall noted that "its architectural proportions make it a handsome addition to the line of splendid buildings enclosed by itself at the north end and by the Palmer House at the south" ("The Music Hall," *Chicago Tribune,* 1 December 1879, 6).

153. "Chicago Real Estate," *Chicago Tribune,* 22 January 1888, 7.

154. Rand McNally, *Bird's-Eye Views and Guide to Chicago,* 87.

155. The rise in the Central Music Hall's stock to 1890 was noted in *Industrial Chicago,* 1:238. The value and sale of Adler's stock was noted in "Petition of Dila K. Adler, Executrix of the Last Will and Testament of Dankmar Adler, 18 May 1900," Probate Court of Cook County, General no. P20–7056, docket 57, p. 10, Probate Records, Estate of Dankmar Adler (Clerk of the Circuit Court of Cook County Archives, Chicago, Illinois).

156. On efforts of Field, Leiter, and others to create the Chicago City Railway in 1882, see Ronald J. Weber, "Rationalizers and Reformers: Chicago Local Transportation in the Nineteenth Century" (Ph.D. diss., University of Wisconsin, 1976), 92–101. On Field and Leiter as investors in State Street properties, see Berger, *They Built Chicago,* 77–84. Field, Leiter, and Company began to acquire large amounts of real estate only in 1879. Two years later, Field's and Leiter's individual properties were publicly disclosed (to Field's surprise) at the time Leiter left the firm. See "Leiter Leaves," *Chicago Times,* 27 January 1881, 5.

157. Adler, paraphrased in "Western Association of Architects," *American Architect and Building News* 20 (2 November 1886): 253. On Adler's praise for Post, see chapter 4, 228. On Post's Western Union Building, see Landau and Condit, *Rise of the New York Skyscraper,* 78–83. In 1889 Adler and Sullivan added a clock tower to the Chicago Inter Ocean Building on the northwest corner of Madison and Dearborn Streets. See Flinn, *Chicago, the Marvelous City of the West,* opposite 144.

158. On the decline of the Socialist Labor Party in 1879–1880, see Avrich, *Haymarket Tragedy,* 44–45. See also Currey, *Chicago: Its History and Its Builders,* 2:381, and Schneirov, *Labor and Urban Politics,* 91–94. On election fraud against socialists, see "The History of the Development of the Labor Movement in Chicago," *Vorbote,* 4 and 18 May 1887, translated and excerpted in Keil and Jentz, *German Workers in Chicago,* 233–236.

CHAPTER 2

1. Sullivan, *Autobiography of an Idea,* 308, 304.

2. On Adler and Sullivan's theater remodelings in Chicago before the Auditorium, see Morrison, *Louis Sullivan,* 65–67; Twombly, *Louis Sullivan,* 138, 141–142, 144–147, 149–157; Van Zanten, "Sullivan to 1890," 13, 43–48; Gregersen, *Dankmar Adler,* 13–15, 50–51, 55–59; Grimsley, "Contributions of Dankmar Adler," 130–184, 199–210; and Van Zanten, *Sullivan's City,* 23–25.

3. "The Music Hall," *Chicago Tribune,* 5 December 1879, 6.

4. "Amusements," *Chicago Tribune,* 17 August 1865, 4, quoted in "McVicker's Theatre," 25. Attendance at Chicago's theaters was reported in *Chicago Tribune,* 4 June 1866, 4.

5. Edwin Booth, quoted in Smith, *American Gothic,* 235. On Booth's Theater of 1869, see also T. Allston Brown, *A History of the New York Stage from the First Performance in 1732 to 1902,* 3 vols. (New York: Dodd, Mead, 1903), 3:94–145; Donald C. Mullin, *Development of the Playhouse: A Survey of Theatre Architecture from the Renaissance to the Present* (Berkeley: University of California Press, 1970), 129–131; Loren Hufstetler, "A Physical Description of Booth's Theatre, New York, 1869–1883," *Theatre Design and Technology* 46 (winter 1976): 1–18, 38; Boyer, *Manhattan Manners,* 70–72; and Stern, Mellins, and Fishman, *New York 1880,* 665–67.

6. *New York Tribune,* 18 November 1868, quoted in Young, *Documents of American Theater History,* 1:195. Booth's Theater opened on 3 February 1869.

7. "Amusements: Opening of McVicker's Theatre," *Chicago Tribune,* 30 August 1871, 4, quoted in Ludwig, "McVicker's Theatre," 27. On McVicker's before the fire, see "Building Improvements: McVicker's New Theatre—an Elegant Structure," *Land Owner* 3 (February 1871): 44; *Chicago Times,* 28 May 1871, 2; and Andreas, *History of Chicago,* 2:597–601.

8. James B. Runnion, "Amusements, Arts, and Science," *Lakeside Monthly* 8 (October 1872): 320–321, quoted in Ludwig, "McVicker's Theatre," 70. Edwin Booth as creditor for the rebuilding of 1872, and McVicker's subsequent bankruptcy in 1878, were discussed in "J. H. McVicker," *Amusement World* 7 (3 August 1878): 1.

9. On the Mark Gray incident, see "Edwin Booth," *Chicago Tribune,* 24 April 1879, 1–2; and Levine, *Highbrow/Lowbrow,* 72–73. On McVicker's postfire productions, see Andreas, *History of Chicago,* 3:662–665, and Ludwig, "McVicker's Theatre," 73–87.

10. *Indicator* 6 (28 May 1885): 6. On the combination system, see Andreas, *History of Chicago,* 3:661–663, and Jack Poggi, *Theater in America: The Impact of Economic Forces, 1870–1967* (Ithaca: Cornell University Press, 1968), 4–11, 245–254. McVicker's views on the system appeared in *Chicago Tribune,* 28 December 1878, 3, quoted in Ludwig, "McVicker's Theater," 90–91.

11. McVicker, quoted in "Theatres as Educators," *Chicago Tribune,* 1 April 1888, 27. See also Ludwig, "McVicker's Theater," 104.

12. Andreas, *History of Chicago,* 3:658.

13. Harold C. Shiffler, "The Chicago Church-Theater Controversy of 1881–1882," *Journal of the Illinois State Historical Society* 53 (winter 1960): 361–375. See also Herrick Johnson, *A Plain Talk about the Theater* (Chicago: F. H. Revell, 1882), and Andreas, *History of Chicago,* 3:658–661. Johnson continued a local clerical tradition of attacking the theater that went back at least to the Civil War. Earlier critiques included the Reverend Robert M. Hatfield's address delivered at the Clark Street Methodist Episcopal Church, 11 December 1865, and published as *The Theater: Its Character and Influence* (Chicago, 1866). Hatfield argued "that the Theater has been a moral pest wherever it has existed during all this period of 2500 years" (10); "that the character of the Theater is indicated by the effect produced in the neighborhood in which one is located" (19); "that the Theater has affinities for corruption, and thrives best where vice and crime are most prevalent" (28); and "that we have no reason to hope for any radical reformation of the Theater . . . for the reason that it is largely and chiefly supported by a class of persons who are attracted by its objectionable features" (29). McVicker, and Unity Church, defended the theater against these attacks. More broadly, see Abe Laufe, *The Wicked Stage: A History of Theater Censorship and Harassment in the United States* (New York: F. Ungar, 1978). On related issues in Victorian Britain, see John Russell Stephens, *The Censorship of English Drama, 1824–1901* (New York: Cambridge University Press, 1980).

14. James H. McVicker, *The Press, the Pulpit, and the Stage* (Chicago: Western News, 1883), 34, 37.

15. *Observanda: McVicker's New Theatre, Chicago* (Chicago: W. J. Jefferson Press, 1891) (Chicago Historical Society).

16. *Chicago Tribune,* 3 May 1884.

17. *Observanda: McVicker's New Theatre.*

18. Mrs. Duane Doty, *The Town of Pullman, Illustrated: Its Growth with Brief Accounts of Its Industries* (Pullman, Ill.: T. P. Struhsacker, 1893), 14, 16. See also "The Pride of Pullman," *Chicago Inter Ocean,* 10 January 1883.

19. Doty, *Town of Pullman,* 14.

20. "Amusements: A Description of the Beautiful New Opera House at Pullman," *Chicago Inter Ocean,* 25 November 1882, 13. See also Stanley Buder, *Pullman: An Experiment in Industrial Order and Community Planning, 1880–1930* (New York: Oxford University Press, 1967), 63–64.

21. *New York Dramatic Mirror,* 31 January 1880, quoted in Young, *Documents of American Theater History,* 1:212. The Madison Square Theater was on Twenty-fourth Street just west of Fifth Avenue. See John C. Edwards, "A History of Nineteenth-Century Theatre Architecture in the United States" (Ph.D. diss., Northwestern University, 1963), 213–22, 399–446, and Stern, Mellins, and Fishman, *New York 1880,* 672–674.

22. Adler, "Paramount Requirements of a Large Opera House," 45, also referred to the stage mechanism of New York City's Madison Square Theater. On this apparatus, see "Movable Theater Stages," *Scientific American,* n.s., 50 (5 April 1884): 207–208. See also Young, *Documents of American Theater History,* 1:212–216; Boyer, *Manhattan Manners,* 72–75; and Percy MacKaye, *Epoch: The Life of Steele MacKaye, Genius of the Theater, in Relation to His Times and Contemporaries,* 2 vols. (New York: Boni and Liveright, 1927), 1:297–329. For MacKaye, Tiffany also designed the Lyceum Theater's hall, which opened in April 1885. See Alice C. Frelinghuysen, "Louis Comfort Tiffany at the Metropolitan Museum," *Metropolitan Museum of Art Bulletin,* summer 1998, 18–20. On American reports of the premiers at Bayreuth, see note 165.

23. Orear, *Commercial and Architectural Chicago,* 55.

24. On Adler and Sullivan's renovations of the Chicago Opera House (1880) and Hooley's Theater (1882), see Twombly, *Louis Sullivan,* 99–100, 144–145, and Gregersen, *Dankmar Adler,* 50–51, 56. On the Grand Opera House, see also Sullivan, "Development of Construction" (1916), in *Louis Sullivan: The Public Papers,* ed. Twombly, 213. Its role as a model for Beman's Pullman Opera House was noted in "Amusements: A Description of the Beautiful New Opera House at Pullman," *Chicago Inter Ocean,* 25

November 1882, 13. The dating of Adler and Sullivan's McVicker's design to spring 1883 was noted in "Synopsis of Building News," *Inland Architect and Builder* 4 (January 1885): 82.

25. "McVicker's New Theatre," *Indicator* 6 (26 September 1885): 783.

26. "Amusements: McVicker's Renovated Theatre," *Chicago Tribune,* 19 June 1885, 5.

27. McVicker, *Press, the Pulpit, and the Stage,* 67.

28. "Amusements: McVicker's Renovated Theatre," *Chicago Tribune,* 19 June 1885, 5. The 1885 renovation of McVicker's was documented in a fifty-page illustrated booklet titled *McVicker's Observanda Acceuil,* noted in Orear, *Commercial and Architectural Chicago,* 55–56. No existing copies of this booklet are known. A later publication, *Observanda: McVicker's New Theatre,* which documents Adler and Sullivan's rebuilding of 1890, is in the Chicago Historical Society. On their 1885 renovation, see also *Inland Architect and Builder* 5 (May 1885): 68; "The New McVicker's," *Chicago Inter Ocean,* 2 July 1885, 5; "Amusements" and "McVicker's Theatre," *Chicago Tribune,* 2 July 1885, 5, 7; "Opera and Drama," *Indicator* 6 (4 July 1885): 553; "McVicker's Theatre: A Thespian Temple Worthy of Chicago," *Real Estate and Building Journal* 27 (18 July 1885): 347–348; "McVicker's New Theatre," *Indicator* 6 (26 September 1896): 783; Clarence H. Blackall, "Notes of Travel: Chicago," *American Architect and Building News* 22 (24 December 1887): 299–300; and Adler and Sullivan, letter, "The Decoration of McVicker's Theater," *American Architect and Building News* 23 (11 February 1888): 70–71, in *Louis Sullivan: The Public Papers,* ed. Twombly, 41–45. There (43) Adler and Sullivan noted that the ornamental carver was James Legge, whose firm also did the ornamental plaster relief in the Auditorium.

29. "Amusements: McVicker's Renovated Theatre," *Chicago Tribune,* 19 June 1885, 5. On the proscenium arch, see "McVicker's Theater," *Chicago Times,* 1 July 1885, 3.

30. "McVicker's New Theatre," *Indicator* 6 (26 September 1885): 783.

31. On the Madison Square Theater's system, see James Hogg, "On the Ventilation of Public Buildings," *Scientific American Supplement,* no. 250 (16 October 1880): 3980–3982.

32. "McVicker's Theatre: System of Ventilation Employed," *Indicator* 6 (26 December 1885): 24. See also "McVicker's Theatre," *Real Estate and Building Journal* 27 (18 July 1885): 347.

33. "The New McVicker's," *Chicago Inter Ocean,* 2 July 1885, 5. Sullivan, "Development of Construction" (1916), in *Louis Sullivan: The Public Papers,* ed. Twombly, 214–215, recalled that in the 1885 renovation of McVicker's Theater he had invented "the first decorative use of the electric lamp . . . placing the lamps in a decoration instead of clustering them in fixtures." This departed from gas chandeliers and wall-hung gaslights. On electrification of Chicago's theaters in the 1880s, see Harold L. Platt, *The Electric City: Energy and the Growth of the Chicago Area, 1880–1930* (Chicago: University of Chicago Press, 1991), 37–38. Jefferson Williamson, *The American Hotel: An Anecdotal History* (New York: Alfred A. Knopf, 1930), 68, notes electric light for the Palmer House's two main dining rooms from 1882. Charles H. Taylor, *History of the Board of Trade of the City of Chicago,* 3 vols. (Chicago: R. O. Law, 1917), 2:618, notes that Chicago's first electric arc light plant was installed in 1881 at the department store of Willoughby, Hill, and Company, on Madison and Clark Streets.

34. "Opera and Drama," *Indicator* 6 (4 July 1885): 553.

35. "New McVicker's," *Chicago Inter Ocean,* 2 July 1885, 5.

36. "Amusements," *Chicago Tribune,* 10 May 1885, 14.

37. "McVicker's Theater," *Chicago Times,* 1 July 1885, 3.

38. Sullivan, "Characteristics and Tendencies of American Architecture" (1885), in *Louis Sullivan: The Public Papers,* ed. Twombly, 2, 8.

39. "McVicker's Theater," *Chicago Times,* 1 July 1885, 3.

40. Sullivan, on his ornament for the remodeled interior of Hooley's Theater, in *Chicago Inter Ocean,* 12 August 1882, 13, quoted in *Louis Sullivan: The Public Papers,* ed. Twombly, 2.

41. "McVicker's New Theater," *Chicago Inter Ocean,* 21 June 1885, 13.

42. MacKaye, *Epoch,* 1:329. On London's Royal Panopticon remodeled as the Alhambra Theater, see Gerald S. Bernstein, "In Pursuit of the Exotic: Islamic Forms in Nineteenth-Century American Architecture" (Ph.D. diss., University of Pennsylvania, 1968), 115–116. English architects also used an Islamic style for Turkish baths, such as George S. Clarke's "Hammam" of 1862 on Jermyn Street, London. See Michael Darby, *The Islamic Perspective: An Aspect of British Order and Design in the Nineteenth Century* (London: Leighton House Gallery, 1983), and Mark Crinson, *Empire Building: Orientalism and Victorian Architecture* (London: Routledge, 1996). Chicago theaters with "moresque decoration" included the Windsor, on Clark Street near Division on the Near North Side ("One Dozen Theatres," *Chicago Sunday Herald,* 30 May 1886, 16).

43. Prominent adaptations of the Moorish style in Chicago included Kinsley's Restaurant (once a tenant in Crosby's Opera House) on the north side of Adams Street west of Dearborn, opposite the United States Custom House and Post Office. Designed by F. L. Charnley in 1885, this structure, catering to various groups, included an inexpensive lunchroom on its ground floor. There Frank Lloyd Wright recalled having gone for his first meal after being hired by architect Joseph L. Silsbee in 1886. The second floor housed two cafés, one for gentlemen and the other for ladies or ladies with escorts. The third floor had rentable private dining rooms, and the fourth was divided into two grand banqueting and ballrooms for catered parties. Among the private dining rooms was the popular German room, where Chicago architects frequently met, notably during the early stages of planning the World's Columbian Exposition. The building's interior "is on a scale of magnificence rarely equaled outside of Oriental domains," while the facade's style was "moresque, after the famous Alhambra at Granada" (Orear, *Commercial and Architectural Chicago,* 51–52). Its bay windows of stained and plate glass were framed in copper work in repoussé, with gilded columns, while other surfaces such as the cornice were of terra cotta in unique designs. Kinsley's south-facing street front appropriated Moorish architecture's connotations of pleasurable consumption. See *H. M. Kinsley, Caterer, Season of 1885–'86* (Chicago Historical Society); Vynne, *Chicago by Day and Night,* 188; Wright, *Autobiography* (1932), 68; David Lowe, *Lost Chicago* (Boston: Houghton Mifflin, 1978), 188; and Duis, *Challenging Chicago,* 148. On Kinsley's earlier quarters, see Cropsey, *Crosby's Opera House,* 59–61, who cites a booklet, *Kinsley's* ([1867?]), at the Newberry Library, Chicago. Sullivan, in *Autobiography of an Idea,* 251, wrote that by about 1876 "he had made a reputation as a worker, and consorted now with a small aristocratic group of the highest paid draftsmen. They met at lunch in a certain favorite restaurant." Connely, *Louis Sullivan,* 91, identified the site as Kinsley's before it moved to its building of 1885.

In Sullivan's period the Alhambra was seen as "the very summit of perfection of Moorish art, as is the Parthenon of Greek art." The Moorish tradition provided a model for harmony of ornament and color in public interiors, such as decorator H. J. Milligan's Oriental Masonic Hall, completed by early 1884 in a building of 1873 on LaSalle Street for the use of many different bodies in Chicago's then vast Masonic fraternity. This was not a space for public commercial entertainment, but rather a room for semiprivate rituals. Praised as "perhaps the best exponent of oriental decoration in the West," the city's central Masonic Hall exemplified those aesthetic principles of the Moors, who "ever regarded as true, what we of the present day hold to be the first principle in architecture,—*to decorate construction, never to construct decoration.* In Moorish architecture, not only does the decoration arise naturally from the construction, but the constructive idea is carried out in every detail of the ornamentation." The Moors "ever regard the useful as a vehicle for the beautiful, and in this they do not stand alone; the same principle was observed in all the best periods of art" ("Mooresque Decoration," *Inland Architect and Builder* 3 [February 1884]: 4). The development of ornamentation from construction and utility as a basis of aesthetics were central to Sullivan's theoretical program. On the Oriental Lodge's Masonic Hall on LaSalle Street, see Andreas, *History of Chicago,* 2:654–655, 3:616. On rooms of this kind, see William D. Moore, "From Lodge Room to Theatre: Meeting Spaces of the Scottish Rite," in *Theatre of the Fraternity: Staging the Ritual Space of the Scottish Rite of Freemasonry, 1896–1929* (Jackson: University Press of Mississippi, 1996), 30–51. See also Irving K. Pond, "European Sketches, Part II—the Alhambra," *Inland*

Architect and Builder 4 (January 1885): 78–79. On Sullivan and Islamic sources, see Dimitri Tselos, "The Chicago Fair and the Myth of the 'Lost Cause,'" *Journal of the Society of Architectural Historians* 26 (December 1967): 259–268, and Menocal, *Architecture as Nature,* 34–42.

44. "The Alcazar Casino," *Real Estate Record and Builders' Guide* 20 (18–25 November 1882): 84, quoted in Stern, Mellins, and Fishman, *New York 1880,* 676.

45. Dankmar Adler and Louis Sullivan, "The Decoration of McVicker's Theater, Chicago," *American Architect and Building News* 23 (11 February 1888): 70, quoted in *Louis Sullivan: The Public Papers,* ed. Twombly, 42.

46. "McVicker's Theatre," *Real Estate and Building Journal* 27 (18 July 1885): 348. The allusion to the passage from Genesis 1 may relate to teachings of Adler's father, Rabbi Liebman Adler, whose analytical sermons on the Bible began with the Creation in Genesis. See Liebman Adler, *Sabbath Hours* (Philadelphia, 1893), and chapter 4, note 37.

47. Rand McNally, *Bird's-Eye Views and Guide to Chicago,* 83.

48. "McVicker's Theater," *Chicago Inter Ocean,* 21 June 1885, 13. Even then New York playhouses such as the Madison Square Theater still had their own stock companies.

49. Wilton Lackaye, letter, n.d. (1896?), Department of Archives and Manuscripts, Chicago Historical Society.

50. "Drama," *Indicator* 6 (22 August 1885): 685.

51. "Building Improvements: McVicker's New Theatre—an Elegant Structure," *Land Owner* 3 (February 1871): 44.

52. Andreas, *History of Chicago,* 3:643–644, and Davis, *Opera in Chicago,* 32–37. On the New Adelphi (later Haverly's) Theater, see Andreas, *History of Chicago,* 3:666. On Mapleson's tours of 1879–1883, see also Ffrench, *Music and Musicians in Chicago,* 28–29. James H. Mapleson, *The Mapleson Memoirs,* ed. Harold Rosenthal (New York: Appleton-Century-Crofts, 1966), 121–123, 135, 142, noted his Chicago tours of 1879–1881. Seating capacities of Chicago theaters were noted in John B. Jeffery, *Jno. B. Jeffery's Guide and Directory to the Public Halls, etc., of the Cities and Towns of the Western, Southern and Middle States of America* (Chicago, 1878), Chicago Historical Society.

53. Andreas, *History of Chicago,* 3:300.

54. Ibid., and Mapleson, *Mapleson Memoirs,* 164. Mapleson had returned to Haverly's original theater in winter 1880 and 1881 and to a newly constructed building also called Haverly Theater early in 1882.

55. Mapleson, *Mapleson Memoirs,* 118–121, gives an account of his first operatic season at the New York Academy of Music. See also Michael J. Pisoni, "Operatic War in New York City, 1883–84: Colonel James H. Mapleson at the Academy of Music vs. Henry E. Abbey at the Metropolitan Opera House" (Ph.D. diss., Indiana University, 1975), 44–60.

56. On the Met's founding, see "The Metropolitan Opera House," *Nation* 37 (25 October 1883): 348–349; [Montgomery Schuyler], "The Metropolitan Opera-House," *Harper's New Monthly Magazine* 67 (November 1883): 877–889; Mariana G. van Rensselaer, "The Metropolitan Opera House, New York," *American Architect and Building News* 15 (16 and 23 January 1884): 76–77, 86–89; Henry E. Krehbiel, *Chapters of Opera* (New York: Henry Holt, 1911), 86–88; Frank Merkling et al., *The Golden Horseshoe: The Life and Times of the Metropolitan Opera House* (New York: Viking Press, 1965), 13–21; Quaintance Eaton, *The Miracle of the Met: An Informal History of the Metropolitan Opera, 1883–1967* (New York: Meredith, 1968), 43–53; Irving Kolodin, *The Metropolitan Opera, 1883–1966: A Candid History* (New York: Alfred A. Knopf, 1968), 3–6; John Briggs, *Requiem for a Yellow Brick Brewery: A History of the Metropolitan Opera* (Boston: Little, Brown, 1969), 6–17; Martin Mayer, *The Met: One Hundred Years of Grand Opera* (New York: Simon and Schuster, 1983), 15–23; Paul E. Eisler, *The Metropolitan Opera: The First Twenty-five Years, 1883–1908* (Croton-on-Hudson, N.Y.: North River Press, 1984), 9–19; Dizikes,

Opera in America, 214–221; Kathleen A. Curran, *A Forgotten Architect of the Gilded Age: Josiah Cleave-land Cady's Legacy* (Hartford, Conn.: Watkinson Library and Department of Fine Arts, Trinity College, 1993), 16–20; and Stern, Mellins, and Fishman, *New York 1880,* 681–688.

57.   Edith Wharton, *The Age of Innocence* (1920), in *Edith Wharton: Novels,* ed. R. W. B. Lewis (New York, 1985), 1017. On the house for William K. Vanderbilt, see Paul R. Baker, *Richard Morris Hunt* (Cambridge:MIT Press, 1980), 274–288; John Foreman and Robbe P. Stimson, *The Vanderbilts and the Gilded Age: Architectural Aspirations, 1879–1901* (New York: St. Martin's Press, 1991), 21–45; and Stern, Mellins, and Fishman, *New York 1880,* 591–596.

58.   "The Opera's New Home," *New York Times,* 24 May 1883, 1.

59.   On New York opera before the Met, see chapter 1, note 31.

60.   On moral concerns in New York City about operas of Verdi and Offenbach in the 1850s and 1860s, see Dizikes, *Opera in America,* 171–173, 193–194. On New Yorkers' reception of Italian opera in this period, see Ahlquist, *Democracy at the Opera,* 160–181.

61.   Schuyler, "Metropolitan Opera-House," 880. Eidlitz's old Brooklyn Academy of Music, on Montague Street, was destroyed by fire in 1904. See Schuyler, "A Great American Architect: Leopold Eidlitz" (1908), in Montgomery Schuyler, *"American Architecture" and Other Writings,* ed. William H. Jordy and Ralph Coe (Cambridge: Harvard University Press, 1961), 1:167–169. Curran, *Forgotten Architect,* 19, noted that while designing the Met, Josiah Cleaveland Cady sought to study the Brooklyn Academy of Music.

62.   On meanings of "metropolitan," see John F. Sprague, *New York the Metropolis* (New York, 1893), and Herbert Croly, "New York as the American Metropolis," *Architectural Record* 13 (March 1903): 193–206. Calvin Tomkins, *Merchants and Masterpieces: The Story of the Metropolitan Museum of Art,* rev. ed. (New York: Henry Holt, 1989), 27–28, noted that the museum grew from the Metropolitan Art Fair of 1864. Early supporters of the museum and the Metropolitan Opera House included John J. Astor, August Belmont, J. Pierpont Morgan, Cornelius Vanderbilt, and Darius Ogden Mills.

63.   On the architectural competition for the Metropolitan and Cady's selection, see Briggs, *Yellow Brick Brewery,* 8–9; Mayer, *Met,* 16–19; Eisler, *Metropolitan Opera House,* 9–10; and Curran, *Forgotten Architect,* 16–17. The original site proposed had been a block bounded by Vanderbilt and Madison Avenues and Forty-third and Forty-fourth Streets, yet leases on parts of this plot contained clauses "whereby the erection of any other buildings than residences on the property was prohibited" ("A Site for the Opera-House," *New York Times,* 9 March 1881, 5). The leaseholders were two of the city's churches, whose leaders opposed a building for entertainment on their land. Schuyler, "Metropolitan Opera-House," 881, noted that "the adjoining owners held under a guarantee that the plot in question should not be occupied for certain specified uses, among which prohibited uses was the erection of any place of public amusement, and that satisfactory waivers could not in all cases be obtained, even in the cause of Italian opera."

64.   Egisto P. Fabbri, chairman, Committee on Building, Metropolitan Opera House Company, quoted in Mayer, *Met,* 15.

65.   Berg (1856–1913), born in New York City as the son of an organist and composer, studied architecture at Stuttgart's Royal Polytechnical School and was a civil engineer. See Milton Stansbury, "Romance in the Opera House," *Opera News* 5 (10 March 1941): 4–9.

66.   Josiah Cleaveland Cady, "The Essential Features of a Large Opera House," *Inland Architect and News Record* 5 (October 1887): 46–48, reprinted in *American Architect and Building News* 22 (29 October 1887): 208.

67.   Ibid., 47.

68.   Schuyler, "Metropolitan Opera-House," 884, noted that the boxes in the first two tiers were distributed among the stockholders, while the *baignoire* boxes and those on the third tier were rented at

the manager's discretion. Briggs, *Yellow Brick Brewery,* 22–23, recalled newspaper diagrams of the Metropolitan's boxes published on the day of its opening, 22 October 1883. On the shape of Cady's plan, see van Rensselaer, "Metropolitan Opera-House," 86–87. On its name, see Mayer, *Met,* 16. On La Scala and Barry's Covent Garden, see chapter 1, note 33. Among Paris's larger theaters was Gabriel Davioud's Théâtre du Châtelet, seating 3,000 and completed in 1862, not for opera but for popular events like circuses. Davioud's adjacent Théâtre Lyrique, seating 1,700 and completed in the same year, was planned as a "théâtre de luxe" meant to house opera. See César Daly and Gabriel Davioud, *Les théâtres de la Place du Châtelet: Théâtre du Chatelet, Théâtre Lyrique* (Paris: Librairie Générale de l'Architecture et des Travaux Publics, 1874).

69. Schuyler, "Metropolitan Opera-House," 883. On the form of the Metropolitan's proscenium, see also van Rensselaer, "Metropolitan Opera-House," 76, who noted that New York's Madison Square Theater (1880) also had a square proscenium. She emphasized that the Metropolitan's creators had sought "a building in which each and every stockholder should have an equal chance of seeing—and of being seen. No variations of plan were to be allowed the architect in favor of architectural effect which would be at the expense of this perfect equality. All the boxes were to be of the same character and the same size, and, in so far as it was possible to human skill, all were to be equally advantageous as regards seeing the stage, and being seen by the rest of the audience."

70. Schuyler, "Metropolitan Opera-House," 883.

71. At the Metropolitan's opening, "much disappointment was caused by the comparative failure of the acoustic properties of the Auditorium . . . . In the upper rows of the boxes and in the balcony only the high voices were distinctly heard. Nor were the facilities for seeing much better in some portion of the auditorium than the facilities for hearing" ("The New Opera House," *New York Times,* 23 October 1883, 1). See also "Metropolitan Opera-House," *Nation* 37 (25 October 1883): 848–849. After a first season it was noted: "The Metropolitan Opera-house season has been financially a disastrous failure." Only consistently sold-out performances would have enabled a profit, yet "the house is never full, and never can be, because there is such a large part of it in which no one can see or hear" ("Patti Will Go to London," *New York Times,* 16 February 1884, 5).

In 1893, after the fire of August 1892, McElfatrick replanned the interior, eliminating the half tier of *baignoire* boxes and transforming the uppermost full tier of boxes into row seating to accommodate a larger general audience. See William H. Birkmire, "The Planning and Construction of American Theaters: Part I," *Architecture and Building* 21 (13 October 1894): 175–179. On the Met's remodeling after another ruinous fire in spring 1903, see Curtis C. Blake, "The Architecture of Carrère and Hastings" (Ph.D. diss., Columbia University, 1976), 301–302. Briggs, *Yellow Brick Brewery,* 15, and Eisler, *Metropolitan Opera,* x, noted later praise for the Met's acoustics.

72. Editorial, "Mr. Abbey's Retirement," *New York Times,* 14 February 1884, 4. Cady's care for sight lines was noted in "A Grand Temple of Music," *New York Times,* 14 October 1883, 5. Briggs, *Yellow Brick Brewery,* 15–16, and Mayer, *Met,* 40–41, noted unresolved difficulties with sight lines up to the old Metropolitan's demolition in 1966.

73. Letter, "Its Boast and Its Snare," *New York Times,* 4 May 1884, 4.

74. Van Rensselaer, "Metropolitan Opera House," 88. Other accounts of Cady's interior include "A Grand Temple of Music," *New York Times,* 14 October 1883, 5; Schuyler, "Metropolitan Opera-House," 886–887; and Krehbiel, *Chapters of Opera,* 86–88.

75. Plans for redoing interior colors were noted in "Improving the New Opera-House," *New York Times,* 30 October 1883, 8. This remodeling, designed by Francis Lathrop, was described in "The German Opera Season," *New York Times,* 2 October 1884, 4.

76. On Francis Lathrop's murals for the Metropolitan's original interior, see van Rensselaer, "Metropolitan Opera-House," 88. On the iconographic program for the Paris Opera, see Christopher C. Mead, *Charles Garnier's Paris Opera: Architectural Empathy and the Renaissance of French Classicism*

(New York: Architectural History Foundation and MIT Press, 1991), 175–193. On Vienna's opera house, see Eduard van der Null and August Siccard von Siccardsburg, *Das K. K. Hofoperntheater in Wien* (Vienna, 1894), and Hans-Christophe Hoffmann, Walter Krause, and Werner Kitlitschka, *Das Wiener Opernhaus,* Das Wiener Ringstrasse, vol. 8 (Wiesbaden, 1972). On the elaborate program of sculpture and painting in second Dresden Hoftheater (1870–1878), see Harry Francis Mallgrave, *Gottfried Semper, Architect of the Nineteenth Century: A Personal and Intellectual Biography* (New Haven: Yale University Press, 1996), 346–352.

77. Van Rensselaer, "Metropolitan Opera House," 88. On theater fires in Europe and the United States from 1797 to 1897, see Sachs and Woodrow, *Modern Opera Houses and Theatres,* vol. 3, suppl. 2, "Theatre Fires," 85–140. Dankmar Adler, "The Tall Business Building: Some of Its Engineering Problems," *Cassier's Magazine* 12 (November 1897): 210, recommended the writings of William Paul Gerhard (1854–1927), whose many works included *Theater Fires and Panics: Their Causes and Prevention* (New York: John Wiley, 1896). Adler wrote on methods of fire prevention in "Paramount Requirements of a Large Opera House," 46, and "Theater Building for American Cities: Second Paper," 823–827. In 1887 Adler, with architect John Wellborn Root, was a member of the Committee on Theatres and Public Halls, created by the Citizens' Association of Chicago, which published its reports in January 1882, October 1883, October 1885, and October 1887.

78. Schuyler, "Metropolitan Opera-House," 887.

79. Cady, "Essential Features of a Large Opera House," 47.

80. James Roosevelt, first president of the Metropolitan Opera House Company, acknowledged: "We never expected that it would pay. None of us went into it with the idea that we would ever get our money back, but simply for the enjoyment to be derived from having a first-class opera-house. No opera-house in the world has ever paid as an investment, and none will ever pay" ("The Opera-House Scheme," *New York Times,* 14 March 1882, 1). Van Rensselaer, "Metropolitan Opera House," 76, noted that the corner masses on Broadway, built in January 1884 after the theater opened in October 1883, were "to contain shops below, above large ball-rooms and restaurants, and above these again bachelors' apartments." A special committee of the Metropolitan's board of directors reported that "the advantage in finishing would be that the plans of the corners included the building of reception and supper-rooms, which would enable the Directors to rent the house for balls" ("The Opera's New Home," *New York Times,* 24 May 1883, 1).

81. Van Rensselaer, "Metropolitan Opera House," 76.

82. On the Casino Theater, see "The New Casino Opened," *New York Tribune,* 23 October 1882, and "The Casino Opened," *New York Times,* 31 December 1882, republished in Young, *Documents of American Theater History,* 1:223–225; *American Architect and Building News* 18 (27 August 1885): 102; James Taylor, "The History of Terra-Cotta in New York City," *Architectural Record* 2 (October–December 1892): 136–148; Montgomery Schuyler, "The Works of Francis H. Kimball and Kimball and Thompson," *Architectural Record* 7 (April–June 1898): 494, 496, 497; Lloyd Morris, *Incredible New York: High Life and Low Life of the Last Hundred Years* (New York: Random House, 1951), 189, 267; Robert A. M. Stern, Gregory Gilmartin, and John M. Massengale, *New York 1900: Metropolitan Architecture and Urbanism, 1890–1915* (New York: Rizzoli, 1983), 206–207, 220–221; Stern, Mellins, and Fishman, *New York 1880,* 674–677; and Nasaw, *Going Out,* 34–36. In his novel *Sister Carrie* (1900), Theodore Dreiser staged his title character's theatrical debut in New York City as a member of the Casino Theater's chorus line. See Dreiser, *Sister Carrie,* Pennsylvania Edition (Philadelphia, 1981), 385–393, 553. Evelyn Nesbit became a consort of architect Stanford White, whose father, Richard Grant White, had been New York's leading opera critic when the Metropolitan was built across Broadway from the Casino. See Charles C. Baldwin, *Stanford White* (New York: Dodd, Mead, 1931), 16–30, and Paul R. Baker, *Stanny: The Gilded Life of Stanford White* (New York: Free Press, 1989).

83. "The New Casino Opened," *New York Tribune,* 23 October 1882, quoted in Young, *Documents of American Theater History,* 1:224.

84. On the Casino Theater's roof garden, see Robert H. Montgomery, "The Roof Gardens of New York," *Indoors and Out* 2 (August 1906): 214–219.

85. Dankmar Adler, "The Chicago Auditorium," *Architectural Record* 1 (April–June 1892): 415.

86. On the first Socialist Revolutionary Congress in 1881, see Avrich, *Haymarket Tragedy,* 55–61, and Pierce, *History of Chicago,* 3:256. On Chicago's labor press in the period, including the *Arbeiter-Zeitung,* see Keil and Jentz, *German Workers in Chicago,* 242–250, and Nelson, *Beyond the Martyrs,* 115–126.

87. Quoted in *Liberty* (Boston and New York), 12 November 1881.

88. International Working People's Association, *To the Workingmen of America* (New York, 1883). On the Pittsburgh Congress and the founding of the IWPA, see Avrich, *Haymarket Tragedy,* 68–78.

89. On Parsons, see Lucy Parsons, ed., *Life of Albert R. Parsons* (Chicago, 1889), and Philip S. Foner, ed., *Autobiographies of the Haymarket Martyrs* (New York: Humanities Press, 1969). On the anarchist ideal, see Albert R. Parsons, *Anarchism: Its Philosophy and Scientific Basis as Defined by Some of Its Apostles* (Chicago, 1887; reprint, Westport, Conn.: Greenwood Press, 1970). For the local reactionary view, see also Charles C. Bonney, *The Present Conflict of Labor and Capital* (Chicago, 1886), and Schaack, *Anarchy and Anarchists.*

90. Richard T. Ely, *The Labor Movement in America, 1854–1943* (New York: T. Y. Crowell, 1886), 219. See also Samuel Rezneck, "Patterns of Thought and Action in an American Depression, 1882–1886," *American Historical Review* 61 (January 1956): 284–307. On the "Chicago idea," see John R. Commons et al., *History of Labour in the United States,* 4 vols. (New York: Macmillan, 1918–1935), 2:290–300, and Samuel Yellen, *American Labor Struggles, 1877–1934* (New York: Harcourt, Brace, 1936), 46–47.

91. Taylor, *Board of Trade;* Jonathan Lurie, *The Chicago Board of Trade, 1859–1905: The Dynamics of Self-Regulation* (Urbana: University of Illinois Press, 1979); and William G. Ferris, *The Grain Traders: The Story of the Chicago Board of Trade* (East Lansing: Michigan State University Press, 1988). On the Board of Trade's fundamental role in managing Chicago's grain trade, see Cronon, *Nature's Metropolis,* 114–119.

92. On the urban impact of the Board of Trade's relocation to LaSalle and Jackson Streets, see Taylor, *Board of Trade,* 2:614–616; Hoyt, *Land Values in Chicago,* 135–136; and Gerald Larson, "Chicago's Loop, 1830–1890: A Tale of Two Grids," in *Fragments of Chicago's Past: The Collection of Architectural Fragments at the Art Institute of Chicago,* ed. Pauline Saliga (Chicago: Art Institute of Chicago, 1990), 72–75. See also "Real Estate: Rapid Rise of Values Near the New Board of Trade," *Chicago Tribune,* 24 July 1881, 16; "Real Estate: The New Wholesale District," *Chicago Tribune,* 28 October 1883, 16; and "Office Buildings Near the Board of Trade," *Chicago Tribune,* 21 November 1886, 7. On the Board of Trade's acquisition of its site, see "A Triumphal March," *Chicago Inter Ocean,* 28 April 1885, 10. On nearby commercial buildings, see H. T. Sudduth, "LaSalle Street, Chicago," *Harper's Weekly* 34 (3 May 1890): 346–347.

93. Ericsson, *Sixty Years a Builder,* 68. On the Bricklayers and Stonemasons Union, see Royal E. Montgomery, *Industrial Relations in the Chicago Building Trades* (Chicago: University of Chicago Press, 1927), 23; Pierce, *History of Chicago,* 3:262–263, 537; *Illinois Bureau of Labor Statistics, Fourth Biennial Report, 1886* (Springfield, Ill., 1886), 172, 179, 196, 369; George Beaumont, "Brickwork," and the Bricklayers Union Committee to Beaumont, 8 April 1886, *Inland Architect and Builder* 7 (May 1886): 61–64.

94. On the 1883 strike, see [United States Industrial Commission], *Report of the Industrial Commission on the Chicago Labor Disputes of 1900, with Especial Reference to the Disputes in the Building and Machinery Trades* (Washington, D.C., 1901), 219–245, 366, 476–480. See also "The Labor Situation,"

Chicago Times, 8 May 1883, 8, and editorials in *Inland Architect and Builder* 1 (March 1883): 15–16; (April 1883): 32; (May 1883): 48; (June 1883): 62; 2 (August 1883): 89, and "Review of Chicago Building for 1883," 2 (January 1884): 154–155. See also Schneirov, *Labor and Urban Politics,* 153.

95.   Philip Peck had bought the lands that became the site of the Grand Pacific Hotel on the north side of Jackson Boulevard from Clark Street to LaSalle for $5,000 ("Ferdinand Peck, Widely Known Chicagoan, Dies," *Chicago Tribune,* 5 November 1924, 19). There he had a home and garden when Ferdinand was born in 1848. In 1851 Philip Peck had sold the west half of this property, facing LaSalle Street, to Northwestern University, which established a school there. When the university moved to Evanston it leased this west property to investors who built the first Grand Pacific Hotel on this site plus the lot to the east, which they leased from Philip Peck, who supported the project by agreeing to long and liberal lease terms ("Death of P. F. W. Peck," *Chicago Tribune,* 26 October 1871, 2). The second or post-fire Grand Pacific Hotel was built in 1873. In 1886, the year after the Board of Trade Building opened across Jackson Boulevard, the Peck estate sold the Grand Pacific site's east half (which Philip Peck had acquired for half of $5,000, or $2,500) to Levi Leiter for $577,000, over two hundred times the elder Peck's purchase price and over three times the land's value in 1870 ("Chicago Real Estate: The Sale of the Grand Pacific Hotel Lot," *Chicago Tribune,* 28 November 1886, 7).

96.   Michael Schwab, quoted in Lucy E. Parsons, comp., *The Famous Speeches of the Eight Chicago Anarchists in Court,* rev. ed. (Chicago: L. E. Parsons, 1910), 26. See *Report of the Committee on Tenement Houses of the Citizens' Association of Chicago* (Chicago, 1884). See also Keil and Ickstadt, "Elements of German Working-Class Culture," 86–87.

97.   *Report of the Committee on Tenement Houses of the Citizen's Association of Chicago* (Chicago, 1884), 4. The other members of the committee were realtor Henry Waller Jr. and Arthur C. Ducat, Chicago agent for the Home Life Insurance Company of New York City, both of whom represented sources of capital for new housing construction. Ducat had been chairman of the committee that framed the city's new building law after the Great Fire, and he then wrote the elaborately detailed law with Frederick Baumann. See *Album of Genealogy and Biography, Cook County, Illinois,* 2d ed., 417. A former Civil War officer, Ducat also organized the Illinois National Guard from 1875 and directed its activities in Chicago during the Great Railroad Strike of July 1877. See Collins, *History of the Illinois National Guard,* 31–57, 65–83, and Turnbaugh, Ethnicity, Civic Pride, and Commitment," 114–119. In his position with the Home Insurance Company, Ducat also helped get approval of William Le Baron Jenney's technically innovative design for the company's Chicago office building in 1883 (Theodore Turak, "Remembrances of the Home Insurance Building," *Journal of the Society of Architectural Historians* 44 [March 1985]: 62–63).

98.   Pliny B. Smith and Joseph Frank, paraphrased in "Homes for the Masses," *Chicago Tribune,* 13 April 1887, 1. See also "Earnings, Expenses and Conditions of Workingmen and Their Families," *Illinois Bureau of Labor Statistics, Third Biennial Report* (Springfield, Ill., 1884), 135–414.

99.   *Report of the Committee on Tenement Houses of the Citizen's Association of Chicago* (Chicago, 1884), 4. On employment patterns in 1884, see Keil and Ickstadt, "Elements of German Working-Class Culture," 85.

100.   Royal J. Melendy, "The Saloon in Chicago," *American Journal of Sociology* 6 (November 1900): 294. On the local reform effort of 1880–1883 to raise saloon license fees, see Schneirov, *Labor and Urban Politics,* 163–165.

101.   Klaus Ensslen, "German-American Working-Class Saloons in Chicago: Their Social Function in an Ethnic and Class-Specific Cultural Context," in *German Workers' Culture in the United States,* ed. Keil, 157–180.

102.   "The Talk of the Day," *Vörbote* (weekly edition of *Chicagoer Arbeiter-Zeitung*), 16 December 1891, translated in Keil and Jentz, *German Workers in Chicago,* 369. In November 1891 a union meeting at Grief's Hall was the target of a violent and destructive police raid that aroused much protest among workers.

103. Testimony of William Seliger, trial of Haymarket conspirators, Chicago, 1887, quoted in Schaack, *Anarchy and Anarchists,* 425. One of Albert Parsons's allies, George Schilling, recalled of Chicago socialist meetings in the mid-1870s: "Oft-times, after posting bills and paying for advertising, we were also compelled to contribute our last nickel for hall rent, and walk home instead of ride" (quoted in Parsons, *Life of Albert R. Parsons,* xxiv, and Floyd Dell, "Socialism and Anarchism in Chicago," in Currey, *Chicago: Its History and Its Builders,* 2: 370).

104. On the Metropolitan Opera-House Company's first tour of Chicago in January 1884, see Andreas, *History of Chicago,* 3:644; Ffrench, *Music and Musicians in Chicago,* 29; Quaintance Eaton, *Opera Caravan: Adventures of the Metropolitan on Tour* (New York: Da Capo Press, 1957), 8–13; and Davis, *Opera in Chicago,* 35–36. On Mapleson and Abbey at Chicago in the winter of 1884, see Pisoni, "Operatic War in New York City," 347–354.

105. "The Abbey Opera Company," *Indicator* 4 (19 January 1884): 62.

106. [Orrin L. Fox?], Editorial, *Indicator* 4 (9 February 1884): 96.

107. [Orrin L. Fox?], Editorial, *Indicator* 4 (2 February 1884), 80. See also "Wanted—an Opera House," *Chicago Tribune,* 21 January 1883, 4. On the Cincinnati opera festivals of 1881 and 1882, see Mapleson, *Mapleson Memoirs,* 142–143, 150–152. In the 1880s Chicago's trade papers for music and theater were *Amusement World* (1878–?), *Chicago Amusement News* (1886–1897), *Chicago Music and Drama* (1885–? edited by S. C. Griggs); *Chicago Musical Times* (1881–1926; Frank D. Abbott, 1881–1891); *The Indicator: Art and Music* (1878–1930; Orrin L. Fox); *Music and Drama* (1884–? William S. B. Matthews); and *Presto* (1884–1937; Frank O. Abbott to 1900). See William J. Weichlein, *A Checklist of American Music Periodicals, 1850–1900* (Detroit: Information Coordinators, 1970). Chicago's main organ makers were W. W. Kimball Company (incorporated 1882; 12,000 built annually); Estey Organ Company (11,000); Mason and Hamlin Organ and Piano Factory (10,000); and the Sterling Company (10,000) ("The Big Four," *Indicator* 4 [12 July 1884]: 499, and "W. W. Kimball Organs," *Indicator* 6 [21 February 1885]: 165). On local piano makers in the 1890s, see Craig H. Roell, *The Piano in America, 1890–1940* (Chapel Hill: University of North Carolina Press, 1989), 148–149.

108. [Orrin L. Fox?], Editorial, *Indicator* 4 (2 February 1884): 80.

109. Ibid.

110. Garczynski, *Auditorium,* 20. Gregersen, "History of the Auditorium Building," 14, noted Fairbank's offer of 1880 to donate $100,000 toward a permanent opera house.

111. Sullivan, "Development of Construction" (1916), in *Louis Sullivan: The Public Papers,* ed. Twombly, 215.

112. Sullivan, *Autobiography of an Idea,* 292.

113. *Indicator* 4 (26 January 1884): 65. On the Chicago Opera House, see Andreas, *History of Chicago,* 3:668–669; Orear, *Commercial and Architectural Chicago,* 57; Marquis, *Marquis' Hand-Book of Chicago,* 240; Flinn, *Chicago, the Marvelous City of the West,* 121–122; Vynne, *Chicago by Day and Night,* 34–36; Rand McNally, *Bird's-Eye Views and Guide to Chicago,* 82, 136; Condit, *Chicago School,* 59–60; and Twombly, *Louis Sullivan,* 156–157, 158.

114. Committee on Public Buildings, Report of 1 May 1882, in *Proceedings of the City Council of the City of Chicago for the Municipal Year 1881–82* (Chicago, 1882), 556–559, and Report of 3 December 1883, in *Proceedings of the City Council of the City of Chicago for the Municipal Year 1883–84* (Chicago, 1883), 256–257. See *Report of the Committee on Theatres and Public Halls of the Citizens' Association of Chicago, October, 1883* (Chicago, 1883). See also chapter 1, note 126, and note 77 above.

115. "Is Haverly's Theater Safe?" *Indicator* 4 (26 January 1884): 65.

116. Rand McNally, *Bird's-Eye Views and Guide to Chicago,* 142, reprinted in Randall, *Building Construction in Chicago,* 206. The site was valued at $331,200 in 1872 ("Inventory of the Real and Personal Estate of Philip F. W. Peck, late of the City of Chicago, in the County of Cook and State of Illinois, deceased," filed 7 February 1872, County Court of Cook County, docket A, p. 5; Probate Records, Estate of

Philip Ferdinand Peck [Clerk of the Circuit Court of Cook County Archives, Chicago, Illinois]; Cook County Clerk of the Court, book 2, pp. 143–152, Cook County, Clerk of the Court, Probate Archives). On the Chicago Opera House's financing, see Gerald W. Kuhn, "A History of the Financing of Commercial Structures in the Chicago Central Business District, 1868–1914" (Ph.D. diss., Indiana University, 1969), 44. In the depression of the 1890s, the Chicago Opera House paid neither dividends to stockholders nor interest to its stockholders ("Will Not Pay July Interest," *Economist* 18 [3 July 1897]: 10). Peck's Auditorium met the same financial end, as is noted in the epilogue, 389–391.

117.   On Peck's family as lessor of the site, see "A Question of Dollars," *Chicago Tribune*, 20 June 1889, 10.

118.   Flinn, *Chicago, the Marvelous City of the West*, 121. On Henderson, see Andreas, *History of Chicago*, 3:669.

119.   Rand McNally, *Bird's-Eye Views and Guide to Chicago*, 82.

120.   Flinn, *Chicago, the Marvelous City of the West*, 121.

121.   "Mosaics," *Inland Architect and Builder* 5 (June 1885): 79. See "Inspecting the New Opera-House," *Chicago Tribune*, 19 June 1885, 5, and "Chicago Opera-House," *Chicago Times*, 16 August 1885, 6.

122.   "Inspecting the New Opera House," *Chicago Tribune*, 19 June 1885, 5.

123.   "Amusements," *Chicago Tribune*, 19 August 1885, 5. See also "Opening of the New Opera House," *Chicago Times*, 19 August 1885, 5.

124.   Andreas, *History of Chicago*, 3:669.

125.   "Drama," *Indicator* 6 (22 August 1885): 685.

126.   "Chicago Opera House," *Indicator* 7 (14 August 1886): 721. On Adler and Sullivan's renovation, see also "Among Architects and Builders," *Chicago Tribune*, 4 April 1886, 7; "The Chicago Opera-House," *Chicago Tribune*, 6 June 1886, 17; "Foyer Gossip," *Chicago Tribune*, 1 August 1886, 3; "Downing in 'The Gladiator,'" *Chicago Tribune*, 15 August 1886, 11. Adler and Sullivan's Chicago Opera House interior was destroyed by fire in December 1888, with no loss of life ("A Theatre Burned Out," *Chicago Tribune*, 13 December 1888, 1).

127.   C. H. Blackall, "Notes of Travel: Chicago—III," *American Architect and Building News* 23 (25 February 1888): 90. See also Blackall, "Notes of Travel: Chicago—II," *American Architect and Building News* 22 (31 December 1887): 314. On the neo-Renaissance Chicago City Hall and Cook County Courthouse, see Bluestone, *Constructing Chicago*, 159–164. In Manhattan, an earlier smaller theater set within a commerical block was the Park Theater of 1873–1874 on the southeast corner of Broadway and Twenty-third Street, designed by Frederic Diaper, a former partner of Alexander Sältzer. See Stern, Mellins, and Fishman, *New York 1880*, 667–670.

128.   Rand McNally, *Bird's-Eye Views and Guide to Chicago*, 82.

129.   Wright, *Autobiography* (1932), 64. In "The Coming Week," *Chicago Tribune*, 29 August 1886, 18, it was noted: "At the Chicago Opera-House Kirafly Brothers 'Sieba' will be given with all the gorgeousness that spectacularism in these days demands." Varied subsequent accounts of Wright's arrival in Chicago include Robert C. Twombly, *Frank Lloyd Wright: His Life and His Architecture* (New York: John Wiley, 1979), 16–18; Brendan Gill, *Many Masks: A Life of Frank Lloyd Wright* (New York: Putnam, 1987), 57–59; Meryle Secrest, *Frank Lloyd Wright: A Biography* (New York: Alfred A. Knopf, 1992), 82–83; and Siry, *Unity Temple: Frank Lloyd Wright and Architecture for Liberal Religion* (New York: Cambridge University Press, 1996), 15. An arrival date of August 1886 would be consistent with Wright's recollection (*Autobiography*, 1932, 69) that he first saw his uncle Rev. Jenkin Lloyd Jones's church as a "nearly completed building," implying that he had first visited it shortly before its dedication in October 1886.

130.   Vynne, *Chicago by Day and Night*, 36.

131.   Rose Fay Thomas, ed., *Memoirs of Theodore Thomas* (New York: Moffat, Yard, 1911), 258. See Thomas, *Musical Autobiography;* Charles E. Russell, *The American Orchestra and Theodore Thomas*

(Garden City, N.Y.: Doubleday, Page, 1927; reprint, Westport, Conn.: Greenwood Press, 1971); Theodore C. Russell, "Theodore Thomas: His Role in the Development of Musical Culture in the United States, 1835–1905" (Ph.D. diss., University of Minnesota, 1969); and Schabas, *Theodore Thomas.*

On Chicago's May Music Festivals of 1882 and 1884, see "Music," *Chicago Tribune,* 14 May 1882; *Chicago Tribune,* 21 May 1882, 20; *Chicago Tribune,* 28 May 1882; "The City," *Chicago Tribune,* 5 March 1884, 8; "The Coming May Festival," *Indicator* 4 (26 April 1884): 286; "The May Festival," *Indicator* 4 (17 May 1884): 342; "The May Festival," *Chicago Tribune,* 31 May 1884, 3; "Amusements," *Chicago Tribune,* 1 June 1884, 6; "Thomas Festivals and Wagner Programmes," *Indicator* 4 (7 June 1884): 412–413; Andreas, *History of Chicago,* 3:649–651; Upton, *Musical Memories,* 208–210; Ffrench, *Music and Musicians in Chicago,* 29–31; and Horowitz, *Culture and the City,* 39–40. See also the *Program: First Musical Festival* (Chicago Historical Society).

132. See William Weber, *Music and the Middle Class: The Social Structure of Concert Life in London, Paris and Vienna* (New York: Holmes and Meier, 1975). On the Sydenham concerts, see Michael Musgrave, *The Musical Life of the Crystal Palace* (Cambridge: Cambridge University Press, 1995). On Patti at Albert Hall, see Herman R. Klein, *The Reign of Patti* (New York: Century, 1920), 235–241, 315–320, 335–336, 341–342. See generally John R. Thackrah, *The Royal Albert Hall* (Lavenham, Suffolk: T. Dalton, 1983), 1–31. Chicago's Auditorium Theater was later described as "more capacious than the Albert Hall of South Kensington" (*Album of Genealogy and Biography, Cook County, Illinois,* 2d ed., 340). On the Trocadéro Theater, see Daniel Rabreau et al., *Gabriel Davioud: Architecte, 1824–1881* (Paris: Délégation à l'Action Artistique de la Ville de Paris, 1981), 89–102. In New York City, Thomas had led concerts at Irving Hall and the Academy of Music before inaugurating Steinway Hall in 1866. William Steinway commissioned this structure for Thomas, siting it across Fourteenth Street from Irving Hall and the Academy of Music and adjacent to showrooms of Steinway and Sons, America's leading piano manufacturer. Steinway Hall was renovated in 1868, when Thomas began summer concerts at Central Park Gardens, which he gave until 1875 (Schabas, *Theodore Thomas,* 32–33, 37–38).

133. Wirt Dexter et al. to Theodore Thomas, 27 July 1877, in Thomas, *Musical Autobiography,* 1:70. See also Schabas, *Theodore Thomas,* 45–46, 81–83.

134. Theodore Thomas to Wirt Dexter et al., 28 July 1877, in Thomas, *Musical Autobiography,* 1:70–71, and Thomas, *Memoirs of Theodore Thomas,* 132.

135. On Thomas's festivals of 1882 at New York, Cincinnati, and Chicago and those of 1884 at Cincinnati and Chicago, see Schabas, *Theodore Thomas,* 114–120, 128–136.

136. [Orrin L. Fox?], Editorial, *Indicator* 4 (8 March 1884): 160. Pierce, *History of Chicago,* 3:490, notes that Maro L. Bartlett founded a church choral union in 1884. A more formal organization of the same name was founded in 1888 to give citywide instruction in reading music and to elevate standards of congregational singing. While serving on the Chicago Board of Education from 1886 to 1890, Ferdinand Peck chaired the Committee on Music, which promoted teaching music reading and choral singing to children throughout the city. See *Proceedings of the Board of Education of the City of Chicago, September 1887 to September 1888* (Chicago, 1888), 101, 207; ibid., September 1888 to 9 August 1889 (Chicago, 1889), 14, 27, 39–40.

137. "Music," *Chicago Tribune,* 21 May 1882, 20.

138. "Music," *Chicago Tribune,* 28 May 1882.

139. Thomas, *Musical Autobiography,* 1:69.

140. "Music," *Chicago Tribune,* 28 May 1882.

141. Margaret F. Sullivan, "Music Festival—1882," *Dial* 3 (1882): 35–36. Adler and Sullivan's role as architects for the 1882 festival was noted in "A Mammoth Opera House," *Inland Architect and Builder* 5 (March 1885): 25. See also *Inland Architect and Builder* 7 (August 1886): 3.

142. *Inland Architect and News Record* 3 (June 1884): 64. On Adler and Sullivan's remodeling of the Exposition Hall's north end for the festival of 1884, see also "The City," *Chicago Tribune,* 6 March 1884,

8; "Chicago's May Festival," *Chicago Morning News,* 28 May 1884; "May Music," *Chicago Tribune,* 28 May 1884; "The May Festival," *Chicago Tribune,* 29 May 1884; *Chicago Daily News* (morning edition), 30 May 1884; *Chicago Times,* 30 May 1884; *Chicago Tribune,* 30 May 1884; "Musical Matters," *Chicago [Saturday Evening] Herald,* 31 May 1884; "The May Festival," *Chicago Tribune* (31 May 1884): 3; *Chicago Herald,* 1 June 1884; "Amusements," *Chicago Tribune,* 1 June 1884, 6; "The May Festival," *Chicago Evening Journal,* 2 June 1884. The seating plan of the Inter-state Industrial Exposition Building's north end for the Republican convention of 1884 appeared in "The Delegates," *Chicago Tribune,* 31 May 1884, 16. The hall's seating plan for the Democrats appeared in "The Convention," *Chicago Tribune,* 8 July 1884, 9. On the convention hall of 1884, see also Gregersen, *Dankmar Adler,* 55, and Twombly, *Louis Sullivan,* 147. The building's original architect, William Boyington, remodeled the hall for the Republican convention of 1880. See "The New Amphitheatre for the Republican National Convention," *American Architect and Building News* 7 (5 June 1880): 248. See also Sauter and Burke, *Inside the Wigwam,* 34–54.

143.   "The May Festival," *Indicator* 4 (17 May 1884): 342.

144.   "Amusements," *Chicago Tribune,* 1 June 1884, 6.

145.   Joseph Gruenhut, *Progressive Age,* 10 September 1881, quoted in Schneirov, *Labor and Urban Politics,* 139. On the Knights of Labor in the 1880s, see Schneirov, *Labor and Urban Politics,* 119–138; Pierce, *History of Chicago,* 3:263–266; and Schneirov, "The Knights of Labor in the Chicago Labor Movement and in Municipal Politics, 1877–1887" (Ph.D. diss., Northern Illinois University, 1984). On Harrison, see Michael L. Ahern, *The Political History of Chicago* (Chicago, 1886); Claudius O. Johnson, *Carter Harrison I: Political Leader* (Chicago: University of Chicago Press, 1928); and Schneirov, *Labor and Urban Politics,* 140–144, 162–168.

146.   Quoted in Commons et al., *History of Labor in the United States,* 2:388. On the new Central Labor Union, see Avrich, *Haymarket Tragedy,* 91–94.

147.   *Discussion über das Thema: "Anarchismus oder Communismus?" Geführt von Paul Grottkau* [state communist] *und Johann Most* [revolutionary anarchist], *am 24. Mai 1884 in Chicago* (Chicago, 1884). On this debate, see Avrich, *Haymarket Tragedy,* 94–95.

148.   "The Lake Front," *Alarm* 1 (25 October 1884). On the IWPA American Group's Sunday meetings at the lakefront from 3 May 1885, see Avrich, *Haymarket Tragedy,* 108–110. At the trial of the Haymarket conspirators, Joseph Gruenhut testified that, for mass meetings of socialist organizations in 1885, "there are only three or four places where you can hold such a meeting; either the lake front or Market Square or the Haymarket" (Schaack, *Anarchy and Anarchists,* 447–448).

149.   Testimony of John J. Ryan, trial of Haymarket conspirators, Chicago, 1887, quoted in Schaack, *Anarchy and Anarchists,* 435.

150.   On threats to Marshall Field's, see testimony of Marshall H. Williamson, trial of Haymarket conspirators, Chicago, 1887, quoted in Schaack, *Anarchy and Anarchists,* 432.

151.   Prof. Charles Orchardson, "Salvation from Poverty," quoted in Schaack, *Anarchy and Anarchists,* 666. Parsons reported that the open air mass meetings on the lakefront at the foot of Van Buren Street on two consecutive Sundays, 3 and 10 May 1885, each drew "between 1,000 and 1,500 persons" ("The Lake Front," *Alarm* 1 [16 May 1885]: 1). Police detective Ryan reported, "The largest number of persons I ever saw attend any of these meetings was not more than 150" (Schaack, *Anarchy and Anarchists,* 435).

152.   On anarchist activities and capitalist preparedness to 1885, see Henry David, *The History of the Haymarket Affair: A Study in the American Social-Revolutionary and Labor Movements,* 3d rev. ed. (New York: Collier, 1963), 137; Avrich, *Haymarket Tragedy,* 109; and Schneirov, *Labor and Urban Politics,* 173–179. Conservatives opposed Harrison's reelection in 1887 because he tolerated anarchism and vice. See Flinn, *History of the Chicago Police,* 349, and Bonney, *Present Conflict of Labor and Capital,* 25.

153.   Andreas, *History of Chicago,* 3:406. Bruce Grant, *Fight for a City: The Story of the Union League Club of Chicago and Its Times, 1880–1955* (Chicago: Rand McNally, 1955), 120–123, noted the

club's support for the opera festival. On the club's campaign for electoral reform to 1885, see Roberts, "Businessmen in Revolt," 39–69. See also "Influence of Clubs on Politics and Society," *Chicago Evening Journal,* 21 January 1887, 4; Flinn, *Chicago, the Marvelous City of the West,* 246; and George D. Bushnell, "Chicago's Leading Men's Clubs," *Chicago History* 11 (summer 1982): 78–88.

154. "The Union League Club," *Graphic* (Chicago) 12 (22 March 1890): 182. Architects Adler, Daniel Burnham, Adolph Cudell, William Le Baron Jenney, Louis Sullivan and his older brother Albert, Peter B. Wight, and builder Victor Falkenau were all members, as were the three Peck brothers and Ferdinand Peck's father-in-law, William A. Spalding. See *The Union League Club of Chicago: June, 1885* (Chicago Historical Society).

155. Silas G. Pratt, ed., *First Chicago Grand Opera Festival at the Exposition Building* (Chicago: Skeen and Stuart, 1885). See also Andreas, *History of Chicago,* 3:647; Mapleson, *Mapleson Memoirs,* 219–220, 230–234; Ffrench, *Music and Musicians in Chicago,* 31–32; Davis, *Opera in Chicago,* 42–43; and Dizikes, *Opera in America,* 250–251.

156. Sullivan, *Autobiography of an Idea,* 293.

157. Peck, quoted in "The Collegians," *Chicago Inter Ocean,* 5 January 1889. Grant, *Fight for a City,* 119, and Berger, *They Built Chicago,* 94, both noted Peck's earlier European travels as the basis of his enthusiasm for grand opera. See also "The Auditorium and the Italian Opera Revival," *Chicago Tribune,* 17 November 1889, 5, and "The Dedication of the Auditorium," *Chicago Tribune,* 8 December 1889, 12.

158. Philo A. Otis, *Impressions of Europe, 1873–1874: Music, Art and History* (Boston: R. G. Badger, 1922). See also Otis, *The Chicago Symphony Orchestra: Its Organization, Growth and Development, 1891–1924* (1924; reprint, Freeport, N.Y.: Books for Libraries Press, 1972). Bluestone, *Constructing Chicago,* 22, noted traveled Chicagoans' awareness of cultural amenities in Europe as an inspiration for improvement.

159. On Patti, see H. Sutherland Edwards, *The Prima Donna: Her History and Surroundings from the Seventeenth to the Nineteenth Century,* 2 vols. (London: Remington, 1888), 2:64–124; Klein, *Reign of Patti;* and Dizikes, *Opera in America,* 223–230.

160. Edwards, *Prima Donna,* 72–73. Another impetus for the idea of democratic access to high culture may have come to Peck from the Reverend David Swing, who preached that "the humblest classes . . . should not be treated to poor music and a spectacular drama because they are unable to appreciate good music and the high histrionic art" (Swing, "A Plea for the Better Classes," in *Truths for Today,* 2d ser. [Chicago, 1876]).

161. On the development of commercial theaters in Paris after 1789, see Giuseppe Radicchio and Michèle Sajous D'Oris, *Les théâtres de Paris pendant la Révolution* (Bari, 1990), and Anthony Sutcliffe, *Paris: An Architectural History* (New Haven: Yale University Press, 1993), 67–68. On the Opéra National, see Jane Fulcher, *The Nation's Image: French Grand Opera as Politics and Politicized Art* (New York: Cambridge University Press, 1987), 113–121, 171. On Garnier's design for the circulation of different classes of operagoers, see Mead, *Garnier's Paris Opera,* 113–127.

162. Daly and Davioud, *Théâtres de la Place du Châtelet,* and Mead, *Garnier's Paris Opera,* 128–129. See also T. J. Walsh, *Second Empire Opera: The Théâtre Lyrique, Paris, 1851–1870* (London: Calder, 1981). On these theaters, and Davioud's unbuilt project for a new Orphéon Municipal (1864–1867), see also Rabreau et al., *Gabriel Davioud,* 54–75, 76–83. On Davioud's and Bourdais's related unbuilt project of 1875 for a "People's Opera House" in Paris, see Izenour, *Theater Design,* 93.

163. Geraniotis, "German Design Influence in the Auditorium Theater," 47–54. Descriptions of Bayreuth's Festspielhaus include Sachs and Woodrow, *Modern Opera Houses and Theatres,* 1:19–31; Albert Lavignac, *The Music Dramas of Richard Wagner and His Festival Theatres in Bayreuth,* trans. Esther Singleton (New York: Dodd, Mead, 1904), 54–67; Pevsner, *History of Building Types,* 86–87; Izenour, *Theater Design,* 75–82; Forsyth, *Buildings for Music,* 179–182; Heinrich Habel, *Festspielhaus und Wahnfried: Geplante und ausgeführte Bauten Richard Wagners* (Munich: Prestel-Verlag, 1985); and Frederic

Spotts, *Bayreuth: A History of the Wagner Festival* (New Haven: Yale University Press, 1994), 38–54. Peck included the Bayreuth Festspielhaus among those theaters that Adler was to examine during his trip of 1888 (see chapter 4, note 143). Adler presumably knew of the building earlier. In his paper "Stage Mechanisms," *Inland Architect and News Record* 13 (March 1889): 42, he referred to Carl Brandt's work as a theatrical engineer in connection with stage equipment for the Opera House in Frankfurt-am-Main, built 1873–1880.

164. On Semper's first Hoftheater at Dresden, see Mallgrave, *Gottfried Semper,* 117–129. On the seating in Schinkel's Schauspielhaus at Berlin, see Barry Bergdoll, *Karl Friedrich Schinkel: An Architecture for Prussia* (New York: Rizzoli, 1994), 60. On these buildings, and on August Sturmhöfel's unbuilt project of 1888 for a *Volkstheater,* or People's Theater, see Geraniotis, "German Design Influence on the Auditorium Theater," 54–55, 58–62. On Semper's unbuilt designs for Munich's Festspielhaus and their relation to Wagner's dramatic theory, see Mallgrave, *Gottfried Semper,* 251–267. On Wagner's interest in ancient Greek drama as a model for his art, see Brian Magee, *Aspects of Wagner* (New York, 1988), 5–9, and Dieter Borchmeyer, *Richard Wagner: Theory and Theatre,* trans. Stuart Spencer (1982; New York: Oxford University Press, 1991), esp. 59–86.

165. On Americans at Bayreuth, see *Presto* 6 (31 August 1889): 6, and Joseph Horowitz, *Wagner Nights: An American History* (Berkeley: University of California Press, 1994), 138–152. Among American reports of Bayreuth's opening were those by Leopold Damrosch, the Metropolitan Opera's future conductor of German opera, who wrote "To Day's Musical Wonder," *New York Sun,* 13 August 1876, 2, and "The Twilight of the Gods," *New York Sun,* 23 August 1876, 2. See also the editorial, "Wagner, the Art Revolutionist," *New York Sun,* 19 August 1876, 2. Financial losses from the inaugural performance of Wagner's operatic cycle *Der Ring des Nibelungen* kept the Festspielhaus closed to 1882. Architects Potter and Robertson's nonwinning design for the Metropolitan Opera House included a lowered orchestra pit, adapted from the one at Bayreuth. See "Competitive Designs Prepared for the Metropolitan Opera House, New York, N.Y., Messrs. Potter and Robertson, Architects, New York, N.Y.," *American Architect and Building News* 8 (13 November 1880): 234–235. In 1890 McKim, Mead, and White's theater at New York's Madison Square Garden was "to be built upon the plan of that at Bayreuth which Wagner caused to be built according to the most approved plans" ("New York's Auditorium," *Chicago Tribune* [25 January 1889], 2). On the Metropolitan's German seasons, see Krehbiel, *Chapters of Opera,* 109–138, 155–212; Kolodin, *Metropolitan Opera,* 87–105; Eaton, *Miracle of the Met,* 66–74; Briggs, *Yellow Brick Brewery,* 30–38; Mayer, *Met,* 48–64; Eisler, *Metropolitan Opera,* 55–171; and Dizikes, *Opera in America,* 238–246. By the end of the Metropolitan's seven Wagner seasons in spring 1891, the popularity of Bayreuth's performances for American tourists had declined. See "Bayreuth's Reign Over," *Chicago Tribune,* 6 September 1891, 11.

166. "The May Festival," *Chicago Tribune,* 31 May 1884, 3.

167. On Mapleson's demise at the Academy of Music after the season of 1883–1884, see Pisoni, "Operatic War in New York City," 460–462, 474–475 n. 39. Early in his career, Mapleson had worked in London for Edward T. Smith, who had sought to bring Italian opera to a broad urban populace. See chapter 2, 105, and Mapleson, *Mapleson Memoirs,* 18–30.

168. "The Chicago Opera Festival," *Chicago Tribune,* 1 June 1884, 6.

169. Editorial, "Music: The Operatic Festival," *Chicago Tribune,* 29 March 1885, 12.

170. On Peck's musical tastes, see "Ferdinand Peck, Widely Known Chicagoan, Dies," *Chicago Tribune,* 5 November 1924, 19. In his later years, Peck had attended every opening night at the Auditorium Theater.

171. Pisoni, "Operatic War in New York City," 13.

172. Percentages of German and Bohemian anarchists in Chicago in 1880–1886 are noted in Melvin G. Holli and Peter D'A. Jones, eds., *Ethnic Chicago: A Multicultural Portrait,* 4th ed. (Grand Rapids: William B. Eerdmans, 1995), 95. On perceived links between German ethnicity and radical

politics, see Schaack, *Anarchy and Anarchists,* 44–73; Carol Poore, "German-American Socialist Culture," *Cultural Correspondence,* special issue (spring 1978): 13–20; Hartmut Keil and Heinz Ickstadt, "Elemente einer deutschen Arbeiterkultur in Chicago zwischen 1880 und 1890," *Geschichte und Gesellschaft* 5 (1979): 103–124; Hartmut Keil and John Jentz, "German Working-Class Culture in Chicago," *Gulliver: Deutsch-Englische Jahrbucher* 9 (1979): 128–147; John Jentz and Hartmut Keil, "From Immigrants to Urban Workers: Chicago's German Poor in the Gilded Age and Progressive Era, 1883–1908," *Vierteljährschrift für Sozial- und Wirtschaftsgeschichte* 68 (1981): 52–97; Hartmut Keil, "The German Immigrant Working Class of Chicago, 1875–90: Workers, Labor Leaders, and the Labor Movement," in *American Labor and Immigration History, 1877–1920s: Recent European Research,* ed. Dirk Hoerder (Urbana: University of Illinois Press, 1983), 156–176; Avrich, *Haymarket Tragedy,* 84–85, 218–219; Nelson, *Beyond the Martyrs,* 15–23; and Hirsch, *Urban Revolt,* 144–170.

173. "The Grand Opera Festival," *Real Estate and Building Journal* 27 (4 April 1885): 160–161.

174. William Penn Nixon, quoted in "Music for the People," *Chicago Tribune,* 3 May 1885, 6.

175. Sullivan, *Autobiography of an Idea,* 292. Peck's and McVicker's addresses were noted in Rand McNally, *Bird's-Eye Views and Guide to Chicago,* 261. On Adler and Sullivan's remodeling of the Exposition Building's north end for the opera festival, see "Synopsis of Building News," *Inland Architect and Building News* 5 (February 1885): 14; "Building News," *Real Estate and Building Journal* 27 (21 February 1885): 89; "A Mammoth Opera House," *Inland Architect and News Record* 5 (March 1885): 25; "The Opera Festival," *Chicago Tribune,* 1 March 1885, 7; "The Operatic Festival," *Chicago Tribune,* 28 March 1885, 12; "The Grand Opera Festival," *Real Estate and Building Journal* 27 (4 April 1885): 160–161; Editorial, "The Opera Festival," *Chicago Tribune,* 5 April 1885, 4; *Chicago Tribune,* 12 April 1885, 27. See also Morrison, *Louis Sullivan,* 67–71; Denson, "History of the Chicago Auditorium," 30–34; Yvonne Shafer, "The First Chicago Grand Opera Festival: Adler and Sullivan before the Auditorium," *Theater Design and Technology* 13 (March 1977): 9–13, 38; Grimsley, "Contributions of Dankmar Adler," 184–189; Twombly, *Louis Sullivan,* 147–149; Gregersen, *Dankmar Adler,* 15–16, 55, 60–61; Frei, *Louis Henry Sullivan,* 64–65; and Dizikes, *Opera in America,* 250–251.

176. "The Opera Festival," *Chicago Tribune,* 1 March 1885, 7.

177. "The Opera Festival," *Chicago Tribune,* 30 March 1885, 9.

178. "The Opera Festival," *Chicago Music and Drama,* 11 April 1885, 4.

179. Mapleson, *Mapleson Memoirs,* 230. On opening night another account of the festival noted: "Away back in the rear portion of the gallery it was rather difficult at times to hear the solo singing and the recitatives . . . . Even in the dress circle and the rear portion of the parquet Mme. Patti's voice seemed smaller than usual, and there appeared to be among members of the audience who were not in close proximity to the stage an impression that the performance would have been more enjoyable in an ordinary-sized theater" ("Patti and Salchi," *Chicago Tribune,* 7 April 1885, 5).

180. Sullivan, *Autobiography of an Idea,* 293.

181. Peck, quoted in "A Week of Music," *Chicago Tribune,* 12 April 1885, 12.

182. On the festival's opening, see "Patti and Salchi," *Chicago Tribune,* 7 April 1885, 5. Guarantors were listed in Silas G. Pratt, ed., *First Chicago Grand Opera Festival at the Exposition Building* (Chicago: Skeen and Stuart, 1885). See also "Bidding for Boxes," *Chicago Tribune,* 13 March 1885, 8. On courtesies to Patti, see "A Day in the City," *Chicago Tribune,* 4 April 1885, 3, and "Patti's Last Night," *Chicago Tribune,* 18 April 1885, 2.

183. "The Opera Audience," *Chicago Tribune,* 10 April 1885, 5.

184. Andreas, *History of Chicago,* 3:651. One editorial had predicted, "Socially, as well as financially and musically, the festival will be a success, and in this regard it will recall palmy days of opera in the Crosby Opera House" ("The Opera Season," *Chicago Tribune,* 29 March 1885, 4).

185. "Amusements," *Chicago Tribune,* 12 April 1885, 27.

186. "Amusements," *Chicago Tribune,* 19 April 1885, 26. In the 1880s Chicago's panoramas were mounted inside large circular or polygonal structures; after paying a small admission fee, visitors climbed to a platform in the center of the building, from which they viewed the surrounding realistic mural, called a cyclorama. To heighten the illusion, real objects and elements of landscape were set in the foreground between the viewing platforms and the surrounding painting. Prominent local cycloramas included "Jerusalem on the Day of the Crucifixion" and the "Battle of Gettysburg" in two buildings on the southeast and southwest corners of South Wabash and East Balbo Avenues, just a block west of Michigan Avenue. In 1892 the Chicago Fire Cyclorama was installed in a dodecagonal building at 127–132 South Michigan Avenue between Madison and Monroe Streets, across Michigan Avenue from the Inter-state Industrial Exposition Building's site. Created for the World's Columbian Exposition, this cyclorama drew 144,000 visitors a year. The Jerusalem, Gettysburg, and Chicago Fire cycloramas were noted in Rand McNally, *Bird's-Eye Views and Guide to Chicago,* partially reprinted in Randall, *Building Construction in Chicago,* 110, 170. See Perry R. Duis and Glen E. Holt, "Chicago as It Was: Cheap Thrills and Dime Museums," *Chicago* 26 (October 1977): 104–108, and Duis, *Challenging Chicago,* 205–208. See also Frances Stover, *The Panorama Painters' Days of Glory* (Milwaukee: Milwaukee County Historical Society, 1969), and Esther Sparks, "A Biographical Dictionary of Painters and Sculptors in Illinois, 1808–1945" (Ph.D. diss., Northwestern University, 1971), 16–18. See also Stephan Oettermann, *The Panorama: History of a Mass Medium,* trans. Deborah Lucas Schneider (1980; New York: Zone Books, 1997).

187. "A Mammoth Opera House," *Inland Architect and Builder* 5 (March 1885): 25. On Wright's recollection of Sullivan's Wagnerian enthusiasms, see chapter 4, 233.

188. Pratt, *First Chicago Grand Opera Festival.*

189. "To Hear Patti," *Chicago Tribune,* 15 April 1885, 5.

190. Peck, quoted in "The Opera Is Over," *Chicago Tribune,* 19 April 1885, 12. On attendance and revenue, see "Close of the Opera Festival," *Chicago Tribune,* 19 April 1885, 4; "Music for the People," *Chicago Inter Ocean,* 3 May 1885, 6; and Andreas, *History of Chicago,* 3:652–653.

191. Keil and Ickstadt, "Elements of German Working-Class Culture in Chicago," 94–95. On local politicized workers' culture, see Avrich, *Haymarket Tragedy,* 136–140; Bruce C. Nelson, "Culture and Conspiracy: A Social History of Chicago Anarchism, 1870–1900" (Ph.D. diss., Northern Illinois University, 1985)," 280–338; Nelson, "Dancing and Picnicking Anarchists," in *Haymarket Scrapbook,* ed. David Roediger and Franklin Rosemont (Chicago: Charles H. Kerr, 1986), 76–79; and Nelson, *Beyond the Martyrs,* 127–151.

192. "The International Working People's Association Organizes a Demonstration and a Picnic," *Chicagoer Arbeiter-Zeitung,* 30 June 1884, translated in Keil and Jentz, *German Workers in Chicago,* 257–259. One labor paper editor wrote that "what we understand by *picnic* today, however,—an out-of-door festivity—is not so much a remnant of the tradition brought over from England, but rather much more something preserved by the Germans, and especially by the German societies" ("The Origin of Picnics," *Chicagoer Arbeiter-Zeitung,* 27 June 1883, translated in Keil and Jentz, *German Workers in Chicago,* 206).

193. "The Paris Commune," *Vorbote,* 25 March 1876, translated in Keil and Jentz, *German Workers in Chicago,* 279.

194. "Unsere Commune-Feier," *Chicagoer Arbeiter-Zeitung,* 20 March 1882, discussed by Christine Heiss, "Popular and Working-Class German Theater in Chicago, 1870 to 1910," in *German Workers' Culture in the United States,* ed. Keil, 194.

195. "Vive la Commune!" *Alarm* 1 (4 April 1885): 1.

196. "Both Pleasant Affairs," *Chicago Tribune,* 13 April 1887, 1. On entertainments of nonradical trade unions, many held in *Turnhalle,* see, for example, "Theatrical Folks' Hop" and "The Stone-Cutters' Ball," *Chicago Tribune,* 8 December 1887, 2. On the city's low-priced commercial entertainments of the

period, see Perry R. Duis, "Whose City? Public and Private Places in Nineteenth-Century Chicago, Part Two," *Chicago History* 12 (spring 1983): 18–21; Lewis A. Erenberg, "'Ain't We Got Fun?'" *Chicago History* 14 (winter 1985–1986): 4–21; Susan E. Hirsch and Robert I. Goler, *A City Comes of Age: Chicago in the 1890s* (Chicago: Chicago Historical Society, 1990), 129–132; and Duis, *Challenging Chicago*, chap. 7.

197. George Wharton James, *Chicago's Dark Places* (Chicago: Craig Press, 1891). See also William Stead, *If Christ Came to Chicago! A Plea for the Union of All Who Love in the Service of All Who Suffer* (London: Review of Reviews, 1894). On Stead, see Dennis B. Downey, "William Stead and Chicago: A Victorian Jeremiah in the Windy City," *Mid-America* 38 (1986): 153–166. On vice in the period, see, retrospectively, Hyde Park Protective Association, *A Quarter Century of War on Vice in the City of Chicago* (Chicago, 1918); Herbert Asbury, *Gem of the Prairie: An Informal History of the Chicago Underworld* (New York: Alfred A. Knopf, 1940); and Miller, *City of the Century*, 505–513.

198. "A Triumphal March," *Chicago Inter Ocean*, 28 April 1885, 10.

199. Andreas, *History of Chicago*, 3:319. On the monolithic column, see Taylor, *Board of Trade*, 2:676. On the Board of Trade building, see "The Board of Trade," *Chicago Tribune*, 28 April 1885, 9; "The Board of Trade Home," *Chicago Tribune*, 3 May 1885, 3; Marquis, *Marquis' Hand-Book of Chicago*, 261–262; *Industrial Chicago*, 1:177; Flinn, *Chicago, the Marvelous City of the West*, 259–260; Rand McNally, *Bird's-Eye Views and Guide to Chicago*, 16, 143; "Architectural Aberrations," *Architectural Record* 3 (July–September 1893): 96–100; Tallmadge, *Architecture in Old Chicago*, 165; Randall, *Building Construction in Chicago*, 108; and Bluestone, *Constructing Chicago*, 131, 141.

200. "Razing the Chicago Board of Trade Tower," *Graphic* (Chicago), n.s., 10 (24 March 1894): 233. On the Phoenix columns in Boyington's Board of Trade Building, see Gerald Larson and Roula Geraniotis, "Toward a Better Understanding of the Iron Skeleton Frame in Chicago," *Journal of the Society of Architectural Historians* 46 (1987): 46–47. On the later Board of Trade Building, see Earl J. Reed Jr., "Some Recent Work of Holabird & Root, Architects," *Architecture* 61 (January 1930): 21, and Robert Bruegmann, *Holabird and Roche and Holabird and Root: An Illustrated Catalog of Works, 1880–1940*, 3 vols. (New York: Garland, 1991), vol. 3, entry 1200, pp. 23–39.

201. "A Triumphal March," *Chicago Inter Ocean*, 28 April 1885, 10. Taylor, *Board of Trade*, 2:638, noted Boyington's selection over architect E. S. Jennison and over Burnham and Root.

202. "A Triumphal March," *Chicago Inter Ocean*, 28 April 1885, 10.

203. "Our Vampires," *Alarm* 1 (2 May 1885): 1. On the dinner, see "The Board of Trade," *Chicago Tribune*, 29 April 1885, 3. On the new building's opening, see also Taylor, *Board of Trade*, 2:710–716. On workers' threats to loot grocery stores, see Testimony of Marshall H. Williamson, trial of Haymarket conspirators, Chicago, 1887, quoted in Schaack, *Anarchy and Anarchists*, 432. On the idea of sacking the Board of Trade, see Schaack, *Anarchy and Anarchists*, 590. On private property as the plundering of labor, see Keil and Jentz, *German Workers in Chicago*, 360–362.

204. "Our Vampires," *Alarm* 1 (2 May 1885): 1. See also "They Want Blood," *Chicago Tribune*, 29 April 1885, 2; Schaack, *Anarchy and Anarchists*, 80–81; and Avrich, *Haymarket Tragedy*, 146–149.

205. Prosecutor Julius S. Grinnell, description of anarchist Samuel Fielden, trial of Haymarket conspirators, Chicago, 1887, in Schaack, *Anarchy and Anarchists*, 572. See "The Eight-Hour Movement," in *Illinois Bureau of Labor Statistics, Fourth Biennial Report* (Springfield, Ill., 1886), 466–498. On the Easter Sunday demonstration, see "Prometheus reckt sich," *Chicagoer Arbeiter-Zeitung*, 28 April 1886; David, *History of the Haymarket Affair*, 183; and Keil and Ickstadt, "Elements of German Working-Class Culture," 81–82. On Parsons's May Day march, see Avrich, *Haymarket Conspiracy*, 186. For strike statistics, see United States Commissioner of Labor, *Third Annual Report of the United States Commissioner of Labor, 1887: Strikes and Lockouts* (Washington, D.C., 1887), 100–171, cited in Schneirov, *Labor and Urban Politics*, 183.

206. Accounts of the clash and its aftermath include David, *History of the Haymarket Affair*, 182–235; Avrich, *Haymarket Tragedy*, 181–239; Smith, *Urban Disorder and the Shape of Belief*, 101–176;

and Schneirov, *Labor and Urban Politics,* 183–205, who stresses problems of overproduction, deflation, and mechanization as root economic causes for disturbances of 1886. Local accounts of Haymarket from the period unsympathetic to labor included "A Hellish Deed," *Chicago Tribune,* 5 May 1886, 1–2; Bonney, *Present Conflict of Labor and Capital;* and Schaack, *Anarchy and Anarchists.*

207. Robert Herrick, *The Memoirs of an American Citizen* (1905; reprint, Cambridge: Harvard University Press, 1963), 66.

208. Rev. David Swing, quoted in Ericsson, *Sixty Years a Builder,* 235. For Swing's and other clerics' first reactions to Haymarket, see "Denounced from Pulpit," *Chicago Tribune,* 10 May 1886, 1–2. See also Lewis F. Wheelock, "Urban Protestant Reactions to the Chicago Haymarket Affair, 1886–1893" (Ph.D. diss., University of Iowa, 1956). Haymarket had major national resonance, attracting widespread condemnation of radicals and inciting aggressive policing in other major United States cities. See, for example, Lester C. Hubbard, *The Coming Climax in the Destinies of America* (Chicago: C. H. Kerr, 1891).

CHAPTER 3

1. "The Opera Festival," *Chicago Tribune,* 5 April 1885, 4. See "Close of the Opera Festival," *Chicago Tribune,* 19 April 1885, 4. On the project of the Trades and Labor Assembly for a general union hall on the lakefront, see Schneirov, *Labor and Urban Politics,* 164.

2. [Orrin L. Fox?], Editorial, *Indicator* 6 (9 May 1885): 394. On lower-income public amusements, see Perry R. Duis and Glen E. Holt, "Chicago as It Was: Cheap Thrills and Dime Museums," *Chicago,* October 1977, 104–108; and Duis, *Challenging Chicago,* 208–209. Generally, see Robert Bogdan, *Freak Show: Presenting Human Oddities for Amusement and Profit* (Chicago: University of Chicago Press, 1988). On Chicago as vice-ridden, see Herbert Asbury, *Gem of the Prairie: An Informal History of the Chicago Underworld* (New York: Alfred A. Knopf, 1940), and Curt Johnson and R. Craig Sautter, *Wicked City: Chicago from Kenna to Capone* (Chicago: December Press, 1994).

3. "Music for the People," *Chicago Inter Ocean,* 3 May 1885, 6. On Parsons's lakefront rally of 3 May, see "The Lake Front," *Alarm* 1 (16 May 1885): 1.

4. "A Futile Opera House Scheme," *Chicago Tribune,* 8 November 1885, 4; "Dearborn Park," *Chicago Tribune,* 8 November 1885, 10.

5. Peck, address to Chicago Commercial Club, 29 May 1886, paraphrased in "New Grand Opera House," *Chicago Tribune,* 12 June 1886, 9. Peck's speech was published verbatim in "Seats for a Multitude," *Chicago Evening Journal,* 29 January 1887, 1.

6. See Vilas Johnson, *A History of the Commercial Club of Chicago* (Chicago: Commercial Club of Chicago, 1977), 120. See also John J. Glessner, *The Commercial Club of Chicago: Its Beginning and Something of Its Work* (Chicago: privately printed, 1910), reprinted in Johnson, *Commercial Club,* 9–83; and Thomas J. Schlereth, "Big Money and High Culture: The Commercial Club of Chicago and Charles L. Hutchinson," *Great Lakes Review* 3 (1976): 15–27. On the Chicago Manual Training School, see Flinn, *Chicago, the Marvelous City of the West,* 268.

7. Commercial Club presidents John W. Doane (1879–1880) and Albert A. Sprague (1882) were guarantors of the Opera Festival, as were four others of the club's thirty-nine charter members: Edson Keith, George M. Pullman, John B. Drake, and Charles M. Henderson. See Glessner, *Commercial Club,* in Johnson, *Commercial Club,* 13–14, and Pratt, *First Chicago Grand Opera Festival.* On Richardson's nonextant house for MacVeagh, see Jeffrey Karl Ochsner, *H. H. Richardson: Complete Architectural Works* (Cambridge: MIT Press, 1982), 391–393. Richardson's better known and still extant residence in Chicago was built at the same time for John J. Glessner, later the author of the Commercial Club's first history. For accounts of this building, see note 184 below.

8. Peck, in "New Grand Opera House," *Chicago Tribune,* 12 June 1886, 9. The idea of a capacious hall as an enabling location for varied cultural events is discussed in Michael Musgrave, *Musical Life of the Crystal Palace,* 3–6.

9. Peck, in "New Grand Opera House," *Chicago Tribune*, 12 June 1886, 9. On national political conventions in Chicago from 1860 through 1884, see Sautter and Burke, *Inside the Wigwam*, 2–65.

10. Ibid.

11. Edward H. Taylor, Testimony, Chicago Auditorium Association vs. Mark Skinner Willing and the Northern Trust Co. as Trustees, etc., et al., in United States Circuit Court of Appeals for the Seventh Circuit, October Term, A.D. 1925, no. 3733, 212–213 (Auditorium Collection, Roosevelt University Archives). On the Studebaker Building, see Introduction, 3–4 and note 5.

12. "Real Estate," *Chicago Tribune*, 31 May 1885, 3.

13. R. Floyd Clinch, Testimony, Chicago Auditorium Association vs. Mark Skinner Willing, 227. See also "Real Estate: The Future of State Streeet and Wabash Avenue," *Chicago Tribune*, 5 May 1878, 10.

14. Edward H. Taylor, Testimony, Chicago Auditorium Association vs. Mark Skinner Willing, 210, 211.

15. Peck, in "New Grand Opera-House," *Chicago Tribune*, 12 June 1886, 9. See also "The Sale of the Scammon Properties," *Chicago Tribune*, 28 March 1886, 13, and "The Auditorium Building," *Economist* 2 (9 February 1889): 97–98. On the leasing agreement, see "The Auditorium in Luck," *Economist* 6 (25 July 1891): 157. On the original financing agreement, see "The Auditorium," *Economist* 7 (30 April 1892): 650. On Walker, see Flinn, *Hand-Book of Chicago Biography*, 375. On his role as client for Holabird and Roche's Tacoma Building, see Bruegmann, *Architects and the City*, 73–78.

16. Peck, in "New Grand Opera-House," *Chicago Tribune*, 12 June 1886, 9.

17. Ibid.

18. This was a limited liability corporation created for publicly beneficial purposes under the laws of the state of Illinois. The association's purposes were described in Records of the Chicago Auditorium Association, Originally Chicago Grand Auditorium Association, December 11, 1886 to November 7, 1906, 2 (Auditorium Collection, Roosevelt University Archives). On limited liability corporations as legal frameworks for building in Chicago during this period, see Bruegmann, *Architects and the City*, 71–72.

19. Ffrench, *Music and Musicians in Chicago*, 32. Original stockholders and their amounts are in Records of the Chicago Auditorium Association, 5, and in the Chicago Auditorium Association, List of Stockholders on 1 February 1888 (Auditorium Collection, Roosevelt University Archives). On Peck's fund-raising, see "Subscribers to the Grand Opera Hall," *Chicago Tribune*, 26 September 1886, 7; "The 'Grand Auditorium,'" *Chicago Tribune*, 28 November 1886, 7; "A Magnificent Enterprise," *Chicago Tribune*, 5 December 1886, 15; and "The Grand Auditorium," *Chicago Tribune*, 10 December 1886, 1. See also Morrison, *Louis Sullivan*, 86, and Twombly, *Louis Sullivan*, 164–165.

20. "The Grand Auditorium," *Chicago Tribune*, 10 December 1886, 1.

21. Peck, Annual Report of the President to the Stockholders of the Chicago Auditorium Association, 1 December 1888 (Auditorium Collection, Roosevelt University Archives). Waterman, *Chicago and Cook County*, 3:924, similarly wrote of Peck: "It was his plan that the undertaking should not be an affair of the few but of the many, and he desired that the stockholders should represent as many classes as possible."

22. "Something for Nothing," *Economist* 44 (9 July 1910): 57. See Berger, *They Built Chicago*, 97. In 1892 it was noted that "the association has seen the poorest financial years in its history, and that it will hereafter be a dividend-paying concern, although, as Mr. Peck has often stated, it is not primarily a moneymaking organization, but a center of music, art and education" ("The Auditorium Association," *Economist* 8 [10 December 1892]: 825). In 1893 the sole dividend paid on Auditorium stock was noted in Records of the Chicago Auditorium Association, 228, and "The Auditorium Association," *Economist* 12 (8 December 1894): 622.

23. On the Rookery's financing, see "A Great Building," *Chicago Tribune*, 4 December 1885, 3; Gerald W. Kuhn, "A History of the Financing of Commercial Structures in the Chicago Loop,

1868–1934" (Ph.D. diss., University of Indiana Business School, 1969), 51–52; Berger, *They Built Chicago,*
62–65; and Bruegmann, *Architects and the City,* 70–71.

24. "The Grand Auditorium," *Chicago Tribune,* 10 December 1886, 1.

25. Peck, Annual Report of the President to the Stockholders of the Chicago Auditorium Association, 12 December 1891 (Auditorium Collection, Roosevelt University Archives).

26. See chapter 2, 106, and note 162.

27. "The Auditorium Building," *Economist* 1 (24 November 1888): 4. Peck stated that "it is the wish
of the projectors that the Auditorium shall eventually come to be the great art center of America"
("The Pride of Chicago," *Chicago Daily News,* morning edition, 9 December 1889). Similar themes recurred in speeches at the theater's opening. See "Dedicated to Music and the People," *Chicago Tribune,*
10 December 1889, 1–2.

28. Adler, "Paramount Requirements of a Large Opera House," 45.

29. Peck, Annual Report of the President to the Stockholders of the Chicago Auditorium Association, 12 December 1891 (Chicago Historical Society), noted: "The main source of revenue—the Hotel—
has had a prosperous year . . . . The Auditorium will always be an uncertain factor with respect to its
revenue." On the site's acquisition and initial plans for its use as a hotel surrounding the theater proper,
see "The Convention Hall," *Chicago Tribune,* 1 August 1886, 13.

30. See chapter 2, 84, and note 80.

31. Adler, "Chicago Auditorium," 415. Henry E. Krehbiel, *Chapters of Opera* (New York: Henry
Holt, 1911), 91, cited a claim by John B. Schoeffel, a partner of Henry Abbey, the impresario who managed the Metropolitan in its first season (1883–1884), that Abbey lost $600,000. See also Briggs, *Yellow
Brick Brewery,* 22, 28–29; Mayer, *Met,* 43–47; and Eisler, *Metropolitan Opera,* 50–53. Garczynski, *Auditorium,* 20, noted that, in contrast to Cincinnati, "New York, with a far greater population, and with infi-
nitely superior wealth, had built the Academy of Music, and still more recently the Metropolitan Opera
House, with no better financial result than the obligation of the owners of these temples of the Muses
to pay annual assessments for the maintenance of these structures, and to lose all prospect of interest
upon the millions invested."

32. See chapter 2, 79, and note 62.

33. Sullivan, *Autobiography of an Idea,* 293–294. Peck had included the term *grand public auditorium* in his proposal to the Chicago Commercial Club, 29 May 1886, quoted in "New Grand Opera
House," *Chicago Tribune,* 13 June 1886, 9.

34. Birgitta Tamm, *Auditorium and Palatium: A Study on Assembly-Rooms in Roman Palaces
during the First Century B.C. and the First Century A.D.,* Stockholm Studies in Classical Archaeology 2
(Stockholm: Almquist och Wiksell, 1963), 7–24.

35. Editorial, "The Auditorium Opening," *Chicago Inter Ocean,* 9 December 1889, 4.

36. On acquisition of the Auditorium's full site and the city council's repeal of the ordinance
bisecting it, see "The Convention Hall," *Chicago Tribune,* 1 August 1886, 13. Peck recalled that "it was
originally contemplated by the projectors that a great public hall and a hotel should be built on a site
not including the corner of Wabash ave. and Congress st. and the north lot of the Michigan ave.
frontage, which were not then obtainable. From that your building has grown to cover the entire site
now occupied" (Annual Report of the President to the Stockholders of the Chicago Auditorium Association, 1 December 1888 [Auditorium Collection, Roosevelt University Archives]). Adler, "Chicago Auditorium," 415, similarly recalled: "When the design of the Auditorium Building was first intrusted to its
architects only two thirds of the ground and less than one-half of the money finally absorbed by the
work were placed at their disposal. But, little by little, the enthusiasm of Mr. Ferd. W. Peck, the chief
promoter of the enterprise, met with such response from the business men of Chicago as to warrant
the acquisition of greater area for the building site and expansions of scope and scale far beyond the
limits contemplated in the conception and development of the original design." Sullivan, "Development

of Construction" (1916), in *Louis Sullivan: The Public Papers,* ed. Twombly, 216, also recalled that "the board of directors of the Auditorium were constantly enlarging their own ideas and amplifying them."

37. Editorial, "Combined Theatres and Hotels," *Hotel Mail* 25 (21 December 1889). Earlier one of the Auditorium's supporters noted that the building would "provide the largest European hotel we have any knowledge of anywhere" ("The Biggest on Earth," *Chicago Evening Journal,* 2 November 1886, 2). Marquis, *Marquis' Hand-Book of Chicago,* 267–274, notes the plan options of some of the city's major hotels of the period. Hotels that included room and board in one daily charge operated on the "American plan." New York City's major hotels were then rapidly converting from the American to the European plan. Chicago's Palmer House offered both plans, while the rival Grand Pacific Hotel was still conducted on the American plan. On these hotels, see chapter 5, 274–286.

Benjamin Latrobe had designed a project for a theater combined with a hotel and other facilities for Richmond, Virginia, in 1797–1798 (Talbot Hamlin, *Benjamin Henry Latrobe* [New York: Oxford University Press, 1955], 86–87, 117–120). In San Francisco, Elias J. Baldwin opened the Baldwin Hotel in 1877 and later the adjacent Baldwin Theater, both destroyed by fire in 1898 (Williamson, *American Hotel,* 95–96, 291). One account of Adler and Sullivan's second design for the Auditorium noted: "Over the two-story entrances the building face will be relieved by swell fronts, something after the style of the Baldwin House in San Francisco" ("A Monumental Edifice," *Chicago Evening Journal,* 9 December 1886, 1).

38. "Music and the Drama," *Chicago Herald,* 26 September 1886, 12.

39. "Chicago Real Estate: Subscribers to the Grand Opera Hall," *Chicago Tribune,* 26 September 1886, 7. On Lautrup, see *Inland Architect and Builder* 5 (March 1885): 25.

40. On the Auditorium's siting and urban visibility, see Garczynski, *Auditorium,* 41–49.

41. "Music and the Drama," *Chicago Herald,* 26 September 1886, 12.

42. Wright, *Genius and the Mobocracy,* 48. On development of the Auditorium's exterior design, see Morrison, *Louis Sullivan,* 86–89; Twombly, *Louis Sullivan,* 164–170; Gregersen, "History of the Auditorium Building," 18–24; and Carroll W. Westfall, "From Homes to Towers: A Century of Chicago's Best Hotels and Tall Apartment Buildings," in *Chicago Architecture,* ed. Zukowsky, 272–275.

43. Paul Mueller, Testimony, Chicago Auditorium Association vs. Mark Skinner Willing and the Northern Trust Co., in Kaufmann, "Wright's 'Lieber Meister,'" 49. Mueller, cited in Tallmadge, *Architecture in Old Chicago,* 198–199, recalled that Sullivan's exterior design was prepared in collaboration with the Northwestern Terra Cotta Company, although the Tacoma Building's cladding system was developed from ideas of Sanford Loring at the Chicago Terra Cotta Company. On the Tacoma Building's design, see Bruegmann, *Architects and the City,* esp. 74–86.

44. Henry Van Brunt, "John Wellborn Root," *Inland Architect and News Record* 16 (January 1891): 86, quoted in *Industrial Chicago,* 1:68. On Burnham and Root's Insurance Exchange Building, see "Insurance Exchange Building," *Chicago Tribune,* 12 April 1885, 12; George Beaumont, "Brickwork," *Inland Architect and News Record* 7 (May 1886): 61–64; Charles H. Blackall, "Notes of Travel: Chicago—III," *American Architect and Building News* 22 (February 1888): 89–90; *Industrial Chicago,* 1:184–185; Robert C. McLean, "The Passing of the Woman's Temple," *Western Architect* 31 (1922): 14; and Hoffmann, *Architecture of John Wellborn Root,* 43–45. On Sullivan's admiration for Root, see Sullivan, *Autobiography of an Idea,* 286–288; Wright, *Autobiography* (1932), 101; and *Genius and the Mobocracy,* 54.

45. Pfeiffer's design for what was originally to be the Plaza Apartment House appeared in *American Architect and Building News* 16 (5 July 1884). Pfeiffer disavowed a link to the Plaza Hotel that was later built on the same site to the designs of McKim, Mead, and White (*American Architect and Building News* 19 [6 March 1886]: 119). See Lydia S. Dubin, "The Hotels of New York City, 1885–1900" (M.A. thesis, Pennsylvania State University, 1969), 42–44; Leland M. Roth, *McKim, Mead and White, Architects* (New York: Harper and Row, 1983), 138; and Stern, Mellins and Fishman, *New York 1880,* 529–530. On English Victorian railway hotels, see Derek Taylor and David Bush, *The Golden Age of British Hotels* (London: Northwood, 1974).

46. Marquis, *Marquis' Hand-Book of Chicago,* 272. The earlier hotel on the same site had been known as Burke's European Hotel, of which McCoy had become manager in 1879. See Andreas, *History of Chicago,* 3:358.

47. Rand McNally, *Bird's-Eye Views and Guide to Chicago,* 72.

48. "A New Area [Era] in Building," *Chicago Journal of Commerce* 44 (19 March 1884): 1, 3. On the Pullman Building, see also *Inland Architect and News Record* 3 (February 1884): 6, and *Inland Architect and News Record* 3 (May 1884): 47; *Building News,* 11 April 1884; Randall, *Building Construction in Chicago,* 100; Thomas J. Schlereth, "Solon Spencer Beman: The Social History of a Midwest Architect," *Chicago Architectural Journal* 5 (1985): 16–18; Schlereth, "Solon Spencer Beman, Pullman, and the European Influence on and Interest in His Chicago Architecture," in *Chicago Architecture,* ed. Zukowsky, 181–182; Berger, *They Built Chicago,* 74–75; and Bluestone, *Constructing Chicago,* 117, 118, 149, 150. On the large square lots for Chicago's tall office buildings, see Carol Willis, *Form Follows Finance: Skyscrapers and Skylines in New York and Chicago* (New York: Princeton Architectural Press, 1995), 59–63.

49. Editorial, "The New Era in Building," *Chicago Journal of Commerce* 44 (19 March 1884): 11. On Chicago's iron and steel industries of the time, see "Industrial Chicago," *Chicago Journal of Commerce* 44 (2 April 1884): 1, and George W. Cope, *The Iron and Steel Interests of Chicago* (Chicago: Rand McNally, 1890).

50. Richardson's Ames Memorial Town Hall, North Easton (1879–1881), was published in *Monographs of American Architecture,* no. 3 (Boston, 1886), which Sullivan owned. Richardson's unbuilt competition project for Brookline's town hall (1870) and his Albany City Hall (1880–1883) appeared in Mariana G. Van Rensselaer, *Henry Hobson Richardson and His Works* (Boston, 1888; reprint, New York: Dover, 1969), also owned by Sullivan, but postdating his 1886 Auditorium design. See Andrew, *Louis Sullivan,* appendix 2: Inventory of Sullivan's Library, 167–169, from Williams, Barker and Severn Company, Auction Catalogue no. 5533 (Chicago, 29 November 1909), Burnham Library, Art Institute of Chicago.

51. Connely, *Louis Sullivan,* 112. On the Paris Hôtel de Ville in the sixteenth century, see Cathryn Steeves, "The Hôtel de Ville of Paris, 1529–1628" (Ph.D. diss., Columbia University, 1992). See also David Thomson, *Renaissance Paris: Architecture and Growth 1475–1600* (Berkeley: University of California Press, 1984), 73–77; and Jean-Marie Pérouse de Montclos, *Histoire de l'architecture française de la Renaissance à la Revolution* (Paris: Mengès, 1989), 70–72. Open cupolas crowned Francis I's chateau at Chambord (1519–1547). On Sullivan's admiration for this period, see *Autobiography of an Idea,* 231.

52. On the Paris Hôtel de Ville's history through the nineteenth century, see Victor Calliat, *Hôtel de Ville de Paris, mesuré, dessiné, gravé et publié par Victor Calliat,* 2 vols. (Paris, 1844, 1856); Théodore Ballu, *Reconstruction de l'Hôtel de Ville de Paris* (Paris, 1884); and Louis de Harcour, *L'Hôtel de Ville de Paris à travers les siècles* (Paris, 1900). See also Henry Russell Hitchcock, *Architecture: Nineteenth and Twentieth Centuries,* 4th ed. (New York: Penguin Books, 1977), 81–82, and David Van Zanten, *Building Paris: Architectural Institutions and the Transformation of the French Capital, 1830–1879* (New York: Cambridge University Press, 1994), 90–92.

53. *Alarm* 3 (20 March 1886). See also "Vive la Commune!" *Alarm* 1 (4 April 1885): 1. On the Commune's significance for Chicago Anarchists, see Avrich, *Haymarket Tragedy,* 138–140; Keil and Jentz, *German Workers in Chicago,* 263–270; and Nelson, *Beyond the Martyrs,* 142–146. More generally, see Samuel Bernstein, "The Paris Commune and American Labor," *Science and Society* 15 (spring 1951): 144–162; Philip M. Katz, "Americanizing the Paris Commune, 1871–1877" (Ph.D. diss., Princeton University, 1994); and Bernstein, *From Appomattox to Montmartre: Americans and the Paris Commune* (Cambridge: Harvard University Press 1999).

54. "Seats for a Multitude," *Chicago Evening Journal,* 29 January 1987, 1.

55. "The Biggest on Earth," *Chicago Evening Journal,* 2 November 1886, 2.

56. "The 'Grand Auditorium,'" *Chicago Tribune,* 28 November 1886, 7. On the stockholders' organizational meeting, see "A Magnificent Enterprise," *Chicago Tribune,* 5 December 1886, 15, and Records of Chicago Auditorium Association, 7–9 (Auditorium Collection, Roosevelt University Archives).

57. By-Laws, adopted 11 December 1886, in Records of Chicago Auditorium Association, following 23. Peck and the original directors were elected on 4 December 1886. Henry Field was an Auditorium director from December 1886 to his death in December 1890. See Records of Chicago Auditorium Association, 7–8, 26, 175; "Death of Henry Field," *Chicago Tribune,* 23 December 1890, 1, and Robert W. Twyman, *History of Marshall Field & Co., 1852–1906* (Philadelphia: University of Pennsylvania Press, 1954), 62. See also Minutes of Executive Committee of Chicago Auditorium Association, May 3, 1887 to December 11, 1907 (Auditorium Collection, Roosevelt University Archives).

58. Sullivan, *Autobiography of an Idea,* 29. On Burnham and Root's office building for Counselman (northwest corner, LaSalle and Jackson; 1883–1884), their Art Institute (1885–1887) for Hutchinson, and their Reliance Building (southwest corner, State and Washington; 1889–1891/1894–1895) for Hale, see Hoffmann, *Architecture of John Wellborn Root,* 39–43, 49–54, 177–185. On Hale, see also Berger, *They Built Chicago,* 49–58. Hale had been a member of the Citizens' Association's Committee on Theatres and Public Halls, which had submitted its report in October 1883.

59. "Seats for a Multitude," *Chicago Evening Journal,* 29 January 1887, 1.

60. "The Grand Auditorium," *Chicago Tribune,* 10 December 1886, 1.

61. Mueller, Testimony, Chicago Auditorium Association vs. Mark Skinner Willing, in Kaufmann, "Wright's 'Lieber Meister,'" 49.

62. "The Grand Auditorium," *Chicago Tribune,* 10 December 1886),1.

63. Ibid.

64. *Industrial Chicago,* 1:195.

65. John McGovern, quoted in Ffrench, *Music and Musicians in Chicago,* 32.

66. On comparison of the Board of Trade's tower to the Washington Monument, see "A Triumphal March," *Chicago Tribune,* 28 April 1885, 2. On the Washington Monument, see *The Dedication of the Washington National Monument* (Washington, D.C., 1885). Later references are noted in Richard G. Carrott, *The Egyptian Revival: Its Sources, Monuments, and Meaning, 1805–1858* (Berkeley: University of California Press, 1978), 140. The Washington Monument was first opened to the public in October 1888, after which 150,000 people went to the top in the first ten months, and many groups inserted plaques in the staircase walls. The view from the top, the highest man-made point other than the Eiffel Tower, was a tourist attraction at the inauguration of Benjamin Harrison in March 1889 ("Washington and the Inauguration," *Presto* 6 [20 March 1889]: 6–7).

On Egyptian motifs in Adler and Sullivan's wholesale clothing store for E. R. Rothschild and Company at 210 West Monroe Street, commissioned in December 1880 and completed by December 1881, see Morrison, *Louis Sullivan,* 58–59. Van Zanten, "Sullivan to 1890," 35, noted a local account of Sullivan's interior decoration of Chicago's Sinai Temple in 1876 as "the only church edifice in the city decorated in the Egyptian Style." In 1909 Sullivan auctioned these books on ancient Egypt and the Near East: J. Gardner Wilkinson, *A Popular Account of the Ancient Egyptians* (New York, 1878); George Rawlinson, *Ancient Monarchies,* 5 vols. (possibly George Rawlinson, *The Five Great Monarchies of the Ancient Eastern World,* 2 vols., 2d ed. [New York: Scribner, Welford, 1871], and *The Seven Great Monarchies of the Ancient Eastern World, or The History, Geography and Antiquities of Chaldea, Assyria, Babylon, Media, Persia, Parthia, and Sassanian or New Persian Empire,* 3 vols., 2d ed [New York: J. B. Alden, 1885]), and *History of Phoenicia* (London: Longmans, Green, 1889); Ernest Babelon, *Manual of Oriental Antiquities* (London, 1889); Gaston Maspero, *Manual of Egyptian Archaeology and Guide to the Study of Antiquities in Egypt* (London); and James H. Breasted, *A History of Egypt* (New York, 1905). See Andrew, *Louis Sullivan,* appendix 2: Inventory of Sullivan's Library, from Williams, Barker and Severn Company, Auction Catalogue no. 5533 (Chicago, 29 November 1909), Burnham Library, Art Institute of Chicago.

67. *Industrial Chicago,* 1:13.

68. Sullivan, *Autobiography of an Idea,* 309.

69. "A Magnificent Enterprise," *Chicago Tribune,* 5 December 1886, 15.

70. J. S. Runnells, quoted in "Dedicated to Music and the People," *Chicago Tribune,* 10 December 1889, 2. Earlier accounts of the building in progress stressed that the "high purpose" underlying the project was "the desire to promote a sentiment of fraternity among sixty millions of people by providing a common place of assembly equally for the deliberation and amusement of vast representative bodies of men" (Charles H. Ham, "The Chicago Auditorium Building," *Harper's Weekly* 31 [2 July 1887]: 471).

71. "Chicago Real Estate: Among Architects and Builders," *Chicago Tribune,* 19 December 1886, 7.

72. "McVicker's Theater," *Chicago Tribune,* 2 July 1885, 7.

73. Sullivan, *Autobiography of an Idea,* 294.

74. Records of the Chicago Auditorium Association, 37 (Auditorium Collection, Roosevelt University Archives).

75. "The Convention Hall," *Chicago Tribune,* 30 January 1887, 17, which noted: "The drawings of Adler and Sullivan have recently been supervised by Eastern experts, one of them being Prof. Wier [*sic*] of Columbia College, and in the main approved, though the Board of Directors has not yet adopted any plans."

76. On Ware's teaching at MIT, see especially Van Zanten, "Sullivan to 1890," 15–18, and John E. Chewning, "William Robert Ware and the Beginnings of Architectural Education in the United States" (Ph.D. diss., Massachusetts Institute of Technology, 1986).

77. Mueller, Testimony, Chicago Auditorium Association vs. Mark Skinner Willing, in Kaufmann, "Wright's 'Lieber Meister,'" 49.

78. Louis H. Sullivan to his brother, Albert W. Sullivan, 20 January 1887 (Sullivaniana Collection, box 1, folder 2, Ryerson and Burnham Libraries, Art Institute of Chicago), reprinted in Connely, *Louis Sullivan,* 113–115. Ware's meeting with the board of directors was noted in Records of the Chicago Auditorium Association, 57–58. Pike later asked Burham and Root to design the Great Northern Hotel (northeast corner, Jackson and Dearborn; 1889–1891). See Hoffmann, *Architecture of John Wellborn Root,* 150–154.

79. Records of the Chicago Auditorium Association, 61. Another account noted: "The architects in charge of the great enterprise are Messrs. Adler and Sullivan, of Chicago. But Professor Ware, the distinguished incumbent of the chair of Architecture of Columbia College, was consulted both as to the grand elevation and the execution of plans" (Ham, "Chicago Auditorium Building," 471). The board authorized Adler and Sullivan's first payment of $10,000 on 18 January 1887 (Records of the Chicago Auditorium Association, 59). On their fee, see chapter 4, note 5.

80. Mueller, Testimony, Chicago Auditorium Association vs. Mark Skinner Willing, in Kaufmann, "Wright's 'Lieber Meister,'" 49. On Ricker, see Roula M. Geraniotis, "The University of Illinois and German Architectural Education," *Journal of Architectural Education* 38 (1985): 15–21.

81. Ware, paraphrased in "Seats for a Multitude," *Chicago Evening Journal,* 29 January 1887, 1.

82. "The Convention Hall," *Chicago Tribune,* 30 January 1887, 17.

83. Dankmar Adler to Albert W. Sullivan, 12 February 1887, quoted in Adler, "Autobiography and Letters of Dankmar Adler," ed. Saltzstein, 19.

84. *Inland Architect and News Record* 9 (April 1887), photogravure edition. Exterior design changes from February to April 1887 are detailed in Gregersen, "History of the Auditorium Building," 18–24.

85. Mueller, Testimony, Chicago Auditorium Association vs. Mark Skinner Willing, in Kaufmann, "Wright's 'Lieber Meister,'" 49.

86. Tallmadge, *Architecture in Old Chicago,* 159–160.

87. Adler, "Paramount Requirements of a Large Opera House," 46.

88. Wright, *Genius and the Mobocracy,* 48.

89. Adler, "Chicago Auditorium," 417.

90. Ibid.

91. Peck, quoted in "The Collegians," *Chicago Inter Ocean,* 5 January 1889. On the Field Store's chronology, see James F. O'Gorman, "The Marshall Field Wholesale Store: Materials toward a Monograph," *Journal of the Society of Architectural Historians* 37 (October 1978): 175–194. Report of the exterior's crown in place appeared in "Big Business Palaces," *Chicago Evening Journal,* 8 November 1886, 3. The Field building opened for business on 20 June 1887. See *Chicago Tribune,* 18 June 1887, 8, and "Center of the Wholesale District," *Chicago Herald,* 18 June 1887, 5. See also Twyman, *History of Marshall Field,* 96–97.

92. Henry Hobson Richardson to his son, John C. Hayden Richardson, October [1885?], quoted in O'Gorman, *H. H. Richardson and His Office, a Centenniel of His Move to Boston, 1874—Selected Drawings* (Boston, 1974), 115. On this trip, see O'Gorman, *H. H. Richardson: Architectural Forms for an American Society* (Chicago: University of Chicago Press, 1987), 23.

93. Dimensions of both buildings are in Rand McNally, *Bird's-Eye Views and Guide to Chicago,* 64, 104.

94. Richardson, quoted in O'Gorman, *Richardson and His Office,* 29.

95. Edward Atkinson, "Slow-Burning Construction," *Century Magazine* 37 (February 1889): 578, quoted in O'Gorman, "Marshall Field Wholesale Store," 189.

96. Anonymous letter [to Ferdinand Peck?], 8 May 1887 (Auditorium Collection, file box L, Roosevelt University Archives).

97. "The Building Department," *Real Estate and Building Journal* 29 (9 April 1887): 181.

98. On materials in Richardson's building, see O'Gorman, "Marshall Field Wholesale Store," 180–181. The decision to use limestone cladding for the Auditorium's upper walls was recorded in Chicago Auditorium Association, Board of Directors, Meeting of 7 May 1887, Records of the Chicago Auditorium Association, 71 (Auditorium Collection, Roosevelt University Archives). See also below, 166.

99. H. H. Richardson to the Allegheny County Commissioners, January 1884, quoted in James D. Van Trump, *Majesty of the Law: The Court Houses of Allegheny County* (Pittsburgh: Pittsburgh History and Landmarks Foundation, 1988), 54–55. On Chicago's smoke nuisance, see Lewis, *Early Encounter with Tomorrow,* 30–34. Ironically, the Auditorium Building itself, with its large coal-fueled heating plant, was cited as one of the chief offenders. See *Report of the Smoke Committee of the Citizens' Association of Chicago, May 1889* (Chicago: Chicago: George E. Marshall, 1889).

100. *Industrial Chicago,* 4:481.

101. Adler, paraphrased in "The Western Association of Architects," *American Architect and Building News* 20 (27 November 1886): 253. O'Gorman, "Marshall Field Wholesale Store," 189, noted Field's and Richardson's visits to Florence.

102. On Field's acquisition of the site for Richardson's building, see O'Gorman, "Marshall Field Wholesale Store," 177, and *H. H. Richardson: Architectural Forms for an American Society,* 76. Field commissioned the new building because he needed a larger facility and his earlier wholesale store at Madison and Market streets stood on rented ground whose leases were soon to expire. See "Real Estate," *Chicago Tribune,* 30 September 1885, 3. On the wholesale district, see "Real Estate," *Chicago Tribune,* 28 October 1883, 18. On Van Osdel's Farwell Wholesale Block, see Marquis, *Marquis' Hand-Book of Chicago,* 294–295; Rand McNally, *Bird's-Eye Views and Guide to Chicago,* 105–106; and Randall, *Building Construction in Chicago,* 112, 123. On Farwell and his company, see Andreas, *History of Chicago,* 2:694, and Twyman, *History of Marshall Field,* 42, 47, 55.

103. *Industrial Chicago,* 4:481.

104. Harold I. Cleveland, "Fifty-five Years in Business: The Life of Marshall Field—Chapter XI," *System* 11 (May 1907): 459. On the Auditorium and Chicago residential hotels, see chapter 5, 287, and note 41.

105. "Marshall Field & Co.'s New Store," *Chicago Tribune,* 12 June 1887, 16.

106. Louis Sullivan, Kindergarten Chat 6, "An Oasis," reprinted in *"Kindergarten Chats" and Other Writings,* ed. Isabella Athey (New York: Dover, 1947), 30. On theories of type and character at the École from the time of Quatremère de Quincy, see Donald Drew Egbert, *The Beaux-Arts Tradition in French Architecture* (Princeton: Princeton University Press, 1980), 121–135.

107. *Industrial Chicago,* 1:25. This view of Romanesque as having evolved directly from Roman architecture followed the opinion of such European historians as Edouard Corroyer, chapters of whose *L'architecture romane* (Paris, 1888) were translated by the Chicago architect William A. Otis. Educated at the École des Beaux-Arts, Otis designed Peck's house of 1887 on South Michigan Avenue (fig. 82). See Corroyer, "Romanesque Architecture," *Inland Architect and News Record* 13 (March 1889): 39–40; (April 1889): 51–53; (May 1889): 65–68; (June 1889): 83–86; (July 1889): 95–96; 14 (August 1889): 3–6; (September 1889): 18–19; (November 1889): 48–50; (December 1889): 73–76; (January 1890): 90–92; 15 (February 1890): 3–5; (March 1890): 31; (April 1890): 43–45; (May 1890): 55–57. Another contemporaneous view of the relation of Roman to Romanesque architecture appeared in Montgomery Schuyler, "The Romanesque Revival in New York" (1891), in Schuyler, *"American Architecture" and Other Writings,* ed. Jordy and Coe, 1:191–195. On Otis, see Henry F. Withey and Elsie R. Withey, *Biographical Dictionary of American Architects (Deceased)* (1956; Los Angeles: Hennessey and Ingalls, 1970), 450, and Art Institute of Chicago, *Chicago Architects Design: A Century of Architectural Drawings from the Art Institute of Chicago* (New York: Rizzoli, 1982), 44. On Richardson's photographs of Roman aqueducts, see O'Gorman, "Marshall Field Wholesale Store," 190, and Jordy, *American Buildings and Their Architects,* 4:34–37.

108. Garczynski, *Auditorium,* 54. On American artists' interest in the Aqua Claudia, see William L. Vance, *America's Rome,* 2 vols. (New Haven: Yale University Press, 1989), 1:68–71. Chicagoans knew of contemporaneous studies on ancient Roman aqueducts, including Rome's own underground conduits. These studies included John H. Parker, *The Archaeology of Rome,* vol. 8, *The Aqueducts* (London, 1876). See also "Old Roman Aqueducts," *Chicago Tribune,* 27 July 1877, 12. On Americans at the Pont du Gard, see "Notes from Over the Water, Nîmes—II," *Chicago Record,* 28 August 1894, 4.

109. Peck, quoted in "No Equal in the World," *Chicago Tribune,* 2 December 1888. Peck's implicit invocation of Roman models for the Auditorium was also consistent with the pride that some Anglo-Americans of the period took in the works of the Romans as the founders of those republican political institutions that the English had revived in the United States. See William W. Stowe, *Going Abroad: European Travel in Nineteenth-Century American Culture* (Princeton: Princeton University Press, 1994), 133–134.

110. Kirkland and Kirkland, *Story of Chicago,* 2:362.

111. Ham, "Chicago Auditorium Building," 471. See "The Center of Empire," *Economist* 10 (9 December 1893): 616. See also Olivia Mahoney, *Go West: Chicago and American Expansion* (Chicago: Chicago Historical Society, 1999).

112. Statistics of the Auditorium Building's weight, cubic volume, and material quantities appeared in a brochure given to visitors to the Auditorium Tower, titled "Auditorium Building, Chicago: Interesting Information," and in J. W. Taylor, "Souvenir of Auditorium," 1890 (both in Auditorium Collection, Roosevelt University Archives). Such statistics also appeared in *Industrial Chicago,* 1:194; Louis Schick, *Chicago and Its Environs: A Handbook for the Traveler* (Chicago: L. Schick, 1891), 199–200; Flinn, *Chicago, the Marvelous City of the West,* 138–139; Rand McNally, *Bird's-Eye Views and Guide to Chicago,* 64; Condit, *Chicago School,* 69; and Twombly, *Louis Sullivan,* 160.

On pile and caisson foundations in New York City's tall buildings after 1870, see Charles Sooy-smith, "Concerning Foundations for Heavy Buildings in New York City," *Transactions, American Society of Civil Engineers* 35 (July 1896): 459–483, and his "Foundation Construction for Tall Buildings," *Engineering Magazine* 13 (April 1897): 20–33; Frank W. Skinner, "The Development of Building Foundations," *Engineering Record* 57 (4 April 1908): 412–422; and Landau and Condit, *Rise of the New York Skyscraper,* 23–26, 179–182.

On Chicago building foundations, see "Chicago," *American Architect and Building News* 24 (20 October 1888): 185–186; *Industrial Chicago,* 1:466–480; "Steel Foundations," *Engineering News and American Railway Journal* 26 (8 August 1891): 116–117; William Sooy Smith, "Chicago Buildings and Foundations," *Engineering News and American Railway Journal* 28 (13 October 1892): 343–346; "Pile Foundations in Chicago," *Engineering News and American Railway Journal* 30 (21 September 1893): 228–230; and "Development of Shallow and Deep Foundations for Chicago Buildings," *Engineering News* 52 (22 December 1904): 560–562, with references to additional earlier articles on the topic in this journal. See also James W. Hatch, "Foundations for Large Buildings," *Construction News* 19 (10 June 1905): 431–432; *Construction News* 19 (17 June 1905): 451–452; *Construction News* 19 (24 June 1905): 471; *Construction News* 20 (1 July 1905): 494; Edward C. Shankland, "Chicago Foundations," *Construction News* 20 (21 October 1905): 312–313, and his "Foundations," in *A Half Century of Chicago Building: A Practical Reference Guide,* ed. John H. Jones and Fred A. Britten (Chicago, 1910); Ralph B. Peck [no known relation to Ferdinand Peck], *History of Building Foundations in Chicago,* Bulletin 373 (Urbana: University of Illinois Engineering Experiment Station, 1948); and Randall, *Building Construction in Chicago,* 18–19.

113. Ferdinand Peck, quoted in "Owners of Earth," *Chicago Tribune,* 31 January 1890, 2. The Auditorium Tower's foundational area (100 x 71 = 7,100 square feet) was greater than its floor area in plan (70 x 41 = 2,870 square feet). On problematic foundations at the Cook County Court House and City Hall, and the United States Post Office and Customs Building, see Adler, "Foundations," *Economist* 26 (27 June 1881): 1136–1138, and Peck, *Building Foundations in Chicago,* 27–29. On these buildings, see also Marquis, *Marquis' Hand-Book of Chicago,* 61–68; Randall, *Building Construction in Chicago,* 102–104; and Bluestone, *Constructing Chicago,* 159–164. On the Board of Trade Building, see "Is The Tower Insecure?" *Chicago Tribune,* 4 August 1888, 1, and Peck, *Building Foundations in Chicago,* 33–35.

114. On Baumann's pamphlet and its influence, see William Le Baron Jenney, "The Chicago Construction, or Tall Buildings on a Compressible Soil," *Inland Architect and News Record* 18 (January 1891): 41; "Illinois State Association," *Inland Architect and News Record* 7 (February 1886): 15–16; Sullivan, "Development of Construction" (1916), in *Louis Sullivan: The Public Papers,* ed. Twombly, 212; and Sullivan, *Autobiography of an Idea,* 245. See also "Obituary: Frederick Baumann," *Journal of the American Institute of Architects* 9 (August 1921): 281–282; Tallmadge, *Architecture in Old Chicago,* 142–143, 154–155; Peck, *Building Foundations in Chicago,* 14–17; Condit, *Chicago School,* 83; Roula Geraniotis, "German Architectural Theory and Practice in Chicago, 1850–1900," *Winterthur Portfolio* 21 (1986): 293–306; and Gerald Larson and Roula Geraniotis, "Toward a Better Understanding of the Iron Skeleton Frame in Chicago," *Journal of the Society of Architectural Historians* 46 (March 1987): 46–48.

115. Frederick Baumann, *The Art of Preparing Foundations, with Particular Illustration of the "Method of Isolated Piers," as Followed in Chicago* (Chicago, 1873), from revised and enlarged edition by George T. Powell, in *Foundations and Foundation Walls,* ed. Powell (New York: W. T. Comstock, 1884), 148–149.

116. Baumann, *Art of Preparing Foundations,* 149–150. On premodern pier and other types of foundations, see Sheila Bonde, Clark Maines, and Rowland Richards Jr., "Soils and Foundations," in *Architectural Technology up to the Scientific Revolution: The Art and Structure of Large-Scale Buildings,* ed. Robert Mark (Cambridge: MIT Press, 1993), 16–51.

117. Sullivan, "Development of Construction" (1916), in *Louis Sullivan: The Public Papers,* ed. Twombly, 213. The Borden Block's innovative foundations were noted in Mueller, Testimony, Chicago

Auditorium Association vs. Mark Skinner Willing, in Kaufmann, "Frank Lloyd Wright's 'Lieber Meister,'" 49. See "The Borden Block," *Chicago Tribune,* 5 September 1880, 16; Morrison, *Louis Sullivan,* 57–58; Condit, *Chicago School,* 38; Van Zanten, "Sullivan to 1890," 12–13; and Twombly, *Louis Sullivan,* 99–101.

118.   William Le Baron Jenney (?), in "Our Illustrations," *Inland Architect and Builder* 4 (September 1884): 24. See also Jenney, "The Chicago Construction, or Tall Buildings on a Compressible Soil," *Inland Architect and Builder* 18 (November 1891): 41; Jenney, "The Construction of a Heavy Fire-Proof Building on a Compressible Soil," *Sanitary Engineer* 13 (10 December 1885): 32–33; and Ralph Peck, *Building Foundations in Chicago,* 19–20. On this structure see Theodore Turak, "Remembrances of the Home Insurance Building," *Journal of the Society of Architectural Historians* 44 (March 1985): 60–65; Turak, *William Le Baron Jenney: A Pioneer of Modern Architecture* (Ann Arbor: UMI Research Press, 1986), 237–263; Larson and Geraniotis, "Toward a Better Understanding of the Iron Skeleton Frame in Chicago," 39–48; and Larson, "The Iron Skeleton Frame: Interactions between Europe and the United States," in Zukowsky, *Chicago Architecture,* 39–56.

119.   Root, in "Illinois State Association," *Inland Architect and Builder* 7 (February 1886): 16. See also Root, "A Great Architectural Problem," *Inland Architect and Builder* 15 (June 1890): 68. On foundations for the Montauk Block and the Rookery, see Harriet Monroe, *John Wellborn Root: A Study of His Life and Work* (Boston: Houghton, Mifflin, 1896), 116–118; Ralph Peck, *Building Foundations in Chicago,* 21–23; Randall, *Building Construction in Chicago,* 95; Condit, *Chicago School,* 54–55; and Hoffmann, *Architecture of John Wellborn Root,* 26–28, 68. Harry Lawrie noted dimension stone's high cost in a paper on Chicago foundations, read at the Chicago Architectural Sketch Club in 1885 (*Industrial Chicago,* 1:469).

120.   Adler, "Foundations of the Auditorium Building, Chicago," *Inland Architect and News Record* 11 (March 1888): 32. Ferdinand Peck similarly wrote: "The foundations under your building have been carefully and scientifically considered. Every square yard of the ground was first tested by heavy water-tanks" (Annual Report of the President to the Stockholders of the Chicago Auditorium Association, 1 December 1886 [Auditorium Collection, Roosevelt University Archives]). See also "The Auditorium Building, Chicago," *Engineering* (London) 51 (3 April 1891): 395, 490; "Gen. Sooy Smith's System," *Economist* 7 (16 April 1892): 576–578; and "Foundations for Heavy Structures in Chicago," *Economist* 13 (19 January 1895): 73.

121.   Sullivan, "Development of Construction" (1916), in *Louis Sullivan: The Public Papers,* ed. Twombly, 216, and Mueller, Testimony, Chicago Auditorium Association vs. Mark Skinner Willing, in Kaufmann, "Wright's 'Lieber Meister,'" 49.

122.   Lawrie, quoted in *Industrial Chicago,* 1:472. Sullivan, "Development of Construction" (1916), in *Louis Sullivan: The Public Papers,* ed. Twombly, 218–219, wrote: "Attention has been called to some settlements in the Auditorium, but you must consider the fact that there was an added load of over one-third in changing the exterior from brick to stone." On settlement of the outer walls, see epilogue, 391.

123.   Sullivan, "Development of Construction" (1916), in *Louis Sullivan: The Public Papers,* ed. Twombly, 217. Baumann, *Art of Preparing Foundations,* 151, wrote that the normal bearing capacity of Chicago's soils was twenty pounds per square inch, a load that "will compress the hardpan to the extent of about one inch during construction of the building, and about one-half an inch during the next six months following, after which time the load appears to be poised upon the clay."

124.   Sullivan, "Development of Construction" (1916), in *Louis Sullivan: The Public Papers,* ed. Twombly, 217.

125.   Ibid., 218–219, and Sullivan, *Autobiography of an Idea,* 309. On the Monadnock's foundations, see Monroe, *John Wellborn Root,* 120, and Ralph Peck, *Building Foundations in Chicago,* 43–44.

126.   Adler, "The Auditorium Tower," *American Architect and Building News* 32 (4 April 1891): 16. See also Ralph Peck, *Building Foundations in Chicago,* 35–41.

127. Editorial, "Chicago's Foundations Are Solid," *Chicago Inter Ocean,* 20 August 1889. On proposals for an "Eiffel Tower" at the World's Columbian Exposition, see Donald Hoffmann, "Clear Span Rivalry: The World's Fairs of 1889–1893," *Journal of the Society of Architectural Historians* 29 (March 1970): 48–50.

128. "Higher Than Others," *Chicago Tribune,* 5 September 1891, 1. On Adler and Sullivan's Odd Fellows project, see Edward W. Wolner, "Chicago's Fraternity Temples: Building Rhetoric and the First of the World's Tallest Skyscrapers," in *The American Skyscraper,* ed. Roberta Moudry (New York: Cambridge University Press, forthcoming).

129. Quoted in Twombly, *Louis Sullivan,* 302. See also "It's a Serious Problem," and "It Will Be A Great Weight," *Chicago Tribune,* 11 October 1891, 13.

130. Adler, "The Tall Business Building: Some of Its Engineering Problems," *Cassier's Magazine* 12 (November 1897): 197.

131. Sullivan, "Development of Construction" (1916), in *Louis Sullivan: The Public Papers,* ed. Twombly, 217. Sullivan stated that all the Auditorium Building's columns were cast iron, not steel. This was true of many of Chicago's metal frame buildings of the period, including Sullivan's later Schlesinger and Mayer (Carson Pirie Scott) Building, built in 1899 and 1903–1904. See Joseph Siry, *Carson Pirie Scott: Louis Sullivan and the Chicago Department Store* (Chicago: University of Chicago Press, 1988), 105.

132. Mueller, Testimony, Chicago Auditorium Association vs. Mark Skinner Willing, in Kaufmann, "Wright's 'Lieber Meister,'" 46.

133. Dankmar Adler to family, August 1888, in "Autobiography and Letters of Dankmar Adler," ed. Saltzstein, 21. On the 1888 lockout at Carnegie's Braddock Mill, see Paul Krause, *The Battle for Homestead, 1880–1892: Politics, Culture and Steel* (Pittsburgh: University of Pittsburgh Press, 1992), 235–237. See also Leon Wolff, *Lockout: The Story of the Homestead Strike of 1892—a Study of Violence, Unionism, and the Carnegie Steel Empire* (New York: Harper and Row, 1965).

134. Adler, "Tall Business Building," 197–198.

135. Adler, "Chicago Auditorium," 420, wrote: "As a multiplicity of pillars would have been objectionable in the public rooms which occupy the first story of the Congress Street front, and which were intended in the original design to take up all of the second floor of the same, the floors from the first story upward are carried on 140 riveted girders 2 feet high and of 36 feet clear span each . . . . The absence of interior columns resulting from the use of the girder construction permitted a degree of freedom in handling the partitions and the division into rooms that was found quite useful."

136. Sullivan, "Development of Construction" (1916), in *Louis Sullivan: The Public Papers,* ed. Twombly, 219.

137. Jane Bonshek, "The Skyscraper: A Catalyst of Change in the Chicago Construction Industries, 1882–1892," *Construction History* 4 (1988): 59–60. See Adler, "The General Contractor from the Standpoint of the Architect," *Inland Architect and News Record* 33 (June 1899): 38–39; Chad Wallin, *The Builders' Story: An Interpretive Record of the Builders' Association of Chicago, Inc.* (Chicago: [Builders' Association of Chicago], 1966), 5–6; and Sibel Bozdogan Dostoglu, "Towards Professional Legitimacy and Power: An Inquiry into the Struggle, Achievements and Dilemmas of the Architectural Profession through an Analysis of Chicago, 1871–1909" (Ph.D. diss., University of Pennsylvania, 1982), 95–103. On Fuller, see also William A. Starrett, *Skyscrapers and the Men Who Build Them* (New York: Scribner, 1928); *George A. Fuller Company: General Contractors 1882–1937: A Book Illustrating Recent Works of This Organization* (New York, 1937); Raymond C. Daly, *Seventy–five Years of Construction Pioneering: George A. Fuller Company 1882–1957* (New York: Newcomen Society in North America, 1957); and Bruegmann, *Architects and the City,* 81–82, 484 n. 63.

138. Wright, quoted in "Chicago's Auditorium Is Fifty Years Old," 10. Under architects Adler and Sullivan, the consulting engineers, construction superintendents, independent contractors, and fabricators were named in Garczynski, *Auditorium,* 15. Ferdinand Peck noted the number of workers in

"Annual Report of the President to the Stockholders of the Chicago Auditorium Association," 7 December 1889 (Auditorium Collection, Roosevelt University Archives). Sullivan, *Autobiography of an Idea,* 294, noted the project's toll on his and Adler's health.

139.   Wright, *Genius and the Mobocracy,* 60. On Wright's views of Richardson, see O'Gorman, *H. H. Richardson, Architectural Forms for an American Society,* 129–142; and James F. O'Gorman, *Three American Architects: Richardson, Sullivan, and Wright, 1865–1915* (Chicago: University of Chicago Press, 1991), 113–132.

140.   On displays inside Richardson's building, see Samuel H. Ditchett, *Marshall Field and Company: The Life Story of a Great Concern* (New York: Dry Goods Economist, 1922), 103–105.

141.   O'Gorman, "Marshall Field Wholesale Store," 188. Architect George Edbrooke's iron-and-glass fronted, nine-story wholesale clothing store of 1887–1888 for Charles L. Willoughby, at the northwest corner of Franklin and Jackson Streets, a half block south of Richardson's Field store, was a well-lit skeletal building. See Donald Hoffmann, *Frank Lloyd Wright, Louis Sullivan and the Skyscaper* (Mineola, N.Y.: Dover, 1998), 10–13.

142.   Van Rensselaer, *Henry Hobson Richardson,* 120.

143.   Garczynski, *Auditorium,* 24, 25. On the technical debates about masonry bearing walls versus skeletal metal frames in tall buildings of the late 1880s and early 1890s, see Siry, "Adler and Sullivan's Guaranty Building in Buffalo," *Journal of the Society of Architectural Historians* 55 (March 1996): 16–19.

144.   On the building trades strike of 1887, see James C. Beeks, *Thirty Thousand Locked Out: The Great Strike of the Building Trades in Chicago* (Chicago: Franz Gindele, 1887); *Industrial Chicago,* 1:556–581; Schneirov and Suhrbur, *Union Brotherhood, Union Town,* 33–36; and Schneirov, *Labor and Urban Politics,* 249–250. Other reports included Intermediate News Number, *Inland Architect and News Record* 9 (April 1887): 51; "Labor Differences," *Chicago Daily Inter-Ocean,* 12 April 1887, 3; "The Carpenters' Strike," *Chicago Tribune,* 13 April 1887, 3; "National Association of Builders," *Inland Architect and News Record* 9 (June 1887): 79; "The Building Strike" and "Conservative Workmen," *Chicago Tribune,* 15 May 1887, 4; "Chicago Real Estate: A Builder's Opinion of the Lockout," *Chicago Tribune,* 12 June 1887, 4; and "Strike of the Bricklayers," *Chicago Tribune,* 18 June 1887, 4.

145.   *Industrial Chicago,* 1:561. On the decision for the stone superstructure to be built of Bedford limestone and not brick, see note 98 above.

146.   Beeks, *Thirty Thousand Locked Out,* 61–64.

147.   Adler, "Architects and Trade Unions," *Inland Architect and News Record* 27 (May 1886): 32. Adler's ideas on labor and politics appear in "Deliberations of the Architects," *Economist* 6 (21 November 1891): 857–858; "Municipal Building Laws," *Inland Architect and News Record* 25 (May 1895): 36–37; "Open Letter to Chicago Mason Builders," *Inland Architect and News Record* 29 (February 1897): 2–3; and "The General Contractor from the Standpoint of the Architect," *Inland Architect and News Record* 33 (June 1899): 38–39. Estimates of financial losses owing to the lockout were noted in *Industrial Chicago,* 1:560.

148.   Adler, quoted in "Why the Strike Must Fail," *Chicago Tribune,* 17 June 1887, 1.

149.   Adler, paraphrased in Beeks, *Thirty Thousand Locked Out,* 135. At this meeting, both Adler and architect John Wellborn Root expressed support for the builders' association against the striking bricklayers. Another account of this meeting, which makes no mention of the labor discussion, appeared as "Illinois State Association of Architects," *Inland Architect and News Record* 9 (June 1887): 88–90.

150.   *Industrial Chicago,* 1:578.

151.   Ibid., 560, and Beeks, *Thirty Thousand Locked Out,* 3.

152.   Quoted in "To Save the Anarchists," *Chicago Tribune,* 22 September 1887, 2.

153.   "The President's Visit," *Chicago Tribune,* 22 September 1887, 2. See also "Plans Still Unfinished," *Chicago Tribune,* 23 September 1887, 2, and "The President's Visit," *Chicago Tribune,* 27 September 1887, 1.

154. "Chicagoan, Head to Heels," *Chicago Sunday Chronicle,* 28 August 1898. On Cleveland's visit to Chicago, see "He Will Be Here Today," *Chicago Tribune,* 5 October 1887, 2, and "A Glittering Turnout," *Chicago Tribune,* 6 October 1887, 1–3. On the carpenters' response, see "Is He A Friend of Labor?" *Chicago Tribune,* 29 September 1887, 1.

155. Peck assured that the Auditorium would be ready for both national conventions in 1888 ("Pushing the Work on the Auditorium Building," *Chicago Tribune,* 30 November 1887, 8). After the Republicans agreed to come, it was anticipated that the Democrats would follow suit ("Chicago Will Win Again," *Chicago Tribune,* 10 December 1887, 1).

156. "Why the Trade Unions Smile," *Chicago Tribune,* 3 August 1888, 8. On the Socialist Labor Party's willingness to have its members vote Democratic, see "Socialists at Work Reorganizing," *Chicago Tribune,* 23 September 1887, 2.

157. "Chicagoan, Head to Heels," *Chicago Sunday Chronicle,* 28 August 1898.

158. *Building Trades Journal* (St. Louis) 5 (January 1888): 5. On convict labor in Illinois, see Illinois Bureau of Labor Statistics, *Fourth Biennial Report, 1886* (Springfield, Ill., 1886), 1–142. This contains statistical information prepared in support of an amendment to the state's constitution that was to prohibit contract prison labor, whereby the state contracted out the labor of its convicts to private employers. This system was financially successful for the state and for businesses but was strongly opposed by reformers on humanitarian grounds. On the politics of this amendment, which passed in 1886 but did not wholly stop contract prison labor, see Earl R. Beckner, *A History of Labor Legislation in Illinois* (Chicago: University of Chicago Press, 1929), 136–140. In the United States, the use of convict labor for stonecutting went back to at least the early nineteenth century in Boston, where local granites were worked by prisoners of the Commonwealth of Massachusetts. See Louis Dwight, *Reports of the Prison Discipline Society of Boston, 1826–1854* (reprint; Montclair, N.J.: Patterson Smith, 1972), and Robert B. MacKay, "Charles Street Jail: Hegemony of a Design" (Ph.D. diss., Boston University, 1980).

159. Chicago Trades Assembly to Mayor DeWitt C. Cregier, quoted in "Mad at the Auditorium Folks," *Chicago Tribune,* 20 May 1889. On Labor Day demonstrations in Chicago in 1888, see "The Trades Assemblies," *Chicago Tribune,* 3 September 1888, 1, and "Labor's Big Festival," *Chicago Tribune,* 4 September 1888, 1–2. Labor Day was first celebrated in the United States at New York City in 1882, although President Cleveland did not declare it a national holiday until 1894.

160. "Marshall Field & Co's New Store," *Chicago Tribune,* 12 June 1887, 16. O'Gorman, "Marshall Field Wholesale Store," 179, noted labor disruptions during construction of Richardson's building. The prefire armory and precinct headquarters at Adams and Franklin Streets was noted in Flinn, *History of the Chicago Police,* 99.

161. William Le Baron Jenney, "The Building Stones of Chicago," paper read before the Chicago Academy of Sciences, 27 November 1883, published in *Chicago Journal of Commerce* 44 (14 May 1884): 5.

162. "A New Building Stone: New Granite Works in Chicago," *Chicago Tribune,* 29 May 1887, 6. On the Lemont quarries, see Flinn, *Chicago, the Marvelous City of the West,* 314. On strikes of quarrymen at Lemont, Lockport, and Joliet, see Avrich, *Haymarket Tragedy,* 96, and "War! The Military Fire upon and Kill Striking Quarrymen at Lemont, Ill.," *Alarm* 1 (16 May 1885): 1.

163. Garczynski, *Auditorium,* 24. The granite contract was noted in Records of the Chicago Auditorium Association, 7 May 1887, 72. The decision to take over the quarries was noted in Minutes of Executive Committee of Chicago Auditorium Association, 7 January 1888, 33–34 (Auditorium Collection, Roosevelt University Archives). By March 1888 Peck reported that "the granite for the sub-structure (two stories) of the Auditorium Building will now be rapidly set, weather permitting. Your Association under a favorable arrangement made with the contracting company two months ago, has taken possession of the Minnesota quarries and plant and reorganized the working force, and the prospects for prompt delivery are most favorable. It is hoped and believed that the granite and cut stone will be set in the exterior walls of the Building for a height of four stories, and perhaps more, before the Republican

Convention in June" (Peck, letter to the stockholders of the Chicago Auditorium Association, 3 March 1888, "Early History and Press Clippings, Chicago Auditorium Association, Chicago, 1887–1889" [Ryerson and Burnham Libraries, Art Institute of Chicago]).

164. Gregersen, "History of the Auditorium Building," 26.

165. "The Studebaker Building," *Chicago Tribune,* 26 March 1887, 7. On the Hallowell Company's granite quarried in Maine for the Board of Trade Building, see "The Board of Trade Home," *Chicago Tribune,* 3 May 1885, 3.

166. "A New Building Stone: New Granite Works in Chicago," *Chicago Tribune,* 29 May 1887," 6.

167. "Real Estate: Details of the Plans of Marshall Field's Great Warehouse," *Chicago Tribune,* 25 October 1885, 28. Among statements of the period on Chicago's growth as an industrial center, see *Chicago Commerce, Manufactures, Banking, and Transportation Facilities* (Chicago: S. Ferdinand Howe, 1884).

168. Chicago Trades Assembly to Mayor DeWitt C. Cregier, quoted in "Mad at the Auditorium Folks," *Chicago Tribune,* 20 May 1889. On the issue, see also "The Proposed Widening of Congress Street," *Economist* 2 (18 May 1889): 404.

169. Cregier, quoted in "Fitzgerald Is Beaten," *Chicago Tribune,* 21 May 1889.

170. *Industrial Chicago,* 1:194.

171. Garczynski, *Auditorium,* 70. The geological connotations of Richardson's and Sullivan's stonework may recall John Ruskin's interest in the emotions evoked by head-on views of mountain bases and cliffs, as discussed in "The Lamp of Memory," in *The Seven Lamps of Architecture* (1849; reprint, New York, 1979), 183, cited in Lauren S. Weingarden, "Naturalized Nationalism: A Ruskinian Discourse on the Search for an American Style of Architecture," *Winterthur Portfolio* 24 (spring 1989): 63.

172. Garczynski, *Auditorium,* 12. On origins of Chicago's name, see Virgil J. Vogel, *Indian Place Names in Illinois* (Springfield: Illinois State Historical Society, 1963), 24–25; "Mystery of Chicago's Name," *Mid-America* 40 (1958); and John F. Swenson, "Chicagoua/Chicago: The Origin, Meaning, and Etymology of a Place Name," *Illinois Historical Journal* 84 (winter 1991): 235–248.

173. Garczynski, *Auditorium,* 12. Accounts of the massacre dating from the period of the Auditorium included Andreas, *History of Chicago,* 1:79–83; *Marquis' Hand-Book of Chicago,* 10–14; Flinn, *Chicago, the Marvelous City of the West,* 25–28; and Joseph Kirkland, *The Chicago Massacre in 1812, with Illustrations and Historical Documents* (Chicago, 1893). See also "Site of the Massacre," *Chicago Tribune,* 8 March 1890, 11.

174. "Mr. Pullman's Splendid Gift," *Elite* 11 (24 June 1893): 9. See also "Marked by a Statue," *Chicago Tribune,* 18 December 1892, 13; *Ceremonies at the Unveiling of the Bronze Memorial Group of the Chicago Massacre of 1812* (Chicago, 1893); "In Lasting Bronze," *Chicago Tribune,* 23 June 1893, 1, 7; and Smith, *Urban Disorder and the Shape of Belief,* 177–178.

175. Edwin O. Gale, *Reminiscences of Early Chicago and Vicinity* (Chicago: Revell, 1902), 28. Currey, *Chicago: Its History and Its Builders,* 5:355, noted Philip Peck's participation in the Black Hawk War, which moved Native Americans west of the Mississippi. On the war and subsequent treaty, see chapter 1, note 14.

176. Richard S. Slotkin, *The Fatal Environment: The Myth of the Frontier in the Age of Industrialization, 1800–1890* (New York: Atheneum, 1985), 480–489.

177. Theodore Roosevelt, quoted in Richard Drinnon, "'My Men Shoot Well': Theodore Roosevelt and the Urban Frontier," in *Haymarket Scrapbook,* ed. David Roediger and Franklin Rosemont (Chicago: Charles H. Kerr, 1986), 129.

178. "Columbus in Bronze," *Chicago Tribune,* 23 April 1893,: 2. See also "Its Beauty Unveiled," *Chicago Tribune,* 26 April 1893, 2. This statue was not well received and was removed to storage in 1897. Later it was melted down to provide the bronze for a statue of William McKinley after his assassination in 1901. See James L. Riedy, *Chicago Sculpture* (Urbana: University of Illinois Press, 1981), 204, 222, 285.

179. Avrich, *Haymarket Tragedy,* 160–177. See also Schaack, "Dynamite in Politics," in *Anarchy and Anarchists,* 28–43.

180. "Explosives: A Practical Lesson in Popular Chemistry," *Alarm* 1 (4 April 1885): 1.

181. Thomas J. Morgan, quoted in "Strong Words Used," *Chicago Tribune,* 13 November 1893, 1. Morgan spoke at a meeting in Central Music Hall organized by London editor William T. Stead, author of *If Christ Came to Chicago.* In fall 1893, after the onset of the national depression, Morgan, who had worked as a machinist for thirty-seven of his forty-six years and had been a staunch socialist since 1873, had begun a law career. He was active in the American Federation of Labor's convention at Chicago in December 1893. See Ralph W. Scharnau, "Thomas J. Morgan and the Chicago Socialist Movement, 1876–1901" (Ph.D. diss., Northern Illinois University, 1970).

182. Herrick, *Memoirs of an American Citizen,* 66.

183. Emmett Dedmon, *Fabulous Chicago* (New York: Random House, 1953), 114–115. Castellar forms recurred in the house of Harlow Higinbotham, the Marshall Field and Company executive and director of the World's Columbian Exposition, sited at Michigan Avenue and Twenty-ninth Street. See "It Is an Ideal Home," *Chicago Tribune,* 18 December 1892, 11.

184. Thomas Hubka, "H. H. Richardson's Glessner House," *Winterthur Portfolio* 24 (winter 1989): 221. On this building, see also Elaine Harrington, "International Influences on Henry Hobson Richardson's Glessner House," in *Chicago Architecture,* ed. Zukowsky, 188–207; John J. Glessner, *The Story of a House: H. H. Richardson's Glessner House* (1923; Chicago: Chicago Architecture Foundation, 1992); and Elaine Harrington, *Henry Hobson Richardson: J. J. Glessner House, Chicago* (Tübingen: East Wasmuth, 1993).

185. "Costly Dwelling-Houses," *Chicago Tribune,* 5 June 1886, 1. Henry Ives Cobb had designed a baronial mansion for Potter Palmer at 1350 Lake Shore Drive in 1892. A local critic wrote of its castlelike battlements: "In times of war or when Anarchists are out loose the portcullis, or whatever the thing is called, can be barricaded and a Gatling gun fired from one of the turret loopholes" ("Bits of Architecture," *Chicago Tribune,* 7 November 1886, 26).

186. "The President's Party," *Chicago Evening Journal,* 9 December 1889, 2. A rendering of Peck's house was published in *Inland Architect and News Record* 10 (October 1887). Peck and Jenney were members of the Union League Club, whose building of 1886 Jenney designed. On this structure, see chapter 5, 295–296.

187. Louis Sullivan, Kindergarten Chat 5, "An Hotel" (1901), in *"Kindergarten Chats" and Other Writings,* ed. Athey, 28. See Ann Lorenz Van Zanten, "The Marshall Field Annex and the New Urban Order of Daniel Burnham's Chicago," *Chicago History* 11 (fall–winter 1982): 130–141, and Siry, *Carson Pirie Scott,* 50–57. Like Richardson's earlier Marshall Field Wholesale Store, the Marshall Field Annex was a target of labor action during its construction. See "Mechanics Go on a Short Strike," *Chicago Tribune,* 20 April 1893, 7. On Sullivan's view of the contrasts between the eastern and western United States, see Robert Twombly, "A Poet's Garden: Louis Sullivan's Vision for America," in *Louis Sullivan: The Poetry of Architecture,* by Robert Twombly and Narciso G. Menocal (New York: W. W. Norton, 2000), 22–24.

188. Garcyznski, *Auditorium,* 70.

189. "Bits of Architecture," *Chicago Tribune,* 7 November 1886, 26.

190. "Thousands in the Hall," *Chicago Tribune,* 11 June 1888, 11.

191. "Chicago Real Estate," *Chicago Tribune,* 19 August 1888, 18.

192. Rand McNally, *Bird's-Eye Views and Guide to Chicago,* 88. On the Central Depot, see also Flinn, *Chicago, the Marvelous City of the West,* 500–501; Stover, *History of the Illinois Central Railroad,* 76; and Ira J. Bach and Susan Wolfson, *A Guide to Chicago's Train Stations, Present and Past* (Athens: Ohio University Press, 1986), 6–7. On William A. Spalding, see *Album of Genealogy and Biography, Cook County, Illinois,* 2d ed., 381–382.

193. Garczynski, *Auditorium*, 56.

194. Louis Sullivan to Claude Bragdon, 8 November 1903, in Bragdon, "Letters from Louis Sullivan," *Architecture* 64 (July 1931): 9.

195. Garczynski, *Auditorium*, 56.

196. Ibid. On Furness's expressive lithic forms, see most recently Michael J. Lewis, *Frank Furness: Architecture and the Violent Mind* (New York: W. W. Norton, 2001), 97–98.

197. Louis Sullivan, Kindergarten Chat 27, "The Elements of Architecture; Objective and Subjective (I); Pier and Lintel" (1901), in *"Kindergarten Chats" and Other Writings,* ed. Athey, 120. On Sullivan's ideal of individuality of style, see chapter 4, 229–231, 244, and note 168.

198. Montgomery Schuyler, "Glimpses of Western Architecture: Chicago" (1891), in Schuyler, *"American Architecture" and Other Writings,* ed. Jordy and Coe, 1:260.

199. Mueller, Testimony, Chicago Auditorium Association vs. Mark Skinner Willing and the Northern Trust Co., in Kaufmann, "Wright's 'Lieber Meister,'" 51.

200. Theodore Dreiser, *Newspaper Days* (1922; reprint, Philadelphia: University of Pennsylvania Press, 1991), 63–64. The loggia's intended function as a reviewing stand was noted in "The Auditorium Hotel," *Daily National Hotel Reporter* (Chicago), 9 October 1890, in "Early History and Press Clippings, Chicago Auditorium Association, Chicago, 1887–1889" (Ryerson and Burnham Libraries, Art Institute of Chicago). David Lowe, *Chicago Interiors: Views of a Splendid World* (Chicago: Contemporary Books, 1979), 3, noted that the Auditorium Hotel's loggia remained in use for outdoor dining into the 1930s. See also Duis, *Challenging Chicago,* 55. Other Chicago novelists who used the Auditorium Building as a setting included Hamlin Garland, *Rose of Dutcher's Coolly* (1895); Frank Norris, *The Pit* (1903); Will Payne, *Mr. Salt* (1903); and Willa Cather, *Song of the Lark* (1915). See Carl S. Smith, *Chicago and the American Literary Imagination, 1880–1920* (Chicago: University of Chicago Press, 1984), 52–55, 60–61, 68–69, 135–136, 140. Literary focus on the Auditorium Building derived in part from the fact that local writers and artists often met next door in the Fine Arts Building, as the Studebaker Building was known after its remodeling in 1898. See introduction, note 5.

201. *Industrial Chicago,* 1:195.

202. Mme Léon Grandin, *Impressions d'une parisienne à Chicago* (Paris: Librairie Ernest Flammarion, 1894), 117: "En outre, l'élément décoratif, peinture et sculpture, si abondant, trop abondant même en nôtre Académie de musique, fait ici complètement défaut."

203. "The Chicago Auditorium Building," *Harper's Weekly* 31 (2 July 1887): 471.

204. "New Business Buildings of Chicago," *Builder* 63 (9 July 1892): 24. See also "The Studebaker Building," *Chicago Tribune,* 26 March 1887, 7. The stone's lime content was noted in "Bedford Stone," *Chicago Tribune,* 5 May 1878, 11. See also "A Story of Stone," *Inland Architect and News Record* 27 (April 1896): 26–28. In a book that was in Sullivan's library, Sarah M. Burnham, *History and Uses of Limestones and Marbles* (Boston: S. E. Cassino, 1883), 64, noted: "The North Vernon [lime]stone of Indiana, of the Hamilton epoch, is nearly pure carbonate of lime, and . . . will sustain a weight of 15,750 pounds to the square inch, while a cubic foot weighs 165.43 pounds. It is evident therefore, that as a building stone this limestone forms a valuable acquisition to the mineral resources of the State." She noted that the crushing strength of building stones varies from about 6,000 to 16,000 pounds per square inch. The quarries at Bedford were owned by a Chicagoan, David Reed, who was given the contract for preparing the stone and placing it in the Auditorium Building ("The Chicago Auditorium," unidentified clipping [1889?] in "Early History and Press Clippings, Chicago Auditorium Association, 1887–1889" [Ryerson and Burnham Libraries, Art Institute of Chicago]).

205. R. Floyd Clinch, Testimony, Chicago Auditorium Association vs. Mark Skinner Willing and the Northern Trust Co., 232 (Auditorium Collection, Roosevelt University Archives).

206. On pressed brick like that in the Wainwright Building, see Sullivan, foreword to St. Louis Hydraulic-Press Brick Company, *Suggestions in Artistic Brick* (St. Louis, [1910]), reprinted in *Louis Sullivan: The Public Papers*, ed. Twombly, 201. See also *Catalogue of Molded and Ornamental Pressed Brick Made by the Chicago Anderson Pressed Brick Company* (Chicago, 1887), which made the brick for Adler and Sullivan's Troescher Building (1884) and Burnham and Root's Rookery (1885–1887). On the relative advantages of terra cotta, see Siry, "Adler and Sullivan's Guaranty Building," 19–22.

207. Rand McNally, *Bird's-Eye Views and Guide to Chicago*, 106. On William Boyington's Union Station of 1881 (demolished 1925), see Bach and Wolfson, *Chicago's Train Stations*, 12–13.

208. Rand McNally, *Bird's-Eye Views and Guide to Chicago*, 30, 31. On James H. Walker and Company, see *Chicago Inter Ocean*, 6 August 1893, 6. Walker and Company received "probably the largest contract awarded to any one firm" for the Auditorium Hotel, furnishing "the art draperies, all the linen, crockery, bedding, glassware, blankets and bedding" (Garczynski, *Auditorium*, 191). On the Ryerson/Walker Wholesale Store, see "Chicago Real Estate," *Chicago Tribune*, 22 July 1988, 3; "Chicago Real Estate," *Chicago Tribune*, 4 November 1886, 3; *Industrial Chicago*, 1:191; Morrison, *Louis Sullivan*, 114–116; Tallmadge, *Architecture in Old Chicago*, 156; Condit, *Chicago School*, 41–42; Jordy, *American Buildings and Their Architects*, 4:110–111; Twombly, *Louis Sullivan*, 243–244; Van Zanten, "Sullivan to 1890"; and William H. Jordy, "The Tall Buildings," in *Sullivan: The Function of Ornament*, ed. de Wit, 36–37, 70–71, 84–85; and Narciso G. Menocal, "The Iconography of Architecture: Sullivan's View," in *Louis Sullivan: The Poetry of Architecture*, by Robert Twombly and Narciso G. Menocal (New York: W. W. Norton, 2000), 92. An ornamental stone impost block from the Walker Wholesale Store survives in the sculpture court of Madelener House, the Graham Foundation's building in Chicago.

209. *Industrial Chicago*, 1:68.

210. Wright, *Genius and the Mobocracy*, 48. Architect Irving K. Pond recalled: "When sometime after the completion of that building [the Auditorium], Sullivan was called upon to design the Walker Warehouse at Adams Street near the river (and in sight of the Field Wholesale), he remarked in my presence: 'I'm going to show 'em in the Walker building more than Richardson ever knew'" ("Autobiography of Irving K. Pond," manuscript, American Academy of Arts and Letters, New York City, F13–F14, quoted in Van Zanten, "Sullivan to 1890," 36).

211. The Walker Wholesale Store's early design in granite was noted in "The City," *Chicago Tribune*, 22 March 1886, 6. Its dimensions were noted in Rand McNally, *Bird's-Eye Views and Guide to Chicago*, 106. On the ten-story building added to the west in 1905, also built for Martin Ryerson Jr. and designed by Holabird and Roche, see "Big Building in the Wholesale District," *Economist* 31 (16 January 1904): 83–84, and Randall, *Building Construction in Chicago*, 225. A physical description of the original Adler and Sullivan Building made in 1948 by the Chicago realty firm of Arthur Rubloff and Company survives in the Richard Nickel files, Office of John Vinci, AIA, Chicago.

212. Sullivan, "Ornament in Architecture" (1892), in *Louis Sullivan: The Public Papers*, ed. Twombly, 82.

213. Sullivan, "Suggestions in Artistic Brickwork" (1910), in *Louis Sullivan: The Public Papers*, ed. Twombly, 201. See also Siry, *Carson Pirie Scott*, 225–226. Sullivan had written of the pier: "It is in equilibrium—at seeming rest. While it seems aspiring, it seems also solidly founded: it impresses us as static: as timeless. Simple as it seems and is to our sense of sight, it is nevertheless compound; for it is the field of operation of the two synchronous forces—downward and upward" (Sullivan, Kindergarten Chat 27, "Elements of Architecture," 121). On Sullivan's architectural ornament as representation of structural forces, see Vincent J. Scully, "Louis Sullivan's Architectural Ornament: A Brief Note concerning Humanistic Design in the Age of Force," *Perspecta* 5 (1959) 73–75; Jordy, *American Buildings and Their Architects*, 4:131–132; and Siry, "Adler and Sullivan's Guaranty Building," 26–27.

214. Morrison, *Louis Sullivan*, 115.

215. Tallmadge, *Architecture in Old Chicago*, 156.

216. Wright, quoted in "Chicago's Auditorium Is Fifty Years Old," 12.

217. Garczynski, *Auditorium*, 111.

218. Upton, *Musical Memories*, 305.

219. Sullivan, *Autobiography of an Idea*, 303.

220. "A Monumental Edifice," *Chicago Evening Journal*, 9 December 1886, 1. On Ruskin's interpretation of Italian campanile as a source for Sullivan's approach to the design of tall office buildings, see Weingarden, "Naturalized Nationalism," 63–67. On Sullivan's response to the Brattle Square Church, see *Autobiography of an Idea*, 188.

221. Mariana Van Rensselaer, "Recent Architecture in America, III: Commercial Buildings," *Century Magazine* 28 (August 1884), 520. On the New York Produce Exchange, see Landau and Condit, *Rise of the New York Skyscraper*, 116–125; Sarah B. Landau, *George B. Post, Architect: Picturesque Designer and Determined Realist* (New York: Monacelli Press, 1998), 58–64; and Stern, Mellins, and Fishman, *New York 1880*, 460–464.

222. "The Auditorium Building," *Economist* 1 (24 November 1888): 4. Early plans to use the sixteenth floor as an observatory were noted in "The Chicago Auditorium," unidentified clipping (1889?) in "Early History and Press Clippings, Chicago Auditorium Association, 1887–1889" (Ryerson and Burnham Libraries, Art Institute of Chicago).

223. Garczynski, *Auditorium*, 143. Peck proudly noted the United States Signal Service Station on the top floor ("Owners of Earth," *Chicago Tribune*, 31 January 1890, 2). When the service left the building, its equipment's wood housing atop the tower was removed. On the panoramic views from the tower, see "Chicago's Tall Tower," *Chicago Herald*, 14 June 1889; Flinn, *Chicago, the Marvelous City of the West*, 141; and Vynne, *Chicago by Day and Night*, 46. The tower and its vistas were not attractive to one critic of the city's inequities. William Stead, *Chicago To-Day: or The Labour War in America* (London, 1894), 93, wrote: "The last day I was in Chicago, I ascended the Auditorium Tower, which may be regarded as the Chicago substitute for the dome of St. Paul's Cathedral. The Auditorium building, with its observatory tower, is about one of the ugliest pieces of architecture which was ever reared, either in the Old World or the New. There is a tendency on the part of architects in the New World to imitate the Aztecs in the huge savage clumsiness of their edifices. It would, however, be cruel to hold the Aztecs responsible for the monstrous bulk of hewn stone from which the weather man keeps watch and ward over the Lake Shore City."

224. On 1 May 1890, "Architect Adler came in by request and the opportunity was taken to fix upon a basis of rental for the space in the tower occupied by Messrs. Adler and Sullivan. The term was agreed upon as three years from May 1, 90. Rent to begin then." For their offices totaling 2,755 square feet, Adler and Sullivan paid "one half of what the other tenants pay per foot" (Minutes of Executive Committee of Chicago Auditorium Association, 1 May 1890, 224 [Auditorium Collection, Roosevelt University Archives]).

225. George G. Elmslie to William F. McDermott, 17 June 1941 (William Gray Purcell Papers, Northwest Architectural Archives, University of Minnesota, St. Paul).

226. Wright, *Genius and the Mobocracy*, 46. The plan was published in "New Offices of Adler and Sullivan, Architects, Chicago," *Engineering and Building Record* 22 (7 June 1890): 5. On the tower office, Wright's departure, and Sullivan's removal in 1918, see Twombly, *Louis Sullivan*, 182–184, 235–237, 428. See also Meryle Secrest, *Frank Lloyd Wright: A Biography* (New York: Alfred A. Knopf, 1992), 119–123. On the bronze plaque commemorating Wright and Adler and Sullivan on the Auditorium tower's sixteenth floor, see *Canadian Architect* 18 (February 1973): 6–7. Wright was identified as an (independent?) architect in Chicago in an announcement of 12 May 1893 of his success in a competition for a pair of boathouses in Madison. See John O. Holzhueter, "The Lake Mendota and Monona Boathouses," in *Frank Lloyd Wright and Madison: Eight Decades of Artistic and Social Interaction*, ed. Paul E. Sprague. (Madison, Wis.: Elvehjem Museum of Art, 1990), 29.

Sullivan noted 1600 Auditorium Tower as his address in "Louis H. Sullivan, Testimony taken in the Probate Court of Cook County, 2 May 1900, Partial Proof of the Last Will and Testament, in the Estate of Dankmar Adler," Probate Court of Cook County, General no. P20-7056, docket 57, p. 10. Probate Records, Estate of Dankmar Adler (Clerk of the Circuit Court of Cook County Archives, Chicago, Illinois).

227. Sullivan, *Autobiography of an Idea,* 201, 196–197.

228. Wright, "The Art and Craft of the Machine" (1901), in *Frank Lloyd Wright: Collected Writings,* vol. 1, *1894–1930,* ed. Bruce B. Pfeiffer (New York: Rizzoli, 1992), 68–69. On local fiction writers' attachment of symbolic ideas to the city's horizontal and vertical expansion in this period, see Sidney H. Bremer, "Lost Continuities: Alternative Urban Visions in Chicago Novels, 1890–1915," *Soundings* 44 (spring 1981): 33. These writers may have been inspired by the many descriptions of views from the Auditorium Tower, one of which claimed: "The view obtained from the tower of the Auditorium is one of the most magnificent to be seen in the whole country, if indeed it may be equaled . . . . Everywhere the greatest activity is manifest; long trains of cars roll in one continuous stream to the doors of the big warehouses, while others steam away laden with freight for every state in the Union; the long wharves and river are an unbroken line of masts and spars, while the smoke from thousands of manufacturing industries tell of the ceaseless toil that has made the city great" ("The Auditorium Tower," unidentified clipping [1889?] in "Early History and Press Clippings, Chicago Auditorium Association, 1887–1889" [Ryerson and Burnham Libraries, Art Institute of Chicago]). Similarly, George W. Steevens, *The Land of the Dollar,* 4th ed. (Edinburgh: Blackwood, 1900), 145–146, advised readers to take an elevator to the top of the Auditorium Building's tower and view the lake, "then turn round and look at Chicago. You might be on a central peak of the high Alps. All about you they rise, the mountains of building—not in the broken line of New York, but thick together, side by side, one behind the other."

229. Garczynski, *Auditorium,* 54. Wright, *Autobiography,* 105, recalled of Chicago's architecture in the late 1880s: "The romantic Richardson and the susceptible Root were beginning to appear but the Potter Palmer Home on Lake Shore Drive was still supreme. The Palmer Home, Palmer Hotel and the Board of Trade were popular architecture. The Adler and Sullivan buildings stood clean and sharp by comparison. See their Borden block, Gage Building and others in Chicago wholesale district of this early period." In *Genius and the Mobocracy,* 60, Wright wrote that their "buildings if considered on their own in time and place went so far beyond contemporaries in point of enlightened countenance as to prophesy a new integrity so far in advance of the work of the period as to arrest the sentient passerby with prescience of a new world."

230. Sullivan, quoted in "Church Spires Must Go," *Chicago Tribune,* 30 November 1890, 36. Sullivan's position contrasted directly with that of the New York architect Stanford White, who as a decorative artist was perhaps Sullivan's most impressive contemporary. These architects' divergent views appear when Sullivan's Auditorium Tower is contrasted with White's tower for Madison Square Garden, designed from the fall of 1887. Ironically, Professor William R. Ware of Columbia had also been retained as an architectural adviser for this project. Chicago's Auditorium was cited as an impetus for construction of Manhattan's new Madison Square Garden, designed by McKim, Mead, and White. In addition to its capacious hall for horse shows, circuses, exhibits, conventions, and similar events, Madison Square Garden had a separate concert hall and a separate theater for dramatic spectacles. This theater's interior was "to be built upon the plan of that at Bayreuth which Wagner caused to be built according to the most approved plans" ("New York's Auditorium," *Chicago Tribune,* 25 January 1889, 2). From its opening in June 1890, Madison Square Garden's many facilities made it a public success. Yet from White's perspective it was the tower on the building's south side along Twenty-third Street that would be the paramount civic symbol. Unlike the Auditorium Tower, White's tower for Madison Square Garden was based on a specific historical source, the Giralda Tower in Seville, originally a Moslem minaret of the 1300s that became part of the fifteenth-century cathedral built on the mosque's site. Taller than its model, White's tower was 38 feet square and rose 341 feet above the street, a slender height-to-width

ratio of 9:1 that made it appear to soar skyward. Like the walls below, the tower's shaft and multitiered crown were rendered in buff-colored Roman brick trimmed with white terra cotta. The rich silhouette of Madison Square Garden's tower marked Manhattan's new center for public amusement and even hedonistic pleasure as a civic ideal far removed from its religious prototype in Seville. Though New Yorkers acclaimed White's tower as a new landmark, its direct appropriation of the Giralda represented the kind of commercially driven historicism that Sullivan condemned. On White's Madison Square Garden, see Charles C. Baldwin, *Stanford White* (New York: Dodd, Mead, 1931), 199–212; Stern, Gilmartin, and Massengale, *New York 1900,* 202–206, 462 n. 3; Roth, *McKim, Mead and White, Architects,* 158–165; and Stern, Mellins, and Fishman, *New York 1880,* 695–705.

CHAPTER 4

1. Mueller, Testimony, Chicago Auditorium Association vs. Mark Skinner Willing, in Kaufmann, "Wright's 'Lieber Meister,'" 44.

2. Adler, paraphrased in "Western Association of Architects," *American Architect and Building News* 20 (27 November 1886): 254.

3. Address by Mr. Louis H. Sullivan to Illinois Chapter, American Institute of Architects, 8 June 1915, Manuscripts Collection, Chicago Historical Society, published as "Tribute to Solon S. Beman" (1915), in *Louis Sullivan: The Public Papers,* ed. Twombly, 210.

4. Adler, "Chicago Auditorium," 415–417.

5. Mueller, Testimony, Chicago Auditorium Association vs. Mark Skinner Willing, in Kaufmann, "Wright's 'Lieber Meister,'" 44. On 25 January 1889, after Adler and Sullivan had worked on the Auditorium project for over two years, "on motion of Mr. [Charles] Hutchinson it was unanimously voted, to recommend to the Board of Directors, that the architects Messrs. Adler and Sullivan, be paid for their professional services the sum of Twenty-five thousand Dollars ($25,000.00) in addition to the Fifty thousand Dollars ($50,000.00) as originally agreed upon. The whole sum of Seventy-five thousand Dollars ($75,000.00) to be on the basis of Fifty thousand Dollars ($50,000.00) cash and Twenty-five thousand Dollars ($25,000.00) full paid Stock of this Association." The Auditorium Association thus gave Adler and Sullivan an amount of stock equal to the full value of the $25,000 in stock that the firm had initially pledged toward the project, and on which the architects had already paid assessments to the Auditorium Association (Minutes of Executive Committee of Chicago Auditorium Association, 25 January 1889, 79 [Auditorium Collection, Roosevelt University Archives]).

6. Peck to Adler, June 1888, quoted in Rachel Baron, "Forgotten Facets of Dankmar Adler," *Inland Architect,* April 1964, 14, and in Joan Saltzstein, "Dankmar Adler: Part I—the Man," *Wisconsin Architect* 38 (July–August 1967): 19.

7. "Flocking to Low Rates," *Chicago Evening Journal,* 14 January 1887, 2. On the reconstructed Columbia Theater, see Marquis, *Marquis' Hand-Book of Chicago,* 237.

8. "The Convention Hall," *Chicago Tribune,* 1 August 1886, 13. One announcement noted that the auditorium would have "an ordinary seating capacity of 6,000, which can be increased on occasion to fully 10,000" ("The Music Hall and Hotel Scheme Being Vigorously Pushed," *Chicago Tribune,* 3 November 1886, 8).

9. Milward Adams, quoted in "The Pride of Chicago," *Chicago Herald,* 20 October 1889, 1. A number of London theaters in this period had larger seating capacities than the Paris Opera, which was then perceived as the finest European theater from an architectural viewpoint. In the 1880s larger London theaters with their maximum number of spectators included Britannia (2,972), Standard (2,878), Drury Lane (2,731), Her Majesty's (2,444), Astley's (2,407), Covent Garden (2,299), Elephant and Castle (2,283), Alhambra (2,208), and Surrey (2,161). Chicago's Alhambra (2,500), Columbia (2,400), and Chicago Opera House (2,300) were larger than the Paris Opera. See Doty, *Town of Pullman,* 13–14.

10. "The Auditorium Building," *Economist* 1 (24 November 1888): 4. See also Miller and Roth, *Cincinnati's Music Hall,* 21–22, and Clubbe, *Cincinnati Observed,* 250.

11. Pisoni, "Operatic War in New York City," 24–26. See also "Academy of Music: Its Architecture," *New-York Daily Tribune,* 2 March 1867, 5; T. Allston Brown, *A History of the New York Stage from the First Performance in 1732 to 1902,* 3 vols. (New York: Dodd, Mead, 1903), 2:55; and Stern, Mellins, and Fishman, *New York 1880,* 678–681.

12. Mapleson, *Mapleson Memoirs,* 280, noted that his last tour to Chicago in May 1886 concluded with "a benefit tendered to me by most of the prominent citizens. They thus showed their appreciation of my efforts as a pioneer; for I was the first manager who had introduced into their city grand opera worthy of the name." Mapleson (282) particularly appreciated Peck's financial help at this tour's close. The Academy of Music was cited as "the largest theatre in New York City" in "Chicago Notes," *Presto* 7 (17 May 1890): 272.

13. Peck, quoted in "The Great Auditorium," *Chicago Tribune,* 18 June 1888, 7.

14. Peck, quoted in "One of Our Wonders," *Chicago Herald,* 16 September 1888, 17. Adler's account of his European trip appeared in his talk "Stage Mechanisms," in *Inland Architect and News Record* 13 (March 1889): 42–43. See also Saltzstein, "Autobiography and Letters of Dankmar Adler," 20–24; and Geraniotis, "German Design Influences in the Auditorium Theater," 44–47. See also note 143 below.

15. "Palace for Passengers," *Chicago Tribune,* 30 November 1890, 34.

16. Peck, Annual Report of the President to the Stockholders of the Chicago Auditorium Association, 7 December 1889 (Auditorium Collection, Roosevelt University Archives).

17. Garczynski, *Auditorium,* 102.

18. "The Convention Hall," *Chicago Tribune,* 30 January 1887, 17. See also "The Grand Auditorium," *Chicago Tribune,* 10 December 1886, 1.

19. Adler, "Chicago Auditorium," 423, wrote: "The boxes, forty in number, are arranged in two tiers upon each side of the parquette. The lower tier forms an arcade of semi-circular arches with rather light treatment and but little effect of inclosure, while the upper boxes are entirely open. In fact, there is nothing at all of the boxlike and stuffy effect produced by the conventional treatment of the open box." The lower boxes' arches framed their occupants on view yet interfered with their views outward.

20. The Auditorium's boxes were sold for a season. See "An Opera Box for $2,100," *Chicago Tribune,* 23 November 1889, 1. As noted, the Met's first patrons paid $17,500 to permanently own a box; for the first season, nonowned boxes rented for $12,000.

21. Sullivan, quoted in "The Pride of Chicago," *Chicago Daily News,* morning edition, 9 December 1889.

22. Adler, "Theater," 22–23.

23. Ibid., 23.

24. "The Convention Hall," *Chicago Tribune,* 30 January 1887, 17.

25. Adams, quoted in "The Pride of Chicago," *Chicago Herald,* 20 October 1889, 1.

26. Report, Committee on Public Buildings, 1 May 1882, in *Proceedings of the City Council of the City of Chicago; 9 May 1881 to 5 May 1882* (Chicago, 1882), 556–559; Report, Committee on Public Buildings, 3 December 1883, in *Proceedings of the City Council of the City of Chicago, 14 May 1883 to 5 May 1884* (Chicago, 1884), 256–257 (Municipal Reference Library, Chicago Public Library). See also *Report of the Committee on Theatres and Public Halls to the Executive Committee of the Citizens' Association of Chicago, October 1887* (Chicago, 1887). On these committees, see chapter 1, note 126, and chapter 2, notes 77 and 114.

27. Adler, "Chicago Auditorium," 423, wrote: "This unusually great rise of the main floor has also made practicable the arrangement of six entrances, similar to the 'vomitoria' of the Roman

amphitheatre, by which the lower half of the parquette seats are reached without rendering it necessary to climb to the upper level of the main floor." Schuyler, "Glimpses of Western Architecture," 260, saw the Auditorium's entrances as "vomitoria." He wrote (258): "A place of popular entertainment, constructed upon a scale and with a massiveness to which we can scarcely find a parallel since Roman days, would present one of the worthiest and most interesting problems a modern architect could have if he were left to solve it unhampered."

28. "The Pride of Chicago," *Chicago Herald,* 20 October 1889, 1.

29. *Report of the Committee on Theatres and Public Halls of the Citizens' Association of Chicago, October, 1883* (Chicago, 1883), 6. Adler advocated a larger number of narrower aisles in "Paramount Requirements for a Large Opera House," 46, and "Theater Building for American Cities: Second Paper," 815.

30. Garczynski, *Auditorium,* 143.

31. Dankmar Adler, Last Will and Testament, 24 August 1895, wrote: "I bequeath the technical and scientific books of which I may be possessed at the time of my death to my son, Abraham Kohn Adler" (Auditorium Collection, Roosevelt University Archives). Abraham K. Adler graduated from the University of Michigan in 1893, then entered his father's office. He worked with his father again from 1896 to Dankmar Adler's death in 1900 ("Obituary: Abraham K. Adler," *Chicago Tribune,* 30 October 1914, 12).

32. Adler, "Tall Business Building," 209–210, wrote of "the many important engineering problems which are encountered in the design and erection of every modern high business building. The reader who wishes to pursue the subject is referred to the writings of Mr. [William P.] Gerhard, Mr. [Frank E.] Kidder and many other eminent specialist[s] who have enriched the literature of the building arts and sciences." Gerhard (1854–1927) published extensively on fire safety in theaters, including his *Theatre Fires and Panics: Their Causes and Prevention* (New York: John Wiley, 1896). Kidder (1859–1905) published professional manuals that went through numerous editions, including *The Architects' and Builders' Handbook, The Architects' and Builders' Pocket-Book,* and *Building Construction and Superintendence.*

33. On European treatises on architectural acoustics and Scott Russell's studies, see chapter 1, notes 35 and 128.

34. Sullivan, *Autobiography of an Idea,* 293.

35. Sullivan, "Development of Construction" (1916), in *Louis Sullivan: The Public Papers,* ed. Twombly, 213.

36. Lowe, "Monument of an Age," 41. Joan W. Saltzstein, ed., *Liebman Adler: His Life through His Letters* (n.p., 1975), 95, noted that Adler and Sullivan's synagogue for KAM, dedicated by Liebman in 1891, had acoustics by Dankmar that "enabled the sounds of his father's voice to reach to the farthest corner of the balcony." On Liebman Adler and KAM, see Bernhard Felsenthal and Herman Eliassof, *History of Kehillath Anshe Maarabh: Congregation of the Men of the West* (Chicago, 1897); Hyman L. Meites, *History of the Jews of Chicago* (Chicago: Jewish Historical Society of Illinois, 1924); and Jacob J. Weinstein, *A History of Kehilath Anshe Mayriv* (Chicago, 1951).

37. On KAM's buildings, see Lauren Weingarden Rader, "Synagogue Architecture in Illinois," in *Faith and Form: An Exhibition,* Maurice Spertus Museum of Judaica (Chicago: Spertus College Press, 1976), 38–43. These were first a building at the corner of Wabash Avenue and Peck Court (named for the site's original owner, Philip F. W. Peck), in the block just west of where the Auditorium was later built. Kehilath Anshe Ma'ariv worshiped there from 1868 until the building's destruction in the fire of 1874, after which the congregation purchased Plymouth Congregational Church on the southeast corner of Indiana Avenue and Twenty-sixth street. Before he married Dila Kohn, Dankmar Adler recalled living with his father through the Great Fire of 1871 (Dankmar Adler, "Some Notes upon the Earlier Chicago Architects," *Inland Architect and News Record* 19 [May 1892]: 48).

As a leader among local reform congregations, Liebman Adler published his weekly sermons on biblical texts in a volume titled *Sabbath Hours: Thoughts [by Liebman Adler]* (Philadelphia: Jewish Publication Society of America, 1893). Liebman's basic orientation to the Bible appears in his view of the first chapter of Genesis on the creation of the world. He emphasized that this text set the keynote for the early books of the Bible as purely natural history, followed by a historical account of the Jewish people. Liebman Adler's interpretive emphasis was not on mystical dimensions of religion, nor on the Bible's literary character, but on its scientific and historical content. The same rational emphasis pervades his son Dankmar's writings on architecture as a field whose development derived from knowledge both of scientific principles and of evolving conditions of human society. It was in this spirit that Dankmar Adler saw the theater as a type with a telling social history and a future based on the scientific study of its architectural technologies. As noted in chapter 2, one account of Adler and Sullivan's 1885 remodeling of McVicker's Theater noted that their firm's motto was "let there be light." On one level this alludes to Liebman Adler's analysis of the Bible's third verse; on another it implies a general ideal of progress in architecture. In theater design, Adler identified this ideal with acoustics and visibility.

38. Mapleson, *Mapleson Memoirs,* 193–194, 208. Adler's trip to Salt Lake City was noted in Arthur Woltersdorf, "Dankmar Adler," *Western Architect* 33 (July 1924): 75. See also Morrison, *Louis Sullivan,* 288, and Twombly, *Louis Sullivan,* 154–155.

39. On the Mormon Tabernacle, see C. Mark Hamilton, *Nineteenth-Century Mormon Architecture and City Planning* (New York: Oxford University Press, 1995), 59–60, and Kate B. Carter, *The Great Mormon Tabernacle* (Salt Lake City: Daughters of Utah Pioneers, 1968).

40. Adler, "Chicago Auditorium," 421.

41. Gregersen, *Dankmar Adler,* 10, notes that the idea of seating rows' not having curvatures centered on the source of sound followed from the theaters of Adler's early employer, architect Ozia S. Kinney, who died in 1869. The capacity of the Auditorium's orchestra pit was noted in "The Pride of Chicago," *Chicago Herald,* 20 October 1889, 1.

42. Gregersen, *Dankmar Adler,* 11–19.

43. Adler, "Theater Building for American Cities: First Paper," 723.

44. Bart Swindall, Auditorium Theater Council, noted this angle of the upper gallery's slope in a tour of the theater on 13 June 1997.

45. Adler, "Paramount Requirements of a Large Opera House," 46.

46. Ticket prices for the Auditorium's inaugural season of 1889 were noted in Minutes of Executive Committee of the Chicago Auditorium Association, 3 May 1887 to 11 December 1907, 146 (Auditorium Collection, Roosevelt University Archives). On prices for the festival, see chapter 2, 109.

47. "No Equal in the World," *Chicago Tribune,* 2 December 1888. On the Colosseum in Rome, see Adler, "Theater," 22.

48. Mallgrave, *Gottfried Semper,* 123–124. At the end of his discussion on different types of theater plans, Pierre Patte, *Essai sur l'architecture théâtrale* (Paris, 1782), favored the ellipse for acoustic reasons. On Patte's treatise, see Izenour, *Theater Design,* 57–59, and Tidworth, *Theatres,* 102.

49. Vitruvius Pollio, *The Ten Books on Architecture,* trans. Morris Hicky Morgan (Cambridge: Harvard University Press, 1926), bk. 5, chap. 3, p. 138.

50. Matthew Hurff, "The Context of Tradition in the Chicago Auditorium," seminar paper, Wesleyan University, May 1992, noted that Vitruvius (*Ten Books on Architecture,* bk. 5, chap. 3, pp. 138–139) wrote that sound "moves in an endless number of circular rounds, like the innumerably increasing circular waves which appear when a stone is thrown into smooth water" and that Adler ("Theater Building for American Cities: First Paper," 722) wrote: "The sound waves, produced in the open air, travel very much as do the ripples in a pool when a stone is thrown into it."

51. Vitruvius, *Ten Books on Architecture,* bk. 5, chap. 3, p. 139.

52. James Fergusson, *History of the Modern Styles of Architecture,* 3d rev. ed., 2 vols. (1862; New York: Dodd, Mead, 1891), 2:382, quoted in John A. Fox, "American Dramatic Theatres" (part 3), *American Architect and Building News* 6 (2 August 1879): 35.

53. Fox, "American Dramatic Theatres," 36.

54. "Dedicated to Music and the People," *Chicago Tribune,* 10 December 1889, 1. See 252–262 below.

55. Izenour, *Theater Design,* 568–569.

56. Adler, "Theater Building for American Cities: First Paper," 724. One reporter described the Auditorium Theater at its opening: "The design is wonderful because it is the first theater ever built with the interior shaped like a cone or speaking-trumpet. The stage being taken as the apex of a hollow cone, the arched roof and diverging walls retreat in a series of constantly increasing circles, like the waves made when a stone is dropped in still water. This is considered the very acme of acoustic achievement" ("The Pride of Chicago," *Chicago Daily News,* morning edition, 9 December 1889).

57. Adler, "Theater," 24.

58. Ibid.

59. Adler, "Theater-Building for American Cities: First Paper," 724.

60. Adler, "Theater," 23.

61. "The Auditorium Building: A Great and Superb Structure," Auditorium Number, *Graphic* (Chicago), o.s., 11 (14 December 1889). Mallgrave, *Gottfried Semper,* 260–262, noted Semper's innovation of the double proscenium in his unbuilt project for Munich's Festival Theater as the source for the triple proscenium framing the stage at Bayreuth. The spatial depth within the triple proscenium accommodated the orchestra's placement in a deep pit or "mystical abyss" between the audience and stage, an idea important to Wagner.

62. Adler, "Theater-Building for American Cities: First Paper," 724.

63. Wright, quoted in "Chicago's Auditorium Is Fifty Years Old," 12.

64. Adler, "Chicago Auditorium," 429.

65. Garczynski, *Auditorium,* 128.

66. Gregersen, "History of the Auditorium Building," 23.

67. Adler, "Theater," 26.

68. Cady, "Essential Features of a Large Opera House," 47. See van Rensselaer, "Metropolitan Opera House," 88; "Ventilation and Warming of the Metropolitan Opera House, New York," *Sanitary Engineer* 9 (6 and 13 December 1883): 10–13, 40–41; and "The New Metropolitan Opera House," *Sanitary Engineer* 9 (10 January 1884): 135, 137. Geraniotis, "German Design Influences in the Auditorium Theater," 45, noted Cady's and Adler's adaptation of the system in Van der Null and Siccardsburg's Imperial Court Opera House in Vienna. Sullivan owned an illustrated folio volume on this building (see note 102 below).

69. "In the New Opera House," *New York Times,* 22 July 1883, 9. For insights into the ventilation systems of the Metropolitan and the Auditorium, I am indebted to Austin Zinsser, "Class and Ventilation in the New York Metropolitan Opera House and the Chicago Auditorium Theater," seminar paper, Wesleyan University, December 2000.

70. On the Auditorium Theater's system of mechanical ventilation, see Garczynski, *Auditorium,* 32–33, and Adler, "Chicago Auditorium," 431–432. See also Izenour, *Theater Design,* 157 n. 56. On the air intake atop the Allegheny County Court House's main tower in Pittsburgh, see Richardson's description of his competition design of December 1883 in Van Trump, *Majesty of the Law,* 56–57, and Van Rensselaer, *Henry Hobson Richardson,* 91. On earlier systems, see Robert Bruegmann, "Central Heating and Forced Ventilation: Origins and Effects on Architectural Design," *Journal of the Society of Architectural Historians* 37 (October 1978): 143–160.

71. Adler, "Paramount Requirements of a Large Opera House," 46. On the advantages of downward supply of cool air in later theaters, see D. D. Kimball, "Ventilating and Cooling of Motion Picture Theaters," *Architectural Forum* 42 (June 1925): 395–96.

72. "Dance for the Poor," *Chicago Tribune,* 29 December 1890, and "Is Dedicated Anew," *Chicago Tribune,* 10 January 1890, 1. See also "The Charity Ball," *Graphic* (Chicago), n.s., 10 (13 January 1894): 27. On the Metropolitan Opera House as a setting for balls, see "The New-Year's Ball and Mr. McAllister," *Harper's Weekly* 34 (18 January 1890): 51. On 29 April 1889, a great banquet was given at the Metropolitan Opera House as part of the celebration of the Washington Inaugural Centennial ("The Crush at the Ball," *New York Times,* 30 April 1889, 3, 5). On the Versailles Opera House, see André Japy, *L'Opéra royal de Versailles* (Paris: Comité national pour la sauvegarde du château de Versailles, 1958); Izenour, *Theater Design,* 59–60; Christopher Tadgell, *Ange-Jacques Gabriel* (London: A. Zwemmer, 1978), 119–124; and Allan Braham, *The Architecture of the French Enlightenment* (Berkeley: University of California Press, 1980), 42–43. On Barry's Covent Garden, see chapter 1, note 33.

73. Adler, "Theater-Building for American Cities: First Paper," 719, wrote: "We are . . . safe in assuming that for the production of anything except grand opera and great spectacular performances, it is not well to have the auditorium too large; and that a house containing from 1200 to 1500 seats will be more satisfactory than a larger one; further that when its seating capacity exceeds 1800, it will have but little value as a place for rendering comedy, drama or light opera. A certain intimacy of relationship between the actor and the spectator is essential in all the lighter forms of stage production."

74. Johnson, "That Guilty Third Tier: Prostitution in Nineteenth-Century American Theaters," in *Victorian America,* ed. Daniel Walker Howe (Philadelphia: University of Pennsylvania Press, 1976), 111–120; David Grimsted, *Melodrama Unveiled: American Theater and Culture, 1800–1850* (Berkeley: University of California Press, 1987), 55–56; and Timothy J. Gilfoyle, *City of Eros: New York City, Prostitution, and the Commercialization of Sex, 1790–1920* (New York: W. W. Norton, 1992), 109–112. On the "Disciplining of Spectatorship," see Kasson, *Rudeness and Civility,* 215–256. On attempts to control gallery behavior, see also Robert W. Snyder, *The Voice of the City: Vaudeville and Popular Culture in New York* (New York: Oxford University Press, 1989), 30–34.

75. Augustin Daly, "The American Dramatist," *North American Review* 142 (May 1886): 491, quoted in Bruce A. McConachie, "Pacifying American Theatrical Audiences," in *For Fun and Profit,* ed. Butsch, 60. On Daly, see Joseph Francis Daly, *Life of Augustin Daly* (New York: Macmillan, 1917), and Marvin Felheim, *The Theater of Augustin Daly: An Account of the Late Nineteenth Century American Stage* (Cambridge: Harvard University Press, 1956). On Daly's consultation with Adler, see Morrison, *Louis Sullivan,* 104, and Mueller, Testimony, Chicago Auditorium Association vs. Mark Skinner Willing, in Kaufmann, "Wright's 'Lieber Meister,'" 44. On the "family circle" at the New York Academy of Music, see Ahlquist, *Democracy at the Opera,* 148.

76. "Pride of All Chicago: From the Second Balcony," *Chicago Herald,* 10 December 1889. Manager Milward Adams said: "Indeed, our gallery gods are to be well provided for, and if they can't eat peanuts and drink in melody up there in better style than anywhere else I should like to see the gallery that surpasses it" ("The Pride of Chicago," *Chicago Herald,* 20 October 1889, 1). In the theater as first planned, there would be "balcony entrances on Wabash ave." ("The Building Department," *Real Estate and Building Journal* 28 [21 August 1886]: 479). Also, "the 160 feet on Wabash avenue will be devoted to stores and to a gallery entrance" ("Music and the Drama," *Chicago Herald,* 26 September 1886, 12).

77. Adler, "Chicago Auditorium," 423.

78. Ibid., 423–424.

79. Ibid., 432.

80. On Peck's ideas for civic lectures and choral events, see "The Great Auditorium," *Chicago Tribune,* 17 June 1888, 5.

81. "The Week's Amusements," *Chicago Tribune,* 6 April 1890, 27. See "Programme of Lectures by Rev. T. DeWitt Talmage, D.D.," 8 April 1890, in Milward Adams Scrapbooks, Newberry Library, Chicago. See also Chicago Bureau of Popular and Scientific Lectures, "The [Henry H.] Ragan Lectures," Central Music Hall, April 15, 17, 21, 24, and 26, 1890 (Chicago Historical Society).

82. "The Committee's Choice," *Chicago Tribune*, 9 December 1887, 1, 3.

83. "The Great Auditorium," *Chicago Tribune*, 18 June 1888, 7.

84. Ibid.

85. Henry O. Northrop, *The Life and Public Service of Gen. Benj. Harrison* (New York, 1888), 308, quoted in Harry Joseph Sievers, *Benjamin Harrison, Hoosier Statesman: From the Civil War to the White House, 1865–1888* (New York: University Publishers, 1959), 337.

86. Adler, "Paramount Requirements of a Large Opera House," 45. Van Rensselaer, "Metropolitan Opera House," 87, noted the configuration of its house lights. Their technology was described in "Gas-Fitting, and Gas Lighting by Electricity of the Metropolitan Opera-House, New York," *Sanitary Engineer* 9 (27 December 1993): 89–90.

87. On the muslin canopy and temporary decorations, by F. P. Foster of Cincinnati, see "The Great Auditorium," *Chicago Tribune*, 10 June 1888, 13, and "The Decorator at Work," *Chicago Tribune*, 12 June 1888, 1. Northrop, *Harrison*, 308, quoted one account of the convention by an out-of-town reporter that misidentified the unfinished Auditorium Theater as the Inter-state Industrial Exposition Building's interior, used for the 1884 convention.

88. *Report of the Committee on Theatres and Public Halls of the Citizens' Association of Chicago, October, 1883* (Chicago, 1883), 6–7.

89. *Chicago Tribune*, 19 June 1888. Peck's emergency preparations and Sullivan's "original design" were noted in "The Hall Nearly Ready," *Chicago Tribune*, 13 June 1888, 1.

90. On electrification as a mark of empowerment, see Platt, *Electric City*, 22–39.

91. On Adler's halls for the party conventions of 1884 (Republican and Democratic, Chicago), 1888 (Republican, Chicago), 1892 (Democratic, Minneapolis), and 1896 (Republican, St. Louis), see Gregersen, *Dankmar Adler*, 55, 71, 84–85, 88.

92. See Sautter and Burke, *Inside the Wigwam*, and Kathleen Zygmum, "Parades, Protests, and Politics," *Chicago History* 25 (fall 1996): 40–59. On the Republican convention of 1884 in Chicago, see John Tweedy, *A History of the Republican National Conventions from 1856 to 1908* (Danbury, Conn.: J. Tweedy, 1910), 205–229, and Edmund Morris, *The Rise of Theodore Roosevelt* (New York: Coward, McCann, and Geoghegan, 1979), 258–268. By then the practice of packing conventions with many visitors, whose vociferous participation was to help ensure nomination of one candidate or another, had been discredited as unwanted by the delegates. It was also no longer as effective as it once had been, since rival candidates could command equal verbally supportive audiences.

93. Adler, "Convention Halls," 22–23.

94. "The Convention Hall," *Chicago Tribune*, 9 June 1888, 1.

95. Adler, "Convention Halls," 14.

96. Ibid.

97. John Scott Russell, "Elementary Considerations" (1838), in Izenour, *Theater Design*, 599.

98. "The Great Convention Hall," *Chicago Tribune*, 21 June 1888, 4.

99. Lew Wallace, *Life of Gen. Ben Harrison* (Hartford, Conn.: S. S. Scranton, 1888), 269. See Tweedy, *Republican National Conventions*, 231–258.

100. "The Auditorium Building, Chicago," *Engineering* (London) 51 (24 April 1899): 490. One Cincinnatian described the finished Auditorium Theater as "a cross between a church and a theatre, with a dash of railroad station thrown in. Cromo style" ("The Auditorium from Cincinnati's Standpoint," *Indicator* 12 [4 January 1890]: 12). On Sullivan's interest in modern railway bridges, see *Autobiography of an Idea*, 246–248; Condit, "Sullivan's Skyscrapers," 78–93; Condit, *Chicago School*, 168–170; and David E. Nye, *American Technological Sublime* (Cambridge: MIT Press, 1994), 77–87.

101. Garzynski, *Auditorium,* 189, wrote: "So great was the enthusiasm felt over the Auditorium that many merchants gladly seized the opportunity offered by the contracts for furnishing the different parts of the structure, to connect themselves in some way with it; for they desired to above all things to be a part of its record, and in the carrying out of their contracts they undoubtedly favored the Auditorium at their own expense. They certainly deserve to be mentioned as among those who felt the generous flame of patriotism which Ferd. W. Peck excited among all those with whom he came in contact. The feeling among all classes resembled that created by the building of the great Gothic cathedrals in the Middle Ages, when knights and nobles, merchants, farmers and workmen contributed, each one according to his means and in his degree, to the work that excited their enthusiasm."

Adler and Sullivan's unbuilt project for the Odd Fellows Temple in Chicago of 1891, discussed in chapter 3, 159, was described as a solution to the "problem of creating and maintaining, under the conditions and environments of the 19th and 20th Centuries, a monumental structure, illustrating and embodying the aspirations and ideals of its founders, and owing its origin to public and ideal purposes. Five hundred years ago these would have found expression in a great cathedral, a monastery or a guild hall, built upon public ground with material and labor donated by an enthusiastically self–sacrificing public" ("To the Odd Fellows of Chicago and the State of Illinois" [Ryerson and Burnham Libraries, Art Institute of Chicago]).

102. Peck, Annual Report of the President to the Stockholders of the Chicago Auditorium Association, 7 December 1889 (Auditorium Collection, Roosevelt University Archives). Peck noted that the French government had paid the equivalent of over $7,000,000 for the Paris Opera House, plus $2,000,000 for the ground, while Chicago's Auditorium had cost $3,100,000 to build, plus a total ground rent of $1,000,000 for the lease period of ninety-nine years. On Sullivan's window shopping near the Paris Opera, see *Autobiography of an Idea,* 227. On the facade's unveiling and the theater's inauguration, see Mead, *Garnier's Paris Opera,* 184–185, 193–195. On Sullivan's return to the United States, see Twombly, *Louis Sullivan,* 73. In 1909 Sullivan owned Charles Garnier, *Le nouvel Opéra de Paris,* 2 vols. (Paris, 1880); Richard Lucae et al., *Das Opernhaus zu Frankfurt am Main* (Berlin, 1883); and Hans Auer, *Das K. K. Hof-Opernhaus in Wien von van der Null und von Siccardsburg* (Vienna, 1885). See Andrew, *Louis Sullivan,* appendix 2: Inventory of Sullivan's Library, from Williams, Barker and Severn Company, Auction Catalogue no. 5533, "Household Effects, Library, Oriental Rugs, Paintings, etc., of Mr. Louis Sullivan," Chicago, 29 November 1909. On Sullivan and Wagner, see note 129 below. On Americans at Bayreuth, see chapter 2, note 165.

103. "The New Auditorium Building," *Chicago Tribune,* 16 April 1887, 5.

104. Adler, paraphrased in "The Western Association of Architects," *American Architect and Building News* 20 (27 November 1886): 253. On Sullivan's reading of "Inspiration" see also "Western Association of Architects," *Chicago Tribune,* 18 November 1886, 6. A version of Sullivan's 1893 revision of this essay, "Study on Inspiration," is published in Twombly and Menocal, *Louis Sullivan: The Poetry of Architecture,* 161–170.

105. Adler, paraphrased in "Western Association of Architects," 253. On the kind of praise Adler referred to, see D. Arnold Lewis, "Evaluations of American Architecture by European Critics, 1875–1900" (Ph.D. diss., University of Wisconsin, 1962), and Lewis, "A European Profile of American 0Architecture," *Journal of the Society of Architectural Historians* 37 (December 1978): 256–282.

106. T. P. Foster, quoted in "The Decorator at Work," *Chicago Tribune,* 12 June 1888, 1.

107. Sullivan, "Characteristics and Tendencies of American Architecture" (1885), in *Louis Sullivan: The Public Papers,* ed. Twombly, 5. This was also originally a talk given to the Western Association of Architects.

108. Ibid., 3.

109. Sullivan, "Inspiration" (1886), in *Louis Sullivan: The Public Papers,* ed. Twombly, 27.

110. Ibid., 16.

111. Ibid., 26–27.

112. Hippolyte Taine, *The Philosophy of Art* (New York: Holt and Williams, 1873), 74. Sullivan, *Autobiography of an Idea,* 233, recalled that while preparing for the École des Beaux-Arts in 1874, he "had discovered three small volumes by Hippolyte Taine devoted to the Philosophy of Art in Greece, in Italy, and in the Netherlands." These were *Philosophie de l'art en Italie* (1866), *Philosophie de l'art en Grèce* (1869), and *Philosophie de l'art dans les Pays Bas* (1869), all based on Taine's lectures at the École. See Twombly, *Louis Sullivan,* 60, 69, 71–73. Earlier in his autobiography, Sullivan (167) recalled that he had first been introduced to Taine's history of English literature as a student at Boston's English High School, in 1870–1871. Taine's *Philosophie de l'art* was first published in 1865, in French, in both Paris and New York. On Taine's aesthetic theory, see Leo Weinstein, *Hippolyte Taine* (New York: Twayne, 1972); and Thomas H. Goetz, *Taine and the Fine Arts* (Madrid: Playor, 1973).

113. Sullivan, "Style" (1888), in *Louis Sullivan: The Public Papers,* ed. Twombly, 51.

114. Taine, *Philosophy of Art,* 78.

115. Sullivan, "The Artistic Use of the Imagination" (1889), in *Louis Sullivan: The Public Papers,* ed. Twombly, 66.

116. Ibid., 66. On Sullivan and Whitman, see Paul, *Louis Sullivan,* 1–3, 42–45; Jordy, *American Buildings and Their Architects,* 4:162–163; Twombly, *Louis Sullivan,* 214–215; Dizikes, *Opera in America,* 253; Lauren Weingarden, "Naturalized Technology: Louis Sullivan's Whitmanesque Skyscrapers," *Centennial Review* 30 (fall 1986): 480–495; and Weingarden, "A Transcendentalist Discourse in the Poetics of Technology: Louis Sullivan's Transportation Building and Walt Whitman's 'Passage to India,'" *Word and Image* 3 (April–June 1987): 202–221.

117. Sullivan, "The Modern Phase of Architecture" (1899), in *Louis Sullivan: The Public Papers,* ed. Twombly, 124–125.

118. Louis Sullivan, Kindergarten Chat 39, "On the Historic Styles," *Interstate Architect and Builder* 3 (9 November 1901): 6, reprinted in *Roots of Contemporary American Architecture,* ed. Lewis Mumford (New York: Dover, 1952), 78.

119. Louis Sullivan, Kindergarten Chat 42, "What Is an Architect?" *Interstate Architect and Builder* 3 (November 1901): 9–10, in *"Kindergarten Chats" and Other Writings,* ed. Athey, 140–141.

120. "The Great Auditorium," *Chicago Tribune,* 17 June 1888, 5.

121. At the Auditorium Theater's dedication in December 1889, Congressman John S. Runnells said: "This building was born of an idea. It was not the idea of Acropolis, it was not the idea of the pyramids, it was not the idea of the dome of St. Paul's. No; it was a higher idea than that of pyramid, dome, or temple" ("Dedicated to Music and the People," *Chicago Tribune,* 19 December 1889, 2).

122. *Chicago Tribune,* 22 January 1884, 5, quoted in Pisoni, "Operatic War in New York City," 373.

123. *Keynote,* 2 February 1884, 14, quoted in Pisoni, "Operatic War in New York City," 373. As one critic wrote: "To require Abbey to bring the metropolitan opera house scenery is absurd. If he had it he could not use it, for it is twice too big for any stage we have" ("One Week of Opera," *Chicago Evening News,* 26 January 1884, 5).

124. In 1887 Josiah Cady, "Essential Features of a Large Opera House," 47, wrote that the orchestra's "pit should be sunk to such a degree that (with the exception of the leader) it does not intrude its writhing, restless members between the audience and the picture before them." Yet one contemporary noted that Cady's pit for the Metropolitan's orchestra was "not the arrangement devised by Wagner for the theater in Bayreuth, and familiar to all readers of the reports of the performances given there, for the concealment of the players is in that case much more complete" ("A Grand Temple of Music," *New York Times,* 14 October 1883, 5). Gregersen, "History of the Auditorium Building," 24, notes that Adler also initially designed a lowered orchestra pit.

125. On the Metropolitan's German seasons, see chapter 2, 107, and note 165.

126. "Organists and Organs," *Indicator* 11 (23 November 1889): 1–2. Davis, *Opera in Chicago,* 38–39, noted local German support for the opera. On the Metropolitan Company's first Wagnerian tour of Chicago in 1885, see Editorial, *Chicago Tribune,* 4 January 1885, 4; "Amusements," *Chicago Tribune,* 18 January 1885, 6; "The Damrosch German Opera at the Columbia Theatre," *Indicator* 6 (28 February 1885): 180; "The German Opera," *Indicator* 6 (7 March 1885): 201–202; "German Opera at the Columbia," *Indicator* 6 (14 March 1885): 224–225; Quaintance Eaton, *Opera Caravan: Adventures of the Metropolitan on Tour* (New York: Da Capo Press, 1957), 21–27; and Dizikes, *Opera in America,* 249–250. On Thomas's Wagner concerts, see Schabas, *Theodore Thomas,* 16–17, 29, 59–63.

127. Sullivan, *Autobiography of an Idea,* 208–209. On Walt Whitman's knowledge of and response to Wagner, apart from Whitman's liking for Italian opera, see Robert D. Faner, *Walt Whitman and Opera* (Philadelphia: University of Pennsylvania Press, 1951), 52–53, and Horowitz, *Wagner Nights,* 244.

128. Sullivan, *Autobiography of an Idea,* 208–209. On Hans Balatka, see Andreas, *History of Chicago,* 2:593, and Ffrench, *Music and Musicians in Chicago,* 129.

129. Wright, *Genius and the Mobocracy,* 49, 54–56. On Sullivan and Wagner, see also Connely, *Louis Sullivan,* 128–131; Jordy, *American Buildings and Their Architects,* 4:161, 165; Dizikes, *Opera in America,* 255–256; and Horowtiz, *Wagner Nights,* 243–245.

130. Editorial, "Wagner, the Art Revolutionist," *New York Sun,* 19 August 1876, 2.

131. Walter Damrosch, "The Twilight of the Gods," *New York Sun,* 23 August 1876, 2. For Sullivan on Michelangelo's Sistine Chapel, see *Autobiography of an Idea,* 233–236.

132. John Wellborn Root, "The Art of Pure Color," *Inland Architect and Builder* 2 (September 1883): 106, reprinted in *The Meanings of Architecture: Buildings and Writings,* ed. Donald Hoffmann (New York: Horizon, 1967), 186, and cited in Lauren Weingarden, "The Colors of Nature: Louis Sullivan's Architectural Polychromy and Nineteenth-Century Color Theory," *Winterthur Portfolio* 20 (1985): 248.

133. *Industrial Chicago,* 2:487, cited in Weingarden, "Colors of Nature," 248 n. 15. On the *Gesamtkunstwerk,* see Wagner's essays "The Artwork of the Future" (1849) and "Opera and Drama" (1850–1851), in *Wagner on Music and Drama,* ed. Albert Goldman and Evert Sprinchorn, trans. H. Ashton Ellis (New York: E. P. Dutton, 1964).

134. Ferdinand Peck, quoted in "One of Our Wonders," *Chicago Herald,* 16 September 1888, 17.

135. Ibid. Gregersen, "History of the Auditorium Building," 58, states that the smaller stage had prompted Peck to explore the installation of the hydraulic lifts of the Asphaleia system, presumably to make it easier to change scenery vertically from beneath the stage. Adler, "Chicago Auditorium," 425, gave the stage dimensions as 100 feet wide by 70 deep feet. Initially the stage was to be the world's widest at 120 feet, thus surpassing the stage of the San Carlo Theater in Naples, whose width was 116 feet ("The Convention Hall," *Chicago Tribune,* 30 January 1887, 17). On comparative dimensions of theaters and their stages, see Cady, letter, "The Metropolitan Opera House," *New York Tribune,* 12 November 1883, 5.

136. Briggs, *Yellow Brick Brewery,* 12–15, emphasizes that backstage storage space was nonexistent at the Met, whose sets had to be transferred in and out six to eight times weekly to five warehouses around New York City. Cady had planned for storage in the space beneath the stage. A municipal ordinance at the time forbade constructing space for storage or other purposes above a theater because it increased the risk of fire.

137. "The Chicago Auditorium," unidentified clipping (1889?) in "Early History and Press Clippings, Chicago Auditorium Association, 1887–1889" (Ryerson and Burnham Libraries, Art Institute of Chicago). See also Ham, "Chicago Auditorium Building," 471. On the Auditorium's initial complement of scenery, see "Auditorium Supplement," *Chicago Inter Ocean,* 11 December 1889. The drops from Vienna were noted in "The Auditorium in Readiness," *Indicator* 11 (7 December 1889): 2. Grimsley, "Contributions of Dankmar Adler," 284, notes these storage spaces for the theater's scenery: the drop storage rack on the backstage wall extending beneath the stage through its basement and subbasement;

two storage areas level with the stage upstage left and right; the fly galleries above the stage; a large room (25 [mult] 100 feet) above the auditorium and below the banquet hall; and additional basement space.

138. Lilli Lehmann, *My Path through Life* (New York: G. P. Putnam, 1914), 342. One account of the Metropolitan after its first season noted that "the stage arrangements and accommodations for the artists are such as to interfere seriously with the success of the performances." The house "must have been designed by a novice in theatre building. The scenic arrangements are such that no change can be made without lowering the curtain and losing time. The scenery itself is in so many places that thirty-five well-paid men instead of a dozen are able to manage it" ("Its Boast and Its Snare," *New York Times,* 4 May 1884, 4).

139. Briggs, *Yellow Brick Brewery,* 23. Gounod's *Faust* was selected for the Met's opening night of 22 October 1883.

140. Adler, "Paramount Requirements of a Large Opera House," 45.

141. Ibid.

142. On the Asphaleia Gesellschaft's system of stage building and machinery, see Edwin O. Sachs, "Modern Theatre Stages, No. XVII," *Engineering* (London), 25 September 1896, 387–390, and Sachs and Ernest, *Modern Opera Houses and Theatres,* vol. 3, supplement 1, *Stage Construction,* 42–55. On the Auditorium stage's counterweights, Adler, "Chicago Auditorium," 428, wrote that all the drops extending across the entire stage for scenic effects as well as the border lights are counterbalanced so that they can be raised or lowered from the stage floor and not from the fly galleries. There were sixty sets of steel counterweight lines over the Auditorium's stage. See also *Presto* 7 (16 November 1889): 4; "A Stagehand Remembers," *Talmanac,* November 1964, 8; and Grimsley, "Contributions of Dankmar Adler," 281–283. Adler, "Stage Mechanism," 42, wrote that some twenty years earlier theatrical engineer Carl Brandt of Darmstadt had "invented a system of balancing scenery with counterweights, which was used in Germany, but to the best of my knowledge nowhere else." Geraniotis, "German Design Influences in the Auditorium Theater," 45, noted Brandt's design of stage equipment for Frankfurt-am-Main's Opera House (1873–1880), about which Sullivan owned a folio (see note 102 above).

143. "Chicago's Tall Tower," *Chicago Herald,* 14 June 1889. Earlier Peck had stated: "We intend to have the most complete stage in the world, with the best appliances. During my recent visit to Europe, I examined a number of stages with this end in view, and Mr. Adler, one of our architects, is there now, with Mr. Bairstow, the chief stage carpenter, who has an experience of thirty years at McVicker's. Mr. Adler, too, is there for the purposes of examining and getting detailed plans of the finest stages in Europe, especially those of Buda-Pesth, Frankfurt, Vienna, Dresden, Baireuth, and La Scala, at Milan . . . . it was for the purpose of seeing [the details of the stage mechanisms] with our own eyes that we made a trip through Europe" ("One of Our Wonders," *Chicago Herald,* 16 September 1888, 17).

Adler, in a letter to Dila Adler, 29 August 1888, noted his initial personal contact with the Kautsky brothers (the founders of the Asphaleia Gesellschaft) while in London. There they were working on the Drury Lane Theater's stage. Adler and James H. Mapleson, the impresario who had staged the Chicago Grand Opera Festival in 1885, "had quite a talk with [the Kautskys] about the application of their methods to the Auditorium" ("Autobiography and Letters of Dankmar Adler," ed. Saltzstein, 22, 23).

144. Adler, "Chicago Auditorium," 432. Another account confirmed that "as if by magic the entire stage can be cleared or set in a few moments without involving the service of more than a dozen stage hands" ("The Pride of Chicago," *Chicago Herald,* 20 October 1889, 1). Adler wrote (424): "The ingenuity of American builders of hydraulic elevators and the special conditions prevailing in this building have, however, caused the introduction of many improvements and modifications of the European apparatus." Leacroft, *Development of the English Playhouse,* 278, noted the rapid action of the Chicago Auditorium's hydraulic lifts.

145. Sachs, "Modern Theatre Stages," 389–390. See also Adler, "Chicago Auditorium," *Chicago Tribune,* 7 December 1889, 428, and Adler, "The Auditorium Stage," *Chicago Tribune* 7 December 1889, 12. On the Theatrical Mechanics Association, see Andreas, *History of Chicago,* 3:557.

146. "Modern Stage Setting," *Chicago Tribune,* 21 July 1889.

147. Wright, quoted in "Chicago Auditorium Is Fifty Years Old," 12.

148. George G. Elmslie to William F. McDermott, 17 June 1941 (William Gray Purcell Papers, Northwest Architectural Archives, University of Minnesota, St. Paul, Minn.).

149. Dizikes, *Opera in America,* 243.

150. Louis Sullivan, "Plastic and Color Decoration of the Auditorium," in *Louis Sullivan: The Public Papers,* ed. Twombly, 74. On a mean between light and dark colors in theaters, see Adler, "Theater Building for American Cities: Second Paper," 816–817.

151. Adler, "Paramount Requirements of a Large Opera House," 45. Van Rensselaer, "Metropolitan Opera House," 87, noted the configuration of its house lights. On their technology, see "Gas-Fitting, and Gas Lighting by Electricity of the Metropolitan Opera House, New York," *Sanitary Engineer* 9 (27 December 1883): 89–90. On the old Met's first interior, see also "A Grand Temple of Music," *New York Times,* 14 October 1883, 5; Schuyler, "Metropolitan Opera-House," 886–887; and Henry E. Krehbiel, *Chapters of Opera* (New York: Henry Holt, 1911), 86–88.

152. Garczynski, *Auditorium,* 128.

153. "Opera and Drama," *Indicator* 6 (4 July 1885): 553.

154. "The Chicago Auditorium," *Architect* (London) 43 (21 February 1890): 126. Peck wrote: "The plan of decoration is consistent and elegant throughout the building, the Auditorium and main rooms of the hotel being finished mostly in gold and ivory tone of color. This has been costly, the quality of the gold leaf being exceptionally fine (23 carats), but it is permanent and grows more beautiful with age, and therefore is wise economy as well as effective in beauty" (Peck, Annual Report of the President to the Stockholders of the Chicago Auditorium Association, 7 December 1889 [Auditorium Collection, Roosevelt University Archives]). Sullivan wrote: "a single idea or principle is taken as a basis of the color scheme, that is to say, use is made of but one color in each instance, and that color is associated with gold" ("Plastic and Color Decoration of the Auditorium" [1889], in *Louis Sullivan: The Public Papers,* ed. Twombly, 74).

155. "Our New Auditorium," *Chicago Sunday Herald,* 8 December 1889. I thank historian Kathleen Cummings, Chicago, for bringing this reference to my attention.

156. *Newark Advertiser,* 9 December 1889. One observer wrote that the decoration throughout the building proceeded on the principle of "the conservation of embellishment within structural consistency" ("The Chicago Auditorium," *Architect* [London] 43 [21 February 1890]: 126). Sullivan, "Plastic and Color Decoration of the Auditorium" (1889), in *Louis Sullivan: The Public Papers,* ed. Twombly, 74, wrote: "The plastic and color decorations are distinctly architectural in conception. They are everywhere kept subordinate to the general effect of the larger structural masses and subdivisions, while lending to them the enchantment of soft tones and of varied light and shade." In "Ornament in Architecture" (1892), in *Louis Sullivan: The Public Papers,* ed. Twombly, 82, Sullivan wrote that in general "there exists a peculiar sympathy between the ornament and the structure . . . . Both structure and ornament obviously benefit by this sympathy; each enhancing the value of the other. And this, I take it, is the preparatory basis of what may be called an organic system of ornamentation."

157. "Our New Auditorium," *Chicago Sunday Herald,* 8 December 1889.

158. "Dedicated to Music and the People," *Chicago Tribune,* 10 December 1889, 1. Another editor wrote: "The entire interior is decorated in a delicate creamy white relieved with gold, and the appearance is one of simple elegance and chaste art in design. A better, a more appropriate plan of decorations could not have been devised. The freedom from garish coloring is the chief charm of the hall" (Editorial, *Indicator* 11 [7 December 1889]: 2).

159. "The Pride of Chicago," *Chicago Herald,* 20 October 1889, 1. Healy and Millet's contract for the Auditorium Building's stained glass was noted in "Mosaics," *Inland Architect and News Record* 2 (July 1888): 89. The following March, "Architect Sullivan read a proposal from Messrs. Healy and Millet

to furnish complete expert services in connection with the decorating of the main hall and its appendages for the sum of Twenty-two hundred fifty dollars ($2250). Healy & Millet to act as purchasing agents of material and labor, make sketches and working drawings, and to superintend the execution of the work in all its details; to keep all acounts and time sheets; on the basis of a total expenditure not exceeding $15,000.00 inclusive of above fees; which proposal was accepted" (Minutes of Executive Committee of Chicago Auditorium Association, 5 March 1889, 86 [Auditorium Collection, Roosevelt University Archives]). See Kathleen R. Cummings, "Sullivan and Millet: Stained Glass in Chicago's Auditorium Building," *Style 1900* 14 (spring/May 2001): 44–48. On restoration of the Auditorium Building's art glass, see "Artful Glass," *Chicago Tribune,* 27 November 2000.

160. "Chicago's Tall Tower," *Chicago Herald,* 14 June 1889, 2. English theater architect Ernest A. E. Woodrow wrote: "Plaster is a valuable fire resisting agent; it is light and resists fire for an indefinite period; it adapts itself to the entire enrichment and decoration of the auditorium; from ceiling and proscenium frame to circle fronts and private boxes" ("Views of an English Architect on Theater Construction, Part IV, Materials," *Inland Architect and News Record* 16 (October 1890): 27).

161. Adler, "Theater-Building for American Cities: Second Paper," 817. Adler was allocated funds to cover the "amount paid to ascertain efficiency of workmen preliminary to selecting contractor for ornamental plastering; the several artisans having prepared specimens from drawings by Mr. Sullivan" (Minutes of Executive Committee of Chicago Auditorium Association, 8 September 1888, 56 [Auditorium Collection, Roosevelt University Archives]). In 1889 the committee authorized direct payments to Schneider and Legge on 26 June (125), 22 July (131), and 31 August (144). On James Legge as contractor for ornamental plastering at McVicker's Theater, see Dankmar Adler and Louis Sullivan, "Decoration of McVicker's Theatre" (1888), in *Louis Sullivan: The Public Papers,* ed. Twombly, 43. See Martin V. Reinhart, "Norwegian Born Sculptor Kristian Schneider, His Essential Contribution to the Development of Louis Sullivan's Ornamental Style," Lecture to the Symposium on the Norwegian-American Life of Chicago, Norway Center, November 1982, Burnham Library, Art Institute of Chicago. See Siry, *Carson Pirie Scott,* 174–175. On Legge and Schneider, see also the catalog for the exhibition at the Arts Club of Chicago, curated by Timothy Samuelson and John Vinci, titled *Conflict and Creativity: Architects and Sculptors in Chicago, 1871–1937. Selections from the Semour H. Persky Collection* (Chicago: Arts Club of Chicago, 1994. Nine hectograph prints (30 by 40 inches) of original working drawings for the Auditorium Building's ornamental plaster work survive in the Ernest R. Graham Study Center for Architectural Drawings, Department of Architecture, Art Institute of Chicago, Accession nos. 1988.236.1–10.

162. "The Pride of Chicago," *Chicago Herald,* 20 October 1889, 1.

163. Garczynski, *Auditorium,* 114, 128. Bart Swindall, Auditorium Theater Council, noted the milkweed pod motif in the course of a theater tour on 13 June 1997. The motif recurs on newel posts at the base of the Auditorium Hotel's main stairway (fig. 145). On the relation of botanical and historical sources for Sullivan's ornament, see Lauren Weingarden's work, especially her essays: "Louis H. Sullivan's Ornament and the Poetics of Architecture," in *Chicago Architecture,* ed. Zukowsky, 229–250; "Naturalized Nationalism: A Ruskinian Discourse on the Search for an American Style of Architecture," *Winterthur Portfolio* 24 (spring 1989): 43–68; "Louis Sullivan's *System of Architectural Ornament,*" in *Louis H. Sullivan: A System of Architectural Ornament* (New York: Rizzoli, 1990). See also Siry, *Carson Pirie Scott,* 153–157.

164. "What the Ladies Wore," *Chicago Tribune,* 10 December 1889, 2. James Mapleson wrote: "A lady has no inducement to wear a handsome toilette at a London Opera-house, where the high fronted boxes with their ridiculous curtains prevent the dresses from being seen. At the American Opera houses the boxes are not constructed in the Italian, but in the French style. They are open in front, that is to say, so that those who occupy them can not only see, but be seen" (*Mapleson Memoirs,* 217).

165. Mapleson, *Mapleson Memoirs,* 217. On the tradition of women seated in boxes around the parquet, see Kasson, *Rudeness and Civility,* 218, 225. On New York City's Park Theater in the early nine-

teenth century, where this tradition prevailed, see Richard Grant White, "Opera in New York," *Century Magazine* 23 (April 1882): 869.

166. "A Hall for the People," *Chicago Inter Ocean,* 10 December 1889, 1.

167. Garczynski, *Auditorium,* 129.

168. On Sullivan's father, see Sullivan, *Autobiography of an Idea,* 11–17, 77–90, and Twombly, *Louis Sullivan,* 2–6. Sullivan's major statement on individuality was his 1888 essay "Style." Earlier he asserted that "it is within the souls of individual men that art reaches its culminations" (Sullivan, "What is the Just Subordination, in Architectural Design, of Details to Mass?" [1887], in *Louis Sullivan: The Public Papers,* ed. Twombly, 34).

169. "Dedicated to Music: Occupants of the Private Boxes," *Chicago Morning News,* 10 December 1889. On visiting between the Auditorium's boxes, see, for example, the Francis Glessner Journals for the period 1892–1895, Manuscripts and Archives Division, Chicago Historical Society, quoted in Helfrich, *Apollo Chorus of Chicago,* 32.

170. "Pride of All Chicago," *Chicago Herald,* 10 December 1889. On the relative prices of boxes in the Auditorium's upper and lower box tiers, see "An Opera Box for $2,100," *Chicago Tribune,* 23 November 1889, 1. On French impressionist paintings of Parisian women in theater boxes, see Robert L. Herbert, *Impressionism: Art, Leisure, and Parisian Society* (New Haven: Yale University Press, 1988), 93–107, and Tamar Garb, "Gender and Representation," in *Modernity and Modernism: French Painting in the Nineteenth Century,* ed. Francis Frascina et al. (New Haven: Yale University Press, 1993), 219–230, 257–267.

171. "Will Shine Like Gold," *Chicago Tribune,* 12 February 1896, 10, quoted in Tim Samuelson and Jim Scott, "Auditorium Album," *Inland Architect,* September–October 1989, 71. Soon after the old Met opened, plans for its remodeling were noted in "Improving the New Opera-House," *New York Times,* 30 October 1883, 8. This remodeling's purpose was to improve the boxes' decor. The scheme, devised by Francis Lathrop (a painter who contributed murals to the original interior) was described in "The German Opera Season," *New York Times,* 2 October 1884, 4. On later remodelings, see chapter 2, note 71.

172. George G. Elmslie to William F. McDermott, 17 June 1941 (William Gray Purcell Papers, Northwest Architectural Archives, University of Minnesota, St. Paul, Minn.).

173. "Auditorium Supplement," *Chicago Inter Ocean,* 11 December 1889. Gelert was paid for this work as a subcontractor of James Legge (Minutes of Executive Committee of Chicago Auditorium Association, 23 July 1889, 132 [Auditorium Collection, Roosevelt University Archives]). Gelert first studied in Copenhagen in the wake of Thorwaldsen and, after apprenticeships in Paris and Berlin, later carved statues for Copenhagen's Dagmar Theater. Having assisted one of his Berlin instructors with an equestrian monument to George Washington in Philadelphia's Fairmount Park, Gelert emigrated to the United States. See "Art Notes," *Graphic* (Chicago) 5 (28 November 1891): 356, and Sparks, "Biographical Dictionary of Painters and Sculptors in Illinois," 389. On the organ, see Garczynski, *Auditorium,* 122–127; Clarence Eddy, "The Great Auditorium Organ," *Indicator* 11 (23 March 1889): 436–437; and Eddy's letter published as "Clarence Eddy on the Organ," *Presto* 7 (22 February 1890): 3. Eddy (1851–1937), who had studied organ in both the United States and Berlin, traveled widely and was familiar with organ design in Europe ("Organs and Organists," *Indicator* 11 [23 November 1889]: 1–2). He gave the dedicatory recital on the Auditorium's newly finished organ on 29 October 1890. The opening number, "Fantaisie Triomphale," had been especially composed for the Auditorium's dedication by his friend Theodore Dubois, organist of the Church of the Madeleine, Paris ("Chicago," *Presto* 8 [1 November 1890]: 523). In 1942, after the theater closed, the Auditorium's organ was sold at the auction of the building's contents to pay back taxes. See epilogue, 397, and note 33.

174. Sullivan, *Autobiography of an Idea,* 208–209.

175. Adler, "Chicago Auditorium," 428–429. Sullivan's foliate ornament as a frame for naturalistic stage imagery recurred in his studies for the proscenium and curtain of the Pueblo Opera House

(1888–1890). See Lloyd C. Engelbrecht, "Adler & Sullivan's Pueblo Opera House: City Status for a New Town in the Rockies," *Art Bulletin* 67 (June 1985): 287, 290.

176. Sullivan, "Plastic and Color Decoration of the Auditorium" (1889) in *Louis Sullivan: The Public Papers,* ed. Twombly, 75–76. The title Sullivan had originally selected for the poem "Inspiration" was "Growth and Decadence." See Twombly, *Louis Sullivan,* 224–225.

177. Period sources include Gabriel Davioud, *Le Palais du Trocadéro* (Paris, 1878); Davioud, *Le Palais du Trocadéro: Le coteau de Chaillot, le nouveau palais, les dix-huit mois de travaux, renseignements techniques* (Paris, 1878); and Davioud, *Monographie des palais et constructions diverses de l'exposition universelle de 1878* (Paris, 1882). See also Rabreau et al., *Gabriel Davioud,* 89–102. On Lameire, see Lawrence Madeline "Un peintre-décorateur, Charles Lameire (1832–1910): Le fonds Lameire au musée d'Orsay," *Revue du Louvre et des Musées de France* 39 (1989): 172–179.

178. William F. McDermott, "Artist Restores Beauty of Old Auditorium," *Chicago Daily News,* 28 October 1932. Sullivan recorded his response to the Sistine Chapel in his *Autobiography of an Idea,* 233–235. See also Menocal, *Architecture as Nature,* 17–18. Peck and his colleagues "voted to authorize Architect Sullivan to have figures placed over the proscenium arch of the Auditorium, the cost thereof not to exceed $2,000, and the design subject to the approval of this committee" (Minutes of Executive Committee of Chicago Auditorium Association, 5 June 1889, 111 [Auditorium Collection, Roosevelt University Archives]). On Holloway's training and his other works in Chicago, see "Worthy of the City," *Chicago Inter Ocean,* 20 March 1892, 17. There he was credited with "the great window in St. Paul's Universalist Church, the mural work in oil upon canvas in Mr. [Harlow] Higinbotham's stately residence, the stained glass in the Garrett Biblical Institute, the huge ceiling in the shop of Carson, Pirie & Co., [and] the glass in Mr. Potter Palmer's castle on the Lake Shore drive." See also Sparks, "Biographical Dictionary of Painters and Sculptors in Illinois," 438. Holloway designed silverware for the Columbian Exposition, discussed in Bob Corson, "A Mystery Solved," *Silver* 28 (September–October 1996): 20–22.

179. Sullivan, "Plastic and Color Decoration of the Auditorium" (1889), in *Louis Sullivan: The Public Papers,* ed. Twombly 75–76. On the figures in Holloway's murals, see "The Auditorium Building: A Great and Superb Structure," Auditorium Number, *Graphic* (Chicago), o.s., 11 (14 December 1889), and "In a Glare of Glory," *Chicago Times,* 10 December 1889.

180. Garczynski, *Auditorium,* 114.

181. "Pride of Chicago," *Chicago Daily News,* morning edition, 9 December 1889.

182. Ibid.

183. At their meeting of 28 August 1889, Peck and his colleagues resolved "that the architects and the decorative contractor [Healy and Millet] proceed with landscape paintings for the side arches in the Auditorium—the cost thereof not to exceed two thousand dollars ($2,000). It being fully understood that if not satisfactory they are to be taken down at the expense of Healy and Millet . . . the landscapes to be subject to modification in the original designs and subject to the approval of the Executive Committee" (Minutes of Executive Committee of Chicago Auditorium Association, 141 [Auditorium Collection, Roosevelt University Archives]). See *Graphic* (Chicago), n.s., 6 (6 June 1892); Francis E. Towne, "Albert Fleury, Painter," *Brush and Pencil* 12 (April–September 1903): 201–208; Sparks, "Biographical Dictionary of Painters and Sculptors in Illinois," 376; and Mary Lackritz Gray, *A Guide to Chicago's Murals* (Chicago: University of Chicago Press, 2001), 6–7. On Healy and Millet, see David Hanks, "Louis J. Millet and the Art Institute of Chicago," *Bulletin of the Art Institute of Chicago* 67 (1973): 13–19, and on Millet, see Sparks, 389. On Sullivan's friendship with Millet and Fleury in Chicago, see Connely, *Louis Sullivan,* 206. On Fleury's murals, see Garczynski, *Auditorium,* 130–132. Fleury also painted the twelve murals in oil, each showing a different American regional scene, in the Auditorium Hotel's banquet hall. See chapter 5, 318–319, and notes 119, 120. He soon became an instructor in mural painting at the Art Institute of Chicago and completed a number of later such commissions. Fleury wrote of his approach to painting open-air scenes in "Picturesque Chicago," *Brush and Pencil* 6 (September 1900): 273–281.

184. Towne, "Albert Fleury," 204.

185. "Pride of Chicago," *Chicago Daily News*, morning edition, 9 December 1889. On Peck's affinity for vactions in Wisconsin's woodlands, see Dean, *World's Fair City*, 69–70.

186. Sullivan, "Plastic and Color Decoration of the Auditorium" (1889) in *Louis Sullivan: The Public Papers*, ed. Twombly, 75–76.

187. Sullivan, "Inspiration" (1886), in *Louis Sullivan: The Public Papers*, ed. Twombly, 12–13.

188. Sullivan, *Autobiography of an Idea*, 300.

189. "Dedicated to Music," *Chicago Morning News*, 10 December 1889. The trade-off of high-priced boxes and low-priced seats for the masses was noted in *Presto* 7 (30 November 1889): 4. The scale of prices for the opera season in December was agreed on as follows:

SECTION	SINGLE SEATS	SEASON TICKETS
main floor/1st section balcony	$3.50	$60.00
2nd section balcony	$3.00	$50.00
3rd section balcony	$2.50	$40.00
2nd balcony	$2.00	$30.00
family circle	$1.00	$20.00
admission	$1.00	
boxes	$30.00	$500.00

(Minutes of Executive Committee of Chicago Auditorium Association, 4 November 1889, 159 [Auditorium Collection, Roosevelt University Archives]).

190. "In a Glare of Glory: Scenes on the Street," *Chicago Times*, 10 December 1889. See also "A Mob Worthy of the Occasion," *Chicago Tribune*, 10 December 1889, 2–3. In 1890–1891, Auditorium Theater programs listed "theatre trains" of the Illinois Central and other railroads departing from 11:20 to 11:40 P.M. (Chicago Theatre Programs Collection, Auditorium, 1890–1914, box AUD 1, Chicago Theater Collection, Chicago Public Library).

191. "Pride of All Chicago: Seen from the Housetops," *Chicago Herald*, 10 December 1889.

192. Frank Norris, *The Pit: A Story of Chicago* (New York: Doubleday, Page, 1903), 5–7.

193. "The Opening of the Auditorium," *Indicator* 11 (30 November 1889): 1. On scagliola, see chapter 5, 300, and note 86. The allegorical figures in the art glass lunettes were identified in "The Auditorium Building: A Great and Superb Structure," Auditorium Number, *Graphic* (Chicago), o.s., 11 (14 December 1889).

194. Garczynski, *Auditorium*, 113.

195. "Peerless Patti Sang," *Chicago Herald*, 11 December 1889.

196. "Auditorium Manager Adams was authorized to make a contract with Marshall Field & Co. as follows for 2300 yards more or less 5-frame Bigelow Witten [*sic*] carpets . . . etc." (Minutes of Executive Committee of Chicago Auditorium Association, 8 August 1889, 135 [Auditorium Collection, Roosevelt University Archives]). Garczynski, *Auditorium*, 116, noted that the upper foyer's carpets were woven by W. and J. Sloan Company of New York City.

197. "Peerless Patti Sang," *Chicago Herald*, 11 December 1889.

198. See "Dedication of the Auditorium," in Milward Adams Scrapbooks, Newberry Library, Chicago, and note 74 above. In his Manhattan Opera House of 1906, Oscar Hammerstein attempted to channel entering boxholders through the stage door. He thought such patrons would like this behind-the-scenes route. Instead, boxholders objected that they could not be seen making their entrances from a large foyer with a grand staircase, as in traditional opera houses. See Jay R. S. Teran, "The New York Opera Audience: 1825–1974" (Ph.D. diss., New York University, 1974), 81.

199. Quotation from "Dedicated to Music and the People," *Chicago Tribune*, 10 December 1889, 1. On the English idea of the theater as a town, see Buckley, "'To the Opera House,'" 120–121.

200. "President Peck's Report," *Chicago Daily News,* morning edition, 9 December 1889.

201. Peck, Annual Report of the President to the Stockholders of the Chicago Auditorium Association, 7 December 1889 (Auditorium Collection, Roosevelt University Archives). On boxes for royalty on the forestage or inside the proscenium of seventeenth- and eighteenth-century European theaters, see Carlson, *Places of Performance,* 146–147.

202. "Dedicated to Music and the People," *Chicago Tribune,* 10 December 1889, 1.

203. Editorial, "The Intellectual Growth of Chicago," *Indicator* 12 (25 January 1890): 21. Earlier, "A memorandum Agreement between Henry E. Abbey and the Chicago Auditorium Association, bearing date February 23, 1889 for a season of Italian Opera in the Auditorium, was read by the President, and his action in the premises approved" (Minutes of Executive Committee of Chicago Auditorium Association, 5 February 1889, 86 [Auditorium Collection, Roosevelt University Archives]). On Peck's negotiations with Abbey, see "The Italian Opera Co., To Return to the Auditorium in March," *Presto* 7 (8 January 1890): 7. On Milward Adams's travels, see, for example, *Indicator* 11 (23 March 1889): 426. The Auditorium's inaugural Italian opera season was "to be the most remarkable in the history of music in this country." The thirteen works performed were *Roméo et Juliette* (Gounod), *William Tell* (Rossini), *Faust* (Gounod), *Il Trovatore* (Verdi), *Lucia di Lammermoor* (Donizetti), *Aida* (Verdi), *Semiramide* (Rossini), *Martha* (Flotow), *Les Hugenots* (Meyerbeer), *La traviata* (Verdi), and *La sonnambula* (Bellini), *Il barbiere di Siviglia* (Rossini), and *Otello* (Verdi). *Lakmé* (Delibes), *Lohengrin* (Wagner), and *Mefistofele* (Boito) were originally scheduled but not performed ("The Auditorium in Readiness," *Indicator* 11 [7 December 1889]: 2, and "Chicago Music, Drama, and Miscellany," *Presto* 7 [8 January 1890]: 5). *Faust* and *Il trovatore* were among Peck's favorites ("Ferdinand Peck, Widely Known Chicagoan, Dies," *Chicago Tribune,* 5 November 1924. 19).

204. "Dedicated to Music and the People," *Chicago Tribune,* 10 December 1889, 1. Mme Patti's fee was noted in "Auditorium Anecdotes," *Chicago Daily News,* 21 June 1941. On Patti in the United States through the 1880s, see Mapleson, *Mapleson Memoirs,* 149–245; Klein, *Reign of Patti,* 202–214, 238–241; and Dizikes, *Opera in America,* 223–230. Klein (162, 237) noted the central place of "Home, Sweet Home" in Patti's repertoire when singing at London's Albert Hall. On this song's genre in earlier American cultural history, see Nicholas Tawa, *A Music for the Millions: Antebellum Democratic Attitudes and the Birth of American Popular Music* (New York: Pendragon Press, 1984), 83–89. See also "The Home of John Howard Payne," *Presto Music Times* 6 (20 December 1888): 7–8. Jenny Lind had sung "Home, Sweet Home" to Payne in person at a concert in Washington, D.C., on 17 December 1850 ("Home, Sweet Home," *Chicago Evening Journal,* 11 December 1886, 11).

205. "Pride of All Chicago," *Chicago Herald,* 10 December 1889. H. Sutherland Edwards, *The Prima Donna: Her History and Surroundings from the Seventeenth to the Nineteenth Century,* 2 vols. (London: Remington, 1888), 1:68, noted Patti's adoption of "Swiss Echo Song" composed by Karl Anton Florian Eckert (1820–1879) and its earlier role in Lind's repertoire.

206. "Patti on the Auditorium," *Chicago Tribune,* 12 December 1889, 1. One editor later wrote that in its acoustics "the Metropolitan is deficient. The superiority of the Auditorium was proved during the recent opera season, when at times during the performances the faintest notes of instrumental solos were heard with surprising distinctness in the most remote part of the house" ("Chicago Music, Drama and Miscellany," *Presto* 7 [22 January 1890]: 5). One account of the Auditorium Theater's opening noted that in the center of the orchestra there "was a phonograph, placed there by the North American Phonograph Company and operated by W. S. Gray, to preserve the oral, vocal, and instrumental performances of the evening for future generations" ("Pride of All Chicago," *Chicago Herald,* 10 December 1889). The wherabouts of this recording, if it survives, are unknown.

207. Henry T. Tuckerman, *Essays, Biographical and Critical, or Studies of Character* (Boston, 1857), 234. The composer Giacomo Meyerbeer also wrote to Germany after hearing Lind in London in 1847: "What shall I say of Jenny Lind? I can find no words adequate to give you any real idea of the impression

she has made. Independently of the fact that the language of panegyric is exhausted, this wonderful artist stands too high in my judgment to be dragged down by commonplace complimentary phrases" (quoted in Edwards, *Prima Donna,* 1:27).

208. Ralph Waldo Emerson, Journal 41 (1850), *Journals of Ralph Waldo Emerson, with Annotations,* ed. Edward Waldo Emerson and Waldo Emerson Forbes, 10 vols. (Boston: Houghton Mifflin, 1912), 8:129.

209. De Witt Cregier, quoted in "Dedicated to Music and the People," *Chicago Tribune,* 10 December 1889, 2. Segments of speeches were also quoted in "The Auditorium Opened," *Indicator* 11 (14 December 1889): 2–3.

210. Peck, quoted in "Dedicated to Music and the People," *Chicago Tribune,* 10 December 1889, 2.

211. "A Temple of Song," *Chicago Globe,* 10 December 1889.

212. Garczynski, *Auditorium,* 132.

213. Schuyler, "Critique of the Works of Adler and Sullivan," in *"American Architecture"* and Other Writings, ed. Jordy and Coe, 2:384–385.

214. Paul Bourget, *Outre-Mer* (Paris: Lemerre, 1895), 1:161–162, translated in Schuyler, "Critique of the Works of Adler and Sullivan," in *"American Architecture" and Other Writings,* ed. Jordy and Coe, 2:380. Bourget in this context was discussing the exteriors of Chicago's tall commercial buildings. See Jordy, *American Buildings and Their Architects,* 4:52–53. On Taine and Bourget (1852–1935), see Weinstein, *Hippolyte Taine,* 23, 145, 153 nn. 31, 35.

215. Schuyler, "Critique of the Works of Adler and Sullivan," in *"American Architecture" and Other Writings,* ed. Jordy and Coe, 2:384–385.

216. George Bernard Shaw, in *Dramatic Review,* 27 June 1885, in *Shaw's Music: The Complete Musical Criticism in Three Volumes,* ed. Dan H. Laurence, 3 vols. (London: Max Reinhardt, 1981), 1:272, quoted in Musgrave, *Musical Life of the Crystal Palace,* 124.

217. William Tomlins to the Ladies and Gentlemen of the Apollo Club, 1 January 1889, published in Helfrich, *Apollo Chorus of Chicago,* 44. Music for the poor in European cities was noted in "Chicago, Music, Drama, and Miscellany," *Presto* 7 (22 January 1890): 4.

218. Tomlins to Apollo Club, 1 January 1889, in Helfrich, *Apollo Chorus of Chicago,* 45.

219. Editorial, "The Apollo Club's New Move," *Indicator* 11 (18 May 1889): 684.

220. William S. B. Mathews, quoted in Helfrich, *Apollo Chorus of Chicago,* 45. See also "The Apollo Club and the Wageworkers," *Indicator* 11 (28 December 1889): 9.

221. Editorial, "The Apollo Club's New Move," *Indicator* 11 (18 May 1889): 684. See also Editorial, *Indicator* 11 (2 November 1889): 5, which noted that the wageworkers' concerts were "to minister to a popular and useful purpose . . . at prices so low that the masses will have no excuse for remaining away."

222. "Fulfilling Its Mission," *Chicago Tribune,* 29 December 1889, 3. See also "Six More Performances," *Chicago Tribune,* 29 December 1889, 27. When the Apollo Club initiated these concerts at the Auditorium Theater in December 1889, "applications for seats are coming in in large numbers, showing that the offer of the club is accepted in the spirit in which is made" ("Amusements," *Chicago Inter Ocean,* 8 December 1889, 13). See also "Music for the Masses," *Indicator* 12 (4 January 1890): 2–3.

223. "Fulfilling Its Mission," *Chicago Tribune,* 29 December 1889, 3.

224. Ibid.

225. Frank Brown, John Lundie, and John Lindgren, [Committee on Workingmen's Concerts?], Apollo Club, Annual Report, 1890–1891, quoted in Helfrich, *Apollo Chorus of Chicago,* 46.

226. Quoted in Otis, *Chicago Symphony Orchestra,* 38, 41. On the Beethoven concert, see "Honors the Master," *Chicago Tribune,* 18 December 1892, 4.

227. "Music and Drama," *Chicago Tribune,* 31 January 1893, 4. See also Otis, *Chicago Symphony Orchestra,* 33, 42, who noted Thomas's workingmen's concert in February 1892. On the Apollo Club's

Workingmen's Concert, see "Light Opera Again," *Chicago Tribune,* 18 December 1892, 37, and "Melody for Toilers," *Chicago Tribune,* 22 December 1892, 1. On workers' resale of tickets to their concerts, see Helfrich, *Apollo Chorus of Chicago,* 47.

228. James, *Chicago's Dark Places,* 54. Chicago's institutional churches and YMCAs of the period also sought to fulfill the need James identified. See Joseph M. Siry, "The Abraham Lincoln Center in Chicago," *Journal of the Society of Architectural Historians* 50 (September 1991): 235–265. Chicago's fourteen-story YMCA building designed by Jenney and Mundie in 1893, on LaSalle Street between Madison and Monroe, was a national model. See Paula R. Lupkin, "YMCA Architecture: Building Character in the American City, 1869–1930" (Ph.D. diss., University of Pennsylvania, 1997), 156–165.

229. "Chicago Music, Drama and Miscellany," *Presto* 7 (22 January 1890): 4.

230. "Chicago Schmierentheater," *Westen* (Sunday edition of *Illinois Staats-Zeitung*), 23 October 1892, quoted and translated in Heiss, "Popular and Working-Class German Theater in Chicago," 188. Information in this paragraph is from Heiss's essay and its cited sources and from Keil and Jentz, *German Workers in Chicago,* 212–220.

231. The Auditorium's directors "recommended to the stockholders that for the purpose of completing the building of the Association, bonds secured by mortgage be issued," to a maximum amount of $900,000, bearing 5 percent interest, and payable in forty years, from 1 February 1889 (Special Directors' Meeting, Chicago Auditorium Association, 23 November 1888, in Records of the Chicago Auditorium Association, 119 [Auditorium Collection, Roosevelt University Archives]).

232. "Something for Nothing," *Economist* 44 (9 July 1910): 57.

233. "The Chicago Auditorium," unidentified clipping (1889?) in "Early History and Press Clippings, Chicago Auditorium Association, 1887–1889" (Ryerson and Burnham Libraries, Art Institute of Chicago). The decision to complete the office building by 1 May 1889 and the Chicago Conservatory of Music and Dramatic Art's lease from that date were noted in Minutes of Executive Committee of Chicago Auditorium Association, 22 September 1888, 55 (Auditorium Collection, Roosevelt University Archives). Peck then rented space on the fourth floor to the Illinois Humane Society (Minutes, 9 March 1889, 89). Decoration of the Chicago Conservatory's quarters by Healy and Millet was noted in Minutes, 10 June 1890, 234. On this suite of rooms, see Garczynski, *Auditorium,* 140–142, and "In Their New Quarters," *Chicago Tribune,* 14 July 1889, 1. The Conservatory's annexing of the Recital Hall was noted in "Chicago," *Presto* 8 (1 November 1890): 523. On the building's offices, see "Will Soon Be Finished," *Chicago Tribune,* 25 January 1889, 8; "Widening Congress Street," *Chicago Tribune,* 10 February 1889, 6; and "Real Estate," *Chicago Tribune,* 24 March 1889, 30.

234. Peck, quoted in "Recital Hall Opened," *Chicago Tribune,* 13 October 1889.

235. "Chicago Conservatory Concerts," *Chicago Tribune,* 20 October 1889. See "The Conservatory Recital," *Presto* 6 (23 October 1889): 5. Garczynski, *Auditorium,* 142, wrote: "The arrangement of the seats resembles that of an operating theatre in a medical Lyceum, almost all rising above the stage, in a horseshoe form." Such an analogy would have been consistent with the announced aim of holding scientific lectures in the Recital Hall. A secondary skylight was set over the north side tier of seating. The hall's size, tiered seating, and beamed ceiling with skylights may have influenced Frank Lloyd Wright's later designs for the auditoriums in Chicago's Abraham Lincoln Center (1897–1903) and Oak Park's Unity Temple (1905–1909). See Siry, *Unity Temple,* 32–50, 88–108.

236. "Dedicating a Dainty Hall," *Chicago Inter Ocean,* 13 October 1889. The arch was elliptically shaped, like those of the Auditorium Theater. Garczynski, *Auditorium,* 142, described the rear freestanding columns as having "the most extraordinary abacuses that resemble inverted pyramids. The capitals of the columns are round, and have for decorative motive the expanded flowers of the lotus, with leaves at the corners, very richly gilt." Such allusion to Egyptian ornamental forms in the Recital Hall would be consistent with their proposed use on the Auditorium's exterior, as discussed in chapter 3, 140–141.

237. "Chicago Conservatory Concerts," *Chicago Tribune,* 13 October 1889.

238. "Dedicating a Dainty Hall," *Chicago Sunday Inter Ocean,* 13 October 1889.

239. Ibid. See Gerald Carson, "In Chicago, Cruelty and Kindness to Animals," *Chicago History* 3 (winter 1974–1975): 151–158; Louis Covotsos and Virginia Marciniak, *The Illinois Humane Society, 1869 to 1979* (River Forest, Ill.: Rosary College, Graduate School of Library Science, 1981); and Duis, *Challenging Chicago,* 14–15. New York City's Humane Society had been founded in 1866.

240. "Dedicating a Dainty Hall," *Chicago Sunday Inter Ocean,* 13 October 1889.

241. Ibid.

242. Jane Addams, *Twenty Years at Hull-House* (New York: Macmillan, 1910), 177–178.

CHAPTER 5

1. Tallmadge, *Architecture in Old Chicago,* 76–77. On statistics for local hotels, see "The Hotel Business of 1876," *Hotel World* 2 (18 January 1877): 1. On Chicago's hotels as semipublic places in the later nineteenth century, see Duis, "Whose City? 2–27, and Duis, *Challenging Chicago,* 35–36.

2. On the origins of bus service from Chicago's hotels to the city's railway stations, see Weber, "Rationalizers and Reformers," 10–16; Williamson, *American Hotel,* 80; and Duis, *Challenging Chicago,* 10. On Chicago's railways and hotels in 1893, see Marquis, *Marquis' Hand-Book of Chicago,* 267–274; Flinn, *Chicago, the Marvelous City of the West,* 352–361; and Rand McNally, *Bird's-Eye Views and Guide to Chicago,* 50–63. On Manhattan's hotels in this period, see Stern, Mellins, and Fishman, *New York 1880,* 514–530. See also Taylor and Bush, *Golden Age of British Hotels;* Pevsner, *History of Building Types,* 188–190; Michael Schmitt, *Palast-Hotels: Architektur und Anspruch eines Bautyps, 1870–1920* (Berlin: Mann, 1982); David Watkin, *Grand Hotel: The Golden Age of Palace Hotels, an Architectural and Social History* (New York: Vendome Press, 1984), 15–17; and Elaine Denby, *Grand Hotels: Reality and Illusion, an Architectural and Social History* (London: Reaktion Books, 1998).

3. On the Tremont House of 1850 and Sherman House of 1861, see *Chicago before the Great Fire* (Chicago, n.d.); Andreas, *History of Chicago,* 2:501; Randall, *Building Construction in Chicago,* 38, 43; and Steven M. Davis, "'Of the Class Denominated Princely': The Tremont House Hotel," *Chicago History* 11 (spring 1982): 26–36, who notes that the twelve-year-old Adelina Patti first sang in Chicago there in 1853. Lowe, *Chicago Interiors,* 1, noted the first Republican convention of 1856 at the Tremont House.

4. A contemporaneous view of Palmer's activity on State Street, quoted in Mayer and Wade, *Chicago: Growth of a Metropolis,* 54. On Palmer's trip to Europe, see Twyman, *History of Marshall Field,* 22.

5. *Land Owner* 3 (April 1871): 103. See Chicago Bureau of Statistics and Municipal Library, "The Making of State Street," *Chicago City Manual* 5 (1912), 56–59; Hoyt, *Land Values in Chicago,* 89–90; Pierce, *History of Chicago,* 3:138–139; Perry R. Duis and Glen E. Holt, "The Many Faces of State Street," *Chicago* 27 (June 1978): 100; and Siry, *Carson Pirie Scott,* 16–18.

6. J. M. Wing, *The Palmer House, Chicago, Illustrated* (Chicago: J. M. Wing, 1876), 13.

7. On Paris's Grand Hôtel de la Paix, see "Édifices de l'industrie privée," *Revue Générale de l' Architecture et des Travaux Publics* 20 (1862): 284–285; Pevsner, *History of Building Types,* 188; David Van Zanten, *Building Paris: Architectural Institutions and the Transformation of the French Capital, 1830–1879* (New York: Cambridge University Press, 1994), 18, 25, 33–34; and Denby, *Grand Hotels,* 80–88. This building followed the Grand Hôtel du Louvre (for the exposition of 1855) in the rue de Rivoli, of which Armand was coarchitect, and was followed by the Hôtel Continental (for the exposition of 1878) by Henri Blondel. On Palmer's view of the Grand Hôtel de la Paix, see Everett R. Chamberlain, *Chicago and Its Suburbs* (Chicago: A. T. Hungerford, 1874, reprint, New York: Arno Press, 1974), 233. Adler wrote to his wife in Chicago from this hotel in September 1888. See, "Autobiography and Letters of Dankmar Adler," ed. Saltzstein, 23.

8. Boston architect Gridley J. F. Bryant to Jury for Competition for Boston Free Hospital, April 12, 1861, in Documents of the City of Boston, document 34, 2:31, quoted in Bainbridge Bunting, *Houses of Boston's Back Bay: An Architectural History, 1840–1917* (Cambridge: Harvard University Press, 1967), 64.

9. "Dry Goods: Grand Opening Last Evening by Field, Leiter & Co.," *Chicago Tribune,* 13 October 1868, 4. On New York's Grand Hotel and Grand Central Hotel, see Landau and Condit, *Rise of the New York Skyscraper,* 59–60, and Stern, Mellins, and Fishman, *New York 1880,* 521–524. See also William Hutchins, "New York Hotels: The Hotels of the Past, I," *Architectural Record* 12 (October 1902): 459–471. On Broadway's ornate architecture, see *The 1866 Guide to New York City: New York as It Is, or Stranger's Guide-Book to the Cities of New York, Brooklyn, and Adjacent Places* (1866; reprint, New York: Schocken Books, 1975), 22.

10. "The New Palmer House," *Land Owner* 2 (October 1870): 267. On the prefire Palmer House, see Andreas, *History of Chicago,* 2:509, and Randall, *Building Construction in Chicago,* 54.

11. On the prefire Grand Pacific Hotel, see "The Pacific Hotel," *Land Owner* 2 (April 1870): 82–83; "Building Improvements: The Grand Pacific Hotel, Chicago—Its New Elevations and Revised Plans," *Land Owner* 3 (March 1871): 72–73; Andreas, *History of Chicago,* 2:509; and Randall, *Building Construction in Chicago,* 77. Its initial promotion was noted in "Death of P. F. W. Peck—Another One of the Old Settlers Gone," *Chicago Tribune,* 23 October 1871, 2. On the postfire building, see "The Grand Pacific Hotel," *Chicago* 3 (December 1874): 130–131. On the property's value, see chapter 2, note 95.

12. "The Pacific Hotel," *Land Owner* 2 (April 1870): 82–83. Plans and views of the projected structure were in demand from all parts of the country even before its foundations were laid in fall 1870 ("Building Improvements: The Grand Pacific Hotel," 73). Philip Peck's lease with the Grand Pacific Hotel Company was noted in "Inventory of the Real and Personal Estate of Philip F. W. Peck, late of the City of Chicago, in the County of Cook and State of Illinois, deceased," filed 7 February 1872, Cook County Clerk of the Court, book 2, pp. 143–152, Cook County, Clerk of the Court, Probate Archives.

13. On the Rookery, see Condit, *Chicago School,* 63–65; Jordy, *American Buildings and Their Architects,* 4:73–76; Hoffmann, *Architecture of John Wellborn Root,* 65–83; Meredith L. Clausen, "Paris of the 1880s and the Rookery," in *Chicago Architecture, 1872–1922,* ed. Zukowsky, 156–171; and Deborah Slaton, "Burnham and Root and the Rookery," in *Midwest in American Architecture,* ed. Garner, 76–97.

14. "Building Improvements: The Grand Pacific Hotel," 73.

15. *Industrial Chicago,* 1:60.

16. Chamberlain, *Chicago and Its Suburbs,* 233. In addition to the Grand Hôtel de la Paix and the Grand Hôtel du Louvre in Paris, Potter Palmer and architect Charles M. Palmer visited the Langham Hotel (1865) in London and the Beau Rivage d'Angleterre (1865) and Grand Hôtel de la Paix (1872) in Geneva. See "Our Great Hotels: The Palmer House," *Land Owner* 5 (June 1873): 115, quoted in Carol W. Westfall, "From Homes to Towers: A Century of Chicago's Best Hotels and Tall Apartment Buildings," in *Chicago Architecture,* ed. Zukowsky, 269. Paris hotels, such as the Hôtel Continental opened for the exhibition of 1878, remained the standard of comparison for American hotels like San Francisco's Palace Hotel and Chicago's Palmer House, which claimed to be the "equal in size, splendor and cost, to the best hotel in Paris" (Mammoth Caravansaries," *Hotel World* 7 [17 August 1878]: 4).

17. Sir John Leng, *America in 1876* (Dundee, 1877), quoted in Pierce, *As Others See Chicago,* 221. On hotels built just after the fire, see Andreas, *History of Chicago,* 3:353–354; Flinn, *Chicago, the Marvelous City of the West,* 352–358; Rand McNally, *Bird's-Eye Views and Guide to Chicago,* 15–16, 51, 58, 116–117, 148; and Westfall, "From Homes to Towers," 267–269. On the Sherman House, see *Land Owner* 4 (March 1872): 33, 38. On the Tremont, see Davis, "'Of the Class Denominated Princely,'" 34–36.

18. Wing, *Palmer House, Chicago,* 8. On its registrations in 1876, see "The Hotel Business of 1876," *Hotel World* 2 (18 January 1877): 1. The 350-room postfire Commercial Hotel stood at the southeast corner of Lake and Dearborn, the site of the original Tremont House. See "The Commercial Hotel," *Hotel World* 2 (10 May 1877): 1. On Palmer as host in his hotel, see Carroll W. Westfall, "The Development of

American Apartment Houses from the Civil War to the Depression, III: Chicago's Better Tall Apartment Buildings, 1871–1923," *Architectura* 21 (1991): 185. On his and Leiter's prefire residence at the Sherman House, see Lloyd Wendt and Herman Kogan, *Give the Lady What She Wants! The Story of Marshall Field & Company* (Chicago: Rand McNally, 1952), 16–17, 70.

19. "Palmer's Grand Hotel," *Land Owner* 5 (March 1873): 82, quoted in Westfall, "From Homes to Towers," 269. On Stewart's Working Women's Hotel (1869–1873), designed by John B. Kellum, on the west side of Fourth Avenue between East Thirty-second and East Thirty-third Streets, see Stern, Mellins, and Fishman, *New York 1880*, 524–525.

20. *Industrial Chicago,* 1:60.

21. Ibid.

22. *Hotel Mail* (New York) 21 (24 September 1887). On the metalwork of the postfire Palmer House's storefronts, see Chamberlain, *Chicago and Its Suburbs,* 233. Other accounts are in "Rebuilt Chicago—Palmer's Grand Hotel," *Land Owner* 4 (January 1872): 1, and Rand McNally, *Bird's-Eye Views and Guide to Chicago,* 46, 47, 53, 55.

23. "Our Great Hotels: The Palmer House," *Land Owner* 5 (June 1873): 115. On Peck's opera quarters, see "A Day in the City," *Chicago Tribune,* 4 April 1885, 3. On the hotel's interiors, see Wing, *Palmer House, Chicago;* and Wing, *Seven Days in Chicago* (Chicago: J. M. Wing, 1876), both in the Chicago Historical Society. Hotels of this period lavished decorative attention on public rooms, while sometimes leaving guest rooms with bare walls ("Hotel Decoration: A Hint to Hotel Men," *Hotel World* 2 [7 September 1876]: 5).

24. Wing, *Palmer House, Chicago,* 7, 9, 30. Flinn, *Chicago, the Marvelous City of the Great West,* 356, noted how this space "most of the time day and night is a sort of rendezvous for the merchants of Chicago or their representatives and visiting buyers."

25. Chamberlain, *Chicago and Its Suburbs,* 234. On this dining room, see also Lowe, *Chicago Interiors,* 126.

26. Wing, *Palmer House, Chicago,* 16. As in the prefire Palmer House, both the restaurant and the grand dining room in the postfire hotel were staffed mostly by African American waiters. In 1890 the local hotel and restaurant industry employed about 1,800 black waiters, out of Chicago's African American population of about 5,000. See Estelle H. Scott, *Occupational Changes among Negroes in Chicago* (Chicago: Work Projects Administration, 1939), 20–23, 41; St. Clair Drake and Horace R. Cayton, *Black Metropolis: A Study of Negro Life in a Northern City* (1945; New York: Harper and Row, 1962), 47; and Duis, *Challenging Chicago,* 261–270.

27. The stonecutters' banquet was at McCoy's European Hotel, and their ball later that evening was at the West Side's Vorwärts Turner Hall on Twelfth Street. See "The Stone-cutters' Ball," *Chicago Tribune,* 8 December 1887, 2. That same evening Chicago's Theater Mechanics Association had its annual social gathering at North Side Turner Hall. See "Theatrical Folks' Hop," *Chicago Tribune,* 8 December 1887, 2. On the Iroquois Club, see Andreas, *History of Chicago,* 3:401–404. In 1894 the Iroquois Club moved out of its floors in the Columbia Theater and into newly converted quarters in the Brunswick Hotel on Michigan Avenue at Adams Street. See "The Iroquois Club," *Economist* 11 (20 January 1894): 66. It was at the Palmer House that "the prominent political leaders of the Democratic party congregate to exchange views and discuss topics of political moment," while the Grand Pacific was "the principal headquarters of the Republican party, and has been the scene of many exciting political events" (Marquis, *Marquis' Hand-Book of Chicago,* 268, 270). See also Miller, *City of the Century,* 187–188. On the banquet for the Society of the Army of the Tennessee staged to honor Ulysses S. Grant, see "The Tennessee," *Chicago Tribune,* 14 November 1979, 1–3. On Grant's impressive reception in Chicago, for which Loop buildings along an extended parade route bore patriotic decorations, see "He Is Here," *Chicago Tribune,* 13 November 1879, 1–8. The world tour was designed to promote Grant as a presidential candidate again in 1880.

28. "Braves at the Banquet," *Chicago Tribune,* 18 November 1886, 1–2.

29. "The Grand Pacific," *Hotel World* 2 (16 November 1876): 5. See *The Grand Pacific Hotel Twenty-ninth Annual Game Dinner, 22 November 1884* (Chicago Historical Society); Pierce, *History of Chicago,* 3:470; Lowe, *Chicago Interiors,* 14–15; Davis, "'Of the Class Denominated Princely,'" 32; and Duis, *Challenging Chicago,* 147. On the Chicago Grand Opera Festival Association's annual banquet, see "Music for the People," *Chicago Inter Ocean,* 3 May 1885, 6. Peck's hand-drawn seating plan for the Union League Club's banquet for Harrison on 9 December 1889 survives in the Auditorium Dedication Volume, Newberry Library, Chicago.

30. Rudyard Kipling, *From Sea to Sea: Letters of Travel; Part II* (New York, 1906), in *As Others See Chicago,* ed. Pierce, 251. See William S. Peterson, "Kipling's First Visit to Chicago," *Journal of the Illinois State Historical Society* 63 (fall 1970): 290–301. Other visitors were struck with the silver dollars inlaid in the floor of the Palmer House's barbershop, a promotional idea of its tenant manager. See Williamson, *American Hotel,* 83.

31. Norris, *Pit,* 278–279, 315, 318, 325, 348.

32. "Thank Our 'Lord-s,'" *Alarm* 1 (22 November 1884): 1.

33. "The Black Flag!" *Alarm* 1 (29 November 1884): 1.

34. Population figures are from Flinn, *Chicago, the Marvelous City of the West,* 352. The Gardner Hotel was acquired and remodeled by the Leland family in 1881.

35. "Unpatriotic Hotel Titles," *Hotel Mail* 24 (30 March 1889).

36. Flinn, *Chicago, the Marvelous City of the West,* 357. On the Richelieu Hotel, see also Andreas, *History of Chicago,* 3: 355, and Westfall, "From Homes to Towers," 271–272.

37. Rand McNally, *Bird's-Eye View and Guide to Chicago,* 32. On Patti at the Richelieu, see "Patti the Divine," *Chicago Tribune,* 8 December 1889, 1. Vynne, *Chicago by Day and Night,* 26, noted that actresses Sarah Bernhardt and Lillie Langtry stayed at the Richelieu.

38. Garczynski, *Auditorium,* 42. Vynne, *Chicago by Day and Night,* 24–25, noted that by 1892 first-time visitors to Chicago often preferred the Auditorium Hotel. Such tourists came to the city from the east by trains, some of which interrupted their otherwise rigorous timetables to stop for twenty minutes at Niagara Falls so passengers could look out on this national geologic wonder. The journey west offered an encounter with the natural beauty of the country's landscapes. Such a trip would culminate at Chicago's lakefront, where passengers would ride past the front of the Auditorium Building just before arriving at the city's Central Depot. In this period domestic and foreign travel was promoted by illustrated lectures, like those of traveler Henry T. Ragan at the Central Music Hall, 15–24 April 1890 (Chicago Bureau of Popular and Scientific Lectures, *The Ragan Lectures,* Central Music Hall, April 15, 17, 21, 24 and 26 [Chicago Historical Society]).

39. Sullivan, "Development of Construction" (1916), in *Louis Sullivan: The Public Papers,* ed. Twombly, 219.

40. Ferdinand Peck to Auditorium Hotel Co., 14 March 1890, in Minutes of Executive Committee of Chicago Auditorium Association, 3 May 1887 to 11 December 1907, 209 (Auditorium Collection, Roosevelt University Archives).

41. "The Auditorium Hotel," *Daily National Hotel Reporter* (Chicago), 9 October 1890, in "Early History and Press Clippings, Chicago Auditorium Association, Chicago, 1887–1889" (Ryerson and Burnham Libraries, Art Institute of Chicago). Mr. and Mrs. Walter L. Peck, Mrs. P. F. W. Peck, and Mrs. Martin Ryerson were among the original residents ("The Auditorium Hotel," *Chicago Sunday Inter Ocean,* 16 March 1890, 9). On Sheridan at the Palmer House, see Leslie Dorsey and Janice Devine, *Fare Thee Well: A Backward Look at Two Centuries of Historic American Hostelries, Fashionable Spas and Seaside Resorts* (New York: Crown, 1964), 205. See also Duis, *Challenging Chicago,* 81, 84. On residential hotels for both the wealthy and others in the later nineteenth century, see Paul Groth, *Living Downtown:*

The History of Residential Hotels in the United States (Berkeley: University of California Press, 1994), 26–89. On Sullivan's Chicago addresses, see Twombly, *Louis Sullivan,* 207, 209–210, 358, 397–398.

42. "The City: Another Hotel Scheme," *Chicago Tribune,* 22 March 1886, 6.

43. Garczynski, *Auditorium,* 42. On Lake Shore Drive's development, see John W. Stamper, "Shaping Chicago's Shoreline," *Chicago History* 14 (winter 1985–1986): 44–55.

44. Peck, quoted in "Its Beauty Unveiled," *Chicago Tribune,* 26 April 1893, 2. For Peck, public control over lakefront lands, designated by the federal government in the 1830s to be forever free and clear, was a requisite complement to the Auditorium. Lake Front Park did become a large civic landscape, renamed Grant Park in 1901. This park remains an indispensable amenity for Michigan Avenue, whose large-scale development did begin with the Auditorium. See Lois Wille, *Forever Open, Free and Clear: The Historic Struggle for Chicago's Lakefront* (Chicago: Henry Regnery, 1972), 71–94; Joan Pomeranc, "Grant Park and Burnham Park," in *AIA Guide to Chicago,* ed. Alice Sinkevitch and Laurie McGovern Petersen (New York: Harcourt Brace, 1993), 39–42; and Dennis Cremin, "Chicago's Front Yard," *Chicago History* 27 (spring 1998): 22–43.

45. Peck, quoted in "The Collegians," *Chicago Inter Ocean,* 5 January 1889.

46. Franklin H. Head, "The Heart of Chicago," *New England Magazine* 6 (July 1892): 566. Warner, *Studies in the South and West,* 192, had noted sixty trains a day.

47. "The Lake-Front," *Chicago Tribune,* 13 February 1886, 2. On this meeting, see also Andreas, *History of Chicago,* 3:190–192. On the Illinois Central's rights to land along the lakefront, see Douglas Schroeder, *The Issue of the Lakefront: An Historical Critical Survey* (Chicago: Chicago Heritage Committee, 1964); Wille, *Forever Open, Free, and Clear,* 26–37; and John F. Stover, *History of the Illinois Central Railroad* (New York: Macmillan, 1975), 179–181, 298–299.

48. "The Lake-Front," *Chicago Tribune,* 13 February 1886, 2.

49. "The City: Mr. Leland and the Lake Front," *Chicago Tribune,* 3 January 1887, 8. See also "Clear the Lake-Front," *Chicago Tribune,* 4 August 1889, 10. On Leland's view of the Exposition Building, see "War on the Horizon," *Chicago Tribune,* 1 March 1890, 1. Demolition of the Exposition Building began in May 1891 in preparation for construction on the site of the monumental classical edifice that would be the Art Institute of Chicago. At this time most citizens favored Lake Front Park as the site of the World's Columbian Exposition rather than Jackson Park, much farther south on the lake, which was soon chosen as the site ("Lake-Front Advocates," *Chicago Tribune,* 2 March 1890, 3). The protesting property owners along Michigan Avenue filed their bill with Chicago's federal circuit court on 2 July 1890, as noted in "Columbian Exposition," *Presto* 8 (20 December 1890): 88.

50. Warner, *Studies in the South and West,* 187. See also "Boulevards and Streets: Michigan Boulevard," *Chicago Tribune,* 23 October 1881, 17, and Flinn, *Chicago, the Marvelous City of the West,* 607–608. Views of drives are in *Tally-Ho: Coaching through Chicago's Parks and Boulevards* (Chicago, 1888).

51. Grant, *Fight for a City,* 56.

52. William W. Howard, "The New Chicago," in "The City of Chicago," supplement to *Harper's Weekly,* 23 June 1888, 451.

53. Warner, *Studies in the South and West,* 187.

54. Ibid., 194–195.

55. Garczynski, *Auditorium,* 46. See George Bushnell, "When Chicago Was Wheel Crazy," *Chicago History* 4 (fall 1975): 167–175; Susan E. Hirsch and Robert I. Goler, *A City Comes of Age: Chicago in the 1890s* (Chicago: Chicago Historical Society, 1990), 133–137; and Duis, *Challenging Chicago,* 178–193. On the national phenomenon, see "The World Awheel," *Munsey's Magazine* 15 (May 1896): 130–159, and Richard Harmond, "Progress and Flight: An Interpretation of the American Cycle Craze of the 1890s," *Journal of Social History* 5 (winter 1971): 235–257. On the club buildings of Chicago's cycling and other athletic groups, see "Homes of the Athletes," *Chicago Tribune,* 19 January 1891, 25. On Henry Ives Cobb's

building for the Chicago Athletic Association, sited on Michigan Avenue north of the Auditorium, see "Model Club House," *Chicago Evening Post,* 10 September 1892, 5; "Home of Athletics," *Chicago Tribune,* 25 December 1892, 11; and John Hipwell, "The Chicago Athletic Club," *Outing* 33 (November 1898): 145–152.

56. Editorial, "The Sale of the Lake Front," *Chicago Tribune,* 3 July 1889, 2. Claims of Chicagoans about their port's traffic were noted in William W. Howard, "The New Chicago," in "The City of Chicago," supplement to *Harper's Weekly,* 23 June 1888, 451.

57. Peck, quoted in "The Lake-Front," *Chicago Tribune,* 13 February 1886, 2. On the recreational activity along the city's shoreline in this period, see "Seen on the Lake Front," *Chicago Tribune,* 4 August 1889, 25. On commercial boats along the lake, see "Queer Craft in Port," *Chicago Herald,* 20 September 1886, 11. Philip F. W. Peck's petitions to the city council regarding wharfage from 1833 to 1839 are noted in Robert E. Bailey et al., eds., *Chicago City Council Proceedings Files, 1833–1871: An Index* (Springfield, Ill.: Illinois State Archives, 1987), 2552–2553.

58. Garczynski, *Auditorium,* 46. On the new thirty-foot, gasoline-powered vessels noted and illustrated in Garczynski, see "A Thousand Miles in a Naphtha Launch," *Forest and Stream* 35 (9 October 1889): 227–228; (16 October 1889): 258–259. Chicago then lacked breakwaters sufficiently extensive to provide a harbor for yachts as shelter from storms on Lake Michigan. See E. C. J. Cleaner, "Why There Is No Yachting at Chicago," *Forest and Stream* 34 (12 June 1890): 422. Such breakwaters were a prominent feature of Burnham and Bennett's proposals for the lakefront in their overall urban plan for Chicago of 1909. On Peck's recreational sailing, see Dean, *World's Fair City,* 72. One obituary noted that Peck "was one of the first locally to take up yachting as a sport and he is credited with having done more than any individual to make this pastime popular on the Great Lakes." He "was called 'commodore' by all who knew him. The title was given to him as the commodore of the Chicago Yacht Club" ("Pioneer's Life Given to City's Uplift," *Chicago Herald American,* 5 November 1924).

59. The Auditorium Association's executive committee sought authorization from the board of directors "to fix an average annual sum of one hundred thousand dollars ($100,000.00) for five (5) years as the rental for the Hotel" (Minutes of Executive Committee of Chicago Auditorium Association, 2 October 1888, 57 [Auditorium Collection, Roosevelt University Archives]). In this period it was rumored that Peck was asking the nationally reputed John B. Drake, then managing both the Grand Pacific and the Sherman House, to run the Auditorium Hotel. This was plausible "in the first place, because the Auditorium would draw more of its patronage from the Grand Pacific than from any other hotel, owing to the class of trade that the latter enjoys; and in the second because the Grand Pacific is no longer a new and first-class structure" ("Notes about Town," *Hotel Mail* [New York] 24 [7 September 1889]). Rumor of Drake as manager had appeared earlier in "The Auditorium Hotel," *Chicago Tribune,* 22 September 1888, 1.

60. Gregersen, "History of the Auditorium Building," 30.

61. "The Auditorium Hotel," *National Hotel Reporter* (Chicago), 7 February 1889, in "Early History and Press Clippings, Chicago Auditorium Association, Chicago, 1887–1889" (Ryerson and Burnham Libraries, Art Institute of Chicago).

62. On 22 January, Peck "made an exhaustive report of the details and conclusion of the negotiations for leasing the hotel," which the executive committee unanimously approved, whereupon Breslin and Southgate met with the committee on 4 February (Minutes of Executive Committee of Chicago Auditorium Association, 78, 84 [Auditorium Collection Roosevelt University Archives]). A preliminary leasing agreement was reached on 6 February, and the final agreement was executed on 18 April 1889 (Special Directors' Meeting, Chicago Auditorium Association, 8 February and 20 April 1889, Records of the Chicago Auditorium Association, 135, 138 [Auditorium Collection, Roosevelt University Archives]). On Breslin and Southgate, see Garczynski, *Auditorium,* 52. On the Gilsey House, see "Big Bonanza Buildings," *Real Estate Record* (New York) 17 (8 April 1876): 255–256; Boyer, *Manhattan Manners,* 31–32;

Williamson, *American Hotel,* 39–40, 262; and Stern, Mellins, and Fishman, *New York 1880,* 522–523. On New York's Brunswick Hotel, see Williamson, *American Hotel,* 271–272. On the Congress Hall of 1868 in Saratoga, see Jeffrey Limerick, Nancy Ferguson, and Richard Oliver, *America's Grand Resort Hotels* (New York: Pantheon Books, 1979), 37. Southgate went to live in Chicago to manage the Auditorium Hotel, whose original staff came from well-known hotels in both Chicago and New York City ("The Auditorium, Chicago," *Hotel Mail* 25 [15 March 1890]).

63. "The Auditorium, Chicago," *Hotel Mail* 25 (15 March 1890). The national meeting's inspection of Adler and Sullivan's building was noted in *Hotel Mail* 24 (18 May 1889). The Auditorium's directors agreed that "a Banquet Hall for the use of the Hotel lessees be built, and that the proposal of the Auditorium Hotel Co. under date of April 17, 1889, as to the minimum rent to be paid for the same be accepted" (Special Directors' Meeting, 20 April 1889, Records of the Chicago Auditorium Association, 139). James H. Breslin to Ferdinand W. Peck, 17 April 1889, wrote of "our conversation relative to Banquet Hall, which for many reasons we consider very important to the Hotel as well as a feature we feel will be appreciated by our patrons, your citizens . . . . The necessity of having this Banquet Hall is growing more urgent as we find we are going to be much crowded for Dining Room capacity without it" (Chicago Auditorium Association, Copies of Documents, 224 [Auditorium Collection, Roosevelt University Archives]).

64. *Real Estate Record and Guide* (New York) 43 (26 January 1889): 105, quoted in Stern, Gilmartin, and Massengale, *New York 1900,* 254.

65. Stanford White's dining room for the Plaza Hotel replicated a salon of Marie Antoinette, the bar a room from Lord Randolph Churchill's chateau, and the main corridor a fresco from the Vatican. On the dining room, see Dubin, "The Hotels of New York City," 43. On the Plaza's opening, see "A Handsome New Hotel," *New York Times,* 30 September 1890, 5. The Plaza Hotel as built transformed the earlier unbuilt project for Plaza Apartments on the same site, whose architect at one point was Carl Pfeiffer, as noted in chapter 3. See Stern, Mellins, and Fishman, *New York 1880,* 529–530. The Imperial's exterior adapted motifs from the Italian and Spanish Renaissance. See Montgomery Schuyler, "D. H. Burnham and Company," *Great American Architect Series for the Architectural Record* (1899; reprint, New York, 1977), 59–61. On the Imperial and other later Manhattan hotels of the 1890s, see Robert Stewart, "The Hotels of New York," *Munsey's Magazine* 22 (November 1899): 281–295, and William Hutchins, "New York Hotels, II: The Modern Hotel," *Architectural Record* 12 (November 1902): 621–635.

66. Louis Sullivan, Kindergarten Chat 5, "An Hotel," *Interstate Architect and Builder* 3 (16 March 1901): 8; reprinted in *"Kindergarten Chats" and Other Writings,* ed. Athey, 27.

67. Peck, speech at annual banquet of Chicago Real Estate Board, quoted in "Owners of Earth," *Chicago Tribune,* 31 January 1890, 2.

68. Kipling, paraphrased in Garczynski, *Auditorium,* 11. Others responded to counter Kipling's views of Chicago. See Elizabeth L. Banks, letter to editor, *London Times,* 6 December 1892, in "As Ourselves See Us," *Chicago Tribune,* 17 December 1892, 14.

69. Garczynski, *Auditorium,* 11.

70. Garczynski, *Auditorium,* 57.

71. "A Visit to the States," article 30, *London Times,* 24 October 1887, quoted in Pierce, *As Others See Chicago,* 240.

72. "The Union League Club," *Graphic* (Chicago), o.s., 1 (12 June 1886): 235. On the Union League Club's building of 1886, see "Stories of Smart Men," *Chicago Herald* (2 May 1886): 3; "The Union League Club," *Chicago Tribune,* 11 June 1886, 1–2; *The Chicago Clubs Illustrated* (Chicago: Lanward, 1888), 58–62; "The Union League Club," *Graphic* (Chicago), o.s., 12 (22 March 1890): 180–182; Charles B. Jenkins, "W. L. B. Jenney and W. B. Mundie," *Architectural Reviewer* (Chicago) 1 (February 1897): 2–9; Grant, *Fight for a City,* 81–95; and Bushnell, "Chicago's Leading Men's Clubs," *Chicago History* 11 (summer 1982): 82. Its interiors were noted among Healy and Millet's works in *Industrial Chicago,* 2:708.

73. "The Black Flag!" *Alarm* 1 (29 November 1884): 1. On the Union Club, see *Chicago Clubs Illustrated*, 63–66.

74. "The Union League Club," *Graphic* (Chicago), o.s., 12 (22 March 1890): 182. See also "Opening Its Annex," *Chicago Tribune*, 8 December 1889, 1. On the metaphorical reuse of Custer's story, see Richard S. Slotkin, "The Last Stand as Ideological Object, 1876–1890," in Slotkin, *The Fatal Environment: The Myth of the Frontier in the Age of Industrialization, 1800–1890* (New York: Atheneum, 1985), 433–532.

75. "The Union League Club," *Chicago Tribune,* 11 June 1886, 1.

76. See *The Standard Club's First Hundred Years, 1869–1969* (Chicago, 1969). On Adler and Sullivan's building of 1887–1888, see Morrison, *Louis Sullivan,* 113, and Twombly, *Louis Sullivan,* 238–241.

77. Adler, "Chicago Auditorium," 420, wrote: "In its construction the hotel presents many interesting features. As a multiplicity of pillars would have been objectionable in the public rooms which occupy the first story of the Congress street front, and which were intended in the original design to take up all of the second floor of the same, the floors from the first story upward are carried on 140 riveted girders 2 feet high and of 36 feet clear span each. The front on which these girders occur is 360 feet long and being but 40 feet deep, is given lateral stiffness by four heavy brick walls extending from bottom to top of the building. The absence of interior columns resulting from the use of the girder construction permitted a degree of freedom in the handling of partitions and the division into rooms that was found quite useful."

78. Gregersen, "History of the Auditorium Building," 40–41. See also epilogue, 397. Garczynski, *Auditorium,* 57, noted that "the ladies' entrance is on the left-hand half of the first arch," the southernmost of three opening from Michigan Avenue. He described the barber shop (65–66) as having an entresol with facilities for both men and women.

79. Garczynski, *Auditorium,* 25.

80. Ibid., 169.

81. "A Visit to the States," article 30, *London Times,* 24 October 1887, quoted in Pierce, *As Others See Chicago,* 240–241.

82. Garczynski, *Auditorium,* 56: "Of the men who obtained contracts for various parts of this noble structure not a few were inspired by the patriotic character of the undertaking, and found themselves kindled to such a pitch of ardor by the contagious fire of Ferdinand Peck's enthusiasm that they turned out the very best work which was possible regardless of all money considerations . . . . These gentlemen for the most part looked upon the Auditorium as a specimen of what Chicago enterprise and patriotism could accomplish, and in consequence made the fulfillment of their contracts a veritable labor of love." On Sullivan's ornament in the Auditorium Building's public interiors, see also Weingarden, "Louis H. Sullivan's Ornament and the Poetics of Architecture," in *Chicago Architecture,* ed. Zukowsky, 240–245; Weingarden, "Naturalized Nationalism," 55–63; and Weingarden, "Louis H. Sullivan's *System of Architectural Ornament*," in *Louis H. Sullivan: A System of Architectural Ornament* (New York: Rizzoli, 1990), 27.

83. Garczynski, *Auditorium,* 61.

84. Burnham, *History and Uses of Limestones and Marbles,* iii, vii. Burnham wrote (113): "The most beautiful and interesting formation of Mexico is the so-called Onyx marble, a calcareous alabaster, the result of chemical agencies, which equals, if it does not surpass, in beauty, the antique Onyx marble of Algeria. Its translucency, its soft, delicate lines of stratification, its deep orange and light green spots or clouds, and its exquisite polish, render it one of the most attractive of ornamental marbles." Less public interiors on the Auditorium Building's upper floors were lined with white Georgia marble, which, among American marbles, had a chemical composition said to be like the pentelic marble of monuments on the Athenian Acropolis. See Siry, *Carson Pirie Scott,* 90–91.

85. Wright, unpublished version of "The Art and Craft of the Machine" (Frank Lloyd Wright Archives, MS 2401.007, pp. 13–15). See Joseph M. Siry, "Frank Lloyd Wright's 'The Art and Craft of the

Machine': Text and Context," in *The Education of the Architect: Historiography, Urbanism, and the Growth of Architectural Knowledge,* ed. Martha Pollak (Cambridge: MIT Press, 1997), 3–36.

86. Garczynski, *Auditorium,* 169. To create scagliola, first the column shaft would be coated with a cement and sand mortar to yield a strong, hard surface. Over this would be applied a soft wash coat made of cement and marble dust to act as a paste. Simultaneously an oilcloth, which would actually carry the marblelike pattern, was laid out smooth and straight on a flat horizontal surface. A white mixture of cement and water was prepared, as were mixtures of cement, water, and other colors. These colors were then applied to the oilcloth with bunches of silk strands, which left lines like those of marble veining. After further preparation of the color fields on the oilcloth, it was applied to the column, where its colors bonded with the column's paste coating. Once the colors were bonded, after about an hour, the oilcloth was removed. While the colors dried and afterward, polishing and finishing over three weeks brought out the marblelike sheen of the finished surface. See Felicien Van den Branden and Mark Knowles, *Plastering Skill and Practice* (Chicago: American Technical Society, 1953), 212–226, and Vinci-Kenny, Architects, *Adler & Sullivan's Auditorium Building: Architectural Guidelines for Its Preservation and Restoration for Roosevelt University* (Chicago, 1977), 76–77.

87. Garczynski, *Auditorium,* 62. Sullivan, *Autobiography of an Idea,* 303, wrote of the Auditorium Building: "Louis's heart went into this structure."

88. "The Auditorium Hotel," *Daily National Hotel Reporter* (Chicago), 9 October 1890, in "Early History and Press Clippings, Chicago Auditorium Association, Chicago, 1887–1889" (Ryerson and Burnham Libraries, Art Institute of Chicago).

89. Adler, "Chicago Auditorium," 421, noted that a forty-foot trussed girder spanned the hotel's main staircase. He had preferred pillars supporting shorter spans.

90. Garczynski, *Auditorium,* 63. Sullivan developed similar electroliers to flank the northwest entrance to Adler and Sullivan's later Guaranty Building in Buffalo (1894–1896). See Bush-Brown, *Louis Sullivan,* fig. 60, and Siry, "Adler and Sullivan's Guaranty Building," 7 (fig. 1). On the Palmer House's electric lights, see Williamson, *American Hotel,* 68. On the Grand Pacific's, see Flinn, *Chicago, the Marvelous City of the West,* 354.

91. Frank Lloyd Wright, *Drawings for a Living Architecture* (New York: Horizon, 1959), 154. Sprague, *Drawings of Louis Henry Sullivan,* 35, notes that Crombie Taylor, the restoration architect of the Auditorium Hotel's banquet hall in the 1950s, said that Wright told him that the newel post was his first assignment after joining Adler and Sullivan.

92. Wright, *Genius and the Mobocracy,* 55.

93. Sprague, *Drawings of Louis Henry Sullivan,* 6.

94. William H. Burke, in *Industrial Chicago,* 2:553. Sullivan, "Development of Construction" (1916), in *Louis Sullivan: The Public Papers,* ed. Twombly, 219, presumably referred to Burke when he wrote of the Auditorium: "The floors throughout the building, in the main part, were changed from wood to mosaic. Mosaic work, as far as I know, was unknown until about that time when an Englishman was the first to introduce it, and almost contemporaneously with its introduction it was used in the Auditorium. There are 9,832,716 little pieces of mosaic used in that building."

95. William H. Burke, in *Industrial Chicago,* 2:555.

96. Garczynski, *Auditorium,* 76.

97. James, *Chicago's Dark Places,* 40. On ladies' entrances to bars of this period, see Madelon Powers, *Faces along the Bar: Lore and Order in the Workingman's Saloon, 1870–1920* (Chicago: University of Chicago Press, 1998), 32–33.

98. Garczynski, *Auditorium,* 70. On Boston's segregation-of-sexes laws, see Perry Duis, *The Saloon: Public Drinking in Chicago and Boston, 1880–1920* (Urbana: University of Illinois Press, 1983), 276–777. Joanne J. Meyerowitz, *Women Adrift: Independent Wage Earners in Chicago, 1880–1930*

(Chicago: University of Chicago Press, 1988), 80, emphasizes efforts by the YWCA to encourage lone women to spend evenings at home and not to seek amusements in the unsupervised world of restaurants and dance halls. On amusements associated with alcohol, and attempts at their control, see Melendy, "Saloon in Chicago." See also James, *Chicago's Dark Places*, 30–53.

99.   James, *Chicago's Dark Places*, 42.

100.   Garczynski, *Auditorium*, 72.

101.   Ibid. On Gallé's contemporaneous glasswork, see Philippe Garner, *Émile Gallé* (New York: St. Martin's Press, 1976), 92–109.

102.   "Gunther's New Building," *Chicago Tribune*, 15 May 1887, 17. Gunther's ice cream and soda parlor previously had been in the street level of the McVicker's Theater.

103.   Garczynski, *Auditorium*, 66. Wright, *Genius and the Mobocracy*, 49, later wrote of "the great, wide, unique Auditorium bar, which I had to design for the great building owing to last-moment pressure on L.H.S. himself. This item may indicate how well versed in the technique of the master 'his pencil' had become."

104.   "Feeding the Masses," *Chicago Tribune*, 18 December 1892, 26. See also Lewis, *Early Encounter with Tomorrow*, 49–50, and Duis, *Challenging Chicago*, 152–163.

105.   "The Auditorium Hotel," *Daily National Hotel Reporter* (Chicago), 9 October 1890, in "Early History and Press Clippings, Chicago Auditorium Association, Chicago, 1887–1889" (Ryerson and Burnham Libraries, Art Institute of Chicago).

106.   Garczynski, *Auditorium*, 67. While a student in the 1870s, Sullivan made precise drawings of the Tuscan and Doric orders. See Martha Pollak, "Sullivan and the Orders of Architecture," in *Chicago Architecture*, ed. Zukowsky, 250–265.

107.   On the Union League Club, see Stern, Mellins, and Fishman, *New York 1880*, 204–213; Wheaton Holden, "Robert Swain Peabody of Peabody and Stearns in Boston: The Early Years, 1870–1886" (Ph.D. diss., Boston University, 1969), 111–114, 346–348; and "Some of the Union League Decorations," *Century Magazine* 23 (March 1882): 745–752. On 6 July 1888, for the Auditorium Hotel, Adler was "instructed to arrange the Building so that the Dining Room and Kitchen of the Hotel shall be on the tenth floor of the building" (Minutes of Executive Committee of Chicago Auditorium Association, 6 July 1888, 50. The spectacular view presumably inspired a later proposal of 1898 for a roof garden over the dining room (Minutes of Executive Committee of Chicago Auditorium Association, 18 April 1898, 436 [Auditorium Collection, Roosevelt University Archives]). This proposal was also noted in the *Economist* 20 (29 October 1898): 509; *Chicago Tribune*, 23 October 1898, 34; and *Construction News* 7 (2 November 1898): 493. I am indebted to architectural historian Kathleen Cummings, Chicago, for these references.

108.   "The Hotel System of London," *Hotel Mail* (New York) 21 (1 October 1887).

109.   Garczynski, *Auditorium*, 86.

110.   Minutes of Executive Committee of Chicago Auditorium Association, 8 September 1888, 56 (Auditorium Collection, Roosevelt University Archives). See also "Chicago Auditorium Electric Light and Power Plant," *Western Electrician* 5 (12 October 1889), 191–193. On the Ponce de León Hotel, see Carl Condit, "The Pioneer Concrete Buildings of St. Augustine," *Progressive Architecture* 52 (September 1971): 128–133; Blake, "Architecture of Carrère and Hastings," 99–111; and Limerick, Ferguson, and Oliver, *America's Grand Resort Hotels*, 80–89.

111.   "The Auditorium Hotel," *Daily National Hotel Reporter* (Chicago), 9 October 1890, in "Early History and Press Clippings, Chicago Auditorium Association, Chicago, 1887–1889" (Ryerson and Burnham Libraries, Art Institute of Chicago).

112.   "The Auditorium Building: A Great and Superb Structure," Auditorium Number, *Graphic* (Chicago), o.s., 11 (14 December 1889). See also Gray, *Guide to Chicago's Murals*, 8–9. On the stencils,

see Philip Neuberg, "Unveiling Sullivan's Artistry," *Inland Architect,* September 1979, 14–15, and "The Auditorium Building Dining Room Stencil Patterns and Paints," Chicago: Roosevelt University, 1978 (Auditorium Collection, file box U, Roosevelt University Archives).

113. Orear, *Commercial and Architectural Chicago,* 46.

114. "Art Notes: Oliver Dennett Grover," *Graphic* (Chicago), n.s., 5 (26 September 1891): 202. See also Andreas, *History of Chicago,* 3:422–423, and Sparks, "Biographical Dictionary of Painters and Sculptors in Illinois," 406–408.

115. Garczynski, *Auditorium,* 74. As a Chicagoan abroad in 1873–1874, Philo Otis, *Impressions of Europe,* 33, wrote that the "Hôtel de Ville in Brussels, with the great Banquet Hall and Salle des Mariages, is rich in historical associations." In September 1888 Adler wrote from Brussels that he "went all over the Hotel de Ville, a very fine building containing some exquisitely furnished rooms dating back several centuries . . . . [It] belongs to one of the best periods of Flemish Gothic architecture" ("Autobiography and Letters of Dankmar Adler," ed. Saltzstein, 23). On workers' balls, see, for example, "Both Pleasant Affairs," *Chicago Tribune,* 13 April 1887, 1. See also Richard T. Griffin, "Sin Drenched Revels at the Infamous First Ward Ball," *Smithsonian* 7 (November 1976): 52–61. On working-class dances and dance halls, see Duis, *Challenging Chicago,* 228. On Sherry's ballrooms, see Stern, Mellins, and Fishman, *New York 1880,* 734; Stern, Gilmartin, and Massengale, *New York 1900,* 223–224; Roth, *McKim, Mead and White, Architects,* 223–224; Paul R. Baker, *Stanny: The Gilded Life of Stanford White* (New York: Free Press, 1989), 223–224; and David Lowe, *Stanford White's New York* (New York: Double-day, 1992), 176–178. On the St. Nicholas Hotel, see "Real Estate Interests," *St. Louis Post-Dispatch,* 11 December 1892, 10; Morrison, *Louis Sullivan,* 122–123; and Twombly, *Louis Sullivan,* 276–278.

116. Adler, "Chicago Auditorium," 420, listed the trusses over the banquet hall as the first of "the most daring and conspicuously successful structural features of the hotel."

117. Garczynski, *Auditorium,* 26. In speaking of the structural plans of his firm's later sixteen-story Schiller Building (1890–1892), Adler said: "You will notice what an immense amount of work have [*sic*] been expended on these drawings. Every piece of steel to go into this building is shown here with the exact size, weight, and the arrangement of rivets. To prepare this portion of the plans took the equal of one man's time for one year . . . and for the plans of the Wainwright building in St. Louis, which we designed and which is a plain business structure, was required the equal of one man's labor for eight months. In the Auditorium and the German Theater building provision had to be made for prosceniums, stage supports, etc." (Adler, quoted in "Make the High Buildings Safe," *Economist* 5 [30 May 1891]: 951).

118. Garczynski, *Auditorium,* 99. Some of the hall's windows combined foliate and geometric forms into an image like a peacock's fan of colored feathers. This motif recurred in Garczynski's book on the Auditorium of 1890. Allusion to peacocks as a delicacy consumed at ancient Roman feasts would be consistent with the banquet hall's use.

119. Minutes of Executive Committee of Chicago Auditorium Association, 239 (Auditorium Collection, Roosevelt University Archives).

120. "The Auditorium Hotel," *Daily National Hotel Reporter* (Chicago), 9 October 1890, in "Early History and Press Clippings, Chicago Auditorium Association, Chicago, 1887–1889" (Ryerson and Burnham Libraries, Art Institute of Chicago). The murals' 1950s repainting was described in a letter of Crombie Taylor to the author, 12 May 1999. On their restoration, see "Off-the-Wall Effort Saving Murals," *Chicago Tribune,* 17 October 2000.

121. Adler, "Chicago Auditorium," 418. On the banquet hall capitals, see Van Zanten, *Sullivan's City,* 37–43.

122. Garczynski, *Auditorium,* 102. On Ruskin's assessment of the capitals in the Doge's Palace, see "The Nature of Gothic," and "The Ducal Palace," in *The Stones of Venice,* 3 vols. (London, 1851, 1853), vol. 2. On the hall's birch, see Shirley Lowry, "Electroliers Sought for Perfect Room," *Chicago Tribune,* 15 October 1956), part 1, p. 9/25. On Ruskin's influence in Sullivan's work, see also Weingarden,

"Naturalized Nationalism." Garczynski (102) compared the banquet hall to "any one of the wonderful palaces built by Andulasian architects in Southern Spain for Arab Emirs and for Moorish kings," the most famous of which was the Alhambra. Another contemporary termed the Auditorium Building as a whole "this great Alcazar," referring to this same type of palace, sometimes fortified like the Alhambra at Granada, built by Moorish rulers in Spanish cities ("Chicago Music, Drama, and Miscellany," *Presto* 6 [9 March 1889]: 5).

123. Garczynski, *Auditorium,* 105. Sprague, *Drawings of Louis Henry Sullivan,* 35–36, notes that Sullivan's extant sketches for the hall's capitals dated from April and July 1890.

124. "A Word for the Architect," *Chicago Tribune,* 15 December 1889, 10. On the pace of work for the Auditorium Hotel interiors and Sullivan's exacting supervision, see Van Zanten, *Sullivan's City,* 31.

125. Cope, *Iron and Steel Interests of Chicago,* 7. This booklet, in the Chicago Historical Society, was published by the reception committee for members of the British Iron and Steel Institute and the Verein Deutscher Eisenhüttenleute on their visit to Chicago, 13 and 14 October 1890. On the banquet hall's reception for these Europeans, see "Welcome to the Guests," *Chicago Tribune,* 14 October 1890, 1; "Chicago on Exhibition," *Chicago Tribune,* 14 October 1890, 2; and "They Left with Regret," *Chicago Tribune,* 15 October 1890, 2.

126. "The Auditorium Hotel," *Daily National Hotel Reporter* (Chicago), 9 October 1890, in "Early History and Press Clippings, Chicago Auditorium Association, Chicago, 1887–1889" (Ryerson and Burnham Libraries, Art Institute of Chicago).

127. Sullivan, *Autobiography of an Idea,* 242. See also Adler, letter, "Foundations," *Economist* 5 (27 June 1891): 1136, and "Chicago Elevators," *Chicago Tribune,* 21 November 1885, 13.

128. *Industrial Chicago,* 2:603.

129. Franklin H. Head, "The Heart of Chicago," *New England Magazine* 6 (July 1892): 551.

130. Rev. David Swing, quoted in Editorial, *Indicator* 12 (4 January 1890): 5.

131. Flinn, *Chicago, the Marvelous City of the West,* 387. See Collins, *History of the Illinois National Guard,* 6–26, 58–85; Andreas, *History of Chicago,* 3:586–587; and Turner, *Souvenir Album and Sketchbook.* Workers derisively referred to the regiment's men as "Marshall Field's boys" ("Our Vampires," *Alarm* 1 [2 May 1885]: 1). The parallel, though much older, elite militia unit in New York was the Seventh Regiment, formed in 1806. Its huge fortresslike armory, designed by Charles W. Clinton, was completed in 1880. On this building's architecture and subsequent regimental armories in Manhattan of the 1880s, see Stern, Mellins, and Fishman, *New York 1880,* 238–251.

132. Flinn, *Chicago, the Marvelous City of the West,* 389.

133. Burnham and Root, "The First Regiment Armory," in Turner, *Souvenir Album and Sketchbook,* 18, 19. See also *Inland Architect and News Record* 13 (June 1889): 90; "Was Laid with Pomp," *Chicago Tribune,* 13 July 1890, 1–2; Julian Ralph, "The First Regiment Armory in Chicago," *Harper's Weekly,* 3 December 1892, 1163; Hoffmann, *Architecture of John Wellborn Root,* 139–144; and Robert M. Fogelson, *America's Armories: Architecture, Society, and Public Order* (Cambridge: Harvard University Press, 1989), 81, 146–147, 151, 158–159, 160–162.

134. "Armory Is Burned," *Chicago Tribune,* 25 April 1893, 1–2, and "Appeal to the State," *Chicago Tribune,* 26 April 1893, 3. On the caretakers' entrapment, see William T. Stead, *Chicago To-day, or The Labour War in America* (London: Review of Reviews Office, 1894), 3–5, who took this incident as a metaphor for Chicago's workers caught within the fires of economic disruption then consuming the city as an edifice of commercialism. On Adler and Sullivan's "Trocadero Theater" in the First Regiment Armory, see Gregersen, *Dankmar Adler,* 86–87. On Florenz Ziegfeld Sr., father of the famous twentieth-century showman, see Flinn, *Hand-Book of Chicago Biography,* 395; Charles Higham, *Ziegfeld* (Chicago: Henry Regnery, 1972), 2–3; and Richard E. Ziegfeld and Paulette Ziegfeld, *The Ziegfeld Touch: The Life and Times of Florenz Ziegfeld, Jr.* (New York: Abrams, 1993), 13–17.

135. On the Chicago Citizens' Association's support for the militia, see its "Report of the Operation of the Two Committees Charged with the Collection of Funds and Purchase of Arms and Equipments for the Civic Forces," 1 October 1878, in *[Annual] Reports of the Citizens' Association of Chicago, 1874–5 to 1882–3*. On the Chicago Citizens' Law and Order League, see Andreas, *History of Chicago,* 3:288–290. Benefit concerts for the armory were described in "A Coming Musical Festival," *Indicator* 12 (4 January 1890): 4; Editorial, *Indicator* 12 (11 January 1890): 5; "The First Regiment Concerts," *Indicator* 12 (18 January 1890): 8, 9–10; and Edward C. Moore, *Forty Years of Opera in Chicago* (New York: Horace Liveright, 1930), 18. Earlier discussion between the Auditorium Association and the First Regiment about their sharing Peck's building was noted in "Music for the People," *Chicago Inter Ocean,* 3 May 1885, 6.

136. Garczynski, *Auditorium,* 111.

137. The Reverend Edward I. Galvin to Ferdinand W. Peck, 13 December 1889, in Auditorium, Dedication Volume (Newberry Library). On Galvin and the Chicago Athenaeum, see Andreas, *History of Chicago,* 3:417. On the Athenaeum's headquarters from 1890, see "Warming Its New Home," *Chicago Tribune,* 10 May 1891, 1; *Industrial Chicago,* 1:275; Flinn, *Chicago, the Marvelous City of the West,* 265; and Rand McNally, *Bird's-Eye Views and Guide to Chicago,* 31–32, reprinted in Randall, *Building Construction in Chicago,* 253. See also *Nineteenth Annual Report of the Chicago Athenaeum 1889–'90* (Chicago Historical Society). Planned inclusion of the Athenaeum in the Auditorium Building was noted in "The Chicago Auditorium," unidentified clipping (1889?) in "Early History and Press Clippings, Chicago Auditorium Association, 1887–1889" (Ryerson and Burnham Libraries, Art Institute of Chicago). Another account noted: "Many institutions of a more or less public character will find a home in the vast structure, such as the Athenaeum, the Chicago Conservatory of Music, and the United States Signal Service" (Charles H. Ham, "The Chicago Auditorium Building," *Harper's Weekly* 31 [2 July 1887]: 471). Of these, only the Athenaeum did not rent space in the Auditorium. On the Art Institute's patrons from its founding in 1879, see Andreas, *History of Chicago,* 3:421, and Horowitz, "Art Institute of Chicago."

138. "Widening Congress Street," *Chicago Tribune,* 10 February 1889, 6.

139. "The New Michigan Avenue Hotel," *Economist* 7 (29 March 1892): 424. See also "Chicago Real Estate," *Chicago Inter Ocean,* 20 March 1892, 9. Formerly an architect with Burnham and Root, Warren had previously designed the Lexington Hotel (1891–1892; later the New Michigan Hotel) on the northeast corner of South Michigan Avenue and Twenty-second Street (later Cermak Road), the Metropole (1891) at South Michigan Avenue at Twenty-third Street, the Victoria, and the Virginia (1889–1890; originally the Leander McCormick Apartments) on the northeast corner of Rush and Ohio Streets. Warren later designed the eight-story Plaza Hotel (1891–1892) at 1553 Clark Street on the North Side. On these hotels of Clinton J. Warren, see *Chicago and Its Resources Twenty Years After, 1871–1891: A Commercial History Showing the Progress and Growth of Two Decades from the Great Fire to the Present Time* (Chicago: Chicago Times, 1892), 16–20; Condit, *Chicago School,* 150–156; Westfall, "From Homes to Towers," 275–276; Westfall, "Development of American Apartment Houses," 184–191; and Bruegmann, *Architects and the City,* 317–318.

140. *Economist* 3 (14 June 1890): 765.

141. Ferdinand Peck, Annual Report of the President to the Stockholders of the Chicago Auditorium Association, 10 December 1892 (Auditorium Collection, Roosevelt University Archives). See also "The Auditorium," *Economist* 7 (30 April 1892): 650. On the first design, see "The New Michigan Avenue Hotel," *Economist* 7 (29 March 1892): 424. See also "Will Have No Rival," *Chicago Tribune,* 28 April 1892; "They Secure the Hotel," *Chicago Tribune,* 29 April 1892; and "Magnificent Ten Story Structure to Be Erected at the S.W. Corner of Michigan Avenue and Congress Street, Chicago," *Daily National Hotel Reporter* (Chicago), 30 April 1892, in "Early History and Press Clippings, Chicago Auditorium Association, Chicago, 1887–1889" (Ryerson and Burnham Libraries, Art Institute of Chicago).

142. R. Floyd Clinch, President, Chicago Auditorium Association, Testimony, in the United States Circuit Court of Appeals for the Seventh Circuit, October Term, A.D. 1925. No. 3733, Chicago Auditorium Association, Appellant, vs. Mark Skinner Willing and the Northern Trust Company as Trustees, etc., et al., Appellees, 228 (Auditorium Collection, Roosevelt University Archives). On the four-story building between the Auditorium Annex and the Congress Hotel, see "The Auditorium Annex," *Economist* 9 (1 April 1893): 444. Development of the west side of Michigan Avenue included structures like D. H. Burnham and Company's Railway Exchange Building (now the Santa Fe Center) on the northwest corner of Jackson in 1904. See "Michigan Boulevard," *Economist* 28 (8 November 1902): 625–626.

143. "Widening Congress Street," *Chicago Tribune*, 10 February 1889, 6. Another account of the period similarly noted: "The exterior surroundings of the Auditorium are yet far from resembling the Trocadero in Paris or the Ring in Vienna, but the nucleus is there and the first step toward creating a proper grand approach to the gigantic structure has been taken in the proceedings for widening Congress street" ("Peerless Patti Sang," *Chicago Herald*, 11 December 1889). On the coordinated architectural design of the Paris Opera and nearby buildings, see Van Zanten, *Building Paris*, 6–40, and Christopher C. Mead, "Urban Contingency and the Problem of Representation in Second-Empire Paris," *Journal of the Society of Architectural Historians* 54 (June 1995): 138–174.

CHAPTER 6

1. *Proceedings of the City Council of the City of Chicago for the Municipal Year 1889–90, Being from April 15, 1889 to April 8, 1890* (Chicago, 1890), 313–314, quoted in Francis L. Lederer, "Competition for the World's Columbian Exposition: The Chicago Campaign," *Journal of the Illinois State Historical Society* 65 (1972): 383. Other accounts of the exposition's early organization in 1889–1890 include Ben C. Truman, ed., *History of the World's Fair* (Chicago, 1893), 21–24; Hubert H. Bancroft, *The Book of the Fair* (Chicago, 1895), 37–39; Harlow N. Higinbotham, *Report of the President to the Board of Directors of the World's Columbian Exposition, 1892–1893* (New York, 1898), 7–8; and Rossiter Johnson, ed., *A History of the World's Columbian Exposition*, 4 vols. (New York, 1898), 1:7–18.

2. "Committees Getting Down to Business," *Chicago Tribune*, 6 August 1889, 2, and "Synoptical Resume of Important Events in the History of the World's Columbian Exposition to Date," *Presto* 7 (15 July 1890): 335. Johnson, *World's Columbian Exposition*, 1:13, reported that early in 1890 there were over 28,000 subscribers to the initial capital stock of $5,000,000. In addition to chairing the exposition's finance committee and serving on its executive committee, Peck was the fair's vice president and served on its board of reference and control, committee on legislation, and Special Committeee on Ceremonies. See Flinn, *Chicago, the Marvelous City of the West*, 538–539, and *Album of Genealogy and Biography* (2d ed.), 340.

3. See "The World's Fair," *Economist* 2 (31 August 1889): 764, which noted: "In this city all trades and all classes have been met halfway by the committee of 250 appointed by the Mayor and the various sub-committees. They feel that they are to bear their part in this great enterprise, and have a corresponding degree of interest in it. Thus far every class and people have promised to subscribe the amount alloted to them, and in some cases more." Organization of stock subscriptions by trades was noted in "Chicago the Favorite," *Chicago Tribune*, 7 August 1889, 2. See *List of Subscribers to the World's Exposition of 1892* (Chicago, 1892), at the Chicago Historical Society. Broad-based stock subscriptions began with London's Great Exhibition of 1851, presumably the model for later such efforts in the United States. See Yvonne Ffrench, *The Great Exhibition, 1851* (London: Harville, 1950), 45–47, 55; Patrick Beaver, *The Crystal Palace: A Portrait of Victorian Enterprise* (London: Hugh Evelyn, 1970), 13–14; Utz Haltern, *Die Londoner Weltausstellung von 1851: Eine Beitrag zur Geschichte der bürgerlich-industriellen Gesellschaft im 19 Jahrhundert* (Munich: Aschendorff, 1971), 89–98; and Jeffrey A. Auerbach, *The Great Exhibition of 1851: A Nation on Display* (New Haven: Yale University Press, 1999), 128–137.

4. Mayor Cregier, quoted in "Dedicated to Music and the People: Asked to Visit Chicago in 1892," *Chicago Tribune*, 10 December 1889, 1–2. The Auditorium Association's purchases of stock in the

Columbian Exposition were noted in Minutes of Executive Committee of Chicago Auditorium Association, 30 October and 19 December 1889, 156, 174 (Auditorium Collection, Roosevelt University Archives).

5. Quoted in "Beginning of the End," *Chicago Tribune*, 2 August 1889, 49. On "civic patriotism," especially among descendants of Chicago's pioneer residents like the Pecks, see Roberts, "Businessmen in Revolt," 247–249.

6. On Peck's trip to Washington in 1890, see Jean F. Block, *The Uses of Gothic: Planning and Building the Campus of the University of Chicago* (Chicago: University of Chicago Press, 1984), 3. On his role as a member of the university's first board of trustees, see Thomas W. Goodspeed, *A History of the University of Chicago: The First Quarter-Century* (Chicago: University of Chicago Press, 1916), 95; Goodspeed, *The Story of the University of Chicago, 1890–1925* (Chicago: University of Chicago Press, 1925), 74; and Richard J. Storr, *Harper's University: The Beginnings; a History of the University of Chicago* (Chicago: University of Chicago Press, 1966), 42–43, 67. Peck chaired the finance committee of the University of Chicago's board in 1891. On Chicago's fund-raising for the fair from February to December 1890, when Harrison officially proclaimed the city as the fair's site, see Reid F. Badger, *The Great American Fair: The World's Columbian Exposition and American Culture* (Chicago: Nelson Hall, 1979), 51–52, 55–56.

7. Peck, "The United States at the Paris Exposition in 1900," *North American Review* 168 (January 1899): 30.

8. Ibid.

9. On the labor struggles at the McCormick Reaper Works in the 1880s, see Robert Ozanne, *A Century of Labor-Management Relations at McCormick and International Harvester* (Madison: University of Wisconsin Press, 1967), 3–28. Accounts of the confrontation included "Victory! Sixteen Hundred Proletarians Engaged in a Battle for Bread," *Alarm* 1 (18 April 1885): 1, 3, and "Strikers Show Fight," *Chicago Herald*, 4 May 1886, 1. On overproduction as one cause of Chicago's labor upheaval in 1886, see Schneirov, *Labor and Urban Politics*, 184–191.

10. "Music and Drama," *Chicago Tribune*, 25 June 1889, 4. On the repertoire in the late 1880s, see Ludwig, "McVicker's Theatre," 104–105. On the fire, see "McVicker's Is in Ruins," *Chicago Tribune*, 26 August 1890, 1; "Was It Incendiarism?" *Chicago Tribune*, 27 August 1890, 1–2; Editorial, "The Theater Fire," *Chicago Tribune*, 27 August 1890, 4; "Examining the Ruins," *Chicago Tribune*, 28 August 1890, 8; and "Burning of McVicker's Theater," *Graphic* (Chicago), n.s., 3 (30 August 1890): 658.

11. "To Rebuild McVicker's," *Chicago Tribune*, 5 September 1890, 3, and "M'Vicker Theater Subscriptions," *Chicago Tribune*, 23 September 1890, 3. McVicker's then current production was moved to the Auditorium's stage. See "'Shenandoah' Survives," *Chicago Tribune*, 27 August 1890, 1. Later Paul Mueller, working with Adler and Sullivan in 1891, was said to recall that the remodeling "included no change in the seating and sight lines of the theater for McVicker is quoted as saying to the architects that he would do bodily harm to any man that interfered with or changed the perfect alignment that had been created before this 1890 fire. Mr. Mueller believes that the balcony pitches and the general alignment of the McVicker's auditorium were attributed to Mr. McVicker himself" (Arthur Woltersdorf, letter to Hugh Morrison, 3 August 1932, transcription in Richard Nickel Files, Office of John Vinci, AIA, Chicago). See also Woltersdorf, "Dankmar Adler," *Western Architect* 33 (July 1924): 77.

12. "The New McVicker's," *Chicago Tribune*, 5 October 1890, 37, and *Industrial Chicago*, 1:204. On McVicker's Theater as remodeled in 1890–1891, see *Observanda: McVicker's New Theatre, Chicago* (Chicago Historical Society); "The Restored McVicker's Theater," *Graphic* (Chicago), n.s., 4 (4 April 1891): 212, 224; Morrison, *Louis Sullivan*, 118–121; Twombly, *Louis Sullivan*, 254–255; Grimsley, "Contributions of Dankmar Adler," 338–357; Gregersen, *Dankmar Adler*, 57–58; and Van Zanten, *Sullivan's City*, 34–37.

13. "The Ventilation," in *Observanda: McVicker's New Theatre*.

14. McVicker, quoted in "Low Priced Theaters," *Chicago Evening Journal,* 8 January 1887, 3.

15. "Enter—New McVicker's," *Chicago Tribune,* 22 March 1891, 9. See also Austin Bierbower, *Life and Sermons of Dr. H. W. Thomas* (Chicago: Smith and Fobes, 1880); "Broad in His Faith," *Chicago Evening Post,* 14 April 1891, 9; Thomas W. Goodspeed, *University of Chicago Biographical Sketches* (Chicago: University of Chicago Press, 1922), 335–358; and Bluestone, *Constructing Chicago,* 101–103.

16. "Enter—New McVicker's," *Chicago Tribune,* 22 March 1891, 9.

17. "Electric Lights," in *Observanda: McVicker's New Theatre.*

18. Ibid.

19. Sullivan's surviving drawings for McVicker's ornamental plaster date from December 1890 to February 1891. See Sprague, "Architectural Ornament," 403–405, and *Drawings of Louis Henry Sullivan,* 39–42. See also Twombly and Menocal, *Louis Sullivan: The Poetry of Architecture,* 262–271.

20. "Enter—New McVicker's," *Chicago Tribune,* 22 March 1891, 9.

21. "The Decorations," in *Observanda: McVicker's New Theatre.* See "McVicker's Roosevelt Organ," *Presto* 8 (5 March 1891): 214, which noted that the instrument was to be used, with a six- or seven-piece orchestra, for both theatrical events and religious services.

22. "McVicker's Theatre," in *Observanda: McVicker's New Theatre.*

23. On Albert and Burridge's work at McVicker's, see "The Decorations," in *Observanda: McVicker's New Theatre;* and "Enter—New McVicker's," *Chicago Tribune,* 22 March 1891, 9. Albert's offer of service as a scenic artist for the Auditorium Theater's first season was noted in "Modern Stage Setting," *Chicago Tribune,* 21 July 1889. On Albert and Burridge, see *Chicago and Its Resources Twenty Years After,* 24–25; *Graphic* (Chicago), n.s., 6 (23 January 1892): 61; and Sparks, "Biographical Dictionary of Painters and Sculptors in Illinois," 241, 314–315.

24. "The Decorations," in *Observanda: McVicker's New Theatre* (1891).

25. Orear, *Commercial and Architectural Chicago,* 54.

26. "News of Stageland," *Chicago Evening Journal,* 26 May 1894, 10. Hoffmann, *Architecture of John Wellborn Root,* 166–176, explored the idea of Egyptian motifs in Chicago architecture. For a local view in 1890 of Egyptian architecture, see *Industrial Chicago,* 1:12–20. On sources for Sullivan's approach to conventionalization of natural forms, see Siry, *Carson Pirie Scott,* 153–154, 266 n. 90.

27. See Olson, "German Theater in Chicago," 68–123; Hofmeister, *Germans of Chicago,* 238–250; and Christine Heiss, "Kommerzielle deutsche Volksbühnen und deutsches Arbeitertheater," *Amerikastudien* 29 (1984): 169–182.

28. Bartow Adolphus Ulrich, *The Native Genius of the Germans and Their Destiny in America* (Chicago, 1885), 1, 16 (Chicago Historical Society).

29. "The Schiller Monument," *Chicago Tribune,* 8 November 1885, 16. The program for the statue's dedication included several essays on Chicago's German culture. See Theodor Gerbracht, ed., *Chicago's Schiller Denkmal: Erinnerungsblatt zur Enthüllungsfeier am 8. Mai 1886* (Chicago Historical Society). On the Goethe Monument, see Kaufmann, "Frank Lloyd Wright's 'Lieber Meister,'" 40–41, and Riedy, *Chicago Sculpture,* 190–196. On civic sculpture funded by Chicago's more prosperous ethnic groups during this period, see Bluestone, *Constructing Chicago,* 191–194.

30. On the Germania Club's building, see Rand McNally, *Bird's-Eye Views and Guide to Chicago,* 99, 196; Dominic A. Pacyga and Ellen Skerett, *Chicago, City of Neighborhoods: Histories and Tours* (Chicago: Loyola University Press, 1986); and Alice Sinkevitch and Laurie McGovern Petersen, eds., *AIA Guide to Chicago* (New York: Harcourt Brace, 1993), 170. The building, now known as Germania Place, was renovated for commercial use in 1992–1993 by Harold D. Rider and Nidata, Inc. See Gerard R. Wolfe, *Chicago, in and around the Loop: Walking Tours of Architecture and History* (New York: McGraw-Hill, 1996), 428. The Germania Club's building followed the construction in 1885–1887 of the elaborate building for New York's Arion Society, a German choral club, on the southeast corner of Fourth Avenue

and East Fifty-ninth Street. Its architects were DeLemos and Cordes. See Stern, Mellins, and Fishman, *New York 1880,* 233–234.

31. On Anton C. Hesing and the *Illinois Staats-Zeitung,* and on its relations with both the *Chicago Tribune* and the *Chicagoer Arbeiter-Zeitung,* see Hofmeister, *Germans of Chicago,* 152–164; Willis J. Abbot, "Chicago Newspapers and Their Makers," *Review of Reviews* 11 (January–June 1895): 646–665; David P. Nord, "The Public Community: The Urbanization of Journalism in Chicago," *Journal of Urban History* 11 (1985): 411–441; and John B. Jentz, "Class and Politics in an Emerging Industrial City: Chicago in the 1860s and 1870s," *Journal of Urban History* 17 (May 1991): 227–263. On workers' newspapers after Haymarket, see Nelson, *Beyond the Martyrs,* 211–216.

32. "Der Schauspieldirektor scheint heuzutage nor noch ein Spekulant zu sein, der die Köpfe in Theater and die Dollars in den Kasse zählt." See review of Mannstadt, *Der tolle Wenzel,* in *Illinois Staats-Zeitung,* 13 February 1888, quoted in Olson, "German Theater in Chicago," 96. Olson noted that the principal play staged for the 1889 Schiller festival was *Kabale und Liebe* (Intrigue and love), the same play Chicago's first German theater in Deutsches Haus had opened with in 1858. See chapter 1, 18. Also presented in 1889 was Schiller's drama *Maria Stuart,* on the sixteenth-century queen of Scotland.

33. "The German Theater Project," *Economist* 3 (12 April 1890): 429–430. See also "A Big German Theater," *Chicago Tribune,* 31 March 1890, 3. On Chicago's German population totals, see Townsend, "Germans of Chicago," 16; Pierce, *History of Chicago,* 3:22–23; Hirsch, *Urban Revolt,* 150; and Hofmeister, *Germans of Chicago,* 13–18. On Franz Amberg, see Emil Dietzsch, *Chicago's Deutsche Männer: Erinnerungs-Blätter an Chicago's Fünfzigjähriges Jubiläum Geschichte der Stadt Chicago* (Chicago: M. Stern, 1885), 321–322. On Adler and Sullivan's Schiller Building, see *Industrial Chicago,* 1:223–224; Barr Ferree, "Architecture," *Engineering Magazine* 4 (October 1892–March 1893): 297–298; Ferree, "The Modern Office Building, Part III," *Inland Architect and News Record* 27 (June 1896): 45; "Chicago," *American Architect and Building News* 39 (4 February 1893): 72; Bannister Fletcher, "American Architecture through English Spectacles," *Engineering Magazine* 7 (June 1894): 318–319; George M. R. Twose, "Steel and Terra-Cotta Buildings in Chicago, and Some Deductions," *Brickbuilder* 3 (January 1894): 3; Morrison, *Louis Sullivan,* 156–162; Condit, *Chicago School,* 128–133; Condit, "The Structural System of Adler and Sullivan's Garrick Theater Building," *Technology and Culture* 5 (fall 1964): 523–540; Sprague, "Adler and Sullivan's Schiller Building," *Prairie School Review* 2 (second quarter 1965): 5–20; Weingarden, "Louis H. Sullivan's Search for an American Style," in *Fragments of Chicago's Past,* ed. Saliga, 118–125; Twombly, *Louis Sullivan,* 293–296; Theodore W. Hild, "The Demolition of the Garrick Theater and the Birth of the Preservation Movement in Chicago," *Illinois Historical Journal* 88 (1995): 79–100; Van Zanten, *Sullivan's City,* 37, 57–59; and Twombly, "A Poet's Garden: Louis Sullivan's Vision for America," in *Louis Sullivan: The Poetry of Architecture,* by Twombly and Menocal, 36–38.

34. "Home for the Germans," *Chicago Tribune,* 3 May 1891, 10.

35. "Chicago's New Playhouse," *New York Times,* 30 September 1892, 4. On German comedies in New York, see Marvin Felheim, *The Theater of Augustin Daly: An Account of the Late Nineteenth Century American Stage* (Cambridge: Harvard University Press, 1956), 141–185. On the Germania Theater, see T. Allston Brown, *History of the New York Stage, from the First Performance in 1732 to 1902,* 3 vols. (New York: Dodd, Mead, 1903), 3:307–310, and Henderson, *City and the Theatre,* 139, 141.

36. "The German Theater Project," *Economist* 3 (12 April 1890): 429–430. Hesing stressed the importance of a central location in his speech at the theater's dedication. See "Gewieht! Das Schiller Theater," *Illinois Staats-Zeitung,* 30 September 1892, 5, where Hesing was quoted: "Es war, wie ich wohl wuste, nicht so leicht, im Mittelpunkt der Stadt den geeigneten Bauplatz zu finden, und als sich die Gelegenheit zeigte, diesen Platz, auf dem unser Haus steht, gewinnen zu können, machte ich diejenigen Herren darauf aufmerksam, die sich gleich mir für die Sache interessirten" ("It was, as I well wished, not so easy to find the suitable building site in the middle of the city, and when the opportunity showed itself, that this site, on which our building stands, could be gained, I called it to the attention of these gentlemen, who like me interested themselves in the affair").

37. Ffrench, *Music and Musicians in Chicago*, 52–53.

38. "German Opera House Building," *Economist* 5 (14 February 1891): 253. On the city's German cuisine of the period, see Dietzsch, *Chicago's Deutsche Männer*, 31–32, and Duis, *Challenging Chicago*, 148–149.

39. "German Opera House Building," *Economist* 5 (14 February 1891): 253.

40. On the Deutsches Stadt Theater, see Grimsley, "Contributions of Dankmar Adler," 227–238; Gregersen, *Dankmar Adler*, 76–77; and Van Zanten, *Sullivan's City*, 34.

41. "The German Theater Project," *Economist* 3 (12 April 1890): 430.

42. Dankmar Adler, "Light in Tall Office Buildings," *Engineering Magazine* 4 (November 1892): 183. See also Sullivan, "The High Building Question," *Graphic* (Chicago), n.s., 5 (19 December 1891): 136–138, in *Louis Sullivan: The Public Papers*, ed. Twombly, 76–79; Donald Hoffmann, "'The Setback Skyscraper of 1891': An Unknown Essay by Louis H. Sullivan," *Journal of the Society of Architectural Historians* 29 (May 1970): 181–187; and Twombly, "Poet's Garden," 44–46.

43. "Home for the Germans," *Chicago Tribune*, 3 May 1891, 10.

44. "German Opera House Building," *Economist* 5 (14 February 1891): 253.

45. "Schiller Rings Up: It Is Completely Fireproof," *Chicago Tribune*, 30 September 1892, 5.

46. Ibid. See also Engelbrecht, "Adler & Sullivan's Pueblo Opera House," 289 (figs. 18 and 20).

47. "Mit der endgültigen Abschassung der vielen Ränge, Parterres, Winkelchen and Eckchen aller Art hat die modern Theater-Architectur einen gewaltigen Schritt vörwarts gethan. Denn, der Hauptvortheil den Bereinfachung and Raumvermehrung liegt in der Erhöhung der Sicherheit des Publikums. Der moderne Architect verwandelt das Theater also in einen freien Raum, und stellt sich damit die neue Aufgabe, eine künstleriche und majestätische Wandbefleidung zu schaffen" ("Geweiht! Das Schiller-Theater," *Illinois Staats-Zeitung*, 30 September 1892, 5).

48. Anton C. Hesing, quoted in "Schiller Rings Up," *Chicago Tribune*, 30 September 1892, 1.

49. "Schiller Rings Up," *Chicago Tribune*, 30 September 1892, 1. Stenciling on the balcony ceiling and other interior surfaces was discovered under layers of paint in the course of efforts to preserve fragments of Sullivan's ornament during the Schiller's demolition in 1961 ("Find New Friezes in Garrick Building," *Chicago Sun-Times*, 23 July 1961).

50. "Chicago," *American Architect and Building News* 39 (4 February 1893): 72.

51. "Chicago's New Playhouse," *New York Times*, 30 September 1892, 4.

52. "Chicago," *American Architect and Building News* 39 (4 February 1893): 72.

53. "Er mag sich nun in Musse der Betrachtung der inneren Ausstattung hingehen und wird auch hier in steigenden Bewunderung, bei all dem Goldgeflimmer, Farbenschusser und Bilderschmuck bald eine Idee finden, welche die Anlage des Ganzen zu einer Einheit zusammenschliest" ("Geweiht! Das Schiller-Theater," *Illinois Staats-Zeitung*, 30 September 1892, 5).

54. Hesing, quoted in "Schiller Rings Up," *Chicago Tribune*, 30 September 1892, 1.

55. "Miscellaneous," *Economist* 7 (14 January 1892): 84. See also "Chicago's New Playhouse," *New York Times*, 30 September 1892, 4.

56. Hesing, quoted in "Schiller Rings Up," *Chicago Tribune*, 30 September 1892, 1.

57. The Schiller's interior iconography was noted in "Geweiht! Das Schiller-Theater," *Illinois Staats-Zeitung*, 30 September 1892, 5; and "Schiller Rings Up," *Chicago Tribune*, 30 September 1892, 5. See also Donald P. Hallmark, "Richard W. Bock, Sculptor, Part I: The Early Work," *Prairie School Review* 8 (first quarter, 1971): 9–12, and Dorathi Bock Pierre, ed., *Memoirs of an American Artist: Sculptor Richard W. Bock* (Los Angeles: C. C. Publishing, 1989), 45–47. On Arthur Feudel[l], see *Graphic* (Chicago), n.s., 4 (20 June 1891): 391. On the Greek ideal in German literary thought in the eighteenth and nineteenth centuries, see Eliza M. Butler, *The Tyranny of Greece over Germany: A Study of the Influence Exercised*

by Greek Art and Poetry over the Great German Writers of the Eighteenth, Nineteenth, and Twentieth Centuries (Boston: Beacon Press, 1958).

58. Vynne, *Chicago by Day and Night,* 47. On German parades in Chicago, see Hofmeister, *Germans of Chicago,* 58, 113, and Miller, *City of the Century,* 469.

59. Ferree, "Modern Office Building," 45. At the Schiller's dedication, Hesing "paid eloquent tributes to F. Almenröder, the sculptor of the heads which adorn the façade, to Messrs. Healy and Millett [*sic*], who had charge of decorating the interior, and to Richard W. Bock" ("Schiller Rings Up," *Chicago Tribune,* 30 September 1892, 1).

60. On the Manhattan, see "New Business Buildings of Chicago," *Builder* 63 (9 July 1892): 24; Flinn, *Chicago, the Marvelous City of the West* (1892), 580; Rand McNally, *Bird's-Eye Views and Guide to Chicago,* 80, 81; Ericsson, *Sixty Years a Builder,* 105–108, 237–239, 262–263; Tallmadge, *Architecture in Old Chicago,* 200; Randall, *Building Construction in Chicago,* 120; Condit, *Chicago School,* 91–92; and Turak, *William Le Baron Jenney,* 280–286. On Heisen, see Berger, *They Built Chicago,* 105–112. On the Schiller Building's tower, see also Van Zanten, *Sullivan's City,* 57–58.

61. "German Opera House Building," *Economist* 5 (14 February 1891): 253.

62. Sullivan, quoted in Thomas Cusack, "Lessons from the Home Life Building Fire," *Brickbuilder* 8 (January 1893): 15. On the Northwestern Terra-Cotta Company's working methods, see Sharon S. Darling, *Chicago Ceramics and Glass: An Illustrated History from 1871 to 1933* (Chicago: Chicago Historical Society, 1979), 175.

63. Fletcher, "American Architecture through English Spectacles," 318. Praise for the Schiller Building's exterior also appeared in Jacques Hermant, "L'architecture aux États-Unis et à l'exposition universelle de Chicago: L'architecture en Amérique et à la World's Fair," *L'Architecture* 7 (20 October 1894): 342, and in Karl Hinckeldyn, "Architekten Verein zu Berlin," *Deutsche Bauzeitung* 29 (13 March 1895): 130. See Lewis, *Early Encounter with Tomorrow,* 229–230 n. 53.

64. Fletcher, "American Architecture through English Spectacles," 318. One critic wrote that Burnham and Root's Masonic Temple was meant to "be an honor to Masonry, and do as much to distinguish it as the Auditorium has done to honor its promoters" ("Grand Home for Masons," *Chicago Tribune,* 6 April 1890, 26).

65. Performances of works by Schiller and others in the new theater prompted Chicago's English-language newspapers to concede that local German theater was then ahead of the city's English-speaking stage ("Schiller-Theater," *Der Westen* [Sunday edition of *Illinois Staats-Zeitung*], 9 October 1892, 4, quoted in Olson, "German Theater in Chicago," 99).

66. "Unser deutsches Theater," *Fackel* (Sunday edition of *Chicagoer Arbeiter-Zeitung*), 18 January 1888, translated and quoted in Heiss, "Popular and Working-Class German Theater," 201. On Lyser, see Keil and Ickstadt, "Elements of German Working-Class Culture," 99–101.

67. See "Chicagoer Stadttheater," *Illinois Staats-Zeitung,* 6 September 1896, and on *Ausgewiesen,* "Schillertheater. *Ausgewiesen," Illinois Staats-Zeitung,* 9 January 1893, and "*Ausgewiesen:* Die gestrige Vorstellung im Schillertheater," *Chicagoer Arbeiter-Zeitung,* 9 January 1893, as discussed in Heiss, "Popular and Working-Class German Theater," 189–190, 191–192.

68. On the remodeling of Hooley's, see Lyman Beecher Glover, *The Story of a Theatre* (Chicago, 1898), 35, 44. See also *Economist* 19 (30 April 1898): 498–499. Wilson and Marshall had previously remodeled Adler and Sullivan's interior in 1893 for the theater manager Harry J. Powers, who also commissioned the remodeling of 1897–1898. In 1889 the postfire McCormick Hall north of the Clark Street bridge was remodeled in a neoclassical style. See "New Temple of Drama," *Chicago Tribune,* 21 October 1889, 6. On the Chicago (later Great Northern) Hotel, Office, and Theater, see Flinn, *Chicago, the Marvelous City of the West,* 580; Rand McNally, *Bird's-Eye Views and Guide to Chicago,* 24, 52; *Inland Architect and News Record* 28 (September 1896), special supplement; Randall, *Building Construction in Chicago,* 128; Hoffmann, *Architecture of John Wellborn Root,* 151–154; and Lowe, *Chicago Interiors,* 38–39.

Root, "Architects of Chicago," *Inland Architect and News Record* 16 (January 1891): 92, wrote: "The Auditorium, a really wonderful building, stands as a monument to [Adler's] and Sullivan's talent." Moresque decoration recurred in the Alhambra Theater at State and Twentieth Streets, of 1890 and the Arcade Theater at 156–164 Clark Street, of 1892. See "Chicago," *Presto* 7 (16 August 1890): 403, and Hirsch and Goler, *City Comes of Age*, 130. On later rejection of Sullivan's style, see Sullivan, *Autobiography of an Idea*, 321–326.

69. On the exposition's sponsors' ball at the Auditorium, see "Societies in Parade," *Chicago Tribune*, 21 October 1892, 5. On the Thursday parade as seen from the Auditorium's tower, see "Viewed from Above," *Chicago Tribune*, 10. On crowds at the building's base, see "In Front of the Auditorium," *Chicago Tribune*, 3. On the World's Congress Auxiliary's dedication, see Higinbotham, *Report of the President to the Board of Directors*, appendix A: World's Congress Auxiliary, 328. The order of precedence for the procession on Friday, 21 October, was in *World's Columbian Exposition: Dedicatory Ceremonies; Chicago, Oct[ober] 20th 21st and 22nd, 1892. Official Souvenir Programme*. See also *Dedicatory and Opening Ceremonies of the World's Columbian Exposition, Memorial Volume* (Chicago, 1893).

70. "Amusements," *Elite* 11 (15 April 1893): 18. See also "Opening of 'America' Delayed," *Chicago Tribune*, 16 April 1893, 44. The attraction of *America* meant that "the net profit from the operation of the theatre for the World's Fair year ending November 30, 1893 was $294,227.79 before the charges on the [Auditorium] Association books. That was the most profitable year in the history of the theatre" (Testimony of William W. Gilkenson, in Chicago Auditorium Association vs. Mark Skinner Willing and the Northern Trust Company, as Trustees, etc., et al., in the United States Circuit Court of Appeals for the Seventh Circuit, October Term, A.D. 1925, no. 3733, p. 271). Chicago's wealthy had previously staged a similar production at the Auditorium for charity, titled "The Four Hundredth Anniversary, or the National Pageant," which had also been shown in eastern cities. See "Pictures of Our History," *Chicago Tribune*, 2 March 1890, Part Four; "From Youth to Manhood," *Chicago Tribune*, 19 March 1890, 2; and "Told a Nation's Story," *Chicago Tribune*, 11 September 1891, 2.

71. "In the Playhouses," *Chicago Evening Journal*, 28 April 1894, 10. After its highly successful run at the Auditorium ended, *America* played in New York, Boston, Philadelphia, and other eastern cities before returning to McVicker's Theater on 29 April 1894.

72. "The Exposition Bonds," *Economist* 8 (24 September 1892): 435. On the exposition's costs and receipts, see "The World's Fair," *Economist*, annual number, 10 (1 January 1894): 25; Higinbotham, *Report of the President to the Board of Directors*, appendix C: Report of the Auditor to the President, 30 June 1895, 339–354; and Badger, *Great American Fair*, appendix H, 140.

73. Charles H. Hermann, *Recollections of Life and Doings in Chicago from the Haymarket Riot to the End of World War I* (Chicago: Normandie House, 1945), 109. On attendance, see *Dedicatory and Opening Ceremonies of the World's Columbian Exposition, Memorial Volume* (Chicago, 1893), 37–38, and Badger, *Great American Fair*, 109.

74. "Fair Debt Wiped Out," *Chicago Tribune*, 10 October 1893, 3. See also "713, 646: This Is Chicago Day's Marvelous Record at the Fair," *Chicago Tribune*, 10 October 1893, 2; "Official Chicago-Day Program," *Chicago Tribune*, 10 October 1893, 1; and "From Canoe to Skyscraper," *Chicago Tribune*, 10 October 1893, 18–19. Peck characteristically raised funds for free tickets for poor children to attend the fair that day. See G. L. Dybward and Joy V. Bliss, *Chicago Day at the World's Columbian Exposition: Illustrated with Candid Photographs* (Albuquerque: Book Stops Here, 1997), 20. On Chicago Day, see also Smith, *Urban Disorder and the Shape of Belief*, 266–267.

75. On the choice of Jackson Park, see Higinbotham, *Report of the President to the Board of Directors*, 19–25, and Badger, *Great American Fair*, 63–71.

76. On Burnham's proposal to Adler and Sullivan to design the Music Hall, see David H. Crook, "Louis Sullivan and the Golden Doorway," *Journal of the Society of Architectural Historians* 26 (December 1967): 254–255.

77. Daniel Burnham, *The Final Official Report of the Director of Works of the World's Columbian Exposition: The Book of the Builders,* 2 vols. (1894; reprint, New York: Garland, 1989), 1:9.

78. On the fair's board of architects, see Burnham, "The Organization of the World's Columbian Exposition," delivered before the World's Congress of Architects, Chicago, 1 August 1893, *Inland Architect and News Record* 22 (August 1893): 6. On Sullivan's idea for a Transportation Building, see Crook, "Sullivan and the Golden Doorway," 255.

79. Charles Norman Fay to Philo Otis, 20 October 1916, quoted in Otis, *Chicago Symphony Orchestra,* 28. On Thomas's move to Chicago, see also Schabas, *Theodore Thomas,* 181–187.

80. *Chicago Record,* 22 October 1892, quoted in Lloyd Lewis and Henry J. Smith, *Chicago: The History of Its Reputation* (New York: Harcourt, Brace, 1929), 200. The Special Committee on Ceremonies' detailed planning of this event from August through October 1892 is recorded in *Minutes of the Meeting of the Council of Administration of the World's Columbian Exposition,* 9 vols. (Chicago, 1892), held by the Chicago Public Library. Later accounts of the opening include Otis, *Chicago Symphony Orchestra,* 39–40; Badger, *Great American Fair,* 83–85; Schabas, *Theodore Thomas,* 201–202; and especially Ellen M. Litwicki, "'The Inauguration of the People's Age': The Columbian Quadricentennial and American Culture," *Maryland Historian* 20 (1989): 47–58. On Milward Adams (1857–1923), see Ffrench, *Music and Musicians in Chicago,* 54–55.

81. Peck wrote of the Paris exposition of 1900: "Its architecture was chaste, dignified, and worthy—a reminiscence of the beautiful White City on the shore of Lake Michigan, which was the delight of millions gathered from all quarters of the globe" (*Report of the Commissioner-General for the United States to the International Universal Exposition, Paris, 1900,* 6 (Washington, D.C., 1901), 1:60).

82. On the exposition's Music Hall and Choral or Festival Hall, see Rand McNally, *Handbook of the World's Columbian Exposition* (Chicago: Rand McNally, 1893), 113, 142. The Music Hall as a substitute in Jackson Park for the distant Auditorium was noted in "World's Fair Music Hall," *Presto* 8 (25 March 1891): 252.

83. On Thomas's musical program for the World's Columbian Exposition, see Ffrench, *Music and Musicians in Chicago,* 33–35; Otis, *Chicago Symphony Orchestra,* 44–54; and Schabas, *Theodore Thomas,* 195–212, who (207) reported the Music Hall's poor acoustics. Initial positive reports of the hall's acoustics appeared in "Test of Music Hall: Apollo Club Sings and Critics Present Are Pleased," *Chicago Tribune,* 24 April 1893, 1. The idea of a national chorus was described in "Mr. Pratt's Plan for World's Fair Music," *Presto* 8 (18 June 1891): 1.

84. Rose F. Thomas to Frances Glessner, 3 May 1892, in Frances Glessner Journals, Chicago Historical Society, box 3, 18 October 1891–26 June 1892, 104–105, quoted in Schabas, *Theodore Thomas,* 190–191.

85. "Razing an Elephant," *Chicago Evening Journal,* 12 October 1893, reprinted in Young, *Documents of American Theater History,* 1:307.

86. Subscribers to the Spectatorium as of 24 August were noted in MacKaye, *Epoch,* 2:338. On this project, see Hannon D. Leroy, "The MacKaye Spectatorium: A Reconstruction and Analysis of a Theatrical Spectacle Planned for the World's Columbian Exposition of 1893 with a History of Producing Organizations" (Ph.D. diss., Tulane University, 1970); Turak, *William Le Baron Jenney,* 307–315; and Larry Anderson, "Yesterday's City: Steele MacKaye's Grandiose Folly," *Chicago History* 16 (fall/winter 1987–1988): 104–114.

87. Columbian Celebration Company, press release, 12 March 1893, quoted in MacKaye, *Epoch,* 2:379.

88. "Big Thing for the Fair," *Chicago Times,* August 1892, quoted in MacKaye, *Epoch,* 337.

89. MacKaye, quoted in *Lincoln (Nebr.) State Journal,* 4 April 1893, reprinted in Young, *Documents of American Theater History,* 1:305.

90. McConachie, "Pacifying American Theatrical Audiences," 62–64. See also William Winter, *The Life of David Belasco,* 2 vols. (1925; reprint, New York: B. Blom, 1972).

91. "Razing an Elephant," *Chicago Evening Journal,* 12 October 1893, reprinted in Young, *Documents of American Theater History,* 1:307.

92. Steele MacKaye, Introduction, *Spectatorio: The World Finder,* produced at the Scenitorium, Chicago, 5 February 1894, quoted in MacKaye, *Epoch,* 2:311–312.

93. Steele MacKaye to Mrs. Mary MacKaye (wife), 22 January 1892, quoted in MacKaye, *Epoch,* 2:317.

94. On the Scenitorium, see MacKaye, *Epoch,* 2:438–457. On the Chicago Fire Cyclorama and other cycloramas in the vicinity, see chapter 2, 112, and note 186.

95. There was considerable overlap between the membership of the New York Stock Exchange (listed in Francis L. Eames, *The New York Stock Exchange* [New York: Thomas G. Hall, 1894], 123–139) and the Metropolitan Opera House's patronage. One linking figure between the two institutions was Cornelius Vanderbilt's son, William K. Vanderbilt, who inherited his father's control over the New York Central Railroad. In 1879 William began to work with J. P. Morgan to maintain family control of the railroad by marketing its stock overseas, which Morgan did. William thereby helped begin the rise of investment banking on Wall Street at just the time when he led in organizing the Metropolitan Opera House in 1880. On Vanderbilt and Morgan, see Robert Sobel, *The Big Board: A History of the New York Stock Market* (New York: Free Press, 1965), 108, and Harold U. Faulkner, *The Decline of Laissez Faire, 1897–1917* (New York: Rinehart, 1951), 37–38. On the concept of cultural capital, see John Guillory, *Cultural Capital: the Problem of Literary Canon Formation* (Chicago: University of Chicago Press, 1993), and Pierre Bourdieu, *The Field of Cultural Production: Essays on Art and Literature* (New York: Columbia University Press, 1993).

96. Eames, *New York Stock Exchange,* 88–89. On Kellum's building of 1864–1865 and its transformations, see Deborah S. Gardner, "The Architecture of Commercial Capitalism: John Kellum and the Development of New York, 1840–1875" (Ph.D. diss., Columbia University, 1979), 125–160; Landau and Condit, *Rise of the New York Skyscraper,* 55; and Stern, Mellins, and Fishman, *New York 1880,* 458–460.

97. Eames, *New York Stock Exchange,* 69–70. In the board room of the 1890s, the most active stocks (about twenty in 1893) accounted for over 80 percent of the exchange's total trading volume. Most of these stocks were shares in companies headquartered in New York, so that their operations were well known locally to exchange members. Exchange employees recorded all sales, including price and number of shares, and placed the information with telegraph companies that distributed it nationally and to Europe by means of stock tickers. At certain hours, dealers and brokers in bonds also gathered to trade at an allotted place in this board room. As with stocks, the most active bonds were not those of industrial companies but those of railroads. Most of these railroad companies had main offices in Manhattan, often near the exchange. Also nearby were brokerage offices and banks at which deposits on purchased stocks were made. Roofed trading halls were an innovation of the nineteenth century. Early modern European stock exchanges, like those of London and Amsterdam, had been outdoor courtyards. See Pevsner, *History of Building Types,* 199.

98. North of Post's templelike facade, a twenty-two-story addition on Wall Street was built in 1923. On Post's New York Stock Exchange (1901–1903) and its addition (1923), designed by Trowbridge and Livingston, see Percy C. Stuart, "The New York Stock Exchange," *Architectural Record* 11 (July 1901): 526–552; "Addition to New York Stock Exchange," *Architectural Record* 48 (September 1920): 192; and Stern, Gilmartin, and Massengale, *New York 1900,* 187–189.

99. I. A. Fleming, *The Chicago Stock Exchange: An Historical Sketch with Biographies of Its Leading Members* (Chicago: Excelsior, 1894), and Wallace Rice, *The Chicago Stock Exchange: A History* (Chicago: Committee on Library of the Chicago Stock Exchange, 1923), 15–17. Histories of the Chicago Stock Ex-

change to the opening of Adler and Sullivan's building also appeared in "Temple for Brokers," *Chicago Evening Journal*, 28 April 1894, 5, and "Temple of Finance," *Chicago Evening Post*, 30 April 1894, 3.

100. "Temple for Brokers," *Chicago Evening Journal*, 28 April 1894, 5.

101. A list of the Chicago Stock Exchange's members was published in "Temple of Finance," *Chicago Evening Post*, 30 April 1894, 3. In 1886 the Chicago Stock Exchange was doing so little business that some members wanted to disband it and recover their investment in membership fees ("The Stock Exchange," *Chicago Evening Journal*, 10 November 1886, 1; "The Stock Exchange," *Chicago Evening Journal*, 19 November 1886, 5).

102. "Chicago Industrials," *Economist* 8 (22 October 1892): 579–580.

103. Flinn, *Chicago, the Marvelous City of the West*, 261. During 1893, stocks in forty-six local companies, and bonds of twenty-six firms, were traded on the Chicago Stock Exchange. See "The Year's Business on the Chicago Stock Exchange," *Economist* 10 (1 January 1894): 12. On the various stocks traded and the local impact of the World's Columbian Exposition, see Rice, *Chicago Stock Exchange*, 30–32. See also *Chicago Stock Exchange, Daily Report*, from 1 May 1878 (Chicago Historical Society).

104. Flinn, *Chicago, the Marvelous City of the West*, 261.

105. Ibid. See "Sales at the New York Stock Exchange," in Eames, *New York Stock Exchange*, 95. In 1889 one observer wrote: "In respect to the volume of business the gap between the New York and Chicago exchanges is a wide one, but it will be narrowed in the next few years" ("The Chicago Stock Exchange," *Economist* 7 [2 November 1889]: 996).

106. "The Chicago Stock Exchange," *Economist* 7 (2 November 1889): 996, and Rice, *Chicago Stock Exchange*, 29. On the Chicago Stock Exchange's various quarters before completion of Adler and Sullivan's building, see "Chicago Stock Board: The Exchange about to Move into Its New Quarters on Dearborn Street," *Chicago Evening Journal*, 5 October 1889, 10, and "Temple for Brokers," *Chicago Evening Journal*, 28 April 1894, 5.

107. "Various Real Estate Matters," *Economist* 8 (17 December 1892): 862.

108. On Philip Peck's house of 1837 on the southwest corner of LaSalle and Washington, see chapter 1, 13–15, and note 10. Ferdinand Peck's oldest brother, Walter, was born in this building after the Pecks took possession in 1840. After the Pecks left later in the decade, the house was used as Chicago's police headquarters until it was demolished in 1868. See "Temple of Finance: Building and Exchange Hall," *Chicago Evening Post*, 30 April 1894, 2, and "Temple for Brokers," *Chicago Evening Journal*, 28 April 1894, 5.

109. "The Lease Will Be Changed," *Economist* 8 (9 July 1892): 54.

110. Ibid.

111. "A Great Improvement," *Economist* 8 (10 December 1892): 827. At first the Pecks reportedly wanted a rental of $30,000 a year from the Chicago Stock Exchange for half of their new building's ground floor, a demand reduced later to $10,000 but not accepted by the exchange. It proposed taking the second floor rent-free for twenty years, finally agreeing to rent half the second and third floors for fifteen years at $1 per year ("Temple of Finance: The Building and Exchange Hall," *Chicago Evening Post*, 30 April 1894, 2).

112. "New Stock Exchange Building," *Chicago Tribune*, 13 December 1892, 30, and Rice, *Chicago Stock Exchange*, 34–35.

113. "Various Real Estate Matters: As to LaSalle Street," *Economist* 9 (14 January 1893): 48.

114. "A Loan of $600,000," *Economist* 9 (29 April 1893): 596. On Edward C. Waller as a major investor in the Rookery, see Kuhn, "Financing of Commercial Structures," 49, and Hoffmann, *Architecture of John Wellborn Root*, 66. A resident of suburban Oak Park, Waller was also a friend of Frank Lloyd Wright in the 1890s, as noted in many sources, such as Brendan Gill, *Many Masks: A Life of Frank Lloyd Wright* (New York: Putnam, 1987), 109, 111, and 117.

115.   "A Loan of $600,000," *Economist* 9 (29 April 1893): 596, and "Temple for Brokers," *Chicago Evening Journal,* 28 April 1894, 5.

116.   Flinn, *Chicago, the Marvelous City of the West,* 261. On Adler and Sullivan's Chicago Stock Exchange Building of 1893–1894, accounts other than those in newspapers included *The Chicago Stock Exchange Building* (1894), rental pamphlet (Ryerson and Burnham Libraries, Art Institute of Chicago); Fleming, *Chicago Stock Exchange;* George M. R. Twose, "Steel and Terra-Cotta Buildings in Chicago," *Brickbuilder* 3 (January 1894): 3; "The Chicago Stock Exchange Building," *Economist* 11 (20 January 1894): 71; "Chicago," *American Architect and Building News* 43 (20 January 1894): 31; "Chicago Stock Exchange Building, Chicago," *Ornamental Iron* 2 (July 1894): 7–13; "Recent Brick and Terra Cotta Work in American Cities," *Brickbuilder* 4 (June 1895): 132–133; and Montgomery Schuyler, *Critique of the Works of Adler and Sullivan* (1896), in *"American Architecture" and Other Writings,* ed. Jordy and Coe, 2:389–390. Later accounts include Sullivan, "Development of Construction" (1916), in *Louis Sullivan: The Public Papers,* ed. Twombly, 221–222; Rice, *Chicago Stock Exchange;* Morrison, *Louis Sullivan,* 169–172; Randall, *Building Construction in Chicago,* 137; Condit, *Chicago School,* 136–138; Edward Lee Michael, "Adler & Sullivan's Palace of Trade: The Chicago Stock Exchange Building," seminar paper for Professor Paul E. Sprague, University of Chicago, spring 1972; John Vinci, "The Chicago Stock Exchange Building," *Chicago History* 3 (spring–summer 1974): 23–27; Vinci, *The Trading Room: Louis Sullivan and the Chicago Stock Exchange,* 2d ed. (Chicago: Art Institute of Chicago, 1989); Twombly, *Louis Sullivan,* 313–317; Saliga, *Fragments of Chicago's Past,* 139–141; Frei, *Louis Henry Sullivan,* 110–113; Elia, *Louis Henry Sullivan,* 109–110; Van Zanten, *Sullivan's City,* 64; and Twombly and Menocal, *Louis Sullivan: The Poetry of Architecture,* 40, 98–100.

117.   Adler, "Tall Office Buildings—Past and Future," *Engineering Magazine* 3 (September 1892): 768.

118.   "Chicago Stock Exchange Building," *Economist* 11 (20 January 1894): 71. A crystalline or chipped glass may have been used for the translucent partitions along the office corridors. See Siry, "Adler and Sullivan's Guaranty Building in Buffalo," 29, 30, 36 n. 99.

119.   "New Palace of Trade," *Chicago Record,* 28 April 1894, 3. John H. Jones and Fred A. Britten, eds., *A Half Century of Chicago Building: A Practical Reference Guide* (Chicago, 1910), 39, noted 410 offices at that time, while newspaper accounts of 1894 gave figures of over 400.

120.   William G. Purcell, "Sullivan's Businessman and the Stock Exchange Building (1948)," Louis Sullivan Centennial Exhibition File (1956), Museum Archives, Art Institute of Chicago. On the building's occupancy rate, see Morrison, *Louis Sullivan,* 172, and Condit, *Chicago School,* 137. The building continued to be nearly fully rented to the time of its demolition ("Developers Seek to Raze the Old Stock Exchange Building," *Chicago Sun Times,* 1 December 1969, 66).

121.   Purcell, "Sullivan's Businessman and the Stock Exchange Building (1948)." Sullivan, "Tall Office Building Artistically Considered" (1896), wrote: "Whether it be the sweeping eagle in his flight or the open apple-blossom, the toiling work-horse, the blithe swan, the branching oak, the winding stream at its base, the drifting clouds, over all the coursing sun, form ever follows function, and this is the law. Where function does not change form does not change" (*Louis Sullivan: The Public Papers,* ed. Twombly, 111). By 1909 Sullivan owned Eadweard Muybridge, *Animal Locomotion* (Philadelphia: University of Pennsylvania, 1887).

122.   Adler, letter, 11 June 1891, in "Lofty Buildings Again," *Economist* 5 (13 June 1891): 1039. On the Chicago Stock Exchange's lack of wind bracing, see Ferree, "Modern Office Building," 24, and Condit, *Chicago School,* 137. See also "Foundations of the Stock Exchange," *Economist* 10 (5 August 1893): 137–138; "Foundations of the Chicago Stock Exchange Building," *Railroad Gazette,* 27 April 1894, 302; and Peck, *Building Foundations in Chicago,* 53–54.

123.   "Temple for Brokers," *Chicago Evening Journal,* 28 April 1894, 5.

124. Sullivan, "Ornament in Architecture" (1892), in *Louis Sullivan: The Public Papers,* ed. Twombly, 80.

125. Twose, "Steel and Terra-Cotta Buildings in Chicago," 4.

126. On D. H. Burnham and Company's Ashland Block, see Flinn, *Chicago, the Marvelous City of the West,* 396–397; Rand McNally, *Bird's-Eye Views and Guide to Chicago,* 116, 135; Randall, *Building Construction in Chicago,* 131; Condit, *Chicago School,* 102–103; Hoffmann, *Architecture of John Wellborn Root,* 219 n. 29; and Lewis, *Early Encounter with Tomorrow,* 61–63. On Robert A. Waller, see Berger, *They Built Chicago,* 127–132. On the earlier postfire Ashland Block, designed by Frederick and Edward Baumann on part of the site, see *Land-Owner* 4 (August 1872): 125–126, 130, and Duis, *Challenging Chicago,* 92.

127. "New Palace of Trade," *Chicago Record,* 28 April 1894, 3.

128. On the Chicago window, see Giedion, *Space, Time and Architecture,* 381–389; Condit, *Chicago School,* 80, 110; and Bruegmann, *Architects and the City,* 124. Sullivan's Chicago windows in his Schlesinger and Mayer Store, designed in 1898, may relate to its client David Mayer's familiarity with them in the Chicago Stock Exchange Building, where he had an office. See "Nearing Completion," *Chicago Evening Journal,* 23 April 1894, 54.

129. Sullivan, "Tall Office Building Artistically Considered" (1896), in *Louis Sullivan: The Public Papers,* ed. Twombly, 106–107.

130. Twose, "Steel and Terra-Cotta Buildings in Chicago," 5.

131. Ibid.

132. "Miscellaneous," *Economist* 10 (23 December 1893): 667. Before construction, the Chicago Stock Exchange's exterior was projected to be "entirely in stone or terra-cotta, light blue or buff in color" ("New Stock Exchange," *Chicago Tribune,* 25 February 1893, 6).

133. "Chicagoan, Head to Heels," *Chicago Sunday Chronicle,* 28 August 1898.

134. "Chicago," *American Architect and Building News* 43 (20 January 1894): 31. On the changed rondel inscription in the entrance arch's spandrel, see Vinci, *Trading Room,* 19. The name "Chicago Stock Exchange" also appeared on the center lintels in the three arches rising through the second and third stories to the south of the central front entrance, marking precisely the location of the trading room. This inscription is faintly visible in figure 195.

135. "Chicago," *American Architect and Building News* 43 (20 January 1894): 31. The working drawings for the Chicago Stock Exchange Building (including cornice details) are recorded in the Burnham Library/University of Illinois Architectural Microfilming Project, microfilm roll 6: Adler and Sullivan, frames 40–161, Art Institute of Chicago. The loggia motif may recall that along the crowning story of Holabird and Roche's Tacoma Building one block to the south. See Bruegmann, *Architects and the City,* 93.

136. "Nearing Completion," *Chicago Evening Journal,* 23 April 1894, 54. On Peck's idea for a two-story room, see "Temple of Finance," *Chicago Evening Post,* 30 April 1894, 2.

137. "Temple for Brokers," *Chicago Evening Journal,* 28 April 1894, 5.

138. On the rejected site, see Fleming, *Chicago Stock Exchange.* On the use of the room's east side, see "Exchange in a New Home," *Chicago Daily News,* 30 April 1894, 1, and "Temple of Finance," *Chicago Evening Post,* 30 April 1894, 2. On the use of prismatic glass, see Vinci, *Trading Room,* 30–31. On this room's later remodeling as a banking hall, see Dietrich Neumann, "'The Century's Triumph in Lighting': The Luxfer Prism Companies and Their Contribution to Early Modern Architecture," *Journal of the Society of Architectural Historians* 54 (March 1995): 36, 37. On Chicago's smoky air, see chapter 3, 146–147, and note 99.

139. "Temple for Brokers," *Chicago Evening Journal,* 26 April 1894, 5. The builder of the Chicago Stock Exchange Building was Victor Falkenau and Brothers, an earlier collaborator and client of Adler and Sullivan and recently the builder of the Congress Hotel. The structural ironwork was begun on 15

August 1893, and the roof was placed on 29 December. One account recorded the labor troubles: "In the beginning the enamel bricks which were to have lined the courts could not be furnished because all the coal mines in England were stopped by the great coal miners' strike of 1893. Next came the carpenters' strike. Next followed, April 2, the plumbers' strike, and, April 3 the painters' strike, besides the marble-setters' strike in February. In order to make up for the time thus lost, the contractors were compelled to lay brick by night by electric light, and with the aid of salamanders, as the temperature was about zero" ("The Building and Exchange Hall," *Chicago Evening Post,* 30 April 1894, 3). On the strikes, see also "New Palace of Trade," *Chicago Record,* 28 April 1894, 3, and "Temple of Finance," *Chicago Evening Post,* 30 April 1894, 2.

140.   On the Chicago Stock Exchange's memberships during the construction of Adler and Sullivan's building, see *Economist* 10 (9 December 1893): 616, and address of Charles Henrotin, president, at the dedication of 30 April 1894, in Fleming, *Chicago Stock Exchange.* Eames, *New York Stock Exchange,* 20, 42, described its early methods of election by secret ballot and subsequent sale of memberships. See also "Center of Finance," *Chicago Evening Post,* 30 April 1894, 9.

141.   "Various Real Estate Matters: The Peck Enterprise on LaSalle Street," *Economist* 9 (7 January 1893): 15.

142.   "Temple for Brokers," *Chicago Evening Journal,* 28 April 1894, 5. As in the Auditorium Building, the Pecks gave local firms the major contracts for the Chicago Stock Exchange Building's materials and equipment. See "Nearing Completion," *Chicago Evening Journal,* 23 April 1894, 54.

143.   Purcell, "Sullivan's Businessman and the Stock Exchange Building." On the Bower-Barff process, see Vinci-Kenny, *Adler & Sullivan's Auditorium Building,* 81.

144.   "New Palace of Trade," *Chicago Record,* 28 April 1894, 3. On the trading room's users, see "The Building and Exchange Hall," *Chicago Evening Post,* 30 April 1894, 2. On the restoration, in addition to Vinci's accounts, see Donald Hoffmann, "Out of Time, Out of Place," *Progressive Architecture* 58 (November 1977): 62–65.

145.   "Warming the House," *Chicago Tribune,* 1 May 1894, 12.

146.   Fleming, *Chicago Stock Exchange,* and Rice, *Chicago Stock Exchange,* 11.

147.   David A. Hanks, "Louis J. Millet and the Art Institute of Chicago," *Bulletin of the Art Institute of Chicago* 67 (1973): 14; and Darling, *Chicago Ceramics and Glass,* 104–108. The letting of the contract to Healy and Millet for the trading room's decoration was noted in "Various Real Estate Matters," *Economist* 11 (10 February 1894): 148.

148.   "Opened for Trading," *Chicago Inter Ocean,* 1 May 1894, 7.

149.   "Sullivan and the Art of Stenciling," in Vinci, *Trading Room,* 44.

150.   Ibid., and Hanks, "Louis J. Millet and the Art Institute of Chicago," 14.

151.   Fleming, *Chicago Stock Exchange.*

152.   Ibid.

153.   "New Mart of Finance," *Chicago Herald,* 1 May 1894, 4, quoted in Michael, "Adler & Sullivan's Palace of Trade," 7. The original creators of the Chicago Stock Exchange in 1882 were also commodities dealers on the Board of Trade, where the exchange first met on 21 March. After moving to other quarters, the exchange returned to the Board of Trade Building after it opened in 1885. On its daily activity, see "Betting on the Clock," *Chicago Herald,* 2 May 1886, 13. Later in 1886, the exchange moved to the Chicago Opera House before relocating to the northeast corner of Dearborn and Monroe Streets in May 1890. See Fleming, *Chicago Stock Exchange,* and Rice, *Chicago Stock Exchange,* 16–19, 24–31.

154.   Sullivan, *Democracy: A Man-Search,* ed. Elaine Hedges (1908; reprint, Detroit: Wayne State University Press, 1961), 103–104.

155.   Sullivan to Carl K. Bennett, National Farmers' Bank, Owatonna, Minnesota, 1 April 1908, in quoted in Vinci, *Trading Room,* 47, and Larry J. Millet, *The Curve of the Arch: The Story of Louis Sullivan's*

Owatonna Bank (St. Paul: University of Minnesota Press, 1985), 85. Sullivan was not alone among Chicagoans in his appreciation of color in the city's natural surroundings. See, for example, "The Study of Color," *Chicago Tribune,* 24 October 1885, 12. On the Stock Exchange trading room, see also Weingarden, "Colors of Nature," 255–257.

156. Sullivan, "The Artistic Use of the Imagination" (1889), in *Louis Sullivan: The Public Papers,* ed. Twombly, 63.

157. Ibid., 62.

158. "Chicago Stock Exchange Building, Chicago," *Ornamental Iron* 2 (July 1894): 9, 11.

159. Ruskin, "The Influence of Imagination in Architecture" (1857), in *The Two Paths: Being Lectures on Art, and Its Application to Decoration and Manufacture* (New York, 1859); republished in E. T. Cook and Alexander Wedderburn, *The Works of John Ruskin* (London, 1905), 16:347.

160. Ibid., 348. Garczynski, *Auditorium,* 8, also highlighted a quotation from Ruskin at the start of his monograph: "He is the greatest artist who has embodied the greatest number of the greatest ideas."

161. "Chicago Stock Exchange Building, Chicago," *Ornamental Iron* 2 (July 1894): 11.

162. Sullivan, *Autobiography of an Idea,* 70, 83–84, 96–97.

163. Ibid., 118–120.

164. Montgomery Schuyler, "Opening of Booth's Theatre," *New York World,* 4 February 1869, 5, quoted in Stern, Mellins, and Fishman, *New York 1880,* 667.

165. Peck, address at dedication of Chicago Stock Exchange Building, 30 April 1894, in "Hegira of Brokers," *Chicago Evening Journal,* 30 April 1894, 1; "Temple of Finance," *Chicago Evening Post,* 30 April 1894, 2; and Fleming, *Chicago Stock Exchange.*

166. On the fire destroying the World's Columbian Exposition's major buildings, see "White City Burned," *Chicago Tribune,* 6 July 1894, 7, and "The Burning of the World's Fair Buildings," *Harper's Weekly* 28 (21 July 1894): 687. Because of the wind's direction on that night, Adler and Sullivan's Transportation Building was not then destroyed by the fire. On the subsequent Pullman strike, see Pullman's and other statements before the U.S. Strike Commission, published as *The Strike at Pullman* (Chicago, 1894); William T. Stead, *Chicago To-Day, or The Labour War in America* (1894; reprint, New York: Review of Reviews Office, 1969); Almont Lindsey, *The Pullman Strike: The Story of a Unique Experiment and of a Great Labor Upheaval* (Chicago: University of Chicago Press, 1942); Buder, *Pullman,* 145–201; Smith, *Urban Disorder and the Shape of Belief,* 232–266; and Schneirov, *Labor and Urban Politics,* 335–343.

167. Charles H. Bebb to Thomas Burke, 12 June 1893; quoted in Jeffrey Karl Ochsner and Dennis Alan Andersen, "Adler and Sullivan's Seattle Opera House Project," *Journal of the Society of Architectural Historians* 48 (September 1989): 230. Morrison, *Louis Sullivan,* 175, noted the peak size of Adler and Sullivan's office staff.

168. "An Important Letter from Mr. Dankmar Adler," *Inland Architect and News Record* 25 (July 1895): 61. On Adler's departure, see also "Yields to Big Salary: Adler Goes to a Corporation," *Chicago Times Herald,* 16 July 1895, 3; Morrison, *Louis Sullivan,* 174–176; Wright, *Genius and the Mobocracy,* 70–71; Twombly, *Louis Sullivan,* 322–326; and Gregersen, *Dankmar Adler,* 6.

EPILOGUE

1. Peck, Annual Report of the President to the Stockholders of the Chicago Auditorium Association, 12 December 1891 (Auditorium Collection, Roosevelt University Archives).

2. "The Auditorium in Luck: Ground Leases Extended a Hundred Years," *Economist* 6 (25 July 1891): 157–158.

3. Peck, Annual Report of the President to the Stockholders of the Chicago Auditorium Association, 12 December 1891 (Auditorium Collection, Roosevelt University Archives).

4. "The Auditorium," *Economist* 7 (30 April 1892): 650.

5. R. Floyd Clinch, President, Auditorium Association, Testimony, in Chicago Auditorium Association vs. Mark Skinner Willing and the Northern Trust Co. as Trustees, etc., et al., in the United States Circuit Court of Appeals for the Seventh Circuit, October Term, A.D. 1925, no. 3733, 231 (Auditorium Collection, Roosevelt University Archives). On the Auditorium and Wabash Avenue's development, see Carol Baldridge and Alan Willis, "The Business of Culture," *Chicago History* 19 (winter–spring 1990): 32–51.

6. "The New Michigan Avenue Hotel," *Economist* 7 (29 March 1892): 424. On the Auditorium Hotel's functional deficiencies, see Gregersen, "History of the Auditorium Building," 33.

7. On payment of dividends, see "The Auditorium Association," *Economist* 8 (10 December 1892): 825, and *Economist* 12 (8 December 1894): 12. On Peck's resignation as president of the board of directors, see Gregersen, "History of the Auditorium Building," 34. On Adler's concern about the settlement of outer walls, see Mueller, Testimony, Chicago Auditorium Association vs. Mark Skinner Willing (1925), in Kaufmann, "Wright's 'Lieber Meister,'" 47–49. From the Auditorium's completion in 1890 up to Adler's death a decade later, he "was called on to rearrange rooms or solve mechanical and structural problems (Tim Samuelson and Jim Scott, "Auditorium Album." *Inland Architect* [September–October 1989]: 65). On the outer walls' settlement and exterior fire escapes, see Henry Diblee, Annual Report of the President to the Stockholders of the Chicago Auditorium Association, December 1901. On the fire walls added to the foyer after 1903, see Gregersen, "History of the Auditorium Building," 35. On the Iroquois Theater fire, see *Chicago Record-Herald*, 31 December 1903, and John Lloyd Wright, *My Father Who Is on Earth* (New York, 1946), 45–48.

8. Denson, "History of the Chicago Auditorium," 144–148. On the Auditorium's programs to 1910, see also Moore, *Forty Years of Opera in Chicago*, 18–50, and Davis, *Opera in Chicago*, 54–77.

9. *Chicago Tribune*, 21 September 1902, sec. 4, p. 1.

10. "Searching for the Real Chicago: A Few Imperishable Words from Frank Lloyd Wright, Rudolf Ganz, Nelson Algren, and Archibald Macleish," *Chicago*, January 1983, 127, quoted in Robert McColley, "Classical Music in Chicago and the Founding of the Symphony, 1850–1905," *Illinois Historical Journal* 78 (winter 1985): 298. Another account noted: "One of the most serious handicaps of this enterprise is the size of the main hall, which is unavailable for most dramatic performances because the ordinary spoken voice cannot be heard nor the facial expression of actors be seen in the distant parts of the house" ("The Auditorium," *Economist* 25 [12 January 1901]: 38). See also "Needs of the Auditorium," *Economist* 23 (31 March 1900): 372; "Thomas Orchestra," *Economist* 29 (21 February 1903): 233, and "Orchestra and Auditorium," *Economist* 29 (21 March 1903): 376.

11. On Thomas and Orchestra Hall, see Thomas, *Theodore Thomas: A Musical Autobiography*, 1:101–103; Otis, *Chicago Symphony Orchestra*, 137–153; and Hines, *Burnham of Chicago*, 227–230. See also "Chicago Orchestra," *Economist* 28 (6 December 1902): 767; "Auditorium and Orchestra," *Economist* 29 (11 April 1903): 471; "New Building Planned for the Chicago Orchestra," *Chicago Tribune* (9 June 1904): 3; "The New Thomas Music Hall," *Architectural Record* 16 (August 1904): 160–164; "Special Steelwork in Orchestra Hall, Chicago," *Engineering News* 52 (3 November 1904): 394–399; Charles E. Russell, *The American Orchestra and Theodore Thomas* (Garden City, N.Y.: Doubleday, Page, 1927; reprint, Westport, Conn.: Greenwood Press, 1971), 199–200, 292, 297, 301; and Forsyth, *Buildings for Music*, 243–244.

12. Sullivan's drawing was listed as a "Design for a Theatre-Front," *Catalogue of the Seventeenth Annual Exhibition of the Chicago Architectural Club* (Chicago: Chicago Architectural Club, 1904), 32, and reproduced in the *Catalogue of the Twenty-sixth Annual Exhibition of the Chicago Architectural Club* (Chicago: Chicago Architectural Club, 1913), 25, and in Roy A. Lippincott, "The Chicago Architectural Club: Notes on the Twenty-sixth Annual Exhibition," *Architectural Record* 33 (June 1913): 570. Elmslie later claimed that "it was a purely imaginative sketch and had nothing to do with Orchestra Hall" (Burnham Library of Architecture to Hugh Morrison, 18 August 1943, transcribed in Richard Nickel

Files, Office of John Vinci, AIA, Chicago). Unpublished recollections of this design as a project for the Orchestra Hall front include Andrew N. Rebori to Mrs. T. M. Hofmeister Jr., 19 September 1956, and William G. Purcell to Burnham Library of Architecture, 7 January 1957 (Louis Sullivan Centennial Exhibition File [1956]; Museum Archives, Art Institute of Chicago); and William G. Purcell, "Chicago Orchestra Hall: Design Project by Louis H. Sullivan," 16 December 1960, Purcell and Elmslie Collection, Northwest Architectural Archives, University of Minnesota, St. Paul. Elmslie's recollection of Sullivan as consultant for Orchestra Hall's acoustics appeared in a letter to the editor, *Chicago Daily News,* 29 July 1941. Frank Lloyd Wright's memory of Sullivan's being called in to assess the hall was noted in Mary Dougherty, "Mary-Go-Round," *Chicago Sun-Times,* 11 June 1950.

13. The Libby Prison Museum had been a warehouse in Richmond, Virginia, used by the Confederate government as a prison for Union soldiers during the Civil War. In 1889 the Chicago candy manufacturer and restaurateur Charles Gunther had the prison dismantled, transported to Chicago, and reerected as the museum devoted to display of his collection of Civil War memorabilia. This museum failed financially and was encased to become the Chicago Coliseum, serving as a multipurpose structure for fairs, expositions, and entertainment until its demolition in 1982–1983. The Coliseum's origins as the Libby Prison presumably gave it a symbolic appeal as a venue for the Republican Party's conventions. The Auditorium Hotel served as headquarters for several of these conventions ("Plan to Raze the Auditorium as Obsolete," *Chicago Tribune,* 16 February 1923, 1). On the Coliseum, see Clement M. Silvestro, "The Candy Man's Mixed Bag," *Chicago History* 2 (fall 1972): 86–99; Hirsch and Goler, *City Comes of Age,* 131–132; Alice Sinkevitch and Laurie McGovern Petersen, eds., *AIA Guide to Chicago* (New York: Harcourt Brace, 1993), 143; and Kathleen Zygmun, "Parades, Protests, Politics," *Chicago History* 25 (fall 1996): 43.

14. On oratory at the Auditorium Theater, see Denson, "History of the Chicago Auditorium," 159–160, 163, 169, and Lowe, "Monument of an Age," 47. On the Republican and Progressive Party conventions at Chicago in 1912, see Henry L. Stoddard, *Presidential Sweepstakes: The Story of Political Conventions and Campaigns* (New York: Putnam, 1948), 138–144. The Auditorium also hosted the Progressive Party's convention in 1916 ("Plan to Raze the Auditorium as Obsolete," *Chicago Tribune,* 16 February 1923, 1).

15. "Old Auditorium Is Restored to Former Glory," *Chicago Tribune,* 11 December 1932, pt. 1, p. 8. On Moody at the Auditorium, see Gilbert, *Perfect Cities,* 188. In presenting his proposal for the building in 1886, Peck had noted: "The recent revival meetings addressed by Sam Jones, Sam Small, and Rev. D. L. Moody, have been held in temporary skating-rinks unsuitable for the purpose" ("Seats for a Multitude," *Chicago Evening Journal,* 29 January 1887, 1). In 1889, before the theater opened, the Auditorium's directors approved the Reverend George C. Lorimer's plan for regular religious services in the theater, provided "that the services should be undenominational and liberal in spirit, and that there shall be no admission charged" (Minutes of Executive Committee of Chicago Auditorium Association, 11 January 1890, 182 [Auditorium Collection, Roosevelt University Archives]). Peck's discussions with Lorimer as "the Auditorium preacher" were noted in Editorial, *Indicator* 12 (18 January 1890): 2. Nondenominational religious services were proposed in *Chicago Evening Herald,* 8 February 1890, 7.

16. On Klaw and Erlanger's plans, see "Get Lease of Auditorium," *Chicago Tribune,* 6 July 1907. Denson, "History of the Chicago Auditorium," 158, notes attempts to promote vaudeville in Chicago about 1907 and resistance to it at the Auditorium. One potential manager proposed a combination of grand opera, drama, and vaudeville for year-round operations ("Auditorium Theater," *Economist* 37 [13 April 1907]: 718). The Chicago Opera House, Haymarket Theater, and Olympic Theater by then staged vaudeville shows exclusively. On the 1905 production of *Ben Hur* at the Auditorium, featuring a cast of four hundred, five chariots, and twenty horses, see *Chicago Tribune,* 27 February 1905, 9. On the 1901 performance of *Uncle Tom's Cabin,* see *Chicago Tribune,* 28 May 1901, 6. On other spectacles of the period, see Denson, "History of the Chicago Auditorium," 153–158. On Milward Adams (1857–1923), see Moore, *Forty Years of Opera in Chicago,* 17–18, and Otis, *Chicago Symphony Orchestra,* 364. Adams

compiled scrapbooks on performances in the Auditorium from the time of its opening in 1889. These scrapbooks, which continue to the time of the theater's closing in 1941, are in twenty-six volumes in the Department of Special Collections, Newberry Library.

17. "Auditorium Theatre May Be Torn Out and Great Structure Remodeled at Cost of $3,000,000," *Real Estate and Building Journal* 42 (15 February 1908): 11. See also *Chicago Tribune,* 14 February 1907, 1, and Gregersen, "History of the Auditorium Building," 35–36. In 1906 the owners of the Auditorium Annex tried to expand their hotel building southward by buying all the frontage on Michigan Avenue from Congress south to Harrison Street, but they were unable to acquire the southernmost plot ("Various Real Estate Matters: A Check to the Auditorium Annex," *Economist* 36 [25 August 1906]: 286).

18. On Holabird and Roche's Hotel LaSalle and Sherman House, see Bruegmann, *Architects and the City,* 325–335.

19. See chapter 3, note 230.

20. On Adler (and Sullivan?) as consultant for Carnegie Hall, see "The Architectural League of New York," *Inland Architect and News Record* 17 (March 1891): 25; *Industrial Chicago,* 1:605; Arthur Woltersdorf, "A Portrait Gallery of Chicago Architects, II: Dankmar Adler," *Western Architect* 33 (July 1924): 77; Twombly, *Louis Sullivan,* 249–251; Saltzstein, "Autobiography and Letters of Dankmar Adler," 20; and Stern, Mellins, and Fishman, *New York 1880,* 691. Carnegie Hall as New York City's answer to Chicago's Auditorium was noted in "New York Is Following Suit," *Indicator* 11 (30 March 1889): 459, and Editorial, *Indicator* 11 (30 March 1889): 462.

21. See Frederick Cone, *Oscar Hammerstein's Manhattan Opera Company* (Norman: University of Oklahoma Press, 1966), and Teran, "New York Opera Audience," 75–94.

22. Giulio Gatti-Casazza, *Memories of the Opera* (New York: Scribner's, 1941), 9, quoted in Teran, "New York Opera Audience," 95. On Kahn's proposal, see Mary J. Matz, *The Many Lives of Otto Kahn* (New York: Macmillan, 1963), 97–102.

23. C. J. Bulliet, *How Grand Opera Came to Chicago* (Chicago, 1940); Moore, *Forty Years of Opera in Chicago,* 51–55; and Davis, *Opera in Chicago,* 78–82.

24. Denson, "History of the Chicago Auditorium," 173.

25. Wright, in "Searching for the Real Chicago," *Chicago,* January 1983, 127, quoted in McColley, "Classical Music in Chicago," 298. In April 1910 the Illinois Supreme Court had upheld a decision to require the Auditorium Association to pay increased annual rent on the north portion of the theater's site leased from the Studebakers in 1886, based on a reappraisal of the land's increased value twenty-five years after the original lease. This decision presumably added urgency to the project of profitably remodeling the theater ("Various Real Estate Matters: Auditorium Must Pay Increased Ground Rent," *Economist* 43 [23 April 1910]: 822). On Marshall's remodeling of the Auditorium Theater, see Moore, *Forty Years of Opera in Chicago,* 36. Resulting reduction of the theater's seating capacity was noted in R. Floyd Clinch, President, Auditorium Association, Testimony, in Chicago Auditorium Association vs. Mark Skinner Willing and the Northern Trust Co. as Trustees, 233 (Auditorium Collection, Roosevelt University Archives). Prints of several of Marshall's drawings for the remodeling, including studies of sight lines, survive in the Auditorium Collection, Roosevelt University Archives. On Marshall, see Berger, *They Built Chicago,* 161–170.

26. Moore, *Forty Years of Opera in Chicago,* 334. On the Chicago Opera Association, and the Chicago Civic Opera Company to 1929, see also Davis, *Opera in Chicago,* 110–178, and Denson, "History of the Chicago Auditorium," 175–182.

27. On Insull and the Chicago Civic Opera House, see Moore, *Forty Years of Opera in Chicago,* 335–352; Davis, *Opera in Chicago,* 179–184; and Sally A. Kitt Chappell, *Architecture and Planning of Graham, Anderson, Probst and White, 1912–1936: Transforming Tradition* (Chicago: University of Chicago Press, 1995), 14–23, 218–222. On Insull's career, see Platt, *Electric City.* On the Auditorium Theater's

acoustics (meaning reverberation time, echo diminution, and projection of sound to distant seats) as a standard for the acoustic design of the Civic Opera House, see Paul E. Sabine, "Acoustics of the Chicago Civic Opera House," *Architectural Forum* 52 (April 1930): 599–604.

28. Gregersen, "History of the Auditorium Building," 35–36.

29. Ibid., 36–37. Increases in property taxes were noted in "Plan to Raze the Auditorium as Obsolete," *Chicago Tribune*, 16 February 1923, 1, and in R. Floyd Clinch, President, Auditorium Association, Testimony, in Chicago Auditorium Association vs. Mark Skinner Willing and the Northern Trust Co. as Trustees, 234 (Auditorium Collection, Roosevelt University Archives). On the legal disagreement between the Auditorium Association and Mark Skinner Willing, son of Henry J. Willing, who had been the original lessor of 80 percent of the site, see "The Auditorium Building," *Economist* 77 (11 June 1927): 1561, and "May Review Auditorium Lease," *Economist* 78 (1 October 1927): 824.

30. Denson, "History of the Chicago Auditorium," 191.

31. On Holabird and Roche's 1932–1933 renovation, see "Old Auditorium Is Restored to Former Glory," *Chicago Tribune*, 11 December 1932, pt. 1, p. 8, and "Artist Restores Beauty of Old Auditorium," *Chicago Daily News*, 28 October 1932. On the theater's programs of 1932–1941, see Denson, "History of the Chicago Auditorium," 192–198.

32. On the decision to close the Auditorium Building, see "Famed Auditorium Theater and Hotel to Close June 30," *Chicago Daily News*, 29 May 1941, 3; "Chicago Leaders Map Campaign to Save Auditorium," *Chicago Tribune*, 1 June 1941, pt. 1, p. 15; "Propose to Save Auditorium for a Civic Center," *Chicago Daily News*, 4 June 1941, 3; "Propose City Take Over Auditorium as Civic Building," *Chicago Tribune*, 5 June 1941, 23; "Architects Join Civic Effort to Save Auditorium," *Chicago Daily News*, 6 June 1941, 39; "The Auditorium," *Chicago Tribune*, 6 June 1941, 14; Edward Barry, "Closing of Auditorium Recalls Joys It Brought," *Chicago Tribune*, 8 June 1941, pt. 6, pp. 1,3; "Show Producers Join in Move to Save Auditorium," *Chicago Daily News*, 11 June 1941, 19; "Propose to Save Auditorium by Moving Civic Opera Back," *Chicago Daily News*, 12 June 1941, 9; William F. McDermott, "Parthenon of Chicago Faces Ruin," *Chicago Daily News*, 14 June 1941, 5; "F. Lloyd Wright Advises City to Run Auditorium," *Chicago Daily News*, 21 June 1941, 1, 3; "Auditorium Anecdotes," *Chicago Daily News*, 21 June 1941, 19; "Auditorium Hotel Will Close Tomorrow: Farewell Party," *Chicago Daily News*, 30 July 1941, 6; "Chicago Says Farewell to Auditorium," *Chicago Tribune*, 1 August 1941, 1; "Opening Night at Auditorium Lives in Memory," *Chicago Tribune*, 17 August 1941, part 3, pp. 1, 2; "Campaign Opens for $400,000 to Save Auditorium," *Chicago Tribune*, 18 August 1941, 11; and "Public Subscription to Save Auditorium, Plan of Leaders," *Chicago Daily News*, 5 September 1941, 5. On the Auditorium Building Corporation, see Gregersen, "History of the Auditorium Building," 38–39.

33. On the Auditorium Music Foundation, see "Grant Reprieve for One Month to Auditorium," *Chicago Tribune*, 14 June 1941, 7; "Legal Maneuver Aims to Rescue the Auditorium," *Chicago Daily News*, 16 June 1941, 7; "Charter Issued for Auditorium Music Center," *Chicago Daily News*, 24 June 1941, 5. On the auction of the theater and hotel contents, see William Shaw, "Memories of Auditorium in Its Glory," *Chicago Daily News*, 27 June 1942, 17; "Hold Preview for Big Auction at Auditorium," *Chicago Daily News*, 3 July 1942, 3; "Auditorium Gives Its Final Show," *Chicago Sun*, 6 July 1942, 4; Leonard Castle, "Auction Hammer Raps Out Knell for Old Auditorium," *Chicago Sun*, 8 July 1942, 7, and "Auditorium's Organ Saved from Junk Pile," *Chicago Sun*, 11 July 1942, 12. On the building's use as a servicemen's center and interior changes, see "Sullivan's Auditorium Inducted," *Journal of the Society of Architectural Historians* 2 (July 1942): 33, and Perlman, *Auditorium Building*, 23.

34. On Roosevelt University's original plans for the building, see the booklet *Roosevelt University Announces Plans for the Restoration of Adler & Sullivan's Auditorium Building, Including the Auditorium Theatre and the Former Auditorium Hotel and Office Building Which Now Houses the University* (Chicago, 1946). On the university's acquisition of the building, see *Chicago Tribune*, 5 October 1946, 27 February 1947, and 17 April 1947. On the widening of Congress Street, see *Progress* (Roosevelt University newspaper), November 1955, 1–3, and Perlman, *Auditorium Building*, 24.

35. "Restoring the Auditorium," *Talmanac,* November 1964, 21; and Wilbert H. Hasbrouck, "Chicago's Auditorium Theater," *Prairie School Review* 4 (third quarter 1967): 12. See also "Roosevelt U. Hopes to Restore Once-Magnificent Auditorium," *Chicago Sun-Times,* 18 April 1957, and "Hike Estimate of Auditorium Theater Cost," *Chicago Daily News,* 4 April 1962. On Crombie Taylor's restoration of the banquet hall as the Rudolf Ganz Recital Hall, see Shirley Lowry, "Electroliers Sought for Perfect Room," *Chicago Tribune,* 15 October 1956, pt. 1, p. 25.

36. Beatrice Spachner, Interview, 27 February 1973, quoted in Denson, "History of the Chicago Auditorium," 262. See also Mary Kerner, "Behind the Scenes: Spachner Restored the Stars to Sullivan's Auditorium Theatre," *North Shore* 2 (March–April 1979): 38–39.

37. Crombie Taylor to author, 12 May 1999. On Taylor's recovery of stencils, see "A System of Stencil Ornament," *Prairie School Review* 4 (third quarter 1967): 18–19.

38. Denson, "History of the Chicago Auditorium," 253–260. Evanston artist Judy Hendershot repainted the box stencils in 1978–1979 (Marilyn R. Abbey, "Behind the Scenes: Stenciling Adds New Glitter," *North Shore* 2 [March–April 1979]: 40–41).

39. "The Auditorium Returns to Life," *Chicago Daily News,* 7 August 1965; "Rebirth in Chicago," *Architectural Forum* 123 (November 1965): 29; "The Auditorium: A Restoration," *Architectural and Engineering News* 8 (January 1966): 42–43; and "An Autumn Night's Dream," *Architectural Forum* 127 (December 1967): 47. See also *Chicago Daily News,* 31 August 1967; Jack Altman, "Curtain Rises at Auditorium," *Chicago Sun-Times,* 1 November 1967, 27; "Hard Facts Behind a Triumph," *Chicago Sun-Times,* 5 November 1967, 2; and William Leonard, "City Greets Auditorium Gala Opening," *Chicago Tribune,* 1 November 1967, 3. See also "The Auditorium Theatre," *Interior Design,* May 1968, 142–145, 206.

40. "Auditorium Building Getting Older but Better," *Roosevelt University Magazine* (winter–spring 1979–1980): 10–12. See also Nory Miller, "Roosevelt University and the Auditorium: What Do You Do with a Great Landmark?" *Inland Architect* 17 (April 1973): 7–13.

41. John A. Burns, "Structure and Mechanics Viewed as Sculpture," *American Institute of Architects Journal* 72 (April 1983): 44–49.

42. Vinci-Kenny, *Adler & Sullivan's Auditorium Building.*

43. Judith Kiriazis, "Living with a Landmark Campus: Roosevelt's Auditorium," *Inland Architect,* September 1979, 12–15. See Lawrence Biemuller, "Slowly and Deliberately, Roosevelt U. Is Restoring One of the Masterpieces of American Architecture," *Chronicle of Higher Education,* 13 March 1991, B6–7.

44. "F. Lloyd Wright Advises City to Run Auditorium," *Chicago Daily News,* 21 June 1941, 1. Accounts of the building's centennial included John von Rhein, "A Hall's Lasting Mark," *Chicago Tribune,* 3 December 1989; Connie Lauerman, "Bravo! Bravo! The Auditorium Theater Takes a Bow for a Hundred Years of Multifaceted Service to the City," *Chicago Tribune Magazine,* 3 December 1989; and M. H. Newman, "The Auditorium Theatre: A Centennial Celebration," *Chicago Sun-Times,* 3 December 1889. Since 1994 Roosevelt University has attempted to wrest control over the Auditorium Theater (and its revenues) from the Auditorium Theater Council. In 1998 the Cook County Circuit Court ruled in Roosevelt's favor, ordering the council to turn over control of the theater to the university. The circuit court's decision was appealed. See "Theatre Getting Its Day in Court," *Chicago Tribune,* 9 June 1998; "Roosevelt Wins Control of Auditorium," *Chicago Tribune,* 29 September 1998; "Court Delays Roosevelt's Takeover of Auditorium," *Chicago Tribune,* 30 September 1998; and "New Trial Ordered in Auditorium Suit," *Chicago Tribune,* 31 March 2001. Continuing restoration efforts on major interiors were noted in "Tuning Sullivan's 'Color Symphony,'" *Chicago Tribune,* 28 May 2000.

SELECTED BIBLIOGRAPHY

ARCHIVAL SOURCES AND UNPUBLISHED DOCUMENTS

Auditorium Dedication Volume. Newberry Library, Chicago.

The Central Church of Chicago, Illinois. Record, from December 4, 1875. Department of Archives and Manuscripts, Chicago Historical Society.

Chicago Athenaeum. Annual Reports for 1873–1877, 1878–1879, 1881–1887, and 1888–1890. Chicago Historical Society.

Chicago Auditorium Association vs. Mark Skinner Willing and the Northern Trust Co. as Trustees, etc., et al., in United States Circuit Court of Appeals for the Seventh Circuit, October Term, A.D. 1925, No. 3733. Auditorium Collection, Roosevelt University Archives.

Chicago Auditorium Association. Copies of Documents. Auditorium Collection, Roosevelt University Archives.

———. Early History and Press Clippings: Chicago Auditorium Association, Chicago, 1887–1889. Ryerson and Burnham Libraries, Art Institute of Chicago.

———. Minutes of Executive Committee of Chicago Auditorium Association, May 3, 1887, to December 11, 1907. Auditorium Collection, Roosevelt University Archives.

———. Records of the Chicago Auditorium Association, Originally Chicago Grand Auditorium Association, December 11, 1886, to November 7, 1906. Auditorium Collection, Roosevelt University Archives.

Chicago Auditorium Building, Chicago, Adler and Sullivan, Architects. Sixty-five sheets of plans and working drawings [April 1887]. Ryerson and Burnham Libraries, Art Institute of Chicago.

Chicago Auditorium Building. Nine prints of working drawings for ornamental plaster work. Department of Architecture, Art Institute of Chicago.

Chicago City Clerk. Assessment rolls for property taxes in 1849–1850. Manuscripts and Archives Collection, Chicago Historical Society.

Chicago Theater Programs Collection. Chicago Theater Collection, Special Collections and Preservation Division. Chicago Public Library.

Gregersen, Charles E. "History of the Auditorium Building" and "Architectural Description of the Auditorium Building." In Addendum to Historic American Buildings Survey, Survey ILL-1007: Auditorium Building (1980).

Historic American Buildings Survey. Survey ILL-1007: Auditorium Building. 1960. Addendum, 1980.

Milward Adams Scrapbooks, Auditorium Theater, 1889–1941. 26 vols. Department of Special Collections, Newberry Library, Chicago.

Peck, Ferdinand. Annual Reports of the President to the Stockholders of the Chicago Auditorium Association, 1 December 1886, 1 December 1888, 7 December 1889, 12 December 1891, 10 December 1892. Auditorium Collection, Roosevelt University Archives.

Louis Sullivan Centennial Exhibition File [1956]. Museum Archives, Art Institute of Chicago.

John Van Osdel Account Books. 2 vols. Vol. 1, 1856–1868; vol. 2, 1868–1886. Manuscripts and Archives Collection, Chicago Historical Society.

William Gray Purcell Papers. Purcell and Elmslie Collection. Northwest Architectural Archives, University of Minnesota, St. Paul.

Williams, Barker and Severn Company. Auction Catalogue no. 5533. "Household Effects, Library, Oriental Rugs, Paintings, etc., of Mr. Louis Sullivan." Chicago, 29 November 1909. Ryerson and Burnham Libraries, Art Institute of Chicago.

THESES AND DISSERTATIONS

Bernstein, Gerald S. "In Pursuit of the Exotic: Islamic Forms in Nineteenth Century American Architecture." Ph.D. diss., University of Pennsylvania, 1968.

Blake, Curtis C. "The Architecture of Carrère and Hastings." Ph.D. diss., Columbia University, 1976.

Buckley, Peter G. "'To the Opera House': Culture and Society in New York City, 1820–1860." Ph.D. diss., State University of New York at Stony Brook, 1984.

Buettinger, Craig. "The Concept of Jacksonian Aristocracy: Chicago as a Test Case, 1833–1857." Ph.D. diss., Northwestern University, 1982.

Denson, Wilbur T. "A History of the Chicago Auditorium." Ph.D. diss., University of Wisconsin, Madison, 1974.

Dubin, Lydia S. "The Hotels of New York City, 1885–1900." M.A. thesis, Pennsylvania State University, 1969.

Elstein, Rochelle S. "The Architectural Style of Dankmar Adler." M.A. thesis, University of Chicago, 1963.

Grimsley, Charles E. "A Study of the Contributions of Dankmar Adler to the Theatre Building Practice of the Late Nineteenth Century." Ph.D. diss., Northwestern University, 1984.

Kann, Kenneth L. "Working Class Culture and the Labor Movement in Nineteenth-Century Chicago." Ph.D. diss., University of California at Berkeley, 1977.

Kaplan, Fredda. "The Architecture of New York City Hotels from 1860 until 1885." M.A. thesis, Pennsylvania State University, 1970.

Kavenaugh, James V. "Three American Opera Houses: The Boston Theatre, the New York Academy of Music, the Philadelphia American Academy of Music." Ph.D. diss., University of Delaware, 1967.

Kuhn, Gerald W. "A History of the Financing of Commercial Structures in the Chicago Central Business District, 1868–1914." Ph.D. diss., Indiana University, 1969.

Ludwig, Jay F. "McVicker's Theatre, 1857–1896." Ph.D. diss., University of Illinois, 1958.

Mazzola, Sandy R. "When Music Is Labor: Chicago Bands and Orchestras and the Origins of the Chicago Federation of Musicians, 1880–1902." Ph.D. diss., Northern Illinois University, 1984.

Nelson, Bruce C. "Culture and Conspiracy: A Social History of Chicago Anarchism, 1870–1900." Ph.D. diss., Northern Illinois University, 1985.

Neuberg, Phillip. "The Auditorium Building Dining Room Stencil Patterns and Paints." 1978. Auditorium Collection, Roosevelt University Archives.

Pisoni, Michael J. "Operatic War in New York City, 1883–84: Colonel James H. Mapleson at the Academy of Music vs. Henry E. Abbey at the Metropolitan Opera House." Ph.D. diss., Indiana University, 1975.

Roberts, Sidney I. "Businessmen in Revolt: Chicago, 1874–1900." Ph.D. diss., Northwestern University, 1960.

Scharnau, Ralph W. "Thomas J. Morgan and the Chicago Socialist Movement, 1876–1901." Ph.D. diss., Northern Illinois University, 1970.

Schultz, Rima L. "The Businessman's Role in Western Settlement: The Entrepreneurial Frontier, Chicago, 1833–1872." Ph.D. diss., Boston University, 1985.

Sparks, Esther. "A Biographical Dictionary of Painters and Sculptors in Illinois, 1808–1945." Ph.D. diss., Northwestern University, 1971.

Sprague, Paul E. "The Architectural Ornament of Louis Sullivan and His Chief Draftsmen." Ph.D. diss., Princeton University, 1968.

Teran, Jay R. S. "The New York Opera Audience: 1825–1974." Ph.D. diss., New York University, 1974.

Townsend, Andrew J. "The Germans of Chicago." Ph.D. diss., University of Chicago, 1927.

Weber, Ronald J. "Rationalizers and Reformers: Chicago Local Transportation in the Nineteenth Century." Ph.D. diss., University of Wisconsin, 1976.

BOOKS

Abbott, Carl. *Boosters and Businessmen: Popular Economic Thought and Urban Growth in the Antebellum Middle West.* Westport, Conn.: Greenwood Press, 1981.

Adler, Liebman. *Sabbath Hours: Thoughts [by Liebman Adler].* Philadelphia: Jewish Publication Society of America, 1893.

Ahlquist, Karen. *Democracy at the Opera: Music, Theater, and Culture in New York City, 1815–60.* Urbana: University of Illinois Press, 1997.

Album of Genealogy and Biography, Cook County, Illinois. 1st ed. Chicago: Calumet Book and Engraving, 1895.

Album of Genealogy and Biography, Cook County, Illinois. 2d ed. Chicago: Calumet Book and Engraving, 1895.

Andreas, Alfred T. *History of Chicago.* 3 vols. Chicago, 1884–1886. Reprint, New York: Arno Press, 1975.

Andrew, David S. *Louis Sullivan and the Polemics of Modern Architecture.* Urbana: University of Illinois Press, 1985.

Art Institute of Chicago. *Chicago and New York: Architectural Interactions.* Chicago: Art Institute of Chicago, 1984.

Avrich, Paul. *The Haymarket Tragedy.* Princeton: Princeton University Press, 1984.

Badger, Reid F. *The Great American Fair: The World's Columbian Exposition and American Culture.* Chicago: Nelson Hall, 1979.

Baumann, Frederick. *The Art of Preparing Foundations for All Kinds of Buildings, with Particular Illustrations of the "Method of Isolated Piers," as Followed in Chicago.* Chicago: J. M. Wing, 1873. Revised and enlarged by George T. Powell, in Powell, *Foundations and Foundation Walls.* New York: W. T. Comstock, 1884.

Beeks, James C. *30,000 Locked Out: The Great Strike of the Building Trades in Chicago.* Chicago: F. Gindele, 1887.

Berger, Miles L. *They Built Chicago: Entrepreneurs Who Shaped a Great City's Architecture.* Chicago: Bonus Books, 1992.

The Biographical Dictionary and Portrait Gallery of Representative Men of Chicago, Minnesota Cities and the World's Columbian Exposition. Chicago: American Biographical Publishing, 1892.

Bluestone, Daniel. *Constructing Chicago.* New Haven: Yale University Press, 1991.

Boyer, M. Christine. *Manhattan Manners: Architecture and Style, 1850–1900.* New York: Rizzoli, 1985.

Briggs, John. *Requiem for a Yellow Brick Brewery.* Boston: Little, Brown, 1969.

Bruce, Robert V. *1877: Year of Violence.* Indianapolis: Bobbs-Merrill, 1959. Reprint, Chicago: Quadrangle Books, 1970.

Bruegmann, Robert. *The Architects and the City: Holabird and Roche of Chicago, 1880–1918.* Chicago: University of Chicago Press, 1997.

Buder, Stanley. *Pullman: An Experiment in Industrial Order and Community Planning, 1880–1930.* New York: Oxford University Press, 1967.

Burnham, Sarah M. *History and Uses of Limestones and Marbles.* Boston: S. E. Cassino, 1883.

Bush-Brown, Albert. *Louis Sullivan.* New York: George Braziller, 1960.

Butsch, Richard, ed. *For Fun and Profit: The Transformation of Leisure into Consumption.* Philadelphia: Temple University Press, 1990.

Carlson, Marvin. *Places of Performance: The Semiotics of Theatre Architecture.* Ithaca: Cornell University Press, 1989.

Carter, Kate B. *The Great Mormon Tabernacle.* Salt Lake City: Daughters of Utah Pioneers, 1968.

Chamberlain, Everett R. *Chicago and Its Suburbs.* Chicago: A. T. Hungerford, 1874. Reprint, New York: Arno Press, 1974.

Chappell, Sally A. Kitt. *Architecture and Planning of Graham, Anderson, Probst and White, 1912–1936: Transforming Tradition.* Chicago: University of Chicago Press, 1995.

Chicago and Its Resources Twenty Years After, 1871–1891: A Commercial History Showing the Progress and Growth of Two Decades from the Great Fire to the Present Time. Chicago: Chicago Times, 1892.

The Chicago Clubs Illustrated. Chicago: Lanward, 1888.

Chicago Directory of Picnic Grounds and Public Halls. Chicago: Stromberg, Allen, 1899.

The Chicago Stock Exchange Building (1894), rental pamphlet. Ryerson and Burnham Libraries, Art Institute of Chicago.

Citizens' Association of Chicago. *Addresses and Reports of the Citizens' Association of Chicago: 1874 to 1876.* Chicago: Hazlitt and Reed, 1876.

———. *Report of the Committee on Tenement Houses of the Citizens' Association of Chicago.* Chicago: George K. Hazlitt, 1884.

———. *Report of the Committee on Theatres and Public Halls of the Citizens' Association of Chicago, January, 1882.* Chicago: George K. Hazlitt, 1882.

———. *Report of the Committee on Theatres and Public Halls of the Citizens' Association of Chicago, October, 1883.* Chicago: Jonathan B. Jeffrey, 1883.

———. *Report of the Committee on Theatres and Public Halls to the Executive Committee of the Citizens' Association of Chicago, October 1887.* Chicago: Citizens' Association, 1887.

———. *Report of the Smoke Committee of the Citizens' Association of Chicago, May 1889.* Chicago: George E. Marshall, 1889.

Clubbe, John. *Cincinnati Observed: Architecture and History.* Columbus: Ohio State University Press, 1992.

Colbert, Elias. *Chicago and the Great Conflagration.* Cincinnati: C. F. Vent, 1872.

Collins, Holdridge O. *History of the Illinois National Guard, from the Organization of the First Regiment in September, 1874, to the Enactment of the Military Code, in May 1879.* Chicago: Black and Beach, 1884.

Condit, Carl W. *The Chicago School of Architecture: A History of Commercial and Public Building in the Chicago Area, 1875–1925.* Chicago: University of Chicago Press, 1964.

———. *The Rise of the Skyscraper.* Chicago: University of Chicago Press, 1952.

Connely, Willard. *Louis Sullivan as He Lived: The Shaping of American Architecture.* New York: Horizon Press, 1960.

Cope, George W. *The Iron and Steel Interests of Chicago.* Chicago: Rand McNally, 1890.

Cronon, William. *Nature's Metropolis: Chicago and the Great West.* New York: W. W. Norton, 1991.

Cropsey, Eugene H. *Crosby's Opera House: Symbol of Chicago's Cultural Awakening.* Cranbury, N.J.: Fairleigh Dickinson University Press, 1999.

Crosby's Opera House: Inauguration Season of the Grand Italian Opera; Director, J. Grau; 17 April 1865. Chicago Historical Society.

Crosby Opera House Art Association: Its Plan and Objects. Chicago, 1866. Chicago Historical Society.

Curran, Kathleen A. *A Forgotten Architect of the Gilded Age: Josiah Cleaveland Cady's Legacy.* Hartford, Conn.: Watkinson Library and Department of Fine Arts, Trinity College, 1993.

Currey, Josiah Seymour. *Chicago: Its History and Its Builders, a Century of Marvelous Growth.* 5 vols. Chicago: S. J. Clarke, 1908–1912.

Daly, César, and Gabriel Davioud. *Les théâtres de la Place du Châtelet: Théâtre du Chatelet, Théâtre Lyrique.* Paris: Librairie Générale de l'Architecture et des Travaux Publics, 1874.

Darling, Sharon S. *Chicago Ceramics and Glass: An Illustrated History from 1871 to 1933.* Chicago: Chicago Historical Society, 1979.

David, Henry. *The History of the Haymarket Affair: A Study in the American Social-Revolutionary and Labor Movements.* 3d rev. ed. New York: Collier, 1963.

Davis, Ronald L. *Opera in Chicago.* New York: Appleton-Century, 1966.

Dean, C. *The World's Fair City and Her Enterprising Sons.* Chicago: United, 1892.

de Wit, Wim, ed. *Louis Sullivan: The Function of Ornament.* New York: W. W. Norton, 1986.

Dizikes, John L. *Opera in America: A Cultural History.* New Haven: Yale University Press, 1993.

Doty, Mrs. Duane. *The Town of Pullman, Illustrated: Its Growth with Brief Accounts of Its Industries.* Pullman, Ill.: T. P. Struhsacker, 1893.

Duis, Perry. *Challenging Chicago: Coping with Everyday Life, 1837–1920.* Urbana: University of Illinois Press, 1998.

———. *The Saloon: Public Drinking in Chicago and Boston, 1880–1920.* Urbana: University of Illinois Press, 1983.

Eames, Francis L. *The New York Stock Exchange.* New York: Thomas G. Hall, 1894.

Einhorn, Robin L. *Property Rules: Political Economy in Chicago, 1833–1872.* Chicago: University of Chicago Press, 1991.

Eisler, Paul E. *The Metropolitan Opera: The First Twenty-five Years, 1883–1908.* Croton-on-Hudson, N.Y.: North River Press, 1984.

Elia, Mario Manieri. *Louis Henry Sullivan.* New York: Princeton Architectural Press, 1996.

Ericsson, Henry L. *Sixty Years a Builder: The Autobiography of Henry Ericsson.* Chicago: A. Kroch, 1942. Reprint, New York: Arno Press, 1972.

Ffrench, Florence. *Music and Musicians in Chicago.* Chicago: Florence Ffrench, 1899.

Fleming, I. A. *The Chicago Stock Exchange: An Historical Sketch with Biographies of Its Leading Members.* Chicago: Excelsior, 1894.

Flinn, John J. *Chicago, the Marvelous City of the West: A History, an Encyclopedia, and a Guide.* 2d ed. Chicago: Standard Guide, 1892.

———. *The Hand-Book of Chicago Biography.* Chicago: Standard Guide, 1893.

———. *History of the Chicago Police from the Settlement of the Community to the Present Time.* Chicago: Police Book Fund, 1887. Reprint, Montclair, N.J.: Patterson Smith, 1973.

Foner, Philip S. *The Great Labor Uprising of 1877.* New York: Monad Press, 1977.

Forsyth, Michael. *Buildings for Music: The Architect, the Musician, and the Listener from the Seventeenth Century to the Present.* Cambridge: MIT Press, 1985.

Frei, Hans. *Louis Henry Sullivan.* Zurich: Verlag für Architektur, 1992.

Fulcher, Jane F. *The Nation's Image: French Opera as Politics and Politicized Art.* Princeton: Princeton University Press, 1976.

Garczynski, Edward R. *The Auditorium.* New York: Exhibit, 1890.

Garner, John S., ed. *The Midwest in American Architecture.* Urbana: University of Illinois Press, 1991.

Giedion, Sigfried. *Space, Time and Architecture.* 5th ed., rev. and enl. Cambridge: Harvard University Press, 1982.

Gilbert, James. *Perfect Cities: Chicago's Utopias of 1893.* Chicago: University of Chicago Press, 1991.

Gilbert, Paul T., and Charles L. Bryson. *Chicago and Its Makers.* Chicago: F. Mendelsohn, 1929.

Glessner, John J. *The Commercial Club of Chicago: Its Beginning and Something of Its Work.* Chicago: privately printed, 1910.

Grandin, Mme Léon. *Impressions d'une parisienne à Chicago.* Paris: Librairie Ernest Flammarion, 1894.

Grant, Bruce. *Fight for a City: The Story of the Union League Club of Chicago and Its Times, 1880–1955.* Chicago: Rand McNally, 1955.

Gray, Mary Lakritz. *A Guide to Chicago's Murals.* Chicago: University of Chicago Press, 2001.

Gregersen, Charles. *Dankmar Adler: His Theaters and Auditoriums.* Athens: Swallow Press and Ohio University Press, 1990.

Habel, Heinrich. *Festspielhaus und Wahnfried: Geplante und ausgeführte Bauten Richard Wagners.* Munich: Prestel-Verlag, 1985.

Haiko, Peter. *Architecture of the Early XX. Century.* New York: Rizzoli, 1989. Selections from *Die Architektur des XX. Jahrhunderts—Zeitschrift für moderne Baukunst.* Berlin: Ernst Wasmuth, 1901–1914.

Helfrich, Mary C. *Apollo Chorus of Chicago: Celebrating 125 Years, 1872–1997.* Chicago: Apollo Chorus of Chicago, 1997.

Henderson, Mary C. *The City and the Theatre: New York Playhouses from Bowling Green to Times Square.* Clifton, N.J.: James T. White, 1973.

Herbert, Gilbert, and Mark Donchin. *Speculations on a Black Hole: Adler and Sullivan, and the Planning of the Chicago Auditorium Building.* Haifa: Architectural Heritage Research Centre, 1998.

Herrick, Robert. *The Memoirs of an American Citizen.* 1905. Reprint, Cambridge: Harvard University Press, 1963.

Hirsch, Eric L. *Urban Revolt: Ethnic Politics in the Nineteenth Century Chicago Labor Movement.* Berkeley: University of California Press, 1990.

Hirsch, Susan E., and Robert I. Goler. *A City Comes of Age: Chicago in the 1890s.* Chicago: Chicago Historical Society, 1990.

Hoffmann, Donald. *The Architecture of John Wellborn Root.* Baltimore: Johns Hopkins University Press, 1973.

Hofmeister, Rudolf A. *The Germans of Chicago.* Champaign, Ill.: Stipes, 1976.

Holli, Melvin G., and Peter D'A. Jones, eds. *Ethnic Chicago: A Multicultural Portrait.* 4th ed. Grand Rapids: William B. Eerdmans, 1995.

Horowitz, Helen L. *Culture and the City: Cultural Philanthropy in Chicago from the 1880s to 1917.* 1976. Reprint, Chicago: University of Chicago Press, 1989.

Horowitz, Joseph. *Wagner Nights: An American History.* Berkeley: University of California Press, 1994.

Hoyt, Homer N. *One Hundred Years of Land Values in Chicago: The Relationship of the Growth of Chicago to the Rise in Its Land Values, 1830–1933.* Chicago: University of Chicago Press, 1933.

Hurlburt, Henry H. *Chicago Antiquities.* Chicago: Fergus, 1881.

Illinois Bureau of Labor Statistics. *Ninth Annual Report of the Illinois Bureau of Labor Statistics: Subject, Franchises and Taxation, 1896.* Springfield, Ill., 1897.

Industrial Chicago. 6 vols. Vols. 1 and 2, *The Building Interests.* Vol. 4, *The Commercial Interests.* Chicago: Goodspeed, 1891–1896.

In Memory of George Benedict Carpenter, Died January 7, 1881. N.p., n.d. Chicago Historical Society.

The Inter-state Exposition Souvenir: Containing a Historical Sketch of Chicago; also a Record of the Great Inter-state Exposition of 1873. Chicago: Van Arsdale and Massie, 1873.

Izenour, George C. *Theater Design.* New York: McGraw-Hill, 1977.

Jaher, Frederic Cople. *The Urban Establishment: Upper Strata in Boston, New York, Charleston, Chicago, and Los Angeles.* Urbana: University of Illinois Press, 1982.

James, George Wharton. *Chicago's Dark Places.* Chicago: Craig Press, 1891.

Janssen, Theodor. *Geschichte der Chicago Turn-gemeinde.* Chicago: M. Stern, 1897.

Johnson, Claudius O. *Carter Henry Harrison I: Political Leader.* Chicago: University of Chicago Press, 1928.

Johnson, Herrick. *A Plain Talk about the Theater.* Chicago: F. H. Revell, 1882.

Johnson, Vilas. *A History of the Commercial Club of Chicago.* Chicago: Commercial Club of Chicago, 1977.

Jordy, William H. *American Buildings and Their Architects.* Vol. 4, *Progressive and Academic Ideals at the Turn of the Twentieth Century.* 1972. Reprint, New York: Oxford University Press, 1986.

Kasson, John F. *Rudeness and Civility: Manners in Nineteenth-Century Urban America.* New York: Hill and Wang, 1990.

Keil, Hartmut, ed. *German Workers' Culture in the United States, 1850 to 1920.* Washington, D.C.: Smithsonian Institution Press, 1988.

Keil, Hartmut, and John B. Jentz, eds. *German Workers in Industrial Chicago, 1850–1910: A Comparative Perspective.* De Kalb: Northern Illinois University Press, 1983.

———. *German Workers in Chicago: A Documentary History of Working-Class Culture from 1850 to World War I.* Urbana: University of Illinois Press, 1988.

King, Moses. *King's Handbook of New York City.* 2d ed. 2 vols. Boston: Moses King, 1893. Reprint, New York: Benjamin Blom, 1972.

Kirkland, Joseph, and Caroline Kirkland. *The Story of Chicago.* 2 vols. Chicago: Dibble, 1892–1894.

Klein, Herman R. *The Reign of Patti.* New York: Century, 1920.

Landau, Sarah B., and Carl Condit. *The Rise of the New York Skyscraper, 1865–1913.* New Haven: Yale University Press, 1996.

Leacroft, Richard. *The Development of the English Playhouse.* Ithaca: Cornell University Press, 1973.

Levine, Lawrence W. *Highbrow/Lowbrow: The Emergence of Cultural Hierarchy in America.* Cambridge: Harvard University Press, 1988.

Lewis, Arnold. *An Early Encounter with Tomorrow: Europeans, Chicago's Loop, and the World's Columbian Exposition.* Urbana: University of Illinois Press, 1997.

Limerick, Jeffrey, Nancy Ferguson, and Richard Oliver. *America's Grand Resort Hotels.* New York: Pantheon Books, 1979.

Lowe, David. *Chicago Interiors: Views of a Splendid World.* Chicago: Contemporary Books, 1979.

———. *Lost Chicago.* Boston: Houghton Mifflin, 1978.

McCarthy, Kathleen D. *Noblesse Oblige: Charity and Cultural Philanthropy in Chicago, 1849–1929.* Chicago: University of Chicago Press, 1982.

McIlvaine, Mabel. *Reminiscences of Chicago during the Forties and Fifties.* Chicago: Lakeside Press, 1913.

MacKaye, Percy. *Epoch: The Life of Steele MacKaye, Genius of the Theater, in Relation to His Times and Contemporaries.* 2 vols. New York: Boni and Liveright, 1927.

McVicker, James H. *The Press, the Pulpit, and the Stage.* Chicago: Western News, 1883.

———. *The Theatre: Its Early Days in Chicago.* Chicago: Knight and Leonard, 1884.

Mallgrave, Harry Francis. *Gottfried Semper, Architect of the Nineteenth Century: A Personal and Intellectual Biography.* New Haven: Yale University Press, 1996.

Mapleson, James H. *The Mapleson Memoirs.* Edited by Harold Rosenthal. New York: Appleton-Century-Crofts, 1966.

Marquis, Albert N. *Marquis' Hand-Book of Chicago: A Complete History, Reference Book and Guide to the City.* Chicago: A. N. Marquis, 1887.

Mayer, Harold M., and Richard C. Wade. *Chicago: Growth of a Metropolis.* Chicago: University of Chicago Press, 1969.

Mayer, Martin. *The Met: One Hundred Years of Grand Opera.* New York: Simon and Schuster, 1983.

Mead, Christopher C. *Charles Garnier's Paris Opera: Architectural Empathy and the Renaissance of French Classicism.* New York: Architectural History Foundation and MIT Press, 1991.

Mendelsohn, Felix. *Chicago Yesterday and Today.* Chicago: F. Mendelsohn, 1932.

Menocal, Narciso G. *Architecture as Nature: The Transcendentalist Idea of Louis Sullivan.* Madison: University of Wisconsin Press, 1981.

Miller, Donald L. *City of the Century: The Epic of Chicago and the Making of America.* New York: Simon and Schuster, 1996.

Miller, Ross. *American Apocalypse: Chicago and the Myth of the Great Fire.* Chicago: University of Chicago Press, 1990.

Miller, Zane L., and George F. Roth. *Cincinnati's Music Hall.* Virginia Beach, Va.: Jordan, 1978.

Millet, Larry J. *The Curve of the Arch: The Story of Louis Sullivan's Owatonna Bank.* St. Paul: University of Minnesota Press, 1985.

Moore, Edward C. *Forty Years of Opera in Chicago.* New York: Horace Liveright, 1930.

Morrison, Hugh. *Louis Sullivan: Prophet of Modern Architecture.* 1935. Reprint, New York: W. W. Norton, 1962.

Moses, John, and Joseph Kirkland, eds. *The History of Chicago, Illinois.* 2 vols. Chicago: Munsell, 1895.

Musgrave, Michael. *The Musical Life of the Crystal Palace.* Cambridge: Cambridge University Press, 1995.

Nasaw, David. *Going Out: The Rise and Fall of Public Amusements.* New York: Basic Books, 1993.

Nelson, Bruce C. *Beyond the Martyrs: A Social History of Chicago's Anarchists, 1870–1900.* New Brunswick, N.J.: Rutgers University Press, 1988.

Newton, Joseph Fort. *David Swing: Poet Preacher.* Chicago: Unity, 1909.

Norris, Frank. *The Pit: A Story of Chicago.* New York: Doubleday, Page, 1903.

Observanda: McVicker's New Theatre, Chicago. Chicago: W. J. Jefferson Press, 1891. Chicago Historical Society.

O'Gorman, James F. *H. H. Richardson: Architectural Forms for an American Society.* Chicago: University of Chicago Press, 1987.

Orear, George W. *Commerical and Architectural Chicago.* Chicago: G. W. Orear, 1887.

Otis, Philo Adams. *The Chicago Symphony Orchestra: Its Organization, Growth, and Development, 1891–1924.* 1924. Reprint, Freeport, N.Y.: Books for Libraries Press, 1972.

———. *Impressions of Europe, 1873–1874: Music, Art and History.* Boston: R. G. Badger, 1922.

Parsons, Albert R. *Anarchism: Its Philosophy and Scientific Basis as Defined by Some of Its Apostles.* Chicago, 1887. Reprint, Westport, Conn.: Greenwood Press, 1970.

Paul, Sherman. *Louis Sullivan: An Architect in American Thought.* Englewood Cliffs, N.J.: Prentice-Hall, 1962.

[Peck, Ferdinand W.] *Report of the Commissioner-General for the United States to the International Universal Exposition, Paris, 1900.* 6 vols. Washington, D.C.: Government Printing Office, 1901.

Peck, Ralph B. *History of Building Foundations in Chicago.* Bulletin 373. Urbana: University of Illinois Engineering Experiment Station, 1948.

Perlman, Daniel H. *The Auditorium Building: Its History and Architectural Significance.* Chicago: Roosevelt University, 1976.

Pevsner, Sir Nikolaus. *A History of Building Types.* Princeton: Princeton University Press, 1976.

Pierce, Bessie L., ed. *As Others See Chicago: Impressions of Visitors, 1673–1933.* Chicago: University of Chicago Press, 1933.

———. *A History of Chicago.* 3 vols. New York: Alfred A. Knopf, 1937–1957. Reprint, Chicago: University of Chicago Press, 1975.

Platt, Harold L. *The Electric City: Energy and the Growth of the Chicago Area, 1880–1930.* Chicago: University of Chicago Press, 1991.

Porter, Rev. Jeremiah. *The Earliest Religious History of Chicago.* Chicago: Fergus, 1881.

Pratt, Silas G., ed. *First Chicago Grand Opera Festival at the Exposition Building.* Chicago: Skeen and Stuart, 1885.

Rabreau, Daniel, et al. *Gabriel Davioud: Architecte, 1824–1881.* Paris: Délégation à l'Action Artistique de la Ville de Paris, 1981.

Randall, Frank A. *History of the Development of Building Construction in Chicago.* Urbana: University of Illinois Press, 1949.

Rand McNally. *Bird's-Eye Views and Guide to Chicago.* Chicago: Rand McNally, 1898.

Rice, Wallace. *The Chicago Stock Exchange: A History.* Chicago: Committee on Library of the Chicago Stock Exchange, 1923.

Riedy, James L. *Chicago Sculpture.* Urbana: University of Illinois Press, 1981.

Rosen, Christine M. *The Limits of Power: Great Fires and the Process of City Growth in America.* New York: Cambridge University Press, 1987.

Roth, Leland M. *McKim, Mead & White, Architects.* New York: Harper and Row, 1983.

Sachs, Edwin O., and Ernest A. F. Woodrow. *Modern Opera Houses and Theatres.* 3 vols. London: B. T. Batsford, 1896–1898. Reprint, New York: Arno Press, 1981.

Saliga, Pauline, ed. *Fragments of Chicago's Past: The Collection of Architectural Fragments at the Art Institute of Chicago.* Chicago: Art Institute of Chicago, 1990.

Sältzer, Alexander. *A Treatise on Acoustics in Connection with Ventilation.* New York: D. Van Nostrand, 1872.

Sautter, R. Craig, and Edward M. Burke. *Inside the Wigwam: Chicago Presidential Conventions, 1860–1996.* Chicago: Wild Onion Books, 1996.

Sawislak, Karen. *Smoldering City: Chicagoans and the Great Fire, 1871–1874.* Chicago: University of Chicago Press, 1995.

Schaack, Michael J. *Anarchy and Anarchists: A History of the Red Terror and the Social Revolution in America and Europe.* Chicago: F. J. Schulte, 1889.

Schabas, Ezra. *Theodore Thomas: America's Conductor and Builder of Orchestras, 1835–1905.* Urbana: University of Illinois Press, 1989.

Schneirov, Richard. *Labor and Urban Politics: Class Conflict and the Origins of Modern Liberalism in Chicago, 1864–97.* Urbana: University of Illinois Press, 1998.

Schneirov, Richard, and Thomas J. Suhrbur. *Union Brotherhood, Union Town: The History of the Carpenters' Union of Chicago, 1863–1987.* Carbondale: Southern Illinois University Press, 1988.

Schick, Louis. *Chicago and Its Environs: A Handbook for the Traveler.* Chicago: L. Schick, 1891.

Schuyler, Montgomery. *"American Architecture" and Other Writings.* Edited by William H. Jordy and Ralph Coe. 2 vols. Cambridge: Harvard University Press, 1961.

———. *A Critique of the Works of Adler and Sullivan, D. H. Burnham and Co., Henry Ives Cobb.* Great American Architects Series 2, Architecture in Chicago. New York: Architectural Record, 1896. Partly reprinted in Schuyler, *"American Architecture" and Other Writings,* ed. Jordy and Coe, 2:377–404, 405–418.

Siry, Joseph. *Carson Pirie Scott: Louis Sullivan and the Chicago Department Store.* Chicago: University of Chicago Press, 1988.

———. *Unity Temple: Frank Lloyd Wright and Architecture for Liberal Religion.* New York: Cambridge University Press, 1996.

Smith, Carl S. *Chicago and the American Literary Imagination, 1880–1920.* Chicago: University of Chicago Press, 1984.

———. *Urban Disorder and the Shape of Belief: The Great Fire, the Haymarket Bomb, and the Model Town of Pullman.* Chicago: University of Chicago Press, 1995.

Smith, Gene. *American Gothic: The Story of America's Legendary Theatrical Family—Junius, Edwin, and John Wilkes Booth.* New York: Simon and Schuster, 1992.

Spotts, Frederic. *Bayreuth: A History of the Wagner Festival.* New Haven: Yale University Press, 1994.

Sprague, Paul E. *The Drawings of Louis Henry Sullivan.* Princeton: Princeton University Press, 1979.

Starring, Helen Swing, comp. *David Swing: A Memorial Volume.* Chicago: F. T. Neely, 1894.

Stern, Robert A. M., Gregory Gilmartin, and John M. Massengale. *New York 1900: Metropolitan Architecture and Urbanism, 1890–1915.* New York: Rizzoli, 1983.

Stern, Robert A. M., Thomas Mellins, and David Fishman. *New York 1880: Architecture and Urbanism in the Gilded Age.* New York: Monacelli Press, 1999.

Sullivan, Louis. *The Autobiography of an Idea.* 1924. Reprint, New York: Dover, 1971.

———. *Democracy: A Man-Search.* 1907; revised 1908. Edited by Elaine Hedges. Detroit: Wayne State University Press, 1961.

———. Kindergarten Chats. First published in *Interstate Architect and Builder* 2 (16 February 1901) to 3 (8 February 1902). Included in *"Kindergarten Chats" and Other Writings,* 1947, ed. Isabella Athey. Reprint, New York: Dover, 1979.

———. *Louis Sullivan: The Public Papers.* Edited by Robert Twombly. Chicago: University of Chicago Press, 1988.

Szarkowksi, John. *The Idea of Louis Sullivan.* Minneapolis: University of Minnesota Press, 1956.

Tallmadge, Thomas E. *Architecture in Old Chicago.* Chicago: University of Chicago Press, 1941.

Tamm, Birgitta. *Auditorium and Palatium: A Study on Assembly-Rooms in Roman Palaces during the First Century B.C. and the First Century A.D.* Stockholm Studies in Classical Archaeology 2. Stockholm: Almquist och Wiksell, 1963.

Taylor, Derek, and David Bush. *The Golden Age of British Hotels.* London: Northwood, 1974.

Thomas, Rose Fay, ed. *Memoirs of Theodore Thomas.* New York: Moffat, Yard, 1911.

Thomas, Theodore. *Theodore Thomas: A Musical Autobiography.* Edited by George P. Upton. 2 vols. Chicago: A. C. McClurg, 1905.

Tidworth, Simon. *Theatres: An Architectural and Cultural History.* New York: Praeger, 1973.

Turak, Theodore. *William Le Baron Jenney: A Pioneer of Modern Architecture.* Ann Arbor, Mich.: UMI Research Press, 1986.

Turner, Henry L. *Souvenir Album and Sketchbook: First Infantry, Illinois National Guard of Chicago.* Chicago: Knight and Leonard, 1890.

Twombly, Robert. *Louis Sullivan: His Life and Work.* New York: Viking/Penguin, 1986.

Twombly, Robert, and Narciso G. Menocal. *Louis Sullivan: The Poetry of Architecture.* New York: W. W. Norton, 2000.

Twyman, Robert W. *History of Marshall Field and Co., 1852–1906.* Philadelphia: University of Pennsylvania Press, 1954.

United States Industrial Commission. *Report of the Industrial Commission on the Chicago Labor Disputes of 1900, with Especial Reference to the Disputes in the Building and Machinery Trades.* Washington, D.C.: Government Printing Office, 1901.

Upton, George P. *Musical Memories: My Recollections of Celebrities of the Half Century 1850–1900.* Chicago: A. C. McClurg, 1908.

Van Rensselaer, Mariana G. *Henry Hobson Richardson and His Works.* Boston, 1888. Reprint, New York: Dover, 1969.

Van Trump, James D. *Majesty of the Law: The Court Houses of Allegheny County.* Pittsburgh: Pittsburgh History and Landmarks Foundation, 1988.

Vinci, John. *The Trading Room: Louis Sullivan and the Chicago Stock Exchange.* 2d ed. Chicago: Art Institute of Chicago, 1989.

Vinci-Kenny, Architects. *Adler and Sullivan's Auditorium Building: Architectural Guidelines for Its Preservation and Restoration for Roosevelt University.* Chicago, 1977.

Vynne, Harold R. *Chicago by Day and Night: The Pleasure Seeker's Guide to the Paris of America.* Chicago: Thomson and Zimmerman, 1892.

Waterman, Arba N. *Historical Review of Chicago and Cook County, and Selected Biography.* 3 vols. Chicago: Lewis, 1908.

Wille, Lois. *Forever Open, Free and Clear: The Historic Struggle for Chicago's Lakefront.* Chicago: Henry Regnery, 1972.

Williamson, Jefferson. *The American Hotel: An Anecdotal History.* New York: Alfred A. Knopf, 1930.

Wing, J. M. *The Palmer House, Chicago, Illustrated.* Chicago: J. M. Wing, 1876.

Wright, Frank Lloyd. *An Autobiography.* New York: Longmans, Green, 1932.

———. *Genius and the Mobocracy.* New York: Duell, Sloan and Pearce, 1949. Reprint, New York: Horizon Press, 1971.

Young, William C. *Documents of American Theater History.*, Vol. 1, *Famous American Playhouses, 1716–1899.* Chicago: American Library Association, 1973.

Zietz, Karyl L. *The National Trust Guide to Great Opera Houses in America.* New York: Preservation Press/John Wiley, 1996.

Zukowsky, John, ed. *Chicago Architecture, 1872–1922: Birth of a Metropolis.* Munich: Prestel-Verlag, 1987.

ARTICLES

"Academy of Music: Its Architecture." *New-York Daily Tribune,* 2 March 1867, 5.

Adler, Dankmar. "Architects and Trade Unions." *Inland Architect and News Record* 27 (May 1896): 32.

———. "The Auditorium Tower." *American Architect and Building News* 32 (4 April 1891): 15–16.

———. "The Autobiography and Letters of Dankmar Adler." Edited by Joan W. Saltzstein. *Inland Architect* 27 (September–October 1983): 20–24.

———. "The Chicago Auditorium." *Architectural Record* 1 (April–June 1892): 415–434.

———. "Convention Halls." *Inland Architect and News Record* 26 (September 1895): 13–14; (October 1895): 22–23.

———. "Engineering Supervision of Building Operations." *American Architect and Building News* 33 (4 July 1891): 11–12.

———. "Foundations." *Economist* 5 (27 June 1891): 1136–1138.

———. "Foundations of the Auditorium Building, Chicago." *Inland Architect and News Record* 11 (March 1888): 31–32.

———. "The General Contractor from the Standpoint of the Architect." *Inland Architect and News Record* 33 (June 1899): 38–39.

———. "An Important Letter from Mr. Dankmar Adler." *Inland Architect and News Record* 25 (July 1895): 61.

———. "The Influence of Steel Construction and of Plate Glass upon the Development of Modern Style." *Inland Architect and News Record* 28 (November 1896): 34–37.

———. "On Inspection of Buildings." *Economist* 5 (30 May 1891): 946–947.

———. "Light in Tall Office Buildings." *Engineering Magazine* 4 (November 1892): 171–186.

———. "The Paramount Requirements of a Large Opera House." *Inland Architect and News Record* 10 (October 1887): 45–46; also published as "Theatres," *American Architect and Building News* 22 (29 October 1887): 206–208.

———. "Slow Burning and Fireproof Construction." *Inland Architect and News Record* 26 (January 1896): 60.

———. "Some Notes upon the Earlier Chicago Architects." *Inland Architect and News Record* 19 (May 1892): 47–48.

———. "Stage Mechanisms." *Inland Architect and News Record* 13 (March 1889): 42–43; also published in *Building Budget* 15 (February 1889): 21–22.

———. "The Tall Business Building: Some of Its Engineering Problems." *Cassier's Magazine* 12 (November 1897): 193–210.

———. "Tall Office Buildings—Past and Future." *Engineering Magazine* 3 (September 1892): 765–773.

———. "The Theater." c. 1900. Edited by Rachel Baron. *Prairie School Review* 2 (second quarter 1965): 21–27.

———. "Theater Building for American Cities: First Paper." *Engineering Magazine* 7 (August 1894): 717–730; Second Paper, September 1894, 815–829.

———. Paraphrased in "Western Association of Architects." *American Architect and Building News* 20 (2 November 1886): 253.

———. Quoted in "Why the Strike Must Fail." *Chicago Tribune* (17 June 1887): 1.

Adler, Dankmar, and Louis Sullivan. Letter, "The Decoration of McVicker's Theater." *American Architect and Building News* 23 (11 February 1888): 70–71. Reprinted in *Louis Sullivan: The Public Papers,* ed. Twombly, 41–45.

"The Art Institute of Chicago Buildings, 1879–1988: A Chronology." *Art Institute of Chicago Museum Studies* 14 (1988): 7–27.

"The Auditorium Building: A Great and Superb Structure." Auditorium Number. *Graphic* (Chicago), o.s. 11 (14 December 1889).

"The Auditorium Building, Chicago." *Engineering* (London) 51 (3 April 1891): 394, 395, 400; (24 April 1891): 488, 489, 490.

"The Auditorium, Chicago." *Hotel Mail* 25 (15 March 1890). New York Public Library.

"The Auditorium Hotel." *Daily National Hotel Reporter* (Chicago), 9 October 1890. In "Early History and Press Clippings, Chicago Auditorium Association, Chicago, 1887–1889." Ryerson and Burnham Libraries, Art Institute of Chicago.

"Auditorium Supplement." *Chicago Daily Inter Ocean,* 11 December 1889.

Baldridge, Carol, and Alan Willis. "The Business of Culture." *Chicago History* 19 (spring–summer 1990): 32–51.

Baron, Rachel. "Forgotten Facets of Dankmar Adler." *Inland Architect,* April 1964, 14–16.

Bennett, Joseph. "An Englishman on Music in Chicago." *Indicator* 6 (18 July 1885): 590–591.

Bonshek, Jane. "The Skyscraper: A Catalyst of Change in the Chicago Construction Industries, 1882–1892." *Construction History* 4 (1988): 53–74.

Bragdon, Claude, ed. "Letters from Louis Sullivan." *Architecture* 64 (July 1931): 7–10.

Brooks, H. Allen. "Chicago School: Metamorphosis of a Term." *Journal of the Society of Architectural Historians* 25 (May 1966): 115–118.

Bruegmann, Robert. "The Marquette and the Myth of the Chicago School." *Threshold* 5–6 (fall 1991): 6–23.

Buettinger, Craig. "Economic Equality in Early Chicago, 1849–1850." *Journal of Social History* 11 (spring 1978): 413–418.

Burns, John A. "Structure and Mechanics Viewed as Sculpture." *American Institute of Architects Journal* 72 (April 1983): 44–49.

Bushnell, George D. "Chicago's Leading Men's Clubs." *Chicago History* 11 (summer 1982): 78–88.

Cady, Josiah Cleaveland. "The Essential Features of a Large Opera House." *Inland Architect and News Record* 10 (October 1887): 46–47; reprinted in *American Architect and Building News* 22 (29 October 1887): 208–209.

Chamberlain, Everett. "The Chicago of the Visitor." *Lakeside Monthly* 10 (October 1873): 272–277.

"The Chicago Auditorium." *Architect* (London) 43 (21 February 1890): 125–126.

"Chicago Auditorium Electric Light and Power Plant." *Western Electrician* 5 (12 October 1889): 191–193.

"Chicago's Auditorium Is Fifty Years Old." *Architectural Forum* 73 (September 1940): 10–12.

"Chicago Stock Exchange Building, Chicago." *Ornamental Iron* 2 (July 1894): 7–13.

Cleveland, Harold I. "Fifty-five Years in Business: The Life of Marshall Field—Chapter XI." *System* 11 (May 1907): 453–463.

Condit, Carl W. "The Chicago School and the Modern Movement in Architecture." *Art in America* 36 (January 1948): 19–36.

———. "The Structural System of Adler and Sullivan's Garrick Theater Building." *Technology and Culture* 5 (fall 1964): 523–540.

———. "Sullivan's Skyscrapers as the Expression of Nineteenth Century Technology." *Technology and Culture* 1 (winter 1959): 78–93.

Crook, David H. "Louis Sullivan and the Golden Doorway." *Journal of the Society of Architectural Historians* 26 (December 1967): 250–258.

Davis, Steven M. "'Of the Class Denominated Princely': The Tremont House Hotel." *Chicago History* 11 (spring 1982): 26–36.

"Death of P. F. W. Peck—Another One of the Old Settlers Gone." *Chicago Tribune*, 26 October 1871, 2.

Duis, Perry R. "'Where Is Athens Now?' The Fine Arts Building 1898 to 1918." *Chicago History* 6 (summer 1977): 66–78.

———. "Whose City? Public and Private Places in Nineteenth-Century Chicago, Part Two." *Chicago History* 12 (spring 1983): 18–21.

———. "Yesterday's City: Dearborn Park." *Chicago History* 15 (winter 1986–1987): 66–69.

Duis, Perry R., and Glen E. Holt. "Chicago as It Was: Cheap Thrills and Dime Museums." *Chicago* 26 (October 1977): 104–108.

"Earnings, Expenses and Conditions of Workingmen and Their Families." In *Third Biennial Report*, 135–414. Springfield: Illinois Bureau of Labor Statistics, 1884.

Egbert, Donald D., and Paul E. Sprague. "In Search of John Edelmann: Architect and Anarchist." *American Institute of Architects Journal* 45 (February 1966): 35–41.

Einhorn, Robin L. "The Civil War and Municipal Government in Chicago." In *Toward a Social History of the American Civil War: Exploratory Essays*, ed. Maris A. Vinovskis. New York: Cambridge University Press, 1990.

———. "A Taxing Dilemma: Early Lake Shore Protection." *Chicago History* 18 (fall 1989): 34–51.

Engelbrecht, Lloyd C. "Adler and Sullivan's Pueblo Opera House: City Status for a New Town in the Rockies." *Art Bulletin* 67 (June 1985): 277–295.

Ensslen, Klaus. "German-American Working-Class Saloons in Chicago: Their Social Function in an Ethnic and Class-Specific Cultural Context." In *German Workers' Culture in the United States, 1850 to 1920*, ed. Keil, 157–180.

Erenberg, Lewis A. "'Ain't We Got Fun?'" *Chicago History* 14 (winter 1985–1986): 4–21.

"Ferdinand Peck, Widely Known Chicagoan, Dies." *Chicago Tribune*, 5 November 1924, 19.

Ferree, Barr. "The Modern Office Building." *Inland Architect and News Record* 27 (February 1896): 4–5; (March 1896): 12–14; (April 1896): 23–25; (June 1896): 45–47.

Fletcher, Bannister. "American Architecture through English Spectacles." *Engineering Magazine* 7 (June 1894): 314–321.

Fox, John A. "American Dramatic Theatres." *American Architect and Building News* 6 (19 July 1879): 20–21; (26 July 1879): 27; (2 August 1879): 35–36; (9 August 1879): 42–44; (23 August 1879): 59–60; (30 August 1879): 68–69; (6 September 1879): 74–75.

Frueh, Erne R. "Retail Merchandising in Chicago, 1833–1848." *Journal of the Illinois State Historical Society* 32 (June 1939): 149–172.

Geraniotis, Roula M. "German Design Influences in the Auditorium Theater." In *Midwest in American Architecture*, ed. Garner, 42–75.

Giacosa, Giuseppe. "Chicago and Her Italian Colony." *Nuova Antologia* 128 (March 1893): 16–28. Translated by L. B. Davis in *As Others See Chicago*, ed. Pierce, 280.

Gmelin, Leopold. "Architektonisches aus Nordamerika: V. Die vielstöckigen Geschäftshäuser [Part 2]." *Deutsche Bauzeitung* 28 (27 October 1894): 532–534.

"The Grand Opera Festival." *Real Estate and Building Journal* 27 (4 April 1885): 160–161.

"A Grand Temple of Music." *New York Times,* 14 October 1883, 5.

Ham, Charles H. "The Chicago Auditorium Building." *Harper's Weekly* 31 (2 July 1887): 471.

Hanks, David. "Louis J. Millet and the Art Institute of Chicago." *Bulletin of the Art Institute of Chicago* 67 (1973): 13–19.

Hasbrouck, Wilbert H. "Chicago's Auditorium Theater." *Prairie School Review* 4 (third quarter 1967): 7–21.

Hansen, Harry. "How to Give away an Opera House." *Journal of the Illinois State Historical Society* 39 (December 1946): 419–424.

Head, Franklin H. "The Heart of Chicago." *New England Magazine* 6 (July 1892): 550–567.

Heiss, Christine. "Popular and Working-Class German Theater in Chicago, 1870 to 1910." In *German Workers' Culture in the United States,* ed. Keil, 181–201.

Hild, Theodore W. "The Demolition of the Garrick Theater and the Birth of the Preservation Movement in Chicago." *Illinois Historical Journal* 88 (1995): 79–100.

Horowitz, Helen L. "The Art Institute of Chicago: The First Forty Years." *Chicago History* 8 (spring 1979): 2–19.

Hutchison, William. "Disapproval of Chicago: The Symbolic Trial of David Swing." *Journal of American History* 59 (June 1972): 30–47.

Jenkins, Charles E. "Messrs. Jenney and Mundie." *Architectural Reviewer* (Chicago) 1 (February 1897): 1–45.

———. "A Review of the Works of S. S. Beman." *Architectural Reviewer* (Chicago) 1 (31 March 1897): 47–101.

Jentz, John B. "Class and Politics in an Emerging Industrial City: Chicago in the 1860s and 1870s." *Journal of Urban History* 17 (May 1991): 227–263.

Johnson, Claudia O. "That Guilty Third Tier: Prostitution in Nineteenth-Century American Theaters." In *Victorian America,* ed. Daniel Walker Howe, 111–120. Philadelphia: University of Pennsylvania Press, 1976.

Jordy, William H. "The Tall Buildings." In *Louis Sullivan: The Function of Ornament,* ed. de Wit, 65–71.

Kaufmann, Edgar J., Jr. "Frank Lloyd Wright's 'Lieber Meister.'" In *Nine Commentaries on Frank Lloyd Wright,* ed. Edgar J. Kaufmann Jr., 37–62. New York: Architectural History Foundation and MIT Press, 1989.

Keil, Hartmut, and Heinz Ickstadt. "Elements of German Working-Class Culture in Chicago, 1880–1890." In *German Workers' Culture in the United States, 1850 to 1920,* ed. Keil, 81–105.

Keyes, Jonathan J. "The Forgotten Fire." *Chicago History* 26 (fall 1997): 52–65.

Kiriazis, Judith. "Living with a Landmark Campus: Roosevelt's Auditorium." *Inland Architect,* September 1979, 12–15.

Larson, Gerald, and Roula Geraniotis. "Toward a Better Understanding of the Iron Skeleton Frame in Chicago." *Journal of the Society of Architectural Historians* 46 (March 1987): 39–48.

Lederer, Francis L. "Competition for the World's Columbian Exposition: The Chicago Campaign." *Journal of the Illinois State Historical Society* 65 (1972): 382–394.

Litwicki, Ellen M. "'The Inauguration of the People's Age': The Columbian Quadricentennial and American Culture." *Maryland Historian* 20 (1989): 47–58.

Lowe, David G. "Monument of an Age." *American Craft* 48 (June–July 1988): 40–47, 104.

McColley, Robert. "Classical Music in Chicago and the Founding of the Symphony, 1850–1905." *Illinois Historical Journal* 78 (winter 1985): 289–302.

McConachie, Bruce A. "New York Operagoing, 1825–50: Creating an Elite Social Ritual." *American Music* 6 (summer 1988): 181–192.

———. "Pacifying American Theatrical Audiences, 1820–1900." In *For Fun and Profit: The Transformation of Leisure into Consumption,* ed. Richard Butsch, 47–70. Philadelphia: Temple University Press, 1990.

McCoy, Amasa. "Appeal for the Fine Arts in the Republic." Address delivered at the Artists' Reception, Crosby's Opera House, 26 March 1866. Chicago Historical Society.

"McVicker's Theatre: A Thespian Temple Worthy of Chicago." *Real Estate and Building Journal* 27 (18 July 1885): 347–348.

"A Mammoth Opera House." *Inland Architect and News Record* 5 (March 1885): 25.

Melendy, Royal L. "The Saloon in Chicago." *American Journal of Sociology* 6 (November 1900): 289–306; (January 1901): 433–464.

"The Metropolitan Opera House." *Nation* 37 (25 October 1883): 348–349.

Michael, Edward Lee. "Adler and Sullivan's Palace of Trade: The Chicago Stock Exchange Building." Seminar paper for Professor Paul E. Sprague, University of Chicago, spring 1972.

Miller, Nory. "Roosevelt University and the Auditorium: What Do You Do with a Great Landmark?" *Inland Architect* 17 (April 1973): 7–13.

Mueller, Paul F. P. Testimony, Chicago Auditorium Association vs. Mark Skinner Willing and the Northern Trust Co., as Trustees, etc., et al., in United States Circuit Court of Appeals for the Seventh Circuit, October [1925] Term, no. 3733, pp. 440–468, mostly reprinted in Edgar J. Kaufmann Jr., "Frank Lloyd Wright's 'Lieber Meister,'" in *Nine Commentaries on Frank Lloyd Wright,* ed. Edgar J. Kaufmann Jr., 42–62. Architectural History Foundation and MIT Press, 1989.

Nelson, Bruce C. "Dancing and Picnicking Anarchists: The Movement below the Martyred Leadership." In *Haymarket Scrapbook,* ed. David Roediger and Franklin Rosemont, 76–79. Chicago: Charles H. Kerr, 1986.

Neuberg, Phillip. "Unveiling Sullivan's Artistry." *Inland Architect,* September 1979, 14–15.

"New Offices of Adler and Sullivan, Architects, Chicago." *Engineering and Building Record* 22 (7 June 1890): 5.

"The New Opera House." *New York Times,* 23 October 1883, 1.

Ochsner, Jeffrey Karl, and Dennis Alan Andersen. "Adler and Sullivan's Seattle Opera House Project." *Journal of the Society of Architectural Historians* 48 (September 1989): 223–231.

O'Gorman, James F. "The Marshall Field Wholesale Store: Materials toward a Monograph." *Journal of the Society of Architectural Historians* 37 (October 1978): 175–194.

Olson, Esther Marie. "The German Theater in Chicago." *Deutsch-Amerikanische Geschichtsblätter* 33 (1937): 68–123.

Peck, Ferdinand. Address to Commercial Club, Chicago, 29 May 1886. Paraphrased in "New Grand Opera House," *Chicago Tribune,* 12 June 1886, 9. Published verbatim in "Seats for a Multitude," *Chicago Evening Journal,* 29 January 1887, 1.

———. "The United States at the Paris Exposition in 1900." *North American Review* 168 (January 1899): 24–33.

Pollak, Martha. "Sullivan and the Orders of Architecture." In *Chicago Architecture, 1872–1922* ed. Zukowsky, 250–265.

Renner, Richard W. "In a Perfect Ferment: Chicago, the Know-Nothings, and the Riot for Lager Beer." *Chicago History* 5 (fall 1976): 161–179.

Root, John Wellborn. "Architects of Chicago." *Inland Architect and News Record* 16 (January 1891): 91–92.

Rykwert, Joseph. "Louis Sullivan and the Gospel of Height." *Art in America* 75 (November 1987): 162–165.

Sabine, Paul. "The Acoustics of the Chicago Civic Opera House." *Architectural Forum* 52 (April 1930): 599–604.

Sachs, Edwin O. "Modern Theatre Stages, No. XVII." *Engineering* (London) 62 (25 September 1896): 387–390.

Saltzstein, Joan. "Dankmar Adler: The Man, the Architect, the Author." *Wisconsin Architect* 38 (July–August 1967): 15–19; (September 1967): 10–14; (November 1967): 16–19.

Samuelson, Tim, and Jim Scott. "Auditorium Album." *Inland Architect*, September–October 1989, 64–71.

Schlereth, Thomas J. "Solon Spencer Beman: The Social History of a Midwest Architect." *Chicago Architectural Journal* 5 (1985): 8–31.

———. "Solon Spencer Beman, Pullman, and the European Influence on and Interest in His Chicago Architecture." In *Chicago Architecture, 1872–1922*, ed. Zukowsky, 172–187.

Schneirov, Richard. "Chicago's Great Upheaval of 1877." *Chicago History* 9 (spring 1980): 3–17.

———. "Class Conflict, Municipal Politics, and Governmental Reform in Gilded Age Chicago, 1871–1875." In *German Workers in Industrial Chicago*, ed. Keil and Jentz, 183–205.

———. "Political Cultures and the Role of the State in Labor's Republic: The View from Chicago, 1848–1877." *Labor History* 32 (summer 1991): 376–400.

Schuyler, Montgomery. "Glimpses of Western Architecture: Chicago." *Harper's Magazine* 83 (August 1891): 395–406. Reprinted in Schuyler, *"American Architecture" and Other Writings*, ed. Jordy and Coe, 1:246–291.

———. "The Metropolitan Opera-House." *Harper's New Monthly Magazine* 67 (November 1883): 877–889.

Scott Russell, John. "Elementary Considerations of Some Principles in Construction of Buildings Designed to Accommodate Spectators and Auditors." *Edinburgh New Philosophical Journal* 27 (April–October 1838): 131–136. Reprinted in *Theater Design*, ed. Izenour, 597–599.

———. "On the Construction of Buildings with Reference to Sound." *Building News* (London), 26 November 1858, 1178; 3 December 1858, 1195–1196; 10 December 1858, 1228.

Scully, Vincent J. "Louis Sullivan's Architectural Ornament: A Brief Note concerning Humanistic Design in the Age of Force." *Perspecta* 5 (1959): 73–80.

Shafer, Yvonne. "The First Chicago Grand Opera Festival: Adler and Sullivan before the Auditorium." *Theater Design and Technology* 13 (March 1977): 9–13, 38.

Shiffler, Harold C. "The Chicago Church-Theater Controversy of 1881–1882." *Journal of the Illinois State Historical Society* 53 (winter 1960): 361–375.

Siry, Joseph M. "The Abraham Lincoln Center in Chicago." *Journal of the Society of Architectural Historians* 50 (September 1991): 235–265.

———. "Adler and Sullivan's Guaranty Building in Buffalo." *Journal of the Society of Architectural Historians* 55 (March 1996): 6–37.

———. "Chicago's Auditorium Building: Opera or Anarchism." *Journal of the Society of Architectural Historians* 57 (June 1998): 2–33.

———. "Frank Lloyd Wright's 'The Art and Craft of the Machine': Text and Context." In *The Education of the Architect: Historiography, Urbanism, and the Growth of Architectural Knowledge*, ed. Martha Pollak, 3–36. Cambridge: MIT Press, 1997.

————. "Louis Sullivan's Building for John D. Van Allen and Son." *Journal of the Society of Architectural Historians* 49 (March 1990): 67–89.

Sprague, Paul. "Adler and Sullivan's Schiller Building." *Prairie School Review* 2 (second quarter 1965): 5–20.

"A Story of Stone." *Inland Architect and News Record* 27 (April 1896): 26–28.

"The Studebaker Building." *Chicago Tribune,* 26 March 1887, 7.

Sullivan, Louis. Address by Mr. Louis H. Sullivan, to Illinois Chapter, American Institute of Architects, 8 June 1915. Manuscripts Collection, Chicago Historical Society. Reprinted as "Tribute to Solon S. Beman" in *Louis Sullivan: The Public Papers,* ed. Twombly, 208–211.

————. "The Artistic Use of the Imagination." *Inland Architect and News Record* 14 (October 1889): 38–39. Reprinted in *Louis Sullivan: The Public Papers,* ed. Twombly, 62–67.

————. "Characteristics and Tendencies of American Architecture." *Inland Architect and Builder* 6 (November 1885): 58–59. Reprinted in *Louis Sullivan: The Public Papers,* ed. Twombly, 2–8.

————. Quoted in "Church Spires Must Go." *Chicago Tribune* (30 November 1890): 36. Reprinted in *Louis Sullivan: The Public Papers,* ed. Twombly, 72–73.

————. "Development of Construction, I." *Economist* 55 (24 June 1916): 1252; 56 (1 July 1916): 39–40. Reprinted in *Louis Sullivan: The Public Papers,* ed. Twombly, 211–222.

————. "Essay on Inspiration." *Inland Architect and News Record* 8 (December 1886): 61–64. Reprinted as *Inspiration: An Essay by Louis H. Sullivan, Architect.* Chicago: Ralph Fletcher Seymour, 1964, and in *Louis Sullivan: The Public Papers,* ed. Twombly, 10–28.

————. "The Modern Phase of Architecture." *Inland Architect and News Record* 33 (June 1899): 40. Reprinted in *Louis Sullivan: The Public Papers,* ed. Twombly, 123–125.

————. "Ornament in Architecture." *Engineering Magazine* 3 (August 1892): 633–644. Reprinted in *Louis Sullivan: The Public Papers,* ed. Twombly, 79–85.

————. "Plastic and Color Decoration of the Auditorium." Originally published as "Harmony in Decoration," *Chicago Tribune,* 16 November 1889, 12. Reprinted in *Industrial Chicago,* 2:490–491, in *Louis Sullivan,* by Sherman Paul, 143–146, and in *Louis Sullivan: The Public Papers,* ed. Twombly, 74–76.

————. "Style." *Inland Architect and News Record* 11 (May 1888): 59–60. Reprinted in *Louis Sullivan: The Public Papers,* ed. Twombly, ed. 45–52.

————. "Suggestions in Artistic Brickwork." Foreword to *Artistic Brick.* St. Louis: Hydraulic Press Brick Company, c. 1910, 5–13. Reprinted as "Artistic Brick," *Prairie School Review* 4 (second quarter 1967): 24–26, and in *Louis Sullivan: The Public Papers,* ed. Twombly, 200–205.

————. "The Tall Office Building Artistically Considered." *Lippincott's Magazine* 57 (March 1896): 403–409. Reprinted in *Louis Sullivan: The Public Papers,* ed. Twombly, 103–113.

————. "What Is the Just Subordination, in Architectural Design, of Details to Mass?" *Inland Architect and News Record* 9 (April 1887): 51–54." Reprinted in *Louis Sullivan: The Public Papers,* ed. Twombly, 34.

Towne, Francis E. "Albert Fleury, Painter." *Brush and Pencil* 12 (April–September 1903): 201–208.

Tselos, Dimitri. "The Chicago Fair and the Myth of the 'Lost Cause.'" *Journal of the Society of Architectural Historians* 26 (December 1967): 259–268.

Turnbaugh, Roy. "Ethnicity, Civic Pride, and Commitment: The Evolution of the Chicago Militia." *Journal of the Illinois State Historical Society* 62 (May 1979): 111–122.

Twose, George M. R. "Steel and Terra-Cotta Buildings in Chicago, and Some Deductions." *Brickbuilder* 3 (January 1894): 1–5.

"The Union League Club." *Graphic* (Chicago), o.s., 12 (22 March 1890): 180–182.

Van Brunt, Henry. "John Wellborn Root." *Inland Architect and News Record* 16 (January 1891): 85–88.

Van Rensselaer, Mariana G. "The Metropolitan Opera House, New York." *American Architect and Building News* 15 (16 January 1884): 76–77; (23 January 1884): 86–89.

Van Zanten, David. "Sullivan to 1890." In *Louis Sullivan: The Function of Ornament,* ed. de Wit, 36–51.

"Ventilation and Warming of the Metropolitan Opera House, New York." *Sanitary Engineer* 9 (6 December 1883): 10–13; (13 December 1883): 40–41.

Vinci, John. "The Chicago Stock Exchange Building." *Chicago History* 3 (spring–summer 1974): 23–27.

Warner, Charles Dudley. "Chicago." In *Studies in the South and West, with Comments on Canada,* by Charles Dudley Warner, 176–232 New York: Harper 1889.

Weingarden, Lauren S. "The Colors of Nature: Louis Sullivan's Architectural Polychromy and Nineteenth-Century Color Theory." *Winterthur Portfolio* 20 (1985): 243–260.

———. "Louis H. Sullivan's Search for an American Style." In *Fragments of Chicago's Past,* ed. Saliga, 118–125.

———. "Naturalized Nationalism: A Ruskinian Discourse on the Search for an American Style of Architecture." *Winterthur Portfolio* 24 (spring 1989): 43–68.

Westfall, Carroll W. "The Development of American Apartment Houses from the Civil War to the Depression, III: Chicago's Better Tall Apartment Buildings, 1871–1923." *Architectura* 21 (1991): 177–208.

———. "From Homes to Towers: A Century of Chicago's Best Hotels and Tall Apartment Buildings." In *Chicago Architecture, 1872–1922,* ed. Zukowsky, 266–289.

Wight, Peter B. "On the Present Condition of Architectural Art in the Western States." *American Art Review* (Boston) 1 (1880): 137–143.

Woltersdorf, Arthur. "A Portrait of Chicago Architects, II: Dankmar Adler." *Western Architect* 33 (July 1924): 75–79.

Wright, Frank Lloyd. "The Art and Craft of the Machine." In *Catalogue of the Fourteenth Annual 0Exhibition of the Chicago Architectural Club.* Chicago: Chicago Architectural Club, 1901. Reprinted in *Frank Lloyd Wright: Collected Writings,* vol. 1, *1894–1930,* ed. Bruce B. Pfeiffer, 53–69. New York: Rizzoli, 1992.

INDEX

Unless otherwise noted, all organizations,
buildings, and sites are in Chicago.